The American School

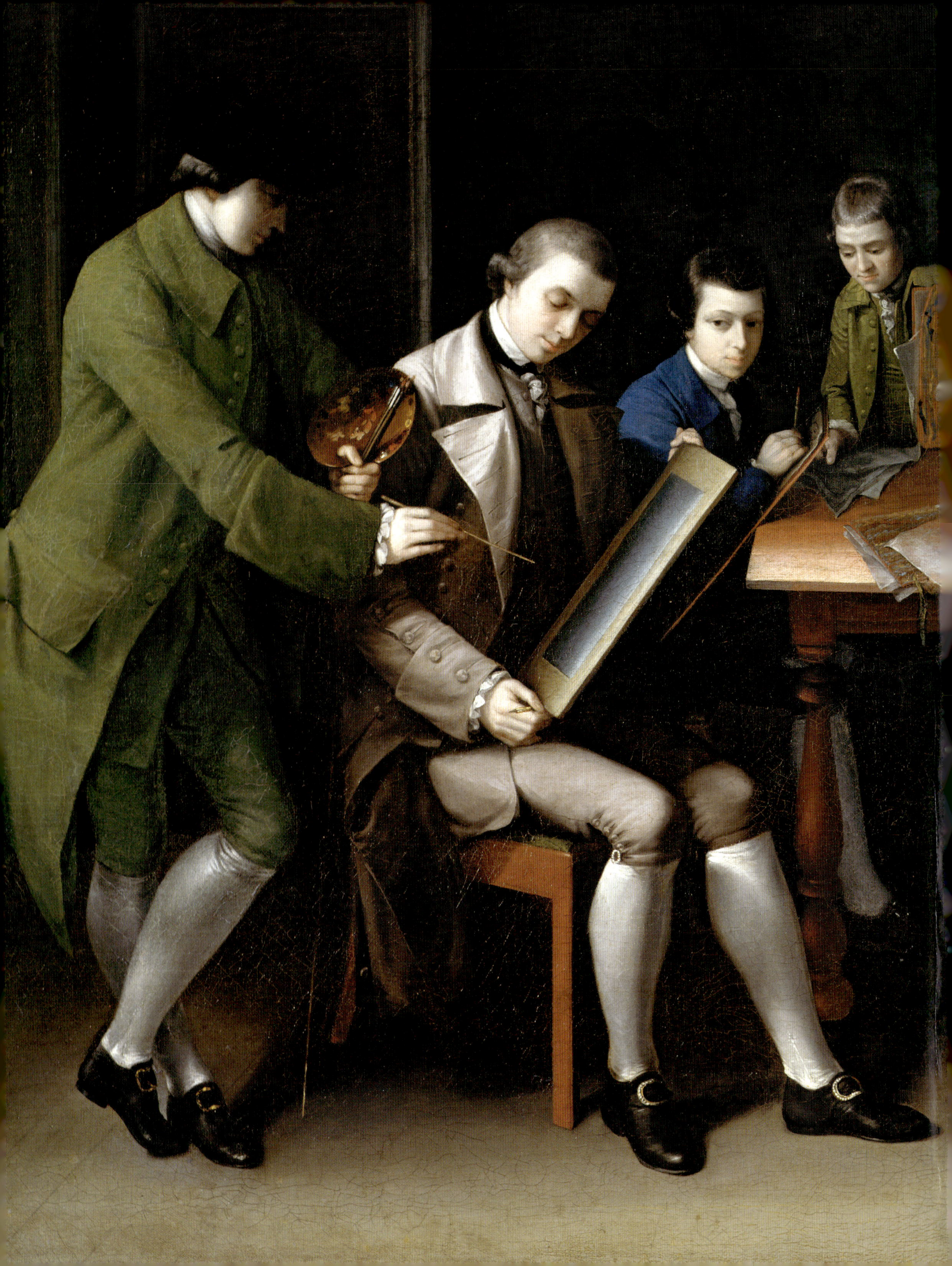

The American School

Artists and Status in the Late Colonial and Early National Era

Susan Rather

PUBLISHED FOR THE PAUL MELLON CENTRE FOR STUDIES IN BRITISH ART BY
YALE UNIVERSITY PRESS • NEW HAVEN AND LONDON

Printed in China
Designed by Emily Lees

Library of Congress Cataloging-in-Publication Data

Rather, Susan, author.
The American school : artists and status in the late colonial and early national era /
Susan Rather.
pages cm
Includes bibliographical references and index.
ISBN 978-0-300-21461-1 (hardback)
1. Artists – United States – Social conditions – 18th century. 2. Artists – United States – Social conditions – 19th century. 3. Art and society – United States – History – 18th century.
4. Art and society – United States – History – 19th century. I. Title.
N6507.R38 2016
709.73'09033 – dc23
2015025662

A catalogue record for this book is available from the British Library

Frontispiece: Matthew Pratt, *The American School*, 1765. Metropolitan Museum of Art, New York, gift of Samuel P. Avery, 1897 (97.29.3), photographed by Geoffrey Clements (detail of fig. 88).

CONTENTS

ACKNOWLEDGMENTS

This book had its genesis decades ago in an informal discussion of Matthew Pratt's painting *The American School* among fellows and staff at the National Portrait Gallery and National Museum of American Art (now Smithsonian American Art Museum). It seemed to me that this well-known work had been misunderstood, and I decided to return to the matter when I had a finished degree and a job. Mission accomplished five years later, I began my inquiries in what I imagined as a circumscribed project, a breather in the course of transforming my dissertation on Paul Manship and archaism into a book about modern and modernistic American and European sculpture of the early twentieth century. I quickly recognized the proverbial tip of the iceberg in issues that Pratt's painting raised about the status of earlier American artists. And so, following a general interest piqued in graduate seminars with Barbara Stafford, I resolved to decamp to the eighteenth century at the earliest opportunity, bypassing entirely the nineteenth-century studies that commanded the attention of most Americanist art historians at that time.

That opportunity came sooner than expected (I was still finishing my first book) when the Winterthur Museum and Library in concert with the National Endowment for the Humanities funded my trial balloon of a grant proposal, affording me a residential fellowship at Winterthur. In that beautiful setting and in productive company with other fellows, including Paul Staiti and David Jaffee, I began a study that has engaged me for longer than I could have imagined. Towards its conclusion, a quite different and newly minted institution, Crystal Bridges Museum of American Art, appointed me senior scholar during the pilot year for the Tyson Scholars of American Art Program. I thank former director Don Bacigalupi for that opportunity, then curator Kevin M. Murphy for perspective and collegiality, and curatorial assistant Ali Demorotski for helping hold everything together. Matt Bailey proved a more agreeable housemate in the "farmhouse" than I could have hoped for. In between, grants from the Center for British Art at Yale University, American Council of Learned Societies, Massachusetts Historical Society, and NEH Summer Stipends Program allowed me to advance different stages of this project. I am also fortunate to have received research and travel funds indirectly from the Kimbell Foundation, through my colleague Professor Jeffrey Smith's Kay Fortson Chair in European Art. My employer, the University of Texas, Austin, stepped in too; while the university does not have a sabbatical program, its other outlets in support of research proved indispensable, notably a Ducloux Family Fellowship from the College of Fine Arts, and several competitive Faculty Research Assignments from the Faculty Development Program. A University of Texas at Austin Subvention Grant awarded by the Office of the President and a grant from the department's Houston Endowment Funds greatly offset my own financial burden in the acquisition of photographs. Finally, the National Endowment for the Humanities brought the process full circle by awarding the fellowship that allowed me to finish what I had started so long ago. The resulting volume would not be what it is without Yale University Press and the Paul Mellon Centre for Studies in British Art. I am exceedingly fortunate that Gillian Malpass took interest in a manuscript that landed unannounced in her offices at the press in London. Her colleague, Emily Lees, a senior editor who designed this volume, showed great patience with my continual tinkering at late stages and was tremendously responsive in trying different layouts for tricky sections. This beautiful book is the result.

I tend to be a fairly solitary worker, so the colleagues and friends who have consistently provided encouragement had only glimpses of the whole, if they saw any of it at all. (Anonymous readers for the press necessarily submitted to the entire manuscript, and I am very grateful for their input.) To say that the shortcomings of a book are an author's alone is as commonplace as true, and I accept mine as true to who I am as a scholar, trusting that readers will find compensating strengths. I so appreciate the faith and forbearance of those who urged me forward at points when I hesitated to pull the strands of this story together. For sustained friendship and support, I am lucky in Stephen Mark Caffey, Katie Robinson Edwards, Angela Miller, Emily Ballew Neff, Glenn Peers, and Richard Shiff. Later on, Sarah Burns and John Davis threw their weight behind the project to great effect, for which I cannot thank them enough. For invitations, opportunities, and interventions at particular moments stretching over all the years of this project, I am grateful as well to the late Lillian Miller and Roger Stein, to Ellen Miles, Carrie Rebora Barratt, Liz Childs, H. Perry Chapman, David Steinberg, Jack Crowley, and Leo Mazow.

Not surprisingly, more than a few graduate students at the University of Texas have been exposed to the developing material, in one form or another. Members of my spring 2011 seminar, in particular, made signal contributions by agreeing to read and comment frankly on the manuscript as it then existed, and so I thank Lynn Bradshaw, Elizabeth Berler Brand, Kara Carmack, Nicole Conti, Claire Howard, Jen Rafferty, and visitor Laura Holzman. At various points, Stephen Caffey, Joshua Fischer, and Lynn Bradshaw served as fine research assistants. It pleases me greatly to here acknowledge my former student Laura Schwartz in her capacity as Head Librarian of the Fine Arts Library at the University of Texas. Her acquisitions over the years have made my work so much easier. Rowena Houghton Dasch, who vowed when starting graduate study that she would finish her Ph.D. before my five-year-old entered college but didn't quite make it, has been around to see how long it took me. She knows well herself that some outcomes cannot be rushed.

My son, Robin, has had to bear having a perfectionistic mother whose editorial meddling, in part, prompted a wry college application essay on how he started college in sixth grade. Fortunately, he turned out wonderfully anyway. My husband, Richard, the island of calm in our household, rescued me from countless technological agonies. Most of all, he has unfailingly given the support and space I needed. I appreciate that more than anything.

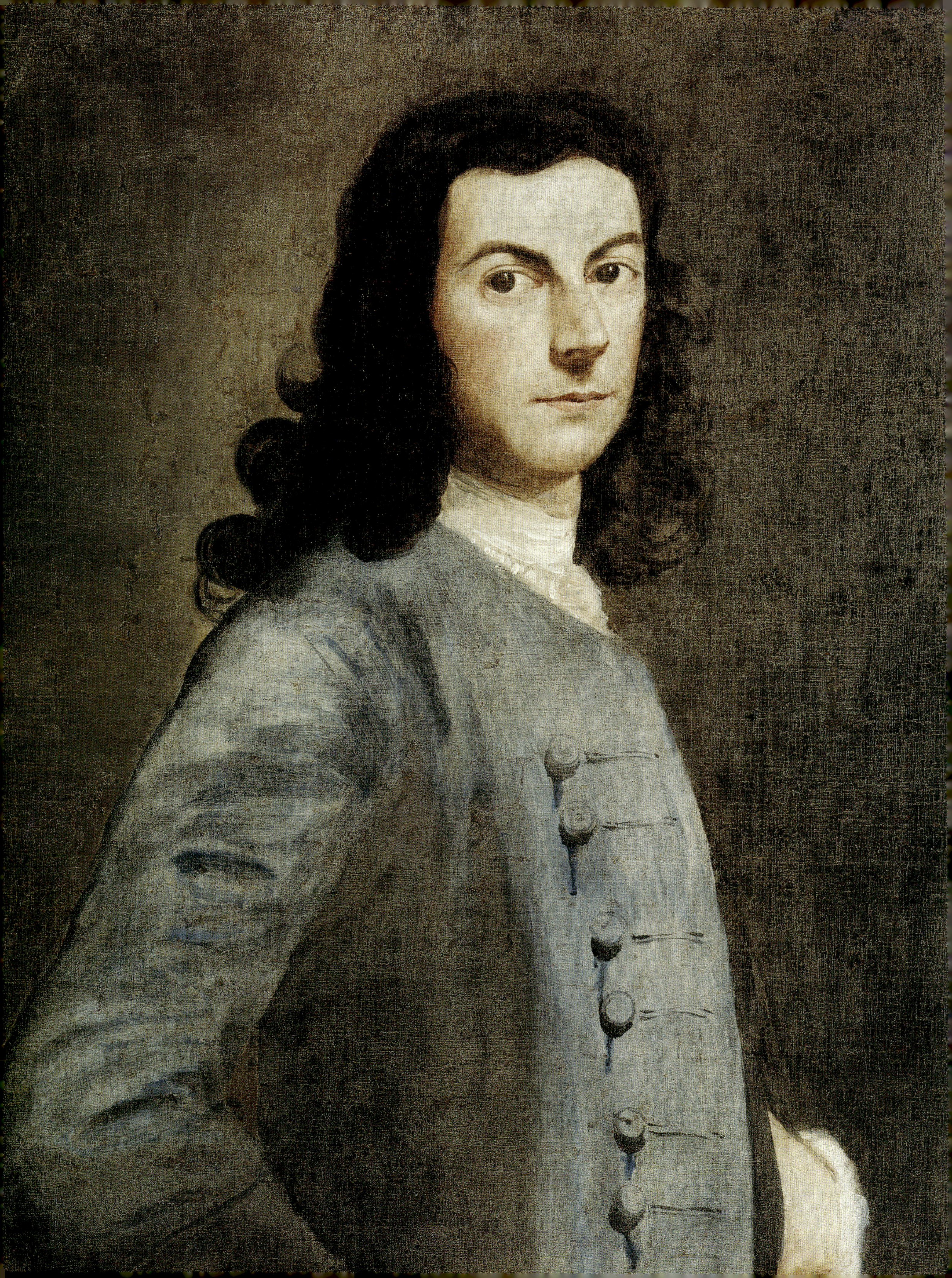

INTRODUCTION

And now a few Words concerning my Picture . . . Tis done by one of the best Hands in England, and is accounted by all Judges here, not only an Exceeding good Likeness, but a very good Piece of Painting: The Drapery is all taken from my own Clothes, & the very Flowers in the lace, upon the Hat, are taken from a Hat of my own . . . I was advised to have it drawn by one Keble . . . but upon seeing his Paintings, I found that though his Likenesses, (which is the easiest Part in doing a Picture,) were some of them very good, yet his Paint seemed to be laid on with a Trowel, and looked more like Plaistering than Painting.

Peter Manigault, 1751

Peter Manigault, in London to study law, penned these lines to his mother back home in Charleston in 1751.[1] His criteria for evaluating portrait and portraitist – he chose Allan Ramsay, a Scot who ranked among the leading artists in mid-eighteenth-century Britain – were commonplace on both sides of the Atlantic and useful for introducing themes central to this book. Manigault's synecdochic characterization of Ramsay as a "hand" reflexively exposes the widely held assumption that painters were manual workers. His repeated use of the words paint and painting draws attention to material and process, a point reinforced by the terms in which Manigault denigrated William Keeble, the portraitist he rejected: his paint "seemed to be laid on with a Trowel," like plastering. Plaster work, in common with all artisan labor, had to be learned, but the skill set necessary to covering a wall paled beside the challenge of applying pigmented oil to canvas in ways that made the raw materials appear as something other than themselves. Strikingly, Manigault considered "likeness," by which he evidently meant representation of a sitter's face, to be the "easiest part" of the process. Eighteenth-century portraitists did not agree; with good reason, they identified their greatest challenge in coloring flesh, a point also made by continental artists and writers. Denis Diderot, the pioneering French art critic, thought "the rest is as nothing in comparison. Thousands of painters have died without acquiring a feeling for flesh, and there will be thousands more who'll die without acquiring it."[2] Perhaps only those well acquainted with painting technique could appreciate the difficulty of representing skin tones, while the evidence suggests that most British and American portrait clients did not much care at a time when other parts of portraits mattered more. Manigault's remarks affirm the greater importance of "drapery" – clothing and fabrics – and of the other material goods that most forcefully communicated social position, a primary function of the eighteenth-century Anglo-American portrait.

The division of labor in later seventeenth- and eighteenth-century British portrait making had potential to diminish

Facing page Detail of fig. 6.

portraitists in the eyes of patrons who agreed with Manigault. "Face-painter," a term then common, aptly describes the work of busy portraitists like Ramsay. He might paint only a sitter's head or even just the face, leaving the remainder of the picture to others. In some cases, bodies were roughed out in advance. An auction at the studio of court portraitist Sir Peter Lely, after his death in 1680, included "14. Halfe lengths outlines" and "whole length postures No. 8 & 1," suggesting a catalogue of poses from which sitters might choose.[3] Portraitists occasionally carried such canvases with them to visit clients, painting head and neck from life. Alternatively, a head could be painted on a separate piece of cloth, easy to affix afterwards to another, larger canvas, with or without a prepared body. According to notes of 1739 made by English engraver, antiquarian, and chronicler of artists George Vertue, the now little-known (but in his time consequential) artist Hamlet Winstanley "traveled about and drew pictures from the life in oyl Colours, often on small peaces of cloth only the face"; these he sent to London "to one Mr. Vanaken . . . [who] stuck them on large strained Cloths as he pleas'd and made postures and draperys. and so made them compleat pictures."[4] Joseph Vanhaeken, until his death in 1749, excelled in a trade then known as "drapery painting," sometimes carried out in a portrait painter's studio by assistants but often performed by men who were, in effect, independent contractors. Such "painter taylors," according to William Hogarth (a rare English artist to shun them), might furnish "nine parts in ten" of a picture.[5] "Phiz-mongers" was Vertue's punning slap to portrait painters who "scarsely coud do any part but the face of a picture," a remark from within the profession that has the effect of supporting Manigault's lay view that painting faces was easy, a matter of rote.[6] Collectively, the remarks of Hogarth, Vertue, and Manigault leave little room for genius in portrait painting, the only genre in which British painters readily found employment. The impossible ideal to which German dramatist, art critic, and philosopher Gotthold Lessing drew attention in a play of 1772 could not even in jest have been applied to an Anglophone painter at mid-eighteenth century: that he might, like Raphael, "have been the greatest genius among painters, even if he had unfortunately been born without hands."[7]

The American School: Artists and Status in the Late Colonial and Early National Era explores the changing status of American artists from hands to minds, from artisans to gentlemen and geniuses, and from colonial Britons to self-identified Americans in the early national period. These binaries were powerful to some artists and not others, some writers and historians and not others, and it is an aim of this book to explore who, when, where, and why. The process of professional status change for artists had unfolded over several hundred years in Europe. Beginning in Italy during the Renaissance, artist-artisans, long associated with trade guilds, sought and attained new definition as practitioners of a liberal, intellectual art. The seventeenth century saw the emergence of select artists as gentlemen-courtiers, before radically changed political, social and economic conditions during the second half of the eighteenth century gave rise to a more independent artist type. In England, somewhat isolated from continental developments until the early seventeenth century, this process began later and proceeded more unevenly, as a sequence of continental painters, starting with van Dyck and Rubens in the 1630s, gained the stature of knighthoods a century and half before the crown bestowed collective recognition on British artists by endorsing the Royal Academy of Arts in 1768. In provincial British North America – where the earliest paintings of colonial manufacture date to the 1660s – the delay was still longer and the pace of change greatly compressed in chronological proximity to conditions of modernity. Focusing on the period from roughly the mid-eighteenth century through the first quarter of the nineteenth, I explore the matter of professional status as illuminated by well-known artists, paintings, and texts as well as non-elite painters, ephemeral images and texts (such as sign paintings and advertisements), and previously unnoticed popular writings about artists in contemporaneous newspapers and magazines.

In its attention to texts concerning artists, my project can be linked to Neil Harris's *The Artist in American Society: The Formative Years, 1790–1860*, published in 1966 when American art history was itself only emerging as a specialization. Harris addressed the subject as a historian, in a sweepingly ambitious study of the place of fine arts in the fundamentally unsupportive culture of a predominantly Protestant, mercantile, and democratic society. The fact that he chose not to attend closely to works of art (his long book had only sixteen illustrations) seems entirely understandable in view of his purpose, disciplinary perspective, and the general state of knowledge concerning American art at that time – or, perhaps, the limited interest in and tolerance for it. Lillian Miller, another historian, independently addressed a closely related topic, with particular attention to institutional history, in *Patrons and Patriotism: The Encouragement of the Fine Arts in the United States, 1790–1860*, also 1966. And, in what proved a banner year for American art history, the art historian Jules Prown brought out two volumes on John

Singleton Copley in America and in England, unprecedentedly weighty treatment of an early American artist and his work.[8] Though all three scholars engaged the eighteenth century (Harris more so than his title suggests), the nineteenth century and especially landscape painting of the antebellum period dominated American art historical writing of the 1970s and 1980s. Yet in a 2003 historiographic essay assessing American art studies of the preceding fifteen years, John Davis hailed the "rejuvenation" of scholarship on the late colonial and federal periods, a "formerly sleepy corner of American art history."[9] My work has been integral to this new wave of scholarly activity.

This book draws together, reconfigures, and expands essays on the subject of artists and status that I began to publish over twenty years ago.[10] At that point, chronologically halfway between Harris's study and the present one, I benefitted from a broader platform in the various disciplines a historian's work may intersect – and a different scholarly temperament, which led me to go deep into the lives of artists, especially painters, their writings, and their works, in fine-grained analysis of individual perspectives on status. During the time I have been engaged in this work, art historians have embraced the Atlantic studies paradigm initiated by historians many decades earlier: a recognition of complex give-and-take in the movement of people, cultures, ideas, and artifacts in the Atlantic world. A boom in scholarship facilitated broadening their initial focus on North America and Western Europe to Africa and Latin America, in full exploration of exchange around the Atlantic rim. For art historians of early America, the objects of study (especially paintings) have somewhat constrained similar expansion, although welcome recent interventions argue for considering the circulation of material things across North America – French and Spanish as well as British colonies and not excluding the participation of enslaved and native peoples. Scholars are also more inclined than before to recognize artistic exchange between Britain (and Europe) and America as a "two-way" traffic.[11] Previously, those writing about art in British North America or even about American artists in Britain emphasized colonial dependence on British or European prototypes, although a lingering counter-model identified a concurrent and distinctive American vision in such artists as Robert Feke and Copley.[12] Benjamin West was the long-acknowledged exception – the American artist whose work made signal contributions to the development of history painting in Great Britain. But even then, questions of artistic influence and reception dominated discussion of his art. Until 1993, when David Solkin paid serious attention to West in his book *Painting for Money: The Visual Arts and the Public Sphere in Eighteenth-Century England*, scholarship on the artist was almost exclusively the province of Americans.[13] Now, scholars are more likely to probe the ways in which colonial American and British artists engaged an Atlantic commerce of ideas, commodities, print culture, and fine art. That is certainly true of my work and its particular concern with the circulation of ideas about artists and the mutability of both artistic and American identities.

Expanding on a literature of earlier American art long devoted to individual artists and their major works, I probe artifacts and texts of all kinds to examine how artists both in and from America conceived of themselves and how others conceived of them during the defining period in the nation's history. Whereas historians have often analyzed objects as products of the forces of social history, in effect illustrating the presence of issues they have already identified, I examine objects and texts that pique my interest to see how they line up with existing understandings. The process encourages observation of anomalies and yields a more diverse and finely textured history, one not always readily subject to generalization. *The American School* joins with other recent scholarship in redressing shortcomings in the literature: lack of interdisciplinarity, insufficiently nuanced reading of texts, inclination to treat more or less realistic pictures as transparent to their subject, failure to make fine distinctions about context, and a tendency to think of eighteenth-century artists in more modernist terms than their situation warranted. My investigation coheres around the problematics of periphery, center, and nation from the perspective of artists and their audiences and in the recurrence of persons and issues. While the work of British artists outside London was considered marginal by metropolitan standards of professional practice, American artists showed greater inclination to use provinciality to their advantage, both before and after independence. Those most likely to do so, paradoxically, attained significant national and international reputations, especially Copley, Benjamin West, and Gilbert Stuart. Other painters featured in this study – William Williams and Matthew Pratt – were less prominent during their lifetimes and more well known now, if sometimes for misguided reasons. Each of these individuals takes center stage in chapters that examine the status of artists from different perspectives and in different geographical locations. Although none of the artists central to this study worked in the South, painters there faced comparable social and professional ambiguities.[14] Major themes include artisanry and professionalism; practice and theory; regional, colonial, and national identities; the democratization of art and portrait painting as a political metaphor; artistic nationalism and naturalism as a presumed American idiom; and the emergent history of American art.

In a narrative that defies neat containment, West exemplifies the shifting guises in which an artist reappears across the book. He is first glimpsed in chapter one through Copley's eyes as exemplar, an American who had successfully reinvented himself in the metropolis of London, a place where Copley imagined artists to enjoy a level of respect and opportunity denied him. The second chapter centers on the intriguing William Williams, whose life might have remained completely obscure were it not for West's late career intervention and his several accounts of a man he acknowledged as his first teacher, testimony that warrants scrutiny for its variations. Chapter three locates West as the key figure – in his own imagination and that of others – in a self-conscious historical drama concerning the status of Anglophone painters, in general, and of the "American" artist, in particular. West is something of a negative model in chapter five, the courtier-artist and academician who would be opposed by his pupil Stuart, the first American embodiment of a more modern, independent and eccentric artist type. Finally, West is the subject of his own chapter in six, which analyzes the artist's efforts, near the end of his long life, to redefine his American-ness, a strategic move intended to secure his reputation for posterity.

This is not a book about West, however. Nor, as his example indicates, does *The American School* offer broad, biographically encompassing assessments of the individual artists and their status, instead focusing on case study works and texts. Chapter two presents the exception in its more comprehensive attention to the life and work of Williams, whose artistic career has been analyzed less productively than has a single striking work of fiction he penned, the annals of a British sailor who spends most of his adult life in Central America. Throughout, my book foregrounds the web of evidence on which historians may draw. That makes impossible any strict chronology or seamless narrative, a neat progression from traditional identification of painter as artisan or mechanic to artist as gentleman-intellectual, to a more modernist conception of the artist as genius-eccentric. These types overlapped in a bumpy and contradictory process of artistic self-formation and social definition.

The account I present, furthermore, might seem at first discontinuous for the period under consideration, since I leave the political revolution – though not politics – largely off-stage. The painters who have always been most closely associated with the American War of Independence are Charles Willson Peale and John Trumbull, neither major subjects here though recurrent characters. They were the only two prominent artists of the time to serve in the military, and both experienced career boosts, sooner or later, from that connection. Peale made portraits of military men while camped with George Washington at Valley Forge, which positioned him perfectly to receive a commission for the first life-size portrait of General Washington (1779) at a point when the conflict turned in favor of the Americans. Trumbull spent two years in the army, attaining the rank of colonel. While in West's studio in the mid-1780s he took up the Revolutionary War subjects that West felt he himself could not engage, given his relationship with George III. This is all well-trodden territory.

In my book, three chapters in part one offer differing geographical and professional perspectives on the 1760s, when Americans had little thought that they were anything other than Britons. Part two, also in three chapters, picks up the story around the time of independence with examination of artists as public figures in the new United States and, in the case of Stuart and West, as American artists outside their native country. Narratives of artists – ostensibly factual or wholly fictional – in newspapers, periodicals, monographs, letters, and diaries receive extended analysis in the second half of this book. In consideration of this sometimes fragmentary and fractured record, I show how the writers, and their subjects (in the cases of actual, rather than invented, persons), grappled with the status and role of artists in the new United States. Throughout, Britain presents a social and cultural force to be reckoned with.

Part one opens with the familiar complaint of colonial America's premier portraitist, Bostonian John Singleton Copley, son of an Irish immigrant and stepson of the London-born and trained mezzotint engraver Peter Pelham. Copley felt professionally sidelined in the colonies, at the mercy of customers who regarded painters, or so he complained, as manual workers. The first chapter explores the implications of artisan status for self-identified fine artists in eighteenth-century America and Britain, where even artists in the capital (though Copley did not realize it) harbored similar grievances. Portraitists, like tailors, made bespoke work that catered to individual patrons, so it is revealing to find tailors as a recurrent negative model in eighteenth-century artist narratives. In an effort to redefine their activity as a gentlemanly and liberal art, painters employed varying strategies. I expose Copley's politics of representation through close examination of his refined self-image and his contemporaneous portrait of silversmith Paul Revere (1768). *Revere*, an unusual painting to feature an artisan and his work, perfectly served the cherished (but anachronistic) legend of the patriot as well as American ideals of egalitarianism yet to be fully enacted. My analysis restores this famous picture's complex period meanings, not identical for subject and painter, whose reasons for showing Revere as he did, I argue, were fundamentally conservative, not radical.

If Copley's idealization of artistic life in London aggravated his social anxieties, the example of William Williams, presented in chapter two, offers compelling evidence that not all colonial artists felt so professionally constrained. Williams, a native of Bristol, England, abandoned a mariner's life for painting in late 1740s Philadelphia. Relatively few works survive, but together with fragmentary textual evidence, they attest to a more varied career than the face painting that occupied most British artists. Williams adapted readily to the requirements of provincial artistic practice. He used newspapers to advertise trade-related services, not limited to picture making, and he marked his place of business with a pictorial sign. Signboards have attracted attention from cultural historians; however, given the limited survival rates for early signs, scholars generally focus on nineteenth-century examples and on reception. Sign painters function much as did tailors in the writings of eighteenth-century British easel painters, as targets for invective, an indication that the boundaries between art and trade remained uncomfortably narrow for some. Relying largely on texts, I explore the practice and implications of sign painting for both trade painters and fine artists. Williams employed two different signs – Hogarth's Head, in Philadelphia, and Rembrandt's Head, in New York – to appeal to distinct American constituencies, in consideration of regional identities and tastes. At the same time, Williams's signs addressed an artistic community in London, especially the printsellers who constituted an important professional resource for painters. Reliable evidence indicates that Williams collected engraved portraits of artists and treatises on art. More tantalizingly, he is documented as having compiled a manuscript of artists' lives, a remarkable enterprise given the limited models in English. Williams offers the example of an artist who remained flexible about working within the constraints of the existing Anglo-American system, without relinquishing a broader idea of who or what an artist might be, even if those ambitions remained essentially private. That is not the usual story told of provincial practice in any part of the British empire, and reconstruction of Williams's diverse artistic career is a significant scholarly intervention of this book.

Benjamin West presents a mirrored opposite to Williams, as the first American painter to study in Italy and to pursue a career in England, as well as for his highly public life as history painter to George III and second president of the Royal Academy of Arts. Chapter three opens with West in Italy, in reconsideration of his famous encounter with the *Apollo Belvedere* and of a mostly overlooked self-portrait drawing in which West weighed his professional options. His relocation to London has always seemed fertile for thinking about what it meant to be an American artist during critical decades for British art and for Anglo-American relations generally. I approach the matter through Matthew Pratt's *The American School* (1765), a painting that projected early optimism about the possibilities. Pratt, who had served a traditional trade indenture in Philadelphia, became the first to study in West's London studio; that space and five artist occupants are the apparent subjects of his picture. Overemphasis on West's later success, along with unproductive efforts to identify participants in the scene, long thwarted understanding of *The American School*. The work is allegory, not documentation. On public exhibition in London, Pratt's *American School* projected an affirmative regionalism. As assertively, it envisioned a leading role for American painters within a British school struggling for self-definition. This chapter asks how study in Britain and on the Continent affected West's and Pratt's self-image and status as artists and as Americans, in addition to considering what Britons and Europeans made of them, topics revisited with regard to later decades in the final two chapters.

In part two, chapter four surveys textual accounts of art and artists published in the early United States, where the role of fine art remained unstable and contested. Unattributed anecdotes about artists peppered American magazines, helping to shape public expectations about painters, while portraits and portraiture provided several men of letters a frame for satirical expression of political concerns. Anecdote, satire, and pointed political end collectively fueled a rare extended example of early writing that engaged the figure of artist, my focus in this chapter. "The Limner" (an archaic term for portraitist) appeared as a series of letters, running from 1804 to 1807, in which the pseudonymous portraitist "Peter Pallet" addresses the editor of the *Balance*, a Federalist weekly published in Hudson, New York. Their author was in fact the paper's editor himself, Harry Croswell, whose motivation to compose "The Limner" arose from his recent conviction for libel against President Jefferson for publications in Croswell's satirical paper, the *Wasp*. In "The Limner," Croswell framed a partisan argument in terms of the issue of truth in portraiture, a matter of abiding interest around 1800. In the process, he reveals much about portrait methods and terminology, sitter expectations and behavior, and the personae of artists.

Without question, the most celebrated artist of the early republic was Gilbert Stuart, an accomplished portraitist whose likenesses of Washington and other political leaders remain lodged indelibly in our national imagination. Yet against his catalog of sober republican faces and at odds with his artistic authority, Stuart toyed with traditional expectations for artists at both ends of the spectrum, from artisan-painter to civic-minded gentleman-artist. In the process, he cultivated a distinctly different identity. Stuart alternately delighted and vexed his acquaintances, who related many stories about him, sometimes repeating tales he told them. While most of these accounts have appeared repeatedly in the secondary literature, chapter five brings critical attention to the thicket of textual and anecdotal evidence surrounding Stuart, an artist who, unlike the other major figures in this study, left almost no firsthand writing (probably having produced very little). He did leave an abundant visual record in hundreds of portraits. These have received varying degrees of scrutiny, often with a focus on the subjects, hardly surprising in view of the artist's illustrious clientele. I offer close examination of a few, with an eye to what they reveal of Stuart's professional and artistic subversions.

William Dunlap's inclusive 1834 *History of the Rise and Progress of the Arts of Design in the United States* noted the contributions to early American art of Williams, Pratt, and their (from his perspective) artisanal brotherhood, while honoring the superior talents of Copley, Stuart, and John Trumbull, if not always their character. Dunlap reserved greatest distinction for West, despite that artist's permanent departure from America in 1760 and his fifty years in service to the British king. The sixth chapter analyzes the process by which West became "American." For Dunlap, once a student of West's, the senior painter's steady mentoring of American artists contributed greatly to his distinction. So did West's lifelong commitment to history painting, the noblest genre according to academic ideals to which Dunlap, an officer in the ambitiously constituted National Academy of Design (founded 1825), fundamentally subscribed. In considering West's resuscitation as American, this chapter focuses on the decisive role played by his biography, *The Life and Studies of Benjamin West, Esq.* (1816), a collaboration between the artist and Scottish writer John Galt. I examine why West, after a lifetime of withholding details about his youth, authorized a book devoted entirely to his formation. His sinking reputation in Britain gave him the motivation, but the initial stimulus came from West's coincidental reencounter with the story of Williams – literally, since what West encountered was not Williams himself but the castaway narrative penned by his versatile former teacher and presumed by West to be at least partly true. I further analyze the value of West's biographical project to its nominal author Galt, a prolific writer of then unfocused talents, who would soon become famous for ironic, fictive autobiographies featuring provincial Scottish characters. Neither Galt nor West, as they were occasionally reminded, was English, and that slightly marginalized position, which they experienced in different ways, drew them together. Finally, I track the reception of the biography in Britain and the United States and trace its effects on West's reputation, beginning with Dunlap's *History* and ending in our own time.

In a book concerned with professional discourses, those with severely limited paths to professional standing have only minor roles. The problematic status of women artists in the profession as it developed in Western Europe during the Renaissance, widely acknowledged by scholars, far exceeds the geographical and chronological boundaries of *The American School*. In eighteenth-century Britain, Swiss native Angelica Kauffmann presents the most visible exception, gaining early admission to the Royal Academy of Arts, as did one other woman, Mary Moser. In a group portrait of the academicians, styled as a conversation piece of artists around a nude male model, Kauffmann and Moser appeared through the surrogate of (imaginary) portraits on the wall. Contemporary notions of decency made their physical presence among the men unthinkable, exposing one of the constraints imposed on women's success in a profession that identified study from life as a foundational practice. Moser, accordingly, specialized in still life painting, a genre of little regard. Male colleagues had more difficulty overlooking Kauffmann, who won commissions as a history painter, placing her in company with West and a select group of others.[15]

The few women in eighteenth-century colonial America who engaged in fine arts practices did so almost exclusively by making portraits, just like their male counterparts, who in that sense were constrained relative to continental fine artists. Women, however, worked disproportionately in pastel or miniature, which required less equipment than painting on canvas in the Old Master medium of oil and had as well much lesser status. In chapter one, when discussing Copley's pastel self-portrait, I reflect on the deleterious gendering of pastels as a female medium. The same could be said for portraiture as a whole, at least from the academic perspective. As a condition of their genre, portraitists necessarily addressed particularities, with no need (or so academic theorists argued) to engage the higher faculty of abstraction, an ability thought deficient in women – and in working men, according to ideas dating to antiquity, also a topic in the first chapter. Yet for women artists, the very act of taking a likeness presented difficulties that both they and male sitters acknowledged. The influential writer and lexicographer Samuel Johnson sat for a portrait to Frances Reynolds, sister of the Royal Academy's first president, Sir Joshua Reynolds, but he nevertheless considered the "Public practice of staring in men's faces . . . inconsistent with delicacy."[16] Miniature portraits, commonly watercolor on ivory, belonged to a more private sphere, often worn close to the body by both women and men. American Polly Rench painted miniatures to help support her widowed mother and young brother, according to her fellow Marylander Charles Willson Peale, who evidently felt compelled to explain why she painted at all. Still, as he recalled, Rench gave up the practice after marrying because it had proved "very disagreable to her to be stare[ing] in the face of gentlemen as she thought it savored of impudance."[17] Among Americans of the time, sculptor Patience Wright stands alone as a woman artist with a public presence, through the entrepreneurial but not entirely dignified or professionally sanctioned display of modeled wax heads on clothed mannequins, a popular amusement at some remove from the more high-toned exhibitions of the Royal Academy and its predecessor institutions.[18] Wright makes an appearance in chapter five, in discussion of the feminizing implications of a portrait that Stuart painted of West when all three were in London. But Wright will not be a major figure here, an exception in numerous respects, even within a narrative that is not always tidy.

Persons of African birth or descent in eighteenth- and early nineteenth-century America were even less likely to become artists than were women. Frederick Douglass appeared to acknowledge as much when, at mid-nineteenth century, he decried the difficulty for a black sitter of obtaining an unexaggerated likeness: "Artists, like all other white persons, have adopted a theory respecting the distinctive features of negro physiognomy."[19] Some surviving portraits of black men and women by white artists in early America show greater sensitivity than Douglass allowed, though he had good reason to complain. Yet Douglass's implicit assumption that only faithful copying of nature yields a good portrait is ironic in view of contrary arguments by portraitists themselves, while physiognomic theories shaped the representation of white sitters too (albeit usually in their favor). More strikingly, Douglass's syntax licenses reading the category of "artists" as subsumed by "all other white persons," as if there were no possibility for non-whites to claim the name of "Artist." In that he was barely exaggerating.

The earliest evidence for a black artist in British colonial North America is both anomalous and anonymous: a Boston advertisement of 1773 for a "Negro Man whose extraordinary Genius has been assisted by one of the best Masters in *London*; he takes Faces at the lowest Rates."[20] The portrait trade in Boston was then monopolized by Copley, who charged high prices but had not yet been abroad, so the man's combined African ancestry and British training (or access to someone trained in London) set him apart as an exotic – and affordable – commodity. The truth and effectiveness of the advertisement cannot be gauged, so long as the identity of the artist remains obscure.[21] In any case, Boston patrons would not have regarded a black man as more than a skilled artisan, an entrenched but undesired connection for white eighteenth-century artists as well, which they sought to disrupt. Stuart revealed key criteria in the definition of "artist" in striking remarks concerning a man of color. As a child in Newport, he had learned to draw by watching an enslaved African named Neptune Thurston chalk facial expressions on the top of a barrel. Thurston himself is supposed to have made the claim locally after Stuart became well known, and Stuart confirmed it late in life, adding: "if that African's mind and natural talent had been properly cultivated, he would have made a much more celebrated artist than his pupil."[22] "Properly cultivated" meant acquisition of professional artistic training and affiliation, somewhat ironic in view of Stuart's posture, when it suited him, of having no other master than nature. That claim had acquired wide value by the later eighteenth century among professionally trained artists, and those who were not trained took advantage of it (as I discuss in chapter four). In an advertisement of 1798, Baltimore artist Joshua Johnson (sometimes Johnston) pronounced himself "a *self-taught genius*, deriving from nature and industry his knowledge of the Art" of portrait painting. Johnson, now believed to be a free man of mixed race, controlled his own labor and presentation and made no mention of his race, except perhaps obliquely in asserting that he had overcome "many insuperable obstacles in the pursuit of his studies" (white artists made such claims as well).[23] Scholars have had considerable difficulty in documenting Johnson's racial identity.[24] Some evidence suggests that contemporaries, including patrons who were overwhelmingly white, assumed Johnson was white as well. If so, they may have literally overlooked him because he was an artist, an unlikely occupation for a black man.

Every center has margins. The most relevant for those who sought professional status as artists in the late colonial and early national era was artisanry – a paradox since artisans vastly outnumbered fine artists and by any other historical measure could hardly be considered marginal. Artisanal producers and productions that impinged on ideals of artists and artistry as developed during these decades therefore play a relatively large role in this book, especially in chapters one, two, and four. Painting as a trade constitutes the near and pervasive background against which American (and British) fine artists sought to distinguish themselves. My book provides no latter-day assistance in shoring up those artists' reputations. Instead, I draw out the instability of professional status and the changing strategies by which artists sought to secure it.

The American artist of this period whose image management has arguably been most transparent, in part because it took so many different forms, is Charles Willson Peale. Peale "seems to have wished to play every part in life's drama," as Dunlap put it, and this has made him irresistible to twentieth- and twenty-first-century historians and art historians.[25] Yet Dunlap thought Peale spread himself too thin and had more the "perseverance and industry" of an artisan than the genius of a true artist; in 1834, he predicted that Peale would "soon be forgotten." For roughly a century he was, until James Thomas Flexner elevated Peale as one of four American "Old Masters," along with the more obvious candidates West, Copley, and Stuart.[26] Flexner did so in part owing to his friendship with Charles Coleman Sellers, a Peale descendant and the artist's would-be biographer, who held a vast trove of family papers. Sellers shared that documentation with Flexner, whose narrative of Peale in *America's Old Masters* (1939) in turn helped Sellers find a publisher for his study.[27] Sellers's eventual gift of the documents to the National Portrait Gallery, Smithsonian Institution, led to establishment in 1974 of an office committed to mining and publishing that material. The Peale papers offered an unmatched resource for the life and times of an eighteenth- and early nineteenth-century artist-entrepreneur and his family, many of whom he groomed as artists. With microfiche availability as of 1980, the floodgates opened to what Peale scholar David Steinberg referred in 2001 as "the interdisciplinary nexus that might be called Peale studies."[28]

Peale's life resonates with most of the themes and persons considered in this book. A sketch of the ways in which that was so will suffice here to reintroduce this familiar artist, who makes appearances in every chapter but on whom I have otherwise chosen not to shine a spotlight. Peale began his working life on solidly artisanal ground, with a traditional trade indenture, though in saddle making not painting. In that sense Peale was more like Williams, the young mariner diverted from a course on which he had initially set, than like Pratt, bound to a painter-in-general at fifteen, or Copley, who at about the same age adopted his recently deceased English stepfather's occupation of artist. Peale broadened his artisanal range to upholstery and metal work and, under financial pressure, took his trades on the road, as he would continue to do during his painting career. The sight of some "miserably done" landscape and portrait paintings in Virginia aroused Peale's can-do attitude and led him to approach the more skilled, second-generation colonial painter John Hesselius with a proposition: a top-quality saddle in exchange for the opportunity to watch Hesselius at work.[29] From that experience, Peale concluded he could become a painter as well. At first, and as part of notices for his saddler's business, he advertised sign painting, an aspect of the trade to which Williams remained open; but Peale quickly decided that portraiture offered better income and prospects for rising in the world. He had already helped himself along by marrying into a prominent Maryland family, an alliance that required all of his ingenuity and perseverance to pull off. That connection proved instrumental to his development as a painter rather than resulting from it, as for Copley, whose prominence and connections as an artist made his advantageous marriage possible. (The widowed Peale's occupation, despite greatly increased stature, did not serve him well in a failed courtship of 1790.) Through his in-laws, young Peale gained benefactors who sent him across the Atlantic in the expectation that metropolitan experience would aid him professionally and financially, while better preparing the artist to serve their interests.

Unlike Copley, who dreamed of fame as a historical painter for two long decades before he left Boston in pursuit of that goal, Peale had no such simmering desire. In London and in West's studio by 1767, soon after Pratt, he gained full exposure to professional possibilities yet initially decided to pursue miniature painting. The decision was not unreasonable. Miniatures were newly fashionable in England during the 1760s, owing much to Queen Charlotte's taste for them, while their relative affordability

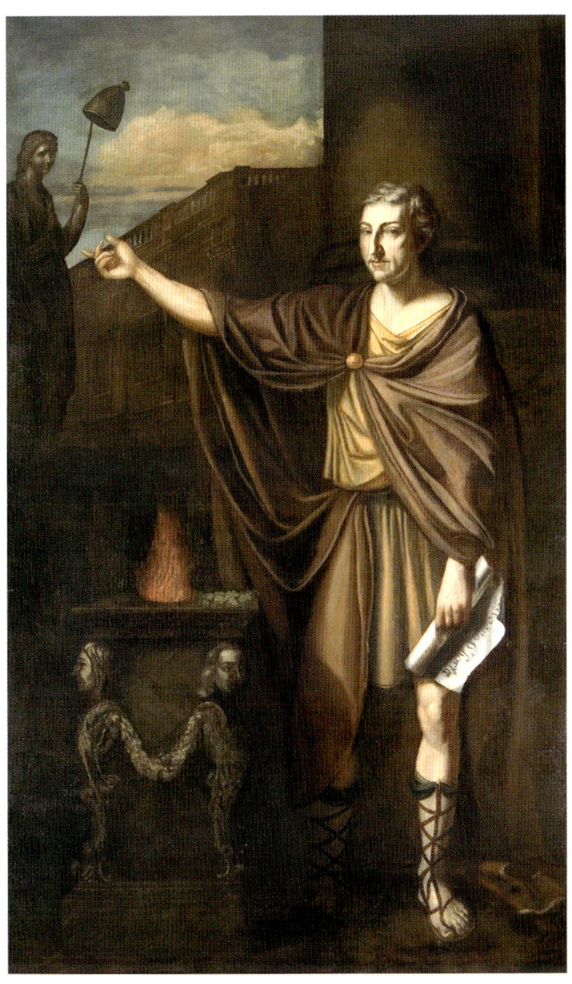

1 Charles Willson Peale, *William Pitt*, 1768. Oil on canvas, 94 × 57 in. (238.76 × 144.78 cm). Collection of the Maryland State Archives, Annapolis (MSA SC 1545–1113).

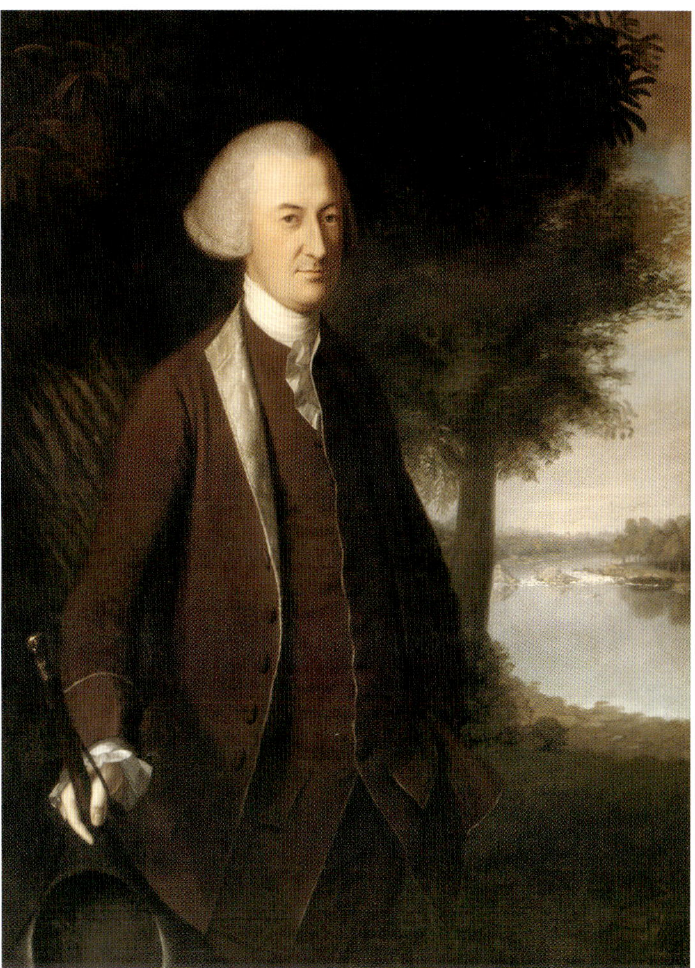

2 Charles Willson Peale, *John Dickinson*, 1770. Oil on canvas, 49 × 39¼ in. (124.46 × 99.69 cm). Courtesy of the Philadelphia History Museum at the Atwater Kent, Historical Society of Pennsylvania Collection.

promised a broader base of customers than for portraits in oil. Peale continued to paint miniatures throughout his career, but his Maryland patrons did not consider such work a good return on their investment in him. They urged him to consider "Larger Portrait Painting" as a "Branch of the Profession that would Turn out to Greater Profit here" and to study history painting, even though it represented "the most Difficult Part of the Profession."[30] Accordingly, in 1768, Peale made a life-size classicizing portrait of William Pitt, British statesman and defender of American liberties (fig. 1). It was his first major painting commission and the basis for a mezzotint engraving, but neither was well received – except by Copley, for whom the print and accompanying broadside (sent him by the artist) offered yet another occasion to lament his own lack of opportunity.[31] Copley did not know that Peale had quickly retreated: upon return home after two years in London, Peale advertised in the *Maryland Gazette* (June 8, 1769) as a "Limner."

With ambitious sitters close at hand, Peale soon resumed making large-scale portraits, now tailored to American tastes for more straightforward and evidently empirical representation. Lawyer John Dickinson – celebrated as the "American Pitt" for defending American rights in letters from "A Farmer" which were widely reprinted in colonial newspapers – appeared in a plain brown suit against a rustic natural setting (fig. 2).[32] "I do not regrett the Loss of the Anticks, or the works of a Raphael and Corregea," Peale explained to a friend and patron, "since I am obliged dayly to portray the finest forms" in nature.[33] Stuart, too, shunned history

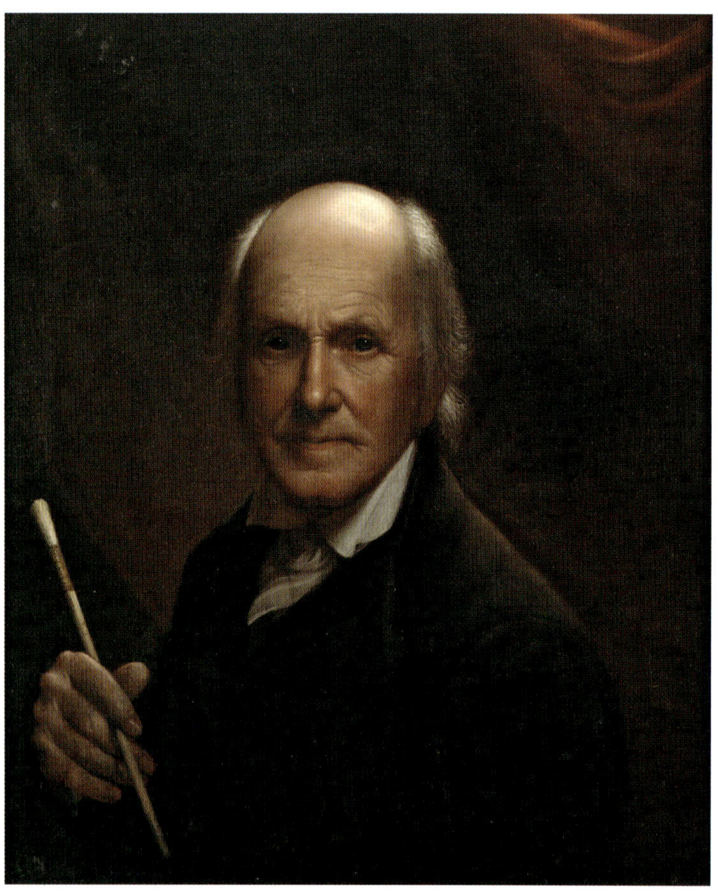

3 Charles Willson Peale, *Self-Portrait in the Character of a Painter*, 1824. Oil on canvas, 26¼ × 22⅛ in. (66.68 × 56.20 cm). Acc. No. 1845.5. Courtesy of the Pennsylvania Academy of the Fine Arts, Philadelphia, gift of the Artist (probably in 1824).

painting for portraiture, avowed nature as a guide, and received high praise from patrons for his ability to capture likeness. But his American career began in 1793, when he returned from seventeen years in England and Ireland. By that time, Peale had produced 686 portraits, including many miniatures, his primary occupation in the contracted marketplace for painters of the revolutionary years. The emergence in the 1780s of the United States, a nation without precedent, prompted Peale to commit himself to systematic portrayal of American "worthies," likenesses displayed in a gallery he built for the purpose. During the period following Copley's departure and prior to Stuart's return, Peale staked out his position as the new nation's leading portraitist. Yet even then, the practical Peale, more than others in this study, accepted the conditions of itinerancy often associated with artisan painters who travelled regionally in search of business.[34] In 1794, he publicly announced retirement from portrait painting, relinquished in favor of his artist sons Raphaelle and Rembrandt Peale and so as to reinvent himself in a larger context, as a naturalist and founder-proprietor of the most significant American museum of the early republic.[35] Desire to expand the range of portraits in his museum eventually led Peale to resume the practice and with something to prove: "I think it important to shew that at the age of 63 I could paint as good a portrait as I could at 50 years of age," Peale wrote in 1804, at a time when Stuart's dominance had raised the bar considerably; "the fire of youth is not equal to matured Idea's in the fine arts."[36]

Peale's late life reckoning with his legacy preoccupied him in both word and image. Between 1821 and 1824, he made six self-portraits, among eighteen spanning his entire career (excluding multi-figure works in which he included himself).[37] Interestingly, Peale had resisted Stuart's proposal, in 1804, to portray him, an offer couched in terms that Peale likely considered boastful: "he believed he would paint a better portrait of me than yet was done – that altho' . . . [I] had often essayed to take my own likeness, yet that done by another artist would give a more faithful expression."[38] Peale did not relish the prospect of being outdone by Stuart. Twenty years later, when making his *Self-Portrait in the Character of a Painter* (1824) – which he gave to the Pennsylvania Academy of the Fine Arts – Peale in effect answered Stuart with a rhetorical question, framed in a letter to his son: "why should I not (in a simple portrait) make as good an imitation as any other man?" (fig. 3).[39]

The artist's relentless self-documentation and self-revision extended to the written record. In 1825 and 1826, Peale composed an autobiographical manuscript that drew on his earlier such account of 1790 and on diaries and correspondence kept and maintained over more than six decades. While he intended the work for publication, Peale felt insecure about his abilities as a writer and expressed a wish that his text – which he called a biography or "novel" – be shaped by "a good penman."[40] Perhaps he hoped to find a Galt, whose life of West bore a title page expressly indicating its basis in materials furnished by the subject. Had he succeeded, Peale would have been only the second American artist to have a monograph devoted to him. His descendant Sellers played biographer a century later. Then, in 2004, historian and deputy editor of the Peale papers David Ward published *Charles Willson Peale: Art and Selfhood in the Early Republic*, a provocative study of Peale's image management.[41] Ward's fine-grained analysis of Peale's constant self-invention and his attentiveness to the performative quality of

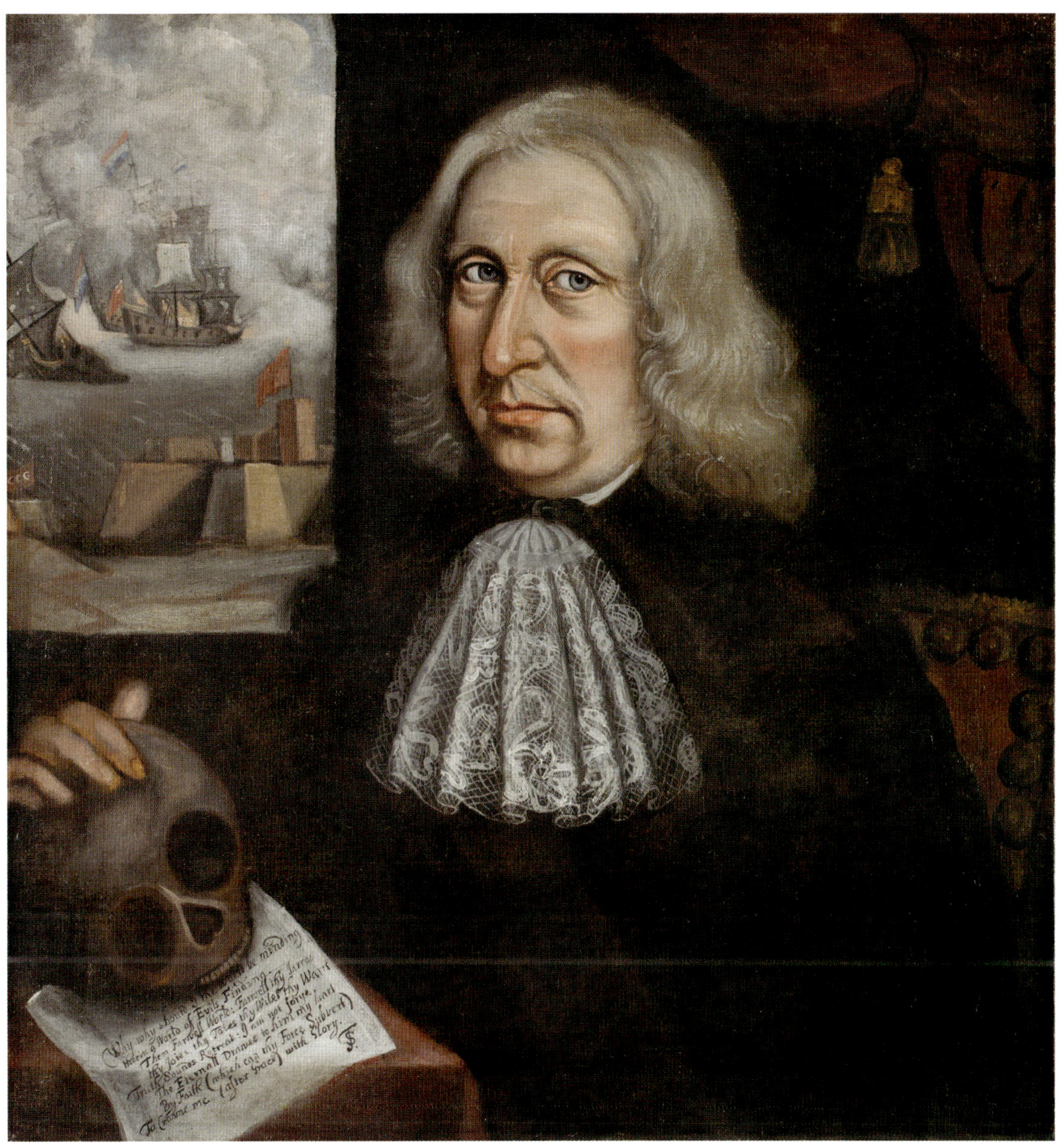

4 Thomas Smith, *Self Portrait*, ca. 1680–90. Oil on canvas, 24¾ × 23¾ in. (62.9 × 60.3 cm). Worcester Art Museum, Worcester, Mass., museum purchase, 1948.19. Image © Worcester Art Museum.

Peale's life makes my task easier. His book, the abundant Peale scholarship, and the published primary source material (the latter my principal source for Peale as he appears in this book) obviate the need to give the artist extended attention. When Peale is not the focus, it may yet be possible to see him from a different perspective, both like and unlike others of his colleagues, as he surfaces in successive chapters of *The American School*.

Although no American artist approached Peale's level of pictorial self-scrutiny, the principal painters in this book all made self-portraits, and these receive due consideration in the course of my broader inquiry into the representation of artists. The history of self-portraiture in British colonial America is almost as old as the documented history of painting. The first American example also represents the first colonial artist for whom we have both work and a name: Thomas Smith (fig. 4). Documents provide names for painters active during the colonial period, but the infrequency of signatures on paintings complicates attribution. Artisan-makers entertained no modernist claims of authorship at a time

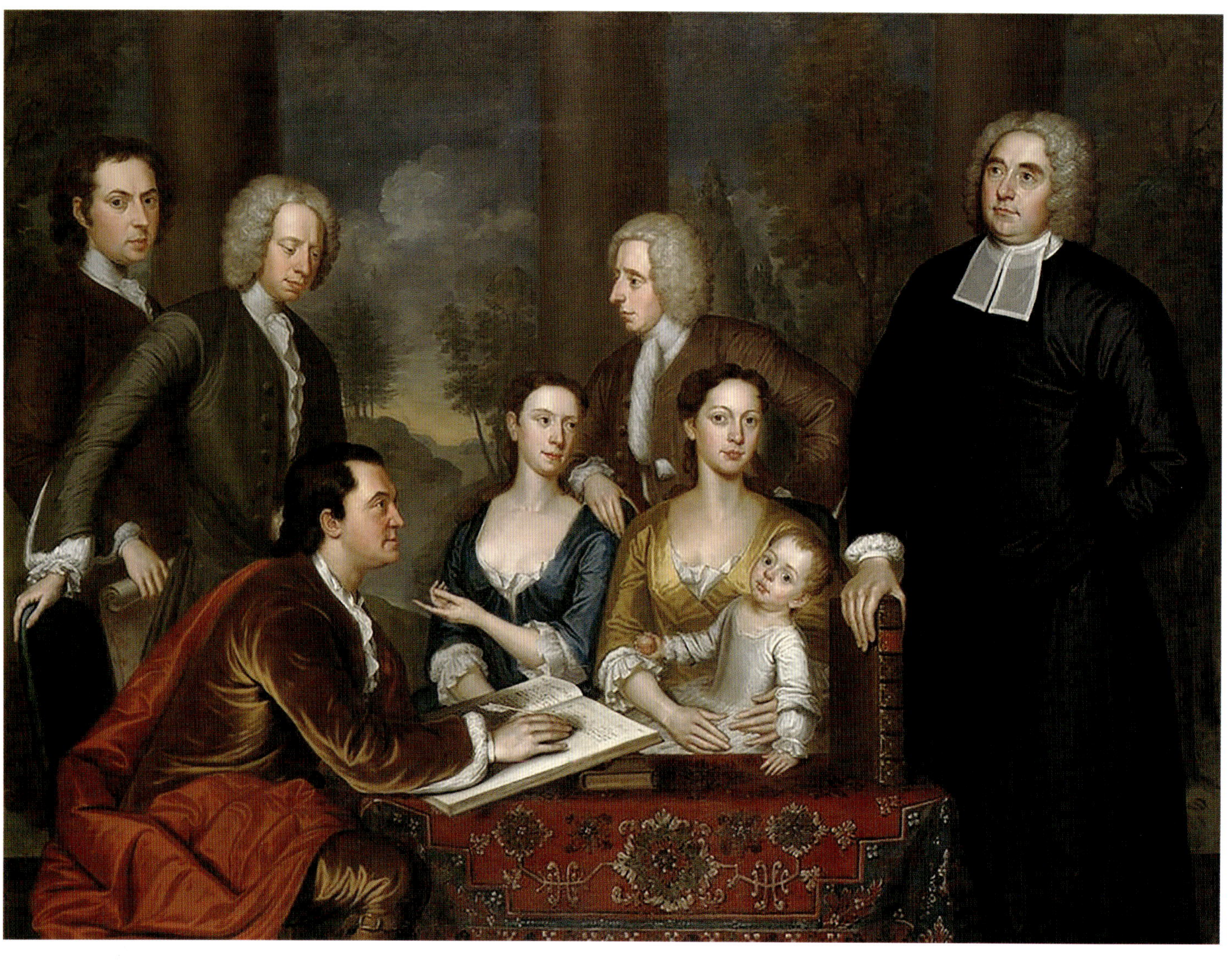

5 John Smibert, *The Bermuda Group (Dean George Berkeley and his Entourage)*, begun 1728, completed 1739. Oil on canvas, 69½ × 93 in. (176.5 × 236.2 cm). Yale University Art Gallery, New Haven, gift of Isaac Lothrop (1808.1).

when portraits were identified much more strongly with sitter-patrons. "Hands" (an appropriate term when names are elusive) can often be distinguished on stylistic grounds, as in the presumed self-portrait and a group of other works made in Boston after 1680, when Harvard College records document payment to a Major Thomas Smith for copying a portrait of Puritan minister William Ames.[42] The initials TS in the self-portrait appear at the end of a poem depicted on a sheet of paper, referring most directly to authorship of that text. As Roger Stein argued, the poem presents a "cognitive map" to this unusually complex painting, with its array of vanitas emblems – most conspicuously a skull – that collectively signal the sitter's preparedness to say "farewell" (a word repeated in the short poem) to his earthly body for eternal life in the Christian hereafter.[43] If the vignette of a maritime battle refers to an experience from Smith's past, it also, Stein proposed, emblematizes the trials of life, both secular and religious, which the poem quite directly addresses. The stylistic currency of Smith's depiction of his own person, painterly and plastic relative to the Elizabethan neo-medieval style of Boston portraits from the preceding decade, belies the conceptual roots of his self-portrait in an older emblematic tradition.[44]

The second quarter of the eighteenth century offered new evidence that artists could be persons of interest and social value in their own right, not coincidentally in connection with painters who also portrayed themselves. John Smibert (1688–1751) underwent traditional trade apprenticeship to a house painter in his native Edinburgh before moving to London. There, in due course, he studied at the first (and relatively short-lived) academy for fine arts in Britain, organized under the aegis of court painter Sir Godfrey Kneller. That German-born, Dutch-trained painter was just one of many continental artists who dominated painting at the highest levels in England from the seventeenth through almost mid-eighteenth century. Smibert's relocation from province to metropolis and his transition from artisan to professional would be repeated by many a British and American painter. His subsequent three years in Italy were then truly uncommon for British artists, forty years before West became the first American-born painter to follow suit. By the early 1720s, Smibert had embarked on a successful portrait practice in London. These distinctions won him an invitation from the Anglican cleric and philosopher Dean George Berkeley to become professor of fine arts at a college Berkeley planned to establish in Bermuda. Berkeley's party made it to Newport, Rhode Island, before funding evaporated, but Smibert, determined to capitalize on an underserved market, decided to remain in New England. He settled in Boston, where his large commemorative group portrait, now known as *The Bermuda Group*, remained on prominent display in his studio until almost the end of the century (fig. 5). Along with Berkeley and six others, Smibert depicted himself, looking out toward the viewer. In his hand, a partially unfurled scroll bears a sketch of trees, a counterpoint to the illusion of the painting, as Margaretta Lovell has compellingly argued, and a reference to the conceptual dimension of the art.[45]

New Englanders took notice of Smibert upon his arrival, the first time an artist had attracted so much attention in the colonies. Mather Byles composed a long poetic tribute in 1730, in the vein of Alexander Pope's epistle to London portraitist Charles Jervas from the 1716 edition of Charles Du Fresnoy's *Art of Painting*, an aesthetic treatise with documented presence in colonial America. Byles's poem appeared in a Philadelphia newspaper before being picked up by a paper in London, from which Smibert had not long been absent.[46] Smibert showed Americans what sophisticated metropolitan artistic practice looked like. He painted in a style that was up-to-date as of the time of his departure from England. He attracted numerous patrons, recording their names, canvas sizes, and prices paid in a notebook that has facilitated identification of a body of work that is rarely signed.[47] Finally, he filled his studio with his painted copies

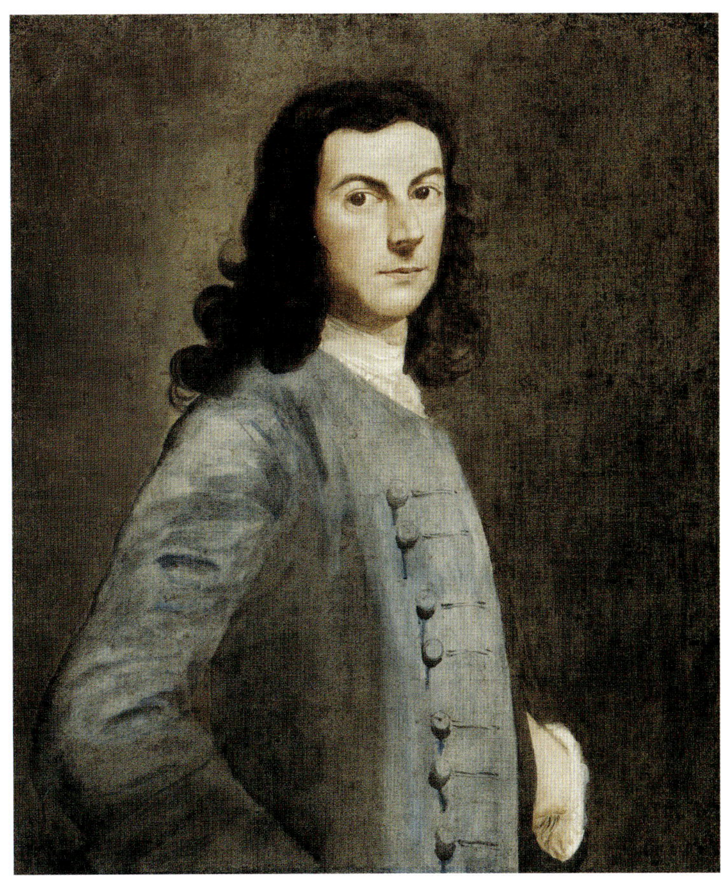

6 Robert Feke, *Self-Portrait*, about 1741–45. Oil on canvas mounted on aluminum, 29¾ × 25⅞ in. (75.56 × 65.72 cm). Museum of Fine Arts, Boston, M. and M. Karolik Fund, 1970.499.

of European masterworks, sculptural casts from the antique, and mezzotint prints – all shipped across the Atlantic for use at the college. Even so, Smibert resorted to trade, running a "color shop" for the sale of painters' materials, which he had to import for his own use but probably found necessary to sell when painting failed to support even him.

After Smibert's activity as a portraitist slowed dramatically in the 1740s, Long Island-born Robert Feke (ca. 1707–ca. 1751) stepped into the breach, working up and down the eastern seaboard during the later part of that decade. Although some sixty portraits are attributed to him, twelve signed, his life remains for the most part a mystery.[48] Yet Feke – who made two self-portraits – has the distinction of being one of the earliest artists to attract description (fig. 6).[49] In 1744, the Scottish physician and travel diarist Dr. Alexander Hamilton met Feke in Newport, Rhode Island. Hamilton thought the painter "the most extraordinary genius ever I knew, for he does pictures tollerably well

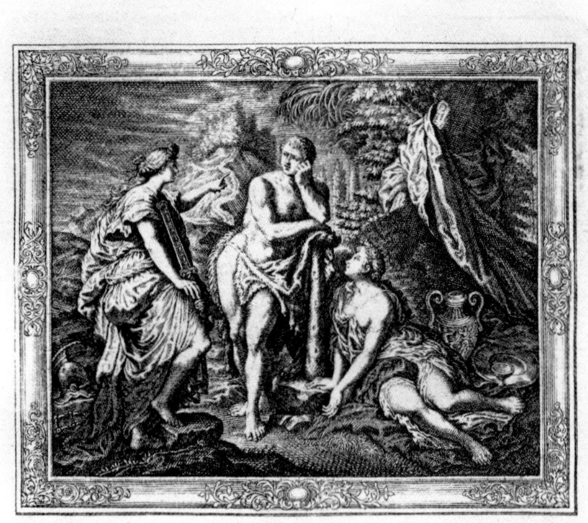

Paulo de Matthæis Pinx: **THE** *Sim: Gribelin ſculps:*

Judgment of *Hercules.*

INTRODUCTION.

(1.) BEFORE we enter on the Examination of our Hiſtorical Sketch, it may be proper to remark, that by the word *Tablature* (for which we have yet no name in *Engliſh*, beſides the general one of *Picture*) we denote, according to the original word TABULA, a Work not only diſtinct from a mere *Portraiture*, but from all thoſe wilder ſorts of Painting which

Vol. 3. [Z 3] are

7 Simon Gribelin after Paolo de Matteis, frontispiece to Shaftesbury, "The Judgment of Hercules," *Characteristicks of Men, Manners, Opinions, Times* (1737, vol. 3). Photo: Harry Ransom Humanities Research Center, University of Texas, Austin.

by the force of genius, having never had any teaching. I saw a large table of the Judgement of Hercules, copied by him from a frontispiece of the Earl of Shaftesbury's, which I thought very well done. This man had exactly the phizz [the look or appearance] of a painter, having a long pale face, sharp nose, large eyes with which he looked upon you stedfastly, long curled black hair, a delicate white hand, and long fingers."[50] Feke's self-portrait seems to show exactly what Hamilton observed, as has been often remarked, but the doctor's comments bear greater scrutiny.

First, Hamilton recognized Feke as an untutored genius. The word genius in this context referred to "natural ability or capacity" more than "exalted" or "extraordinary capacity for imaginative creation," a sense that originated in England at around the time he wrote.[51] Hamilton's reference to Feke's genius acknowledged provincial realities, since formal training was hard to come by. Similarly, an obituary for painter Nathaniel Emmons, of Boston, had noted in 1740 that "his excellent Works were the pure Effects of his own Genius, without receiving any Instructions from Others."[52] Still, the identification of "genius" in those circumstances foreshadows an enduring characterization of American artists (not least by themselves) as unconstrained by isolation or even aided by it, as in the memorable story of West's boyhood that West and Galt crafted in 1816. By that time, as will be evident with Stuart, genius had acquired the more rarefied meaning so often, in the Romantic context, coupled with eccentricity.

Second, in writing of his encounter with Feke, Hamilton made no mention of portraits, any Anglophone artist's bread and butter and the only works by Feke to survive, though most date after their 1744 encounter. What drew Hamilton's attention was a historical "table" copied from the frontispiece to Shaftesbury's "A Notion of the Historical Draught or Tablature of the Judgment of Hercules," as first published in the revised (and often reprinted) edition of *Characteristicks of Men, Manners, Opinions, Times* (1714) (fig. 7). At the start of the essay, Shaftesbury explains his use of the word tablature to distinguish a work of cohesive meaning and design from "mere *Portraiture*." While he concedes that a successful portrait or any other "inferiour" type of painting must have "*Unity of Design*," he identified a much greater challenge in history painting in which "not only *Men*, but *Manners*, and human Passions are represented."[53] The most telling moment in the story of Hercules at the crossroads is when he turns his attention away from the entreaties of Pleasure and toward the argument of Virtue, in a painting that allegorizes civic responsibility. Painters had by long tradition been thought incapable of independent judgment (a matter considered in detail in chapter one), and Shaftesbury intended to dictate every aspect of the tablature of Hercules to the artist he commissioned, Paolo de Matteis; he recognized the Neapolitan history painter as "an eminent master . . . the best now in Italy," but that distinction was still relative to Shaftesbury's own, as a gentleman. Afterwards seeking an autograph copy of the resulting painting, Shaftesbury attempted to flatter de Matteis, calling the first work the product of "your Idea and your hand" despite his own close management of the outcome.[54] Shaftesbury's words, however insincere, indicate that he was not oblivious to the claims of artists – which de Matteis expressed in a number of elaborately conceived self-portraits – even when attempting to impose his own superior ideas. For Shaftesbury, even so, de Matteis and engraver Simon Gribelin, whose print after the tablature of Hercules was made to accompany the earl's text, were hardly more than hands.

For Dr. Hamilton, finally, Feke is both a mind – "extraordinary genius" – and a hand. In his description of the painter, Hamilton did not neglect Feke's "delicate white hand, and long fingers," or other features that made Feke look as Hamilton thought a painter should. That included the steadfast gaze from notably large eyes, which the artist accentuated by illuminating his face fully. Forty years before widespread revival of interest in physiognomy as a way of judging character through analysis of facial and bodily features, the observant physician thought he recognized the "phizz of a painter." Close to mid-century, then, Anglo-American artists began to gain an identity distinct from that of other men.

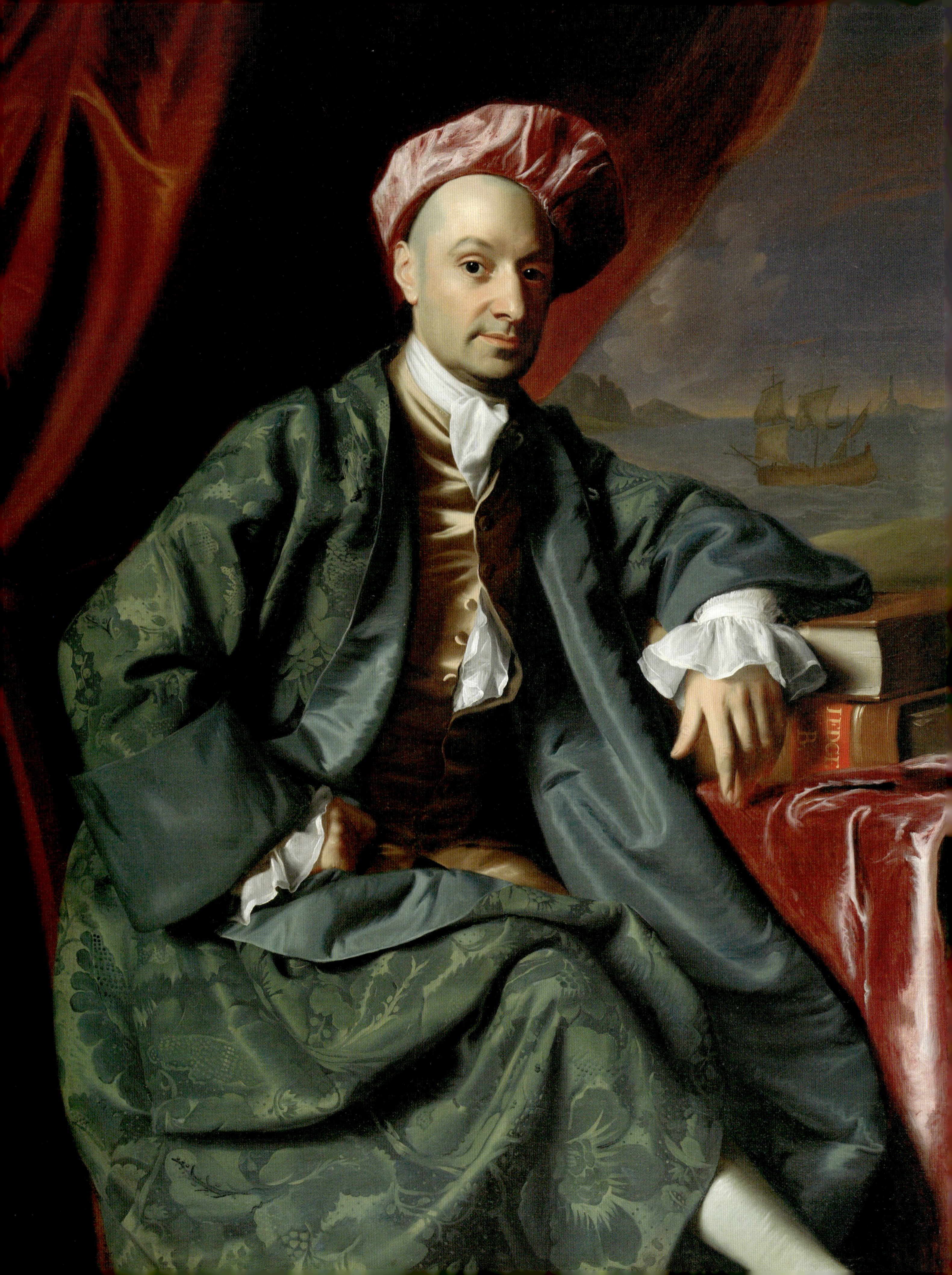

I

PORTRAIT PAINTING AND STATUS IN BOSTON AND LONDON

> We may observe in general, that as the power of INVENTION is the distinguishing ingredient of ORIGINAL GENIUS in all the fine arts, as well as in Science; so, in whatever degree INVENTION is displayed in either of these, in the same degree ORIGINALITY of Genius will always be discovered. This distinction will exclude all PORTRAITS in painting, however excellent, . . . from any pretensions to originality, strictly considered.
>
> [William Duff], *An Essay on Original Genius* (London, 1767)

> A taste of painting is too much Wanting . . . was it not for preserving the resemble[n]ce of perticular persons, painting would not be known in the plac[e]. The people generally regard it no more than any other usefull trade, as they sometimes term it, like that of a Carpenter tailor, or shew maker, not as one of the most noble Arts in the World.
>
> John Singleton Copley, Boston [1767?]

Writing to a correspondent in England, portraitist and Massachusetts native John Singleton Copley (1738–1815) lamented the lack of regard for painting among his fellow Bostonians, who for the most part limited their patronage to the relatively utilitarian art of portraiture.[1] At the same time, he rued their failure to concede that painters might merit higher status than common tradesmen. Such elevation, promoted by art theorists and in elite circles since the Renaissance, rested on the argument that historical subjects (biblical, mythological, historical, and allegorical) required intellect and imagination. Copley's dissatisfaction was a gauge of the ambition that helped to make him colonial America's premier painter, but that also led him, in 1774, to abandon an American career of nearly two decades for what he felt certain would be the artistically more supportive climate of London.

Historically, the American Copley and the English Copley have been considered almost as two different painters (figs. 8, 9). Americanist art historians distinctly preferred his colonial works, typically judged more authentic and American (synonyms for some writers), although they granted quarter to the early history paintings of his London career, notably *Watson and the Shark*, a shocking scene set in the New World (fig. 10). British scholars, by contrast, paid Copley

Facing page Detail of fig. 20.

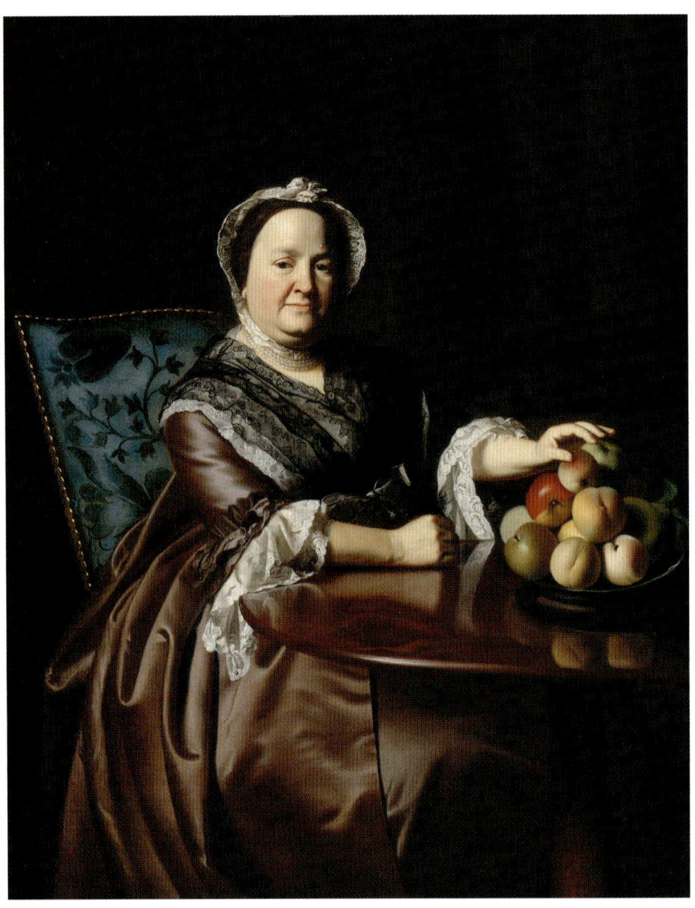

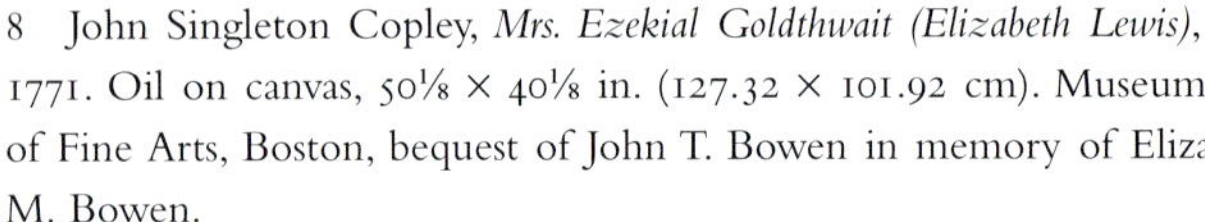

8 John Singleton Copley, *Mrs. Ezekial Goldthwait (Elizabeth Lewis)*, 1771. Oil on canvas, 50⅛ × 40⅛ in. (127.32 × 101.92 cm). Museum of Fine Arts, Boston, bequest of John T. Bowen in memory of Eliza M. Bowen.

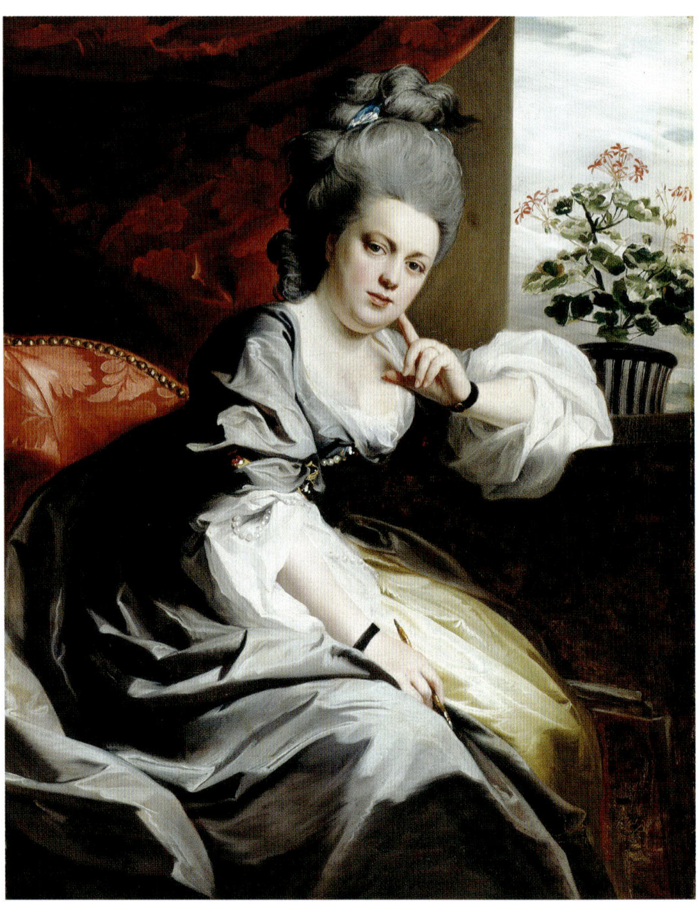

9 John Singleton Copley, *Mrs. Clark Gayton*, 1779. Oil on canvas, 50 × 40 in. (127 × 101.6 cm). Detroit Institute of Arts, gift of Mr. D. J. Healy / Bridgeman Images.

relatively little attention, though his London career lasted twice as long as his working life in Boston, a period of four decades during which he never recrossed the Atlantic.[2] When he left at thirty-five, Copley was formed as a man, and the more competitive artistic environment of the metropolis only allowed his own competitiveness to emerge more fully, ingeniously even, in the single-picture exhibitions he pioneered. As an artist in England, Copley managed to paint history (if less exclusively than he would have liked), but whether he changed much as a painter, subject matter notwithstanding, is open to question.[3] Although Copley's years in England are not at issue in this chapter, his "Englishness" while in America absolutely is.

Copley's complaint about the lack of taste for painting in Boston had foundation, even if he overstated his colonial isolation.[4] In the Anglophone world, until at least the mid-eighteenth century and longer in colonial America, painters held the status of artisans because they worked with their hands. Artisan could mean "artist; professor of art" or "manufacturer; low tradesman," according to Samuel Johnson's contemporaneous English dictionary.[5] Undated verse from the *Guardian* supporting Johnson's first definition identified the artisan-artist with portrait painting: "Best and happiest *artisan*/Best of painters, if you can,/With your many colour'd art,/Draw the mistress of my heart." Cheery as the passage might sound, it exposes two impediments to elevation of this branch of painting. First, portraitists were dependent on clients, whom they needed to please. Second (and more tellingly, since artists of all kinds usually worked for patrons), portrait painting involved imitation and kept the artisan tethered to unimproved nature, limiting freedom to invent. Early in the century, the Earl of Shaftesbury adamantly laid out the ways in which portraiture harmed the painter: "the subjecting of his genius, narrowing of his

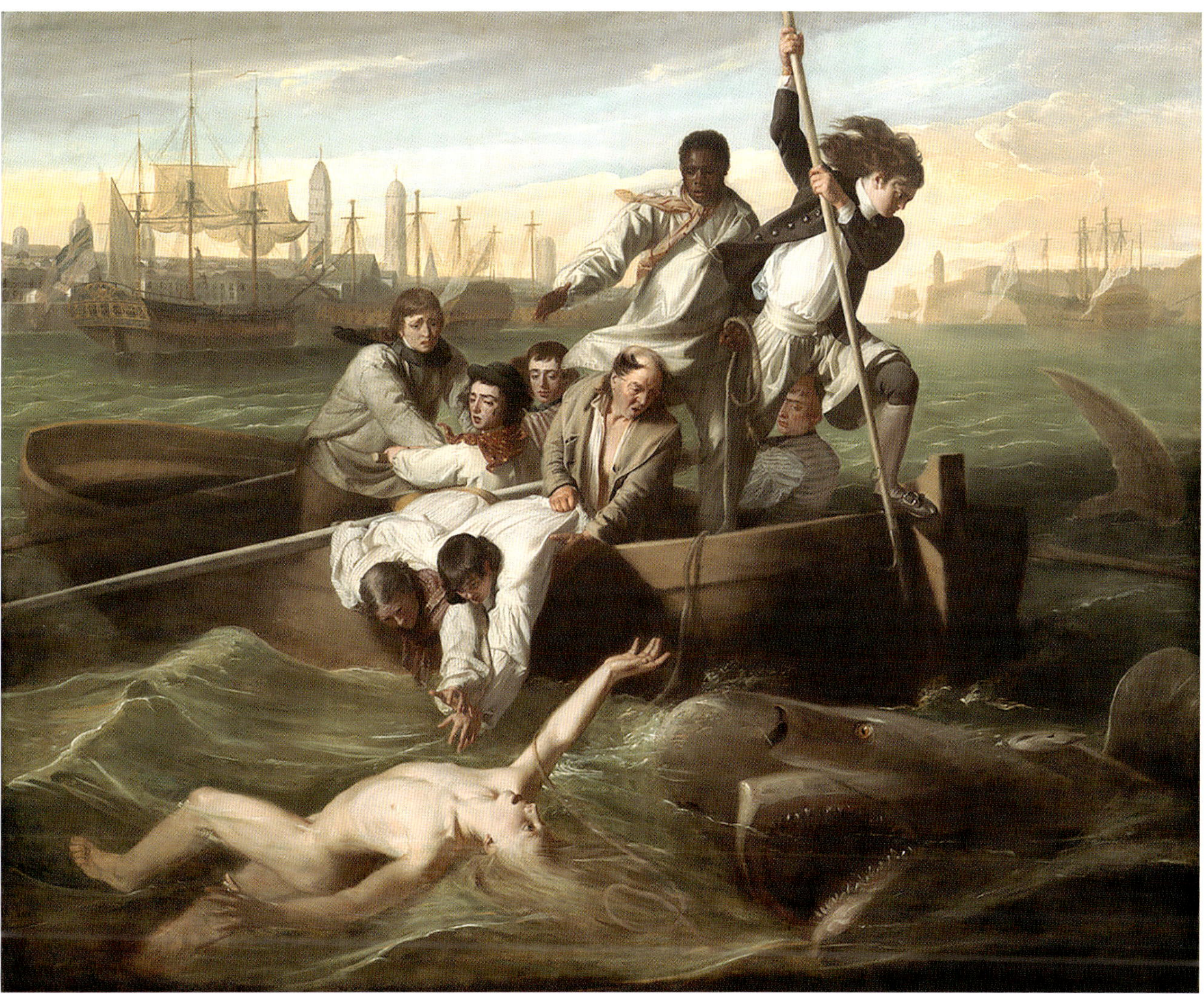

10 John Singleton Copley, *Watson and the Shark*, 1778. Oil on canvas, $71^{11}/_{16} \times 90^{7}/_{16}$ in. (182.1 × 229.7 cm). National Gallery of Art, Washington, D.C., Ferdinand Lammot Belin Fund.

thought, contraction of his idea, deadening of his fancy, constraining of his hand, disaccustomed him in the freedom of his pencil, tying him down to copying, translating, servilely submitting him to the lords and ladies, etc., his originals" (that is, the models he copied).[6] In the first sustained defense of portraitists and argument on behalf of English artists, Jonathan Richardson (who was both) asserted that "the invention of the Painter [portraitist] is exercis'd in the Choice of the Air, the Attitude, the Action, Drapery, and Ornaments, with respect to the Character of the Person."[7] The more persistent point of view remained that expressed by William Duff in *An Essay on Original Genius*, the idea that portraits were merely "COPIES OR RESEMBLANCES of Nature," not requiring invention. In the art treatises to which Copley had access in Boston, portraits were either dismissed or barely mentioned.[8] Whatever his sources of information, Copley understood portraits as a low rather than liberal art.

In choosing the comparison with carpenters, tailors, and shoemakers – members of the lesser artisanry, having meager wages, uncertain prospects for advancement, and little possibility of acquiring property – Copley willfully magnified the insult to his occupation. Artists, along with metalworkers like silversmiths and watchmakers, had considerably greater expectations. Copley saw his fulfilled to a significant degree when in 1769 he married the daughter of a prosperous merchant and purchased a substantial piece of property. But Copley resisted identification with any artisan, a distancing that becomes evident in comparing his self-portrait of that year and his portrait of silversmith Paul Revere from the year before. The portrait of Revere, more subtly than Copley's words, encodes the tensions that plagued him and other colonial painters who were eager to disassociate themselves from the artisan ranks and to redefine their activity as a liberal art. This reading depends first on understanding what it meant to Copley to be ranked an artisan, and why, beyond hyperbole, he singled out the artisans that he did.

Copley may have made a living by a "usefull trade," but he plainly wished to be seen as something more. As the practitioner of a "noble" art, he identified with gentlemen, a designation that, prior to the sixteenth century, had been reserved for persons of noble birth, who did not work.[9] By the eighteenth century, and especially in colonial British America where few held titles, the term had wider application. Birth and parentage still counted for a great deal; so did wealth, though it alone did not make the gentleman, especially if gained in trade. Gentlemen were never defined by what they did, by the usefulness of their trades, but by their quality and condition as men of learning, manners, taste, and character.

The vast majority, by contrast, ranked as the common people, a group that subsumed the "middling" and "lower sort," eighteenth-century terms signifying those in a society who were not gentlemen.[10] No matter how respectable or how wealthy, if they worked for a living – especially if they worked with their hands – they could claim no more than "middling" status. Nor did most aspire to a higher station. The prevailing desire among artisans, Gary Nash has argued, was "not to reach the top but to get off the bottom."[11] Some artisans were nearer the bottom than others, engaged in crafts with limited earning power and, for a variety of reasons, lesser prestige. Tailoring, for example, was thought suitable for the weak because it required little exertion. It also took so little in terms of capital investment in raw materials – needle, thread, tape measure (customers usually supplied their own cloth) – that almost anyone could take up the trade. And at a time when people wore the same clothes over and over, mending, an even lesser aspect of the trade than making, accounted for much of a tailor's work, as also for shoemakers.[12] Shoemaking (sometimes called cordwainery) occupied an even lowlier, less well compensated position. In the colonies, the large number of practitioners further undercut incomes. Seventeenth-century Boston had so many shoemakers that established tradesmen attempted to control access through establishment of a guild, a system that otherwise never took hold in the colonies.[13] Carpentry required considerably more skill and commanded higher wages, but its seasonal nature and potentially greater danger offset relatively greater prestige. The construction industry in Boston, furthermore, stagnated during the 1760s and 1770s, a period of economic decline for that city generally.[14]

Carpenters, tailors, and shoemakers – these were the artisans with whom Copley deplored connection, and he was not alone in expressing contempt for them, though the perspective was more typical of social elites throughout the British North American colonies. William Henry Drayton of South Carolina found inconceivable that gentlemen such as himself should have to accept the participation in government of "men who never were in a way to study" (that is, acquire a liberal education) and who knew little more than how "to cobble an old shoe in the neatest manner, or to build a necessary house."[15] Likewise, the royal governor of Georgia decried the absence of "Gentlemen or Men of Property" among provincial leaders and found the composition of the revolutionary committee in control of Savannah "a Parcel of the Lowest People Chiefly Carpenters, Shoemakers, Blacksmiths &c."[16] What concerned these patricians was fitness for political leadership, which the classical republican tradition – an important eighteenth-century ideal in the Atlantic world – denied working men.[17] (Women, though completely disenfranchised, showed equal inclination to scapegoat the lower sort, as did a Philadelphian who employed irony to condemn the "rascally clergy" in Maryland, charging that "taylors, coblers, blacksmiths, and such fellows" take holy orders "when they cannot live like gentlemen by their trade.")[18] Shoemakers had long been associated with agitation among the downtrodden, and a basis in fact was close at hand: Boston cordwainer Ebenezer MacIntosh led mobs that dismantled the houses of stamp distributor Andrew Oliver and Chief Justice Thomas Hutchinson in demonstrations of August 1765 against the Stamp Act.[19] Blacksmiths and tailors date as figures for the politically engaged lower orders as early as Shakespeare's "smith . . . with open mouth swallowing a tailor's news" – a tailor who, in haste to spread political rumors, could not even get his slippers on the correct feet.[20] English painter Edward Penny envisioned the comic scene in *A Blacksmith Hearkening to a Tailor's News*, shown at the inaugural Royal Academy of Arts exhibition in 1769. Engraved in 1771 and published with the title *The English Politicians*, the work commented derisively on political engagement by the lower sort, who since 1762 had rallied around the controversial House of Commons member John Wilkes.[21]

In classical republican discourse, working men like tailors and shoemakers could never act virtuously and in the public interest. The necessity of plying their trades and engagement with concrete materials inhibited their ability to think in the abstract terms necessary to governance.[22] Only gentlemen, whose fortunes traditionally derived from ownership of land worked by others, were thought capable of holding integrity in public office. They alone satisfied the expectation that leaders be independent and "disinterested." In the absence of a hereditary aristocracy in America, the old notions began to break down and yet the old prejudices lingered. John Adams, writing in 1760, sarcastically called shoemaking "too mean and dimi[nu]tive an Occupation" to satisfy a legal client of his. The shoemaker, who should have "diligently followed his Trade," wanted instead to "rise in the World" and took to "meddling with Law," to his financial ruin. A few months later, Adams vehemently insisted on the "ancient and universal" English division between yeomen and gentlemen in the case of a New England farmer, styled "gentleman" in a writ. The defendant, he wrote in his diary, was "not a Gentleman in any Respect, neither by Birth, Education, Office, Reputation or Employment; . . . [nor] one in Thought, Word, or Deed. He spring[s] from ordinary Parents, he can scarcely write his Name." Adams's scorn is striking given his father's occupations of shoemaking and farming. He, however, had acquired what the shoemaker and yeoman in these legal encounters had not: "the Advantage of a liberal Education," for Adams a prerequisite to leadership and membership in a "natural" aristocracy.[23]

In the literature of art, the shoemaker had long exemplified a man mired in particulars and incapable of judging the whole. Pliny first told the tale of a shoemaker who criticized Apelles's representation of a sandal. Acknowledging the shoemaker's expertise in the matter of footwear, Apelles made the correction; however, he refused to do so when the man returned to criticize his rendering of the leg, that being outside a shoemaker's expertise.[24] For Plato, painters were men of similarly narrow experience. To make his point, he imagined a painter who "can paint us a shoemaker, for example, or a carpenter, or any of the other craftsmen. He may know nothing of any of these skills, and yet, if he is a good painter, from a distance his picture of a carpenter can fool children and people with no judgment, because it looks like a real carpenter."[25] The painter, in other words, may possess imitative skills sufficient to trick an unsophisticated viewer, but he does so without understanding, merely representing appearances. Eighteenth-century writers on art were at pains to refute this view and repeatedly retold Pliny's story, emphasizing the painter's superiority to "ignorant, uneducated" would-be critics.[26] Some painters, they conceded, were too closely bound to the particular. Portraitists, especially, faced this problem. But others transcended that limitation by figuring the ideal, the substance rather than the accidental and irrational appearance of things, and by illustrating noble actions. According to eighteenth-century theory, such an abstract and intellectual art did not address the common person and could not be made by the common person. Artists who engaged historical subjects – that is, subjects with a moral purpose, which promoted virtue by representing virtue – acted, as did gentlemen, for the betterment of mankind and not just for themselves or for particular clients.[27]

Political leadership does not appear to have been Copley's concern, at least not in the narrow sense of partisan politics, to which he maintained a studied neutrality throughout the imperial crisis. But even before he reached his majority, he had clearly consumed, if not entirely digested, European aesthetic treatises that proclaimed the importance and socially redeeming character of historical subjects; such subjects number among his earliest paintings (fig. 11). In the absence of demand, however, history painting could neither provide Copley's living nor, once he was established, support the style of life to which he had become accustomed. He was dependent on, and restricted by, his fellow colonists' preference for portraiture and unavoidably in the position of having to please.

"Painter Taylor"

The importance of flattery and generally ingratiating behavior by a portraitist in dealing with a client accounts for the recurrence of tailors and related clothing tradesmen in eighteenth-century artist narratives. "A man of very middling Talents may easily succeed" in portrait painting, noted William Hogarth, adding with a tinge of Copley's bitterness, "more of artifices and the address of a mercer is required than [the painter's] genious."[28] Mercers, closely allied to tailors, dealt in expensive textiles, especially silks, and assisted clients in selecting fabric for their clothes. Certain "artifices" contributed to a mercer's success, according to *The London Tradesman*, a book published in 1747 to guide parents in selecting trades for their children. The mercer, according to author Robert Campbell, "traficks most with the Ladies, and has a small Dash of their Effeminacy in his Constitution . . . He must be a very polite Man, and skilled in all

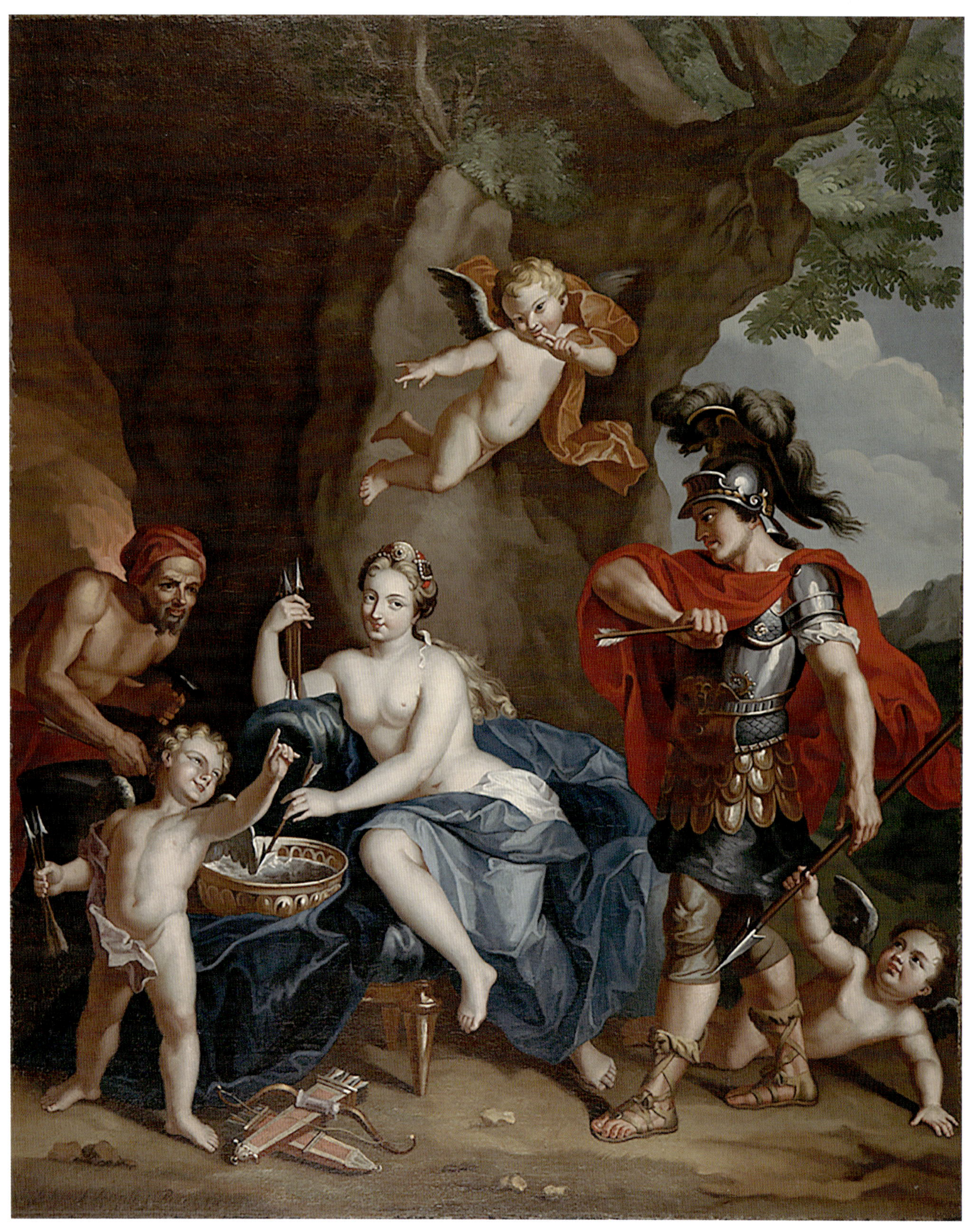

11 John Singleton Copley, *Mars, Venus, and Vulcan: The Forge of Vulcan*, 1754. Oil on canvas, 30 × 25 in. (76.2 × 63.5 cm). Collection of the Kalamazoo Institute of Arts, purchase; acquired through the generosity of an anonymous donor, 2013.20.

the Punctilio's of City-good-breeding . . . He must dress neatly, and affect a Court Air, however far distant he may live from St. *James's* . . . [None are] so fit for that Branch of Business, as that nimble, dancing, talkative Nation the *French*: Our Mercer must have a good deal of the *Frenchman* in his Manners."[29]

The caricatured fawning, foppish Europeans in Hogarth's graphic work make clear his disdain for those who waited on the wealthy and suggest how deeply he abhorred strategic obsequiousness in a portraitist's relationship to patron. West, who found fame in 1760s London, knew enough to shun any connection with such tradesmen, at least according to John Galt's heavily embroidered biography of 1816, in which West as a child refused to play with a boy who wanted to become a tailor. The story – meant to establish West's sense of his own destiny – makes clear that an artist who would become the intimate of a king had no business forming such base associations.[30] West's social purity, however, was somewhat compromised by the tattle that, in preparing to portray George III in 1780, the artist "ascertained the exact proportions of his Majesty with a compass and taylor's measure, from head to foot." The anonymous commentator's remark set up his judgment of West's George III as "a stuffed pillow."[31] Gilbert Stuart, to whom West deflected portrait customers in the early 1780s, was more sporting. When fellow passengers on an English stagecoach wondered about his occupation, he teased them, saying that he made "coats and waistcoats for gentlemen," but that he was not a tailor.[32] When an actual painting was at stake, however, Stuart refused to modify the clothes of dissatisfied patrons, as any tailor would have to do, declaring flatly: "a painter may give up his art, if he attempts to alter to please."[33]

Collectively, these remarks reveal a commonplace arising from shared conditions: like most eighteenth-century tailors and dressmakers, portrait painters made a product on order from an individual customer.[34] Anyone whose work was bespoke encountered considerable pressure to satisfy client desires. The tailor's work had a literally material effect on a client's public persona, since in the burgeoning consumer society of the eighteenth century, individuals negotiated status partly through cloth, a costly consumer item. The title of a book published in Philadelphia in 1772 made the point unequivocally: *The Miraculous Power of Clothes, and Dignity of the Taylors: Being an Essay on the Words, Clothes Makes Men.* (Women were served by mantua makers, the period term for dressmakers, though tailors made ladies' riding habits.) From "a chaos of velvet, brocade, and other rich stuffs," the author explains, the tailor "created illustrious personages, graces, honours, and other worthies."[35] His skill, according to Robert Campbell's *London Tradesman*, lay in sizing up the customer and cutting the cloth to favor him. A master tailor "must be able, not only to cut for the Handsome and Well-shap'd, but to bestow a good Shape where Nature has not designed it . . . His Hand and his Head must go together."[36] The tailor, it is clear, served as an agent of the client's self-interested public presentation. So, too, did the portraitist, and in ways uncomfortably aligned with the tailor given the importance of costume in portraiture generally.[37]

In England, a significant number of portraitists employed specialist drapery painters, including Joshua Reynolds, who in 1768 became first president of the Royal Academy of Arts (and a knight in the process). The practice supports the importance to sitters, borne out by the visual evidence, of being depicted in compellingly rendered fabrics, if not always meticulously detailed costume. A successful drapery painter could earn a living equal or better to that of a successful portraitist, with far less hassle, in Thomas Gainsborough's estimation: "whilst a Face painter is harassed to death the drapery painter sits and earns 5 or 6 hundred a year, and laughs all the while."[38] Yet *The London Tradesman* allowed drapery painters few claims to stature; such an artisan ranked as "the lowest Degree of a liberal Painter," a "workman" with "but a dull Genius, and a mere Mechanic Head."[39] Even though Hogarth had denigrated these "painter taylors," he saved his venom for portraitists who relied on them for "nine parts in ten . . . and perhaps the best [part]" of their pictures.[40] Perhaps portraitists drew criticism for such division of labor because that practice seemed only to affirm the notion that portrait work required little genius to begin with.[41] However, using assistants had been a norm for Old Master painters, who maintained workshops to execute their ideas. Such practices predate "modern" art in the emergent Romantic sense that elevated individual expression, remaining instead traditionally academic in valuing invention over execution, the latter considered merely mechanical and beneath the dignity of a fine artist.

Reynolds, always concerned to elevate the rank of painter, associated artistic dignity especially with history painting, in which the artist addressed general truths rather than the particularities of unrefined nature. Accordingly, in his fourth Discourse before the Royal Academy (1771) – the sequence of lectures and eventual publications that began in 1769 – Reynolds warned that "the historical Painter . . . does not debase his conceptions with minute attention to the discrimination of stuffs. With him, the cloathing is neither woollen, nor linen, nor silk, sattin, or velvet; it is drapery; it is nothing more."[42] One might therefore see unintended irony in William Hayley's verse praising the 1783 William Mason translation of Charles Alphonse Du Fresnoy's *Art of Painting*, for which Reynolds wrote extended notes:

With pride, by envy undebas'd
My English spirit views
How far your elegance of taste
Improves a Gallic Muse.
I thought that Muse but meanly drest
When her stiff gown was Latin;
But you have turn'd her grogram vest
Into fine folds of satin.

The Muse, of course, is the last figure who should appear in satin; in painting, following Reynolds, her garb should be "drapery" and "nothing more."[43] Any portrait painter who wished to enhance both his sitter and his own position, according to Reynolds, will likewise forgo modern costume in favor of dress "with the general air of the antique"; he may, in effect, undo the work of the tailor, who, in Reynolds's alliterative words, distorts, disfigures, disguises, and deforms nature in the service of fashion.[44] His rival Gainsborough characteristically took an opposing point of view. In his *Isabella, Viscountess Molyneux, later Countess of Sefton*, a showpiece for the inaugural Royal Academy exhibition in 1769, Gainsborough featured a spectacular modern dress without robbing the picture of Old Master grandeur (fig. 12). Two years later, responding to Lord Dartmouth's displeasure with his wife's portrait, Gainsborough made his position clear, faulting the "fancied" (or invented) Dress requested by the client: "had I painted Lady Dartmouths Picture, dressd as Her Ladyship goes, no fault (more than in my Painting in general) would have been found with it." Gainsborough proposed to "dress it (contrary I know to Lady Dartmouths taste) in the modern Way," adding in a postscript, "I am very well aware of the Objection to modern Dresses in Pictures, that they are soon out of fashion & look awkward; but . . . we must set it against the unluckiness of fancied Dresses taking away Likenesses, the principal beauty & intention of a Portrait."[45] This was an argument against Reynolds, who practiced what he preached in such works as *Lady Sarah Bunbury Sacrificing to the Graces* (1763–1765; fig. 13). But the strategy left Reynolds and his sitter in that case open to wisecracks. Lady Sarah, one contemporary remarked, "never *did* sacrifice to the Graces . . . she was a cricket player, and ate beefsteaks."[46] Yet Reynolds knew well that the painter who paid too much attention to drapery exposed himself to the charge that Cardinal Albani, the eighteenth-century Roman collector-connoisseur, supposedly made about the master artist Guido Reni, "that he was rather a taylor than a painter."[47]

This slur on Reni appeared in Francesco Algarotti's *Essay on Painting* of 1764, a book Copley had evidently read by November 1766, when he asked West to clarify an unrelated matter. Copley wondered about Algarotti's "five points" governing the disposition of the head, hands, and feet of a figure in painting, presumably for consideration in connection with his portraits, although the Italian author never addressed portraiture.[48] The American painter was even less well informed about continental and English art theory and practice than he himself suspected. He defended the "simplissity in the dress" in a pastel he sent West on the grounds that he had no access to "that variety of Dresses here as in Europe, unless I should put myself to a great expence to have them made."[49] Copley did not recognize that such defensiveness was unnecessary; emphasis on fashion in portraiture was, at that moment in England, increasingly unfashionable, at least among the theoretically inclined (who did not consistently do what they advised). Reynolds, preparing to portray the Duchess of Rutland in 1780, had his sitter try on eleven different dresses before painting her in an invented concoction that she referred to as "that bedgown" (a loosely cut, short jacket worn by fashionable women at home and by working class women at any time).[50] Yet in an age when artists, including Copley, freely copied costumes from prints and other sources, his imagined dependence on the tailor cast Copley as a "painter taylor."[51]

Copley's reading of aesthetic treatises fueled his dissatisfaction with portraiture.[52] He must have noted its absence in Algarotti – especially striking given the author's extended dedication to the Society for the Encouragement of Arts, Manufactures, and Commerce, a new organization based in London, where portraits, above all, sustained the business of painting. For Algarotti, the "ideal Painter . . . alone is a true painter"; his discussion of the elements of painting, its proper models and subjects, left no room for portraiture.[53] But West had broken the mold, and Copley, feeling marooned in provincial Boston, looked to this fellow American as model and mentor. Attempting to position himself as an informed insider, Copley parroted the inflated language of art treatises, writing of West to the artist and entrepreneur John Greenwood (who also had left America to pursue fortune abroad), "I sincerely rejoice in Mr. West's successfull progress towards the summit of that Mighty

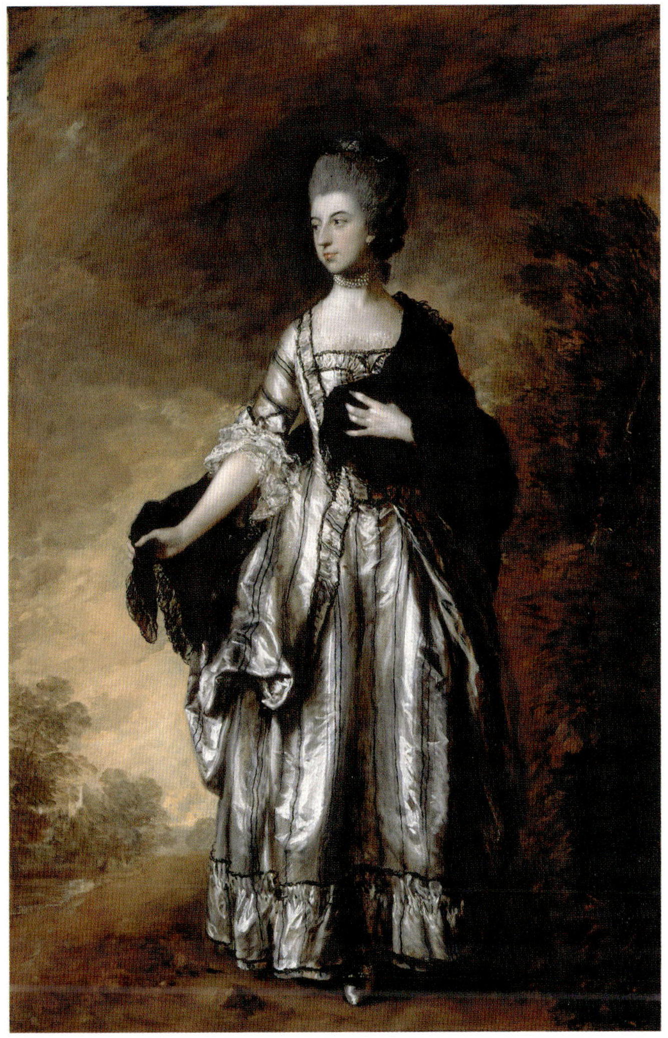

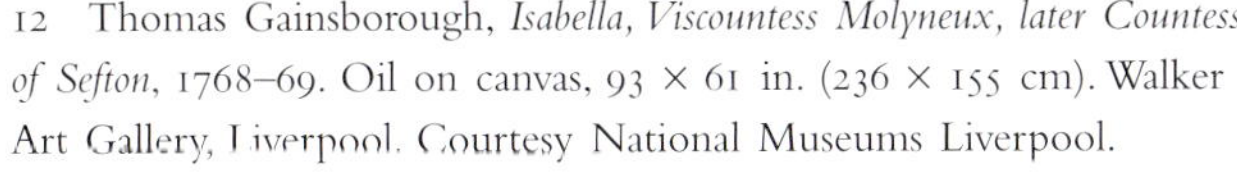

12 Thomas Gainsborough, *Isabella, Viscountess Molyneux, later Countess of Sefton*, 1768–69. Oil on canvas, 93 × 61 in. (236 × 155 cm). Walker Art Gallery, Liverpool. Courtesy National Museums Liverpool.

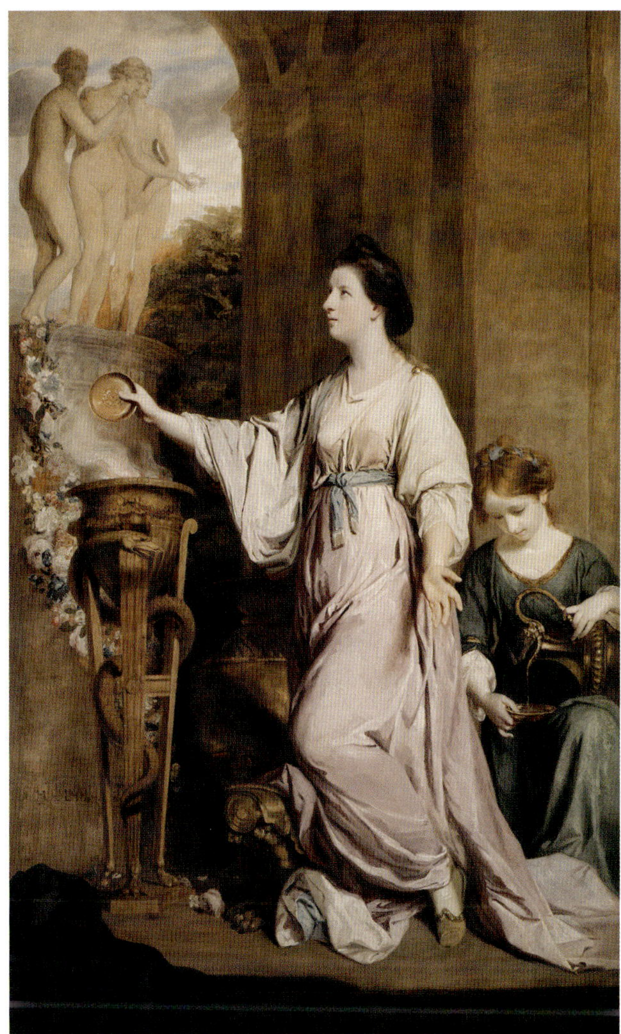

13 Sir Joshua Reynolds, *Lady Sarah Bunbury Sacrificing to the Graces*, 1763–65. Oil on canvas, 95½ × 59¾ in. (242.6 × 151.5 cm). Mr. and Mrs. W. W. Kimball Collection, 1922.4468, Art Institute of Chicago.

Mountain where the Everlasting Lauriels grow to adoarn the brows of those Elustrious Artists that are so favourd of Heaven as to be able to unravel the intricate mazes of its rough and perilous Asent."[54]

Copley's image in this passage conflates Parnassus, home of the Muses, and the mountain that represents "the arduous and rocky way of Virtue" in so many paintings of the Choice of Hercules, a subject valued for dramatizing the moral dilemma of choosing between virtue and vice.[55] After seeing Copley's portrait of his half brother, Henry Pelham (fig. 14), placed at exhibition with the Society of Artists (another new London organization) in 1766, Reynolds had laid out Copley's choice: travel to Europe to study the masters and become "a valuable Acquisition to the Art" (this is the path of virtue) or have his "Manner and Taste corrupted and fixed by working in [his] little way at Boston" (vice).[56] But Reynolds left out what was for Copley an important part of the equation: in Copley's words, "the profits of the art."[57] Should he risk financial instability in the more competitive British or European art market or should he preserve his lucrative colonial portrait practice? "I make as much as if I were a Raphael or a Correggio," Copley boasted, and he saw little point in acquiring European "improvements" only to "bury" them in the colonies. The directness with which Copley addressed the subject of money – he sought West's assurance that he might in London equal his American income of three hundred guineas a year – betrays his provinciality, his marginality to

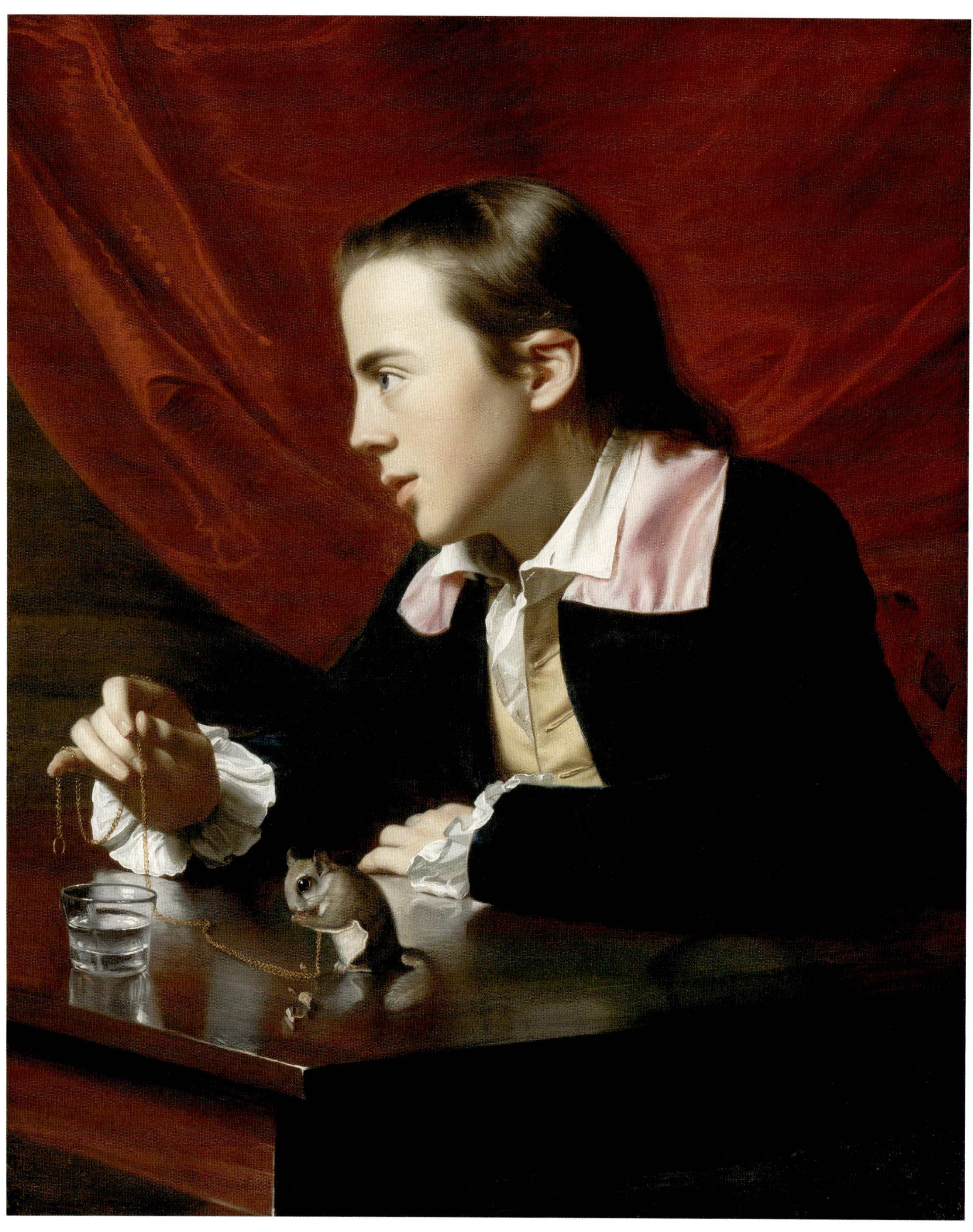

14 John Singleton Copley, *A Boy with a Flying Squirrel (Henry Pelham)*, 1765. Oil on canvas, 30⅜ × 25⅛ in. (77.15 × 63.82 cm). Museum of Fine Arts, Boston, gift of the artist's great-granddaughter, 1978.297.

an elite discourse, suppressing commerce and the material, on the role of the arts in modern British society.[58]

An artist at the center, in London, could always position himself outside that discourse by rejecting it, as Hogarth did. In a defense of writing as a money-making profession, James Ralph cited Hogarth's pronouncement (which rings true in its combativeness) that "till Fame appears to be worth more than Money, [Hogarth] will always prefer Money to Fame."[59] Copley echoed this position, to which virtue has little relevance and, for all his professed disgust with portraiture, faced up to the realities of the marketplace. "Painters cannot Live on Art only," Copley wrote. Unwilling to "purchas[e] fame at so dear a rate," he sacrificed pride to financial security. He made the choice between inspiration and decoration for which David Garrick, the famous English actor and theatrical manager, drew criticism, namely of pandering to a debased public in commercial society. That was the point of an engraving of 1772 showing Garrick between the Muses and the carpenters and tailors, a play on Reynolds's witty portrait *Garrick between Comedy and Tragedy* (1762), itself a parody of innumerable paintings showing the Choice of Hercules (fig. 15).[60] Although in the engraving, Comedy/Vice appears on the same side as her sternly posturing sister Tragedy/Virtue, Comedy's affiliation with the tradesmen as a deleterious influence is figured in their mutually firm grasp of the compromised actor.

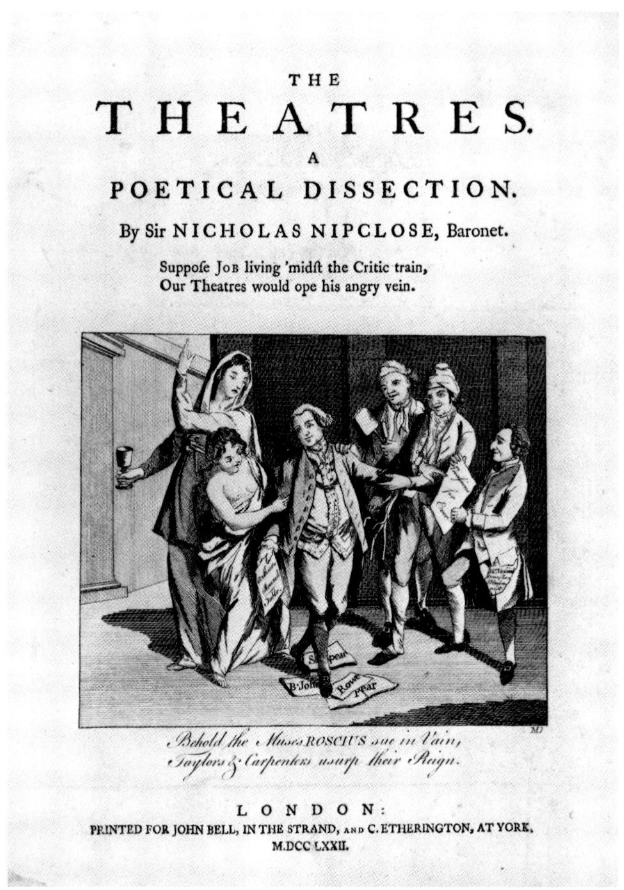
THE
THEATRES.
A
POETICAL DISSECTION.
By Sir NICHOLAS NIPCLOSE, Baronet.
Suppose JOB living 'midst the Critic train,
Our Theatres would ope his angry vein.
Behold the Muses ROSCIUS sue in Vain,
Taylors & Carpenters usurp their Reign.
LONDON:
PRINTED FOR JOHN BELL, IN THE STRAND, AND C. ETHERINGTON, AT YORK.
M.DCC.LXXII.

15 Title page of Sir Nicholas Nipclose [Francis Gentleman], *The Theatres: A Poetical Dissection* (London, 1772). Photo: Harry Ransom Humanities Research Center, University of Texas, Austin.

Garrick (like Hogarth) openly sported with aristocratic and classical forms, as in his prologue to *The Tailors*, a farce first performed July 2, 1767, at the Haymarket:

> This night we add some heroes to our store,
> Who never were as heroes known before:
> No blust'ring Romans, Trojans, Greeks, shall rage;
> No knights arm'd *cap-à-pie* shall croud our stage;
> . . .
> With different instruments our troop appears,
> Needles to thimbles shall, and sheers to sheers.
> With parchment gorgets, and in buckram arm'd
> Cold-blooded Tailors are to heroes warm'd,
> . . .
> Each outside shall belie the stuff within,
> A Roman spirit in a Tailor's skin.[61]

The humor of the prologue and play depended on the relatively low status of tailors. Copley, unlike the sophisticated Garrick, could find nothing funny about his situation in colonial Boston. Yet far more than he would have liked to admit, his frank pursuit of material well-being matched him well to his self-satisfied portrait subjects. By staying in America, Copley in effect allied himself with the tailors as the servant of clients who employed him in their own strategic self-enhancement.[62]

Such had not been the case when he painted Pelham in profile, an uncommissioned work that ignores conventional mid-eighteenth-century terms of likeness, normally fulfilled by showing a sitter's face in frontal or three-quarter view. Copley served verisimilitude with his careful rendering of the boy's distinctively shaped ear, as if instructed by a guide to painting from *Universal Magazine*, a mid-century British periodical committed to the "useful" as well as polite arts: "If a person has any particularities as to the set or motion of the head, eyes, or mouth (supposing it be not unbecoming) these must be taken notice of, and strongly expressed."[63] Pelham's ear in effect guaranteed likeness. But Copley knew that his young brother's identity did not matter in the forum of a London public exhibition; in that context the profile view thwarted consideration of the

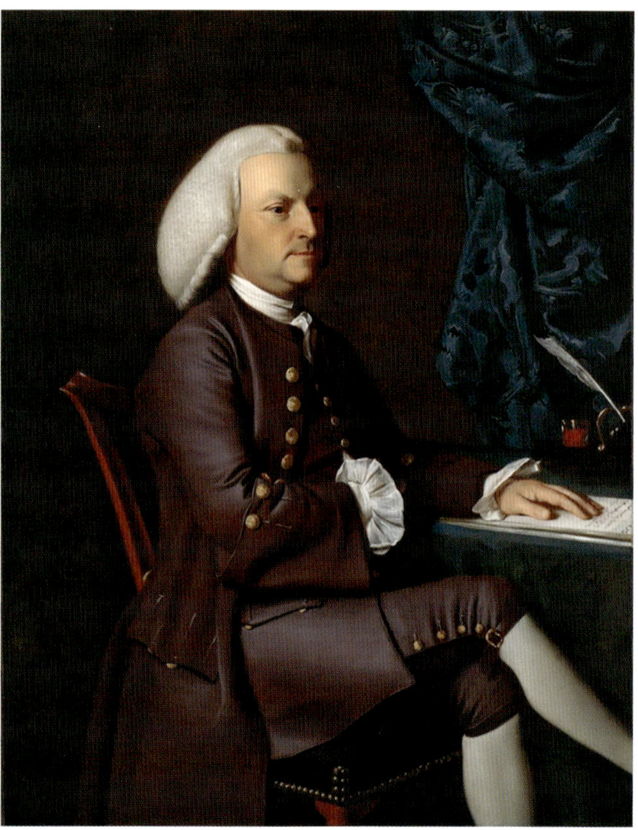

16 John Singleton Copley, *Isaac Smith*, 1769. Oil on canvas, 50⅛ × 40⅛ in. (127.3 × 101.9 cm). Yale University Art Gallery, New Haven, gift of Maitland F. Griggs, B.A. 1896 (1941.74).

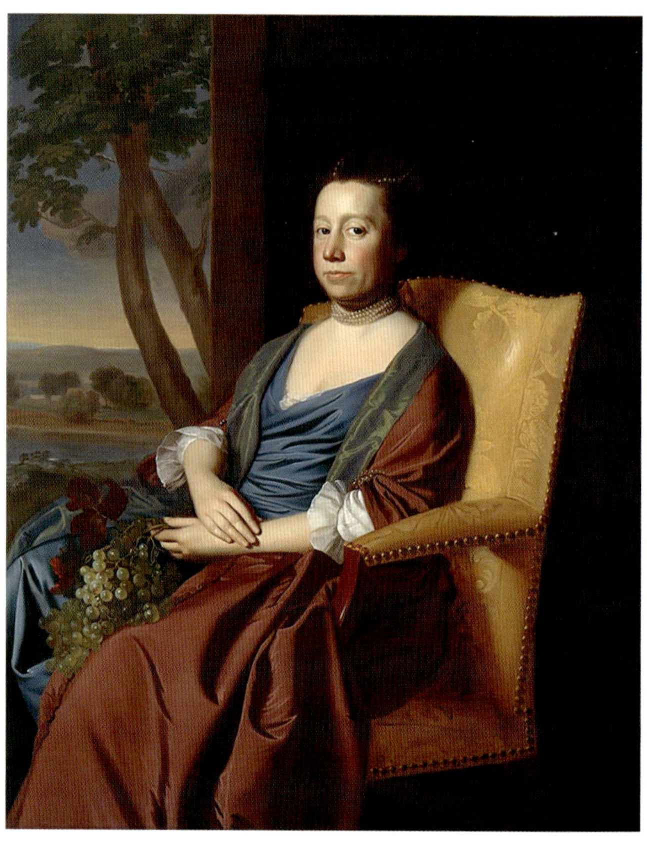

17 John Singleton Copley, *Mrs. Isaac Smith (Elizabeth Storer)*, 1769. Oil on canvas, 50⅛ × 40⅛ in. (127.3 × 101.9 cm). Yale University Art Gallery, New Haven, gift of Maitland F. Griggs, B.A. 1896 (1941.73).

painting as portrait and drew attention instead to Copley's invention and execution. His success in divorcing the work from portraiture is evident from Captain Bruce's assertion that, if Copley wished, he could sell the work in England "to advantage," not normally an option for portraits.[64] The conceit of boy with pet squirrel and various accessories encourages the impression that the glass of water, like so many other details of this work, serves to demonstrate the painter's skill, specifically his ability to render the material quality of different things.[65]

It was a miscalculation. Reynolds observed "an over minuteness" in *Boy with a Squirrel*, while West thought the painting "too liney." What bothered them was Copley's determined representation of things, of mundane particularities rather than the ideal generalities that elevate painting and painter.[66] The idea was hardly new when, in his eleventh Discourse (1782), Reynolds conceded: "There is a Genius particular and appropriated to [the painter's] trade (as I may call it)"; it is, he continued, "the Genius of mechanical performance." The parenthetic qualification indicates Reynolds's discomfort with any reference to trade. Even if he no longer had to defend himself in the most fashionable circles, Reynolds and other artists experienced persistent contempt from gentry. Fanny Burney, a close friend, noted in her diary of 1779 that one such man "spoke of Sir Joshua Reynolds as if he had been upon a level with a carpenter or farrier" (the shoemaker to a horse).[67] But Reynolds, in his Discourse, diverts our attention from the troubling words (trade, mechanical), insisting that the painter's genius consists in capturing the general effect and not "the subordinate and particular beauties or defects" of the subject: "It is certain that a nice discrimination of minute circumstances, and a punctilious delineation of them, whatever excellence it may have . . . never did confer on the Artist the character of Genius." Reynolds makes clear that these conditions should apply to portraiture as well, however singular the subject: "The excellence of Portrait-Painting . . . depend[s] more upon the general effect produced

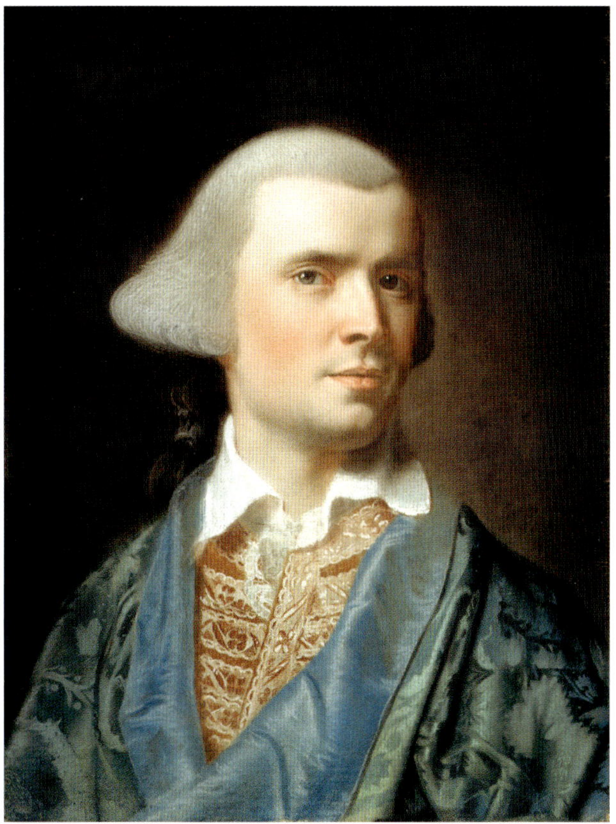

18 John Singleton Copley, *Self-Portrait*, 1769. Pastel on paper mounted on canvas, 23¾ × 17½ in. (60.3 × 44.5 cm). Courtesy Winterthur Museum, gift of Henry Francis du Pont, 1959.1127.

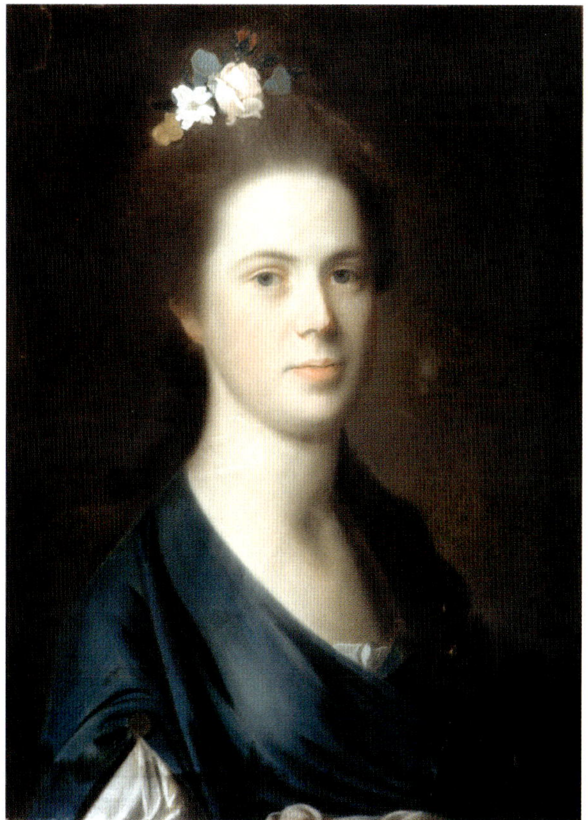

19 John Singleton Copley, *Susanna Clarke Copley (Mrs. John Singleton Copley)*, 1769. Pastel on paper mounted on canvas, 23⅛ × 17¼ in. (58.7 × 43.8 cm). Courtesy Winterthur Museum, gift of Henry Francis du Pont, 1959.1128.

by the painter, than on the exact expression of the peculiarities, or minute discrimination of the parts . . . peculiarities may be reduced to classes and general descriptions; and there are therefore large ideas to be found even in this contracted subject."[68] For Reynolds, only the ability to abstract from experience could earn an artist the name of genius or gentleman.

Copley, as represented in London by *Boy with a Squirrel*, did not succeed on Reynolds's terms. By its "over minuteness," the painting defined him as a mechanic.

The Artist as Gentleman

Even as Copley complained that fellow colonials were disposed to see him as a tradesman, he succeeded in distancing himself in many ways from any artisanal connection. By the late 1760s, his clientele had narrowed to the wealthiest and most prominent residents of Boston and its surrounding communities, including Nicholas and Thomas Boylston, Ezekiel Goldthwait, Jeremiah Lee, Isaac Smith, and their wives (figs. 16, 17). Copley firmly allied himself with these prosperous Bostonians in 1769, when he married Susanna Clarke, daughter of merchant Richard Clarke.

To commemorate this important life event, Copley made portraits in pastel of himself and his bride (figs. 18, 19). Through the late eighteenth century, paired portraits remained the most common format for representing a married couple. Those who commissioned portraits in oil from Copley usually chose canvases of 50 × 40 inches, a size known as half-length, which permitted a view to the knee. Copley's pastels – most dating to the late 1760s – were less than half as large, a constraint imposed by the readily available scale of plate glass needed to protect the powdery surfaces but also conforming to standard sizes of paper. While a figure can be shown at any scale, Copley and his patrons evidently preferred a bust-length presentation. His pastel portraits consequently lack the full array of gender-specific attributes that larger formats accommodated, and they accord equal visual weight to husbands and wives. So it is striking that Copley made his likeness more showy than that of his wife. Other wives wear ermine, pearls, lace, ribbons, or flowers tucked into their bodices; only a few flowers adorn Susanna Copley's hair and plain drapery covers her upper body. Her husband's contrastingly sumptuous attire includes a lace-trimmed waistcoat, a garment of considerable sartorial cachet, as evident from New York tailor John Forest's decision to do business at "the sign of the Gold-Lac'd Waistcoat," where "gentlemen and others, may have either plain, gold or silver lace work, done in a plain, or full laced manner, as compleat, and as much to their satisfaction as in London."[69] Attesting to the social value of such a garment in London at mid-century, Peter Manigault (the young man so pleased with the laced hat in his portrait, from the opening epigraph to this book) wrote his mother of a visit to church: "my Friend had a Laced Waistcoat and hat, [and] he, or rather his Laced Waistcoat, was introduced into a pew, while I, that is, my plain Clothes, were forced to stand up, during the whole time of divine Service."[70] Manigault, who at least displayed a sense of humor about being reduced to a suit of clothes, lost no time in acquiring a laced coat for himself.

Over his fully laced waistcoat, Copley wears a fashionable banyan of glossy blue-green figured silk damask, apparently identical to the one in which he depicted wealthy Boston merchant Nicholas Boylston two years earlier (fig. 20). A loose garment of exotic associations – known variously as an Indian gown, dressing gown, morning gown, or nightgown (as distinguished from bed nightgown) – a banyan replaced a fitted coat in informal circumstances.[71] Despite what the alternate names suggest today, banyans could be worn at home to greet visitors or in the street. Sir Richard Steele, in the *Spectator*, took note of young men in coffeehouses "who rise early for no other Purpose but to publish their Laziness" and who "come in their Night-Gowns to saunter away their time." A half century later, a character created by Oliver Goldsmith reports on the "modern manner of some of the nobility receiving company in their morning gowns."[72] The fashion had taken firm hold in America by then. The son of an Irish tin-plate worker who emigrated to America, William Paterson, recorded how he learned to be a gentleman while a student at Princeton in the early 1760s. He was sensitive to excesses of gentility and railed against "the effeminacy and dissoluteness of modern manners," including the wearing of banyans.[73] The Corporation of Harvard College considered the fashion inappropriate as well, decreeing that no student should "wear any silk night-gowns as being not only an unnecessary expense but inconsistent with the gravity and demeanor proper to be observed."[74] These accounts, if not wholly positive, unequivocally identify banyans with men of leisure, gentility, and education.

These were the associations Copley conjured up by portraying himself in a banyan. The fine fabric and intense color of his garment serve a similar purpose. Seventeenth-century sumptuary laws, although widely ignored in colonial British America, had forbidden common people such sartorial riches, which, even into the eighteenth century, bestowed on the wearer the cachet of birth and wealth. Refined fit, style, color, and material became even more important signifiers of gentility as persons of all social groups began to wear the same types of garments, as Jonathan Prude has shown in analyzing descriptions of dress from eighteenth-century notices of runaway indentured and enslaved persons.[75] Britons were bound up in an empire of goods, with Americans especially hungry for fine textiles imported from England.[76] Benjamin Franklin chose an apt metaphor when he observed that, until the time of the Stamp Act crisis, Americans "were led by a thread."[77] The trappings of status concerned Copley as much as the next person, and he impressed even the "emphatically well-born" (in William Dunlap's phrase) John Trumbull, who recalled their first meeting, around 1772: "We found Mr. Copley dressed to receive a party of friends at dinner. I remember his dress and appearance – an elegant looking man, dressed in a fine maroon cloth, with gilt buttons – this was dazzling to my unpracticed eye!"[78] While Copley evidently did not wear a banyan on that occasion, his elegance in a fine gown is on full display in the self-portrait. For thirteen other portraits of men executed between 1767 and 1770, including Boylston's, Copley or his clients chose the same costume (not always shown in the same colors).[79] Such repetition did not undermine Copley's reputation, since eighteenth-century portrait subjects frequently wear attire appropriated from other works, usually in the service of fashion and status.[80] When an artist's self-image resembles his portraits of other sitters, its self-reference might seem diluted (the concentrated gaze evident here, a frequent sign of self-portrayal, appears in Copley's portraits generally). But when the portraitist's clientele belonged overwhelmingly to upper levels of society, as Copley's did – and as painters themselves rarely did – an inescapable conclusion emerges: Copley has fashioned himself a gentleman.

The same point is made by Copley's carefully dressed and powdered hair, which he elected over the caps that men in banyans often wore on their shaved heads (as in eight of the portraits by Copley).[81] Whether it is his own hair or a wig remains unclear. Large and elaborate wigs are unmistakable, as with Isaac Smith's old-fashioned physical wig, a heavy frizzed type favored by merchants and professionals. Copley also frequently represented the edge of a wig with a distinct line and sometimes a cast shadow, neither of which appears in the self-portrait.[82] Fine wigs were expensive, troublesome and time-consuming to maintain, and they demanded physical poise in the wearer. Their power to communicate status is evident in recollections of the Reverend Devereux Jarratt, looking back on his childhood as a humble carpenter's son in Virginia, ca. 1740: "a *periwig*, in those days, was the distinguishing badge of *gentle folk*," and the mere sight of a man in a wig was then enough to make him run away from these "beings of superior order." As a new schoolmaster in the early 1750s, Jarratt made sure to acquire "an old wig" so as to appear "something more than common."[83] Although evidence suggests that by the 1760s men at any stratum of society in colonial America might wear wigs, only the well-to-do had the means to wear to them well. Wigs declined in favor beginning around 1770, except among professional men (and, in London, among the ultra-fashionable macaroni, whose enormous wigs and feminized over-refinement helped hasten the decline in wig wearing among others).[84] By that time Copley represented more of his sitters with their own hair. Even then, however, it remained common for men to dress and powder natural hair in a manner imitative of wigs. In the self-portrait, Copley hedged his bets. To show himself with a bald head and cap might have seemed excessively informal, inappropriate to a portrait paired with that of his wife in commemoration of their marriage and marking, as well, the new social position he gained with that alliance. A man with a shaved head, furthermore, required a wig in public, but the authority with which he wore it would remain unarticulated in a wigless portrait.[85] Copley eliminates doubt by showing himself, alone among his men in banyans, in a powdered coiffure, a choice that complements his expensive costume to mark him as unmistakably genteel.

The property at which Copley hung his self-portrait represented his status even to persons who never entered. In the year of his marriage and with financial assistance from his father-in-law, Copley paid £860 for several lots, totaling about twenty acres and including a barn and three houses, on Beacon Street, north of the Powder House on Boston Common. By contrast to the dense population center of the North End, where Copley grew up, this was an outlying area, as seen on the map made by William Price in 1769 (fig. 21). On the north side along the Charles River lived prosperous mechanics and tradesmen, seafaring men and laborers. The southern slope, facing the Common, was less settled but more affluent, as signaled by the relative expansiveness of individual landholdings and most especially by the grand house built in 1737 by Thomas Hancock. The site had sufficient importance to be labeled as "Hancock seat" on the Price map, by which time the estate had passed to the original owner's nephew and heir, John Hancock, one of the richest men in America.[86]

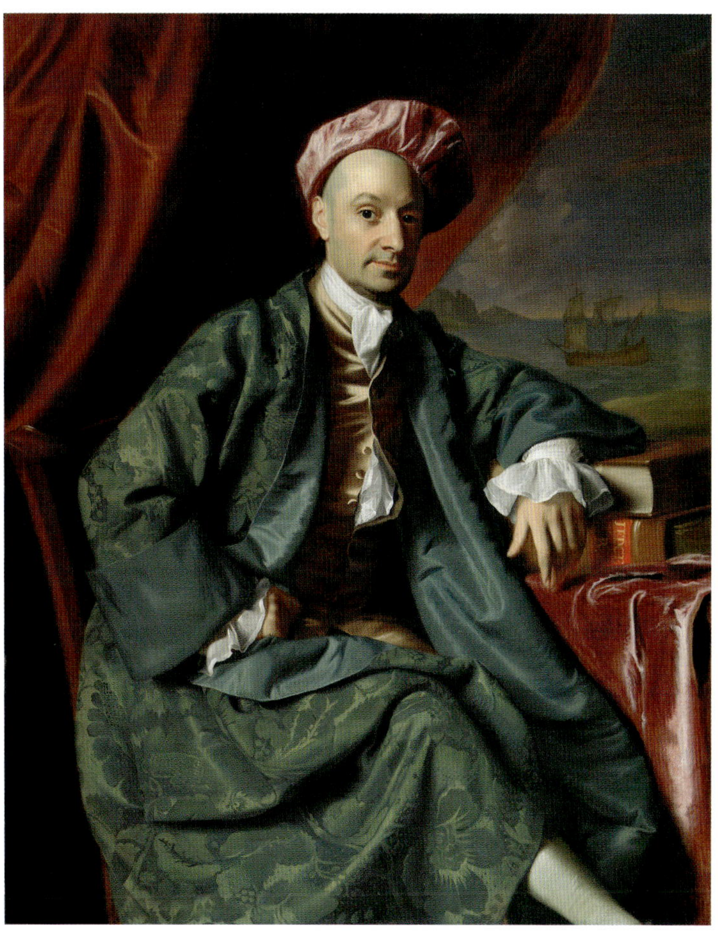

20 John Singleton Copley, *Nicholas Boylston*, 1767. Oil on canvas, 50⅛ × 39¹³⁄₁₆ in. (127.3 × 101.1 cm). Harvard Art Museums / Fogg Museum, Cambridge, Mass., Harvard University Portrait Collection, bequest of Ward Nicholas Boylston to Harvard College, 1828, H90. Imaging Department © President and Fellows of Harvard College.

John Hancock's property figures prominently in a watercolor of Boston Common by Christian Remick, who dedicated this work to the wealthy and powerful merchant (fig. 22). Remick (1726–1773), a fourth-generation British

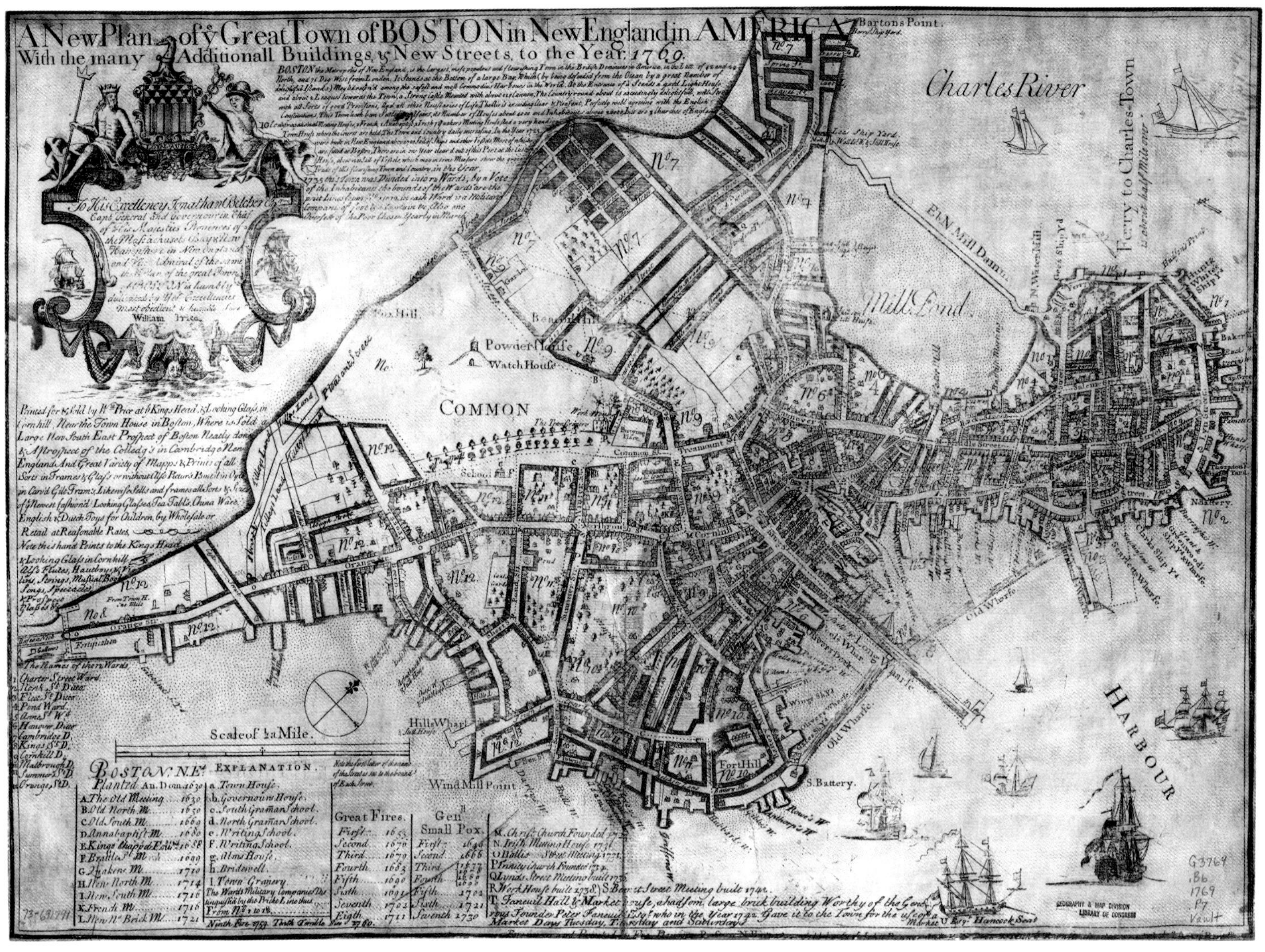

21 William Price, *A New Plan of ye Great Town of Boston in New England in America, with the many additionall buildings & new streets, to the year, 1769*, [1769]. Library of Congress, Geography and Map Division, Washington, D.C.

American and master mariner, advertised watercolor "sea pieces" and perspective views in a Boston newspaper; he was probably a self-taught artist.[87] His views present the landscape equivalent to Copley's portraits (albeit far less polished) in that they had little to do with emergent academic conceptions of landscape art as articulated by Reynolds in 1759 and visually identified at that same time with Richard Wilson's pastoral Italianate landscape compositions. According to Reynolds, the landscape artist must "attend only to the invariable, the great and general ideas which are fixed and inherent in universal nature," eschewing "literal truth and a minute exactness in the details."[88] Remick's drawings emerge instead from seventeenth- and eighteenth-century British empirical practices of mapping and topographical representation, the domain of both military draftsmen and male amateur artists, at least prior to the third quarter of the century.[89]

Remick rendered his view of Boston Common with attention to plausible particularities of the site and in response to a particular event: the arrival of British troops on September 30, 1768, following colonial resistance to taxation under the Townshend Acts and the public rioting in Boston after customs officials impounded Hancock's sloop *Liberty*. Although Remick's contemporaneous *Perspective View of the Blockad[e] of Boston Harbour* expresses blatant politics – at the center, above massed British warships discharging soldiers, appears a banner citing the Magna Carta, the foundational English document of individual rights – his

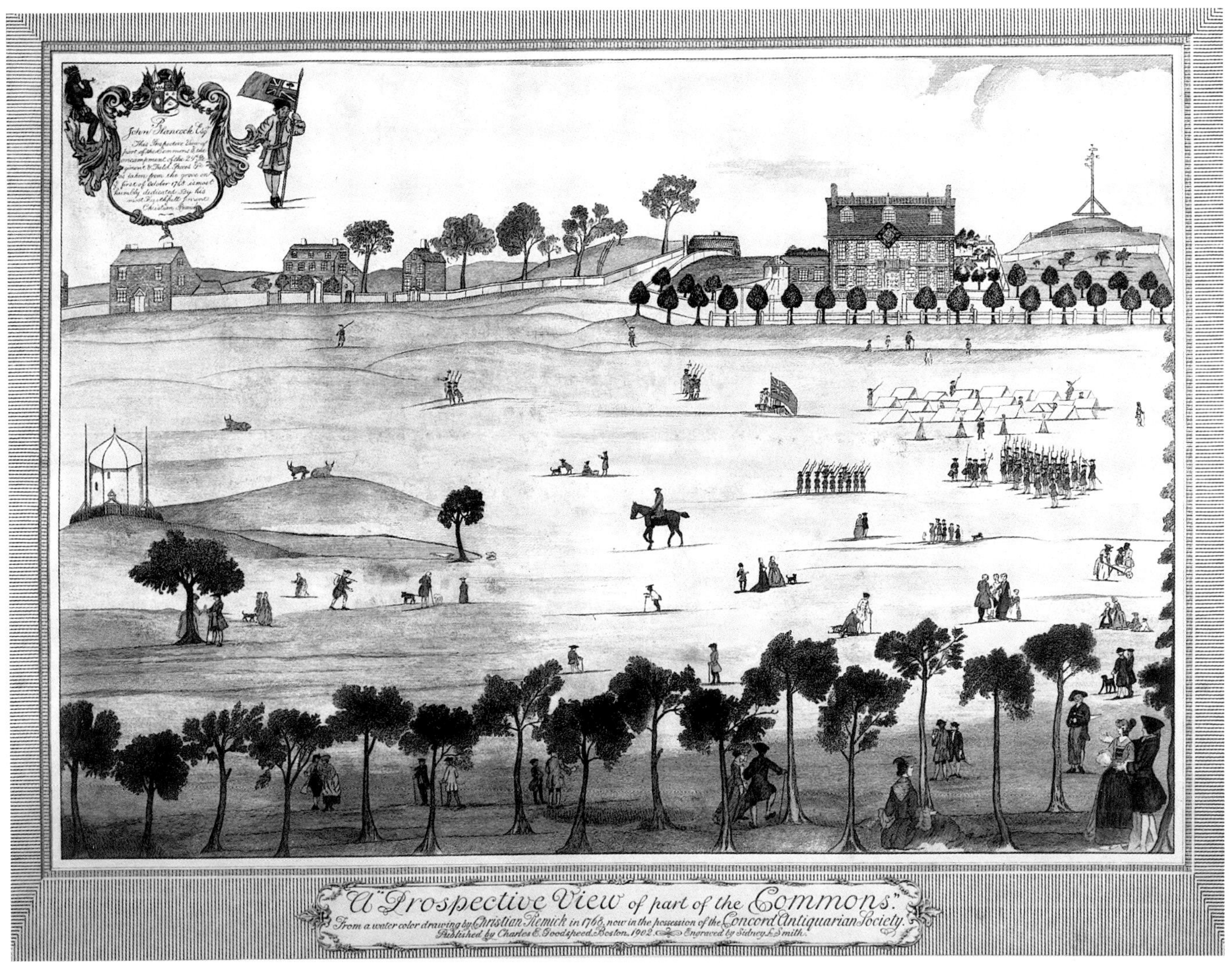

22 Sidney L. Smith, after Christian Remick, *A Prospective View of Part of the Commons*. Engraving from a watercolor of 1768. Charles Goodspeed publisher, Boston, 1902. Concord Museum, gift of Cummings E. Davis, Pi410. Courtesy Concord Museum, Concord, Mass.

view of the Common at first glance projects a sense of civil order and prosperity consistent with traditions of topographic views and maps.[90] A portion of the 29th Regiment musters in front of their encampment on the town's publicly shared open land, also known as the Training Field since it had long been used by local militia. Punctuated by little hillocks and with a small structure at the left, the Common occupies a broad band across the middle 50 percent of Remick's composition. At the lower edge, an allée of trees planted almost fifty years earlier ("The Mall," shown on the 1769 map) shades fourteen men and women, mostly well dressed and in pairs; they function within the composition as staffage, the characteristic foreground component of eighteenth-century views, while also depicting the local social custom of strolling the Mall after teatime.[91] As if on a fine autumnal outing, they appear nonchalantly to observe military proceedings that were a relatively common occurrence, even before those actions were directed at them. The Common was a place shared by Bostonians in all walks of life, and more than two dozen others dot the open field: a gentleman on horseback nearly in the center; people with pets; family groups, including a trio of African-Americans with a wheelbarrow; and a couple of working men, one in shirtsleeves and another shouldering a stick and sack. At the upper left, on rising ground with irregularly spaced trees, two dwellings and a tall outbuilding appear within the neat enclosure of a wall – the properties that Copley purchased the following year. Divided from that area by a lane that disappears over the hill (George Street on the map) stands the imposing Hancock house. Remick carefully detailed the principal elements of its early Georgian architectural style: broad, centered entry door below a second-floor balcony, string course between the two principal floors, third-floor dormers in a high gambrel roof with balustrade, and chimneys at both ends. Above the second floor appears a lozenge-shaped hatchment with family coat of arms, traditionally placed to announce a death in the family. The house rises behind a neat lane of lime (linden) trees, which further reinforces its distinction and enhances its formality. The trees had been lately planted by John Hancock, so Remick exaggerated their size for the picture, at once highlighting Hancock's role as a public benefactor – he also had a music stand erected on the Common to provide amusement for townspeople – and as the holder of a very significant piece of private property, with walled garden and orchard.[92] Beyond, at the upper right of the composition, stands the beacon that gave Copley's Beacon Hill neighborhood its name, originally erected so that neighboring communities could be warned of Indian attack. The structure provided a point of surveillance, as well, and so in effect does Hancock's house, in a work that might be regarded as a metaphorical portrait of an emerging defender of colonial liberties.[93] Still, Hancock's fortune depended on commerce with Britain, and, at that moment, he placed a premium on finding a peaceful resolution of the dispute.

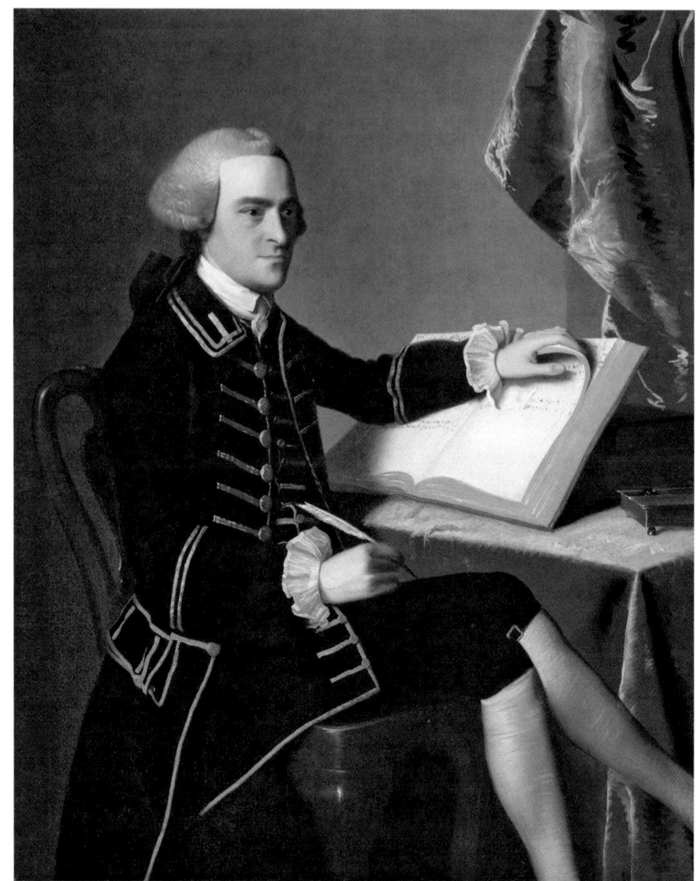

23 John Singleton Copley, *John Hancock*, 1765. Oil on canvas, 49⅛ × 39⅜ in. (124.8 × 100 cm). Museum of Fine Arts, Boston, deposited by the City of Boston, L-R 30.76.d.

Copley and John Hancock had been acquainted at least since 1764, when Hancock commissioned a grandly staged, full-length portrait of his deceased uncle for Harvard College and a more sober presentation of himself with a merchant's ledger, alluding to his new role as the head of an important shipping business (fig. 23). (Some years earlier, Thomas Hancock had commissioned two modest portraits of himself, a pastel and a miniature, from the barely twenty-year-old Copley.) On the evidence of Copley's aspirational writings, it seems somewhat unlikely that the portraitist showed John Hancock the deference expected from an artisan and which, to varying degrees, artisans were conditioned to display. Shoemaker George Robert Twelves Hewes, for one, recalled that as a twenty-one-year-old apprentice, he was scared "almost to death" to pay a bidden visit on New Year's Day 1763 to Hancock, whose shoe he had repaired. This was not a social call between equals, but a custom through which working members of society appeared to acquiesce in their own social subordination, even as some found subtle ways to resist.[94] Copley consented to play no such subordinate role, certainly not in 1769. With firm new ties to another prominent merchant family, the Clarkes, Copley was determined to project an image consistent with that of his nearly exact contemporary and neighbor Hancock. His self-portrait makes clear that he regarded himself as no less a gentleman. Two years later, Copley's extensive remodeling of his residence brought the house into newer fashion than Hancock's, publicizing the artist's taste and success to the upscale clientele he cultivated.[95]

Analyzed in terms of its iconography, Copley's self-portrait projects social assurance and position; however, his use of the pastel medium, when considered in light of the artist's correspondence during the 1760s, exposes a deep vein of insecurity. Without Copley's writings, that condition would be difficult to detect. Crayon painting, as it was then known, enjoyed well-established popularity abroad, practiced by both professional and amateur artists, such as Rhoda Delaval, whose gentleman father paid her London teacher (and portraitist) Arthur Pond a generous one guinea per session (fig. 24).[96] In America, Copley's principal American predecessor, and the isolated American artist working in the medium before mid-century, was Henrietta Johnston, active in Charleston from about 1708 to the late 1720s (fig. 25), contemporaneous with the Venetian artist who is usually credited for launching the eighteenth-century vogue for pastel portraits, Rosalba Carriera.[97] Copley, perhaps unknowingly, had direct familiarity with Johnston's work after being commissioned by Thomas Amory II, in 1770, to copy Johnston's pastel portrait of Amory's father, who had lived in Charlestown until 1720. Copley's earliest pastels date to 1758, but he probably gained exposure to the medium ten years prior, when his widowed mother married the artist Peter Pelham (1695–1751), a London-trained mezzotint engraver. That print-making method, invented in the mid-seventeenth-century and favored for reproducing oil paintings, employed pastel in the process, and many mezzotint artists worked in both media. Copley's other potential sources of information about pastels included art manuals – though these focused more on how to make crayons than on technique – and imported prints "in the crayon manner."[98] John Gore, who sold painters' materials at the Sign of the Painter's-Arms in Queen Street, first advertised "crayons" imported from London in the *Boston Gazette, and Country Journal* on March 9, 1761, so Copley did not have to make his own materials, not a common practice among pastelists in any case. Like other colonial American practitioners of pastel, he probably learned mostly through experimentation, but he became a technically proficient crayon painter and benefited from limited colonial competition.

Copley seized the opportunity presented by his interest in the medium to reach out to a brother artist across the Atlantic. In 1762, the year before he took up pastels in earnest, he drafted a letter to the Swiss-French pastelist Jean-Étienne Liotard (1702–1789). Liotard had enjoyed a run of popularity in mid-1750s London and was known for his colorful persona and uncompromising honesty of por-

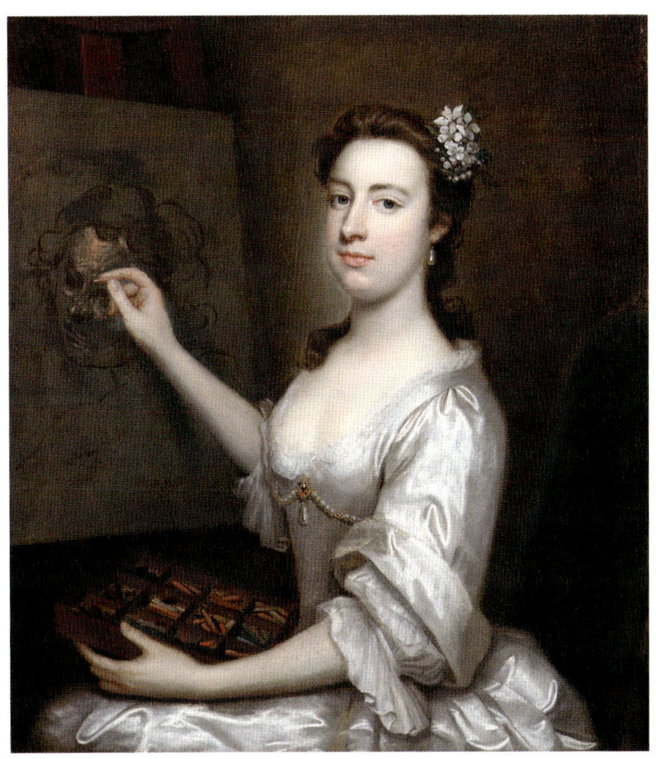

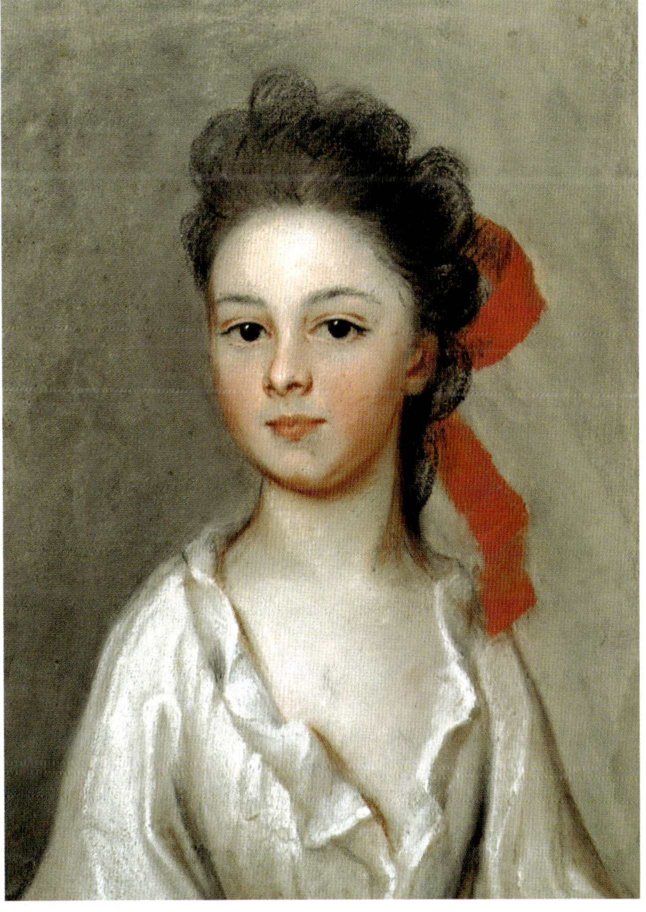

Top 24 Arthur Pond (attrib.), *Rhoda (née Delaval), Lady Astley*, ca. 1750. Oil on canvas, 30¼ × 27 in. (76.8 × 68.6 cm). © National Portrait Gallery, London.

Bottom 25 Henrietta de Beaulieu Dering Johnston, *Henriette Charlotte Chastaigner (Mrs. Nathaniel Broughton, 1700–1754)*, 1711. Pastel on paper, 11⁷⁄₁₀ × 9 in. (29.71 × 24.63 cm). Gibbes Museum of Art, Charleston, gift of Victor A. Morawetz, 1938.020.0004. Image courtesy of the Gibbes Art Museum/Carolina Art Association.

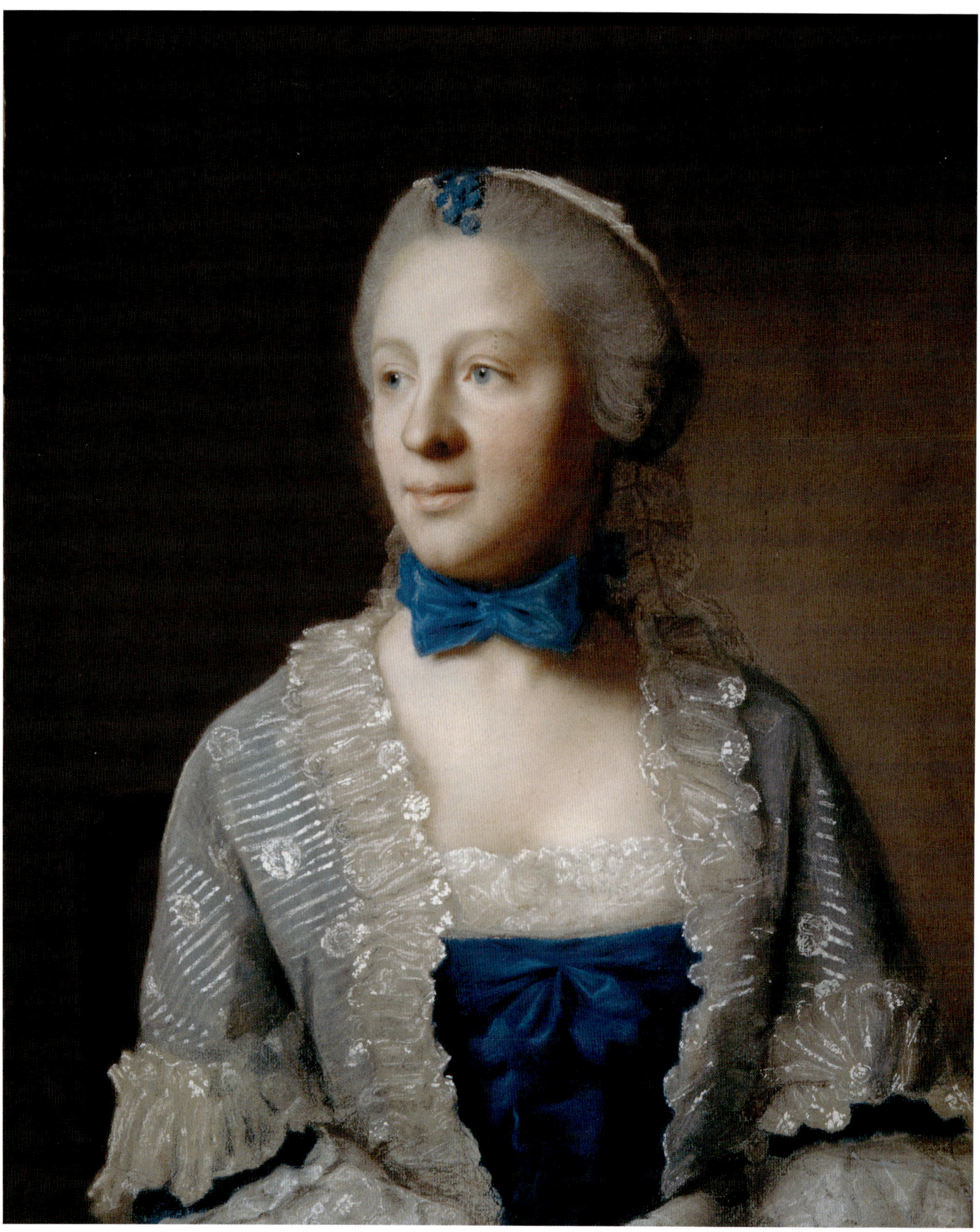

26 Jean-Étienne Liotard, *Eva Marie Garrick*, 1753–55. Pastel on paper, 30½ × 24½ in. (77.5 × 62 cm). © Devonshire Collection, Chatsworth. Reproduced by permission of Chatsworth Settlement Trustees.

trayal (fig. 26). As Copley's letter makes clear, he knew of Liotard by reputation, no more. The American asked Liotard for help in "obtaining a set of the best Swiss crayons for drawing of Portraits . . . the very best kind such as you can recommend [for] liveliness of color and justness of tints." He continued:

> You may perhaps be surprised that so remote a corner of the Globe as New England should have any d[e]mand for the necessary eutensils for practiceing the fine Arts, but I assure You Sir however feeble our efforts may be, it is not for want of inclination that they are not better, but the want of oppertunity to improve ourselves. However America which has been the seat of war and desolation, I would fain hope will one Day become the school of fine Arts and Monsieur Liotard['s] Drawing with Justice be set as patterns for our immitation. not that I have ever had the advantage of beholding any one of those rare peices from Your hand. but [I have] formd a Judgment on the true tast[e] of several of My friend[s] who has seen em.[99]

Alternately insistent, defensive, proud, and ingratiating, the Copley of this letter is also remarkably uninhibited, showing little of the apprehension stirred up by his eventual contact with artists abroad. Notably, his conception of the fine arts at this point imbued pastels (and implicitly portraiture) with importance, a perspective soon to be challenged. Whether Copley even sent the letter to Liotard remains unknown; if he did, and actually received pastels as requested, he probably would have mentioned it in the correspondence he took up a few years later with West (by which time he did have a London supplier for crayons).[100] In any case, the mere fact that Copley composed such a letter in 1762 – a promising moment for Americans within a consolidated British empire – demonstrates the intensity of his desire to make contact with illustrious artists on the other side of the Atlantic, whatever their nationality.

In 1766, Copley learned that some in that community of artists, by then quite real to him and aware of him in turn, frowned on crayon painting. Reynolds "condemned" work in pastel or watercolor (used for miniatures); likewise West, advising Copley on a second submission to the Society of Artists, cautioned him against working in any medium other than oil paint, it having "superiority over all other Painting."[101] The judgment against pastel took blunter form in *An Essay on Perfecting the Fine Arts in Great Britain and in Ireland* (1767), using terms reminiscent of the distinction between artists and artisans. A drawing academy in Ireland had been a springboard for many excellent pastelists, the writer noted, but he cautioned that "to expect Painters from mere Workers in Chalk, would be to expect Philosophers from a Grammar-school."[102] At the periphery himself, Copley found West's injunction baffling and wrote to ask about his disapproval of crayons, adding: "I think my best portraits done in that way."[103] Copley probably would not have made this assertion had not his crayon portraits met particular approval from clients, who must have found them fashionably novel. Those Boston patrons, unlike the artist, remained unaware of (or unmoved by) the criticism directed at pastels by a handful of British artists then attempting to reshape the terms of artistic accomplishment. After querying West, Copley learned that the London-based American artist, curiosity evidently piqued, had received one of his pastels from Captain Bruce.[104] But West seems not to have given Copley any feedback on this work, and the surviving correspondence reveals no specifics of his distaste for the medium.

The greater fragility of pastels was well known – a review of the first Society of Arts exhibition in 1760 questioned Francis Cotes's preference for the medium on those grounds – but that does not alone explain the objection.[105] For a history painter like West and other artists of academic inclination, pastels were damned by their association with small-scale portraits, more of a private than public art, and by their popularity with amateurs, who appreciated the ease of a medium that required no drying, no varnish, little preparation, and few tools (though no little skill). Both factors feminized pastels, a gendering reinforced by the prominence among pastelists of women and French artists generally. Reynolds, for one, reportedly dismissed Liotard, who had studied and worked in Paris, by noting that "his pictures are just what ladies do when they paint for their amusement."[106] Not sensitized to such matters, Copley persisted with West, but more nervously, sending him another pastel in 1768, with a protective explanation: "It is a plain head and the only apology I have to offer is this, that as I never saw any thing done in that way that could possably be esteemd, I am more at a loss to know what will please the Coniseur."[107] Two years later, he abandoned pastels.

Copley's exchanges on the subject of pastels reveal that his use of the medium in 1769 for his self-portrait was freighted with meaning. His skill with crayons was a source of great pride – in that way, he made his "best portraits," he said – and the medium connected him to a European artist of wide experience and success – "fameux peintre" reads part of the drafted address to Liotard (written in another hand, presumably for Copley to copy). But his pastels had been ignored in another quarter that mattered to him very much; as his last statement on the subject to West indicates, Copley felt increasingly insecure, "at a loss," about his efforts. The assured surface, of pastel and painter, begins to break down. In every stroke of Copley's self-portrait lurks a nagging element of doubt.

An Artisan and a Gentleman

> A portrait photographer depends upon another person to complete his picture. The subject imagined, which in a sense is me, must be discovered in someone else willing to take part in a fiction he cannot possibly know about. My concerns are not his. We have separate ambitions for the image. His need to plead his case probably goes as deep as my need to plead mine, but the control is with me.
>
> Richard Avedon, *In the American West, 1979–1984* (1985)

At around the same time that he pictured himself as a gentleman, Copley portrayed silversmith Paul Revere, a fellow Bostonian, as an artisan (fig. 27). The portrait of Revere ranks among the best-known paintings ever produced by an American artist. It speaks to the way Americans mythicize their country as a land of equality and opportunity – first, because Revere appears as a man of the people, and, second, because it concretizes the shadowy horseman of the enduring story, the midnight rider who assisted at the birth of the freedoms Americans hold dear. In his 1994 book *Paul Revere's Ride*, historian David Hackett Fischer validates Copley's portrait for showing the "distinctive individual of strong character and vibrant personality" that those who actually knew Revere described. Performing a physiognomic reading, Fischer sees "a sense of seriousness in his high forehead and strength in his prominent chin." He detects Revere's pedigree in "the austere, old-fashioned [hair]style that gave his English puritan ancestors the name Roundheads," though the "sensual" features recall "his French forebears." All in all, Fischer asserts, the viewer feels "the searching look of an intelligent observer who sees much and misses little; the steady look of an independent man."[108]

Enthralled by Revere, Fischer forgets Copley, a common response to the portrait. Copley may have been America's most important artist of the colonial period, but the American Revolution intervened to make a legend of Revere. Even Dunlap, writing about Revere among other engravers in his *History*, devoted most of his entry to Revere's ride.[109] Lack of primary documentation for Copley's portrait of Revere made the oversight more intractable, discouraging questions about the relationship between the two men. Although a later twentieth-century cleaning of the picture revealed a date of 1768, long approximated on stylistic grounds, no record of a commission exists nor any mention of the portrait in the voluminous papers of either man or of their contemporaries.[110] My arguments about Copley's portrait of Revere are therefore based on circumstantial evidence, but in the absence of hard information, no one can do more than speculate. This has not stopped generations and scores of authors, academic and popular, from writing about the work and no wonder: it is an image of extraordinary power, seductive in its transparency and constituent of Revere's place in the historical imagination. For all these reasons, its maker cannot be disregarded. To restore Copley's agency and to suggest what portraying Revere may have meant to him is a primary concern for the remainder of this chapter. Though Copley would not have been able to articulate it himself, Richard Avedon's characterization of his relationship to photographic subjects applies perfectly to Copley, Revere, and the portrait that will always connect them.[111]

Copley seldom portrayed artisans. Over the course of his American career, from 1753 to 1774, the artist represented only fifteen men (12 percent of his output) who were occupied in "Crafts and Small Retail Business."[112] All but one of these craftsmen or small businessmen – wealthy, Harvard-educated distiller Thomas Amory II – sat for Copley before 1769. The humblest, occupationally, was also one of the first: tailor Thomas Marshall, whose portrait of around 1755 does not reveal his livelihood, except indirectly through his suit, apparently velvet and as such very fine. The sitter for Copley's only earlier known representation of an artisan, an engraver, has not been conclusively identified. Possibly it was a posthumous, idealized portrait of Copley's stepfather, engraver Peter Pelham, who died in 1751, or even a self-portrait, since Copley began his artistic career in 1753 by making mezzotints from previously used plates in Pelham's studio. But the man in the picture appears older than the youth Copley then was and bears little resemblance to the artist as he appears in the 1769 self-portrait, while Copley, sufficiently ambitious at seventeen to make a history painting, seems unlikely to have represented himself with engraver's tools.

Revere, like Copley (three years his junior), inherited his father's fully equipped shop and commenced business in 1754. Following eighteenth-century custom, he referred to himself as a goldsmith, after the most precious material

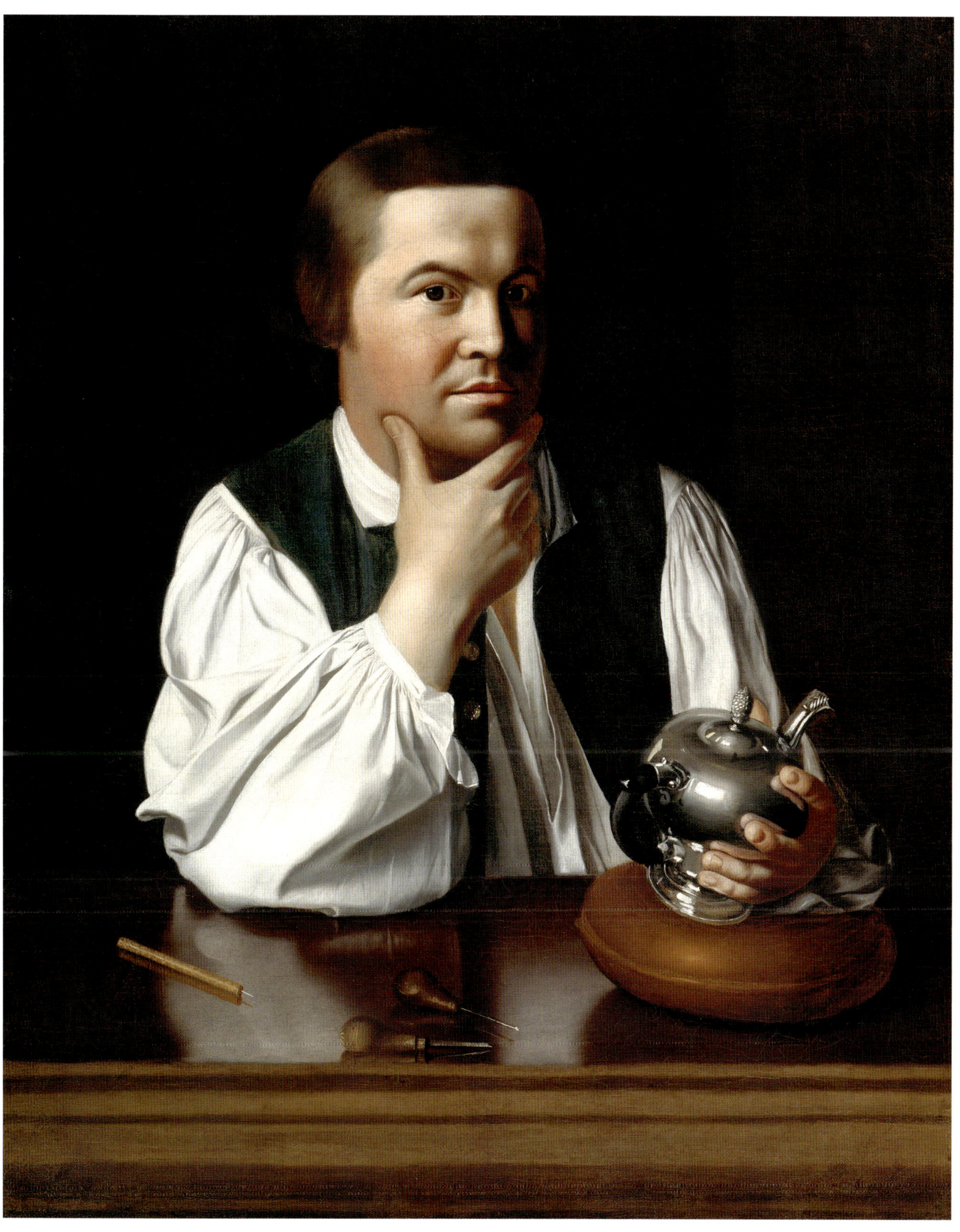

27 John Singleton Copley, *Paul Revere*, 1768. Oil on canvas, 35⅛ × 28½ in. (89.22 × 72.39 cm). Museum of Fine Arts, Boston, gift of Joseph W., William B., and Edward H. R. Revere, 30.781.

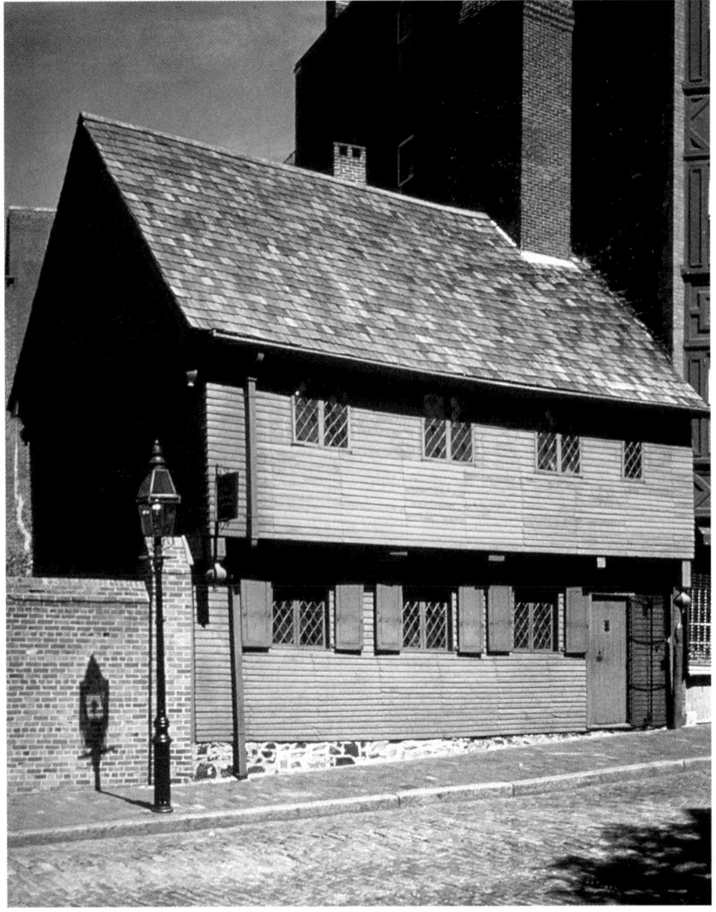

28 Paul Revere House, Boston. Courtesy Paul Revere Memorial Association. Photo: Art of Light.

he worked, usually for small items like buttons or rings; however, the bulk of his business was in silver. Silver was money, so the silversmith's character and integrity mattered to a degree without parallel among artisans. Customers had to trust smiths to work the valuable metal into plate at the sterling standard set by the London Goldsmith's Company (92.5 percent silver to 7.5 percent other metal, usually copper). *The London Tradesman* highlighted this enhanced social position in referring to the goldsmith as "the most genteel of any in the Mechanic Way," status evident from the fact that, during the early eighteenth century, professional men occasionally apprenticed their sons to goldsmiths. Goldsmiths needed better schooling in "a plain English Education" than men destined for "merely mechanical" employment, as their trade required both "a mechanical Hand and Head."[113] Revere demonstrated the latter in meticulous records of business transactions. He entered separate charges for materials (assessed by weight and quality) and labor, sometimes with additional fees noted for extras, like engraving. On February 17, 1762, for example, Revere charged Samuel Treat £6.7.9 for 18.5 ounces of silver, £3.6.8 for making a teapot, £1.6.8 for engraving it, and £0.3.4 for a wooden handle.[114] Treat paid in silver and cash, as did most clients after 1763, when Revere apparently stopped accepting payment in goods, such as cloth. In early 1763, Revere recorded the first of numerous transactions over the next four years with Copley, who purchased gold and silver frames, as well as glass for miniatures; in each case, the artist paid by cash.[115]

Revere experienced ups and downs in his business, with a low period in 1768 when Copley portrayed him.[116] Still, in 1770, after renting for many years, he was able to purchase a three-story wooden house on North Square from Captain John Erving, a merchant and real-estate speculator (fig. 28). Revere took out a mortgage of £160 on the total purchase price of £213.6.8 "Lawful Money" (Massachusetts currency), precisely one-quarter of the sum Copley paid for his property in 1769 and 1770. Revere's house, built in 1680, was considerably smaller than Copley's, even though he had six living children in 1770 and Copley only one, but it was typical in size and date for its solidly residential North Square neighborhood. The silversmith's relative prosperity allowed him to separate his home and place of business, which remained in the waterfront shop where the family had formerly also lived. In North Square, Revere's neighbors included another goldsmith, a baker, a cabinetmaker, an apothecary, a tallow chandler, a housewright, two tailors, and two shoemakers. Five merchants resided in North Square, as did a physician, a minister, several widows (including, by marriage, one of the few titled aristocrats in Boston), and the royal governor, Thomas Hutchinson.[117] Such economic mixing characterized most neighborhoods in eighteenth-century Boston. Revere's household ranked near the bottom third in terms of wealth among thirty-one neighbors assessed taxes in 1771.[118]

According to Fischer, Revere held a new "American attitude toward class" and regarded "the status of gentleman . . . [as] a social rank and a moral condition that could be attained by self-respecting men in any occupation." He found support for more liberal application of the term gentleman in the military commission the goldsmith received from royal governor William Shirley in 1756, addressed "Paul Revere, Gentleman."[119] The wording may be merely conventional, as officers in the British army were defined as gentlemen whatever their actual background. The colonial authorities necessarily made do with what they had, candidates of the "better sort" being relatively scarce (that notwithstanding, Revere never managed to obtain a commission in the Continental army).[120] Revere apparently sat in on meetings of the Long Room Club, a secretive political organization mostly comprising Harvard graduates in the professions of medicine, law, and divinity along with men of independent means. Among them, Revere (perhaps not formally a member) was the lone "mechanic."[121] He must have been comfortable with his station, for he wrote a cousin in France, to whom he might easily have dissembled: "I am in middling circumstances and very well off for a tradesman."[122] Earlier in the century, writing "On the Dignity of Trade in England," Daniel Defoe had proposed that "trade is so far here from being inconsistent with a gentleman, that, in short, trade in England makes gentlemen, and has peopled this nation with gentlemen."[123] Revere is supposed to have once defined a gentleman as a man who "respects his own credit," so he may have seen no contradiction in regarding himself as both an artisan and a gentleman, though not until the late 1780s did Revere style himself "Esquire" on official documents.[124] There is no question that more men than ever before claimed the name of gentleman, but having that claim accepted by others was another matter altogether.[125]

Copley manifestly portrayed Revere not as a gentleman but as a worker, "caught . . . in an unbuttoned moment," according to Fischer, not by the happenstance that wording suggests but by design. Whether Copley followed Revere's wishes or initiated the plan is unknown. His portrait of another goldsmith and engraver, Nathaniel Hurd, painted three years earlier, makes clear that there were options. Hurd was the first of Copley's sitters to be portrayed in the banyan that, in Copley's body of work, is associated with gentlemen. However, a rare unfinished painting by Copley shows Hurd with his sleeves rolled up, the goldsmith's bare arm a startling reminder of how seldom an exposed limb appears in eighteenth-century portraits of men (fig. 29). The conspicuously open collar, preserved in the completed picture, was also unconventional and remained so into the next century, when the Scottish painter David Wilkie chided a fellow artist who thought to portray himself similarly: "Oh don't do that; you'll look as if you were going to be shaved."[126] Hurd's turbaned head in the unfinished work would make sense with a banyan, so perhaps that canvas was a study for the painting as finally executed. Or maybe it was a more daring and rejected initial conception. Either way, it was a novel portrayal and Copley retained the oil study.[127] A few years later, he found in Revere a willing subject for the approach.

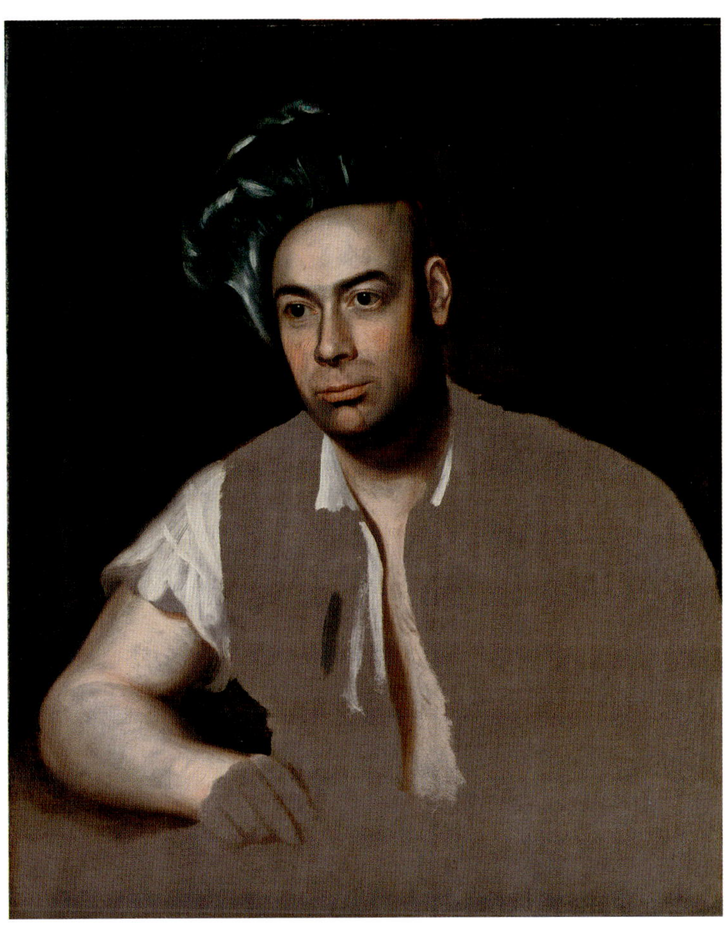

29 John Singleton Copley, *Unfinished Portrait of Nathaniel Hurd*, ca. 1765. Oil on canvas, 29⅜ × 24⅝ in. (74.61 × 62.55 cm). Memorial Art Gallery of the University of Rochester, New York, Marion Stratton Gould Fund.

In the final portrait of Hurd, Copley included two books, the larger volume marked on the spine "Display of Heraldry / I. Guillim" to identify a basic source of information about family coats of arms such as Hurd, a specialist in engraving, and Revere engraved on silver or book plates (fig. 30).[128] In this way, goldsmiths abetted their clients' social aspirations, not only by fashioning fine objects for the owner's use and display but also by representing, in heraldic form, claims to familial distinction that few actually possessed. Hurd fabricated such connections in his capacity as engraver and was not above making his own claims to status, as in commissioning a portrait by Copley. Despite allusions to his occupation in that portrayal, Hurd appears at leisure, an impression the banyan reinforces.

Revere, by contrast, is much more closely identified with his trade: he holds a teapot and appears without a coat and

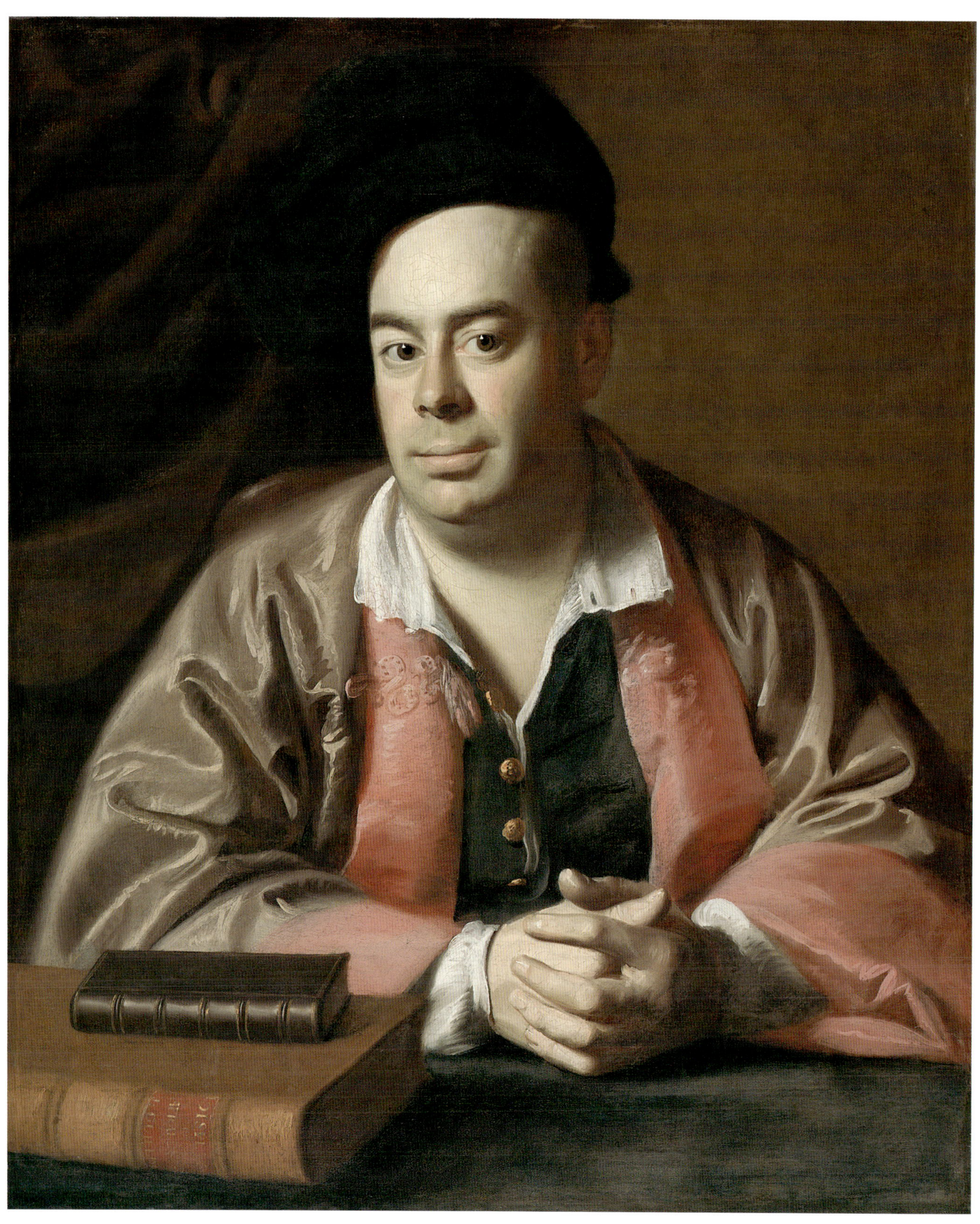

30 John Singleton Copley, *Nathaniel Hurd*, ca. 1765. Oil on canvas, 30 × 25½ in. (76.2 × 64.8 cm). Cleveland Museum of Art, gift of the John Huntington Art and Polytechnic Trust 1915.534. © The Cleveland Museum of Art.

in shirtsleeves, appropriate dress for a man at work but rarely otherwise. But this is not business-as-usual for a craftsman who made his living largely from the production of lower end goods such as flatware and personal accessories.[129] Revere's attire, moreover, is unusually fine for a worker: a dark green silk vest with gold buttons – presumably of his own manufacture and therefore a kind of advertisement – and a spotless and billowing white linen shirt, sign of a clean and healthy body at a time of infrequent bathing.[130] In the earliest known American representation of a goldsmith at his trade, a crude woodcut that formed part of an advertisement for Thomas You of Charleston in 1767, the artisan wears rolled-up shirtsleeves and a protective leather apron over his breeches while working with hammer and anvil (fig. 31).[131] Revere's imminent task is considerably less physical or messy; as Copley portrayed him, he seems at the point of engraving, using tools that Copley has carefully depicted. Yet Revere would not have performed such work at a polished table, risking scratches from a misplaced tool, and that table, with its extremely deep edge, has no correspondence to contemporaneous furniture styles. Compositionally, its gleaming surface balances the burnished teapot while further allowing Copley to demonstrate his skill in painting reflections, as in *Boy with a Squirrel*. The prominent reflections, together with Revere's pose, further invite contemplation of reflection in its metaphorical sense.

Most accounts of the painting assume that Revere himself made the decision to be identified with his trade because he was proud to be an artisan (and, many writers infer, proud to be an American). Even if he dictated the form of the painting, a circumstance impossible to prove, Copley obviously complied. By the same token, it is difficult to imagine that Copley could have compelled Revere to appear as an artisan had the goldsmith not wished it, even if Copley made the work for his own purposes. Surely, the artist and artisan cooperated. At the same time, they may have had distinct agendas, each served by the same portrait.

Neither man can have overlooked the political implications of the portrayal. Revere, when he sat for his portrait, was occupied less by the manufacture and engraving of teapots (a fraction of his business at that time) than by tea itself, the most potent symbol of American grievances against the British government and its perceived unlawful taxation of imported consumer goods.[132] Tea drinking and its equipage had typically been associated with refinement and identified with the domestic sphere and the civilizing agency of women.[133] But Revere's grip on the gleaming

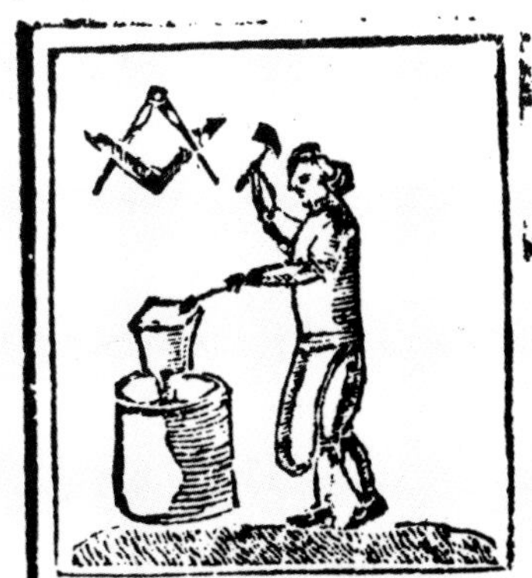

THOMAS YOU,
GOLD-SMITH;
At the Golden Cup in Meeting-ſtreet, next Door to Mr. HOLIDAY's Tavern;

TAKES this Method of returning Thanks to his Friends and Acquaintance for their paſt Favours, & to requeſt a continuance of the ſame. He undertakes the working Part, and hopes the general Satisfaction he has given to thoſe who have already employed him, will be a ſufficient Motive for their kind Recommendation to others: Any Piece of Plate worked up in his Shop, he will warrant as good as Sterling; and if any ſuch Piece ſhould break, he will mend the ſame *Gratis*.——He has for Sale, ſundry Pieces of large Plate and Jewellery, which he will ſell at a low Advance. Country Orders punctually obeyed.
N. B. A back Room to let: Enquire of ſaid YOU.

31 Advertisement of "Thomas You, Gold-Smith," Charleston, *South Carolina Gazette and Country Journal*, Aug. 4, 1767.

orb, stubby fingers spread wide and doubled in the reflection, seems anything but refined. The forceful, tenacious gesture and level gaze, to the contrary, allay contemporaneous concerns over the emasculating effects of luxury and of tea drinking.[134] Revere appears a man of thought and action, one fully prepared to challenge British policy over the colonies. By the time Copley painted him, Revere had already joined with the Sons of Liberty in a successful campaign against the Stamp Act, which sparked violent protests in Boston during the summer of 1765. An English creamware teapot bearing the inscription "No Stamp Act," hand enameled in red, makes the point that tea had become highly politicized by that time, even though the Stamp Act taxed legal and commercial documents and printed materials, not tea (fig. 32).[135]

In 1767, the Townshend Acts imposed duties on a wider variety of items – including glass, painters' colors, oil, lead, paper, and tea – and colonial resistance mounted. A detailed non-consumption list drawn up in the Boston town meeting of October 28, 1767, identified many other British manufactures, such as silverware and imported fabrics, that colonists were urged to spurn in favor of American-made goods, a decision benefiting such local craftsmen as Revere.[136] Tea

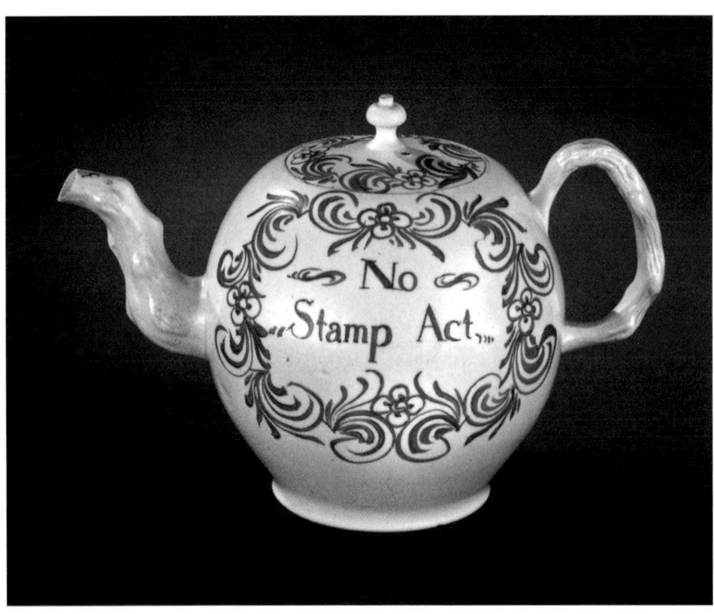

32 "No Stamp Act" teapot, possibly made at the Cockpitt Hill factory, probably Derby, England, 1766–70, refined earthenware (creamware) with red enamel decoration. Colonial Williamsburg Foundation Museum Purchase.

came under renewed scrutiny with the merchant-sponsored non-importation boycott that gathered strength during 1768 and 1769.[137] The anonymous author of a letter published on the front page of the *Boston Gazette* for August 15, 1768, blamed Americans for exposing themselves, in their dependence on tea – "that most pernicious article of luxury" – to the "bait" in England's "snare." Tea, the writer argued, should be shunned not "on account of its physical qualities, but on account of the political diseases & death that are connected with every particle of it." The enforcing presence of British soldiers in Boston beginning in fall 1768 (as recorded in Remick's watercolor of Boston Common) exacerbated a tense situation and eventually exploded in the so-called "Boston Massacre" of March 5, 1770, when British soldiers killed several townspeople. Revere commemorated that event with an engraving (fig. 33), the unauthorized reproduction of a drawing by Henry Pelham, Copley's half brother, who accused Revere of pirating his work in a letter of March 29, 1770.[138] Even after the Boston Massacre, with soldiers withdrawn and the Townshend Acts repealed, a symbolic tax on tea continued. By the late 1760s and continuing into the next decade, abstention from tea drinking had become a political act throughout the colonies.[139]

Between 1767 and 1775, Revere's production of teapots (previously one or two a year) ceased almost entirely, although he continued to engrave plain teapots that clients brought him. During that eight-year period, he produced only two, both in 1773 – the year of the Tea Act, which pushed colonial consumers closer to revolution. One of those sets was the extravagant order, the largest Revere ever filled, for a forty-piece tea and coffee service, for which Dr. William Paine of Worcester paid £108. Paine's commission, in connection with his marriage, conspicuously manifested the loyalist sympathies of a man who, in 1774, joined in strongly worded protest of the "riotous, disorderly, and seditious practices" of those involved in the Tea Party protest of the preceding December.[140] Revere participated in the fateful uprising, yet he was willing to separate business and politics when substantial profit and family ties were at stake, as with the Paine tea set, the patron's wedding gift to his bride, Lois Orne, a distant cousin of Revere's first wife, Sarah. In fact, Revere served clients of both Whig and Tory persuasion, just as Copley did.[141] Still, no one can have mistaken the direction of his political sympathies.

Copley, on the other hand, acutely sensitive to the professional perils of taking sides, made efforts to keep his politics private. For the Society of Artists exhibition of 1771, he considered pairing a subject "in the Evening of Life with one in the Bloom of Youth." He was then engaged on the first work, a portrait of Mrs. Humphrey Devereux commissioned by her son, London auctioneer John Greenwood, formerly a resident of Boston. The second, his portrait of a four-year-old boy (location unknown), was already in London, sent by the boy's father to his son's namesake, John Wilkes, a radical Whig heroic to American Whigs for his defense of English liberties and his outspoken criticism of royal policies, including unjust taxation. Recognizing the passions that Wilkes inflamed, Copley pondered the wisdom of exhibiting that portrait before a London audience; but he dodged responsibility and left the decision in West's hands, declaring himself "desireous of avoideing every imputation of party spir[it], Political contests being neighther pleasing to an artist or advantageous to the Art itself."[142] (For whatever reason, the boy's portrait was not shown.) Given the furor over the tea tax, it is hard to imagine that Copley overlooked – even if he did not initially plan – the political dimension in his portrayal of Revere.[143]

Copley's own self-portrait had political resonance as well, since fine, imported fabrics and trimmings were among the luxuries that many Bostonians resolved not to purchase in the wake of the Townshend Acts. Sixty prominent merchants of the town signed a non-importation agreement on August 1, 1768. The eight resolute non-subscribers – pub-

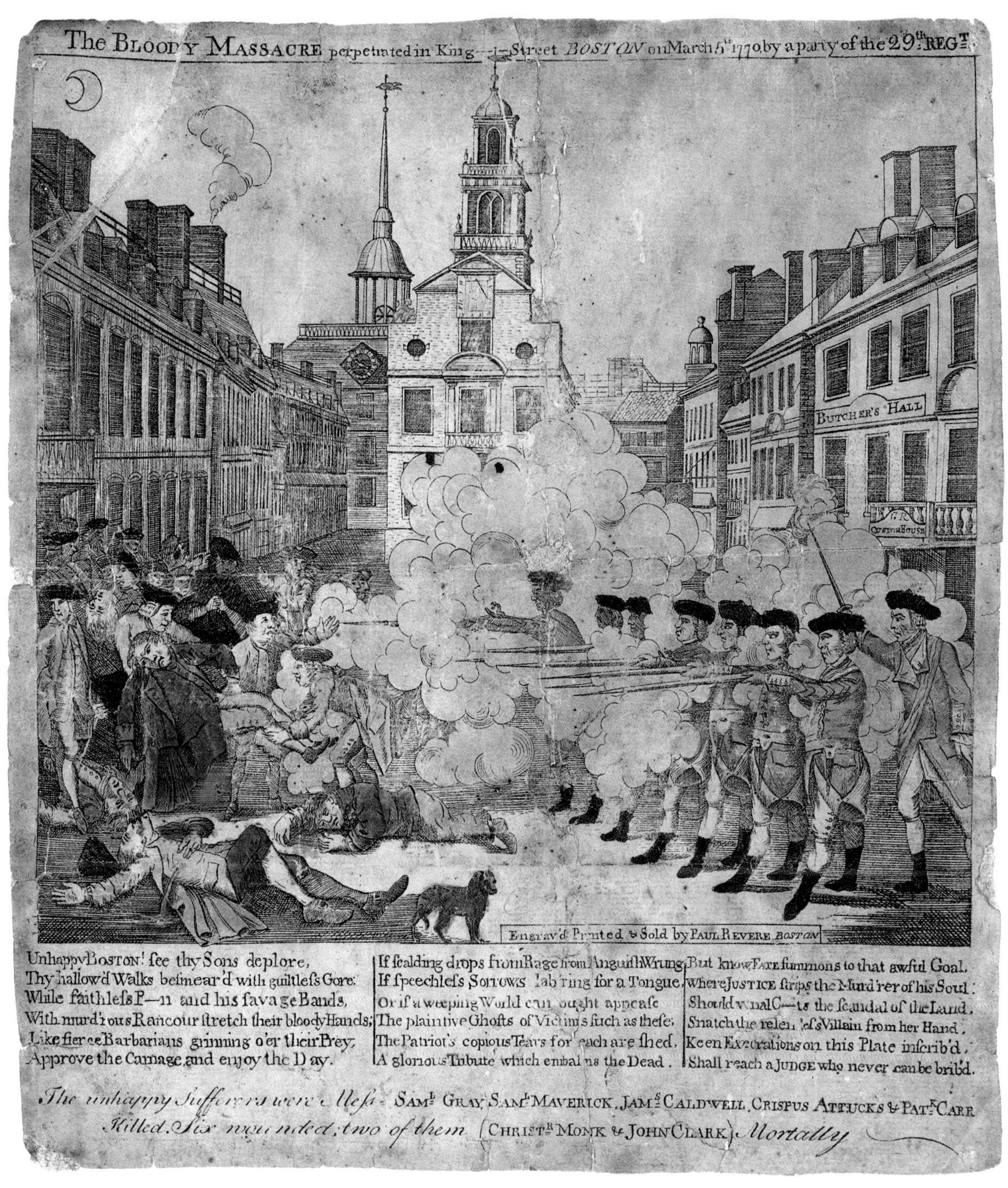

33 Paul Revere, Jr., *The Boston Massacre*, 1770. Engraving, hand colored. Museum of Fine Arts, Boston, gift of Miss Margaret A. Revere, Miss Anna P. Revere, Mr. Paul Revere, and Mr. John Revere Chapin, 62.506.

licly denounced as "enemies to their country" in the *Boston Gazette* (August 14, 1769) – included Richard Clarke, whose daughter Copley wed only a few months later.[144] In the portrait occasioned by his marriage, the splendidly attired Copley pictorially cast his lot with a wealthy and defiantly loyalist merchant family. The artist was hardly alone in clinging to fine stuffs, which remained available for purchase in Boston from inventory built up in anticipation of the boycott. Homespun cloth could be worn as a badge of conscience, and it is tempting to read the expanse of white linen of Revere's shirt as such, even if duties on white lead, among other painters' colors, potentially undercuts the political point (though arguably only to a more limited constituency of persons with trade-specific knowledge).[145] But, in a portrait designed to endure, few were prepared to commemorate what might have been a passing political concern. With posterity to consider, Copley's clients showed no inclination to cast off British finery. They were united, as well, in their patronage of him. The artist's connection to the Clarkes had no discernible impact on his ability to attract commissions from prominent Whigs, just as his portrayal of such radicals as Samuel Adams failed to dissuade Tory patrons. He was, after all, far and away the best portraitist in colonial Boston.

This returns us to the matter of Copley's status and to what his portrait of Revere can tell us on that score. By the terms of colonial British American society, both Copley and Revere were highly skilled, high-rank artisans who produced luxury goods for the market. Their prices suggest intriguing equivalence. An engraved silver teapot similar to the one Revere holds in his portrait brought the artisan £12 in 1762 (such objects were among the more expensive items he made), while Copley, in 1769, charged £9.16 for a quarter-length (30 × 25 inch) portrait, the approximate date and exact size of Revere's; the following year, he received the same amount for a somewhat smaller pastel portrait, roughly the size of his own.[146] These items, however, had different profit margins. Silver accounted for more than half the price of the 1762 teapot, and when clients provided the metal, as they often did, Revere's fee was closer to £5. Copley's sitters, by contrast, supplied no materials for their portraits, and those materials, of relatively low cost, had little inherent value or potential for exchangeability.[147]

English art theorist Jonathan Richardson, in a mercenary vein that somewhat undercut his claims for painting as a liberal art, observed that, relative to other manufactures, an artist's finished product more completely outstripped the value of the raw materials used to make it.[148] How did that product gain value? Campbell, in *The London Tradesman* of 1747, was cynical about the matter: "The good Face-Painter must have the Name of having travelled to *Rome*; and when he comes Home, he must be so happy as to please some great Personage, who is reputed a Connoisseur, or he remains in continual obscurity. If he should paint a Cobler, with all the Beauties of the Art, and the most glaring Likeness, he must paint only Coblers, and be satisfied with their price; but if he draws a Duke, or some dignified Person, though his Features should prove so strong that the mere Signpost Dauber could not fail to hit the Likeness, he becomes immediately famous and fixes what Price he pleases on his Work."[149] Campbell deplores the equation of a painter's merit with a sitter's social position, though he exaggerates to make the point since (Plato's example notwithstanding) cobblers rarely had portraits taken.[150] (His reference to sign painting activated a slur no less common than the comparison of portraitists to tailors, as I discuss in later chapters.) Still, his account suggests that painters charged as much as they could get. Without cynicism, the entry for "painter" in an early nineteenth-century trade manual supports that view: "The earnings of an artist cannot be defined: he is paid according to his talents, and to the celebrity which he has acquired."[151] Accordingly, a friend urged Copley to raise his prices after his second showing at the Society of Artists, in 1767, and his election to its membership.[152] Yet following eighteenth-century custom, canvas size determined portrait prices. In other words, painters received payment commensurate with the amount of time and labor presumed necessary to manufacture a portrait, not according to more elusive measures of talent or genius.

Copley, who chafed at the association of art with trade, had a vested interest in intellectualizing his own artisan labor, and this cause affected his portrait of Revere. The goldsmith, as Copley presented him, strikes a pose that emphasizes the mental rather than manual aspects of his craft, recalling the eighteenth-century description of goldsmithing as an occupation requiring both "a mechanical hand and head." With his right hand, Revere makes a caliper-like gesture, drawing attention to his head (and, it seems, inviting us to take his measure); his spread left hand firmly secures the completed teapot, polished and gleaming.[153] But one task remains – engraving – judging from the tools before Revere. Engraving required intellect, or so some argued, an opinion not universally shared. The founders of the Royal Academy in 1768 initially meant to exclude engravers, on grounds that their work was substantially reproductive. However, the work of engravers subsidized the income of painters, especially history painters, by making their pictures widely marketable, so the decision was quickly relaxed, allowing six Associate Engravers to join the thirty-six founding members (twenty-eight painters, five architects, and three sculptors).[154] Not all were so high handed. "The Principles of this art" of engraving, stated *Universal Magazine* in 1748, ". . . are the same as those of painting." Yet only the engraver who studies the antique, the best masters of oil painting, and perspective and architecture can become "a perfect master of design." In the plate illustrating "The Art of Etching and Engraving," an allegorical figure of "genius" – a winged woman who points

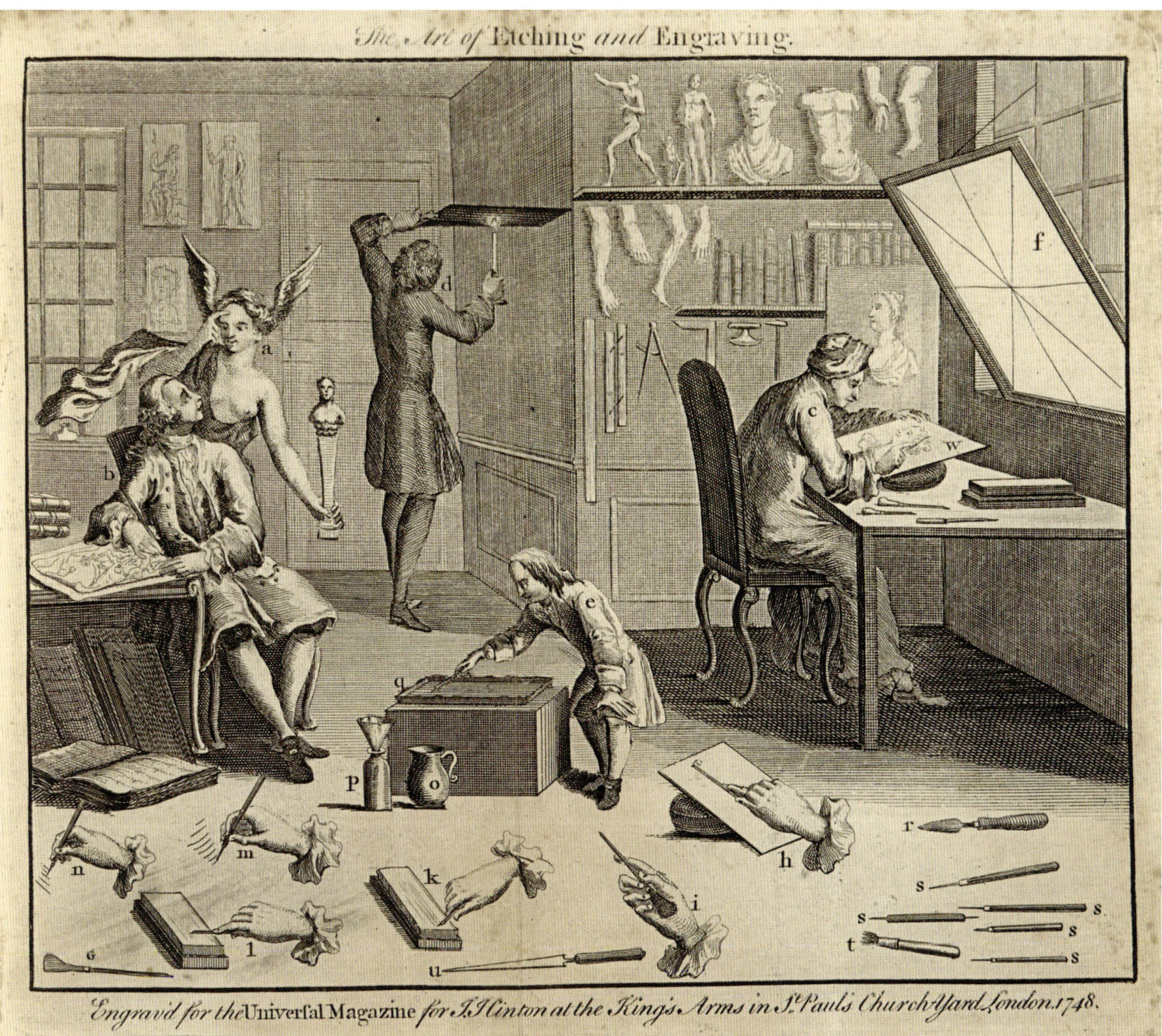

34 "The Art of Etching and Engraving," *Universal Magazine of Knowledge and Pleasure* 3 (Oct. 1748). From the O. Meredith Wilson Library Rare Book Collection, University of Minnesota, Minneapolis.

to her forehead – is shown "inspiring the draughtsman . . . with the design, which he afterward cuts with his graver" (fig. 34).[155] Strikingly, the draftsman wears a gentleman's suit and wig when communing with genius (he twists away from his drawing to look up at her) but a cap and gown while bent over his work table. In the foreground, disembodied hands hold tools that illustrate the materials and processes of engraving, somewhat at the expense of the intellectual dimension brought out by the text. In his portrait of Revere, Copley's decision to highlight engraving as an aspect of the goldsmith's trade (not actually one of Revere's strengths) makes him somewhat like Copley himself: a creator of images on surfaces and a man whose activated mind precedes his engaged hand. The portrait of Revere in that sense functions as a surrogate self-portrait. Revere's level gaze shows him alert and thoughtful, as

Copley would have been in undertaking the work. Perhaps Copley was emboldened by Roger de Piles. In characterizing the manner in which a powerful portrait speaks its subject's distinction, the French painter and theorist chose obvious examples – "I am that invincible king, surrounded with majesty . . . I am that man of letters who is absorbed in the sciences" – and some far less so: "I am that famous artisan, who was so singular in his profession."[156] In the portrait of Revere as an artisan, Copley dared to be more honest about the virtues of artisanry than he was in his contemporaneous self-portrait.

Copley nevertheless had the upper hand on Revere, since engravers of silver usually copied or adapted their designs from books of heraldry, like the one Copley included in his portrait of Nathaniel Hurd. Heraldry, according to Campbell's *London Tradesman*, was "but a dry insipid Study," requiring "no nice Hand, nor exquisite Taste," but only "a slight Resemblance of the Figures designed." Heraldic painters draw "very expeditiously, and execute, after their manner, with two or three rude Strokes of a Pencil, what a judicious Painter would employ some Hours about" – here again, the equation of value with time expended.[157] Although Campbell was writing about heraldic painters not engravers, the meanness of the task extended to any practitioner of heraldry. The painter's job, by contrast, was much more complex, iconographically and pictorially. His genius lay in invention, a point on which eighteenth-century aesthetic treatises insisted.[158] For that reason, George Vertue, in notes on Hogarth of 1729, expressed surprise that an artist "only bred to Grave small works in Silver" had attained "daily success . . . in painting small family peices & Conversations."[159] Copley had himself tried engraving when quite young, using his deceased stepfather's materials. At just as early a date, however, his ambitions had propelled him beyond engraving and beyond portraiture, both considered imitative, into the imaginative realm of history painting, an art of gentlemen. So long as Copley lived in America, history painting (aside from canvases he made for his own purposes) remained an unfulfilled aspiration. His fellow colonials wanted portraits, and he settled for their money, suffering the indignities he perceived in silence.

Privately, Copley retaliated any way he could. He vented steam in correspondence, as scholars have long known. He also, I believe, worked out his feelings in the portrait of Revere, a conclusion that helps explain the rare and puzzling representation of the artisan as an artisan. Artists used their sitters to jockey for position all the time, though generally to advance their position publicly by association with an important sitter. In the case of Revere's portrait, Copley may have aimed to accomplish precisely the reverse: to enhance his position by giving visual definition to the alternative, if only for the sake of private satisfaction in the social distance he had gained from the ranks of tradesmen. If indeed Revere saw no contradiction in calling himself both artisan and gentleman, he may have detected no slight.[160] Copley's ambition, in painting and in society, licensed considerable audacity, and his portrayal of Revere as an artisan was bold and original. Copley's self-portrait, by contrast, is more restrained and conventional, just as his sense of gentility was more traditional and restricted than Revere's, paradoxically more in line with those colonial Americans who, he said, associated painting with trade. However his society may have regarded him, Copley knew he didn't want to share social rank with a goldsmith who frankly described himself as "a tradesman." He never counted himself an artisan or ever, even after his move to England, portrayed himself either at work or with his work, though Reynolds, West, and many others did so.[161]

In the fine banyan and elegant coiffure that immediately distinguish Copley from Revere, the artist appears not as producer but as consumer, traditionally both the gentleman's privilege and his obligation, since in that role he provided work for the common people.[162] A worker who also consumed, and conspicuously so, Copley showed himself fully a product of his time. Following a course unimaginable before the consumer revolution of the eighteenth century, he bought the trappings of gentle status and, through the labor he denied, fixed the image of his own leisure. As a portraitist whose art helped clients assert status, Copley was acutely aware of the power of visual representation. His portrait marks him as a gentleman in almost every respect – except for the fact that he made it, which he elides. At the same time, Copley marshaled his gentlemanly sensibility and used his craft against Revere, fixing on canvas the image of what he at least regarded as a social inferior. For all that Copley may have satisfied Revere, the proud artisan, he did so in a way that underscored their difference at the moment of social ascent commemorated by his self-portrait.

Copley's conflicted need to distance himself from Revere while also, on some unacknowledged level, identifying with him, registers some of the tensions in the eighteenth-century portraitist's position, especially acute for an ambitious artist operating at a distance from the center. Copley wanted to be considered the gentleman that theorists on art told him he might be. When he looked in the mirror, he saw a gentleman. But when he looked at Revere, an unapologetic artisan returned his gaze, as if challenging him to mark their difference. In one sense, Copley did just that, his brushstrokes on the canvas forming the image of a worker who makes objects with his hands. A mimetic tour de force, the painting routinely persuades viewers to overlook Copley's own hand in his work and to see there embodied the ideal American, the common man whose attachment to liberty and justice spurred him to extraordinary deeds.

Ironically, Copley's rendering of Revere, or any other of his sitters for that matter, only demonstrates the strength of his attachment to artisanal values. His meticulous handling and his skill in rendering materials reinforce his identification with the artisan-producers of objects such as he included in his paintings. At the same time, Copley struggled with anatomy, designing figures whose occasionally anomalous proportions counter transparency, pulling the viewer back to the artist at his easel. Without exception, Copley's works betray work – painstaking craftsmanship and labor attested by wearied sitters like Mrs. Thomas Mifflin, who reportedly endured twenty sittings for the double portrait with her husband.[163] *Sprezzatura* – the gentleman's graceful ease and, in art criticism, painting that appears effortless – was neither part of Copley's images nor part of his image.[164] In Italy, where in 1774 he finally traveled to study the Old Masters, Copley did not find painting any easier. Even after working five weeks at a copy of Correggio's *Holy Family with St. Jerome*, Copley expected to spend twice as long again, or so the English painter Joseph Wright told their mutual friend, Ozias Humphry, adding: "It is with infinite labour that he produces what he does, but that is *entre nous*" (an aside indicating the negative connotation of labor).[165]

Only when flashy brushwork became a prominent measure of genius did artists win their battle over craftsmen, because they were freed from adherence to certain manual standards that governed artisan labor. John Neal, one of the first American art critics, made the distinction in 1823, when he contrasted Peale, Copley's contemporary, with Stuart, leader of the next generation. Both artists were near the end of their lives but still painting. Stuart was "careless, bold and confident," Neal pronounced, invoking qualities associated with the man and his art. "He develops character like a magician. He uses little or no material; is authority, in whatever he does." Material in this case means paint, not fabric, though painting fabric could in the hands of Peale or Copley consume material, as Neal made clear. Peale "never seems weary of labour," he wrote. "His drapery is . . . too laboured" and "he never lets [a portrait] go out of his hand, but as a piece of *workmanship*, which will always be worth the money that he has been paid for it."[166] Labor plus materials equals value. This artisanal equation would give way only slowly, and then incompletely, to other means for evaluating the work of fine artists in the new United States.

Copley would not be around to see it. His father-in-law, Richard Clarke, was a consignee of the tea thrown into Boston harbor in December 1773, and the increasingly tense political climate there gave Copley the push he needed to embark on the Italian study that Reynolds and West had urged seven years earlier. He left in 1774 and, with the onset of revolution, his wife, children, and her father fled to England a year later. After Copley rejoined them, the family remained in England, never to return. Copley's son John grew up to a distinguished legal and political career, a knighthood and, upon his first appointment as Lord Chancellor in 1827, elevation to the peerage as Baron Lyndhurst. The younger John Copley, in short, achieved a status his father could hardly have imagined. In America, much had changed by that time, leaving a final irony. In his portrait of Revere, Copley unwittingly gave the revolution a face; the elitist enshrined the heroic plebeian, who still seems to present the possibility that, in America, all things are possible.

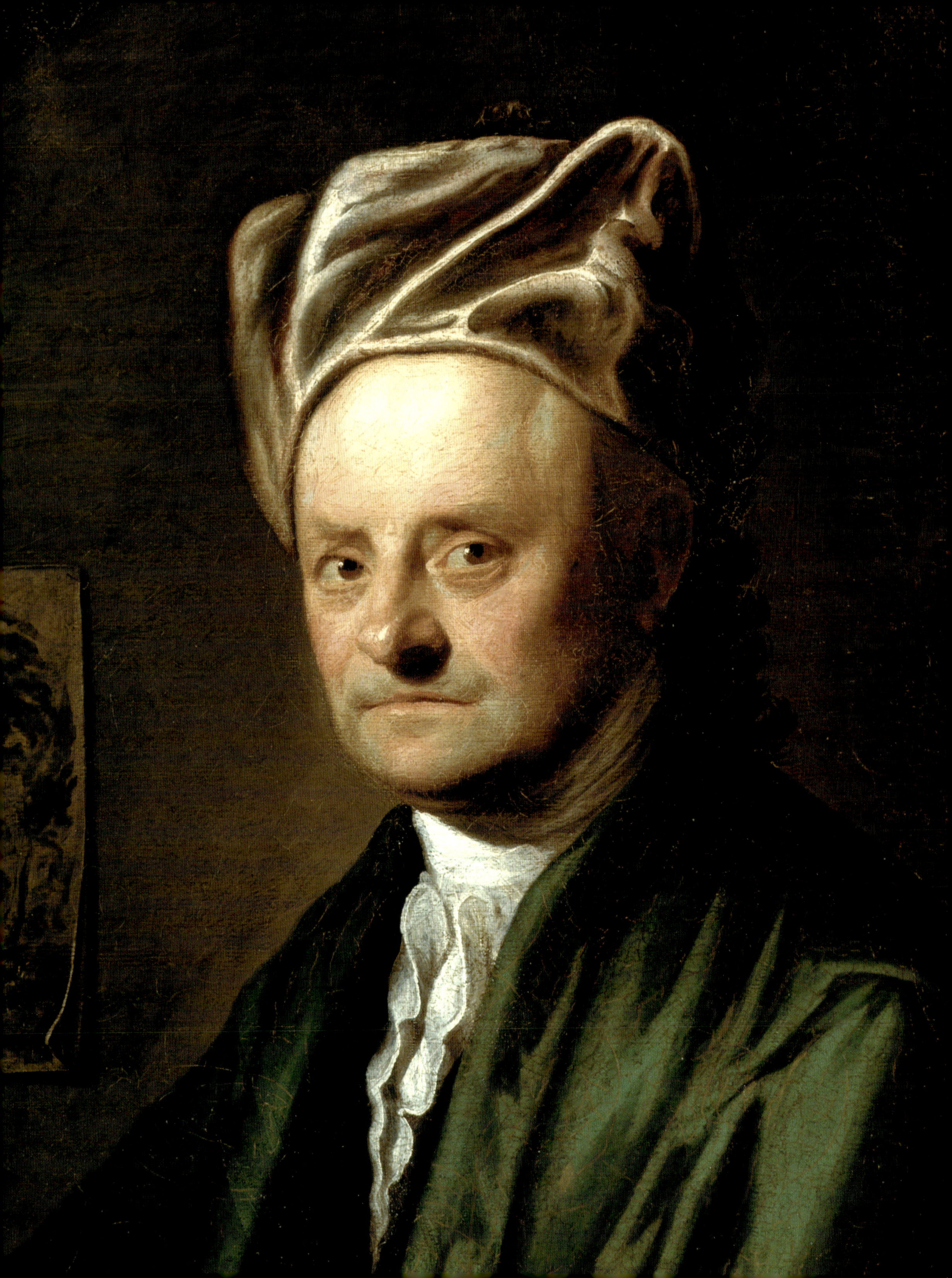

2

THE TRADE OF ART IN PHILADELPHIA AND NEW YORK

William Williams

In the early 1780s, Thomas Eagles, an English gentleman living in Bristol, was approached by a stranger who requested his help in gaining admission to a hospital for indigents. Eagles perceived the supplicant to be no common beggar and invited him to call at his residence. Other visits and financial assistance followed, as Eagles developed a protective interest in the intelligent old man, who gave his name as William Williams. Williams, a native of Bristol, said he had been both a painter and a mariner, and, in due course, Eagles found him a place in the Merchants' and Sailors' Almshouse in that city. Their friendship continued until Williams's death in 1791, but despite the length of the association, Eagles never learned very much about the enigmatic Williams. He was completely unprepared for the grateful artist's bequest, an astonishing collection of personal effects, including a self-portrait, some two hundred books, and a manuscript "Lives of the Artists." Only then, it seems, did Eagles read another manuscript that Williams had entrusted to him some years earlier: a remarkable first-person narrative by the pseudonymous "Mr. Penrose," a shipwrecked sailor who lives nearly three decades among Central American Indians (fig. 35).[1] This novel, probably based on some degree of personal experience, was Williams's most startling legacy.[2] But Eagles had further occasion for surprise. In 1805, Benjamin West, Royal Academy of Arts president and painter to the king, was shown the manuscript of castaway adventure and recognized stories once related to him. More than a half century earlier in America, Williams had been West's first instructor. "Had it not been for him," West declared, "I should never have been a painter."[3]

West's encounter with the Penrose manuscript prompted a flood of memories, and Eagles wanted to hear them. "Perhaps he was the only person in existence who cd. Give any acct. of Wms' life & manners," Eagles noted in his memorandum of West's remarks on that occasion. In 1810, West furnished Eagles – who was having difficulty finding a publisher for the Robinson-Crusoe-like tale – with an elaboration of his earlier recollections, which necessarily also reflected on West's own New World story.[4] That story would be more fully related in the biography of West's youth and travels before his move to England, a collaboration between West and writer John Galt that came out in 1816. In that context, fully explored in chapter six, Williams

Facing page Detail of fig. 66.

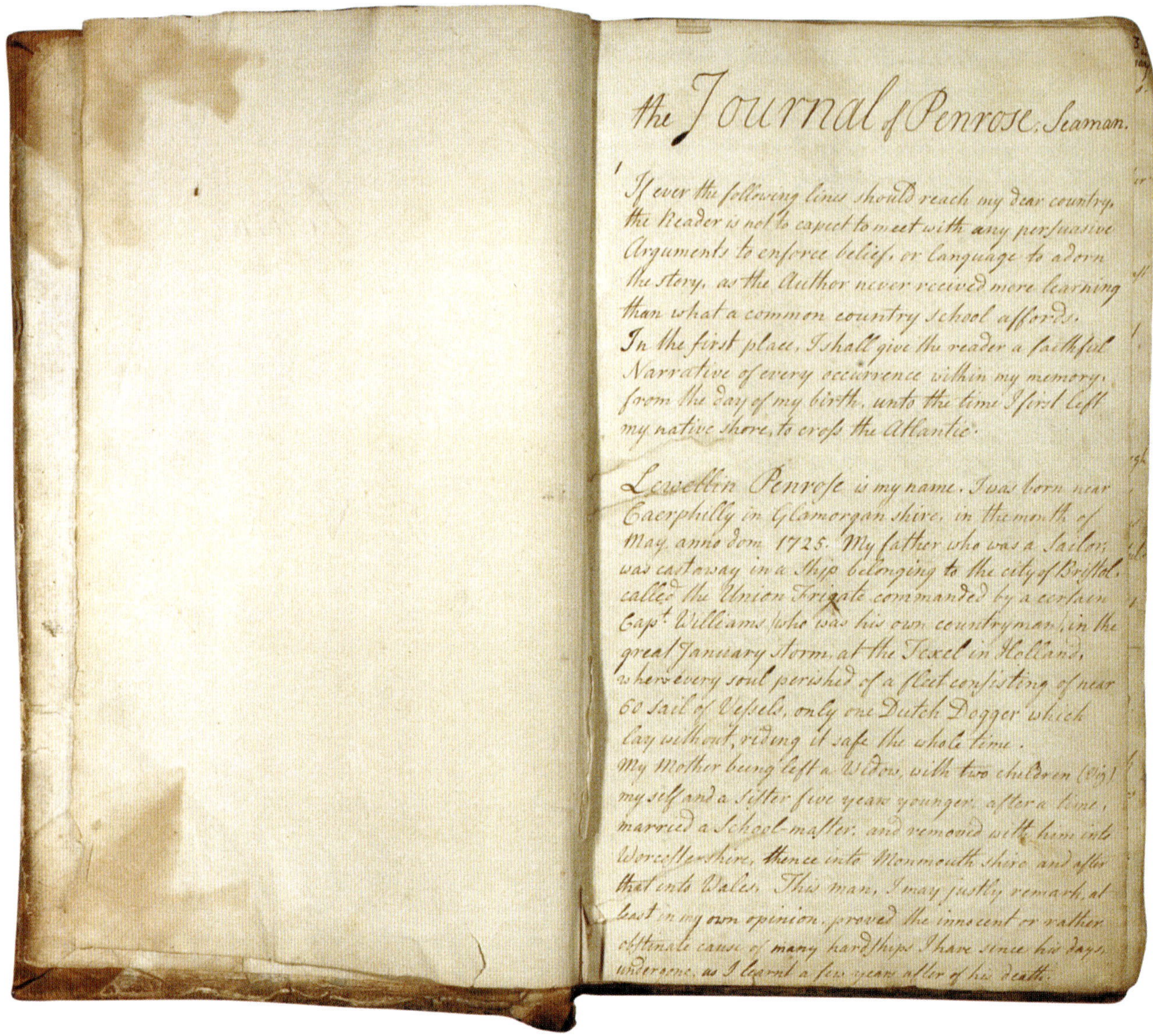
the Journal of Penrose, Seaman.

If ever the following lines should reach my dear country, the Reader is not to expect to meet with any persuasive Arguments to enforce belief, or language to adorn the story, as the Author never received more learning than what a common country School affords.
In the first place, I shall give the reader a faithful Narrative of every occurrence within my memory, from the day of my birth, unto the time I first left my native shore, to cross the Atlantic.

Lewellin Penrose is my name. I was born near Caerphilly in Glamorgan shire, in the month of May, anno dom 1725. My father who was a Sailor, was castaway in a Ship belonging to the city of Bristol, called the Union Frigate commanded by a certain Capt Williams (who was his own countryman) in the great January storm, at the Texel in Holland, where every soul perished of a fleet consisting of near 60 sail of Vessels, only one Dutch Dogger which lay without, riding it safe the whole time.
My Mother being left a Widow, with two children (Viz) my self and a Sister five years younger, after a time, married a School-master, and removed with him into Worcestershire, thence into Monmouth shire and after that into Wales. This man, I may justly remark, at least in my own opinion, proved the innocent or rather obstinate cause of many hardships I have since his days undergone, as I learnt a few years after of his death.

35 [William Williams], "The Journal of Penrose, Seaman." Courtesy Lilly Library, Indiana University, Bloomington.

nearly faded from the picture, reduced to indirect catalyst in West's transformation from natural talent to great artist.

In the case of Williams, the historian is challenged to establish the merest facts, because they seem so firmly embedded in the embellished narrative of another life. Not even a birth date had been established until David Howard Dickason, a literary historian, undertook research that yielded the unexpurgated edition of Penrose in 1969 followed by a biography and impressionistic catalogue of Williams's work in 1970.[5] Dickason concluded that his subject had been born in 1727, which eliminated any possibility that Williams could have lived for long on the Caribbean coast and banished the image of the wise senior artist who sparked West's career. If Williams was in actuality just eleven years older than West and barely more than age twenty when they met, his expertise was only relative. The frequency of the name William Williams in the eighteenth-century record has allowed for continued speculation about West's mentor, whose richly layered and surprising life has been likened to "a series of Russian dolls."[6] I make no attempt to sort out Williams's family tree or other aspects of his personal life and instead focus on what can be determined about his professional life as an artist. This much is clear: during some three decades in America, almost half that time after West's departure, Williams charted a steady course between artisanal practicality and professional aspiration.

The tantalizing glimpses of Williams that can be extracted from the record introduce a more complicated and ambitious American artist than the figure West later recalled. His paintings on canvas, examined in the first part of this chapter, reveal Williams to have been an artist of considerable imagination, in many respects more daring than Copley, however provocative that statement may seem in view of the Bostonian's vastly greater talent and fame. In fact, the art historian is hard pressed to find the variety of works created by Williams among surviving colonial paintings, let alone in the surviving oeuvre of any one artist. While the tally of his known pictures pales by comparison to Copley's, evidence suggests that Williams was at once more willing to branch out artistically and actually successful in securing commissions that allowed him to do so.

Williams used print advertisements to offer his services as a painter "in general," available to perform diverse tasks. Both the medium and the message demonstrate a tradesman-like engagement not sanctioned from the elite, cosmopolitan perspective with which West and Copley identified, however imperfectly, while still in the colonies. That perspective long colored the history of American art and relegated artists like Williams to the sidelines, when instead such persons and practices constituted the norm. The second part of this chapter, accordingly, examines the trade of art, especially as revealed through a range of eighteenth-century print advertisements and sign paintings. Williams's advertisements bear careful consideration as the only known textual representations of his artistic practice that he himself generated. And they point to important missing visual evidence: the signboards that Williams hung at his shops in two different American cities, each a calculated effort to market himself to the public.

At the same time that he adapted to conditions of artistic practice as he found them, Williams demonstrated a level of professional awareness and purpose not strictly necessary to the furtherance of his trade. He was particularly concerned with the representation of the "artist": representing artists on his shop signs, compiling artists' lives, and collecting portrait prints of artists. With these lost, but credibly documented, artifacts of his career, it is difficult to do more than hypothesize. Still, the effort should not be spared and constitutes a short final section of this chapter, together with consideration of Williams's self-portrait. Whatever limitations his colonial situation and native ability imposed, the unavoidable conclusion remains that Williams never relinquished a broader vision of who or what an artist might be.

Williams, Painter

Little in Williams's youth can have prepared him for the career of painter. He was born in Bristol, then the second largest city in England, the country's leading port and a merchant stronghold – but a far cry from London in population or sophistication. From an artistic point of view, Bristol remained a backwater. Exposure to "heads in oil" and landscapes made by an elderly artist of the town inspired Williams; his "greatest wish was to be a Painter," West recalled hearing from his teacher. Williams did not report receiving formal training, however, and found his ambition thwarted when he was bound to a captain in the "Virginia trade," which involved transportation of goods and African captives to North America and return shipment of tobacco to England. He deserted in Norfolk and sailed for the West Indies, where he may have lived a short while, the basis for his story of Penrose. By 1747, if West can be relied on, Williams had resurfaced as a painter in Philadelphia, beginning an association that continued "without interruption" until West's departure for Italy in 1760.[7]

Philadelphia had a population of about 13,500 in 1749 and continued to grow steadily, rivaling Bristol for the place of second largest city in the British empire by the eve of revolution.[8] It was a mercantile center and home to many artisans. Though no American city supported a large population of artists, Philadelphia proved as fertile an environment as any during the 1750s and 1760s. A sufficient number of prosperous citizens commissioned likenesses, and no single artist dominated that market, as Copley did in Boston from the late 1750s. In addition to Williams, about eleven painters can be documented in Philadelphia between 1749 and 1769. A few of them were temporary residents who cherry-picked prominent clientele during painting trips up and down the east coast. The most notable were Robert Feke, a leading American portraitist of the 1740s who disappeared from the records around 1750, and John Wollaston, the professionally trained English painter who (along with Joseph Blackburn) introduced contemporary London style to Americans over the course of the 1750s. Cosmo Alexander, a Scot best known as the young Gilbert Stuart's early employer and mentor, made visits to Philadelphia in the later 1760s. Other artists hailed from the region, some well documented and others much less so and even without attributed work. They included John Hesselius, Benjamin West, Matthew Pratt, Henry Benbridge, James Claypoole, Jr., John Meng, John Green, and Christopher Steele, in whose painting room Charles Peale reported seeing a self-portrait (though no works by Steele are presently known).[9] Hesselius, the eldest of that group (born in the late 1720s, like Williams), had the most secure start among them because his father, Gustavus Hesselius, an émigré from Sweden in 1712, had been an established painter but did not compete with the son, who in any case spent most of his career in Maryland. Claypoole's father was a painter, too, and undoubtedly his teacher, though Claypoole, Sr., engaged the varied livelihood of painter-in-general, which is how his nephew and apprentice Pratt began his own career. West managed a quick start without apprenticeship, as had Copley in Boston. Though he did not develop painting skills so rapidly as Copley, West succeeded in attracting influential patrons who believed in the value of European training and were prepared to fund him in that endeavor, making West the first American artist to study in Italy. Green, of humble origins like West, found his way into the same heady circle of educated Philadelphians but left no pictures before his departure for Bermuda ca. 1765. Meng, for whom only a couple of Philadelphia works are known, including a presumed self-portrait, also went to the British island colonies, where he died at around age twenty. The well-born Benbridge moved in the same company as West and Green and later, after receiving an inheritance, took his place among the first Americans to work in West's London studio. In their Philadelphia midst, and for longer duration, was "Williams Wm Painter," as he appeared in the city's tax list of 1756, with an estate valued at a mere £10, barely over the threshold for taxability.[10]

Williams was more successful, at least over time, than that meager early figure suggests, since he listed 241 paintings at the end of his now lost "Lives of the Artists." That record survives only in the severely condensed version that Eagles appended to West's 1810 letter. Why Eagles made his brief transcription, when he owned the manuscript with the full list, remains open to question, but was likely connected with his plan of using West's letter to persuade a publisher to accept the Penrose manuscript; in that context, the notation supported West's claim to have known Williams in Philadelphia. Williams made one hundred pictures in Philadelphia, each with a specified owner, according to Eagles, though he copied the detail only for a single work connected to the famous Benjamin Franklin. The artist's stay of indeterminate length in the prosperous island colony of Jamaica (ca. 1760–62) resulted in fifty-four yet unlocated paintings, for which Eagles transcribed no specifics at all; however, his notation of the place puts a finer point on where Williams may have been than the broader characterization "West Indies" that appeared in Williams's 1763 advertisement of his return.[11] Williams produced a further eighty-seven works, including eight cited with particulars by Eagles, during roughly seven years in New York (1769–ca. 1776). Only a few painters active in colonial America – Smibert, Wollaston, Copley – have a greater number of recorded or identified pictures, while few named eighteenth-century artists have so scant a surviving body of work as does Williams. Perhaps he embellished his colonial output or perhaps Eagles did so to impress a publisher; either way, the counts are impossible to verify.[12] Yet even the limited evidence makes clear that Williams painted in a wider variety of genres than most colonial artists. He produced portraits, history paintings, landscape and marine subjects, as well as painting scenery for theatrical productions. Based on the surviving works, Williams did not neatly partition these genres, which overlapped and informed one another.

Characteristically for a mid-century Anglophone painter, Williams turned out "innumerable" portraits, as Eagles stated hyperbolically, considering that he had an itemized list. The earliest, from the 1750s, shows Benjamin Lay, a (by then) disowned English Quaker and rabble-rouser (fig. 36). Lay had settled in the Philadelphia area in 1731, after time as a merchant in Bermuda sharpened his antipathy to slavery and prompted him to seek a community more receptive to his campaign against slave holding, an expectation not entirely fulfilled. Through spectacular public denunciations of slavery and other practices he considered immoral (including tea drinking), Lay became a notorious figure, the more so for his physical deformities: he was short and hunchbacked, with spindly limbs, which Williams represented. Eagles, copying Williams's list, identified the picture as "for Dr. Benjamin Franklin." Franklin, a slave owner as of 1735, had published an abolitionist tract by Lay in 1737, but it appears he did not commission the painting, given his query to Deborah Franklin in 1758 soon after his departure for England: "I wonder how you came by Ben. Lay's Picture."[13] Perhaps Williams undertook the work speculatively. As a resident of Bristol, Britain's major port in the slave trade, Williams had not only seen the trafficking of African peoples at first hand but likely abetted that trade during his short years of maritime employment. As Penrose, Williams expressed anti-slavery sentiments, so he must have been fully aware of Lay's abolitionism.[14] That cause, however, does not directly enter the thematics of Lay's portrait, which suggests, more broadly, the ingredients of a healthy, moral, and peaceful existence, as articulated in the book Lay holds, marked "Trion on Happiness." *The Way to Health, Long Life*

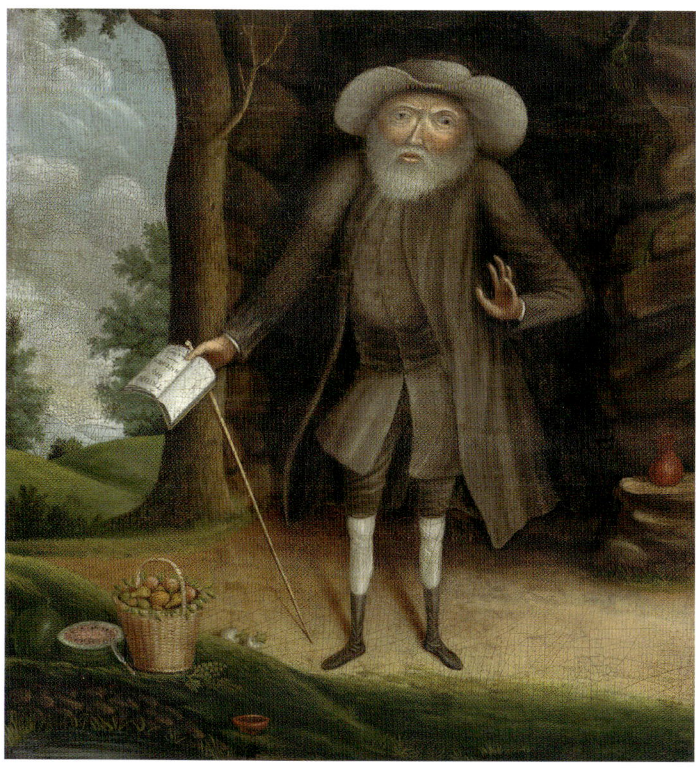

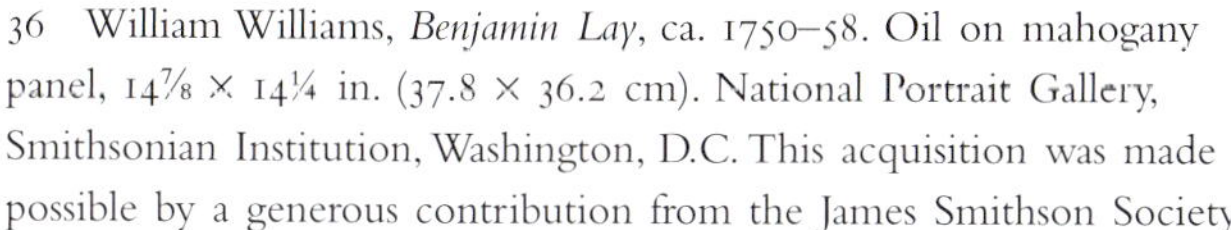

36 William Williams, *Benjamin Lay*, ca. 1750–58. Oil on mahogany panel, 14⅞ × 14¼ in. (37.8 × 36.2 cm). National Portrait Gallery, Smithsonian Institution, Washington, D.C. This acquisition was made possible by a generous contribution from the James Smithson Society.

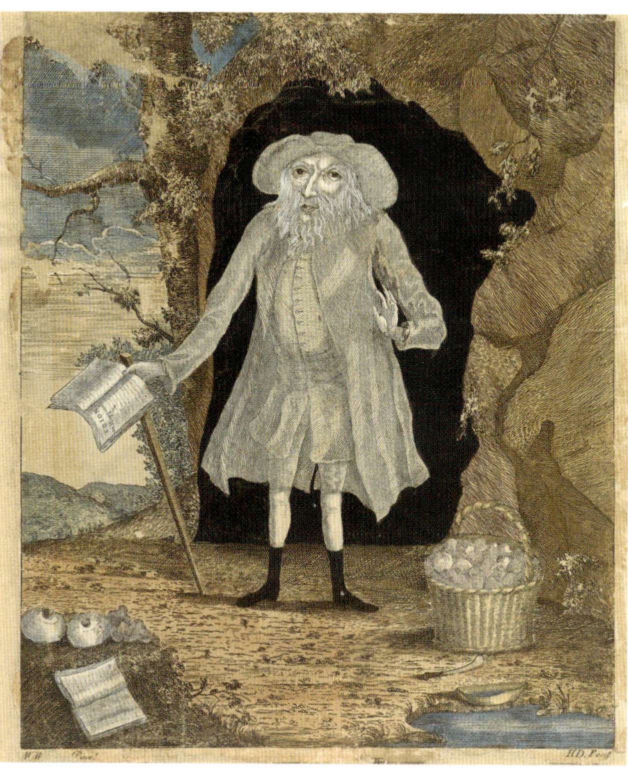

37 Henry Dawkins, *Benjamin Lay*, print from a painting by William Williams, ca. 1760. Etching and engraving. National Portrait Gallery, Smithsonian Institution, Washington, D.C.

and Happiness, by English Quaker Thomas Tryon, advocated temperance, vegetarianism, and retreat from the city, all practiced by Lay and indicated by details of the picture: a spring, fruits and vegetables, and the cave dwelling in which Lay kept his extensive library. The death of this colorful character in 1759 inspired a rare portrait print of colonial manufacture by Henry Dawkins, an English engraver active in Philadelphia by 1757, who took Williams's painting as his model (fig. 37). In the absence of copyright protection for artists, issuance of the print did not depend on consent from the painter. (Nor, for that matter, did the portrait depend on Lay's consent or presence as a sitter.) Yet Williams's value to and possible stake in the enterprise is fully evident: though he did not sign the original portrait, "W. Williams Pinxt." appears inscribed beneath the engraved image.[15]

Colonial painters rarely signed their works, but in the case of a notable portrait commission for printer and bookseller David Hall, Williams elected to do so, a practice he subsequently continued. Hall may have known Williams as a customer; the artist's bequest to Eagles of some two hundred volumes confirms his bibliophilic habit. The most important bookseller in Philadelphia at the time of his 1766 commission to Williams, Hall found the moment auspicious for other reasons.[16] In February, he acquired Franklin's share of the printing business in which they had been partners since 1748, though Hall (a Scot hired by Franklin from London in 1744) had alone managed the business, including publication of the *Pennsylvania Gazette*. In May 1766, he entered a new partnership with William Sellers, his longtime journeyman. Hall, then in his early fifties, chose this time of new promise, independence, and seniority to commission a trio of large, full-length portraits of his children, including two sons who would inherit the business and a daughter approaching marriageable age.[17]

Williams spared no effort in representing Deborah, William, and David Hall. Fourteen-year-old William coolly regards the beholder, left hand assertively on hip, the right on two volumes set atop a marble-surfaced table, while a folio leans against the table's decorative leg (fig. 38). Books were common props in portraits, and here the artist gave

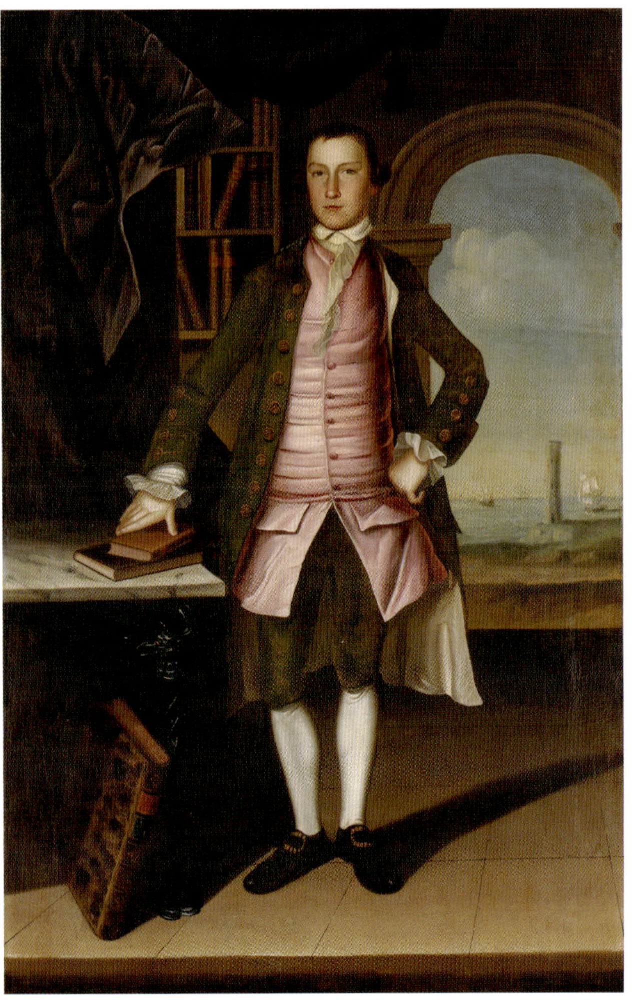

38 William Williams, *William Hall*, 1766. Oil on canvas, 71 × 46 in. (180.34 × 116.84 cm). Courtesy Winterthur Museum, gift of Henry Francis du Pont, 1959.1332.

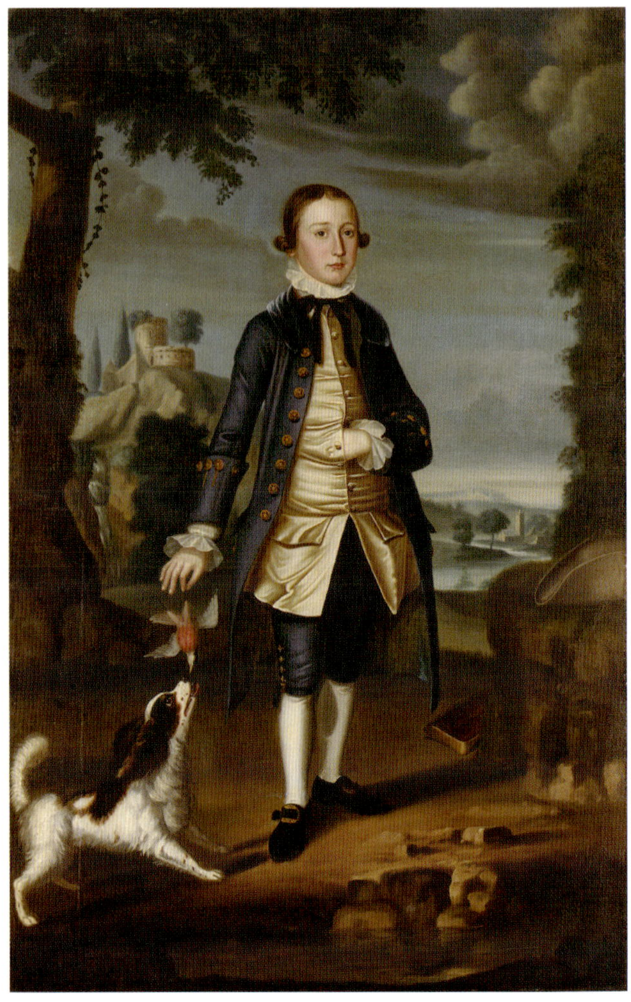

39 William Williams, *David Hall*, 1766. Oil on canvas, 70⅘ × 45⅘ in. (180.02 × 116.52 cm). Courtesy Winterthur Museum, gift of Henry Francis du Pont, 1959.1333.

them an active role. Slight disarrangement of leather bound volumes on the tall case behind William implies his removal of those closer to him, including the first volume of Tobias Smollett's *A Complete History of England*, identifiable by lettering on the spine (Smol Histo Vol 1). Initially published in 1757, the full set included fifteen costly volumes, which David Hall and other Philadelphia booksellers advertised after acquiring sets from London.[18] The collection of books in William Hall's portrait refers at once to his father's career and to the young man's learning and prospects. Williams suggests the power of books to reveal worlds in the right background of the composition, where a heavy rounded arch opens to sky, water, and a tall, slender lighthouse. In positioning young William Hall precisely at compositional midpoint between books and vista, the artist heralds the promising future that the father's success afforded his eldest son. Six years later, as it happened, David Hall's untimely death thrust William and his younger brother David, Jr., into partnership with Sellers in the printing business. As represented by Williams in 1766, eleven-year-old David Hall knew only the pleasures of youth (fig. 39). He has been shooting birds; one tiny prey dangles from the boy's pinched thumb and forefinger, at the maw of an excited spaniel, and the butt of his gun can be glimpsed to the right. A halo of landscape features surrounds David. A small stream or spring occupies the immediate foreground (a compositional device Williams used repeatedly), a twisted tree spreads its lacy canopy of foliage over the boy's head, and vine-covered masses culminate in puffy clouds to the left and right. The distant view presents an array of fanciful landscape and architectural motifs, including a rocky promontory with castle, tumbling waterfall, placid winding river, and building with tall square tower.

By contrast to the open settings in the boys' portraits, Williams placed fifteen-year-old Deborah Hall in front of a substantially enclosed garden, as refined as the young lady herself (fig. 40). Though sitters in British and American portraits often appear in attire specific to portraits, which would never have been worn, Deborah wears an expensive dress at the height of fashion: a lavish *robe à la française* (open robe with sacque back), with ruching on the gown and petticoat, cascading lace at the elbows, lace trim and floral bouquet on the bodice, and a ruffled collar. To Deborah's right, a stone plinth faced with a relief of Apollo and Daphne supports a potted rose plant in full flower – one bloom about to be plucked by the young girl – as well as a pet squirrel, its slack chain elegantly threaded through the girl's fingers. Although a serene body of water can be glimpsed beyond the plinth, the dominant landscape feature is a manicured garden of topiary and clipped islands of grass (comprising three pairs of circular or globular forms) enclosed within a high wall, one section curved and ornamented with niches and statuary. Beyond the wall, softly shaped trees suggest an extended park. To the northwest of Philadelphia, along the "pleasant stream" of the Schuylkill River, country estates featured carefully laid out gardens such as those of John Penn's estate, Springettsbury, begun by his father, William Penn. Ezra Stiles, an English visitor in 1754, approvingly noted the effect of "agreeable variety" produced by the "neat little park," "spruce hedges cut into beautiful figures," "spacious walkway," and "groves." Nearby at Bush Hill, Stiles visited the "very elegant garden" of James Hamilton, in which he saw "7 statues in fine Italian marble curiously wrot," while another riverside garden included statues of Apollo, Diana, Fame, and Mercury.[19] The garden that Williams painted in Deborah Hall's portrait, in other words, did not necessarily spring solely from his imagination. On the other hand, Williams filled the space with emblematic details, likely derived from books, that speak to the importance of patience and virtue in a young woman.[20]

The backgrounds for all three Hall portraits have usually been said to evoke theatrical scenery, which the versatile Williams is known to have made in 1759. In a rare surviving document concerning his career, Williams petitioned Pennsylvania governor William Denny to allow a new theater to open, against opposition from religious opponents, so he could be paid for work already completed. Williams claimed he had yet to receive the "£100 and upwards" it had cost

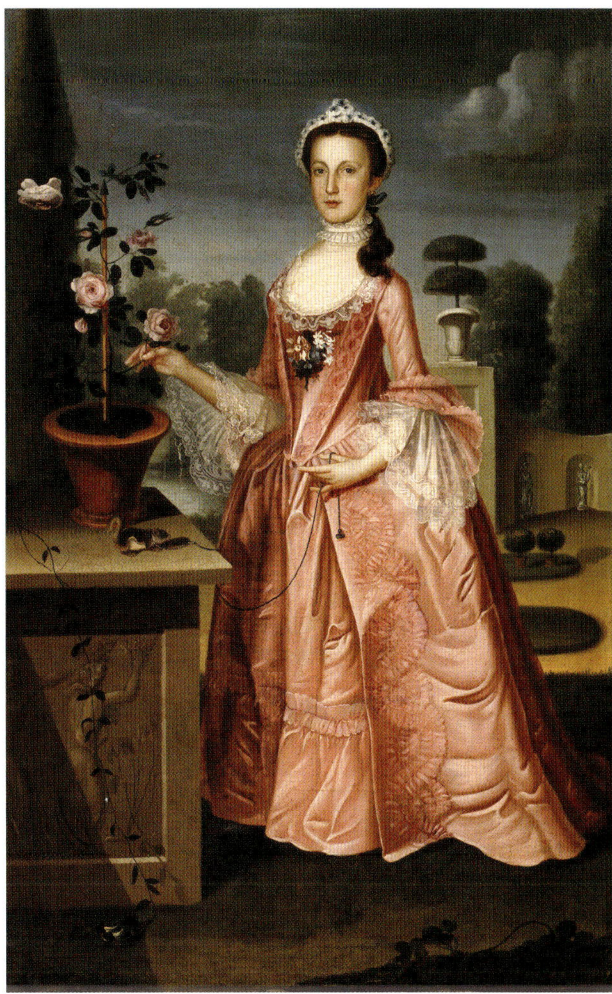

40 William Williams, *Deborah Hall*, 1766. Oil on canvas, 71⅜ × 46⅜ in. (181.3 × 117.8 cm). Brooklyn Museum of Art, New York, Dick S. Ramsay Fund, 42.45.

him to make "a New set of Scenes," and his co-signatory, Alexander Alexander, was out £300 for construction of the building.[21] Considering that prices for half-length (40 × 50 inch) portraits ranged from £8 to £20 between 1750 and 1776, Williams's fee of £100 for scenery does not sound like much, when a single drop for even a small theater measured roughly 25–30 feet wide and 16–20 feet high.[22] On the other hand, portraits required a much higher standard of finish than scenery, and the sum Williams received is consistent with documented compensation to London scene painters who were paid by the piece rather than seasonally. However, incomplete information and variations in the value of currency complicate any analysis of payments for scene painting, a trade with slight documentation prior to 1770.[23] It seems at first remarkable that the theater building cost only three times its scenery. The explanation lies partly in the fact that the painting of imagery, as opposed to houses, was higher status work than carpentry (curiously, the petition identifies Alexander as a smith). Furthermore, the earliest American theaters were quite basic structures, often converted from other spaces.[24] Even when built expressly as playhouses, theaters tended to be abandoned or sold when a season concluded, a pattern followed by the first professional English touring company in the colonies, the London Company of Comedians, managed by Louis Hallam, Sr., and after his death in 1756 by David Douglass. The Society Hill Theatre, for which Williams painted scenes, served the company in 1759 only. Scenery, by contrast, had greater value to a theater troupe, owing to its easy transportability (Hallam arrived in 1752 with scenes "painted by the best Hands in London"), the practice of restaging the same plays in different cities, and the possibility of rehabilitating worn stock.[25] Few productions featured specialized scene paintings, a costly and unnecessary expense at a time when, with few exceptions, scenery served to establish a generalized and generically appropriate locale for a play. Eighteenth-century performances did not depend on stage realism; audiences expected and appreciated artifice.[26]

Williams's paintings indicate that contemporaneous viewers appreciated artifice in portraits as well, notwithstanding an idea widely held throughout the twentieth century that a lack of artifice in Copley's portraits contributed significantly to his popularity. Copley's depiction of sitters' faces, down to warts and moles, look startling in company with the more generic faces seen in most colonial portraits, including those by Williams. But the settings in which Copley placed those sitters and their poses were often transparently artificial. While that has always been obvious in such grandiose portrayals as the full-length pendants of Mr. and Mrs. Jeremiah Lee, commissioned to hang in their impressive mansion in Marblehead, it is equally true of many seemingly more modest works, evident if the viewer will only look away from ostensibly forthright faces that seem to invite connection. The Lee portraits stand out among only a few paintings in which Copley placed his subjects at implied physical remove from the viewer; more typically, he fostered a sense of intimacy. Williams favored distance. In the portrait of William Hall, he made no concessions to the idea that the boy's world and the viewer's are coextensive. Although the artist scored the floor on which young William stands, a conventional way of creating illusory depth, he articulated its forward edge and painted a dark stripe at the bottom perimeter of the composition, above the frame, so the floor reads as a stage-like projection. The arrangement compels the viewer to recognize a similar effect, with a nod in the direction of naturalism, in the companion portraits of David and Deborah Hall as well as in other portraits, in which the artist established a subtle visual barrier between viewer and subject. A decade earlier, for example, close to the time of his commission for scenery, Williams situated Lay in a patch of light beyond a darkened foreground of grass, which at the left rises to a mound above a neat rocky bank bordering a spring. Most of Williams's surviving easel paintings in any genre show pronounced elements of fantasy or, in the case of Lay's cave, present (quasi-) authentic settings that had a fantastical or theatrical air. The sitters in these works are actors on the stage of Williams's imagination, stimulated by his theatrical involvements.

Although no actual scenery and few sketches or prints of scenes survive for British eighteenth-century theater, the idea that Williams's easel paintings draw on his experience in theater finds generalized textual support. *The Case of the Stage in Ireland* (1758) outlined types of scenes a company ought to stock, including temples, tombs, city walls and gates, palace exteriors and interiors, streets, chambers, prisons, gardens, and rural prospects of groves, forests, and deserts; other texts mention caves and waterfalls.[27] Such details punctuate Williams's portraits, while among easel paintings no parallel at all presently exists for Williams's *Imaginary Landscape* of 1772, with an astonishing confection of a tower (fig. 41).[28] The nearest extant counterpart is the decorative painted interior (ca. 1770–80) of an unusual seven-sided drawing room for Marmion, a Virginia plantation house built ca. 1756 (fig. 42). The Marmion overmantel features a windmill perched atop an arched rock formation and a host of other motifs in a caprice that recalls Williams at his most inventive and raises the possibility that he too painted decorative interiors.[29] Such work was within the realm of a painter-in-general, but even those who did not present themselves as such might consider taking on decorative work. Peale accepted a commission for a landscape overmantel from Philadelphia merchant John Cadwalader, presumably because the opportunity to paint a pure landscape intrigued him; his lack of appropriate artisanal training in decorative painting, however, led Peale to abandon the project.[30] Williams's *Imaginary Landscape* hints at his capacity for theatrical spectacle, borne out by the published description of a set first used by Douglass's company for its 1759 season and therefore attributable to Williams. Nathaniel Lee's *Theodosius, or The Force of Love* featured "A grand view of the Temple; The transparent Altar-Piece, shewing the Vision of Constantine the Great, before his Battle against the Christians; the Bloody Cross in the Air; inscribed about in Golden Character, In hoc signo vinces."[31] In addition to Lee's Restoration drama, with its unusually particularized scenery, Shakespeare's *Hamlet* and *Macbeth* also became part of the company repertoire in 1759.[32] With sixteen different mainpieces in Philadelphia that year, as well as afterpieces for each performance (three new), the Douglass company may have required further scenery from Williams. Whatever he produced to earn his £100, Williams's scene paintings continued in use over the next few years for productions in Annapolis, Williamsburg, Newport, New York, Charleston, and elsewhere. Not until summer 1764 did Douglass announce the acquisition of new scenery from London, the company's principal source from that point forward.[33]

Williams's penchant for imaginative scenes found a receptive patron base in the city of New York, to which the artist relocated in 1769. That, at least, is the impression left by the inventory of his paintings as transcribed by Eagles, who pared down the list relative to the reported total of eighty-seven works but nevertheless included far more particulars than he had for Philadelphia. His aim, evidently, was to highlight an intriguing diversity in Williams's production:

An Emblematical piece for ye Corsican Club
A small Moonlight for Lord Rosehill
A small whole length of Lady Rosehill
A Conversation of Mr. Denning & family
A large History of the Good Samaritan for Mr. C. Bush
A History piece of the Repose in Egypt for do. [ditto]
A small Landskip for Mr. J. Minshull
A large Tempest for Capn. A. Rutgers

Only the Denning family portrait survives, but these eight paintings – notable for having named patrons – include one symbolic composition, a pair of New Testament biblical subjects, three pure landscapes of differing types, and two portraits, which Eagles likely chose because something about the notation made them stand out among the "innumerable" other portraits in the full original inventory.[34]

That would be the case with the "small whole length of Lady Rosehill," which, together with the "small Moonlight" for Lord Rosehill, raises immediate questions that threaten to undermine the list's credibility. Not many titled aristocrats spent time in the colonies, and a commission by such persons (as we may imagine them) to a painter-in-general like Williams has a further air of improbability. Yet the assembled evidence leaves little doubt that Williams, prob-

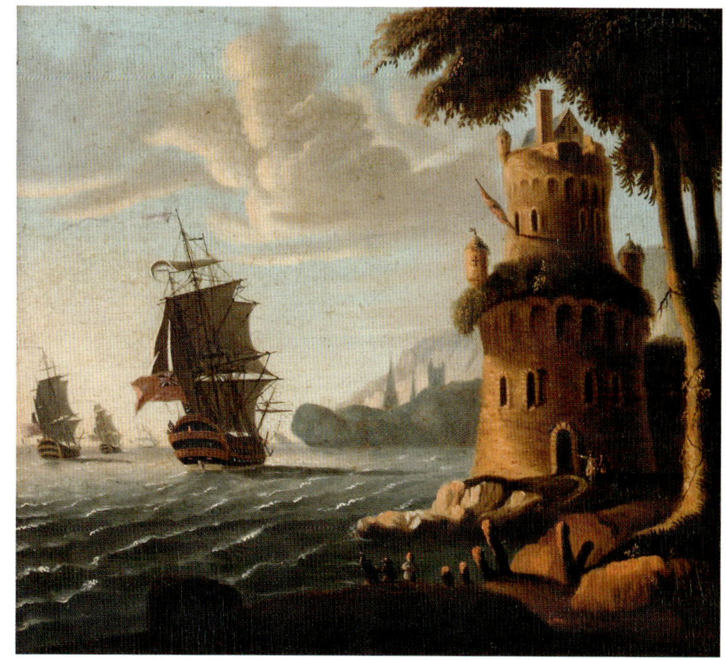

41 William Williams, *Imaginary Landscape*, 1772. Oil on canvas, 16 × 18½ in. (40.6 × 47 cm). Newark Museum of Art, gift of Clara A. Lee, 1922 22.275.

42 Overmantel painting from Marmion, the Fitzhugh family house, Tidewater, Virginia, ca. 1756. Metropolitan Museum of Art, New York, Rogers Fund, 1916.

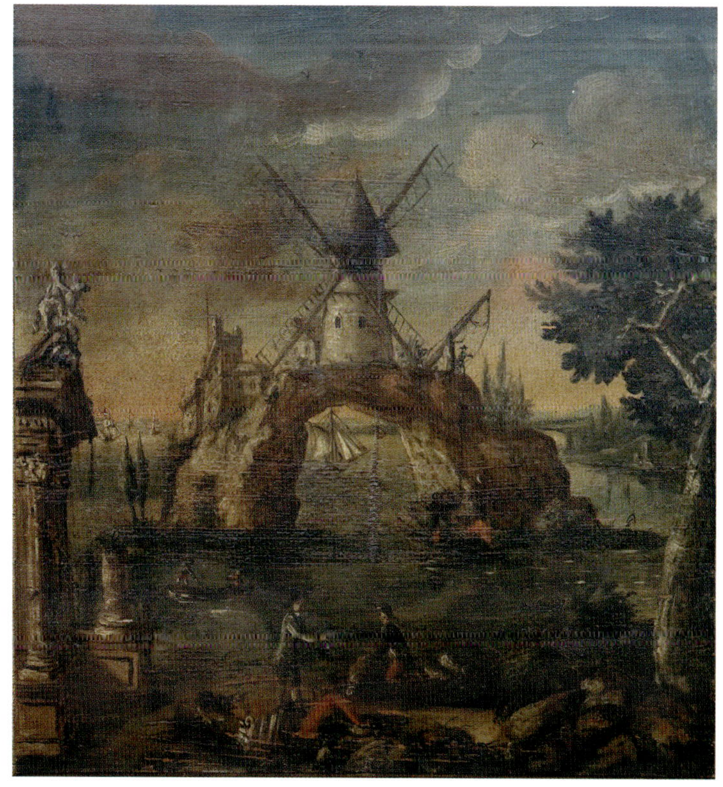

ably early in his New York career, did have such patrons, about whom more can be pieced together, and from a wider range of sources, than for others who commissioned Williams.

A brief notice in the *Pennsylvania Chronicle* of August 29, 1768, provided the key to the patrons' identities: "Last week was married in Maryland, the Right Honourable Lord Rosehill, to Miss Margaret Cheer, a Lady much admired for her Theatrical Performances." "Miss Cheer," as the name appears in contemporaneous playbills and advertisements for Douglass's by then renamed American Company, appeared regularly on American stages between 1764 and 1769. At the time of the actress's Charleston debut, a correspondent remarked: "Mr. Douglass has made a valuable acquisition in Miss Cheer who arrived here from London much about the time that Mr. Douglass arrived with his company. Soon after that, she agreed to go on the stage where she has since appeared in some Chief Characters with great applause . . . Her fine person, her youth, her Voice, & Appearance &c conspire to make her appear with propriety."[35] Miss Cheer's life before that time, her experience as an actor, and the cause of her relocation remain obscure; not so her American success, established by theatrical announcements and commentary in colonial newspapers. Within three years, Miss Cheer had taken on most of the company's leading lady roles, to continuing critical approbation. "Miss Cheer never loses the sweetest Accent, or faulters in the Clearness of expression," wrote one critic, ". . . I am not alone when I pronounce her one of the best Players in the Empire; she appears to me, from that Ease of Behavior which always shines through every Action, to have been much among People of Fashion, for she well fits the highest character she ever assumes."[36]

The prominent actress caught the eye of one such person of fashion, Lord Rosehill, the title born by male heirs to the Earls of Northesk. David Carnegie, his given name, was the eldest son of the 6th Earl of Northesk, a Scottish peer and admiral in the British navy. If aristocrats often entered into romantic and sexual liaisons with actresses, they rarely recast those mistresses as wives. But Rosehill was an impetuous young man, just nineteen years old. He had arrived in the colonies in late 1767 or early 1768, following two years as an ensign in the 25th Regiment of Foot, a Scottish infantry unit of the British army. The circumstances were not auspicious. Lord Rosehill was at odds with his father, having married secretly at age seventeen, in January 1767. Though a priest performed the rite at Fort William in the Scottish Highlands, no witnesses were present or required by Scottish law. The couple consequently acknowledged their new status to various persons, "after which they were bedded." The bride then went to stay with a relative, while Lord Rosehill left Scotland and almost immediately began trying to extricate himself from the marriage. These details come from a process of Declarator of Marriage filed against David Carnegie by Christian Cameron, asserting her status as wife, in 1769.[37]

At least one resident of Philadelphia, English officer Alexander Macrabie, had heard about Rosehill's disgraced circumstances in early 1768, well before the marriage to Miss Cheer: "Here is arrived a young Scotch gentleman, Lord Rosehill, son of Lord Northesk; he is under age, and married without his father's consent, who sends him hither upon a very small allowance to repent at his leisure . . . most people wait on him." If Macrabie knew the details, others likely did as well or eventually would; Philadelphians, the Englishman noted, "are dragons for politicks and scandal."[38] Discretion must have been maintained for some time or the second, unlawful marriage would never have occurred, while the Maryland location for those nuptials, away from Philadelphia or New York society, lends them a certain clandestine quality. The cat must have been out of the bag soon afterward, with the revelation of a wrong that concealment could only compound.

Miss Cheer's continued appearance on the American stage, odd if she had married a titled man with income and expectations, makes sense if he actually had no money; he had in fact been disinherited.[39] The actress's ability to support him must have augmented Miss Cheer's attractions for Lord Rosehill and, for a while at least, her new title had monetary value. On September 19, 1768 – just a month after her marriage – the *Pennsylvania Chronicle* announced that "the Right Honourable Lady Rosehill, (late Miss Cheer) has engaged to perform with Mr. Douglass, in the Theatres of Philadelphia and New-York, for the ensuing Winter, at a Sum much above Ten Pounds per Week, and a Benefit." The generous figure – a departure from the traditional joint-stock system under which the American Company then operated – suggests that Lady Rosehill would draw an audience based on the role she appeared to have assumed in life as well as for the parts she played on stage.

Curiously, when Miss Cheer finally had her benefit performance at New York's John Street Theater, on April 24, 1769, the announcement made no reference to Lady Rosehill, a title never used in a theatrical context or in print after September 1768. Patrons desiring tickets to the benefit (an established way for actors to make extra money, usually

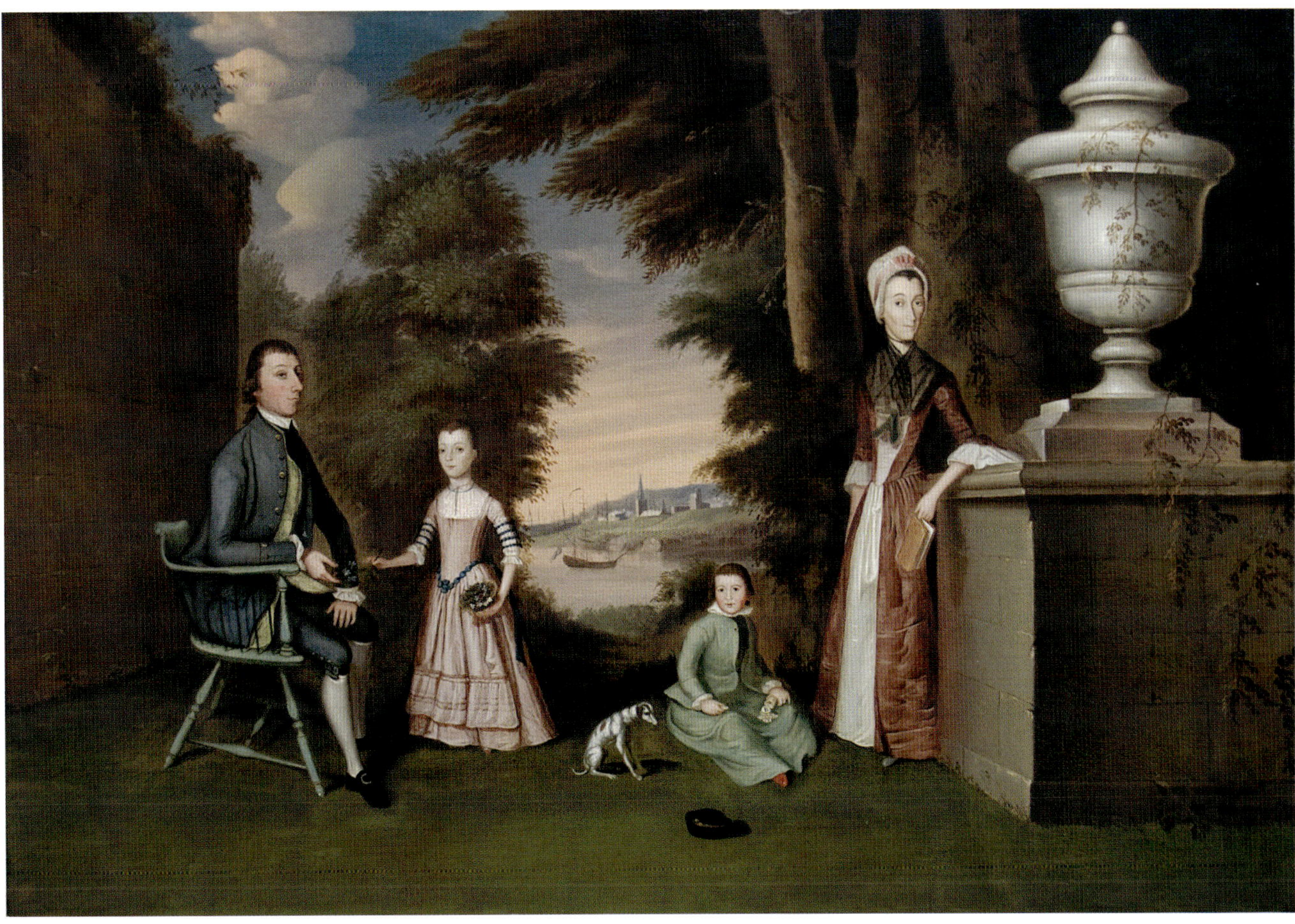

43 William Williams, *The William Denning Family*, 1772. Oil on canvas, 35½ × 52 in. (90.17 × 132.08 cm). Martin and Gracia Andersen Foundation, Orlando, Florida, on loan to the Orlando Museum of Art.

at the close of the season) were directed by advertisement to "Miss Cheer, at Mrs. Allen's, in Bateaux-Street."[40] The one-block-long street lay just across Broadway from John Street and its theater. But it was removed from the center of town, at the city's northwestern perimeter, and populated by humble artisans, not an auspicious address for a young lord of good standing or his lady.

Miss Cheer's address provides the compelling link to Williams, who publicized his availability to patrons at a Batteaux Street address in early May 1769.[41] There Williams must have connected with the actress, or reconnected given his prior employment by Douglass as a scene painter and his residence in Philadelphia during the time of Miss Cheer's great success there.[42] Although Williams's paintings for the lady and her husband (who grew up in a Highland castle full of pictures) have vanished, this ill-fated couple have now sprung more fully and messily to life than have other New Yorkers who commissioned Williams.[43]

The single presently identified work from the New York list is the other portrait Eagles chose to mention, probably because the characterization "conversation" caught his attention.[44] A conversation piece, first of all, was a group portrait – in this case of "Mr. Denning & family," signed and dated 1772 (fig. 43). As Eagles must have deduced from Williams's complete inventory, multi-figure compositions were rare in the colonies. London professional Smibert introduced the type with the *Bermuda Group* (see fig. 5). His large and imposing figures – situated in front of thick columns and a delicate landscape – showcased an approach to group portraiture on the verge of eclipse in Britain.[45] There, during the 1740s and 1750s, patrons favored small-scale canvases with miniaturized groups of figures, shown at full-length in domestic interiors or expansive, naturalistic landscape settings. In the colonies, Williams made the first works of this type or at least the earliest to have survived. American consumers might have resisted an unfamiliar

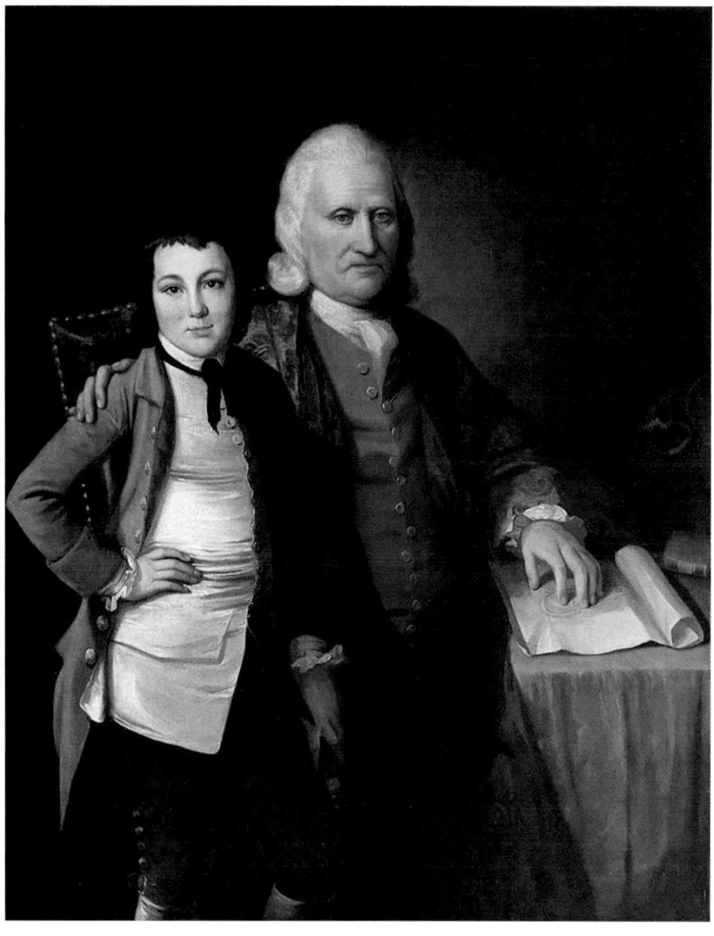

44 Matthew Pratt, *Cadwallader Colden and his Grandson Warren De Lancey*, ca. 1772. Oil on canvas, 50 × 40 in. (127 × 101.6 cm). Metropolitan Museum of Art, New York, Morris K. Jesup Fund, 1969 (69.76).

mode of presentation, or perhaps they felt less pressure than British gentry to make land ownership appear natural.[46] At the same time, few artists in America, even those with English training, had much expertise in rendering landscapes, which was more the province of military draftsmen.[47] Lawrence Kilburn and John Mare, both established in New York prior to Williams's arrival and still active during his residence there, made neither group portraits nor portraits with landscape backgrounds. Two painters who worked in West's London studio during the mid-1760s – Abraham Delanoy and Matthew Pratt – surfaced in New York in 1771–72, but they also worked within prevailing colonial conventions, as in Pratt's double portrait of New York's former lieutenant governor Cadwallader Colden and his grandson Warren De Lancey (ca. 1772) (fig. 44). Copley took a star turn in New York society during the second half of 1771, his only colonial painting tour, for which he had secured patrons in advance; in all, he produced some three dozen single-figure portraits there. "Painting much engages the attention of people in this City," Copley informed his brother; "it takes up much time to finish all the parts of a Picture when it is to be well finishd, and the Gentry of this place distinguish very well, so I must slight nothing."[48] He pleased even himself, judging his painting of Mrs. Thomas Gage "beyond Compare the best Lady's portrait I ever Drew" (fig. 45). Notwithstanding Peale's claim that certain unnamed New Yorkers who visited him in Philadelphia in 1772 thought he was "the best painter of America," one who made "more certain and handsomer Likenesses than Copley," most of Copley's contemporaries knew they were outmatched. Copley might be an unreliable narrator on that account, but his report of Pratt's response to *Mrs. Gage* suggests genuine dispiritedness on the Philadelphian's part: "It will be flesh and Blood these 200 years to come, that every Part and line in it is Butifull, that I must get my Ideas from Heaven, that he cannot Paint etc, etc."[49] Williams could not rival Copley's high level of technical achievement, but he was much more willing to experiment. Even Copley's greatest admirers recognized his self-imposed constraints. William Carson of Newport told Copley he doubted the artist had any superior in Europe but asked why he did not attempt something more than portraiture, "something new." He ventured that Copley was "unknown" even to himself, because he did not test his limits.[50]

In the Denning family and another surviving New York group portrait of John Wiley, his mother, and sisters (fig. 46), Williams went against the colonial grain. He did not confine the landscape to a window-like view or represent it in the abstracted and formulaic manner borrowed from late seventeenth and early eighteenth-century English mezzotints, which artists continued to use at mid-century. Instead – and based on unknown sources, since few English conversation pieces of the mid-century type were engraved – Williams set his figures in the landscape in a manner that recalls work by Arthur Devis, an artist popular among the rising middle class in England and, for a time, the gentry (fig. 47).[51] The resemblance has much to do with the way the two artists represented figures as diminutive, doll-like, and stiff, an effect resulting in Devis's case (and likely that of Williams) from habitual use of a lay figure, common at the time among portraitists, who rarely trained in life drawing. Copley so depended on his mannequin (which in his case did not inhibit convincing corporeality in portraits) that immediately upon arrival in New York he wrote

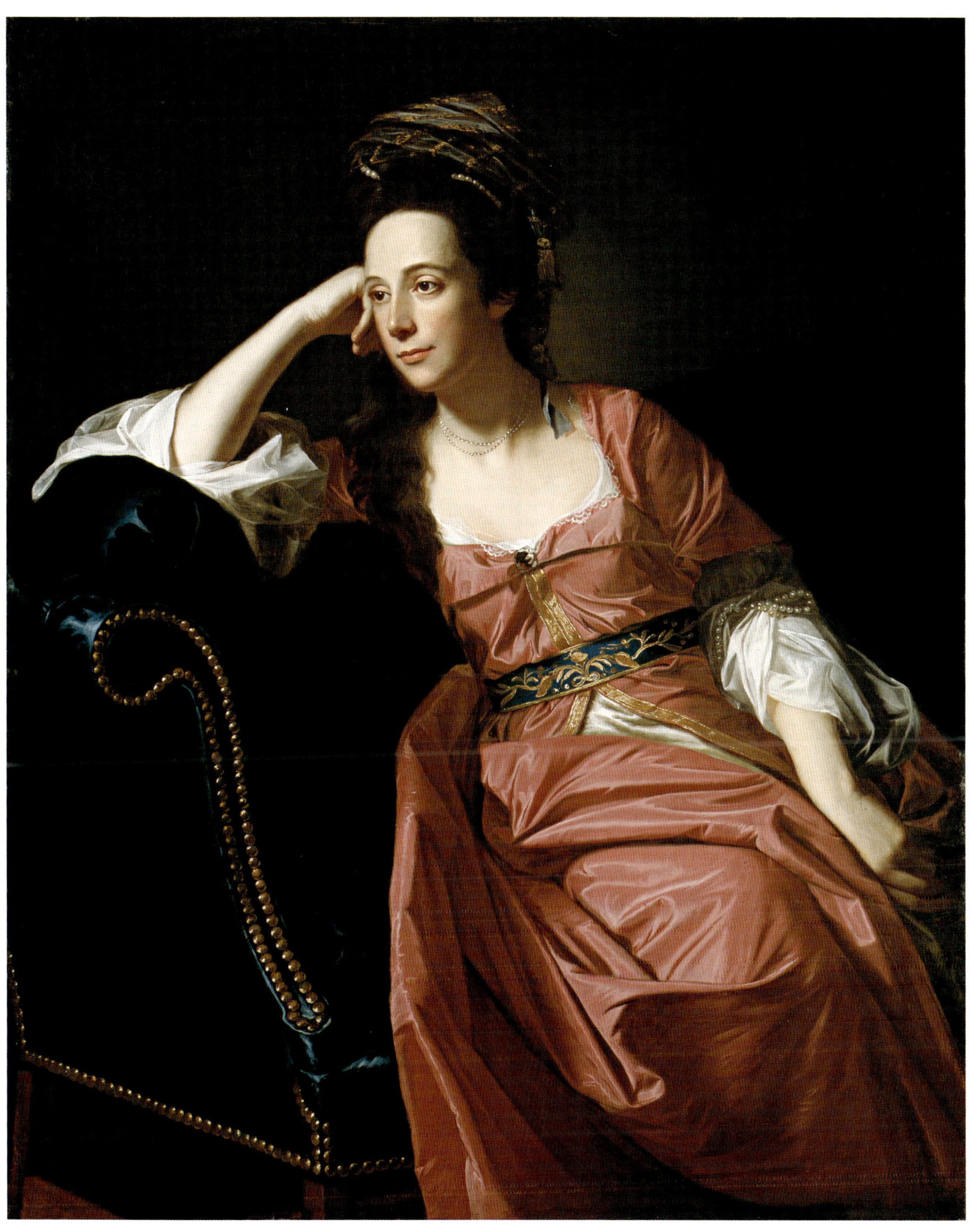

45 John Singleton Copley, *Mrs. Thomas Gage (Margaret Kemble)*, 1771. Oil on canvas, 50 × 40 in. (127 × 101.6 cm). Timken Museum of Art, Putnam Foundation Collection, San Diego.

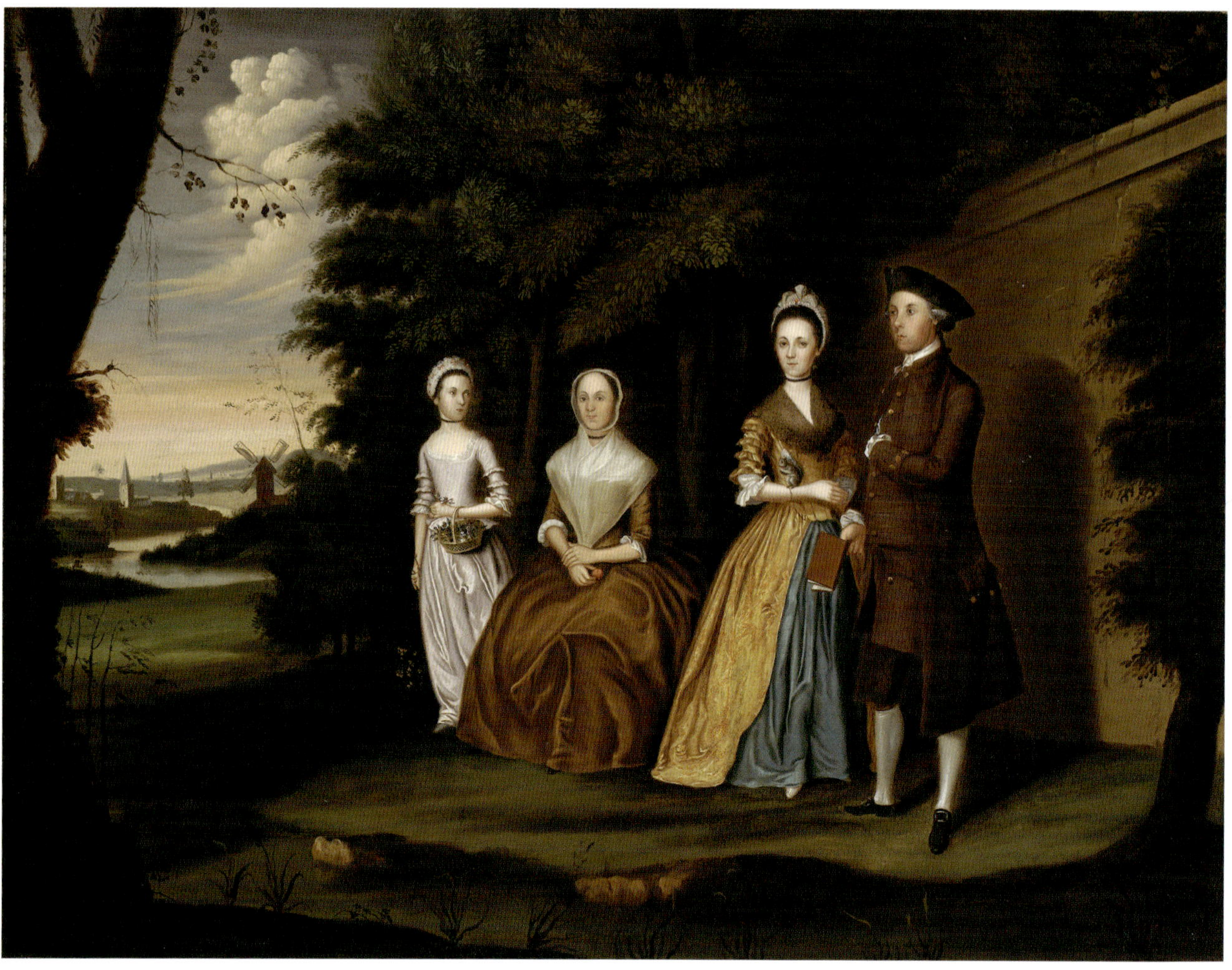

46 William Williams, *The Wiley Family*, 1771. Oil on canvas, 36 × 47½ in. (91.4 × 120.7 cm). Smithsonian American Art Museum, Washington, D.C., gift of Diane and Norman Bernstein.

Pelham asking that it be sent from Boston.[52] Devis's adherence to gestural codes signifying gentility, as presented in contemporaneous conduct manuals, heightens the awkwardness of his figures from our perspective but presumably did not do so in his time.[53] Devis typically placed portrait sitters in open settings, but Williams favored heavily wooded foregrounds, more reminiscent of the outdoor conversations painted around mid-century by English artist Francis Hayman (fig. 48). In the paintings by Williams, massive trees and dense growth plausibly represent the New World locality, the relative wildness remaining in proximity to the city of New York. At the same time, aggressive man-made elements – high masonry walls and an immense urn atop a plinth in the Denning family group – domesticate the forest glade and establish strong orthogonals that direct the eye beyond shadowy foregrounds to bright and distant views.

Williams included recognizably local elements of civilized and cultivated New York in his conversation pieces. In the case of the Dennings, the central vignette offers a view across the East River to the tip of Manhattan, with the spire of Trinity Church and a glimpse of the city's commercial center. Denning was a merchant whose family resided on Wall Street and attended Anglican services, so the scene had personal resonance. Many New Yorkers would have found something with which to identify in the same vista, as the city remained quite compact. Yet for this family the vantage point too had meaning: Sarah Hawxhurst Denning had been born and raised on Long Island, at Oyster Bay (a point too far north to permit the prospect Williams painted). Her father was an affluent merchant to whom Denning was apprenticed not later than 1759, at which time his future wife also assisted in the business, as shown by correspond-

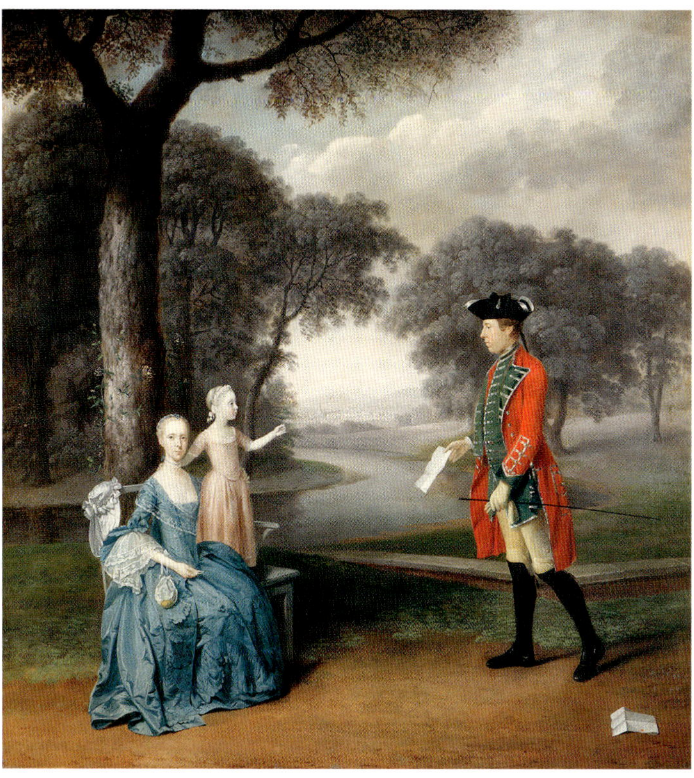

47 Arthur Devis, *Francis Vincent, his wife Mercy and daughter Ann, of Weddington Hall, Warwickshire*, 1753. Oil on canvas, 42 × 39⅜ in. (106 × 100 cm). Harris Museum and Art Gallery, Preston / Bridgeman Images.

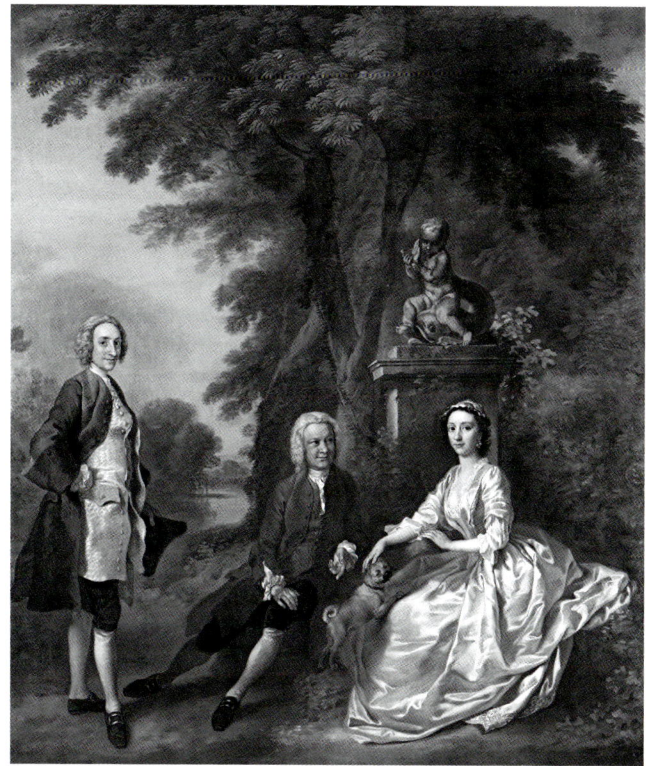

48 Francis Hayman, *Jonathan Tyers, with his Daughter Elizabeth, and her Husband John Wood*, 1750–52. Oil on canvas, 39 × 34 in. (99.1 × 86.4 cm). Yale Center for British Art, New Haven, Paul Mellon Collection.

ence and invoices of that year for "pigg mettle" (a kind of iron) from William Denning, "for my master," and Sarah Hawxhurst, who explained in a postscript: "my Father is not come home from the country yet."[54] Williams's painting conjures the country and, through the garden wall and urns, its improvement. Prosperous landowners had laid out substantial gardens in the village of Brooklyn, roughly the vantage point in the group portrait. On the property of Lodewyck Bamper, according to a nineteenth-century source, "a garden extended, in the rear of the house, to Ferry street; and, under the care of an imported professional gardener, was cultivated and filled with all kinds of fruits and flowers to which the climate was congenial. In the large walks of this garden were placed, in the summer-time, painted wooden statues, life-size, representing grenadiers in full dress and equipments complete, also female figures representing soldiers' wives and children."[55] With some license in terms of geographical coordinates, Williams's depiction of New York from Long Island honored both the Hawxhurst and Denning families.

In the Wiley portrait, the prospect seems at first more fanciful and the composition more calculated, another example of Williams's theatrically arranged pictorial spaces in its sharply demarcated foreground and sequence of framing elements at the sides, like painted wings of playhouse scenery. Yet even if the setting had no real counterpart, many of its elements existed in late colonial Manhattan – dense forest, hills, winding streams, church spires, windmills.[56] The prominent windmill may allude to the distilling business that occupied twenty-three-year-old John Wiley, among his other merchant enterprises. But the persistent idea that the picture represents this family's garden places too much value on factuality as a priority for patron and artist. The success of the mid-eighteenth-century British conversation piece depended less on an artist's realistic portrayal of property or interpersonal dynamics than on his ability to present sitters as persons of civility and refinement. In the Denning and Wiley conversations, Williams allowed the settings, clothing, and studied comportment of family members to speak, in visual articulation of Anglo-American identity.

Williams's sustained interest in landscape – whether as a major component of portraits (unusually, none of his surviving works show sitters in wholly interior spaces) or as independent works, like the nocturne, landscape, and "tempest" on the New York list – sets him apart from painters active in the American colonies or, more precisely, from other painters based on their surviving works. The obituary of 1740 for Boston area painter Nathaniel Emmons mentioned his "admirable Imitations of Nature, both in Faces, Rivers, Banks and Rural Scenes"; an inventory of Smibert's estate shortly after his death in 1751 included "13 Landskips" (only one of which survives); and advertisements placed in colonial newspapers north and south attest to landscape painting as a service some offered, without affording scholars the satisfaction of assessing the results.[57] Among surviving early landscapes are a few decorative paintings from houses and North American city and harbor views, in some cases made for transatlantic audiences. This textual and visual evidence all supports what common sense suggests: Williams cannot have been unique.[58] Yet in his commitment to landscape across painting genres and over several decades, that is exactly how he appears.

Landscape engaged Williams from the very start of his career in the late 1740s, according to West. While carrying a painted landscape in the streets of Philadelphia, Williams met either West himself or, more plausibly, a neighbor of West's cousin, who commissioned a work in that genre from Williams and later arranged an introduction for the artistically inclined boy.[59] Whoever first encountered Williams and his landscape was treated to an arresting public sight that amounted to a portable advertisement. The tactic had more limited duration than customary forms of publicity, such as trade cards (then called shop bills) that employed word and image to represent a vendor's services or newspaper advertisements, which (when illustrated at all) featured crude, stock images. Still, with painting in hand, Williams could show off a product and promote his services in person. West told Eagles in 1805 that he had been impressed from the start by Williams's accuracy as a painter of landscapes and "cattle pieces" and that Williams shared the "secret" of his success, a camera obscura. Handheld cameras were relatively simple to make and popular with untrained artists, which Williams then was, because the user could easily reproduce a landscape by tracing its projected image.[60] The tool helps explain why Williams took up landscape at the outset of his painting career and why West, his pupil, did the same. Two works reasonably considered among West's earliest paintings (variously 1748–53) offer a hint of what Williams's landscapes may have looked like, given the evidence of his later works. Both are thought to have been overmantels that West painted for a house in Philadelphia, work such as a painter-in-general might undertake.[61] More fanciful than the conventional title suggests, *Landscape with Cow* packs three castles, a stone bridge, ship, windmill, waterfall, wooded path, and three figures into an awkward conglomeration, parts of which might have been made with the aid of a camera (fig. 49). *Storm at Sea* probably derived from a print but seems more related to the life experience of Williams than of West himself at that point, notwithstanding his residence in a port city.[62]

Time spent at sea as well as a childhood in Bristol gave Williams experience on which to draw for maritime subjects, like the imaginary landscape with its carefully rendered ships and the "large Tempest" that appeared on Eagles's list of the paintings Williams made in New York. The owner of the latter picture, Captain Anthony Rutgers, Jr., was a New York-based privateer. In 1758, his ship *Boscawen* survived a terrible storm near Bermuda, while the privateer brig *Duke of Marlborough* suffered more gravely, with seven lives lost and the ship's masts destroyed; upon return to the colonial port, a newspaper reported, the vessel still appeared "in a shattered condition."[63] Perhaps the "large Tempest" commemorated the captain's narrow escape on that occasion; at the very least, it evoked the ocean storms that no seafaring man could avoid. Williams's own firsthand knowledge gave him credibility with such a patron, and any need to refresh his memory as to ship architecture could easily be satisfied at dockside. He likely also availed himself of naval prints. An engraving made and published by John Boydell in 1753, after a painting by Charles Brooking, showed another privateer *Boscawen* (named after the British admiral) engaging the French fleet at Martinico in the West Indies (fig. 50). The usefulness of such a print is evident by comparison to the colonial artist's *Imaginary Landscape*. While the military action had no direct applicability to known marines by Williams, the depiction of British men-of-war in *Imaginary Landscape*, as Roger Stein proposed, had nearly unavoidable political resonance in America of 1772.[64]

When Williams began to make landscapes around mid-century, topographical views – ostensibly factual renderings of specific sites – constituted the dominant British approach to landscape representation. The *View of Boston* (ca. 1730s) attributed to Smibert presents an early and rare oil painting of an American topographical subject. Need for such views arose from military contexts and, by the eighteenth century, was largely fulfilled by draftsmen systematically trained in mathematics, surveying, topography, perspective, and map

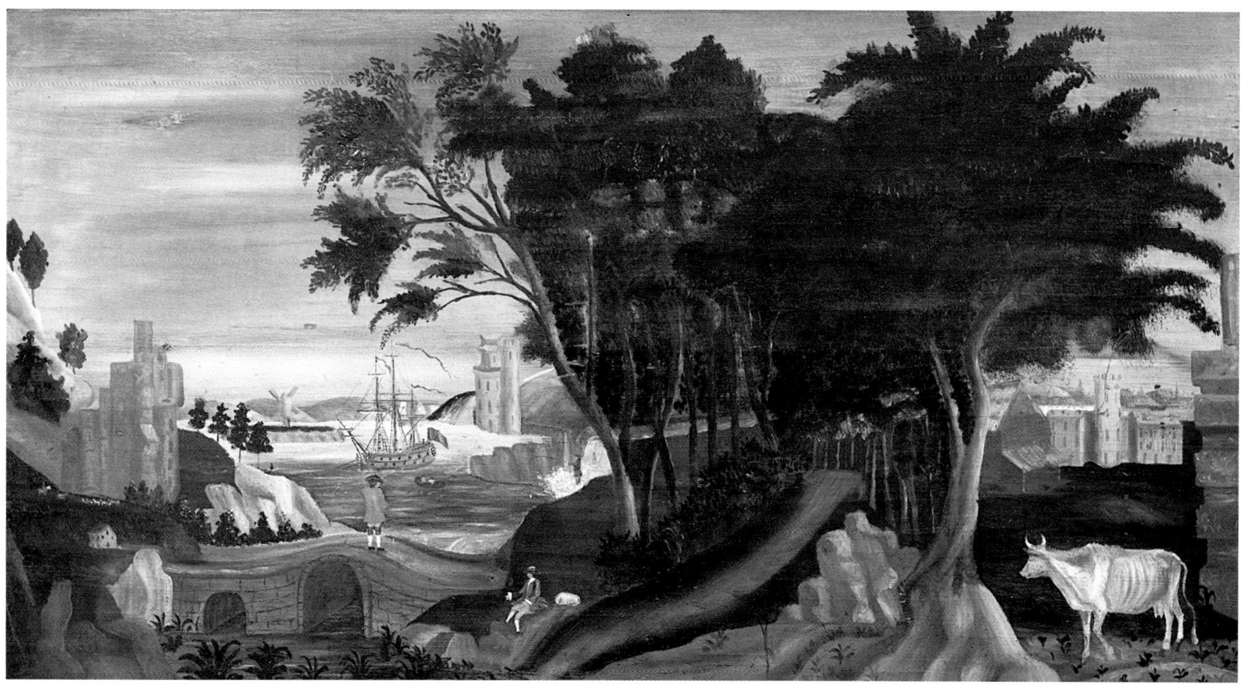

49 Benjamin West, *Landscape with Cow*, ca. 1752–53 (?). Oil on panel, 26¾ × 50¼ in. (68 × 127.5 cm). Courtesy Pennsylvania Hospital Historic Collections, Philadelphia.

50 John Boydell after Charles Brooking, *The Boscawen and Sheerness Privateers*, 1753. Etching and line engraving. Yale Center for British Art, New Haven, Paul Mellon Collection.

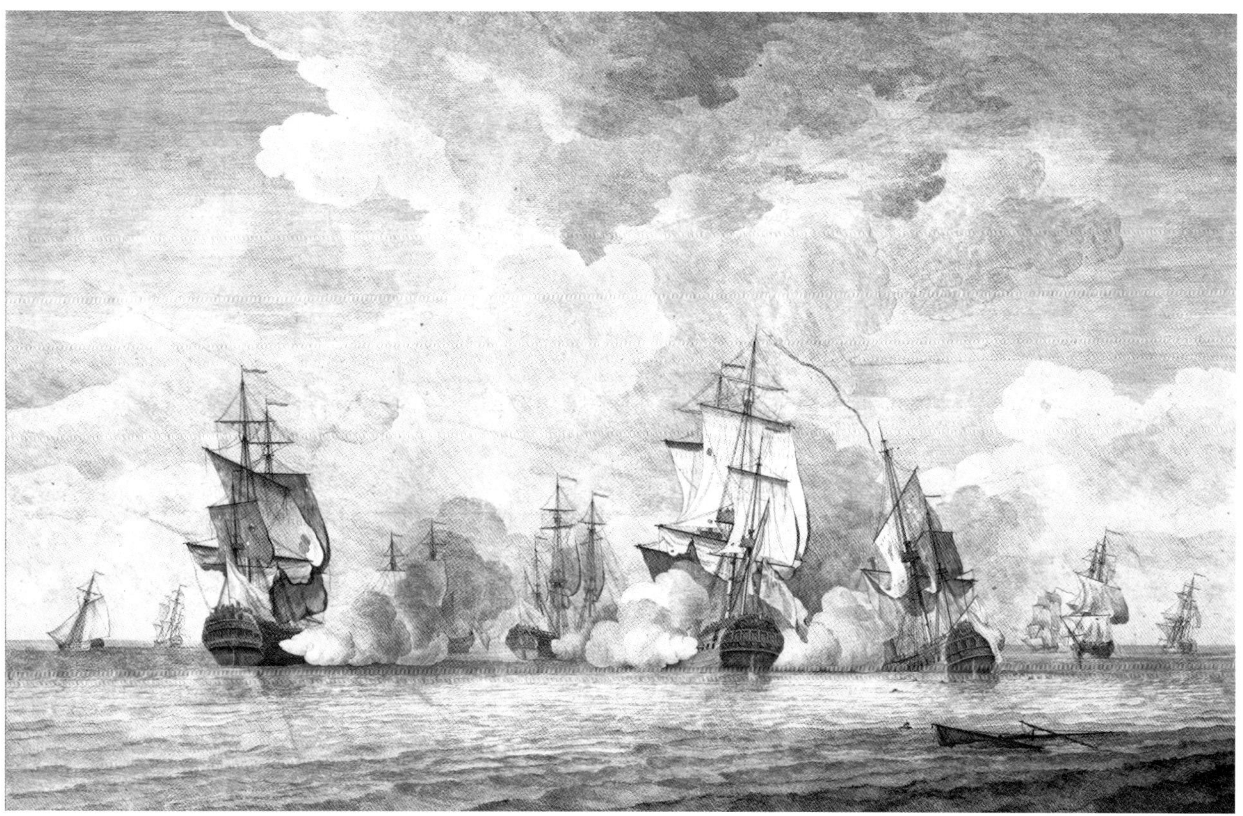

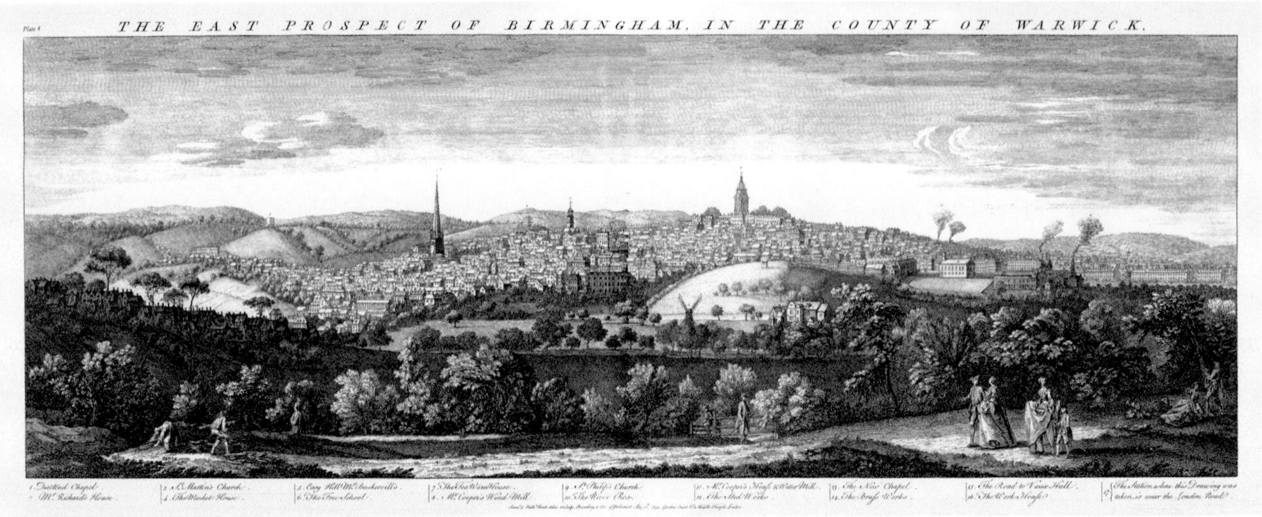

51 Engraving after Samuel and Nathaniel Buck, *East Prospect of Birmingham, in the County of Warwick*, 1753. Marlborough Rare Books, London.

making.[65] Though often unique artifacts, topographical views might also be engraved for a broader audience. With regard specifically to North America, the first major undertaking of this type showcased the new global British landscape as *Scenographia Americana: Or, A Collection of Views in North America and the West Indies. Neatly Engraved . . . from Drawings Taken on the Spot, by Several Officers of the British Navy and Army* (London, 1768). Among twenty-eight impressive plates, six based on Thomas Pownall's drawings of New York, New Jersey, and Pennsylvania locations had previously been published in 1761. Thomas Davies, another trained military draftsman, rendered American scenes from the start of his long service in North America, in 1757, and some of those works were also engraved at an early point. Yet such engravings would have been known in narrow circles at first, and, in any case, little about them corresponds with the various landscape types painted by Williams. Civilian mapping, which became important during the eighteenth century, presents a somewhat closer parallel, as in the series of panoramic prospects of the cities, ports, and towns of Great Britain published from drawings made between 1728 and 1753 by Samuel and Nathaniel Buck.[66] Their *East Prospect of Birmingham, in the County of Warwick* (1753), for example, shows an expansive view with rolling hills, trees, and a windmill surrounding the city, its church spires and industrial chimneys piercing the sky (fig. 51). Although in the Denning and Wiley families Williams did not employ the elevated vantage point characteristic of topographical representations – good for showing cities but unsuitable for portraits – the vistas he included belong more to the tradition of views than of imaginary and symbolic landscapes, as in his earlier Philadelphia portraits.[67] In their mixture of wildness and cultivation, the landscapes in the Denning and Wiley family portraits might seem allied with the British mode of the picturesque. However, the idea and ideals of the picturesque were not widely disseminated, even in England, until the early 1780s (most especially in the writings of the Reverend William Gilpin), and impact on artists working in America does not come into focus until the 1790s.

Finally, in considering possible sources of inspiration for Williams's landscapes, the stylized plants that appear throughout his work may be related to botanical illustration. In the Wiley family portrait, for example, a row of sparse vegetation forms a decorative frieze across the bottom of the canvas, silhouetted against the foreground stream (its bank the place of Williams's signature). Williams must have been a consumer of botanical writing, since he also produced it: his *Penrose* manuscript reveals a precise observer of nature. To make up a story spanning three decades based on actual experience of no more than a year or two (if on any at all), Williams would have had to refresh and expand his understanding of Central American flora and fauna. Philadelphia had a trove of books on voyages and travel, geography, topography, and natural history in the Library Company. Whether Williams had access is unknown, though Benjamin Franklin and other founders of the subscription library in 1731 established it precisely for the benefit of men of modest means. Whatever needs composing the Penrose manuscript may have satisfied for Williams, an interest in natural history was clearly among them.

The career of Williams, painter, held up well during his years in America. The artist's productivity and unusual diversity of output find support in textual evidence, while his existing paintings demonstrate his imagination and inclination to experiment.[68] Reach, more than grasp, characterized Williams's ambition. In his major surviving commission, for example – the Hall portraits of 1766 – elaborately staged landscapes, interiors, and still life elements vie for attention with the figures. The busy, iconographically loaded compositions remain a catalogue of unintegrated detail. To a cosmopolitan contemporary, such characteristics betrayed unmistakable provinciality. When Reynolds, in exactly contemporaneous criticism of Copley's *Boy with a Squirrel*, deplored that picture's "hardness" and "over minuteness," he identified those features as constituent of the American's "little way at Boston," a painting manner that could only be overcome by the acquisition of European experience.[69] Though Copley, after learning of Reynolds's opinion, attempted to modify his style without leaving home, he need not have done so. His patron base continued to expand, and he continued to produce portraits that attest to clients' appetite for details expressive of their values and tastes. Copley's uncommon success spared him any need to earn income except at his easel, but the artist remained dissatisfied with the limitations of portrait painting. Williams, during the same years, managed to find clients for a surprising range of picture types. Yet he was always prepared to adapt, as other evidence of his life in America attests.

Sign Painting and Advertising

William Williams, Painter,
Acquaints the Publick, that he is removed from Chestnut-street to the House next Door to Benjamin Loxly's, near the Draw bridge, where he intends to follow his Business as usual.

N.B. He also instructs young Gentlemen on the German Flute, common Flute, and Hautboy, after an easy Method, and the newest Taste.

Pennsylvania Gazette, April 21, 1757

William Williams Limner &c,
Being lately returned from the West-Indies; desires to acquaint the Publick; that he now Lives in Loxley's Court, at the Sign of Hogarth's Head, his former place of Residence, where he intends to carry on his Business viz. Painting in general.

Also an Evening School, for the Instruction of Polite Youth, in different branches of Drawing, and to sound the Hautboy, German and common Flutes, by their humble servant

William Williams
N.B. Those Gentlemen inclining to Learn, may by applying be informed of the Conditions.

Pennsylvania Journal and Weekly Advertiser, January 13, 1763

William Williams, Painter,
At Rembrandt's Head in Batteaux-street
Undertakes painting in general, viz. History, portraiture, landskip, sign painting, lettering, gilding, and strewing smalt. N.B. He cleans, repairs, and varnishes, any old pictures of value, and teaches the art of drawing. Those ladies or gentlemen who may be pleased to employ him, may depend on care and dispatch.

New-York Gazette, and the Weekly Mercury, May 8, 1769

Advertisements made up roughly half of the content of colonial American newspapers after 1760, with the largest category announcing imported consumer goods and the next comprising notices placed by colonial artisans, including painters.[70] Yet colonial British artists were less likely to advertise than other tradesmen and portrait painters least likely of all, as personal recommendations carried more weight with patrons embarking on so intimate a transaction.[71] Peale advertised as a saddler in 1762, as a saddler and sign painter in 1763, and as a watch repairman in 1764, but he did not place notices of his availability to paint portraits after taking up that occupation. Some portraitists benefited from indirect promotion, for which they themselves presumably supplied content, as when Boston newspapers announced Copley's election as Fellow in the London-based Society of Artists in 1767, his socially advantageous marriage in 1769, and his departure on professional grounds for England in 1774. Williams, by contrast, was direct and his practice diverse (fig. 52).

Williams's advertisements indicate that he, like many other colonial American artists, followed the career of "painting in general." Someone in that line of work, in addition to producing pictures for framed display on walls, repaired paintings and undertook a range of other more

WILLIAM WILLIAMS, Painter,
At REMBRANDT's Head, in Batteaux-ſtreet,

UNdertakes painting in general, viz. Hiſtory, portraiture, landſkip, ſign painting, lettering, gilding, and ſtrewing ſmalt. N. B. He cleans, repairs, and varniſhes, any old pictures of value, and teaches the art of drawing. Thoſe ladies or gentlemen who may be pleaſed to employ him, may depend on care and diſpatch.

Above 52 Advertisement of "William Williams, Painter," *New-York Gazette, and the Weekly Mercury*, May 8, 1769. Courtesy American Antiquarian Society.

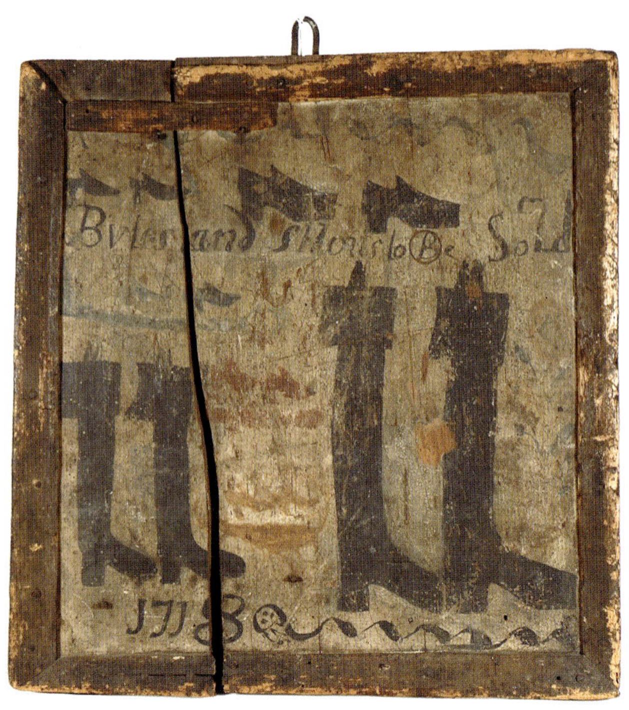

Right 53 "Butes and Shous to be Sold." Trade sign, Providence, Rhode Island, 1718. Paint on wood, iron, 19¾ × 19 in. (50.16 × 48.26 cm). Courtesy Rhode Island Historical Society, RHi X17 1135.

practical jobs that also used oil paint, such as the embellishment of signs, coaches, and houses. (Exterior uses preceded adoption of the oil medium by easel painters.) The designation "limner" in English and American documents, less common as the century progressed, distinguished picture making from house and decorative painting. For that reason, Pratt's apprenticeship papers of 1749 characterized his master, James Claypoole, Sr., as "Limner & Painter in General."[72] Limning especially connoted portrait painting, or "drawing a face in colors," as defined in an article on painting practices for *Universal Magazine* (London) in 1748.[73] Williams, who used both the terms limner and painter, exemplified the artisanal practicality and flexibility necessary for survival in a provincial market – though even in London professional diversification could help keep a career afloat.[74] He relocated in pursuit of new patrons, placed print advertisements to announce his arrival, marked his place of business with a tradesman's sign, and took on whatever work he could find.[75] As his ads attest, Williams did not restrict his services to painting. In Philadelphia, where he lived in a new house off Arch Street, Williams offered instruction in drawing and woodwind instruments, the latter exclusively the province of men (as his 1757 ad indicated).[76] Beyond the additional income that lessons in such genteel pastimes might provide, the activities had the further potential to place Williams in contact with the sort of people inclined to commission paintings.[77] The language of his advertisements, typical for trade and merchant notices of the period, to some extent delimited the "public." While stonecutters, by contrast to artists (and silversmiths), addressed their clientele as "any persons," Williams used terms designed to appeal to those refined by education or wealth: "gentlemen," "polite youth," and, finally, "ladies or gentlemen." As their "humble servant," he placed himself in the role of inferior, desiring above all to please.[78]

Yet some of the services Williams offered targeted working men like himself, artisans and shopkeepers who needed trade signs. Lettering, gilding, and strewing smalt, from the 1769 ad, were all aspects of signboard manufacture. Smalt was blue powdered glass derived from cobalt; it yielded glittery surfaces that made signs more eye-catching. Gilding functioned similarly. Lettering, the dominant feature of nineteenth-century signs, was less important earlier, perhaps consistent with designs common at times of low literacy, even though literacy rates were generally high in British North America. Imagery played a critical role in the days before street numbering, when projecting signs helped customers locate businesses. Benjamin Franklin highlighted the value of pictorial and linguistic economy in his political parable about the hat maker who eliminated words from his trade sign until only his name and the picture of a hat remained.[79] The representational ability that Williams announced in his notices appealed to purchasers of signs as well as of easel paintings.

Imagery on early signboards might seem to have little in common with pictures made for interior display, though

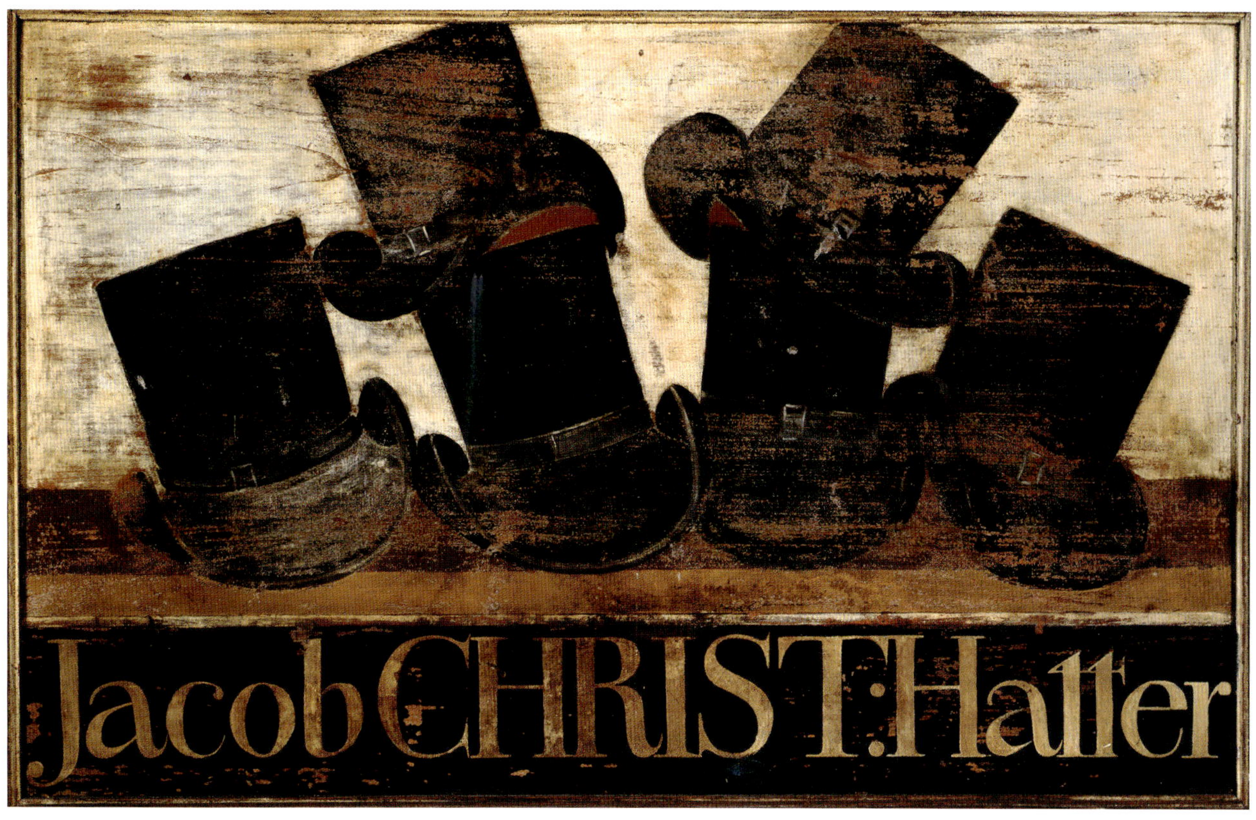

54 Edward Hicks, Jacob Christ: Hatter, shop sign, ca. 1810–40. Oil on panel, 24¾ × 37⅞ in. (62.8 × 96 cm). From the Collection of the Mercer Museum of the Bucks County Historical Society, gift of Henry Chapman Mercer, 1918.

visual evidence is scant; worn-out signs were readily discarded when their wood supports deteriorated from exposure.[80] To forestall that inevitability, sign painters first applied an oil-rich layer, to penetrate and protect the wood, whereas fine art painters used more oil at the conclusion of the process, followed by the varnishing that few signs received; some evidence of varnish on more painterly and detailed signs suggests that they were made by easel painters.[81] The earliest surviving examples, together with references to signs in newspaper advertisements, indicate that most signs bore simplified images, easily legible from a distance, and that certain conventions facilitated identification of the trade carried out at a given address. At their most straightforward, signs illustrated wares made by practitioners of the trade, if not necessarily by the tradesman in any particular shop. Goldsmiths – the tradesmen most likely to hang signs, judging from print advertisements – could be found at the golden cup and crown, the clock, or the teapot, tankard, and earring.[82] Hatters and cordwainers often displayed head- and footwear, as on an extraordinary survival from a shoe shop in Providence, Rhode Island, dated 1718, or a hatter's sign of a century later, unusual in its attribution to a known painter, Edward Hicks (figs. 53, 54). (Despite his later reputation for paintings on the theme of the "peaceable kingdom," Hicks made his living as a decorative painter, not a picture maker, responsible for no fewer than thirty-five known signs, among other practical work.)[83] Joshua Reynolds, early in his distinguished career, invoked the formulaic character of signs to criticize contemporary English portraitists, who, he said, so "indiscriminately" applied "a set of postures . . . that all their pictures look like so many sign-post paintings."[84] Signs did not have to be original to be effective (neither, for that matter, did portraits, though Reynolds was loath to acknowledge as much). Nor did signs rely on the spatial illusionism critical to the definition of painting as a fine art since the Renaissance. The absence or failure of perspective resulted in chaotic illegibility, an effect evident in West's early landscape and parodied by Hogarth in his frontispiece to *Dr. Brook Taylor's Method of Perspective Made Easy* (1755), a revision by Joshua Kirby of an earlier text (fig. 55). Kirby's engagement in the theory of perspective belied his beginnings as a house and sign

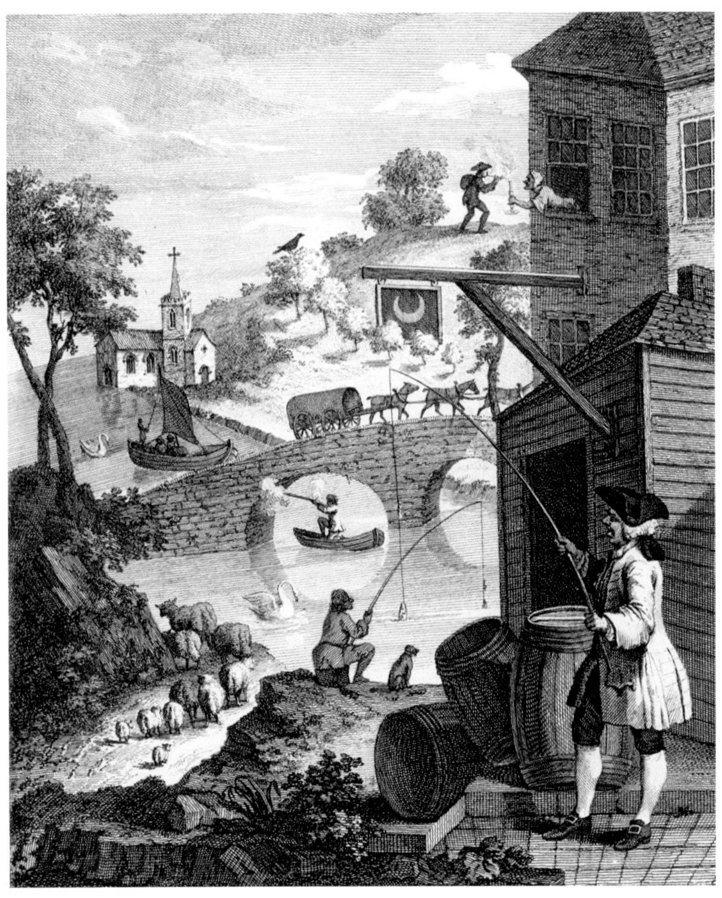

55 Luke Sullivan after William Hogarth, *Satire on False Perspective*, frontispiece to *Dr. Brook Taylor's Method of Perspective Made Easy* by Joshua Kirby, 1755. Etching and engraving, second state of two. Metropolitan Museum of Art, New York, gift of Sarah Lazarus, 1891.

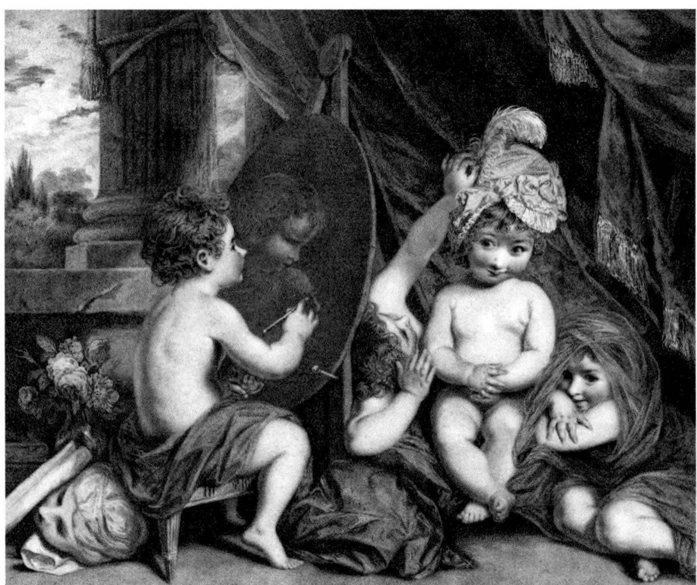

56 Francis Hayward, after Sir Joshua Reynolds, *The Infant Academy*, 1783. Stipple engraving. Yale Center for British Art, New Haven, Paul Mellon Fund.

painter in provincial Ipswich, England. Hogarth, too, started his career modestly, as an engraver of printed ephemera like shop cards, and he maintained a populist outlook. His "Satire on False Perspective" for Kirby's book, understood within the context of Hogarth's career, affectionately evoked the "episodic and egalitarian" imagery of signs, Ronald Paulson proposed, as distinguished from the hierarchical placement of elements in academic paintings.[85]

Yet some American signboards were imitative – of nature and of fine art. Chester Harding, a successful nineteenth-century portraitist who began his career as a sign painter, recalled his youthful association (ca. 1810) with a western Pennsylvanian whose sign united a copy of Reynolds's "Infant Artists" with the legend "Sign, Ornamental, and Portrait Painting executed on the shortest notice, with neatness and despatch."[86] The guarantee of careful and prompt work underscored the advertiser's artisanal identity as readily as did the services offered. The choice of image, moreover, suggests the Pennsylvania painter suffered no illusions about his talents as a portraitist. For Reynolds, *The Infant Academy* commented wryly on a profession in which high-style ambitions (evoked by the classical columns) remained perennially constrained by fashion (represented by the juvenile sitter's elaborate headdress) (fig. 56). In the rustic American setting, that satire invites a more literal reading, as a good-humored acknowledgment of artistic immaturity.

An unusually well-documented Boston sign presents another adaptation from high-style painting, with wholly serious purpose. John Johnston, its maker, grew up in the trade, son of Thomas Johnston – an engraver, japanner, and heraldic painter – and apprentice to John Gore, an ornamental and sign painter who also sold art supplies at the sign of the "Painter's Arms," in Queen Street, Boston.[87] By the late 1780s, however, portraiture had become Johnston's primary business, conducted by the mid-1790s from a rented address distinguished in the history of fine arts in Boston, Smibert's former studio. For decades after his death in 1751, American artists made the pilgrimage to a place that, even as progressively emptied of its contents, retained its aura for the several artists who rented the premises. By Johnston's time, only *The Bermuda Group* remained.[88] The complex composition, however stylistically outmoded, must have been inspiring to Johnston, lately advanced from trade painting to portraiture. Yet in 1797, Johnston took what might seem a professional step backward when he agreed to paint a shop sign for Dr. Thomas Bartlett, whose apothecary had been named as the Boston Dispensary for distribution of medicine to the poor (fig. 57). Seizing an opportunity, Johnston based his design on an engraving after Hogarth's 1736 mural of the "Good Samaritan" for St. Bartholomew's Hospital in London. He was thus able to paint a historical subject, the most respected genre in the academic canon, and to see the work placed before the public in advertisement not only of the Boston Dispensary but also of Johnston's ability to paint a composition of greater complexity and sophistication than the usual shop sign. Similar considerations had motivated Hogarth to donate his services to St. Bartholomew's sixty years earlier.[89]

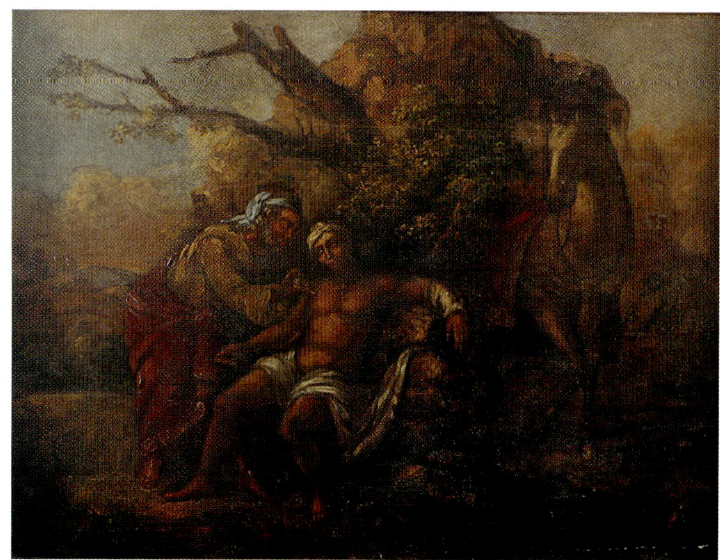

57 John Johnston, *The Good Samaritan*, shop sign for Thomas Bartlett, Apothecary, Boston Dispensary of Medicine for the Poor, 1797. Oil on wood, 41¾ × 46¾ in. (106.04 × 118.74 cm). Tufts Medical Center, Boston.

Passersby might have suspected that the signs of the Good Samaritan and the Infant Academy copied well-known pictures, but few could have named the original artists. Several American signs from the 1760s sought to capitalize more directly on the reputations of famous painters by representing those artists' heads. All have disappeared, so it is impossible to know whether lettering named those personages, as it did General Wolfe on a surviving contemporaneous tavern sign (fig. 58); however, print advertisements supplied the identities.[90] In Boston, Thomas Crafts hung the Sign of Raphael's Head above his shop in 1764, in address to artists and also to signify "quality" – of the products sold within the shop and, by extension, of the work carried out using those goods. Like his competitor John Gore at the Painter's Arms, Crafts sold both "Colours prepared for House and Ship painting" and a wide selection of paints for artists, presumably his principal customers for "the best of London Crown Glass for Pictures" and "an Assortment of Metzotinto Prints."[91]

58 Sign of General Wolfe, ca. 1768, from Israel Putnam's tavern in Brooklyn, Conn. Paint on pine, 30 × 24¼ in. (76.2 × 51.43 cm). Connecticut Historical Society, gift of Rufus S. Mathewson.

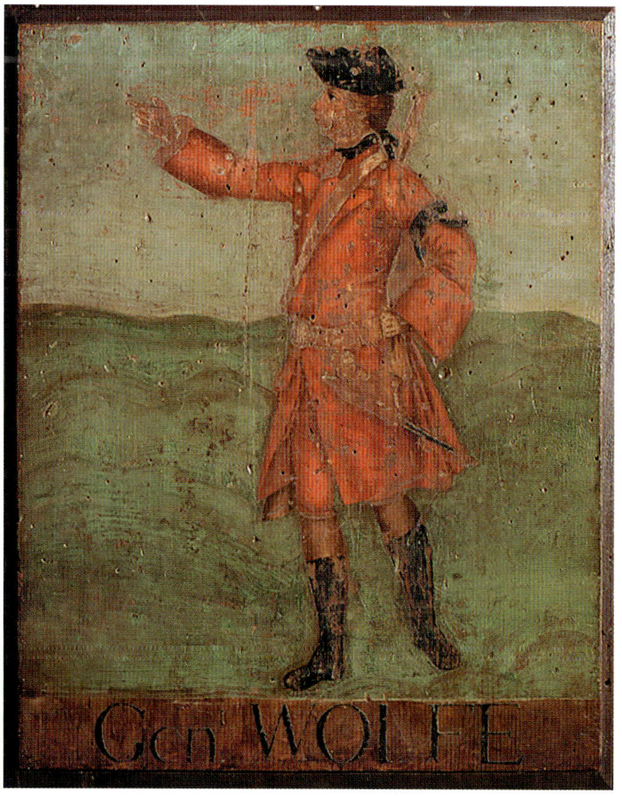

Paint sellers such as Crafts and Gore, known as "colormen," replaced apothecaries as a source of pigments for painters and supplanted ad hoc arrangements, like that of Smibert, who converted the necessity of importing supplies for himself to advantage by selling the same, an activity that supplemented his income from portraiture. Colormen served customers across the full spectrum of painting trades. But not all painters were created equal, according to Campbell's *London Tradesman*, which branded house painters – synecdochically reduced to "hands" – "the dirtiest, laziest, and most debauched set of fellows that are of any trade in and about London" and, as such, unsuitable company for practitioners of "the liberal part of this art."[92] Early colormen were not always sensitive to artists' anxie-

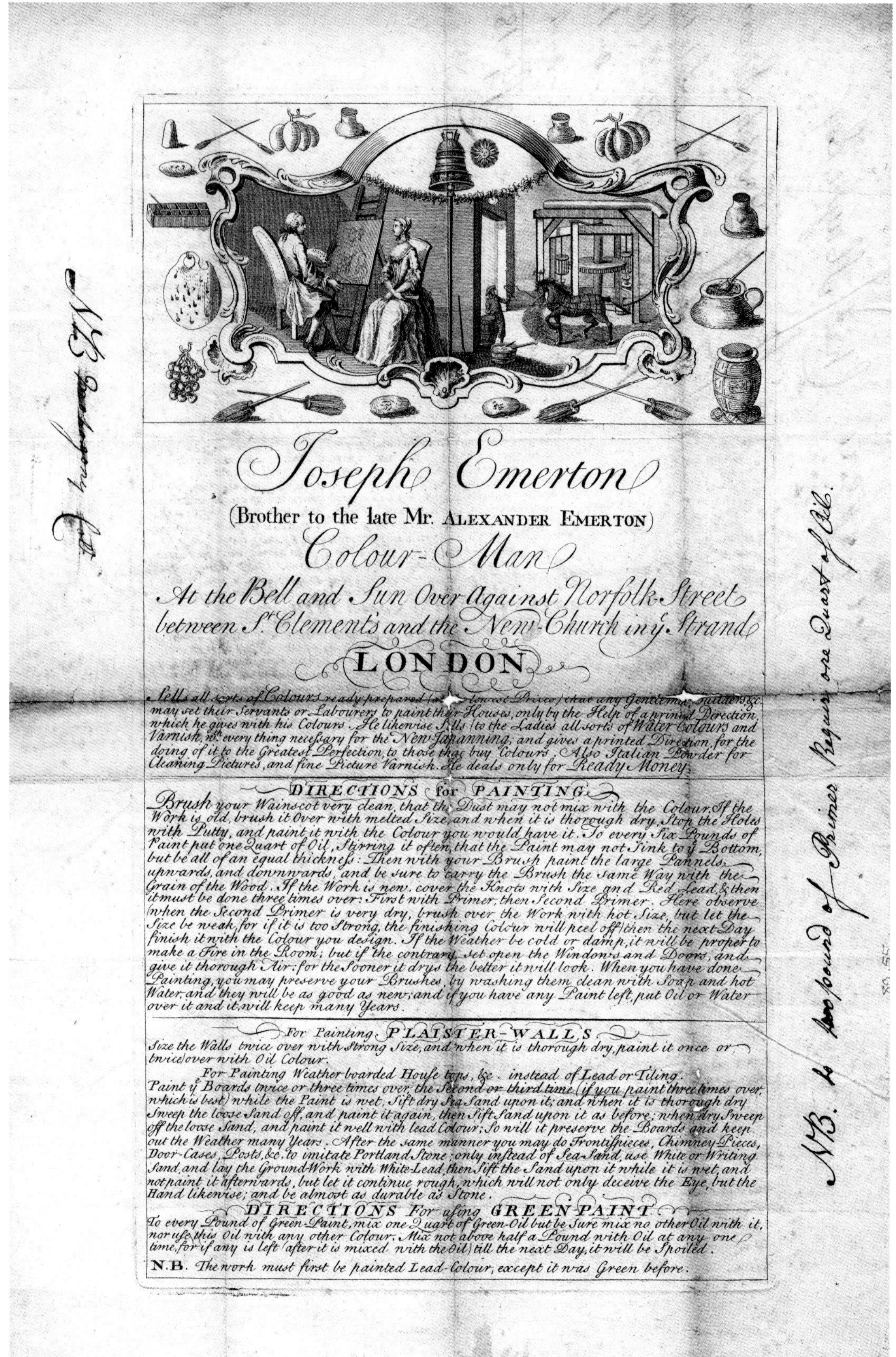

59 Trade card of Joseph Emerton, London, ca. 1744. British Museum, London. © The Trustees of the British Museum.

ties about status. Joseph Emerton of London, one of the first manufacturers of prepared paints for commercial use, had an elaborate trade card (ca. 1744) that paired images of the horse-mill employed for grinding quantities of paint and a fashionable portraitist at the easel – even though the "directions for painting" beneath the cartouche address house painting alone (fig. 59).[93] (Emerton's juxtaposition echoes Thomas Lawrence's much later comment on the drudgery of portraiture as a "dry mill-horse business.")[94] Campbell decried the advent of "Colour-Shops who have set up Horse-Mills to grind Colours and sell them to Noblemen and Gentlemen ready mixed at a low Price, and by the Help of a few printed Directions, a House may be painted by any common Labourer at one Third the Expence," relative to the cost of hiring a house painter trained in the art of "grinding, mixing, and compounding the colours." Eighteenth-century easel painters, similarly, had traditionally compounded dry pigments purchased from color shops in their own studios. Some colormen did make an appeal to fine artists. The trade card of one of the earliest in London, John Calfe at "St. Luke's Head," showed the patron saint of painters – legendary portraitist of the Virgin Mary – with palette and brushes at an easel.[95] But Calfe supplied house painters too, and he also sold snuff, which, like paint mixed with oil, was sometimes stored in bladders. (A grape-like cluster of tied bladders appears on Joseph Emerton's trade card.)

Williams seems both tradesman-like and professionally shrewd and self-aware in his use of shop signs to advertise his place of business: the sign of Hogarth's Head in Philadelphia and Rembrandt's Head in New York. Print advertisements reveal that tradespeople, such as goldsmiths and other metal workers, cabinetmakers, and upholsterers, often employed shop signs, whereas individuals who presented themselves as painters of portraits or other types of pictures rarely did. Among advertisements for painters in New York City, only Williams's notice mentioned a sign.[96] In their search for clients, some artists simply moved about too much to warrant setting up shop; but others, even those with diversified businesses, must have wanted to avoid the association with trade encouraged by the mere act of hanging (and, presumably, making) a sign. Williams, atypical in his use of signboards, at least chose their imagery purposefully, which some tradesmen did not. John Winters, "Painter, from London," carried out his business in Philadelphia in 1740 at the unpromisingly named "Sign of the easy Chair." Tempting as it may be to speculate that Winters chose that image in lighthearted attempt to reassure potential portrait subjects about the rigors of sitting, the absence of portraiture from the more artisanal services he listed rules against it. Instead, Winters appears guilty of one of "those Absurdities which are committed over our Heads," according to the *Spectator*, in not "mak[ing] use of a Sign which bears some Affinity to the Wares in which [the shop] deals."[97]

In Philadelphia, Hogarth's head served Williams by linking him with a resolutely English artist whose work was affordable and accessible through the medium of prints. Hogarth's high profile, in Britain and America, arose especially from circulation of his prints of modern moral subjects. Not surprisingly, he attracted the attention of Philadelphia's famed moralist, Franklin, who wrote to Hogarth in 1764 (the artist died that year, and there is no record of a reply) and in 1768 acquired a complete set of Hogarth's prints for the Library Company.[98] In a practical measure that threatened to compromise his image as a fine artist, Hogarth routinely advertised his engravings in London newspapers, an effective means of reaching a broad potential customer base for prints. A man of multiple talents, he never hesitated to promote himself by any means possible. Hogarth's two self-portraits were part of that effort, given high visibility as frontispieces to folio editions of the artist's prints. In the first, based on a painting of 1745, Hogarth represented his bust-length image on a fictive oval canvas, shown resting on three books, an allusion to the literary dimension of his art – and to Anglophone traditions, since, in the painted original, the volumes are marked Shakespeare, Milton, and Swift (fig. 60). An engraver's burin in front of those volumes signals Hogarth's versatility and, in the context of the folio, his authorship of the prints it contained. To the right, an oval palette dabbed with pigments echoes the shape of the internal canvas and affirms Hogarth's role as painter (in the actual painting, the palette bore no pigments, perhaps because the canvas itself did). More enigmatically, a hovering serpentine figure arcs across the palette beneath the words "the line of Beauty," alluding to the central principle of Hogarth's aesthetics of daily life, articulated in his book *The Analysis of Beauty* (1753).[99] On a more mundane level, Hogarth included his pug dog, a breed associated with England and perhaps a reference to its master's well-known pugnacity. It is tempting to imagine this engraved self-portrait as a model for Williams's sign, since the internal canvas already appears sign-like; that is, Hogarth carefully displayed the picture within the picture at a slight angle to show an edge tacked to the stretcher, affirming its status as artifact: the sign of Hogarth's head.

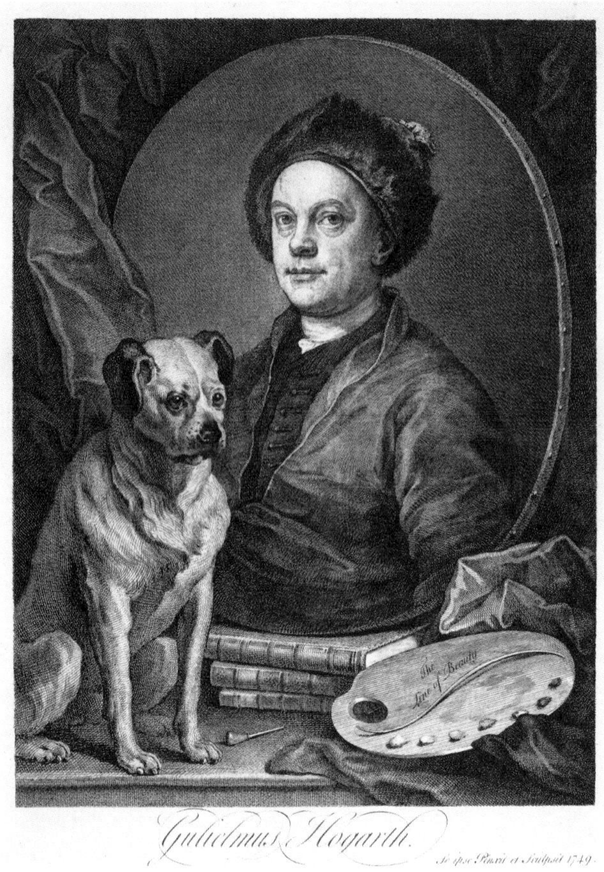

60 William Hogarth, *Gulielmus Hogarth (Self-Portrait)*, 1749. Etching and engraving. Yale Center for British Art, New Haven, Paul Mellon Collection.

61 Pierre Eugène Du Simitière, drawing of old Dutch houses, New York City, ca. 1769. Library Company of Philadelphia.

At the sign of Rembrandt's Head in New York City, Williams strategically targeted a potential clientele, to whom he announced his business in eight advertisements in the *New-York Gazette, and the Weekly Mercury* that appeared between May and June 1769. The city, though by then part of an English colony for over a century, retained elements of its Dutch heritage, attracting the attention of outsiders. Artist, naturalist, and antiquary Pierre Eugène Du Simitière, in New York concurrently with Williams, sketched a Dutch-style dwelling with crow-stepped gable marked 1689 and made note of houses "built with brick, mostly in the dutch taste" (fig. 61).[100] More than just "Odd old Dutch Houses" caught the attention of another observer who, less than ten years before Williams's arrival, found "the People mostly Dutch," while yet another visitor estimated, only somewhat more conservatively, that "more than half . . . are Dutch."[101] The impression is striking given that Dutch and English populations were by then well integrated, affiliated by economic status, with only two-fifths of New York City residents claiming Dutch ancestry in 1750 and one-fifth twenty years later, when the total population climbed to just over 20,000.[102]

Williams became a part of the burgeoning city, which had prospered during King George's War and the French and Indian War of the 1740s and 1750s. Provisioning of troops, privateering, a surge in construction, and increased consumption of all kinds of goods by New Yorkers who made money in these ventures expanded the city physically and economically. The artist settled on a street in the West Ward that had been platted for city lots by landowner Dirck Dey in 1748.[103] These lots were still being developed and marketed in 1770, since the area lay north and west of Wall Street and lower Broadway, the administrative and prime residential centers of British New York. The new Dey (or "Dyes") Street ran west from Broadway and just north of "Van Pelts Rope Walk," established prior to 1724 on open land, as pictured (two blocks south of a planted allée) and labeled on David Grim's hand-drawn map retrospectively representing New York ca. 1742–44 (fig. 62). In the more settled neighborhood shown on the Maerschalk Plan of 1755 (fig. 63), "E. Pels" still ran that business (below the R of river).[104] A ropewalk was a long, straight narrow space, either open or covered, along which a man walked backward to spin hemp fibers into rope, keeping them taut around his waist as they were twisted by a wheel operated by another man at the start of the walk. Evert Pels's ropewalk – 15 feet wide, roughly 675 feet long and apparently covered – benefited from proximity to shipbuilding. Grim's map notated "Batteaux built

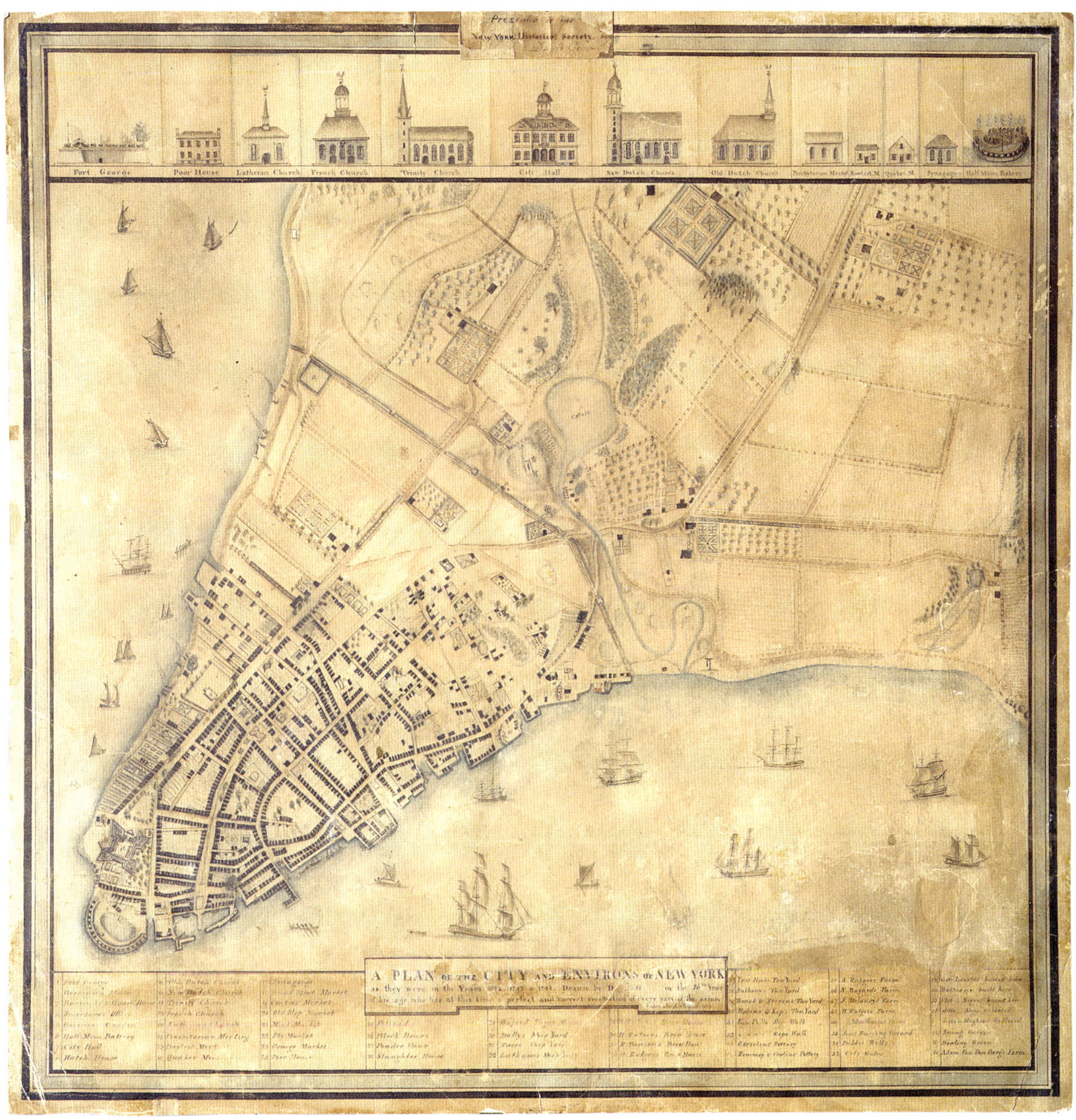

62 *A Plan of the City and Environs of New York as they were in the years 1743 & 1744*, as recalled and drawn by David Grim, Aug. 1813. New-York Historical Society, N-YHS Library maps, call #M2 1.1. Photography © New-York Historical Society.

here" for an area to the immediate north and by the river, near the dock Dey controlled. "Battoes" were flat-bottom boats used in the Indian trade (one appears just offshore from the ropewalk) and the name also served boats constructed for wartime use. Both enterprises necessitated enlargement of wharves and the establishment of an arsenal along the North River between 1730 and 1766.[105] These activities explain why Williams and neighboring artisans who advertised businesses on the street called it Batteaux Street.[106]

A description of Dey Street in 1763, advanced by petitioners for the erection of a market at the river end, characterized it as recently "dug out and paved . . . wide and spacious, . . . [with] a very gradual, easy and equal Descent . . . , which renders it much the best street leading

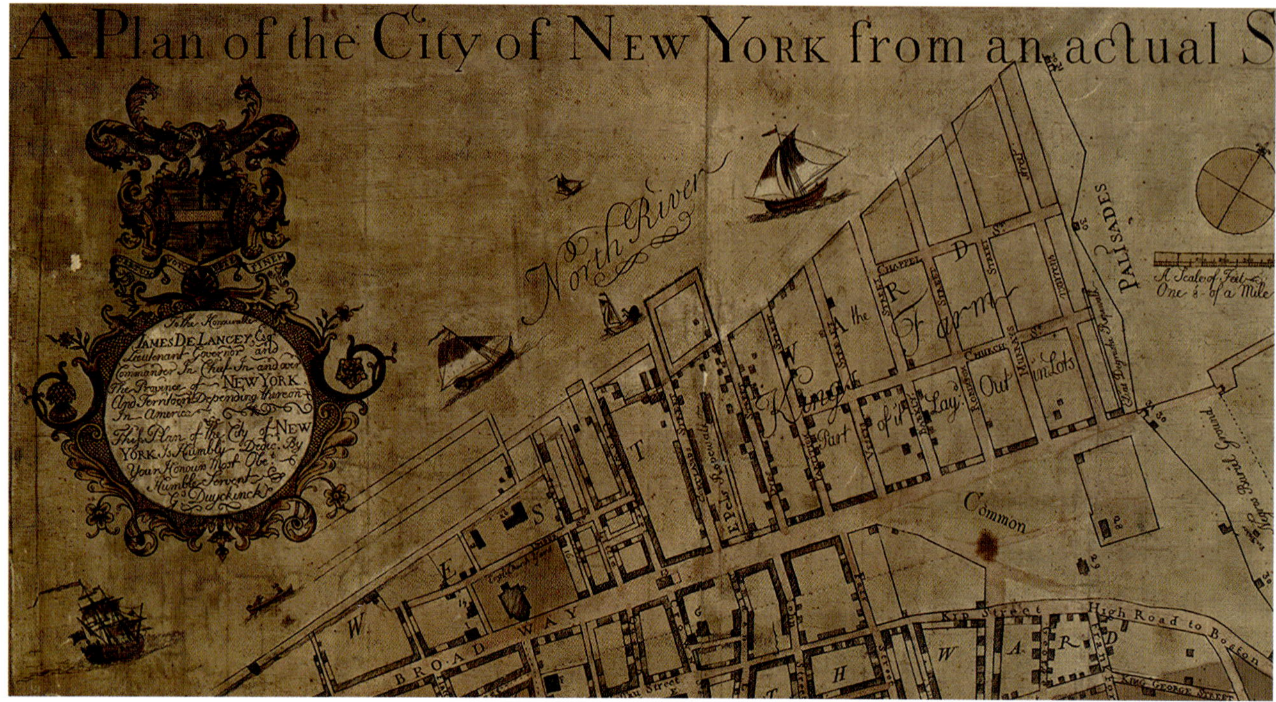

63 *A Plan of the City of New York from an actual Survey*, drawn by Francis Maerschalck, printed, engraved for, and sold by Gerardus Duyckinck, 1755. Detail of new streets west of Broadway including Dey Street, north of E. Pels's Ropewalk. Library of Congress, Washington, D.C., Geography and Map Division.

from the Broadway to the North River as well as for Carts Wagons and other Carriages as for persons to walk on foot."[107] Alexander Hamilton recalled pleasant strolls along the tree-shaded street, during his time as a student at King's (later Columbia) College, founded in 1754 on the former [Trinity] Church Farm in the West Ward, to the north.[108] Even closer at one block north on the Broadway end was St. Paul's Chapel, completed, except for its steeple, in 1766. Robert Morris recorded that a visit to see the elegant new church building took him "into the country."[109] The neighborhood developing around St. Paul's and King's College was less polished than those institutional presences suggest, founded on affordable leases from the church and attractive to persons of limited economic means as well as to "above 500 'ladies of pleasure.'"[110] The long block of Dey/Batteaux was home to a variety of artisans, including many in fairly humble occupations who did not work at their place of residence – carpenters, bricklayers, cartmen – as well as persons who did and catered directly to a genteel clientele – a glove cleaner and dyer, a mender of china and ladies' fans, the painter Williams.[111] William Dunlap, drawing on childhood memories of New York City "as it existed from 1767 to 1774," unfavorably characterized buildings of the neighborhood north of Trinity Church and south of St. Paul's as "mean."[112] Yet all of the houses on Dey were recently built, typically by the initial lessee, and advertisements placed when the properties changed hands present them as well equipped. The one where Williams resided until fall 1770 had a "bake house and oven, very convenient for a baker"; another, where "Mr. Winter, House-Carpenter, now lives," had "7 Rooms and 5 Fire-Places, a very good Cellar and a Kitchen, with a new cistern"; still another was "almost new, two stories high, with a brick front and a good cellar under the whole."[113] These were obviously not the "old Dutch Houses" visitors to the city commented on, and few tenants among Williams's immediate neighbors had names suggesting Dutch ancestry, despite the prevalence of Dutch surnames in New York at the time (even though by this date such names no longer reliably indicated an individual's heritage or cultural identity).[114] References to things or persons as "Dutch" may primarily have meant "not English" and included individuals of Huguenot, Flemish, German, and Scandinavian ancestry. Still, Williams, an Englishman by birth and a recent arrival in New York, may have shared the perception of contemporaneous visitors regarding Dutch presence in the city.

The prospect of a local population with roots in the Netherlands offered painters some cause for optimism, and Williams chose the sign of Rembrandt's head for his Batteaux Street shop and residence accordingly. Seventeenth- and eighteenth-century inventories reveal that persons of Dutch origin or descent had more diversified and, in a few cases, much more substantial collections of pictures than did Anglo-Americans, consistent with middle-class consumption of art in the Netherlands.[115] The Swedish naturalist Peter Kalm, visiting New York in 1748, observed that the walls of New York houses were "quite covered with all sorts of drawings and pictures in small frames."[116] At the Stuyvesant residence in 1768, Du Simitière saw a variety of pictures, including portraits and "a conversation piece in a landskip," while noting "in the windows of the house (which is built in the old dutch taste)" many panes of glass representing family coats of arms, salvaged from a demolished church building.[117] Though the Dutch Reformed Church, as a branch of Calvinism, prohibited placement of religious pictures in churches, it condoned private display of such works, common in the resolutely Dutch communities upriver and perhaps not unusual in New York City. Notably, Williams presented himself to New Yorkers as able to clean and repair "any old picture of value." He also advertised "landskip" and "History" among the types of pictures he made, indicating that he hoped to find clientele for such subjects. His use of the term "landskip" may have been calculated: it derived from *landtschap*, the Dutch word for a genre that the English considered a Netherlandish invention and used in artistic circles until 1770 (even though "landscape" entered common usage in literary contexts much earlier).[118] While the absence of any reference to landscape in Williams's earlier ads leaves the matter open to question, Williams's choice of the Dutch-sounding variation cannot be discounted as part of his marketing effort in New York.

Eagles's list of the paintings Williams made in New York indicates that the artist did find buyers for works other than portraits. His landscapes included the "small Moonlight" for Lord Rosehill, "large Tempest" for Captain Rutgers, and "small Landskip" – plus the extant *Imaginary Landscape*. "History" comprises two biblical subjects for a single client, as well as the "Emblematical piece for ye Corsican Club." A New York counterpart to the London club of that name is undocumented but makes sense for a colonial city that William Smith described in 1762 as "one of the most social places on the continent," where "men collect themselves into weekly evening clubs."[119] Britons showed intense sympathy for the Corsicans in their unsuccessful fight to preserve their independence and democratic liberties against French aggression. Colonial newspapers printed or reprinted hundreds of notices concerning Corsica during the later 1760s, while 1768 saw publication of James Boswell's *An Account of Corsica: The Journal of a Tour to that Island, and Memoirs of Pasquale Paoli*. In its third, 1769 edition, the book bore a frontispiece after the portrait of patriot-general Paoli that Boswell, then just in his late twenties, acquired from his American artist friend Henry Benbridge, a former Philadelphian who, in that year, entered the London studio of West after four years in Italy. Above and beneath the portrait head in its oval, the engraver added a collection of martial motifs – musket, sword, hatchet, canon, drum, banners – on which Williams might have drawn for his "Emblematical piece." Williams's modest success with history in New York registers his persistence, a quality not shown by painter John Durand, who set up in the heart of town, "near the City-Hall, Broad-Street" in 1768, the year before Williams arrived. Durand was adventurous in announcing his presence. He did not take out a standard ad, with his name and occupation at the head, and offered no details of his business. Instead, he made an argument for the importance of history painting and flattered prospective patrons, "gentlemen and ladies," by expressing his hopes for the encouragement that "so elegant and entertaining an Art, has always obtain'd from People of the most improved Minds, and best Taste and Judgment, in all polite Nations in every Age."[120] Six notices in two different newspapers in April and May evidently failed to entice customers; a week after the last one, "John Durand, Portrait Painter" had resurfaced in New Haven, where his new advertisement made no mention of history painting.[121]

Williams understood that Americans of all backgrounds preferred portraits to any other kind of painting, and his calculation in choosing Rembrandt for his sign did not neglect that reality. Writers on art acknowledged Rembrandt's merits as a painter of likenesses, one who stayed close to nature. Peale acknowledged as much to a patron in 1772, when he wrote that, though he had no access to "Greecian and Roman statues," he had a "variety of Characters . . . [and] must paint as Rambrant did [and] make these my Anticks."[122] "Wonderful Strength, Sweetness, and Resemblance" were hallmarks of Rembrandt's portraits, according to the first life of the artist that is attributable to an English author: a short biography in a group assembled by "R. G. Esq." for the 1716 translation of Du Fresnoy's *Art of Painting*, a book Williams owned, according to West.[123] Jonathan Richardson – a writer on art also familiar to Williams – offered tribute that gained authority from his position as theorist, painter, and collector. With a broader view of Rembrandt's production than simply his portraits, Richardson praised the artist for sublimity and invention, along with excellence in expression and composition.[124] Richardson collected Rembrandt's prints and drawings, the best known aspect of the Dutch artist's production during the first part of the eighteenth century. Rembrandt's paintings, by contrast, were barely represented in English collections before 1740. But the market for both his paintings and works on paper grew exponentially after that time, supplemented by reproductive mezzotints; the first made in Britain, in 1747, copied a presumed (but unlikely) early self-portrait.[125] With the head of Rembrandt on his New York sign, Williams – a consumer of prints, reader of art books, and painter in his own right – signaled his awareness of British taste. Paradoxically, ascendant English fashion following British victory in the French and Indian War marginalized Dutch pictures and display customs in New York City. During his 1779 sojourn in the city, Du Simitière, a voracious collector, was able to acquire many Dutch pictures from families who no longer wanted them.[126] Williams may well have overestimated American sophistication in matters of art or misjudged New York preferences, however Dutch the city appeared relative to Philadelphia. His New York ad and shop sign nevertheless constituted a business strategy. Otherwise, the artist could simply have reused the signboard with Hogarth's head that hung at his Philadelphia address in 1763.

Williams's signs of Hogarth's and Rembrandt's heads, along with certain other signboards mentioned in texts, raise questions concerning the role of naturalistic representation in sign painting. A conflicted answer emerges from the incident in Harding's autobiography concerning the associate who did business at the sign of the "Infant Artists." The man painted portraits of "the primitive sort," Harding recalled, but even these inspired the young artisan to try his hand at the art. In his first effort, Harding made a portrait of his wife using materials available, a board and colors from his sign-painters' trade. The painting prompted an epiphany: "I made a thing that looked like her. The moment I saw the likeness, I became frantic with delight: it was like the discovery of a new sense; I could think of nothing else. From that time, sign-painting became odious." (Harding anticipated the reader's skepticism concerning this overestimation of skill; he cut his youthful self down to size in reporting that his colleague at the sign of the Infant Artists pronounced Harding's second portrait of his wife "no more like [her] than like him.") Significantly, Harding did not turn his back on sign painting because he considered it low-status work; even after he took up portraiture, he recalled of those early years, it "never occurred" to him "that it was more honorable or profitable than sign-painting."[127] He was, instead, seduced by illusionism but anticipated no call to perform that particular magic on signboards.

In the case of signs featuring persons of distinction, some painters did trouble to produce naturalistic portraits. Hard evidence exists in a double-sided sign for Bissell's Inn, in Windsor, Connecticut. Each side of the heraldic-shaped board portrayed a hero from the War of 1812, Commodore Oliver Hazard Perry and Captain James Lawrence, the latter based on an engraving after Gilbert Stuart (fig. 64). Stuart ranked as America's foremost portraitist when this sign was made, and a hint of his painterliness informs the work, which has been attributed to Nathaniel Wales, a painter who specialized in both signs and portraits. In Litchfield, Connecticut, Wales advertised "the SIGN PAINTING business, in all its various branches . . . done with neatness and dispatch. Also LIKENESSES . . . if not approved as Likenesses, no pay will be requested."[128] Viewers, not surprisingly, judged portraits on signs by the same criteria they routinely applied to portraits on canvas, that is, by degree of likeness. They quipped about the failures, as painter James Jarves is said to have done of a Cincinnati tavern sign featuring Andrew Jackson: "I'll rub a dog's tail on a pallet and he'll *wag* a better likeness."[129] Among the thirty-eight men represented on an ambitious sign for the "Federal Convention of 1787" Inn, in Philadelphia, the figure of Judge James Wilson attracted particular comment for displaying "that imposing air which was natural to him, and which had strongly impressed the delineator" – as if the figure had been studied from life. Indeed, the writer (casting a backward glance from 1824) asserted that the painter, "one of our neglected sons of genius who reduced by want of patronage to portrait and sign painting for a livelihood, [had] obtained a glimpse of this truly venerable assembly, which he instantly transferred to a sign post that he had been employed to decorate for an ale-house."[130] The comment reveals the nineteenth-century ascendancy of genres other than portraiture, in equating portraiture with sign painting as occupations to which a worthy painter might be "reduced" by patrons insufficiently appreciative of the fine arts. Though the article did not name the artist in question, Dunlap identified him as Pratt, the Philadelphian who began his career in apprenticeship to a "limner and painter in general." Pratt's horizons had expanded consider-

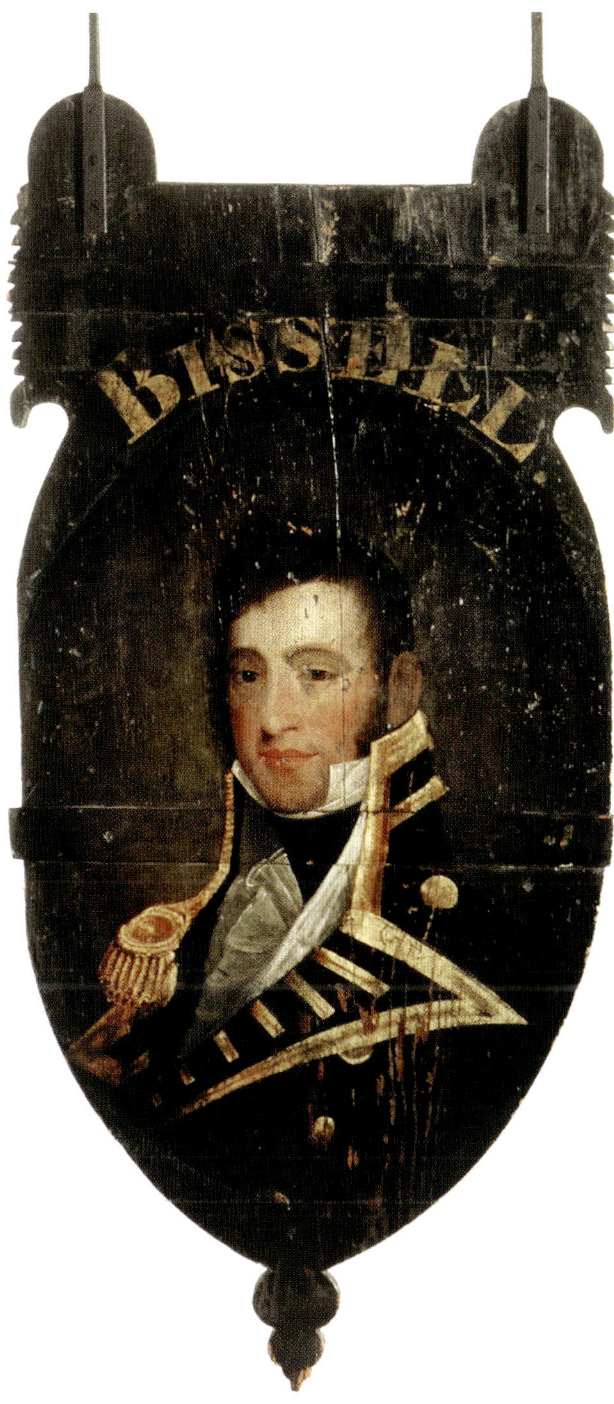

64 Captain James Lawrence, sign for Sill's Inn and Bissell's Inn, ca. 1814. Oil on panel, 55¼ × 22¾ in. (132.7 × 57.8 cm). Windsor Historical Society, Windsor, Conn.

ably by 1764, when he began the sojourn in West's London studio that is a focus of chapter three. Twenty years later, however, the artist was again painting signs. Some were complex history paintings in the guise of group portraits for the man in the street – though brought down to earth, at least figuratively, by the metal and wooden artifacts necessary to signboard display. Relative to the often lavish frames of the fine art object, these materials connoted something quite different, arguably the positive signification of honest craftsmanship. Most of Pratt's signs were as prosaic as their materials, like the cock in a barnyard that he made for a beer house in Spruce Street. According to Dunlap, "the execution of this was so fine, and the expression of nature so exactly copied, that it was evident to the most casual observer that it was painted by the hand of a master." Trying to make the best of the situation, Dunlap conceded: "It is well known that many a good painter has condescended, and many a one been glad, to paint a sign."[131]

Dunlap's use of the verb "condescend" implies that such painters voluntarily, even "gladly," consented to perform a task understood as beneath them. The "good" painters, in other words, were fine artists and sign painting merely trade. Dunlap stretched the point; few artists made signs for reasons other than financial necessity. (The early eighteenth-century French academician Antoine Watteau presents the notable exception with his signboard for art dealer Edmé-François Gersaint, a bit of transparent artifice calculated to appeal to sophisticated Parisians.)[132] Numerous British and American artists made signs early in their careers, when they were either unaware of stratification in the trade and profession of painting, as in the case of Harding, or simply not in a position to advance to the next level. George Romney's first commissioned work, made around 1757, was a postmaster's sign featuring a hand holding a letter. Later famous for his portraits, Romney then lived in Kendal, Cumberland, where, according to his son, "it cannot be supposed that there were many who had acumen sufficient to distinguish, and taste enough to admire, the growing talents of a young artist."[133] Older artists, too, experienced constraints imposed by provinciality or the limitations of their talent. If Pratt made signs towards the end of his career while retaining a measure of respect, Abraham Delanoy could not turn his own relationship with the American-born master West – proclaimed in his advertisement of 1771 – to his advantage. A mere six months after placing that notice, Delanoy was selling groceries, and by the 1780s, according to Dunlap, he was "in 'the sear and yellow leaf' both of life and fortune. He was consumptive, poor, and his only employment sign-painting."[134] Painters who merely began in trade could become successful artists, but those who ended in trade were judged failures. Other painters, like Williams, worked in the trade while also producing pictures for display. In the nineteenth century, when the fine art of painting was better established, easel painters had less need to take on other kinds of work. Yet John Archibald Woodside, Sr., a possible student of Pratt's, appears in Philadelphia directories as an "ornamental" or "sign" painter during the same two decades (1817–1837) that he exhibited at the Pennsylvania Academy of the Fine Arts as a "Painter [of] Animals and Still Life." Dunlap thought that Woodside painted signs "with talent beyond many who paint in higher branches."[135] After Woodside's death in 1852, a newspaper hailed him as "one of the best sign painters in the state, and perhaps in the country, . . . the first to raise this branch of the art to the degree of excellence here which it has now attained."[136]

For many eighteenth- and early nineteenth-century artists, the pursuits of painting as trade and as fine art (or at least of household display) coexisted. Whether from interest, necessity, or obliviousness to distinctions, men such as Williams, Johnston, Harding, and Woodside pursued diversified careers, over the long term or for shorter periods. Though the degree to which they experienced membership in a broader community of artists can be difficult to gauge, the case of Williams – a self-described painter-in-general – offers an intriguing glimpse of professional engagement.

The Lives and Portraits of Artists

Williams's decision to mark his shops with the heads of Hogarth and Rembrandt, however calculated an appeal to potential customers in America, arose from more than purely commercial concerns. Those heads were a means of professional connection, across space and time, vibrantly meaningful for a man known to have assembled narratives and portraits of artists. In his aspiration to more than the trade of art, Williams used trade signs, paradoxically, to affirm ambition, ability, and affiliation.

At one level, Williams's signs employed the language of contemporaries on the other side of the Atlantic and acknowledged a professional resource of sustaining importance to his career: London printsellers. Both J. Jackson and Nathaniel Smith featured Rembrandt's Head on their signs, while John Smith and book- and printsellers Ryall and Withy transacted business at Hogarth's Head, also shown on their trade cards.[137] In the latter case, striking for its projecting ribbons with names of artists and other luminaries, Hogarth's 1745 self-portrait (or more likely, the engraving from it) provided the model, evident from inclusion of the palette with the line of beauty. John Smith's shop sign, more inventively, borrowed its image from the profile self-portrait that Hogarth included at the margins of his painting and print *The Gate of Calais* (1748), inspired by his misadventures in the French port town, where he was arrested while sketching.[138] That detail had been extracted and used in a variety of graphic contexts. On Smith's double cartouche trade card, Hogarth's coarse and stolid appearance in the small upper field provides a witty foil to the refined and dynamic ornamentation of the cartouche as a whole, rendered in the modern French style (later known as rococo) that had been thoroughly absorbed into English decorative arts by the mid-eighteenth century (fig. 65). The lively trade in prints by both Hogarth and Rembrandt established the value of their heads as markers for print shops, almost alone among the clamor of London businesses to feature artists on their signboards.[139] The printsellers' signs also directly addressed painters, a dependable clientele who bought prints as a matter of professional necessity. Reproductive engravings were often the only means of access to works of art and artists, since texts on art that presented esteemed models for emulation rarely featured illustrations. Interested readers had to gather examples for themselves, as Williams apparently did at the outset of his artistic career during the late 1740s, according to West.[140] Such prints connected provincial artists to a world otherwise inaccessible to them and fueled their ambitions: Copley's, for example, when he painted historical subjects as a youth, or Williams's, when he decided to advertise history among his specialties. At a purely practical level, prints were a tool for artists, routinely consulted in the design of pictures. Portrait prints, in particular, constituted an essential resource for face-painters, who, together with their clients, mined mezzotint engravings after noted British portraits for composition, attitude, and fashion.

So long as Williams's needs were relatively ordinary, they could have been met locally by vendors who obtained prints from London, such as bookseller David Hall, whose children Williams portrayed. Rising demand in the colonies after mid-century encouraged the establishment of specialist printsellers in the major cities.[141] Robert Kennedy opened his Philadelphia "Print-Shop" in 1761 and by 1768, in partnership with his brother Thomas, advertised richly varied stock: "pictures in the present English taste . . . –Amongst which are, scriptural, historical, humourous and miscellaneous designs; . . . elegant gardens, landscapes and American Views . . . ; battles by sea and land; horse-racing and hunting, . . . Royal and illustrious personages, ladies of

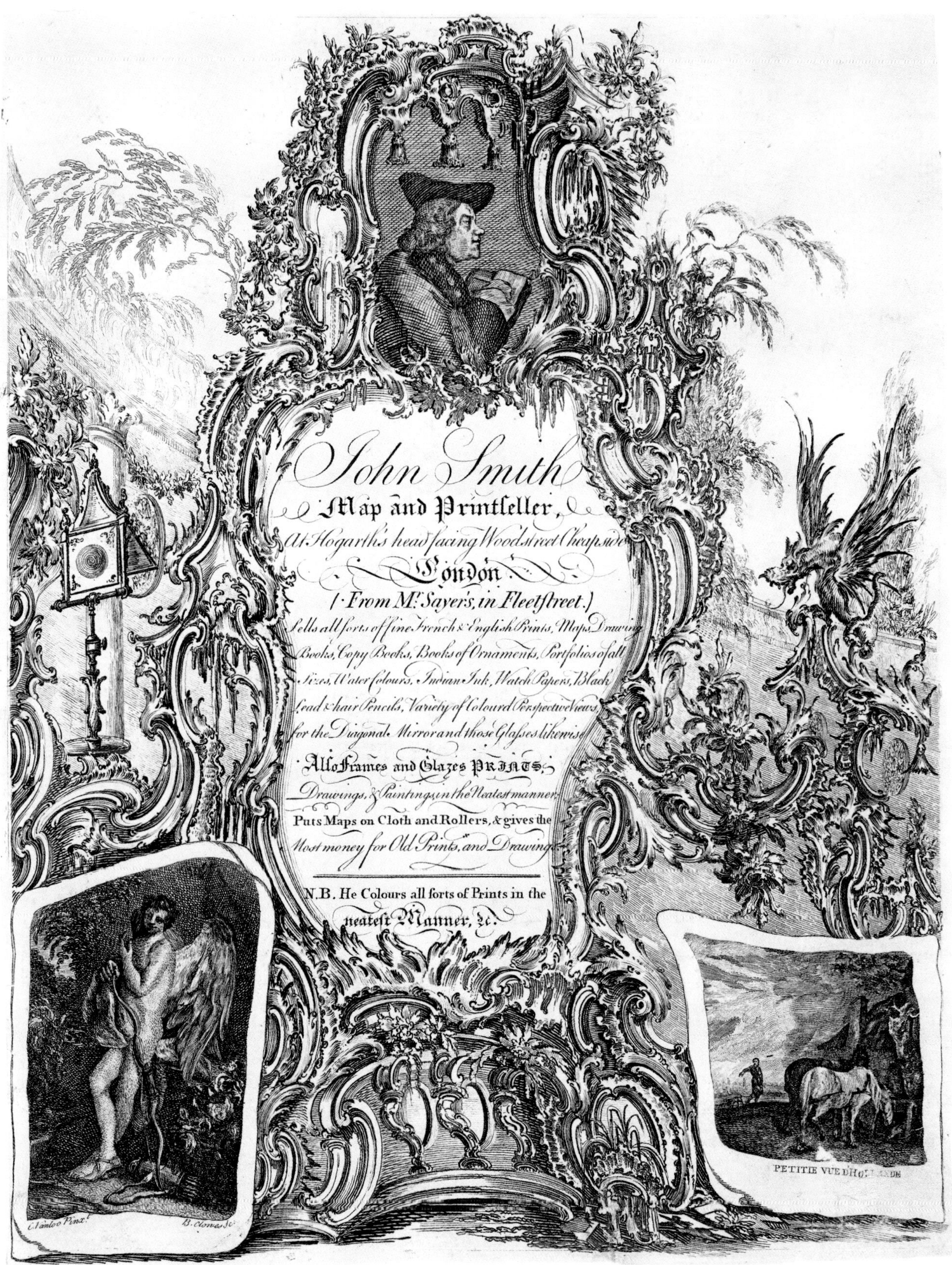

65 Trade card of John Smith, map and printseller, London, ca. 1753. British Museum, London. © The Trustees of the British Museum.

quality and celebrated Beauties, &c." What the Kennedys did not have on hand, they were willing to order for "such as want any thing extraordinary in the print way."[142] Once Williams began assembling portraits of artists, he became a candidate for such assistance. Artist portraits had constituted an important genre of print since the sixteenth century, a development closely tied to the dramatic rise in the status of artists, abetted by laudatory biographical accounts. Giorgio Vasari led the way in 1550 with his three-volume *Lives of the Artists*, which, in its second, enlarged edition of 1568 included dozens of portrait heads. Later publications expanded coverage beyond Vasari's Italian focus, and some gave primacy to the portraits over biographical text.[143] Williams may have contacted London printsellers himself. Nathaniel Smith, at Rembrandt's Head, was a specialist in engraved historical portraits and an intimate of Williams's after the painter's return to England, raising the possibility of a prior association between them. An interest had by then become a passion; according to West's 1810 letter, Williams spent "more than two years in daily pursuit of collecting portrait prints of eminent painters." That activity is born out by inclusion in his will of "two large Folio Volumes entitled Heads of Illustrious Artizans."[144]

Williams's interest in historical artists led him not only to collect prints but also to compile a manuscript of artists' lives, now lost but firmly documented as part of his bequest to Thomas Eagles and in later writing by Thomas and his son, John Eagles.[145] Did Williams begin by collecting artist portraits and then compile accounts of those artists from whatever sources he could find, or did the writing come first? Most likely the latter. West told Eagles in 1805 that after meeting Williams in the late 1740s the Englishman "lent me the lives of the painters," without specifying the form, though Eagles elsewhere refers to a manuscript. In 1810, West implied that he had read accounts of artists in books Williams loaned him by "Richardson & du Fresnoy" (both of which mentioned Vasari's inclusion of heads). Jonathan Richardson's works did not present biographies per se, but Du Fresnoy's *Art of Painting*, in its first two English editions (1695, 1716), included accounts of "the most eminent painters, both ancient and modern," by Richard Graham, based (according to Graham) on the writings of Vasari, Bellori, Félibien, van Mander, and others.[146] By the end of the seventeenth century, it had become common for books of art theory to conclude with lives, reinforcing intellectual claims by and on behalf of artists. Eleven of Vasari's lives appeared in William Aglionby's *Painting Illustrated in Three Diallogues* (1685) and in the retitled 1719 edition of the book, but that remained the only English translation of Vasari until the mid-nineteenth century.[147] Roger de Piles placed much more emphasis on painters in *The Art of Painting, and The Lives of the Painters*, first translated in 1706 and reissued in 1744 and 1754. Significantly, the English edition introduced an "essay towards an English school." The title suggested formation, as did the presence among the one hundred artists included of many Europeans active in England. Nevertheless, the writer, even though unnamed in the first edition, addressed readers from a national perspective, throwing down the gauntlet before "the French author" who did not "do justice to the Painters of our nation."[148] The collector and connoisseur Horace Walpole, benefiting from notes assembled by the engraver George Vertue, was able and willing to be much more comprehensive. Walpole's *Anecdotes of Painting in England* ran to four volumes (issued between 1762 and 1780) and included more than one hundred engraved portraits of artists, of which Walpole was a major collector.[149] The scope of the enterprise suggests that Walpole did not entirely subscribe to his own deflating prefatory assessment of England as "a country which has produced so few good artists" or at least indicates that he saw new possibilities for art and artists in Britain.

Across the Atlantic, in the colonies, Williams had worked hard to expand his artistic and professional range. Similarly, his interest in artists' lives and portraits demonstrates professional awareness and purpose far exceeding the requirements of his occupation, even when judged by metropolitan standards. That engagement allowed the resourceful Williams to cultivate an artistic community far richer than his immediate circumstances afforded. Notably, Williams wrote out a list of his own paintings at the conclusion of his manuscript "lives," thereby appending his own career to an illustrious sequence of artists.[150] This imagined professional community sustained and inspired him.[151]

Williams joined that company in committing his face to canvas in an undated self-portrait (fig. 66). On the basis of the artist's presumed "Alms-House dress," John Eagles (whose father inherited the portrait from Williams) thought it had been made during the 1780s, the decade when Williams came under his father's protection. However, the senior Eagles remained unaware for all of that time that his friend was an artist, suggesting at the very least that Williams no longer painted. The younger Eagles, for that matter, writing about the portrait in the 1850s, conceded that Williams looked more youthful in the picture than the old man he remembered, perhaps a function of Eagles's own maturity.[152] The costume, as E. P. Richardson pointed

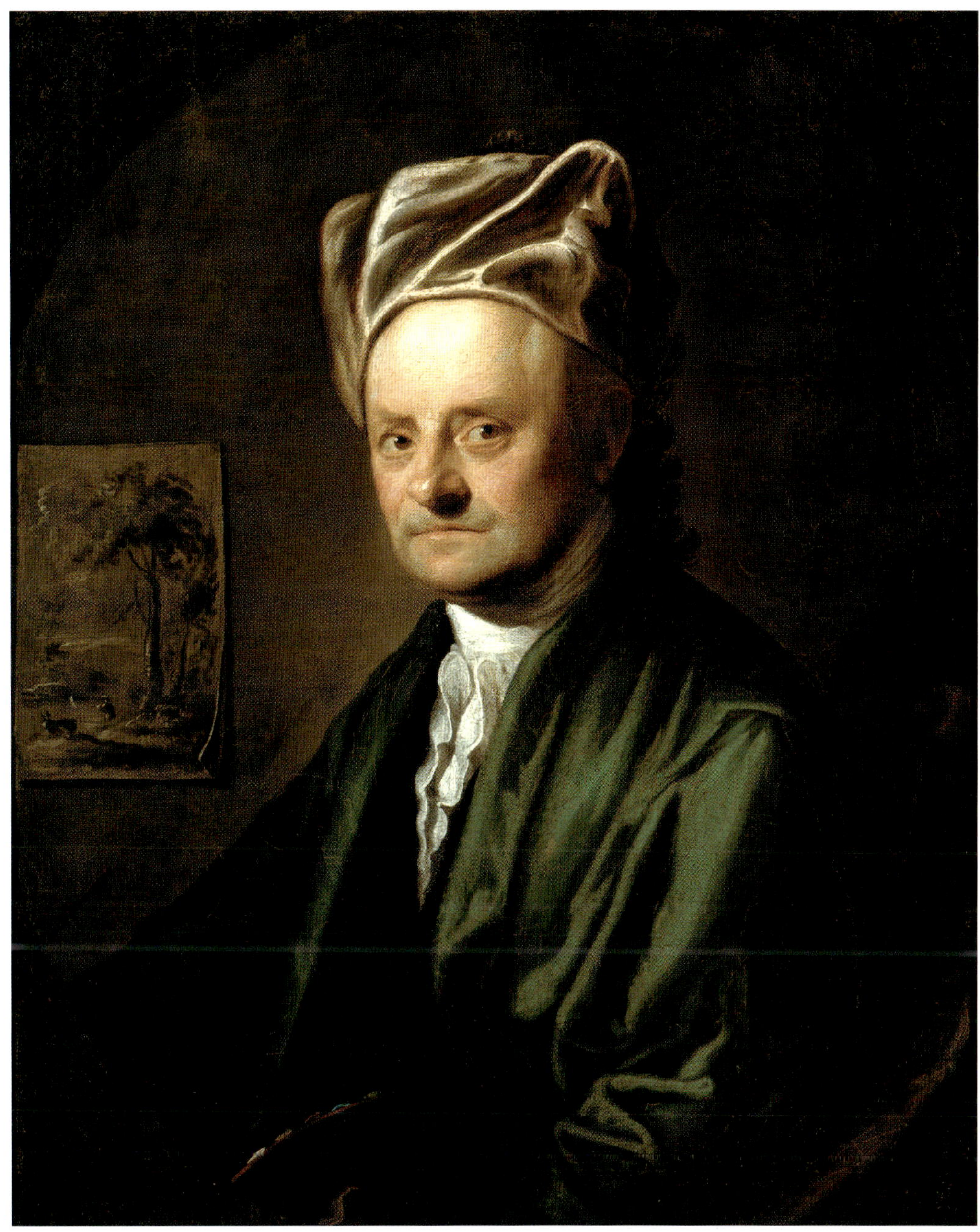

66 William Williams, *Self-Portrait*, before 1791. Oil on canvas, 30 × 25 in. (76.5 × 63.8 cm). Courtesy Winterthur Museum, gift of Henry Francis du Pont, 1964.2202.

out, is less likely almshouse dress than the banyan and cap that constituted informal attire for men throughout the eighteenth century.[153] Banyans, beyond their association with leisure, gentility, and education, as invoked by Copley, also suited those who worked in the privacy of their homes, including writers, scientists, and artists. They were so often portrayed in banyans (and those portraits so often engraved) that the costume acquired value as a sign for creative and intellectual life.[154] Such was Hogarth's life, as announced by his two self-portraits, in which the artist wears a more tailored version of the banyan as well as a cap. The books and palette with the line of beauty in the earlier example assert the intellectual and technical tools of the artist's profession. In the later self-portrait, Hogarth's *Analysis of Beauty* – identifiable by the protruding first plate from that volume – rests against the easel at which the artist sits to paint, summoning the figure of the comic muse from his imagination (see fig. 87). Although no literary reference appears in Williams's self-portrait as finished, radiographic analysis of the canvas shows him holding what appears to be a book in his left hand, while draping his right arm over the back of a chair. The excised book might have indicated a specific text or author that inspired him, like those Hogarth included in his first self-portrait – or like *The Analysis of Beauty* in American John Trumbull's self-portrait of 1777 (see fig. 102). Or it could have been more directly self-referential, an indication of Williams's engagement with writing, most provocatively as the secretive author of *Mr. Penrose*.[155]

In the end, Williams concealed the literary reference to represent himself unambiguously in the professional role that he publicly embraced between the 1750s and 1770s: "Painter." Borrowing a configuration frequently employed for engraved artist portraits, Williams framed his image within a painted oval. Hogarth had toyed with that format inventively in the illusory canvas of his 1745 self-portrait, but Williams was no Hogarth. His own self-portrait is far more conventional, and that in itself is significant. By using a well-understood vocabulary, Williams entered a dialogue with the broader community of artists. In possession of the appropriate tools, he leaves no doubt as to his occupation. An oval palette occupies the immediate foreground, tilted upward by the natural grip of the painter's barely glimpsed left hand, its outer edge accentuated by bright deposits of paint.[156] The butt end of a brush in the unseen right hand intrudes from the left, establishing the position of an easel just outside the depicted space. A sketchy, monochromatic scene of trees with a herdsman and animal appears unframed on the wall behind the artist – one edge of the paper curls up – advertising, as Williams did in print, his abilities as a draftsman and his interest in landscape. All of these details are subsidiary to the painter's face, skillfully brushed and ruddy above the green banyan. Williams's level expression and fixed gaze communicate concentration in his act of self-portrayal, but very little else.

Still, it was a face that fascinated the Reverend John Eagles. Though barely seven when Williams died, Eagles had been strongly impressed by the enigmatic artist. More than sixty years later, in the year of his own death, Eagles composed "The Beggar's Legacy" for *Blackwood's*. It is a curious essay, a "voluntary of vagaries" concerning beggars, thirty pages of "prelude" that, the author concedes, may "be thought impertinent to the simple narrative" to which the title refers. Yet the reader soon recognizes the narrative related in the last twelve pages as anything but simple: Thomas Eagles's encounter with Williams in Bristol, the old man's surprising legacy, Penrose's journal and the many questions it raised, the Royal Academy president's encounter with that manuscript and his memories of Williams, and Eagles's efforts to publish the book, finally fulfilled by his son. "Who knows who a beggar may be?" asks Eagles. "The Beggar's Portrait," the only subheading in the entire essay, introduces Williams's self-portrait (described, not illustrated) and, through it, a limited answer to that question. Eagles notes a similarity to Hogarth's features, without sensing a resemblance in "character . . . for there is no expression of combativeness. It is mild, inquiring, experienced, and meditative upon experiences." The portrait and the man at first appear commonplace, yet "seen a second time," the picture "would arrest attention," revealing "something singular." Above all, for the writer, Williams exhibits "an experienced look [that] is very striking . . . the look of keen observation . . . a strangeness written in many lineaments . . . sensible, shrewd, inquisitive, patient, unimpassioned – as one cognisant of other men's doings and thoughts – uncommunicative of his own."[157] Eagles perceives so much in this relatively inexpressive portrait because he reads into it what he has already surmised regarding Williams's character. Yet it seems accurate because it accords with the Williams who can be excavated, bit by bit, from the historical record.

In 1775 or 1776, Williams joined some 17,000 other civilian New Yorkers (three-quarters of the population) in pre-war exodus from the city, which looked to one observer "as if the Plague had been in it, so many Houses being shut up."[158] The circumstances are known only through the letter West provided Thomas Eagles in 1810 and have never been verified. Williams, by then a widower, lost two sons in battle for the patriot cause, West wrote. "Much dejected," he "availed himself of a friendly proposition made to him by an English gentleman returning from America to embark with him for England – to reside under his roof in Bedfordshire, & to paint there for his amusement the remainder of his life." West said he reconnected with Williams and met the artist's patron (who remains unidentified) when they stopped in London on their way to the countryside. Eighteen months later, the benefactor died and Williams returned to London. The fifty-year-old artist and his former pupil were in frequent contact over the next few years, during which West worked at his large and complex *Battle of La Hogue* (ca. 1775–80). West told Eagles that he "introduced a likeness of Williams in one of the boats, next in the rear of Sir George Rook[e]," and Williams's self-portrait helps

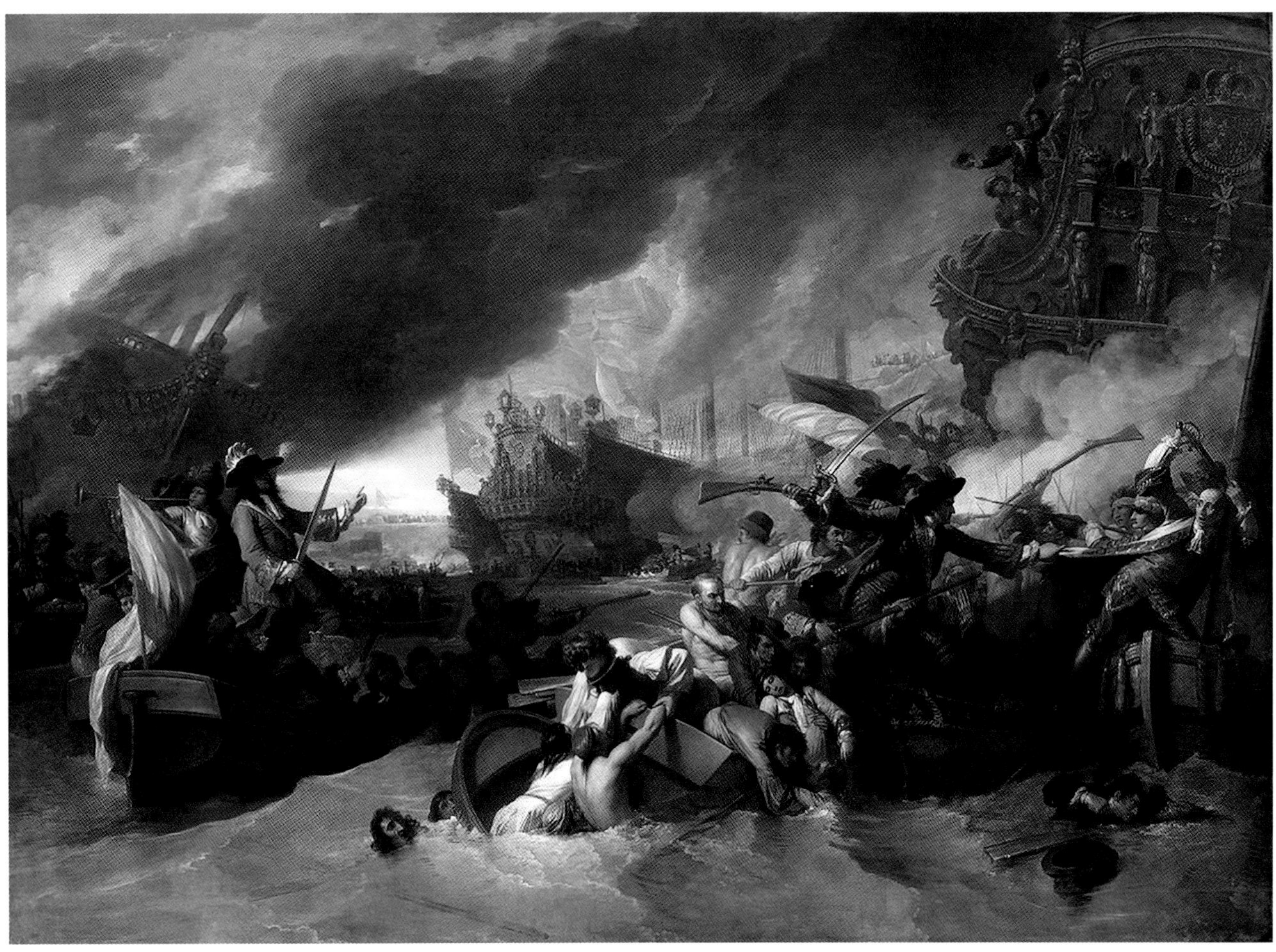

67 Benjamin West, *The Battle of La Hogue*, ca. 1778. Oil on canvas, 60⅛ × 84¼ in. (152.7 × 214 cm). National Gallery of Art, Washington, D.C., Andrew W. Mellon Fund.

identify him as the man at the far left of the composition, wearing a feathered hat (though a shirtless seaman near the center of the picture also resembles him) (fig. 67). During these years in London, Williams was especially close to Nathaniel Smith, the printseller at Rembrandt's Head from whom he bought portrait prints of artists; John Thomas Smith, the printseller's son and future eminent engraver, saw Williams so often that West asked him for information about Williams when collecting his own thoughts for Eagles.[159] By 1781, according to the younger Smith, Williams had returned to his native Bristol, a city to which American loyalist exiles also gravitated, finding it so "like our dear Philadelphia."[160] Just a few years later, Williams encountered Eagles.

The historian's dependence on West for key parts of Williams's story cannot be denied. On the other hand, Williams started and maintained his career completely independent of West, who left America as a young man in 1760, bound for Italy. By the end of the decade, West, permanently settled in London, had become well known; just a few years later, he achieved the rare distinction of historical painter to the king. Strikingly, Williams appears never to have capitalized on his relationship with West, though that scenario would in many ways be easier to understand than West's use of Williams in a late life effort to reform his public identity, the subject of chapter six. Williams, by contrast to Copley and West, presents the example of an artist who remained flexible about working within the constraints of the existing Anglo-American system, while resourcefully nourishing a broader and deeper sense of artistic identity. West's example made that choice seem quaint. His success proved a magnet to artists the same age and younger, so powerful that for the next several generations, artistic ambition could not be separated from experience abroad.

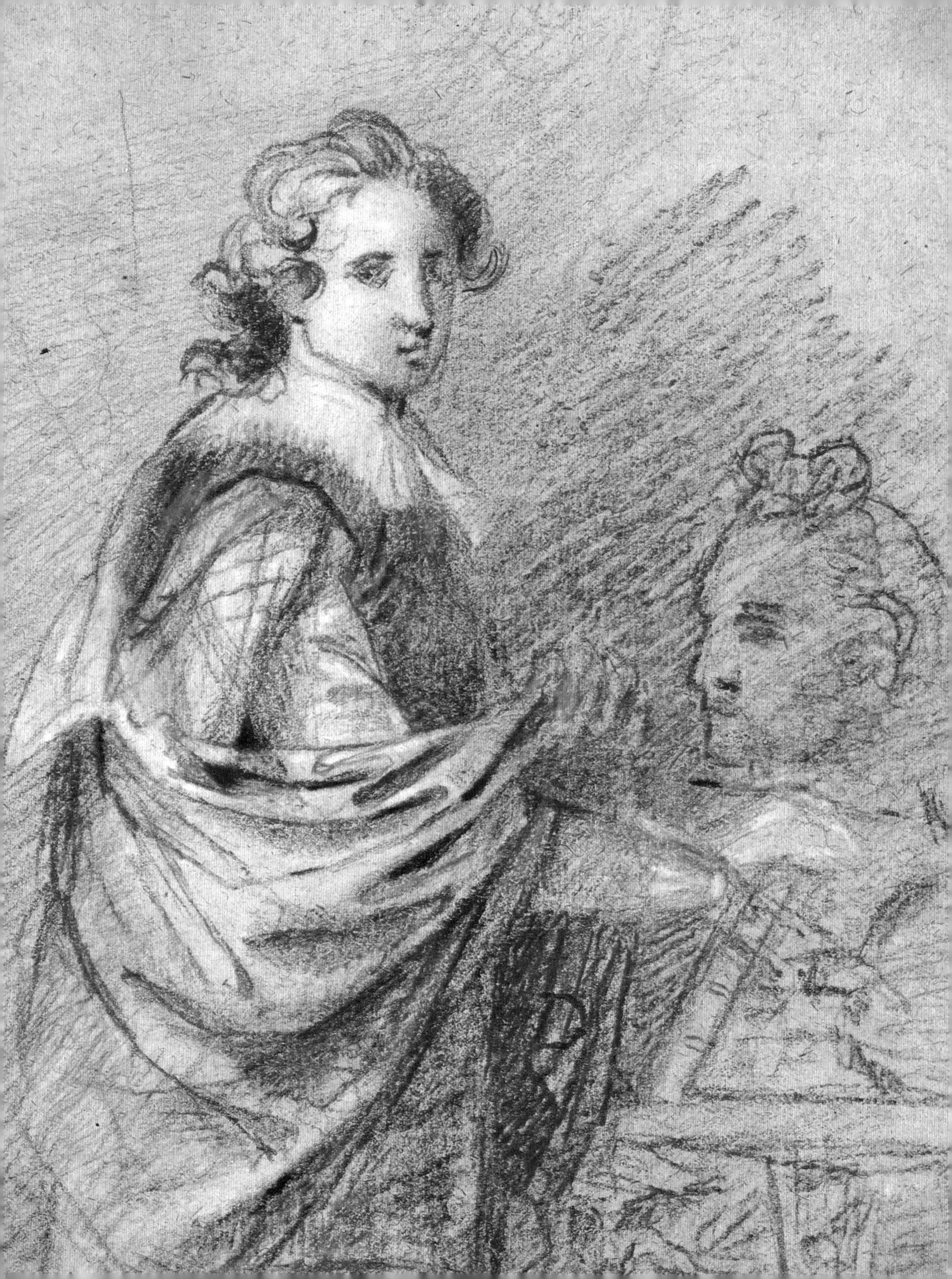

3

THE AMERICAN SCHOOL, ITALY AND LONDON

West's voyage across the Atlantic in 1760 changed his life and the future of American art, even though he never returned to America. In London by 1763, during a critical decade for British artists, he contributed materially to a new conception of British painters and painting, doing as much as anyone to establish the viability of historical subjects. Those outcomes, even considering the high hopes of Philadelphia benefactors who financed West's three-year tour of Italy, cannot have been predicted. His course of study, for one thing, was entirely commonplace. West visited major Italian artistic centers, especially Rome, immersed himself in study of the acknowledged high points in western art, notably of classical antiquity and sixteenth- and seventeenth-century Italy; and painted copies of masterworks, a form of training that also benefited patrons at home, to whom he sent the pictures.[1] British artists who preceded West in Italy, including Reynolds, had not been able to convert that experience into patronage opportunities beyond the customary demand for portraits.

Unusually for a Briton on either side of the Atlantic, West had already received an early commission for a historical subject, the *Death of Socrates*, which he based loosely on an engraving (fig. 68). Then just eighteen and living in frontier Lancaster, Pennsylvania, West was not more than an artisan in the eyes of his patron, gunsmith William Henry. Following a convention in engraving, Henry had his own name, in the implied role of inventor, added to the canvas on which West's name, coupled with the word "pinxit," signified his manufacture.[2] (West signed no other American paintings.) *Death of Socrates* brought West to the attention of influential Philadelphians who afforded him the rudiments of a gentleman's classical education, even as West continued in the prosaic Anglo-American trade of portraiture. The notion that West might become a different kind of painter with significantly altered status in life, however much desired, would not on the face of it seem a realistic expectation.

Neither West nor his patrons can fully have appreciated the impact of his status as an American in an international milieu. At the time of his departure, Americans of English descent considered themselves Britons, and since West's father had left England as an adult, that heritage was recent. Only in the course of the 1760s did an American identity begin to emerge for the colonists, taking firmer shape in Britain before it did in North America. In Italy, an American was more exotic still, and West found his distinction magnified. The artist quickly learned that he stood out, in ways both beneficial and potentially detrimental to the career he was starting to build, conferring advantages at the same time that it required a degree of defensive image management.

Facing page Detail of fig. 71.

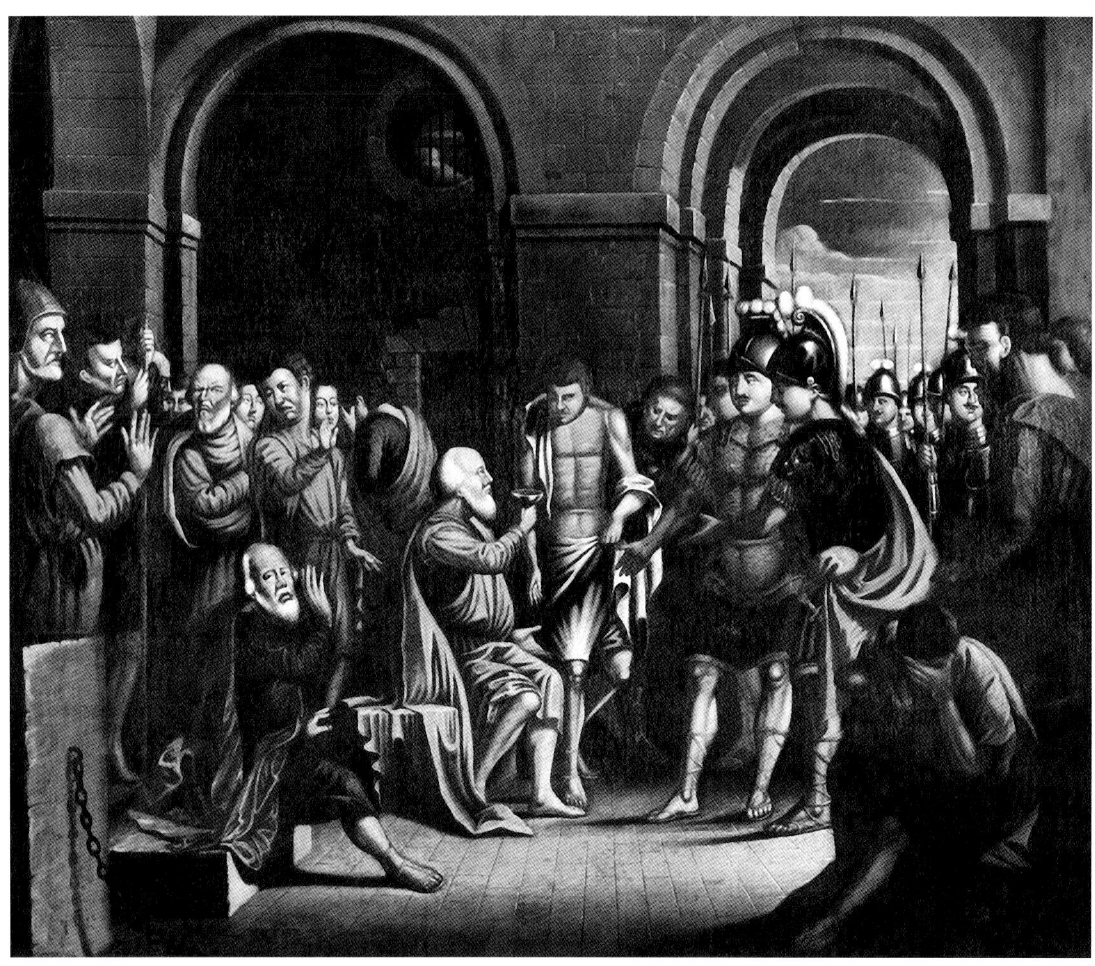

68 Benjamin West, *Death of Socrates*, ca. 1756. Oil on canvas, 34 × 41 in. (86.4 × 104.1 cm). Courtesy of the Philadelphia History Museum at the Atwater Kent, Historical Society of Pennsylvania Collection.

This chapter opens by considering West's models as he sought to define himself as an artist, whether selected in an active process of emulation or attracted despite himself. What he could not at first control, he would manage to seize; that, at least, is how West's biographical collaborator, John Galt, presented the artist's first days in Rome, in the influential book of 1816 that is the subject of my final chapter. The interactions Galt reported, while not subject to proof, can yet be re-examined for probability and meaning. It is particularly important to do so in light of the collaborators' mission of constructing an American identity for West at the end of his life. Conversely, an almost completely overlooked self-portrait drawing that West made toward the end of his Italian sojourn offers a fresh and material opportunity to see him as he then imagined himself. Perhaps the work has been ignored for the very reason that it does not fit with the West that he himself and Galt so persuasively packaged for history. The persona in the Italian drawing, surprisingly tentative, had almost nothing to do with the bold young American who, in Galt's telling, caused a sensation in 1760 (though the drawing offers a corroborative glimmer to that account). In fact, West's American origins figure not at all in a self-portrait that comes across instead as an audition for the multiple parts that, at that moment and hardly before, seemed open to a British artist with continental experience.

West arrived in London from Italy toward the start of an auspicious decade for British artists generally, and he immediately set out to capitalize on the situation. No period in his career has been more thoroughly studied than West's first ten years in London, with understandable emphasis on the artist's centrality to the emergent British genre of history painting. During that time, West painted a number of North American subjects and remained willing to foreground his American-ness or to allow others to do it for him. And so they continue to do: Americanist art historians, especially, have tended to focus on West's American subjects – not surprisingly given the novelty of those works and the success of West's ambitious *Death of General Wolfe* (1770), commemorating the hero who completed Britain's conquest of Canada during the French and Indian War. But that focus has had the unintended effect of giving those subjects greater prominence in West's oeuvre than they warrant. In fact, the artist backed away from such subject matter as tensions between the colonies and Britain mounted in the early 1770s, when a too close identification with his rebellious homeland threatened to compromise West's social and professional position.[3]

West exerted a gravitational force on American artists, who travelled to London to study with him from 1764 until the end of his life. Most became portraitists, the only branch of fine art that could support them, but some experimented with American historical subjects, following West's early example. Copley, guided by West via correspondence beginning in 1766 but never formally his pupil, made his first daring modern history painting – *Watson and the Shark*, set in Havana harbor (see fig. 10) – soon after arriving in London in 1775.[4] John Trumbull of Connecticut followed a path that West contemplated but could not diplomatically pursue in making the American Revolution his subject for a series of paintings beginning in the 1780s. Keeping focus on the professionally momentous years of the 1760s, though, I turn in the second half of this chapter to a more direct form of professional self-definition that American artists, like British counterparts, took up in earnest: portrayal of themselves and fellow artists. Their cognizance of the stakes is fully evident in a canvas of 1765 by the first of West's associates, Matthew Pratt, in which Pratt showed himself, West, and three others collegially engaged in studying and making art. In its evident aim of visually defining the terms of professional artistic practice, the work belongs to a small group of remarkably similar canvases by other British painters. Yet Pratt raised the stakes by publicly exhibiting his painting as *The American School*, suggesting that there was something distinctive about them. The association with West at a key stage in his career – that stature acknowledged in Philadelphia when Kennedy's print shop adopted West's head as its sign – ensured Pratt's painting a canonical place in the history of American art, notwithstanding the artist's failure to thrive professionally.[5] But that is a matter of hindsight. *The American School* is far more than a documentary tribute to West. It demands consideration within the visual, social, and professional contexts of an unusually fertile period of self-definition for Anglophone painters in general and, Pratt implies, for American painters in particular.

West in Italy

AN AMERICAN NATIVE

When West arrived in Italy, study there or anywhere in Europe was no longer rare for a British artist, but an American painter abroad in Italy had no precedent.[6] The prospect of colonial refinement seemed so "extraordinary" that an Englishman in Rome, Thomas Robinson, informed of "an American, and a Quaker, come to study the fine arts," found himself "possessed by an irresistible desire to see" West.[7] (West was not a Quaker, a matter I address later in the chapter, but the identification relative to Robinson's encounter with West served to further distance the American from fine art, which Quakers were known to regard with some suspicion.) In this account by West's biographer Galt, the infinitive verb "to see" suggests the importance of visual appraisal in assessing the newcomer. It also sets the stage for an anecdote concerning the artist's introduction to Rome's most influential collector and connoisseur, Cardinal Albani, blind in old age. Curious about the visiting American's appearance, Albani asks if West is "black." At a time when European categorization of human color was limited to white and black, Albani meant Indian (Galt is explicit on this), not African. The characterization of Native Americans as "red" did not become common until the nineteenth century, notwithstanding Thomas Jefferson's memorable reference to "man, white, red, and black" in *Notes on the State of Virginia* (1784).[8] Colonial Americans were inclined to see Indians as light-skinned, even "white" (and thus assimilable); when they did refer to Indian skin color, they tended to say "tawny" or "copper colored."[9] In England, the slave trade colored perceptions of race, as evident in the confused query to a colonial North American visitor by an Englishwoman who asked "if all the people of my country were white, as she saw I was, for being styled in the general West Indians, she thought we were all black, as she supposed the Indians to be."[10] Cardinal Albani found his presumption corrected. Surprised to learn that his guest is "white," he countered, "as fair as I am?" to the company's amusement given his own "darkest Italian olive" complexion. Under certain conditions, an

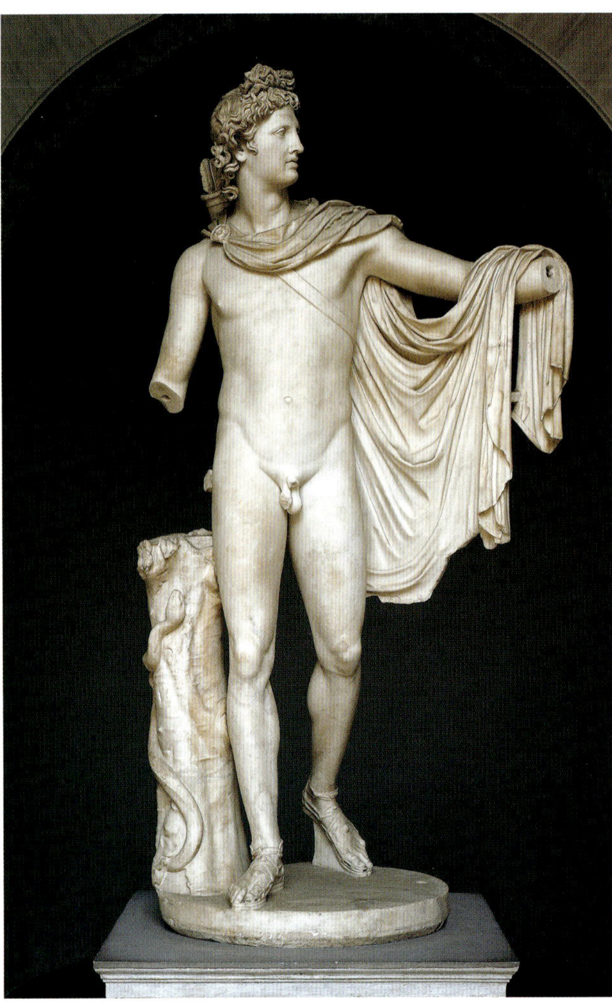

69 Marble statue known as *Apollo Belvedere*, copy after Greek bronze original of the fourth century BC. De Agostini Picture Library/G. Nimatallah/Bridgeman Images.

American of English descent might be appraised as an exotic "other."

West had much to gain from skillful manipulation of European expectations about America. He took immediate advantage of the circumstance in his encounter with the *Apollo Belvedere*, a story best known in Galt's memorable styling, although related by West himself as early as 1794, more than three decades after the purported event.[11] A curious and worldly crowd assembled in the Belvedere Palace sculpture court, at the Vatican, to witness the young artist's first sight of this most famous ancient statue (fig. 69).[12] West did not disappoint. After shutters to a niche containing the Apollo were thrown open, he responded memorably: "My God, how like it is to a young Mohawk warrior!" With these few brilliantly chosen words, West trumped the worldly jades who had gathered for vicarious experience of aesthetic innocence and confirmation of their own superiority. Expected to show awe, West served up privileged recognition, even as his exclamatory invocation of the deity registered surprise, authenticating a response that may have been calculated by some of West's new friends as much as by himself. In accounts by eighteenth-century writers on both sides of the Atlantic, the Mohawk – part of the Iroquois Confederacy whose alliance both the French and British courted as instrumental to their territorial ambitions – "were always esteem'd as the most Desperate, and most Cruel of the Natives of *North-America*"; the name of Mohawk even came to be attached to disorderly behavior by white Britons.[13] West, called upon to explain himself to those affronted by his comparison of the mythic god to a savage, sought to mollify his audience. He described Mohawk Indians as skilled, fleet, and vigorous, qualities worthy of Apollo. "'I have seen them often,' added he, 'standing in that very attitude and pursuing, with an intense eye, the arrow which they had just discharged from the bow.'"[14]

West's response to the *Apollo Belvedere* turned the tables on Albani's supposition that he was "black" or Indian (as did Galt later, in asserting that West, upon initial approach to Rome, found an Italian goatherd "more wild and ferocious than . . . the Indians").[15] The Apollo's unadorned whiteness did not prevent West from seeing black and identifying the physically idealized statue with the athletic perfection of a Native American. Without a hint of academic verbiage, in other words, West cleverly demonstrated his appreciation for pure form, apart from color or ornament. A "godlike human body has no ornament," nineteenth-century American sculptor Horatio Greenough affirmed, while implicitly objecting to West's famous remark; "a naked Apollo is more beautiful than a tattooed and feathered and blanketed savage," Greenough stated.[16] Yet West had demonstrated something important to the British academic art community during the later eighteenth century (and, frankly, to Greenough as well): the ability of superior men, among whom theoretically aware artists counted themselves, to see beyond particularities.

West knew more about Native Americans than most Britons or Europeans, but he cannot have had the familiarity he claimed. Mohawk territory intersected New York, not Pennsylvania. Relatively few Indians remained in eastern Pennsylvania at the time of West's birth in 1738, in Springfield Township, Chester County (now Swarthmore, Delaware County). Lenni Lenape had once lived along the banks of the Delaware – an English name that the English adopted for these Native Americans – and the tributaries of that river in southeastern Pennsylvania. By the late 1720s, they had been pushed west to lands along the Susquehanna and by the 1740s further west still. Conestoga, in Lancaster County, was the closest major Indian settlement to Philadelphia during the first half of the eighteenth century, the site of significant negotiations between the Pennsylvania Provincial Government and various Indian groups; but after the early 1740s, its importance declined precipitously.[17] In 1748, Swedish naturalist Peter Kalm observed that in Philadelphia or even within 120 miles of the eastern seaboard, a colonist could pass six months without ever seeing an Indian.[18] The "settlement," "neighbor," or "tame" Indians who remained in proximity to colonists lived much as did the poorest white settlers and were judged "intirely unacquainted with foreign Indians and their Customs."[19] By 1755 and 1756, when West painted in Lancaster – the closest he ever lived to Indian settlements – relations between whites and Native Americans, even the Delawares (or Lenni Lenape), had deteriorated precipitously.[20] In sum, it seems improbable that he ever observed any Indian hunter with a bow, much less a Mohawk.[21]

A literary model for West's association of Indian and Apollo lay chronologically at hand to the purported event in the 1755 novel *Lydia*, by John Shebbeare, a Tory political satirist whose trial for libel and imprisonment a few years later made him well known in London.[22] He based the novel's hero Cannassatego on the Iroquois (Onondaga) leader who assisted Thomas Penn and the Pennsylvania Proprietors with controversial land acquisitions between 1737 and 1744. Believing "the Natives of his Country ill-treated, deluded, and destroyed alike, by *English* and by *French*," the fictional Cannassatego determines at the outset of the story to travel to London in appeal for justice. If the British are as virtuous as they claim, he tells assembled chiefs, they will listen to reason and make amends. In pursuit of a political point against Britain's Whig administration, Shebbeare created a relatively early Anglophone version of the romanticized Indian. The case for leaders of the Iroquois Confederacy as possessing "bright and noble Genius" had been influentially made by New York governor Cadwallader Colden as early as 1727, but not without contradiction, as in the same sentence he called the Five Nations a "barbarous people, bred under the darkest Ignorance."[23] Shebbeare's protagonist is a superior man whose form and features reveal "Sensibility of Soul" and "Courage and Compassion," among other virtues. In the extended physical description with which the book opens, the narrator compares him to the *Apollo Belvedere*, whose "Air, Attitude and Expression . . . were seen animated in this American the Instant he had discharged his deadly Shaft; and tho' the fair Complexion of the *European* Natives was not to be found in this Warrior, yet his Shape and Countenance hindered you from perceiving the Deficiency." Before his departure, Cannassatego's beloved, herself "form'd like the statue of a *Grecian* sculptor," observes his profile against a black rock and, using the point of an arrow, marks the resemblance on a shell (making light, incidentally, what was not so dark as black after all). She then fashions her own likeness for him, after studying her reflection in placid water. The Indian maiden offers a Native American variant on the story of a potter's daughter in ancient Corinth who traces the shadowed profile of her lover on a wall. A variety of texts dating from antiquity identify the "Corinthian Maid" with the origin of both painting and (through intervention of her father) modeling. The fact that Shebbeare's Indian woman does not trace when representing her lover arguably lends her a greater level of sophistication. Though the mid-eighteenth-century American setting prevents her from being a true origin figure, Shebbeare illogically advances the possibility anyway, with his chapter subhead: "first rise of Drawing faces in America, perhaps in every other Place."[24] Such associations between Indians and classical figures had by West's day a long history in word and image. The commonplace makes clear why the incident in the Belvedere sculpture court had such power to delight. Facing the Apollo, West invested his difference with value, converting his presumed scant knowledge of European culture from a potential liability into a virtue.[25]

Though West's encounter with the Apollo remains unverifiable by contemporaneous texts, a well-documented commission from early in his Italian sojourn resulted from West's distinction as an American while simultaneously reinforcing that identity. In September 1760, only a few months after his arrival in Italy, West received a request from his transatlantic traveling companions, Philadelphians John Allen and Joseph Shippen. The two were by then in Venice, where the British consul John Murray had shown them many courtesies. In demonstration of their gratitude, the young Americans hoped to enlist West, who could hardly refuse the favor since Allen's father provided most of the financial backing for his study. Murray had previously commissioned a painting representing "the 4 parts of the World," but the work could not be completed "for want of knowing the particular Dress of our Indians," Shippen wrote.[26] Having served in the provincial militia at the Pennsylvania

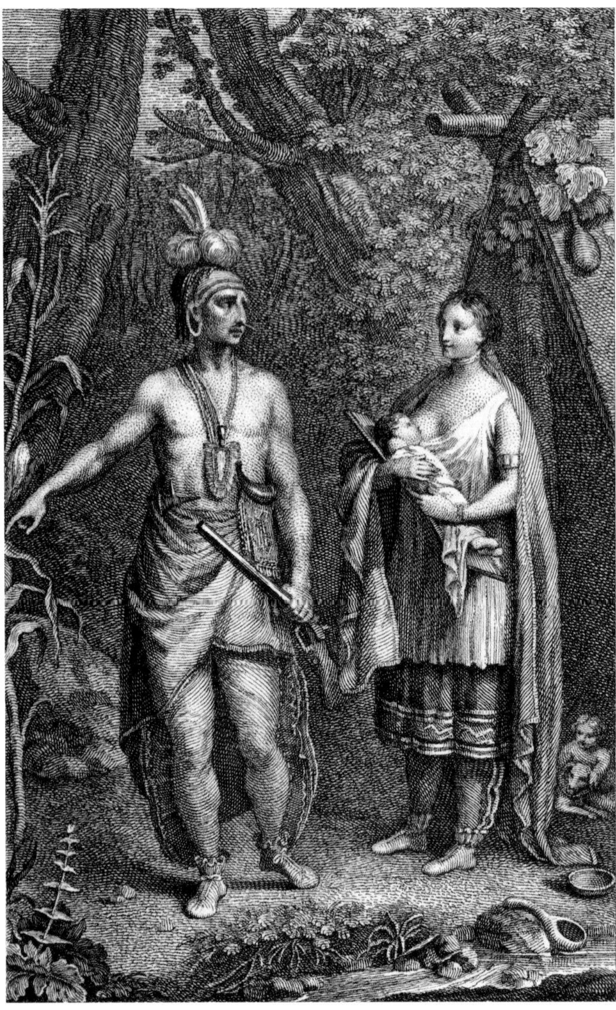

70 Francesco Bartolozzi after Benjamin West, frontispiece to *Storia degli stabilimenti europei in America* (Venice, 1763), the Italian translation of Edmund Burke's *An Account of the European Settlements in America* (1757). Etching with engraving. British Museum, London.

frontier, Shippen offered detailed instructions concerning the desired appearance of the natives, and West followed them carefully in *The Warrior's Family*, which survives in a painted copy by an unidentified artist and in engraving (fig. 70).[27] The result, while not historically correct, was substantially less generic than visions of "America" familiar from European representations of the continents. *Warrior's Family* gained a further measure of historical authority as the engraved frontispiece, with an extensive description, to *Storia degli stabilimenti europei in America* (Venice, 1763), a translation of Edmund Burke's 1757 *An Account of the European Settlements in America.*[28] West continued to include Native Americans in his paintings through the 1760s and, with increasing efforts at accuracy, during the 1770s. In this he was aided by rich collections of Native American material culture in Britain, where the powerful role played by Indians in building the empire, more so than their exoticism, gave them especial potency.[29]

Between Portraits and History

West's unusual status as an American artist in Italy served him well and facilitated his rapid integration into a circle of connoisseurs, collectors, and artists.[30] An international cohort in Rome, both directly and indirectly, encouraged his transformation from portraitist to painter of history. They included German painter Anton Raphael Mengs (whose patron was Albani), Scottish artist Gavin Hamilton and his English colleague Nathaniel Dance, and a select group of Grand Tourists and cognoscenti. Throughout his stay in Italy, West made copies of notable masterworks, a way of educating himself and repaying generous patrons at home, for whom, as for Britons in general, a competent copy had significant value. Eventually, West undertook original historical subjects and began to make his name in London as a history painter. Henry Benbridge's statement in 1769 that West "intends to decline Portrait Painting and to follow that of History" confirms that he had not yet fully done so.[31] Though only five or six oil portraits survive from his time in Italy, the number that followed indicate his continued engagement in this bread-and-butter occupation.[32]

In Italy, West also portrayed himself, a decision that had nothing to do with earning a living and everything with envisioning his place in the world. He had made at least one earlier self-portrait, around 1758, a watercolor-on-ivory miniature which he presented to a young woman with whom he evidently had an attachment.[33] Consistent with its form and purpose, that work makes no statement about West as an artist, except insofar as it demonstrates his skill in a socially valued type of picture making. The Italian self-portrait, by contrast, cannot have been meant for public display, since it is a mere sketch, somewhat clumsily executed and marked by changes in conception (fig. 71). These factors complicate reading and have, seemingly, discouraged attempts at interpretation.[34] Yet the drawing has much to tell us about West's emerging sense of artistic identity.

The young man positioned himself just left of center on the 6 × 7-inch sheet, standing perpendicular to the picture plane, right shoulder out and face turned obliquely toward the viewer, originally himself if he used a mirror, as self-

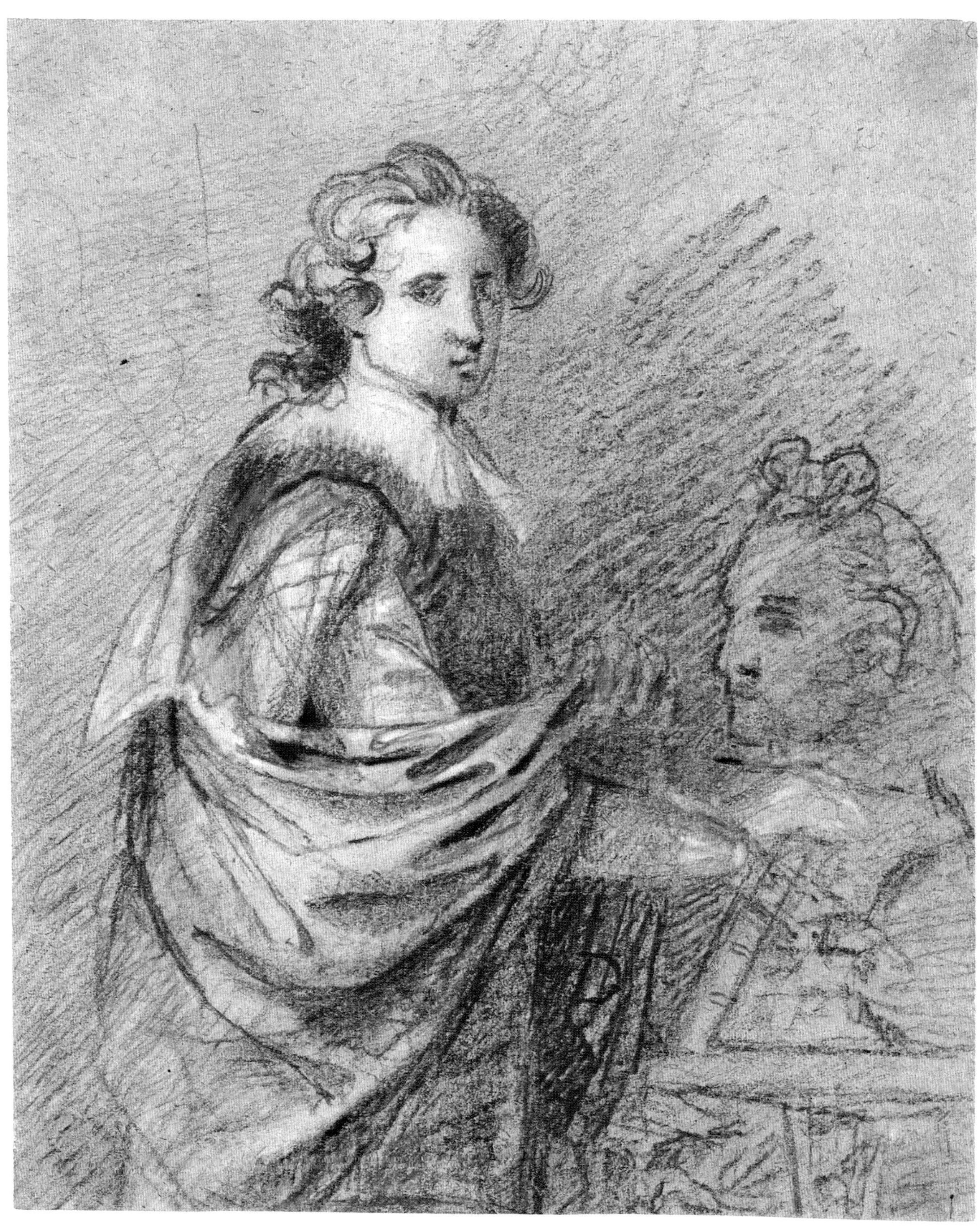

71 Benjamin West, *Self-Portrait*, ca. 1762–63. Drawing. Friends Historical Library of Swarthmore College.

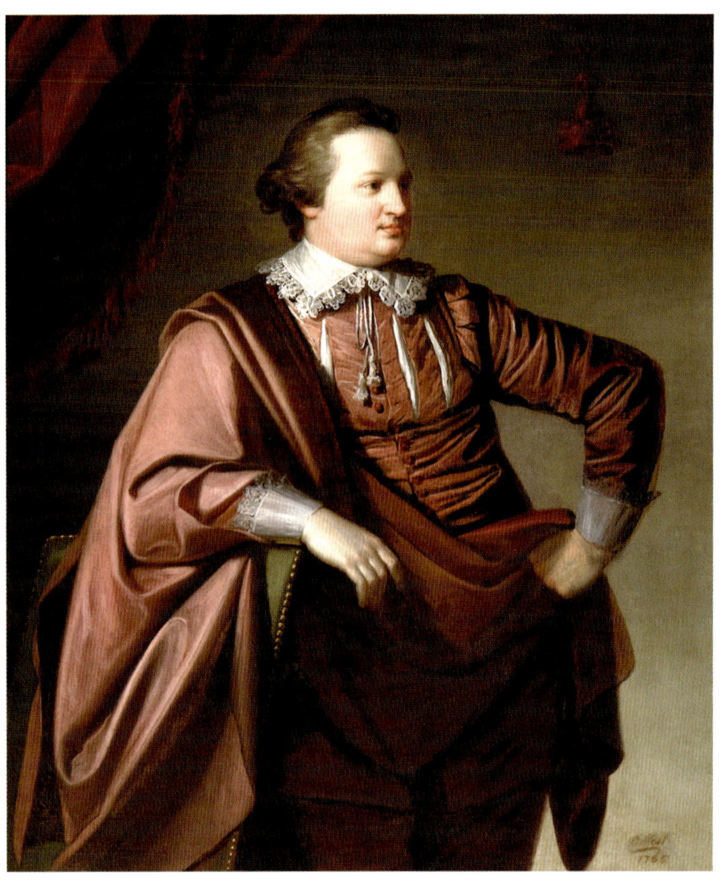

72 Benjamin West, *John Sawrey Morritt*, ca. 1765. Oil on canvas, 50 × 40 in. (127 × 101.5 cm). Private collection.

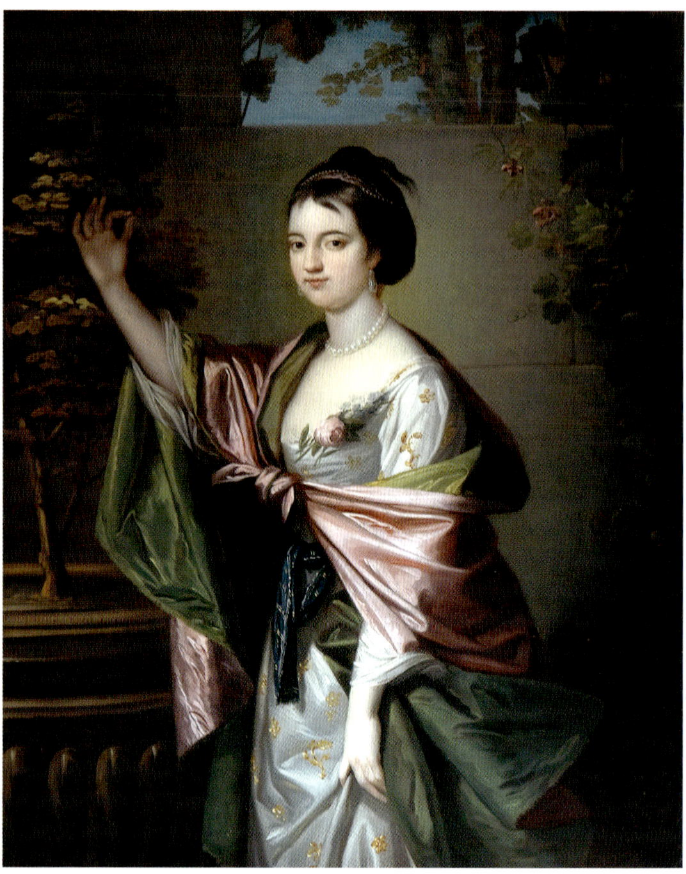

73 Benjamin West, *Mrs. John Sawrey Morritt*, ca. 1765. Oil on canvas, 50 × 39½ in. (127 × 100.5 cm). Private collection.

portraitists customarily did. His bodily orientation and gesture direct the viewer's eye toward the right half of the drawing, where a sculpted bust and other less clearly defined objects appear, presumably atop a table that is not delineated. Rough and heavy lines of charcoal darken much of the paper surface but not the right side of West's face, set off further by the brightness of his broad square collar. The densest passages correspond to West's torso, his garment there tonally differentiated from the one visible sleeve. The figure otherwise remains largely concealed by drapery, a cape that West draws over his outstretched right arm; from the clasped left hand, fabric cascades to the far side of his body.

West's attire bears no relationship to everyday men's clothing yet would have been instantly recognizable to contemporaries as what they called "Vandyke" dress. The look was widely familiar from portraits by, or believed to be by, the Flemish artist Anthony van Dyck, who was active in England during the 1630s. For his aristocratic British sitters, van Dyck concocted variations on contemporary fashion, often greatly simplified, especially in the case of women's clothing.[35] Numerous British men and women just before and after the mid-eighteenth century chose to be portrayed in Vandyke dress, and some also wore such costumes at masquerade parties, then popular in England (but not a custom in the colonies). At one such event in 1742, Horace Walpole encountered "quantities of pretty Vandykes," many no doubt inspired by the famous full-length portrait known as Rubens's wife, attributed to van Dyck when Sir Robert Walpole, Horace's father, purchased it around 1730.[36] West portrayed no female sitters in Vandyke dress. That taste had been generally eclipsed in women's portraits of the 1760s by quasi-classical attire, like that in which West represented two wives whose husbands he showed in Vandyke clothing (figs. 72, 73).[37] Two men among West's three male portrait subjects in Italy appear in Vandyke dress: John Allen, his American traveling companion, and Thomas Robinson, the Englishman who was so curious to see West upon his arrival in Rome.[38] In the Italian context, the outfit constituted a clear

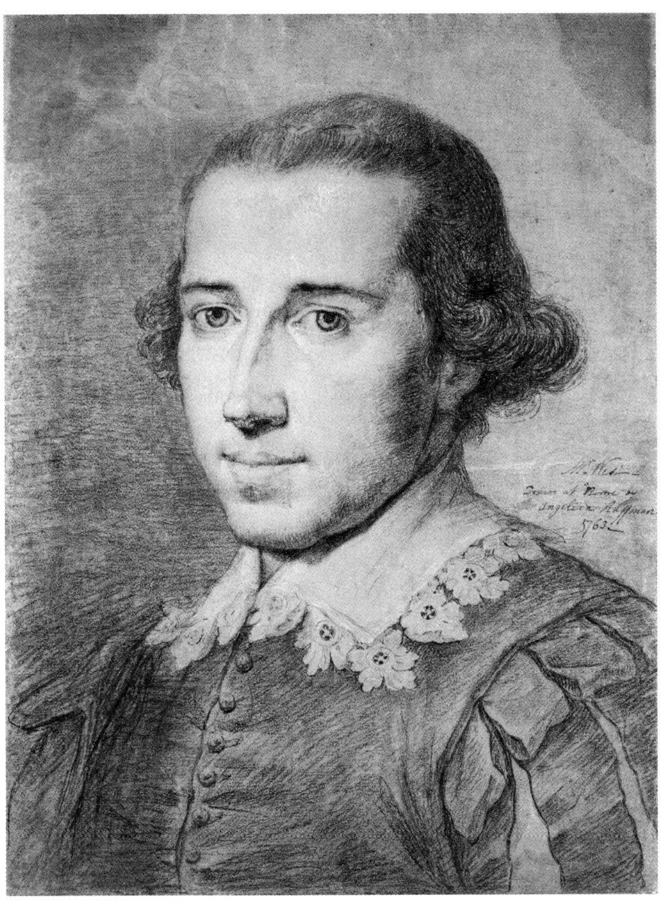

74 Angelica Kauffmann, *Benjamin West*, ca. 1762–63. Drawing. © National Portrait Gallery, London.

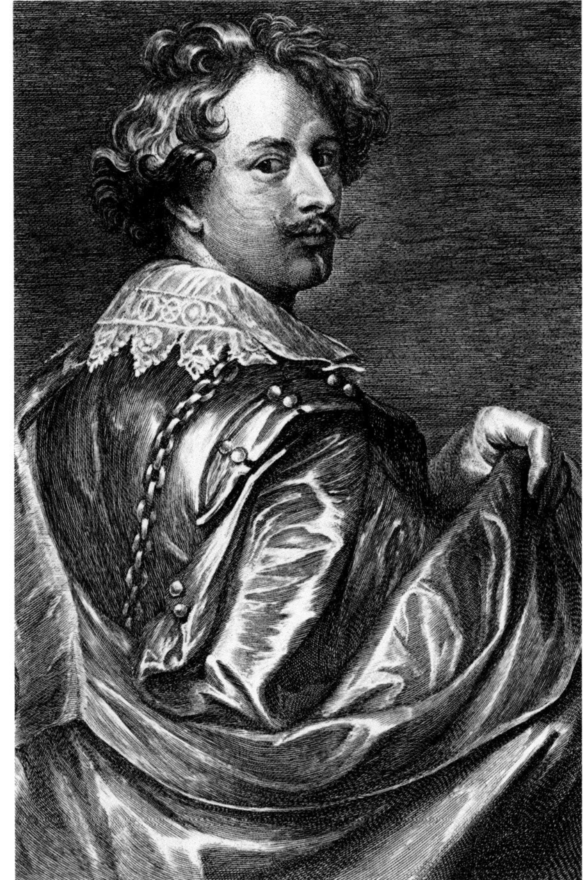

75 Lucas Vorsterman after Sir Anthony van Dyck, *Sir Anthony van Dyck*, mid-seventeenth century. Line engraving. © National Portrait Gallery, London.

marker of British identity, as also employed by Anton Mengs and by leading Roman portraitist Pompeo Batoni, who catered to British Grand Tourists.[39] West himself obviously wears such attire in an unusually refined drawing by Angelica Kauffmann, the twenty-one-year-old, multilingual Swiss whom he met in Florence in June 1762 (fig. 74); he, on the other hand, portrayed her in classicizing drape (see fig. 79).[40] Kauffmann subsequently portrayed Reynolds in Vandyke dress in a painting of 1767, by which time she too had moved to England (see fig. 132). The costume communicated fashionability and social currency, while also connecting British patrons and painters to the founding moment in the modern English portrait tradition, as defined by Jonathan Richardson and others.[41] Van Dyck's continental artistic glamour and sophistication, embraced at the court of Charles I, had completely vanquished a lingering Elizabethan portrait style (still evident in the earliest known colonial American portraits, made in the Boston area around 1670). The king rewarded van Dyck with a knighthood, granting him a status of which most English artists could only dream; later British rulers extended the honorific to their court portraitists, usually also Europeans, including Sir Peter Lely and Sir Godfrey Kneller. By the time of the Hanoverian monarchs, British artists stood ready to claim nobility for themselves, whether bestowed or symbolic, as a quality arising from their self-identification as gentlemanly practitioners of a liberal art.

In his Italian self-portrait drawing, West more fully embodied van Dyck than most male sitters in Vandyke dress. While they routinely sport carefully curled and dressed contemporary hairstyles or wigs, as West does in Kauffmann's portrait, West chose longer tousled locks, like van Dyck's own in a self-portrait then widely known through a print by Lucas Vorsterman (fig. 75). Aspects of West's drawing that are hard to decipher and suggest representational struggles or indecision have a clear model in that work, notably the sweeping collared cape held oddly high before the body and the fold of fabric that falls from mid-shoulder but is not part of the sleeve.

This engraved van Dyck self-portrait had been added, after the Flemish artist's death in 1641, to a large group of his portraits of notable persons in various media that van Dyck arranged to have engraved and published beginning in 1634. A decade later, the set numbered eighty works, fifty-two representing connoisseurs or artists, while an expanded total eventually included more portraits of artists based on other originals by van Dyck. Instead of being identified by tools that refer to the manual aspect of their occupations, most of the painters, sculptors, architects, and engravers in the series appear as do the scholars, in fulfillment of Renaissance ideals of their professional dignity. The accessible model of van Dyck's portraiture in general offered artists from his time through the eighteenth century a sterling example. This gallery of portrait prints, known as the *Iconography*, appeared in multiple editions beginning in 1645. The last, with 132 plates and concise sitter biographies, came out in 1759, just before West's arrival in Italy.[42]

At the Uffizi Gallery in Florence, a city in which he spent many months, West had the chance to see a greater number of painted artist portraits and self-portraits than were available anywhere else in the world. The collection had been systematically assembled after 1664, when Prince (later Cardinal) Leopoldo de' Medici, whose family already owned about fifteen such works, began to commission artist portraits directly and to make purchases through agents. By the time of his death in 1675, he owned some eighty artist portraits, mostly Italian. Cosimo III de' Medici, Leopoldo's nephew, and Filippo Baldinucci, biographer of artists and first custodian of the collection, further enlarged its scope to include artists from all over Europe. By the mid-eighteenth century, approximately 225 artist portraits were on hand.[43] The collection became more widely known with publication of the self-portraits between 1752 and 1766 in the final five (of twelve) illustrated volumes of *Museum Florentinum*, the Italian answer to van Dyck's *Iconography*.[44] Though the Uffizi was not formally opened to the public until 1769, travelers long had access by appointment. West's connections would have made this an easy matter.

Eighteenth-century Britons revered Raphael, whose self-portrait at around age twenty-three (ca. 1506) was in the Uffizi (fig. 76). The artist's close-set eyes, askew in the obliquely turned face, his long slender nose and small cupid's-bow mouth echo in West's drawing. But Raphael's self-portrait was not well liked. Edward Gibbon, whose fourteen visits to the Uffizi in 1764 attest to its availability even in advance of the museum's public opening, noted: "The worst portrait in the collection is that of the first of painters," Raphael, guilty of "bad gothic taste" in this instance.[45] The apparent timidity of the work, not yet expressive of Raphael's mature classicism, might actually have reassured the twenty-four-year-old West. Even the Renaissance master had to become a master.

A then newly identified Raphael self-portrait offered a much more appealing alternative and lay close at hand in the Palazzo Altoviti across town (fig. 77). In fact, it is Raphael's portrait of the banker Bindo Altoviti, as noted somewhat confusingly by Giorgio Vasari: "For Bindo Altoviti he [Raphael] made his portrait when he was young."[46] The ambiguous pronouns led Giovanni Bottari, editor of a sixth edition of Vasari's *Lives of the Artists* (1759–60), to assume that Raphael had given Altoviti his own portrait, a case Bottari made in a long footnote.[47] For Bottari and others, the physical beauty of the sitter and refined artistry of the Altoviti painting, which Vasari called "stupendissimo," made it fully worthy of Raphael. Wishful observers overlooked disparities in hair, eye, and skin coloring between this and Raphael's Uffizi self-portrait. Even more, they chose to disregard the anomaly of the visible hand, which would have been the artist's right, working hand if he were looking at himself in a mirror. From their perspective, the young man's sensitive appearance far better suited artist than banker (whom Raphael depicted as a newly wed husband, a point lost by the eighteenth century). West's loose curls have something in common with Altoviti's flowing locks, much more so than with Raphael's helmet of hair in the Uffizi self-portrait. Altoviti's hair parts above the low neckline at the back of his tunic, in alluring exposure of bare skin, a pale expanse that West's unarticulated seventeenth-century-style collar evokes. The illusion (and allusion) would not have been supported had West included the lacy border seen in the van Dyck self-portrait he emulated, in West's other portraits of men in Vandyke dress, and in the portrait Kauffmann drew of him.

The American's familiarity with the rediscovered Altoviti Raphael "self-portrait" is all but guaranteed by the circumstances of West's stay in Florence. He spent considerable time there, undergoing treatment for an acute leg infection between November 1761 and spring 1762 and then remained until August.[48] In Florence, West lodged close to the Pitti Palace in the house of Ignazio Hugford, an Anglo-Italian painter, collector, connoisseur, dealer, art restorer, and, as of 1762, the highest ranking artist among officers of the Accademia del Disegno in Florence. Hugford's enterprises

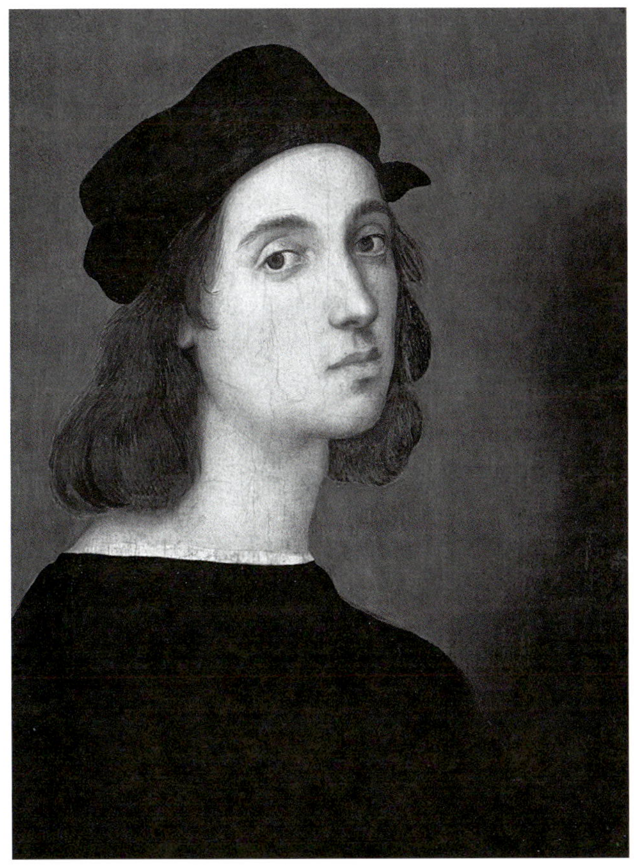

76 Raphael, *Self-Portrait*, ca. 1506. Oil on panel, 17¾ × 13 in. (45 × 33 cm). Galleria degli Uffizi, Florence/Bridgeman Images.

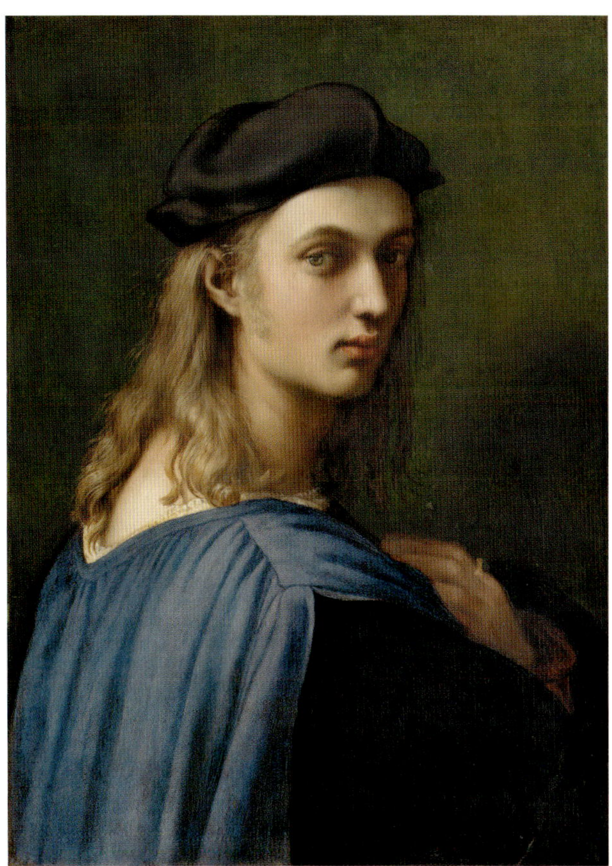

77 Raphael, *Bindo Altoviti*, ca. 1515. Oil on panel, 23½ × 17¼ in. (59.7 × 43.8 cm). National Gallery of Art, Washington, D.C., Samuel H. Kress Collection.

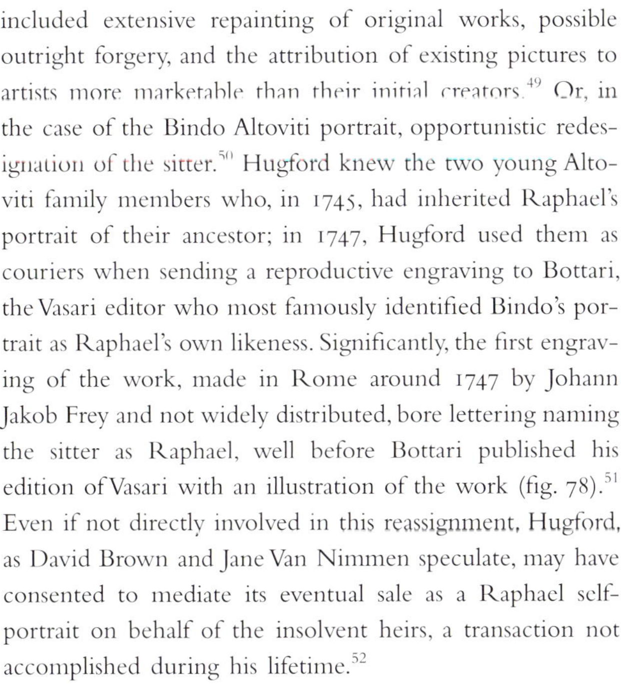

included extensive repainting of original works, possible outright forgery, and the attribution of existing pictures to artists more marketable than their initial creators.[49] Or, in the case of the Bindo Altoviti portrait, opportunistic redesignation of the sitter.[50] Hugford knew the two young Altoviti family members who, in 1745, had inherited Raphael's portrait of their ancestor; in 1747, Hugford used them as couriers when sending a reproductive engraving to Bottari, the Vasari editor who most famously identified Bindo's portrait as Raphael's own likeness. Significantly, the first engraving of the work, made in Rome around 1747 by Johann Jakob Frey and not widely distributed, bore lettering naming the sitter as Raphael, well before Bottari published his edition of Vasari with an illustration of the work (fig. 78).[51] Even if not directly involved in this reassignment, Hugford, as David Brown and Jane Van Nimmen speculate, may have consented to mediate its eventual sale as a Raphael self-portrait on behalf of the insolvent heirs, a transaction not accomplished during his lifetime.[52]

Hugford had close ties to the British community in Florence and a history of generosity to traveling artists. In 1755, for example, he took in English sculptor Joseph Wilton and French painter and architectural draftsman Charles Louis Clérisseau. So his hospitality to the young American merely extended those courtesies. For West, confined to bed during much of his stay, the benefits are likely to have been extraordinary. He might as well have been in a museum, one presided over by a man with deep interest in the history of art, artists, and representation of artists. In 1762, Hugford published a biography of his teacher, Anton Domenico Gabbiani; between 1767 and 1772, he brought out a sixth edition of Vasari; and between 1769 and 1775, he produced some three hundred portraits of artists for yet another collection of lives and likenesses, *Serie degli uomini i più illustri nella Pittura, Sculptura e Architettura, con i loro Elogi e Ritratti*.[53] Though the last two enterprises postdate West's time in Italy, they developed from Hugford's long and not entirely orthodox engagement with art history, which included strong

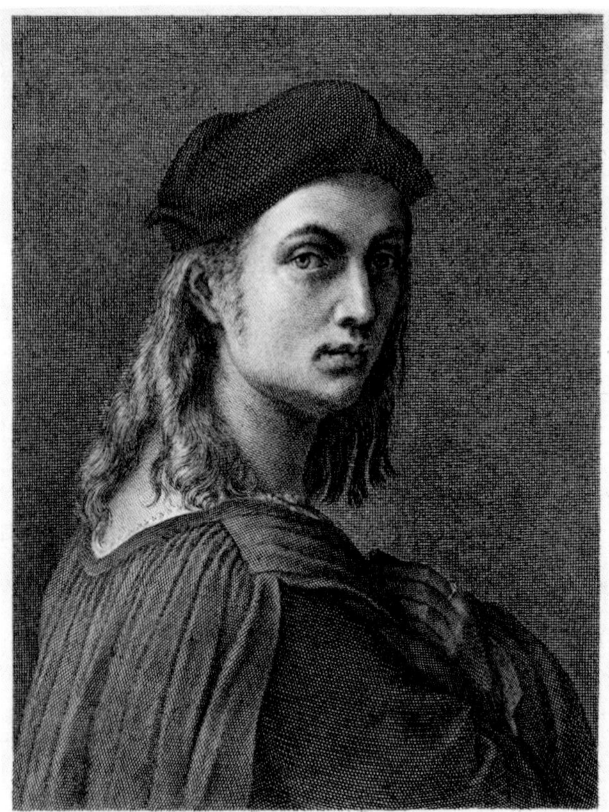

78 Jacob Frey after Raphael, *Bindo Altoviti*, ca. 1747 (as Raphael's self-portrait). Engraving and etching, based on a drawing by Giovan Domenico Campiglia. British Museum, London. © The Trustees of the British Museum.

interest in Italian art before 1500, well before the more general nineteenth-century rediscovery of the so-called Italian primitives.

West must have made use of the substantial visual resources available at Hugford's, since he had a frame constructed to permit drawing and painting while in bed. "He practiced drawing with great assiduity . . . [and] covered the floor of his chamber with his drawings," Peale reported hearing from West, while the artist himself said he had "painted several Ideal pictures as well as Portraits" while bedridden.[54] While it is difficult to imagine him entertaining portrait sitters under the circumstances, West had himself. He may have made the van Dyckian-Raphaelesque self-portrait drawing at that time, inspired by the immediacy of Hugford's own collection and by the hundreds of artist self-representations that clamored for his attention in Florence.

In that city, too, West first met Angelica Kauffmann, who focused on portraits at the start of her career and also showed an early and enduring commitment to self-portraiture.[55] Her signed and dated painting of a man in the Uffizi has plausibly been identified as West on the basis of physiognomic similarities to Kauffmann's two drawings of the American, both probably made later in Rome, where the young artists reconnected in spring 1763.[56] West, in turn, drew Kauffmann (fig. 79). With palette and brushes in hand, classicizing dress and hairstyle (somewhat Bindo- or Raphaelesque), and small mask hanging from a chain around her neck, Kauffmann embodies Pittura, an allegorized representation that she, as a woman, could fully inhabit, an identification that the seventeenth-century Roman artist Artemisia Gentileschi had likewise claimed in a notable self-portrait. West's familiarity with the attributes of Pittura, which artists cherry-picked from Cesare Ripa's extended but unillustrated description in the *Iconologia* (1593), suggests that his thick wavy hair in the self-portrait drawing was more than mere emulation of van Dyck. As for van Dyck himself in the *Self-Portrait with a Sunflower*, West's disordered hair evokes the imaginative energy of Pittura.[57]

Unable as a man to personify painting, West chose to model his self-image on the most esteemed painters: van Dyck, Raphael, and possibly also Nicholas Poussin. He profoundly admired the French painter, whose career-long residence in Rome and veneration for ancient and Italian Renaissance masters redeemed him among the English, otherwise greatly antipathetic to France. Gibbon, for one, lamented the absence of a Poussin self-portrait from the Uffizi. In two self-portraits made for French patrons in 1649–50, Poussin rests his hand on a drawing folio; he holds a drawing implement as well in the first of these. West could at the time only have known the works through print variants. In Albert Clouet's engraved adaptation of Poussin's second self-portrait, like the one made by Charles Errand for inclusion in Giovanni Bellori's *Le vite de' pittori, scultori, ed architetti moderni* (1672), the folio under the artist's hand becomes a book, marked "De lvm[en] et vmb[ra]" to emphasize the science of painting and theoretical concerns over studio practice (fig. 80). West made a similar shift in altering his self-portrait. The lower right portion, difficult to read, suggests that his right arm once extended downward toward the table, where his hand met a curved object, the edge of an oval palette perhaps. West's first depiction of a fellow artist, a small rough sketch of his Philadelphia friend John Green made during the later 1750s, showed that painter with palette and brushes and leaning on a mahlstick,

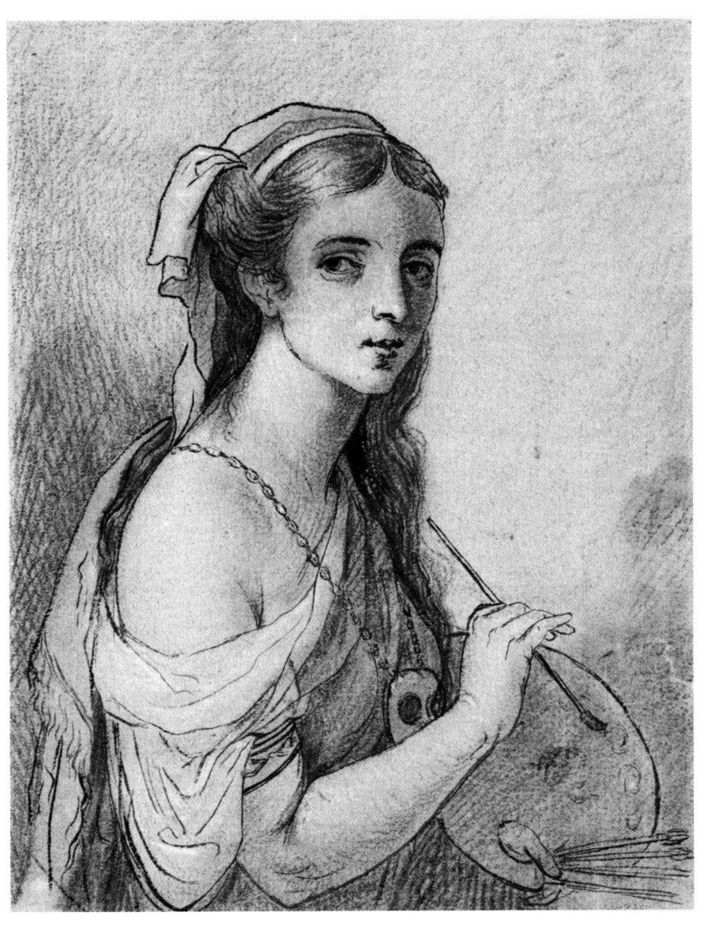

79 Benjamin West, *Angelica Kauffmann*, ca. 1762–63. Drawing. Friends Historical Library of Swarthmore College.

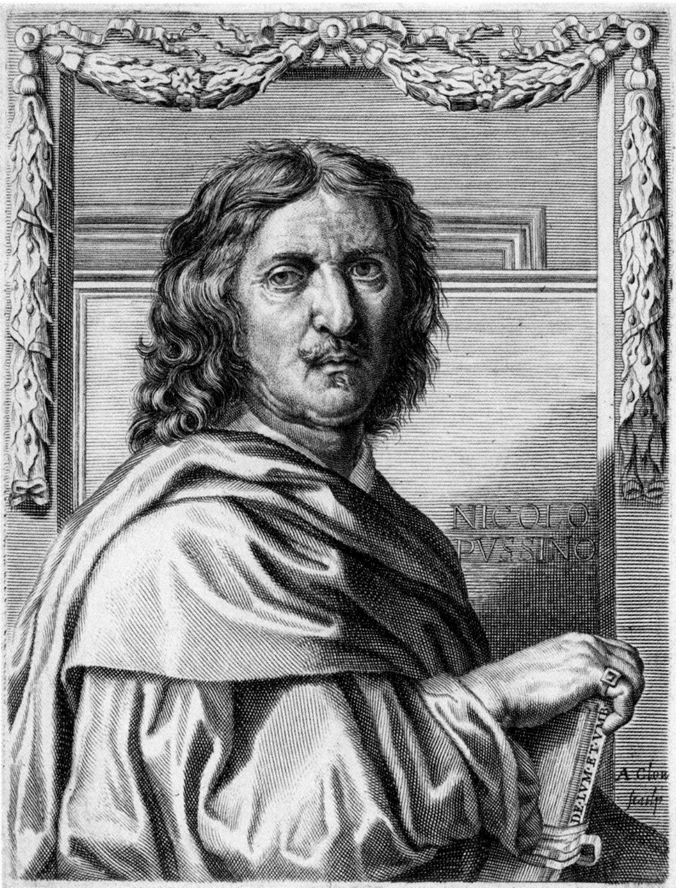

80 Albert Clouet after Nicolas Poussin, *Self-Portrait*, 1649 (Berlin). Engraving. National Gallery of Art, Washington, D.C., gift of John O'Brien.

a tool used by artists to steady the hand while painting (fig. 81).[58] West also gave Kauffmann painter's tools in the drawing contemporaneous with his Italian self-portrait. In revising his gesture, West elevated his depicted right hand so it rests atop an upended volume, seen from the spine and identifiable as a bound book by its relative thickness and raised bands. The motif also appears in van Dyck's portrait of French court painter Simon Vouet, engraved for the *Iconography*, in which the depicted book bears the title "Trattato della nobiltà della Pittura," in reference to Romano Alberti's 1585 book of that title, written for the Accademia di San Luca in Rome (fig. 82). While West preserved allusion to the manual aspect of his practice in the drawing implement threaded through his fingers, his inclusion of the book places equal emphasis on learning to the identity and claimed nobility of the artist.

The most compelling evidence that West had begun to think of himself as something other than a mere portraitist lies in the bust on the table, positioned above the book in terms of the two-dimensional organization of the drawing. The head, slightly larger than West's, appears nearly in profile, with brow, nose, and chin decisively outlined, so the form stands out on the heavily marked paper. Many eighteenth-century portraits include either specific classical busts or generically classicizing examples. In this case, the distinctive topknot of hair makes the bust identifiable beyond doubt as the head of *Apollo Belvedere* (fig. 83). West did not overlook the detail in a contemporaneous drawing of the entire statue.[59] As early as the 1720s, busts of the Apollo could be seen in many Roman collections, according to an English visitor, who remarked on their "female Delicacy," a quality to which the hairstyle, "rais'd like that of Women," contributed.[60] Perhaps this helps explain why, despite that ubiquity and the statue's fame, the bust (as opposed to the full statue) rarely appeared in painted portraits.[61] The presence of Apollo in West's self-portrait lends

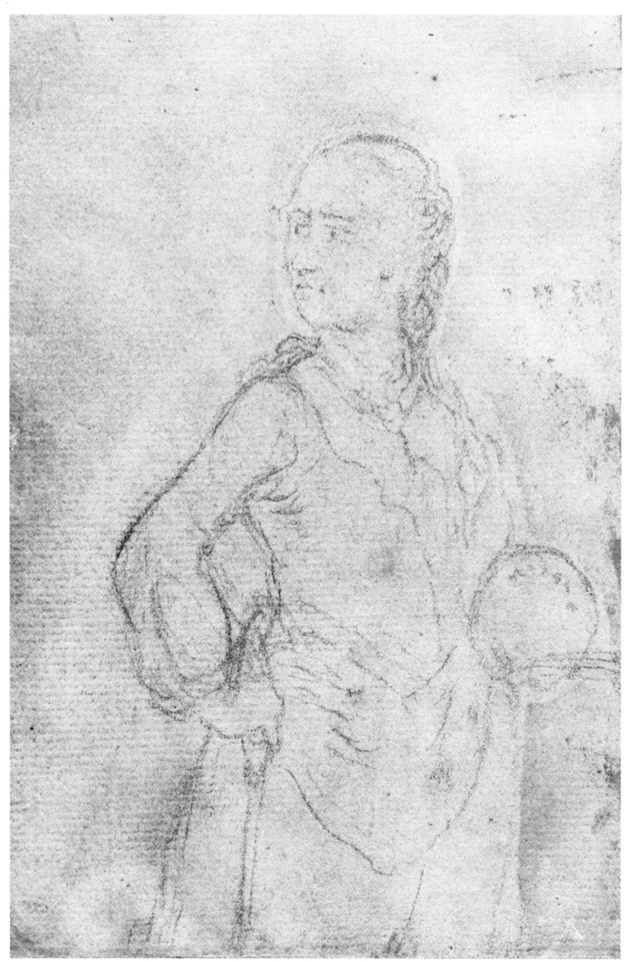

81 Benjamin West, portrait of John Green, drawing from West's sketchbook, ca. 1758–60. Benjamin West drawings and sketchbooks ca. 1790–1807, Historical Society of Pennsylvania, Philadelphia.

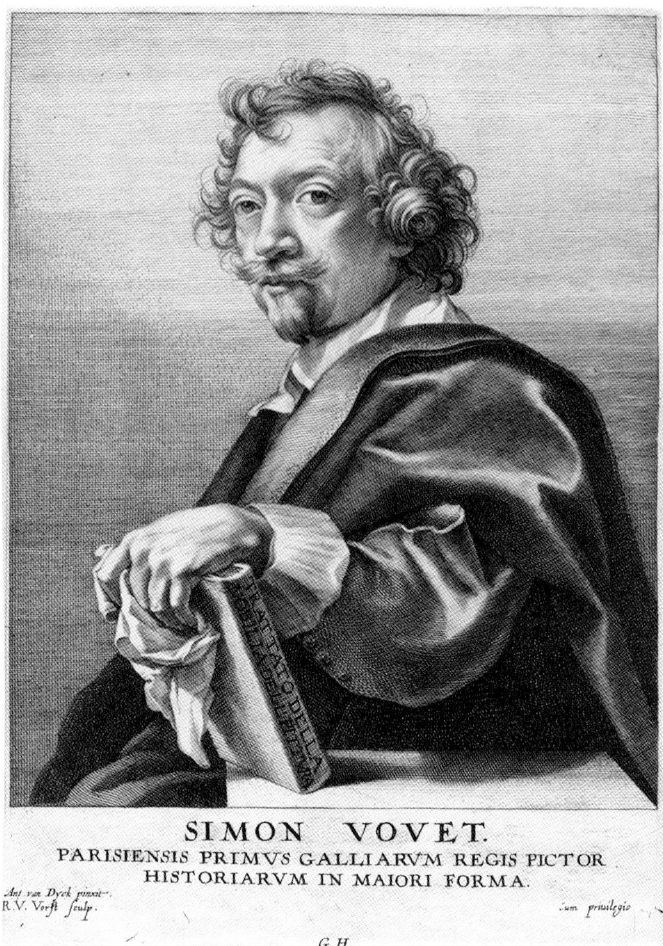

82 Robert van Voerst after Sir Anthony van Dyck, *Simon Vouet*, probably 1626–41. Engraving. National Gallery of Art, Washington, D.C., Rosenwald Collection, 1943.3.8281.

credence to the idea that an encounter with the renowned work, whether or not it transpired as Galt described, played a formative role in the way West defined himself and wished to be seen. The *Apollo Belvedere* links him to the apogee of ancient art for eighteenth-century viewers and to history, a type of subject matter West had been thinking about for a number of years, at least since his *Death of Socrates*. At the same time, the artist's Vandyke dress destabilized that association through its period specificity and firm association with portraiture. Even so, the impression remains that West, nearing the end of his time in Italy, was mulling over options and experimenting in ways that would, in short order, lead to his emergence as a new kind of British artist.

West may have chosen history painting in part for its primacy in the academic hierarchy to which British artists increasingly paid heed. In that case, he had the advantage of good timing since reasons less abstract than practical provided equally strong motivation to pursue history, namely the need to stand out among artists in London. The limitations of West's talent as a portraitist would eventually have sidelined him, but that may not have been a primary consideration for a man who rarely underestimated himself. Still, he hesitated about going on to London rather than home to America, rhetorically asking a friend: "What would I do among the Reynolds and Ramsays?"[62] Reynolds and the Scottish portraitist Allan Ramsay, among others, had seemingly insurmountable advantages over West: established reputation, acknowledged talent, and important connections. Ramsay had just been appointed Principal Painter in Ordinary to George III while Reynolds fueled and benefited from the culture of celebrity that swirled around

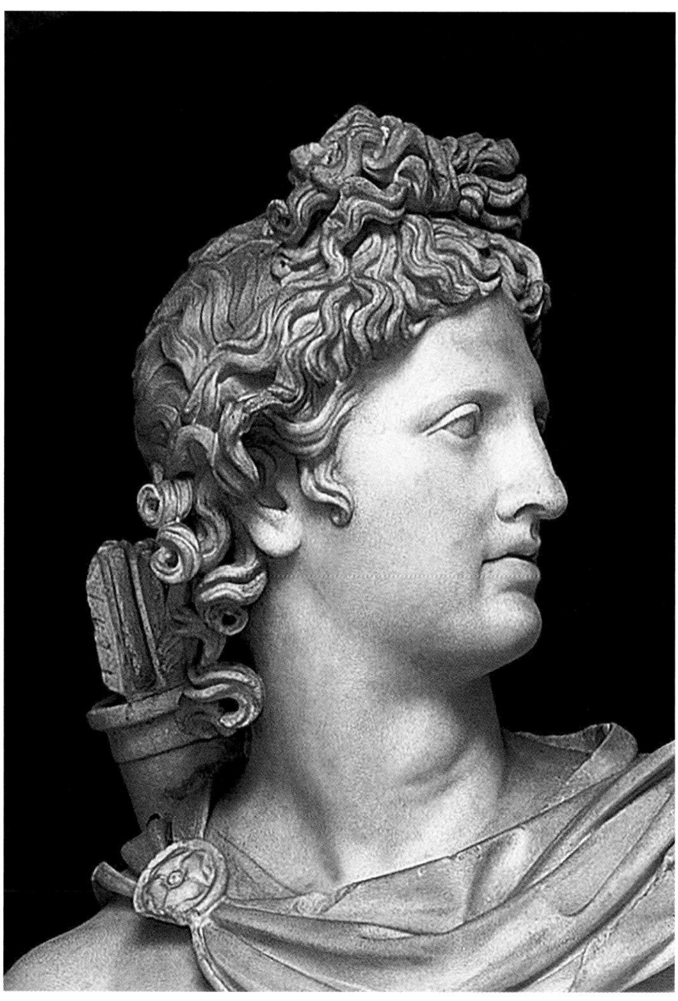

83 Marble statue known as *Apollo Belvedere* (detail), copy after Greek bronze original of the fourth century BC. De Agostini Picture Library/G. Nimatallah/Bridgeman Images.

the aristocrats, authors, actors, politicians, and courtesans who were his clients and, often, friends. Between 1760 and 1768, he showed twenty-seven portraits in the new London forum of the public art exhibition, almost all of persons with well-developed public identities.[63] West did paint and exhibit portraits, but his growing commitment to history made him unusual among the roughly two thousand portraitists in London (Horace Walpole's estimate as of 1759).[64] According to Samuel Sharp, a surgeon who published accounts of travel through Italy in 1765 and 1766, English artists were more likely, upon return to London from Rome, to "quit their works of genius, and be totally absorbed in portrait-painting, the stumbling-block on which all the *English* painters fall."[65] West, the American painter, set out to prove otherwise.

Art and Trade: The Exhibitions of Early 1760s London

> Every Englishman constantly holds a pair of scales, wherein he exactly weighs the birth, the rank, and especially the fortune of those he is in company with, in order to regulate his behavior and discourse accordingly; and on this occasion the rich tradesman is always sure to outrank the poor artist.
>
> André Rouquet, *The Present State of the Arts in England* (1755)[66]

West arrived in London at an opportune time, as British artists sought in earnest to banish the idea of art as trade – rooted not only in its manual basis but in the condition of painting for money – and to establish it instead on a footing with the liberal arts.[67] For the first time, they attacked the problem collectively and publicly, in regular art exhibitions beginning in 1760 and with progressively more honed objectives as different contingents sorted out their priorities and formed themselves into like-minded groups.

1760 saw the first such exhibition, when sixty-nine painters, sculptors, architects, and others showed an eclectic array of works – including models, patterns for ornamental coaches, and designs for bridges and monuments – in space rented from the Society for the Encouragement of Arts, Manufactures, and Commerce. That organization, founded in 1754, had the goal of promoting useful arts and industry, of encouraging artisans (male and female) as well as fine artists.[68] Dissatisfaction with the form of the first exhibition and regulatory control exercised by the Society of Arts, especially its opposition to an entrance fee, led a significant number of participants to form an independent organization more narrowly committed to the fine arts, as indicated by the name the group first thought to adopt, "Free Professors of Painting, Sculpture and Architecture." As the Society of Artists of Great Britain, this group held its first show in 1761, a money-making venture with proceeds committed to future exhibitions and advancement of members' careers but more immediately designed to make the event more exclusive. A philanthropically inclined faction remaining from the exhibitors of 1760 emerged in 1762 as the "Free Society of Artists associated for the Relief of the Distressed and Decayed Brethren and their Widows and Children" – a name that, despite altruistic intent, inadvertently conjured a pathetic image of artists as a collective. Although this group had fewer notable members than the Society of Artists, following the latter's example they narrowed the scope of exhibits so that fine arts took center stage, without completely excluding fancy work, novelties and utilitarian

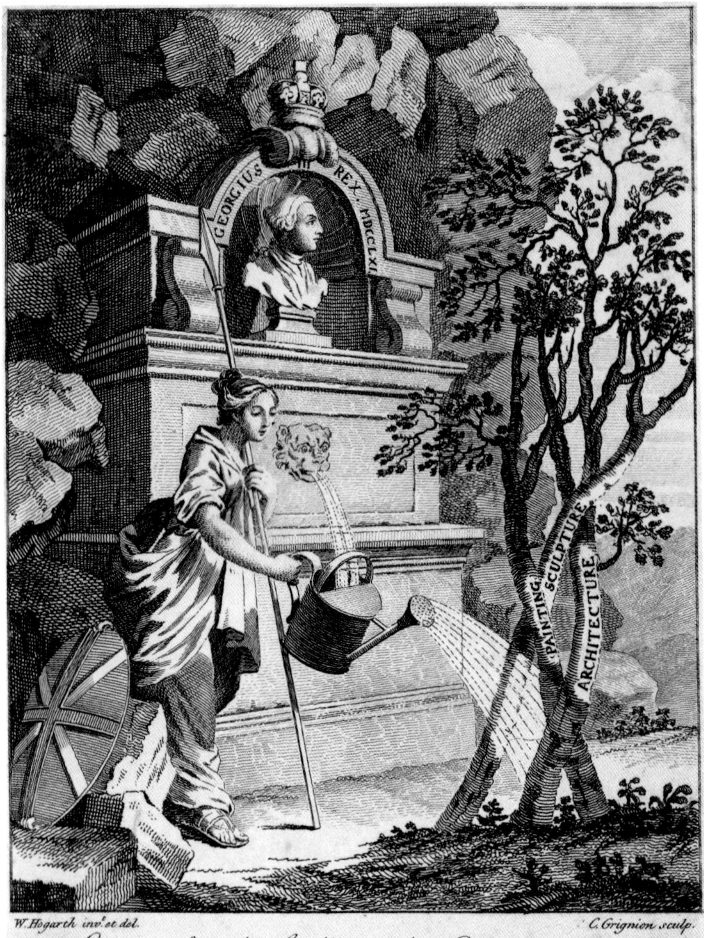

Left 84 Charles Grignion after William Hogarth, frontispiece to *A Catalogue of the Pictures, Sculptures, Models, Drawings, Prints, &c. Exhibited by the Society of Artists in Great Britain*, 1761. Etching and engraving. British Museum, London. © The Trustees of the British Museum.

Above 85 Charles Grignion after William Hogarth, tailpiece to *A Catalogue of the Pictures, Sculptures, Models, Drawings, Prints, &c. Exhibited by the Society of Artists in Great Britain*, 1761. Etching and engraving. British Museum, London. © The Trustees of the British Museum.

productions. Both organizations held annual exhibitions throughout the decade. In 1765, the first group attained the added prestige of a Royal Charter, as the Incorporated Society of Artists. For a powerful cohort, it was not enough; working in some secrecy, they won full backing of George III and announced themselves, in December 1768, as the Royal Academy of Arts. The following spring, the Academy held its first annual exhibition, concurrently with that of the Society of Artists, to which a few influential members remained loyal and overtly resistant to the principles of the Royal Academy.[69]

In all this jockeying for position, the artist who suffered most was Hogarth, whose long campaign to elevate the profession beyond the level of "painter tailor" ran aground on his refusal to acknowledge the authority of continental traditions. Hogarth made the point in a last unstable moment of unity with colleagues, whom he joined in the newly formed Society of Artists. For the group's first exhibition catalogue in 1761, Hogarth designed a frontispiece welcoming a new era for British art under the reign of George III (fig. 84). Britannia, personified as a beautiful young woman, channels water from a fountain adorned with the king's bust onto a trio of thriving saplings rooted in the soil and marked Painting, Sculpture, and Architecture. For the catalogue tailpiece, Hogarth witheringly satirized what he hoped to leave behind (fig. 85). An oblivious monkey, foppishly attired and holding a connoisseur's magnifying glass, waters the desiccated remains of three trees in pots marked Obit 1502, 1600, and 1604 and collectively labeled as "Exoticks." Hogarth, the proud English artist who inserted "Anglus" between his name and the verb "pinxt" when signing a portrait of 1741, wanted nothing more than to close the book on Old Master worship, but he offered no alternatives that colleagues found compelling.

Hogarth identified a native English pictorial tradition with the humble art of sign painting, a characteristically provocative position, which he knew fellow artists would use against him. Such had not been the case for Williams in America, for whom painting and hanging a sign was simply part of conducting business along a customary spectrum of painting activities. At the same time, as I have argued, Williams's signs served a more imaginative and professionally expansive purpose in connecting him to artists and art tradesmen, like the printsellers at Rembrandt's and Hogarth's Head in London. But that does not mean his practices squared with those of metropolitan artists. By mid-eighteenth century, would-be fine artists who actually lived in London were more concerned to avoid connections to trade. Hogarth, who may have practiced sign painting early in his career, hung a sign at his place of business through the 1740s, but he fashioned this "Golden Head" (reportedly a bust of van Dyck) from carved and gilded cork, materially and technically distancing the signboard from his livelihoods in painting and engraving.[70] Still, it compromised his image at a time when very few painters in London displayed shop signs.[71] The ubiquity of signs in Hogarth's paintings and prints of modern life further reinforced his identification with the trade. In *Beer Street* (ca. 1751), he showed the sign painter as well, an emaciated man atop a ladder, holding a palette and positioned in dreamy absorption before his signboard, as if he were a studio painter at the easel (fig. 86). Instead of mocking the sign painter for unsuitable pretension, Hogarth suggests that the man is a stifled talent, the victim of an indifferent public and contemptuous connoisseurs, who pay more attention to "Ancient Painting" – the 1740 book of that title by George Turnbull (marked "Turnbull on Painting") rests in a basket on the right – than to modern English artists.

The sign painter in *Beer Street* gained a voice in a letter to the *Adventurer* in 1752, whose author, literary satirist Bonnell Thornton – a close friend of Hogarth's – declared himself "but an humble journey-man sign-painter in Harp Alley [center of the London sign painting trade], who might have emulated Raphael or Titian were it not for the English prejudice against native artists."[72] A decade later, Thornton ran a burlesque advertisement in *St. James's Chronicle* (May 23–26, 1761) soliciting entries from "Natives of Great Britain" for "the Projected Exhibition of the Brokers and Sign-Painters." The following spring, an act to improve the streets banned projecting signs in English cities and provided fodder for a real exhibition, which opened in April 1762, possibly with input from Hogarth.[73] A celebration of popular and native imagery, the Sign Painter's Exhibition was hardly a benign display of anticipatory nostalgia. Instead, it parodied the contemporaneous show by the Society of Artists, from which Hogarth had severed his connection immediately following its first exhibition, after his historical painting *Sigismunda Mourning over the Heart of Guiscardo*, a scene from Boccaccio's *Decameron*, had been so derided that he withdrew it. The Sign Painter's Exhibition included the Rising Sun, by a "modern Claude Lorraine," and Hogarth's Head, described in the catalogue as a "Portrait of a justly celebrated Painter, though an Englishman and a Modern." Most of the entries were probably real commercial signs, made to signify in new ways through comical juxtapositions and catalogue commentary. In response to outrage from members of the Society of Artists and their supporters, the organizers of the Sign Painter's Exhibition denied satirical intent, claiming as their "sole view . . . to convince foreigners, as well as their own blinded countrymen, that how ever inferior this nation may be unjustly deemed in other branches of the polite arts, the palm for sign painting must be universally ceded to us."[74]

Hogarth was not a sign painter or less ambitious than Reynolds and his associates. But his appointment in 1757 as "Serjeant-Painter to His Majesty" exposed him to their disdain. The title should have been a source of pride. Hogarth's father-in-law, Sir James Thornhill, a pioneering English history painter, had once held the position, with which Hogarth chose to identify himself by inscribing the title on a late state of his engraved second self-portrait, *Hogarth Painting the Comic Muse* of 1758 (1764, fig. 87).[75] The comic muse and the brush and paint pot – tools of the painter in general that do not appear in the painted original – suggest Hogarth's sardonic intent. The position of Serjeant-Painter, listed by the Board of Works among Master Bricklayers, Master Carvers, Master Glaziers, and others, was essentially that of a glorified house painter and entailed all the aspects of painting in general that aspiring artists of the period so wanted to purge from their experience. Although Hogarth personally did not take on such tasks, he received payment for their execution by subcontractors and attracted barbs from fellow artists angered over his resistance to continental models of artistic organization and practice. They called him a "sign painter," suggesting that England had nothing to celebrate in Hogarth and that English traditions offered little of use or value to professional artists. The put-down carried a greater sting than "painter tailor," at a time when the diversified business of painting in general was but narrowly removed from fine art studio practices. (Even the Royal Academy, at its founding in 1768, could neither fill the predetermined membership of forty Academicians, a number modeled on the Florentine and French academies,

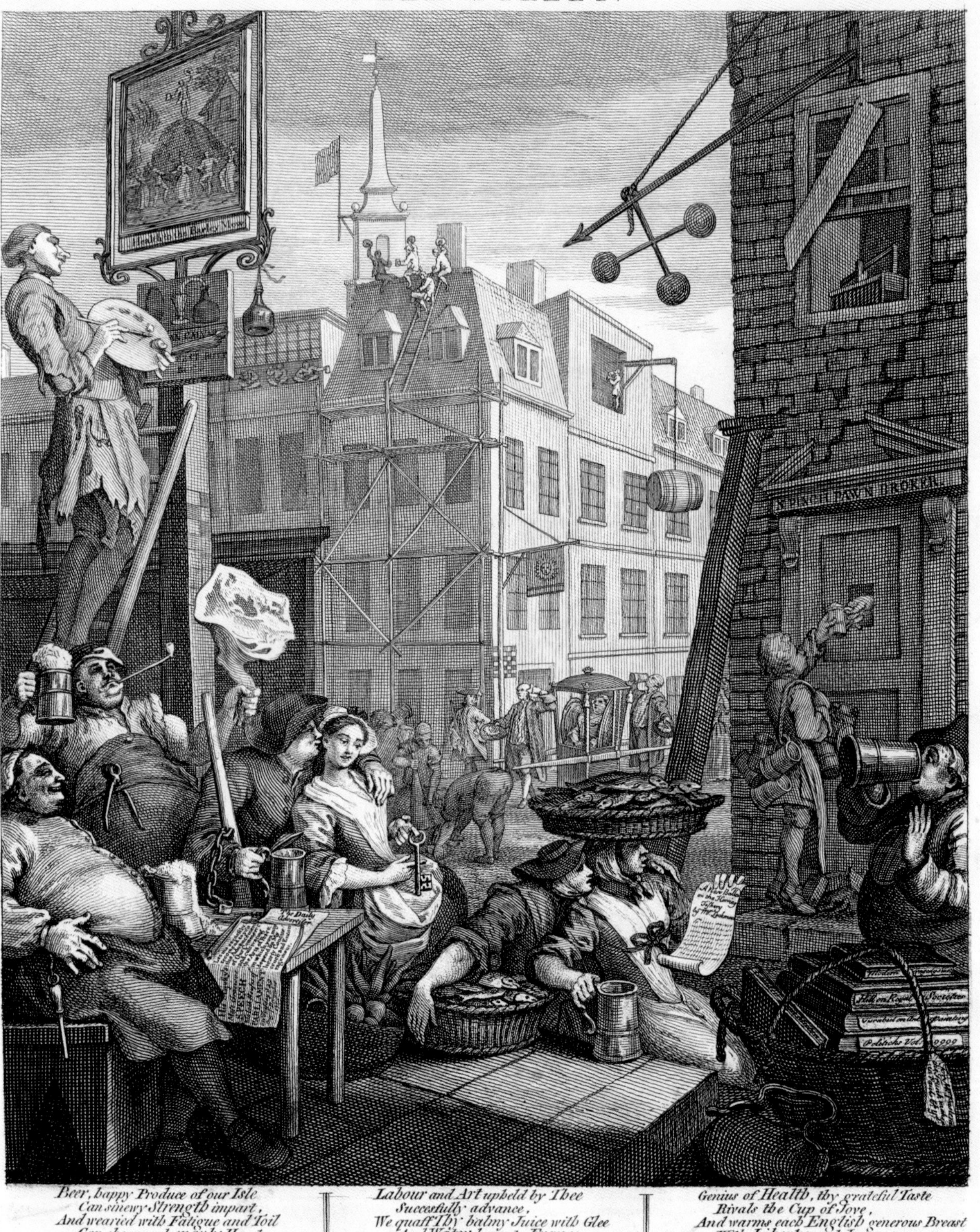

86 William Hogarth, *Beer Street* (undated, ca. 1751). Engraving. Yale Center for British Art, New Haven, Yale Art Gallery Collection, Frederick Benjamin Kaye Memorial Collection.

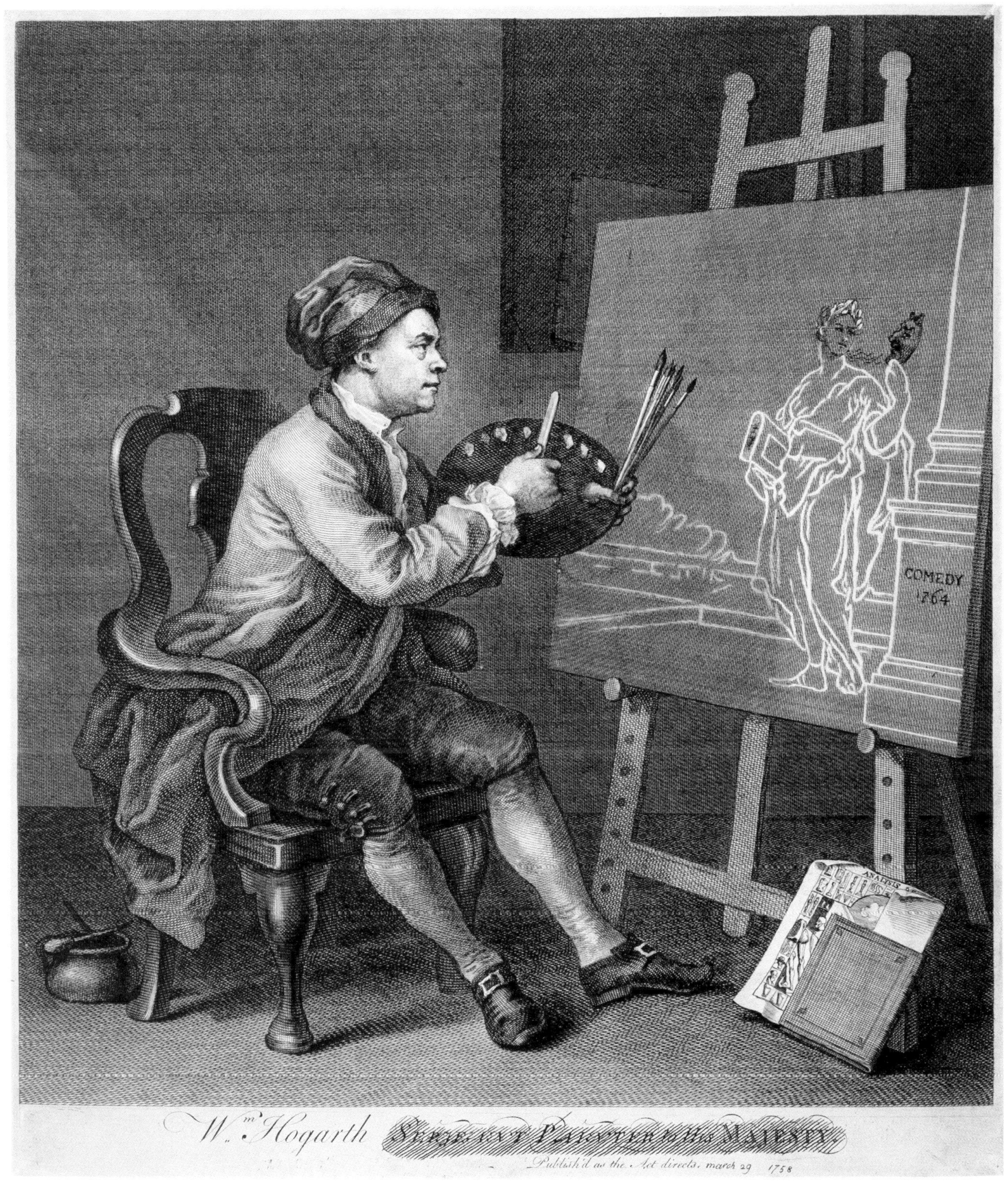

87 William Hogarth, *Hogarth Painting the Comic Muse*, 1764. Engraving. British Museum, London. © The Trustees of the British Museum.

nor avoid naming among the thirty-four founders several who were drapery- and coach-painters.)[76] Hogarth, in the final state of his self-portrait (1764), transformed the comic theatrical mask into a satyr's face, a bitter concession to his enemies and a sober corrective to their fantasy of the dignified, disinterested English painter.

Educating the Artist

In 1764, Hogarth's death removed an irritant to the British art establishment, identified at that moment with the Society of Artists, soon to acquire a royal charter. West became firmly associated with the group in that same year, after deciding to remain in London rather than return to Pennsylvania. Almost immediately, he opened his doors to fellow American artists. Matthew Pratt, the first of many who benefited from West's generosity, in turn publicized West's studio as the locus of a nascent "American School" when he showed a painting under that title with the Society of Artists in 1766. In addition to the work by this painter "of Philadelphia," visitors could also see "A boy with a flying squirrel" by "Mr. William Copely [*sic*]" of "Boston, New England," along with works by West.[77] This was the first exhibition to include three identifiably American painters.

In the histories of American art, *The American School* (1765) holds a position of importance out of all proportion to the regard accorded Pratt, whose reputation rests exclusively on that picture (fig. 88). Its canonical status arose entirely from the association with West, shown at far left with palette in hand and recognizable based on other portrayals of him. Identification by resemblance is always problematic because it fails to account for artistic style; however, an exactly contemporaneous portrait of West by Pratt offers a greater than usual measure of certainty.[78] Determining the identities of the others long preoccupied writers on Pratt's painting, who took for granted that it was fundamentally documentary – a group portrait, in effect, even though in 1765 West had no other known associates than Pratt.[79] Even Pratt could not be pinned down. Most believed he showed himself receiving a critique in drawing from the master, as if physical proximity trumped other criteria Pratt might have applied in representing his relationship to West. In any case, it makes no sense to see the work as homage to West, the teacher, at a time when his half-century of mentoring had barely begun.[80]

An entirely different reading emerges when we consider that Pratt has summoned an American school not yet fully in existence, giving himself a leading role within it as the man at the easel, West's equal. If, from a purely artistic and technical point of view, Pratt's painting seems only to confirm the tentativeness and modesty of the American school during the later colonial period, the artist had an ambitious goal. Rather than simply mirroring an actual situation, Pratt hoped to shape public perception of American art and artists. His painting joined a multiplying number of self-portraits and portraits of artists made and exhibited during the 1760s, a corollary to the formation and reformation of professional societies and evidence of powerful need among artists to take the lead in determining their professional identities. The Society of Artists exhibitions included no fewer than sixteen self-portraits over the course of the decade (a number that dropped precipitously to just two further during its ensuing twenty years of existence), while the Free Society placed eight such works on display – counts that exclude images of artists or art making not strictly classifiable as self-portraits.[81] Pratt's *American School* was one of those. The painting makes sense only in the artistically charged context of metropolitan London. With *The American School*, Pratt predicted a leading role for his countrymen in the British quest to establish parity with the greatest masters and schools in western art.

PAINTER'S PROGRESS

When Matthew Pratt (1734–1805) arrived in London in 1764, he was no novice to the practice of painting. Born in Philadelphia to a goldsmith of English heritage, Pratt had apprenticed at age fifteen and after the death of his father to his maternal uncle, James Claypoole, Sr., whom Pratt described as a "Limner & Painter in general."[82] Limning must not have been a particularly active part of the business, judging from Peale's characterization of Claypoole as a house painter and glazier and from the absence of any identified works.[83] Pratt recorded that he learned to paint portraits while with his uncle, but after release from his indenture in 1755, portraiture alone did not supply his living either. The *Pennsylvania Gazette* for March 5, 1756, carried his advertisement for "Painting, Gilding, Glazing, and Varnishing . . . At the sign of the Sash . . . where may be had good putty and powder blue." Yet in the following year, Pratt went to Jamaica on a trading voyage; he did not begin painting portraits in Philadelphia until 1758.[84] Only two survive from that six-year period before his departure for England, both from around 1760: a likeness of Benjamin Franklin copied after English artist Benjamin Wilson's por-

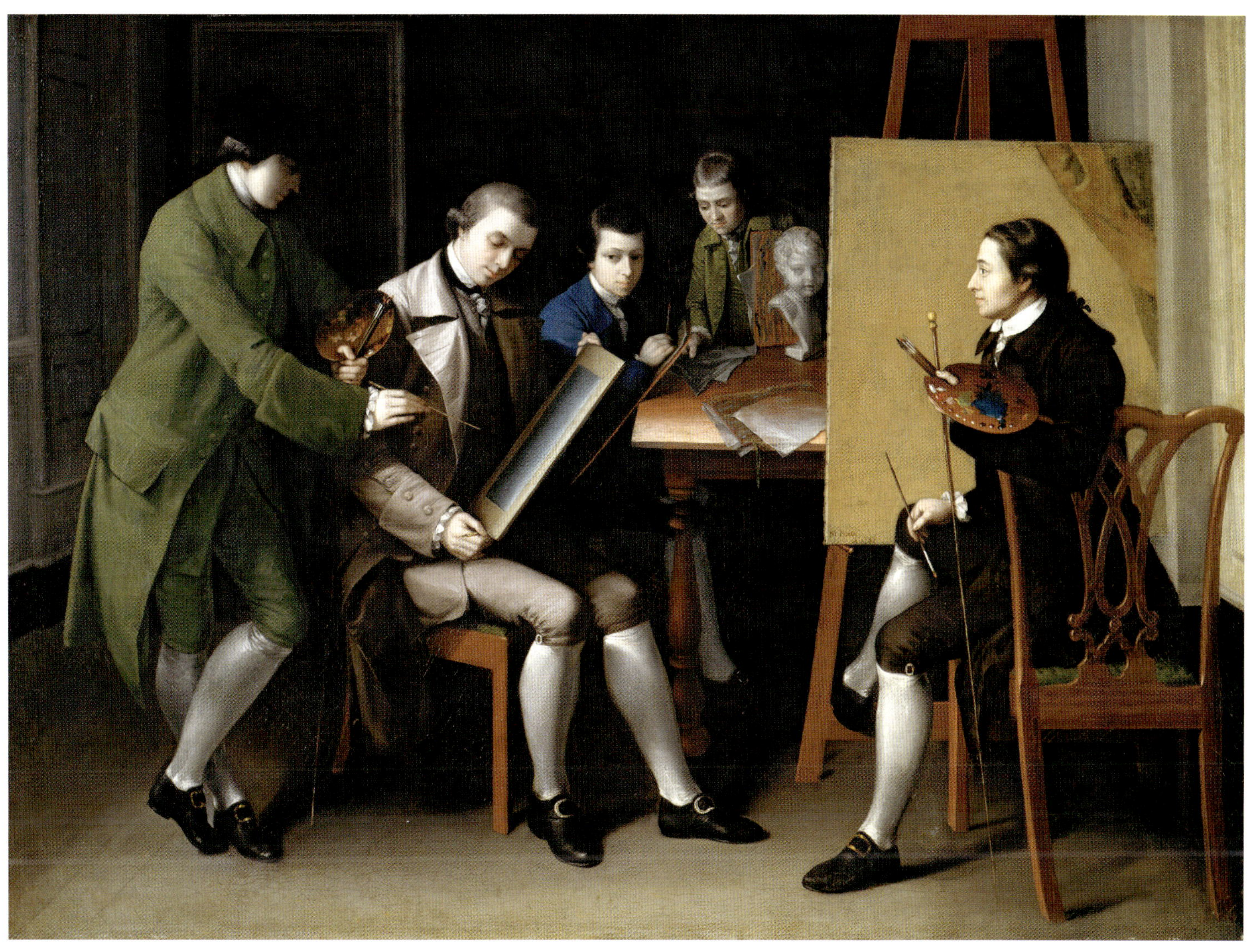

88 Matthew Pratt, *The American School*, 1765. Oil on canvas, 36 × 50¼ in. (91.4 × 127.6 cm). Metropolitan Museum of Art, New York, gift of Samuel P. Avery, 1897 (97.29.3), photographed by Geoffrey Clements.

trait of 1759, which was in Philadelphia, and a portrait of Elizabeth Moore Pratt, the artist's bride. The latter shows that Pratt, like West prior to his departure from America, sought to emulate the work of English painter John Wollaston, who was active in Philadelphia in 1758.[85]

Pratt seized the opportunity for direct engagement with English art when he crossed the Atlantic as escort for his cousin Elizabeth Shewell, West's longtime American fiancée. Soon after arrival in midsummer 1764, Pratt gave his cousin in marriage and then accompanied the Wests on their honeymoon (his own wife had remained in Philadelphia), before moving with them into the town house West had taken that spring in Castle Street, Leicester Fields, near Reynolds and Hogarth, who died in October of that year.[86] Perhaps as a wedding gift, Pratt made pendant portraits of Elizabeth and Benjamin West, in which he shed some of the tentativeness of his earlier Philadelphia work (figs. 89, 90). Living in West's household, he enjoyed constant contact with a painter far more sophisticated than any of his American experience, including Wollaston. With some justification, then, Pratt has been considered the first of West's pupils. Yet Pratt himself did not characterize the association in this way. West, he later recorded, "rendered me every good & kind office . . . , as if I was his Father, friend and brother."[87] Pratt's familial relationship to West, four years his senior, and his prior experience as an artist gave him little

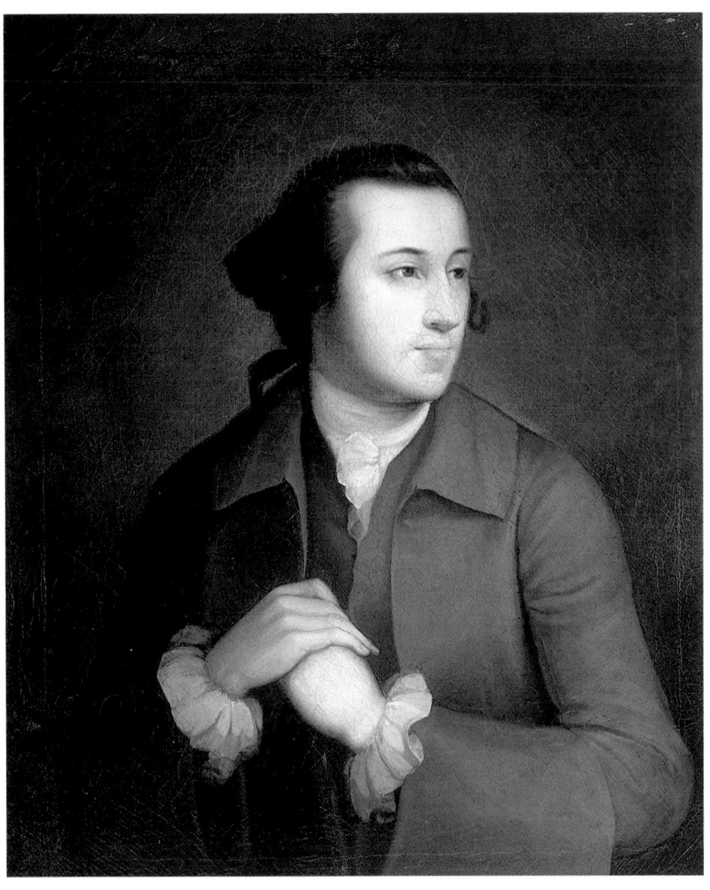

89 Matthew Pratt, *Benjamin West*, ca. 1765. Oil on canvas, 30¼ × 25⅛ in. (76.8 × 63.8 cm). Courtesy of the Pennsylvania Academy of the Fine Arts, Philadelphia, gift of Mrs. Rosalie V. Tiers Jackson.

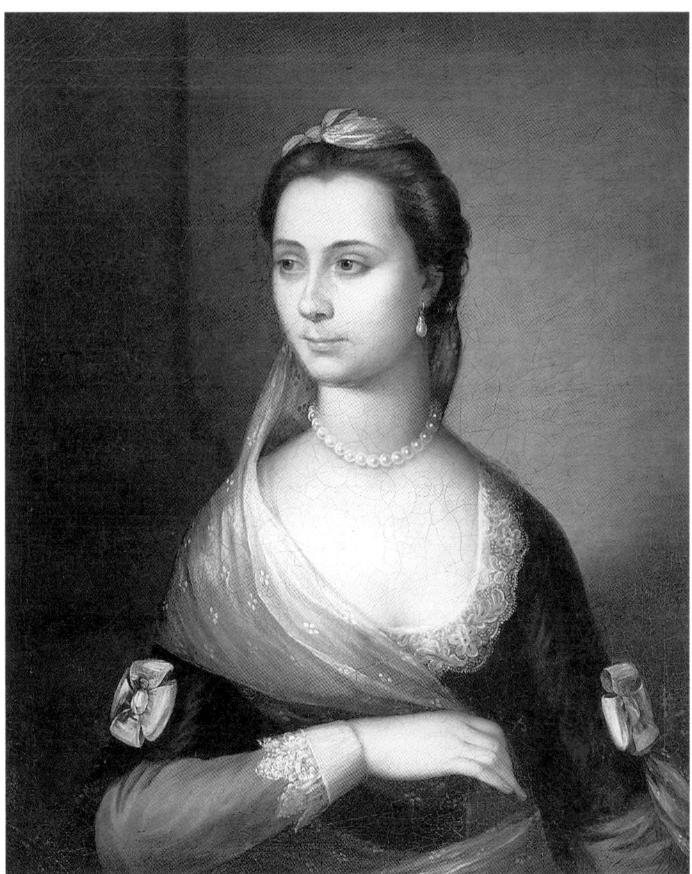

90 Matthew Pratt, *Mrs. Benjamin West*, ca. 1765. Oil on canvas, 30 3/16 × 25¼ in. (76.7 × 64.1 cm). Courtesy of the Pennsylvania Academy of the Fine Arts, Philadelphia, gift of Mrs. Rosalie V. Tiers Jackson.

reason – and apparently no inclination – to overstate his professional debt to West, however great that might have been. Consistent with this view, Elizabeth West, who thought Pratt's talent "merely mechanical," declared in private correspondence that her cousin possessed "a great share of vanity & always overrated his Ability."[88]

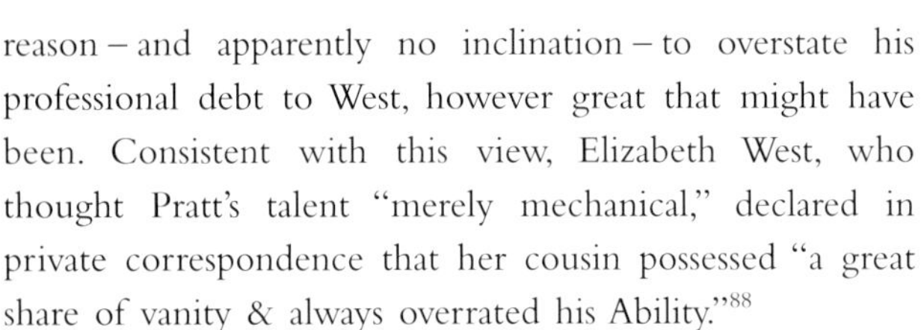

Pratt projected an air of assurance in a self-portrait believed to date early in his London sojourn (fig. 91). He holds a brass porte-crayon (double-ended chalk holder) in what appears, somewhat anomalously, to be the left hand but would actually have been his active right hand in the mirror's reversal. Artists who portrayed themselves holding tools, as opposed to omitting the working hand, almost always corrected the reflection. Angelica Kauffmann's self-portrait drawing of 1771 presents an exception, intended, Angela Rosenthal argued, to underscore the act of making that Kauffmann otherwise more conventionally depicts: pencil to paper and intently focused eyes (fig. 92).[89] But Pratt folds his (overly long) arms as he leans forward at a small table strewn with drawing paper, a relaxed and nonchalant pose that suggests a lack of fastidiousness given the proximity of the crayon to his coat. Clearly, Pratt cannot have sat like that while actually painting himself, not least because he painted in oil, but the question remains whether not switching the working hand was purposeful or whether it betrays an unthinking mimesis. Kauffmann had thwarted any such conclusion by inscribing her headband with the word "Imitatio." A virtue according to eighteenth-century art theory, imitation involved imagination as distinct from copying or reproduction, a lower level of activity.

Pratt took care to make this distinction in *The American School*, in which he visually articulated a course of artistic education that he, by implication, had successfully navigated. It was a public declaration, since Pratt both exhibited the work and marked it with signature and date – unique in his oeuvre – at the lower left-hand corner of the canvas depicted

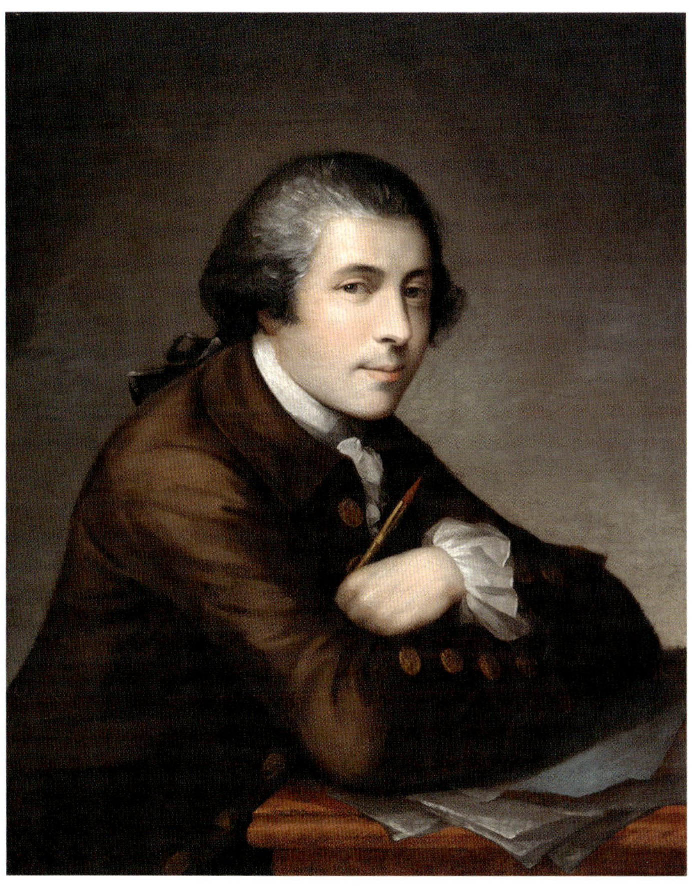

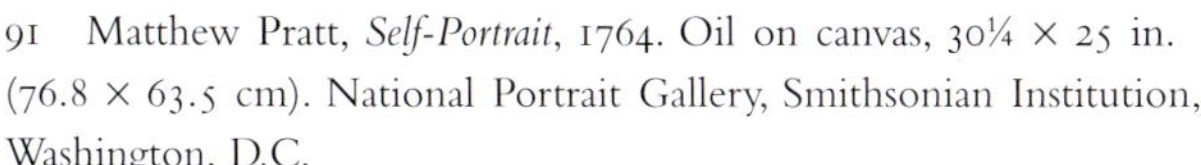

91 Matthew Pratt, *Self-Portrait*, 1764. Oil on canvas, 30¼ × 25 in. (76.8 × 63.5 cm). National Portrait Gallery, Smithsonian Institution, Washington, D.C.

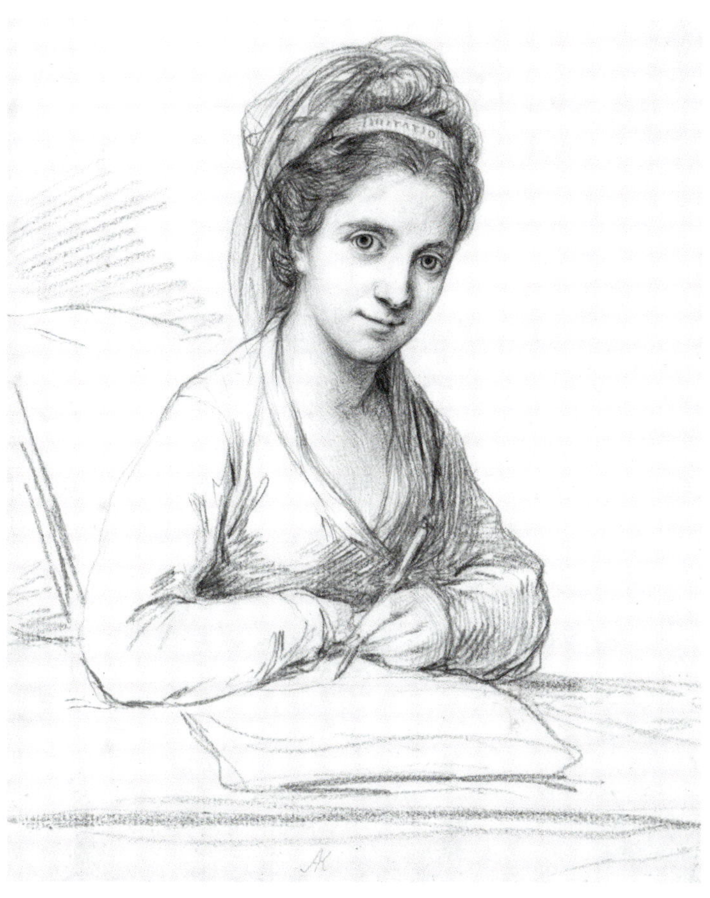

92 Angelica Kauffmann, *Self-Portrait as Imitatio*. Graphite on paper. Yale Center for British Art, New Haven, Paul Mellon Collection.

on the easel. Conservation studies reveal that Pratt added the easel, palettes and brushes, boy with portfolio, and plaster bust to a composition initially conceived as a straightforward indoor conversation piece.[90] In that case, the participants must have corresponded to real persons, who were not necessarily artists. As a multi-figure group, *The American School* constituted a substantially more ambitious offering than Pratt's submission to the Society of Artists the year before, *Fruit Piece*. That work, now lost, would have stood out at exhibition as a still life, but the distinction can only have been unfavorable to Pratt, given the low regard for the genre among academically inclined artists, who considered still life painting mere copying. Pratt distanced himself from that activity when he decided to make art the theme of *The American School*, producing, in effect, an artistic manifesto.

Consider the details of *The American School*. Five male subjects pursue various art-related activities in an interior space. On the far side of the table, the smallest and apparently youngest removes several sheets of paper from a portfolio. The next student, somewhat older and wearing a blue coat, pauses in the act of drawing a bust that rests on the table; its form appears at the exposed corner of his paper. On the one hand, this sculpture refers to the classical past, the wellspring of western art. But here antiquity seems to be looking to the modern age, since the bust is positioned so that it seems to observe the lesson. Significantly, it represents a child considerably younger than any of the students, of an age when the intellect and motor skills remain insufficiently developed to benefit from artistic training such as the painting depicts. So young a person might be regarded as a lump of matter, full of potential, yet to be molded.[91] The boy in blue has not been idly distracted from his drawing but looks on and listens to the critique taking place at his right. The object of discussion is a drawing (now indiscernible) on blue paper held by the seated young man clothed in a buff colored suit. The com-

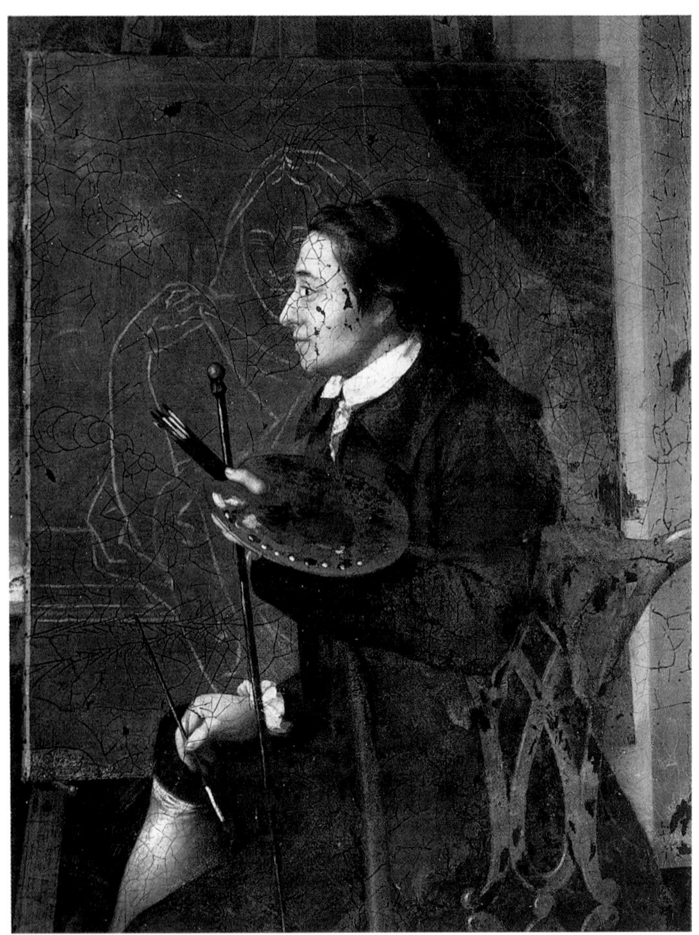

93 Matthew Pratt, *The American School*, 1765 (detail under ultraviolet light). Metropolitan Museum of Art, New York, gift of Samuel P. Avery, 1897 (97.29.3).

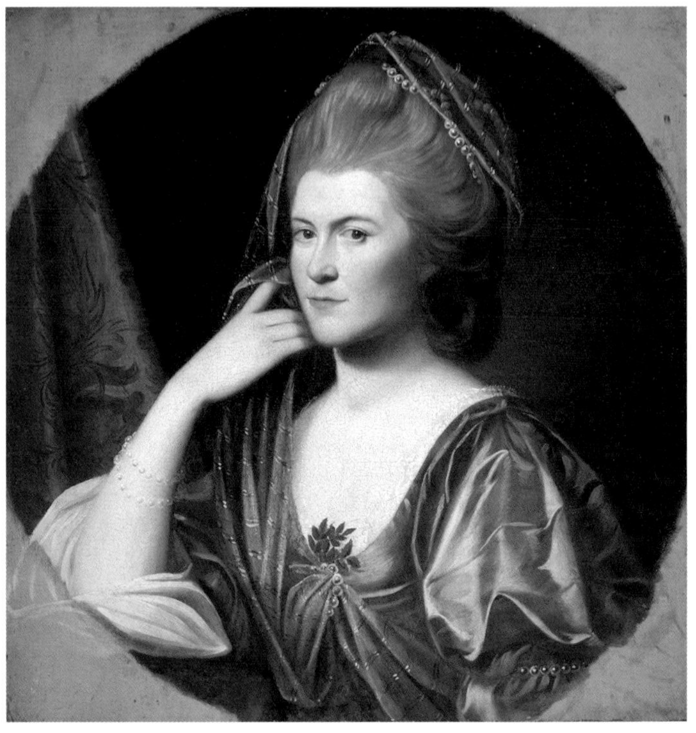

94 Henry Benbridge, *Mrs. Robert Shewell, Jr. (Mary Boyer Shewell)*, ca. 1775. Oil on canvas, 25⅞ in. (65.7 cm). Fine Arts Museums of San Francisco, gift of Mr. and Mrs. John D. Rockefeller 3rd, 1979.7.9.2.

mentator, in green, leans against the chair in a cross-legged stance that signified gentility in English male portraits of the period. An implied serpentine line, extending from the bust on the table to the standing man, knits together these figures, collectively absorbed and engaged in art by touch, sight, and sound.

To the right of the picture, another man, wearing dark brown, sits in a fashionable Marlborough-leg Chippendale chair (see detail on p. 131). Although he watches and listens to the instruction that unites the group on the left, he holds an autonomous position within the work, isolated compositionally in front of the light-colored canvas and narratively in terms of his activity. This man paints. Holding palette, brushes, and mahlstick (like the instructor), he sits at an easel, resting his foot casually on its base, having turned, it seems, only briefly away from his work. In its present state, the depicted canvas appears blank except for a roughed-in bit of drapery in the upper right-hand corner; however, ultraviolet light reveals that it once held the outline of a veiled woman, made transparent by time (fig. 93).[92] The figure recalls innumerable veiled women in portraits of the time, including Pratt's earlier likeness of his wife and wives painted by West to accompany husbands in Vandyke dress. A close parallel exists in a later portrait once attributed to Pratt but now assigned to Henry Benbridge, another Philadelphian with familial ties to West, who made his way to West's studio in 1769 (fig. 94).[93] In *The American School*, Pratt makes no effort to hide the labor of the hand that portraiture or any other kind of art making involves, but he invests that labor with dignity by emphasizing qualities of mind. All of the participants in the scene appear thoughtful and engaged as they look, listen, make, or teach, affirming a point on which academic theorists insisted: intellect drives the painter's skill.[94]

Pratt's *American School* offers condensed visual exposition of the recommendations for artistic education advanced in treatises popular throughout the eighteenth century. Roger de Piles, giving oft-repeated advice, counseled that students should commence at a very young age, training the eye and the hand in graduated exercises in geometry (which "teaches to reason"), perspective, anatomy and proportion, study after the antique and modern masters like Raphael, study of prints and from life.[95] After gaining basic mastery in design through these pursuits, the student learns coloring, again by emulation of the masters and by copying nature. Books such as de Piles's focused on the proper sequence of artistic education and on the theory of art, not the mechanics of art making. Practical manuals, by contrast, provided the "how-to," presenting detailed technical information and even promising that success "may be attained in a short Time without a Master," as announced by the subtitle to *The Compleat Drawing-master*.[96] Artists with little or no access to formal training often had to rely on such books.[97] Few can have considered reading an adequate substitute for study "under the Discipline of a knowing Master," an important advantage for those who could secure it.[98]

In choosing to make the education of artists a subject for painting, Pratt had company. At the 1766 Society of Artists exhibition, *A Boy Deliberating on his Drawing* by Nathaniel Hone resonated thematically with Pratt's work, though in a much simpler composition. More remarkable similarities exist in an apparently unexhibited painting of approximately the same date by John Hamilton Mortimer, a Society of Artists member. The work includes a young man who sits at a legged drawing board (Mortimer himself, based on comparison with his self-portraits), an older man who offers guidance, a boy who watches and listens but does not yet fully participate, and casts after the antique (fig. 95). (Mortimer omitted the instructor from another version of this painting, identical in other respects.) Certain aspects of the scene evoke the Duke of Richmond's gallery, where Mortimer studied soon after its doors opened in late February 1758. This was by design an academy where painters, sculptors, and engravers or, by permission, "any young man or boy, above the age of twelve years" might draw and model using "original plaster casts from the best statues and busts which are now at Rome and Florence", applicants could also request that casts be moved to facilitate study, as appears to be occurring in Mortimer's painting.[99] In response to this new resource, the Society of Arts, then in its fourth year, promptly offered an incentive for "Youths under the Age of Twenty-one" to sharpen their skills: a prize of twenty-five guineas for the best drawing after a work in the duke's gallery, to be awarded in a competition the following spring.[100] Mortimer won for his rendition of Michelangelo's *Bacchus*. He and others who frequented the drawing academy benefited from the weekly presence and advice of two established artists, the sculptor Joseph Wilton and the Italian painter-engraver Giovanni Cipriani, a former pupil of Ignazio Hugford (West's host in Florence), who accompanied Wilton to England in 1755. The older man in Mortimer's painting has been identified as Wilton, though both he and Cipriani had left the Duke of Richmond's gallery by 1761. Mortimer, for that matter, appears older than when he worked there and far more skilled than he would have then been at a point when he had only just, in 1760, graduated to life drawing at the St. Martin's Lane Academy. More likely he made the self-portrait close to the time of his election as a fellow of the Society of Artists in 1765, where, during the 1760s, he primarily exhibited portraits of various kinds. Yet he also won Society of Arts-sponsored prizes for history painting in 1763 and 1764, positioning him as a potential rival to West, then newly arrived in London.[101] Mortimer's self-portrait at a drawing board highlights his skill as painter and grounding in fundamentals of professional practice, which in his case, unlike Pratt's, reflects deeply rooted experience.[102]

At exhibition with the Free Society of Artists in 1766, the rival organization to the Society of Artists, a painting by George Romney featured an even earlier stage of artistic training than did Mortimer and Pratt.[103] Although Romney went on to a highly successful career, unlike Pratt, the two present interesting parallels at this stage. Exact contemporaries, each served a provincial apprenticeship, in Romney's case cancelled in 1757 by master Christopher Steele after just two of four years contracted, when Steele decided to go to Ireland. (This may have been the same Steele whom Peale met in Philadelphia sometime during the earlier 1760s, "a man of considerable talents" who had a self-portrait in his painting room.)[104] Romney followed a provincial painting practice for approximately five years, as had Pratt, before moving to London in 1762. The following year, he entered the Society of Arts competition for a historical subject from British or Irish history, only to see his preliminary second place prize for *The Death of General Wolfe* re-awarded to Mortimer; according to William Hayley, Romney believed that Reynolds was behind this reversal, which left Romney with a conciliatory third.[105] Mortimer,

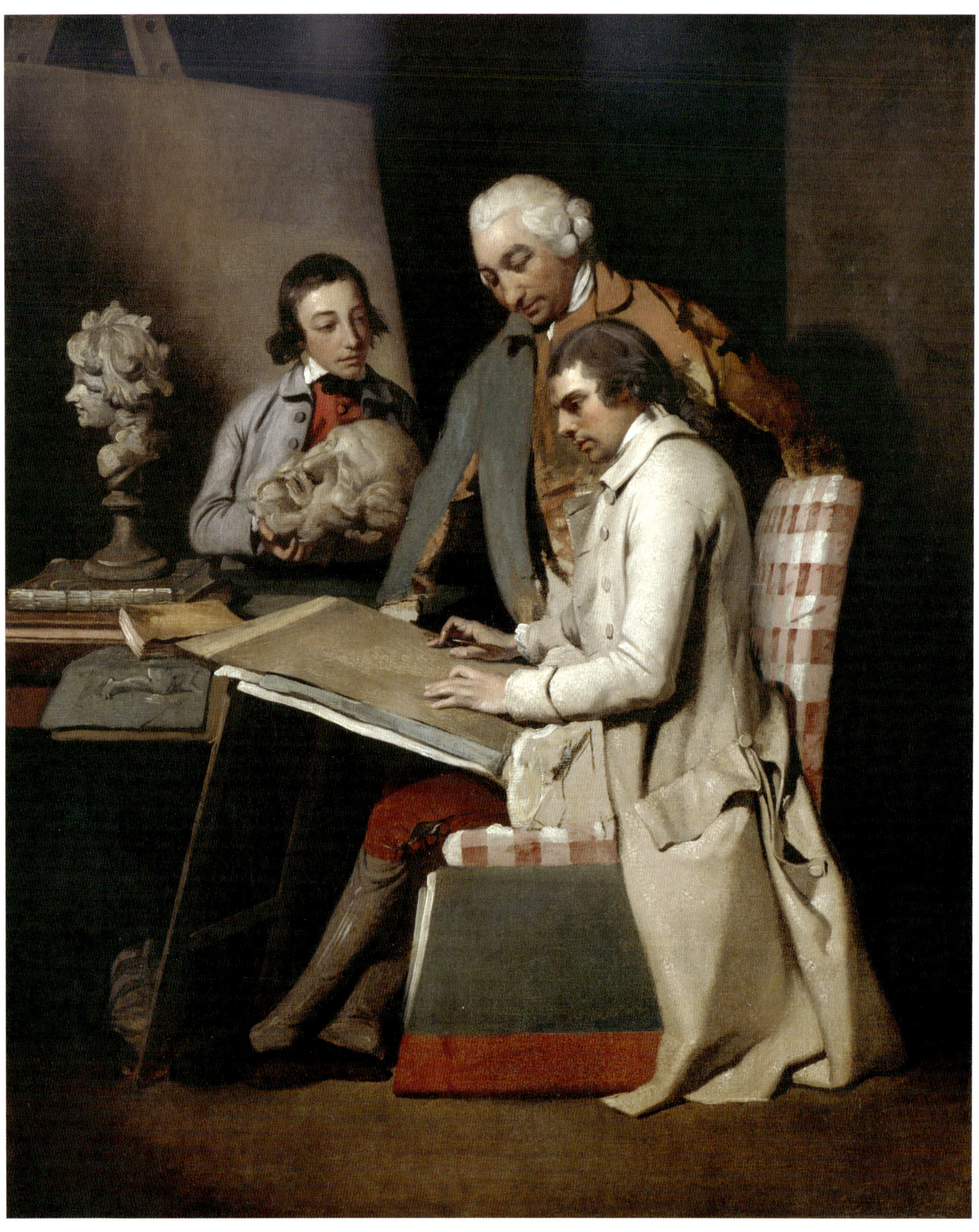

95 John Hamilton Mortimer, *The Artist with Joseph Wilton and a Student*, ca. 1765. Oil on canvas, 30 × 25 in. (76 × 63.5 cm). Royal Academy of Arts, London, given by T. Humphrey Ward, 1889.

for his part, said he thought Romney should have had the prize, not because his work was superior but because he had painted it "in a room so small that he could not examine the effect of the whole at a single view and at a proper distance, and that under this disadvantage his performance was surprising."[106] The backhanded compliment recalls Reynolds's assessment of Copley, marooned (as they both believed) in the provinces.

Romney, as much as Pratt, wished at this point to identify himself with theoretically orthodox artistic training. He made the case for that training at its most fundamental level in a depiction of his younger brothers in an intimate studio setting, exhibited with the Free Society as *A Conversation* (fig. 96). Peter, an aspiring artist, sits with a drawing board on his knees, its outer end propped against a large canvas on an easel. Using the ruler and compass atop his board, Peter has drawn two triangles and a circle; these geometric figures are the focus of his remarks to the attentive James. The lesson serves as a reminder that eighteenth-century British artists still struggled to establish the dignity of painting as a liberal art, a cause in which the science of perspective, with geometry as its basis, played a key role. Virtually every tract on art since the Renaissance, theoretical and practical, made this point. Leonardo da Vinci was a commanding early voice. The first English translation of Leonardo da Vinci's *A Treatise of Painting* (1721), which Romney studied, begins: "Whoever would apply himself to Painting, must, in the first Place, learn Perspective." Leonardo identified perspective as "both the Guide and the Gate, . . . without which, it is Impossible to succeed either in *Designing*, or in any of the Arts depending thereon."[107] Perspective is "the very soul of all painting," asserted Jean Dubreuil in a treatise on the subject in 1726, "and that alone which can make the painter a master."[108] On a more quotidian level, a how-to book that Romney owned counseled: "Make your entrance [to the practice of art] . . . with plain geometrical figures, such as are the circle, square, oval, cone, triangle, cylinder, which at first . . . mark out with your rule and compass, till you can readily do it with your hand."[109]

Peter Romney engages in just such a pursuit, but not as a beginning artist, since he received instruction from George between 1759 and 1762 and was active as a painter by 1766, though without much success. Peter, in his turn, instructs James, consistent with the belief that a liberal art can be passed on by intellectual processes – an idea that *The American School* also endorses. Specifically, Peter gestures at a triangle while looking upward, face in near profile, at James. The exchange demonstrates a lesson from contemporary

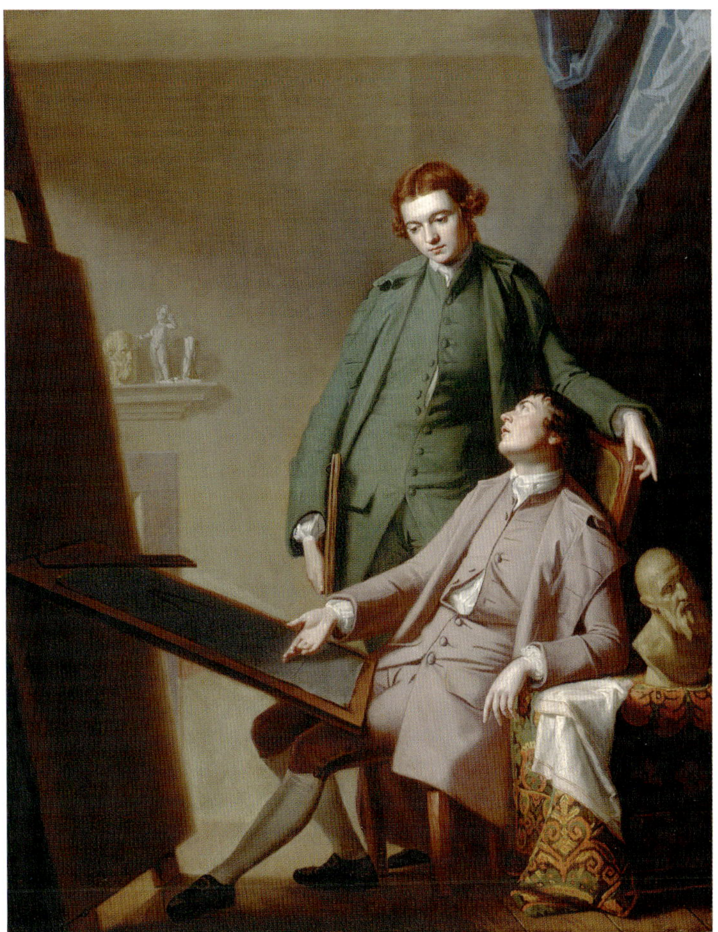

96 George Romney, *A Conversation (Peter and James Romney)*, 1766. Oil on canvas, 43½ × 34½ in. (110.5 × 87.6 cm). Yale Center for British Art, New Haven, Paul Mellon Collection.

drawing manuals: the triangle offers an aid to construction of the half face.[110]

Heads and hands figure prominently in Romney's painting. James's head, brightly illuminated against a neutral background, first attracts the viewer's attention. His gaze directs the eye to Peter's open hand, from which the arm traces an arc to Peter's upturned face; following his glance, the viewer's eye returns to James's face. James drapes his left arm casually across the back of the chair in which his brother sits, and his hand, reversing Peter's gesture, can be read as pointing to the bust on the table. The little group on the mantel echoes the principal figures; a putto mimics James's serpentine stance and, like him, gestures at a plaster head (while touching its own head). This choreography supports an idea important in Pratt's *American School* and to British artists of the period generally. The painter succeeds

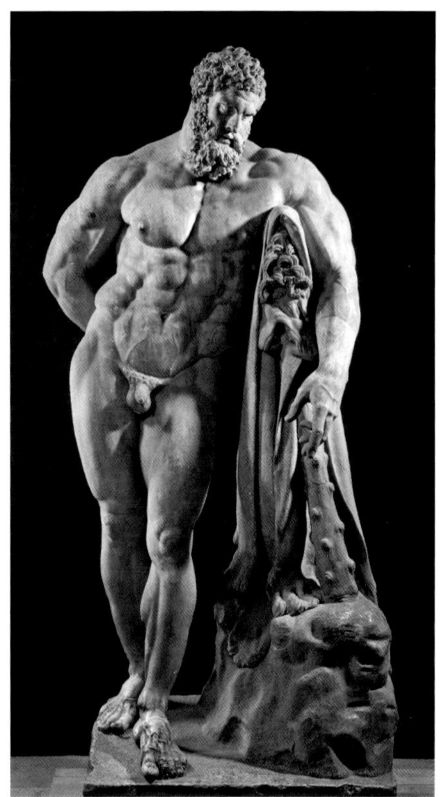

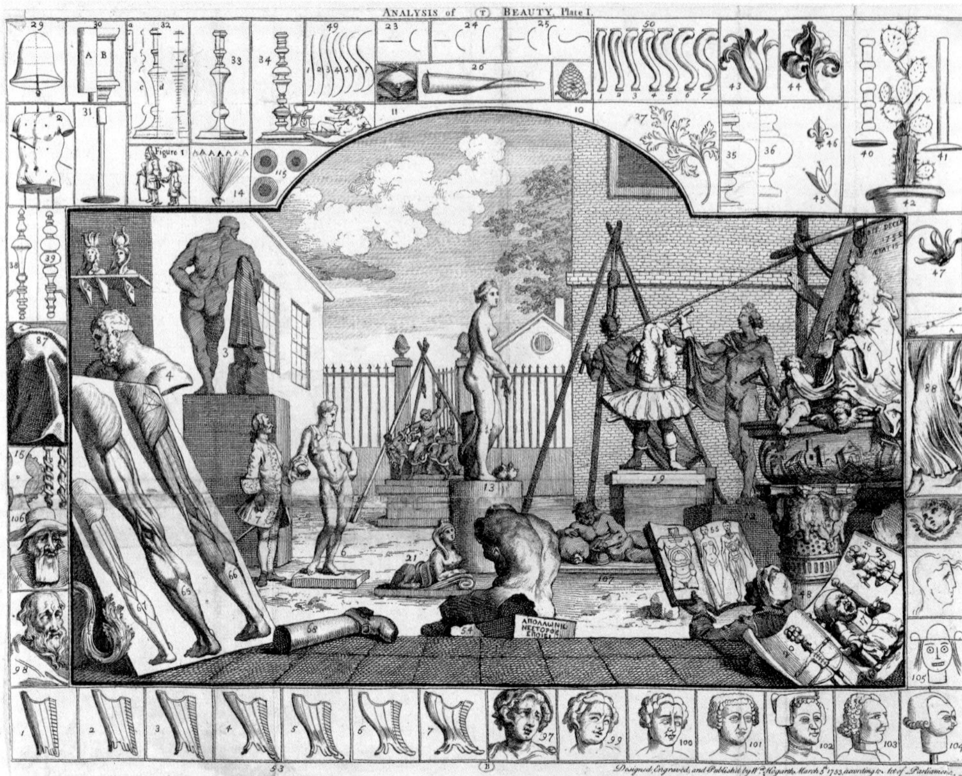

Left 97 The *Farnese Hercules*, Roman copy of Greek marble original, fourth century BC. Museo Archeologico Nazionale, Naples / Bridgeman Images.

Right 98 Hogarth, *Analysis of Beauty*, Plate 1: *A Statuary's Yard*, 1753. Engraving. Yale Center for British Art, New Haven.

not only because of what the hands can do but also by powers of intellect.

To the right on the mantel, an odd sculptural fragment provides further insight into Romney's case for the modern artist. It is a greatly reduced cast of the left leg from the enormous Hercules (over three meters high) then in the Palazzo Farnese in Rome (fig. 97). Discovered in the Baths of Caracalla around 1550, this work quickly became one of the most celebrated ancient sculptures, among "the three finest statues in the world," according to an English travel account published in 1766.[111] The Hercules had been recovered in parts over time. Sixteenth-century Italian writers reported that Michelangelo recommended a younger sculptor for the job of fashioning legs to complete the extant head and torso, a task so admirably accomplished that, even after discovery of the originals, the Farnese family accepted Michelangelo's advice to retain the sixteenth-century limbs "in order to show that works of modern sculpture can stand comparison with those of the ancients."[112] Romney's decision to show the disembodied leg indicates his awareness of that history and raises compelling interpretive possibilities. The leg by itself refers to the classical original, which still stood alone at that date, suggesting that Romney (who had not traveled on the Continent) upheld the superiority of ancient art. Hogarth, though vehemently opposed to the modern academic practice of copying ancient statuary, praised classical artists for their fidelity to the principles of nature. He particularly singled out the Farnese *Hercules* for the way all of its parts communicated the hero's strength, and he included both the full statue, shaded and seen from behind, as well as its head and shoulders in Plate 1 of *The Analysis of Beauty* (fig. 98).[113] In Romney's painting, the heroic leg is so diminished as to be almost comical. The central point of the story involving Michelangelo concerned the possibility that modern artists could achieve parity with the ancients, and this idea had not been abandoned by eighteenth-century theorists. Romney's painting acknowledges the example of ancient sculpture while foregrounding the intergenerational and interpersonal dynamic by which men become artists.

These paintings of artists at work by Pratt, Romney, and Mortimer, among others, staked out positions concerning the education and status of artists, a major preoccupation in London during the 1760s.[114] All three feature a variety of materials considered necessary to artistic education, attest to the importance of both manual and mental skills, and address the transmission of knowledge and experience. In the case of Pratt's *American School*, too much emphasis has been placed on West, whose later prominence as teacher and public figure long obscured the autobiographical aspect of the painting. Visually, West is eclipsed, face masked in shadow, by the man in full illumination at the easel. By the internal logic of the picture, this man is the only plausible candidate for Pratt. He alone appears in the act of painting, the highest level of achievement according to the system of academic education presented in the work itself: a measured progression of drawing engravings and casts after the antique, drawing from life, and, finally, painting. Pratt himself cannot have trained in this way in America and, as a man of thirty when he arrived in London, seems unlikely to have submitted to extensive remedial education. But he hungered for the dignity and authority that such artists as Reynolds and West ascribed to the painter who had pursued a rigorous professional path. In *The American School*, a work resonant with proud authorship, Pratt constructs and condenses an imagined past.

The American School also confidently projects Pratt's future. He shows himself as West's equal, a master in his own right no longer requiring guidance. He is at once the creator of *The American School*, the would-be artist of the canvas on the easel that bears his signature, and to certain degree the subject of that canvas – an impression that time has serendipitously enhanced, since Pratt now appears silhouetted and centered against its blankness. But, as already noted, the canvas once held the outline of a woman who is not present in the studio space. Pratt's emphasis on pedagogy in this work forestalls the presumption that a portrait client sits just outside the field of vision. The artist instead conjures the figure from memory and imagination, using powers of mind, and through technical mastery gives her life on the flat surface of the canvas. He has already painted a decorative swag, a common element in portraits of the period but unlikely at this early stage of a work to be more fully realized than the principal subject. Its role in *The American School* belongs to the larger composition, balancing on the right side the arc and accented highlight of West's shoulder at the left. Significantly, the pigments displayed conspicuously on Pratt's palette do not correspond to the drapery on the depicted canvas; rather, they are the blue and green that figure prominently in *The American School* itself. The parallel spatial relationship of the depicted and actual canvases reinforces their identification with one another. In nearly every possible respect, Pratt distinguishes the seated man at the easel – himself – as creator of *The American School*.

THE AMERICAN SCHOOL

Nineteenth-century references to Pratt's painting as "School of West," "The London School of Artists," and "West's School of Painters in London" identify the work with its most famous subject and its metropolitan locale but not, or only indirectly, with America.[115] The *Catalogue of . . . the Society of Artists of Great-Britain*, however, confirms *The American School* as the original title at exhibition in April 1766. Since colonial Britons in general did not readily distinguish themselves as Americans at the time, it remains on open question whether the title was Pratt's choice or assigned by someone else. Speculation is warranted on a larger issue: what did the word American signify and to whom? Perspective mattered.

Until the eve of revolution, most white colonists of British North America considered themselves British. All shared a common monarch and many were of British descent (Copley, West, and Stuart had parents from Ireland, England, and Scotland, respectively, while Williams was English of Welsh descent). Americans contributed significantly to Britain's North American military victories – over Spain in the Caribbean, during the War of the Austrian Succession (1739–48), and over France in Canada, during the Seven Years' War (1756–63). And colonists were economically bound to Britain, avid consumers of British goods that by mid-century had anglicized colonists of diverse national origin.[116] These colonists took their cultural cues from across the Atlantic to such a degree that, as historian Julie Flavell put it, "London was the capital of America." She estimated the number of Americans in the metropolis during the late colonial period as close to a thousand persons. Most not only blended in but took for granted that they would. The largest group in London, wealthy merchants and planters from the southern mainland and West Indies, assimilated almost seamlessly with the English, much more so, by some accounts, than Scots, whose unpopularity in London soared during the prime ministry of Lord Bute in 1762–63.[117] Scots were all too readily betrayed by their accents, which many worked hard to erase. Conversely, in the opinion of a titled British visitor to the colonies in 1764,

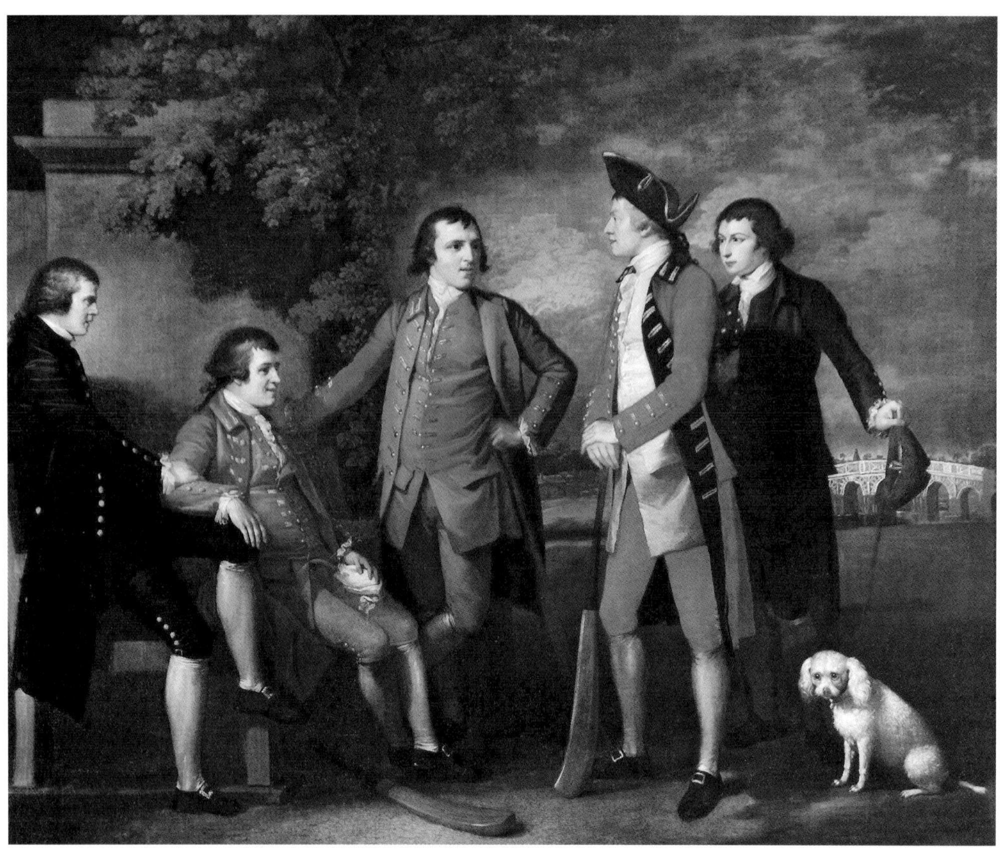

99 Benjamin West, *The Cricketers*, 1764. Oil on canvas, 40 × 50½ in. (101.6 × 128.27 cm). Private collection.

one could find in Philadelphia impressive "propriety of language . . . the English tongue being spoken by all ranks in a degree of purity and perfection, surpassing any but the polite part of London."[118] West had connections to a privileged American cohort in the capital. In a conversation-piece known as *The Cricketers* (1764), he depicted several New World elites, including two of the younger Allens of Philadelphia (from the family that sponsored his study abroad and who commissioned the painting) and Ralph Izard of Charleston, who displayed a second version of the group portrait in his London parlor (fig. 99). Among that general crowd at the time, even among those who became leading patriots, Flavell has asserted, "there is not a whisper of the development of an 'American character.'"[119]

At the same time that Americans felt themselves most fully British, they began to be seen as less so among Britons. Sensitive to a perceived change, an American newspaper contributor countered: "Are not the People of *America*, BRITISH Subjects? Are they not *Englishmen*?"[120] The concept of British nationalism remained unstable and parochial throughout the eighteenth century, with Englishness as a normative condition relative to which Scots, Irish, Welsh, and Americans could be marginalized in varying degrees and on varying terms.[121] They did not necessarily accept such marginalization, and some foresaw an eventual shift in the seat of empire to its geographical periphery in America. Scottish landowner Archibald Grant, for example, recommended investment in America, which he predicted would eventually be "the grand seat of Empire and all its Concomitants."[122] Metropolitan anxieties over the expansion of empire led to an increasing emphasis on central control and to aggressive colonial policies. The Stamp Act of 1765 roused vigorous American protest, prompting review by the British House of Commons – which heard rhetorically brilliant testimony from "Franklin, of Philadelphia" (as the witness identified himself) – and repeal in March 1766, just one month before Pratt "of Philadelphia," as the exhibition catalogue identified him, showed *The American School*. For many Britons, Americans came to be associated "with other groups over which the British state claimed authority," occupying a "midway position between fully-fledged Britons and undoubted foreigners – as fellow-subjects but not quite fellow-nationals."[123] As early as 1763, the English had begun to use the term "American" as a consistent way of differentiating its colonial population; another decade passed before the colonists were ready to adopt the term themselves.[124]

West did refer to himself as an American in a letter of 1763, reporting that he had "at last arrived at the mother country, which we Americans are all so desirous to see."[125] Perhaps he could have said "we Pennsylvanians," since his correspondent hailed from the same colony, but perhaps also he had become accustomed, while in Italy, to the terms by which he was identified on the European continent. The distinction of being American traveled with him from Italy to London, cropping up in press accounts of exhibitions at the Society of Artists, with which West quickly associated and of which he became a director in 1766.[126] It is therefore hard to imagine that Pratt and/or West did not choose the title for Pratt's submission to the Society in 1766, presenting a professional subset in West's studio and calling it (or them) "the American School." At that point, however, an American school had barely begun to take shape, so the painting is less about showing what was than about shaping perception of what might be.

In distinguishing an American school, Pratt may have wished to draw a contrast between the academy he depicted and the practice in Reynolds's studio across Leicester Square. James Northcote, who worked with Reynolds between 1771 and 1776, is the major source of information on that subject, if a somewhat self-contradictory one. Despite his respect for the artist, Northcote thought Reynolds "a very bad master in the Art."[127] "His scholars," Northcote related – referring to Reynolds's assistants, of whom there were four in 1763 (the same number Pratt showed with West) – "were absolute strangers to Sir Joshua's manner of working . . . He made use of colours and varnishes which they knew nothing of, and [they] always painted in a room distant from him."[128]

Northcote had something quite different to say about West: "West was a learned painter, for he knew all that had been done in the art from the beginning; he was exactly what is called 'the schools' in painting, for he did everything by rule, and could give you chapter and verse for every touch he put on the canvas. He was on that account the best possible teacher, because he could tell why and wherefore everything was to be done."[129] Northcote obviously found West pedantic (and developed an intense dislike of him), but he recognized that pedantry had its place.[130] His assessment of West's effectiveness as an instructor is borne out by the testimony of West's three generations of pupils. John Downman, an Englishman who studied with West from 1768 to 1770, retrospectively (after West's death) inscribed his youthful portrait drawing of his "most beloved teacher."[131] John Thomas Smith, future keeper of prints at the British Museum and an astute chronicler of the London art scene, also briefly spent time in West's studio; his statement that there were "very few artists now basking in the sunshine of patronage who have not benefited essentially by his generous and able communications" would seem to attest to West's role in the careers of many other Britons.[132] But the American-born artist is most closely associated with American pupils, who frequently referred to him as "a friend, a brother, or a father."[133] Such coupled references to a benefactor as father or friend attest to the changed model for social relations – from patriarchal to affectional paradigm – that emerged during the later eighteenth century.[134] Pratt himself used such terms in describing West's kindnesses to him but, significantly, placed himself in the paternal role. West's students found him an ideal teacher because he guided by positive example and gave them freedom to exercise their developing skills; the diversity of their production bears out his leniency. West later explicitly denounced pedagogical rigidity and efforts to introduce conformity from a platform that invited comparison with Reynolds: West's first Discourse as president of the Royal Academy, a position in which he succeeded Reynolds in 1792.[135] Directly comparing the two men, Gilbert Stuart (as recorded by one of his pupils) stated that West "was in fact to goodness what Sir Joshua seemed."[136]

As Pratt showed him in *The American School*, West plays a genial supervisory role, differentiated as the only man standing or wearing a hat. This last detail cannot signify that he has just come in from outside since he holds palette, brushes, and mahlstick, tools that suggest he has simply stepped away from an easel close by. Yet men of West's generation no longer wore hats indoors, instead placing them on wall pegs, as seen in numerous paintings of the period and in Pratt's initial version of *The American School*. (Two hats show up under ultraviolet illumination, with one above the centermost boy and the other, still barely visible to the naked eye, just above and to the left of the internal canvas.) The fact that none of the participants wear wigs can be attributed to a short-lived fashion for younger men to show their own hair.[137] Contrarily, West's hat might risk making him appear ill-mannered; at the very least, it presents a puzzle.

An explanation for West's hat arises if a viewer assumes he is Quaker, as many in England did. Quaker men often retained their hats indoors, removing them, whether inside

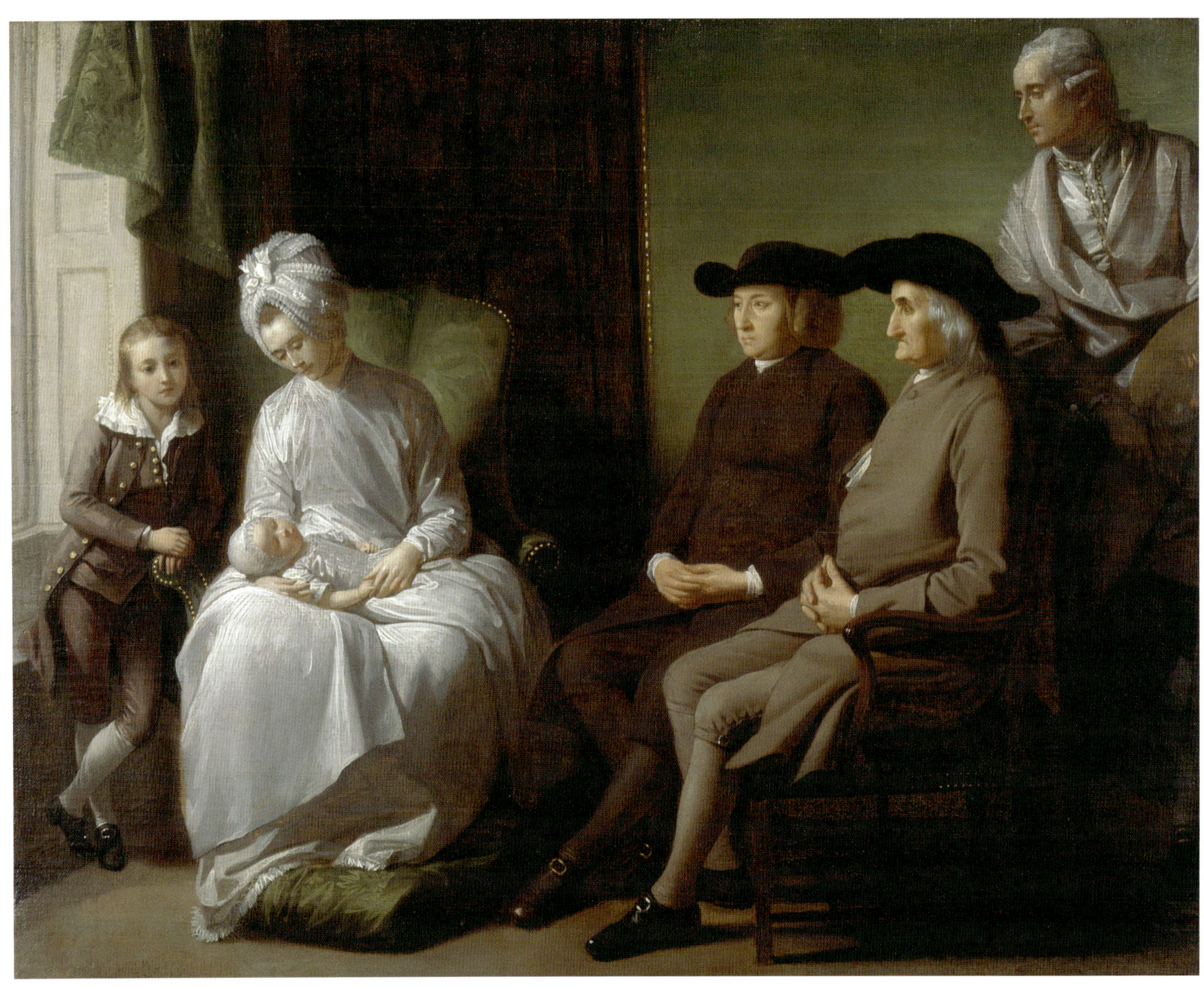

100 Benjamin West, *The Artist and his Family*, ca. 1772. Oil on canvas, 20½ × 26¼ in. (52.1 × 66.7 cm). Yale Center for British Art, New Haven, Paul Mellon Collection.

or out, for no authority except God, as when praying.[138] West drew attention to that custom and to his Quaker heritage in *The Artist and his Family* (ca. 1772; fig. 100), which simultaneously commemorates the birth of West's second son, Benjamin, Jr., reunion with his father, and introduction to his much older, English half brother (born to their father's first wife). The two Quaker men dress in keeping with Quaker commitment to material simplicity, at a time of renewed call for the faithful to avoid ornamentation and extravagance.[139] Wearing plain suits and broad-brimmed hats on their natural hair, they sit erect at the center of the composition, facing Elizabeth West, who cradles her baby while comfortably ensconced in a richly upholstered high-back chair. Mother and child are swathed in white and illuminated from an adjacent window, giving them an air of sanctity but not quite so obvious a religious or art historical reference as when West portrayed Elizabeth and their first-born son, Raphael, in the guise of the famous *Madonna della Sedia* by their son's namesake. In *The Artist's Family* – a composition with strong (but presumably unintended) resonance with *The American School* – Raphael West leans comfortably against the arm of his mother's chair, closing the composition on the left. West himself appears at the far right, holding a palette and wrapped in a light-colored banyan; his easy stance, embroidered vest and fashionably powdered wig cast him as the Quakers' antithesis. The nineteenth-century English writer Leigh Hunt, related to West by marriage, remembered seeing the artist at work in a "white woolen gown." Though Hunt believed West to be "of Quaker origin," he conceded that the Pennsylvania native "had the look of what he was, a painter to a court. His appearance was so gentlemanly, that, the moment he changed his gown for a coat, he seemed to be full-dressed. The simplicity and self-possession of the young Quaker, not having had time to grow stiff (for he went early to study at Rome), took up, I suppose, with more ease than most would have done, the urbanities of his new position. And what simplicity helped him to, favour would retain."[140]

In fact, West was not raised in the Society of Friends, in which his family had a checkered past. His mother had been shunned by the Chester Monthly Meeting prior to her marriage and her future offspring – ten children, with Benjamin the youngest – also barred from membership; West, Sr., had only returned to the faith in 1759, after his wife's death.[141] Even though Benjamin West never was Quaker, his family portrait reveals a stake in the association, something he never discouraged, as Franklin (more removed from the faith even than West) had not while on the Continent, where Quakers were held in higher regard than in England. Thus, the Prince of Parma could be charmed rather than offended when West left his hat on during an audience, since the prince assumed the young American was merely following his faith – although Galt reported that West, at the time, believed he was following English court custom.[142] Misconceptions all around. Pratt knew that West, whose Anglican wedding he had attended, was not Quaker, but possibly he encouraged the identification to evoke Quaker resistance to earthly authority, a sensitive matter in England. In the early years of the faith, Quaker theologian Robert Barclay sought to explain that Quaker refusal to doff hats to social superiors was not to upset the social order but to show proper deference to God. The message seems to have been lost on non-Quakers, who formed judgments based on what they observed.[143] West's hat in *The American School* marks West and the American school over which he and Pratt preside as fundamentally non-deferential, consistent with the general impression created by Pratt's painting of good-natured and open pedagogical exchange.

West guided his pupils in a manner that leading educational theorists of the age would have approved. The critical importance of positive example, especially parental example, dominated John Locke's *Some Thoughts Concerning Education* (1693), so popular that it was reprinted nineteen times before 1761. Even Queen Charlotte, portrayed with her two eldest sons by Allan Ramsay around 1764, saw fit to have a copy displayed beside her. Locke presented the mind at birth as a blank slate to be written on by experience. Only exposure to positive role models resulted in an autonomous and self-reasoning adult. Jean-Jacques Rousseau, the other giant in eighteenth-century pedagogy, disagreed with Locke on the possibility of educating children by reason, a faculty he considered to develop later in the maturation process. In *Émile, ou de l'éducation* (1762), Rousseau placed greater emphasis on the role of experience, arguing that children should be allowed to explore their natural inclinations, guided by the hidden hand of a wise adult.[144] Both mimicry or emulation and experiential training played a role in artistic education. And just as the child needs a good parent, so the art student most benefits from a generous teacher, a desideratum that often went unmet, judging from de Piles's warning that masters should not withhold instruction for fear of being surpassed by pupils.[145] Reynolds, for whatever reason, guarded his method, leaving his "scholars" in the dark, according to Northcote. Little evidence exists that West did the same.

Pratt's *American School* plots a course among different models of practice. By showing artists at varying stages of advancement, voluntarily associated and engaged in intimate and friendly dialogue, he celebrates a path to painting that did not lead through trade apprenticeship and contractual subjugation of apprentice to master, which he had himself experienced. Such collegiality evokes a fundamental founding principle behind the second St. Martin's Lane Academy (1735–68) – shown in an unfinished painting of around 1761, attributed to Johann Zoffany (fig. 101) – a life class to which subscribers paid an entrance fee and worked without regulatory oversight.[146] "This institution is admirably adapted to the genius of the English," wrote Swiss miniaturist Jean André Rouquet in 1755, in a book assessing "the present state of the arts in England": "Each man pays alike; each is his own master; there is no dependence."[147] That had been Hogarth's vision for St. Martin's Lane, but it was already facing challenge when Rouquet's book appeared, as the author, an acquaintance of Hogarth's, undoubtedly knew. An increasingly powerful group involved with St. Martin's Lane and, eventually, the Society of Artists (from which Hogarth resigned following its inaugural exhibition in 1761) supported founding a state academy with an institutional hierarchy and with copying at the foundation of artistic training. Insofar as Pratt showed artists copying, his painting could

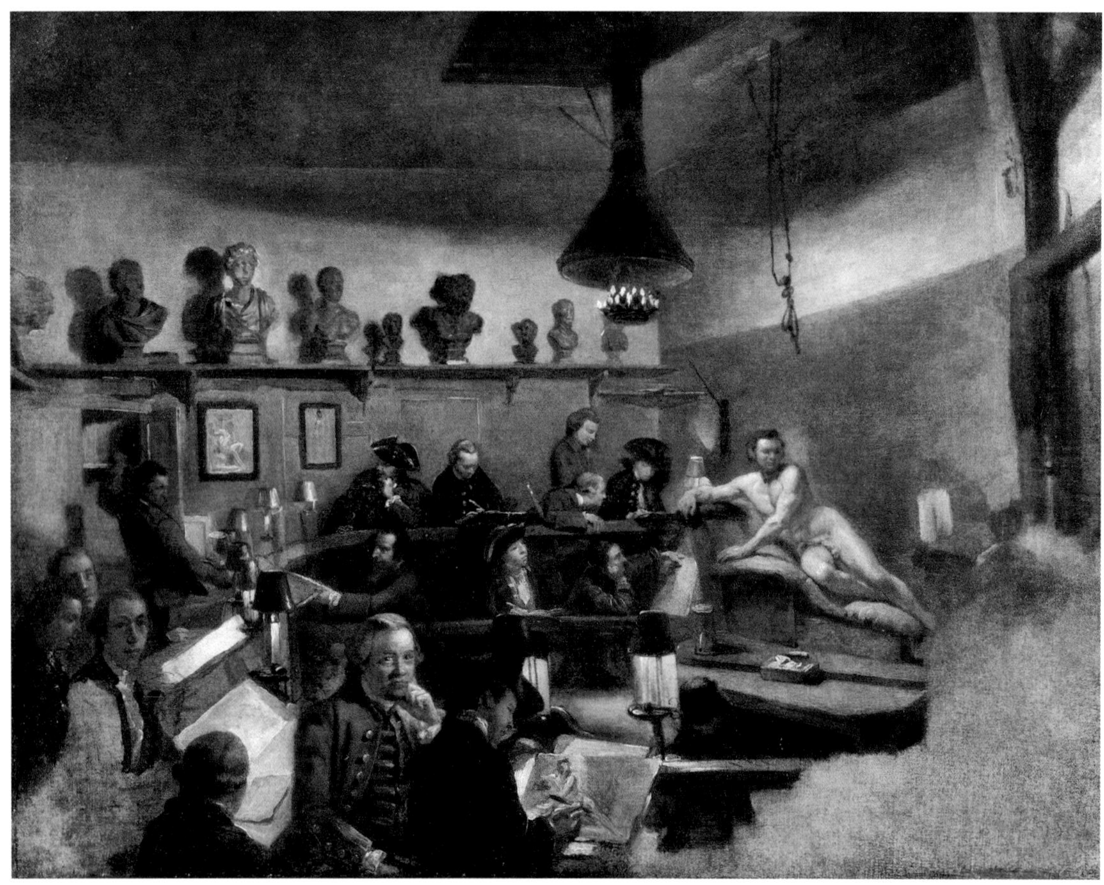

101 Attributed to Johann Zoffany, *A Life Class at St. Martin's Lane Academy*, ca. 1761. Oil on canvas, 19⅞ × 26 in. (50.5 × 66 cm). Royal Academy of Arts, London, given by William Smith, 1871.

be said to position the American school with this ascendant, continentally inclined group of British artists, a cohort that included West. Reynolds, their official leader as first president of the new Royal Academy, conveyed the degree to which he considered that institution's educational model the only one. In his first Discourse, of 1769, he stated (somewhat ironically) that its students and members had an "advantage . . . which no other nation can boast. We shall have nothing to unlearn."[148]

Reynolds exaggerated by omission. Prior to founding of the Royal Academy, St. Martin's Lane had been the established place in London for artists to work from life. West frequented the academy, just a block east of his home in Castle Street and in a quarter traditionally inhabited by artists, book and printsellers, and colormen – a panoply of artistic tradesmen.[149] He, perhaps, as a relative newcomer to London and almost certainly Pratt did not share the vehemence of Hogarth's long-time combatants in the London art world, who lost that target with Hogarth's death in October 1764, only two months after Pratt's arrival in London. Hogarth's profile had been high in their home town of Philadelphia, quite literally so at Hogarth's Head in Loxley's Court, the shop of West's former teacher Williams as of January 1763. Hogarth's prints circulated in the city, and the Library Company of Philadelphia, of which Pratt's father had been a charter member, was among the first public institutions in America to acquire Hogarth's *Analysis of Beauty*.[150] American painters showed Hogarth's treatise more respect than did the London artists who sought to marginalize him. Perhaps they appreciated Hogarth's admonition to artists: "see with our own eyes" – a particularly attractive idea to those with limited access to academically approved models.[151] West reportedly (albeit later) praised Hogarth's book as "of the highest value to every one studying the Art."[152] John Trumbull, a Harvard graduate who was unusually well read in art theory, portrayed himself with one elbow on a copy of Hogarth's *Analysis* in 1777 (fig. 102). And when Charles Peale, after study with West in London

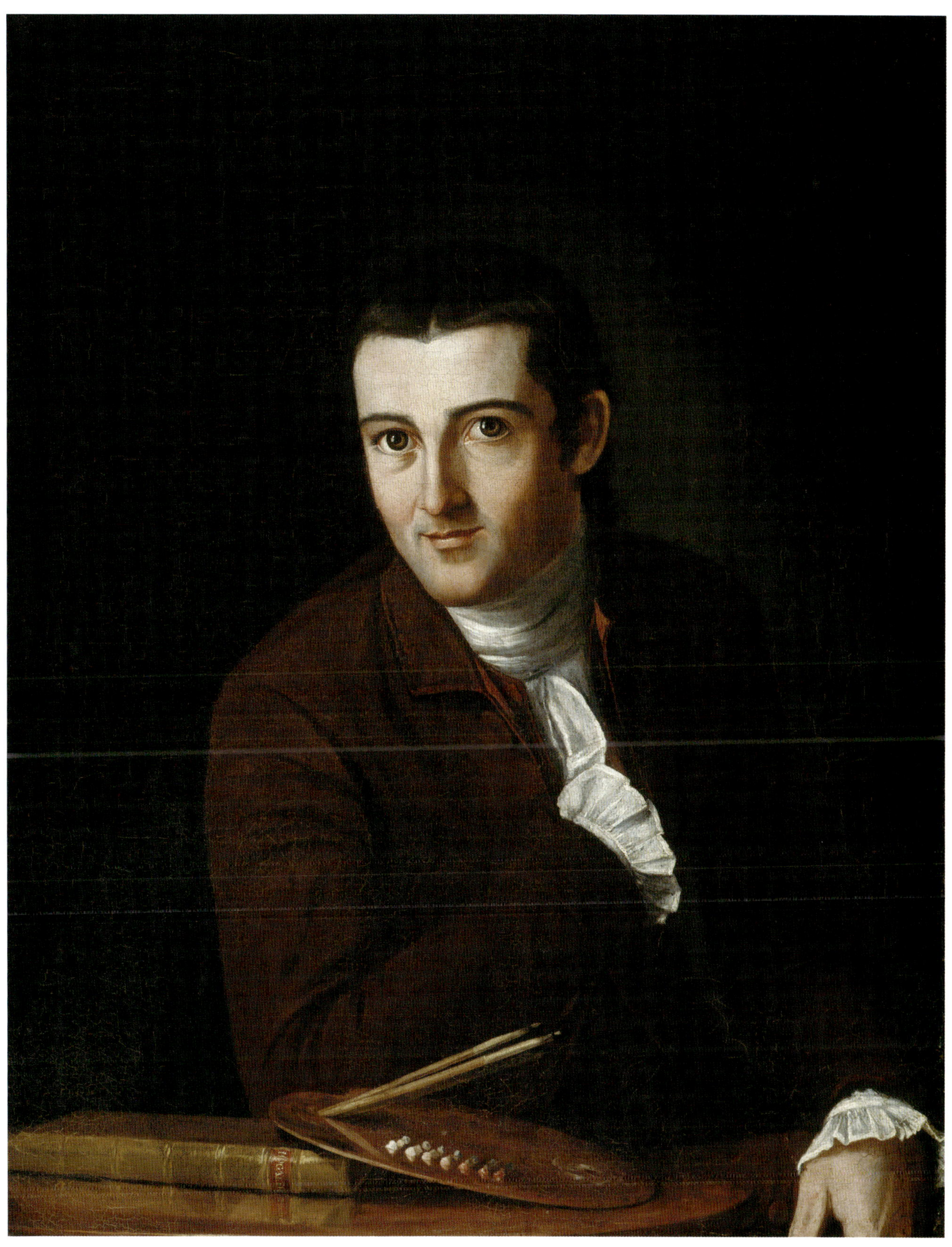

102 John Trumbull, *Self-Portrait*, 1777. Oil on canvas, 30¼ × 24⅛ in. (76.83 × 61.28 cm). Museum of Fine Arts, Boston, bequest of George Nixon Black, 29.791.

between 1767 and 1769, set out to instruct his brother St. George Peale in art, he began with Hogarth's guiding principle, the line of beauty.[153] Pratt's attentiveness to that characteristically Hogarthian device is evident in the serpentine configuration of the left-hand group in *The American School*, which enhances their sense of connectedness.

Pratt's self-portrayal on the right side of *The American School* evokes elements of Hogarth's various self-representations. His decision to frame his body against the canvas – unusual in self-portraiture – recalls Hogarth's more explicit presentation of himself as a work of art in *Self-Portrait with Pug*, in which he also introduced the line of beauty as a figure hovering above the palette, on which it casts a shadow (see fig. 60, after the painting of 1745). In his final self-portrait – its painted original and several states of engraving – Hogarth sits to the left of a fully displayed easel, on which he has drawn a muse (see fig. 87). The absence of a model is significant. Hogarth's critics presented him as a slavish imitator of nature, an easy charge to level at an artist who vigorously advocated for nature as the foundation of an artist's work and who was far more willing than others to represent the baser aspects of modern life. But Hogarth had a system of visual mnemonics, a linear shorthand by which an artist could recall to memory a figure observed in nature.[154] In notes unpublished during his lifetime, Hogarth made clear the importance that such an ability had for him: "Whoever can conceive part [of] a human figure with all its circumstances and variations when absent as distinct as he doth the 24 letters with their combinations is perhaps the greatest painter . . . than ever yet existed."[155] In his late self-portrait, Hogarth appears to do exactly that, affirming his fundamental creativity.

In *The American School*, similarly, the lack of an external referent for the figure depicted on the internal canvas gives primacy to the artist's imagination. Pratt in effect illustrates a passage from the Dryden translation of Du Fresnoy's *Art of Painting*: "At length I come to the Work itself, and at first find only a bare stain'd Canvas, on which the Sketch is to be disposed by the Strength of a happy Imagination; which is what we properly call *Invention*." Invention, the passage continues, "is a kind of Muse."[156] Using powers of invention, Pratt has sketched a figure on the canvas: the Muse herself.[157]

The muse links the participants in *The American School* to a European tradition of history painting to which many British artists of the period strongly wished to connect. In *The Choice of Hercules* (1764), West drew from that deep well, as Ann Abrams demonstrated, while also making a work that she justifiably called "one of the most profound autobiographical statements" of his career (fig. 103).[158] The painting is an allegorical self-portrait that begins to answer the question West posed in his Italian self-portrait drawing: portraiture or history? The drawing was obviously a portrait, in which the artist himself, with his Vandyke dress, embodies portraiture. In West's *Choice of Hercules*, Vice plays that role, not by resemblance but as an evocation of the vanity and "self-love" that too long prevented British artists from reaching their potential, according to a line of argumentation prevalent during the 1750s and 1760s.[159] Apollo's head at right in the self-portrait drawing represents history, as does Virtue, who directs Hercules, West's surrogate, toward Parnassus and the temple of fame – a path West manifestly chose in making this historical canvas. A few years later, West boasted to his old friend John Green (the subject of his casually sketched first artist portrait) that in electing to paint history he had "undertaken to whele [wield] the club of Hercules."[160]

Although West never exhibited *The Choice of Hercules* or his contemporaneous modern history painting *General Johnson Saving a Wounded French Soldier from the Tomahawk of a North American Indian* (1764), he boldly demonstrated his early commitment to history in submissions to the Society of Artists's spring exhibition.[161] In 1764 and 1765, he showed four canvases of literary and mythological subjects and, in 1766, two subjects from ancient Roman literature and history. Pratt was present by time of the second exhibition, at which he showed his still life, and as a guest in West's home he had access to all of the artist's early historical pictures. The new arrival from Pennsylvania and his host would surely have discussed West's commitment to history, his experience of Italy, and the role that Mengs had played in setting West on this path.

West and Mengs met almost immediately after the American's arrival in Rome in 1760, according to Galt, and Mengs asked West to provide "a specimen of his proficiency in drawing." West prepared a painted portrait instead, which Mengs judged so accomplished that he urged West to undertake an immediate study tour and then "paint an historical composition to be exhibited to the Roman public"; in this way, West could "determine the line of [the painting] profession which [he] ought to follow."[162] West's respect for Mengs is easy enough to understand, given the German's ascendancy as a history painter. Less immediately comprehensible is West's reported dislike of Batoni, who been a prolific and accomplished painter of historical subjects for two decades before Mengs even began his career

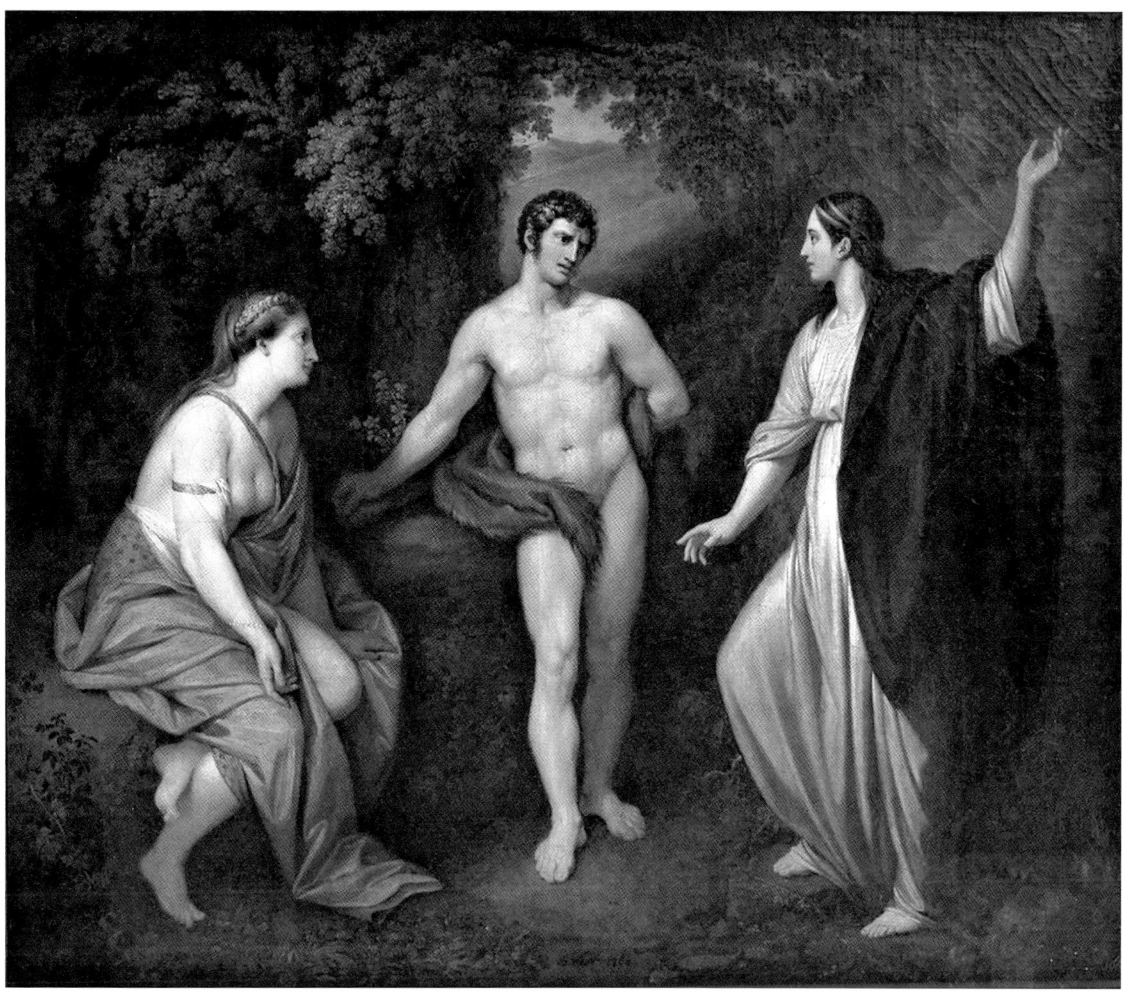

103 Benjamin West, *The Choice of Hercules between Virtue and Pleasure*, 1764. Oil on canvas, 40 × 48 in. (101.5 × 122 cm). Victoria and Albert Museum, London, bequeathed by Mrs. Harrison, 40-1886.

and who ranked as Rome's most inventive and popular portraitist after 1750.[163] Yet Englishman Thomas Robinson, in the same summer that he took West under his wing, judged Mengs superior to Batoni on the basis of their contemporaneous portraits of Pope Clement XIII. Robinson faulted Batoni for excessive attention to particularities at the expense of the whole and praised Mengs for achieving a grander effect with "force" and "Dignity" – exactly the sort of opinion to register on West.[164] In a personal encounter at Batoni's studio, the senior artist was said to have put West off when, after simply touching up a canvas, he trumpeted: "Go! young man; now you have it in your power to say that you have seen Batonni [*sic*] paint!"[165] The examples of Mengs and Batoni – positive and negative, personal and professional – helped forge West's choice. Though he did not begin his first independent historical work until 1763, two years after Mengs left for Spain, West was still then thinking of Mengs, calling him "my favorite master."[166]

The muse in Pratt's painting may allude to Mengs's *Parnassus*, a fresco of Apollo and the Muses that Cardinal Albani commissioned for the reception room ceiling of his new villa outside Rome, underway at just the time of West's arrival in 1760 and completed the following year (fig. 104). Apollo appears at the center, flanked by a muse who rests one elbow on a columnar plinth, hand to face in a gesture like that of the figure on Pratt's canvas; in her other hand, she holds an unfurled scroll. The scroll and diadem identify her as Calliope, the muse of heroic or epic poetry who by tradition crowns the poet on Parnassus, as she does in Poussin's *Parnassus*. But Apollo holds the crown in Mengs's work, so he represents Poetry while Calliope – whose scroll bears Mengs's signature – symbolizes Painting. Not only the poet but also

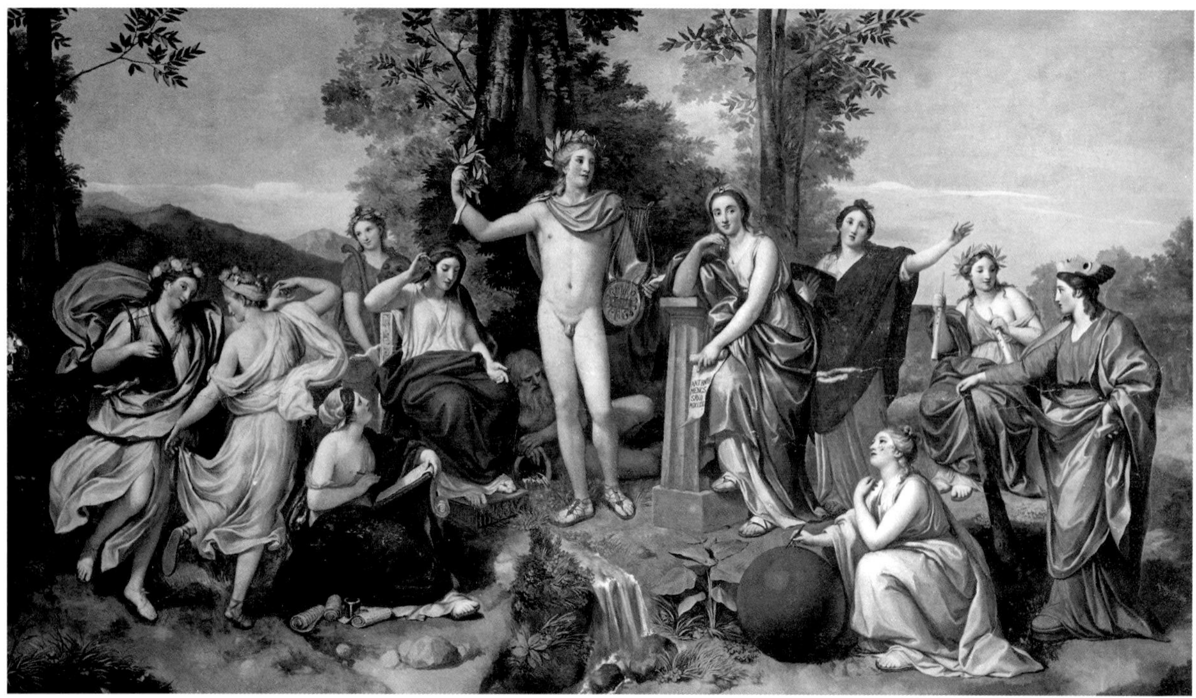

104 Anton Raphael Mengs, *Parnassus*, 1761. Fresco. Museo Torlonia, Rome / Alinari/Bridgeman Images.

the painter merits a crown on Parnassus. Mengs honors himself at the center of the work he created, a painting that visually explicates the doctrine of *ut pictura poesis*, the idea that painting, like poetry, should instruct and delight.[167]

Johann Joachim Winckelmann, Albani's librarian and an important contributor to the decorative program of the new villa, wrote of Mengs's *Parnassus*: "A more beautiful work has not appeared in all modern times; even Raphael would bow to it."[168] In his *History of Ancient Art*, published in German in 1764, Winckelmann went a step further: "The embodiment of all the beauties . . . in the figures of the ancients is found in the immortal works of Antonio Raphael Mengs . . . the greatest painter of his time and perhaps of the following age as well. He has arisen like a phoenix, as it were, out of the ashes of the first Raphael to instruct the world about beauty in art and to achieve in it the highest flight of human powers."[169] Winckelmann then hailed Mengs as "the German Raphael." Mengs agreed that Raphael was "unquestionably the greatest painter" among the moderns.[170] But this did not mean he suspended critical judgment of the Renaissance master. Raphael's art suffered from lack of familiarity with Greek art, Mengs believed, while considering himself to have the advantage in that regard. In Cardinal Albani's *Parnassus*, Mengs sought to improve upon Raphael's treatment of the same subject for the Stanza della Segnatura in the papal apartments by emphasizing sculptural over painterly values – an approach that Winckelmann had recommended to modern artists in *Reflections on the Imitation of Greek Works in Painting and Sculpture* (1755).[171] Through this act of historical rivalry, Mengs earned his inclusion in the *History of Ancient Art*.

Mengs, the German Raphael, had a New World counterpart in West, who had become "known in Italy by the name of the American Raphael," according to the title accompanying an amatory poem first published in French (from a source having nothing to do with West) and then English in the London *Public Advertiser* in 1764.[172] In West's case, as the British art historian Sarah Monks noted, "that moderation of sentiment (Raphael's characteristic quality, in contemporary discourse) and happy indebtedness to example – benefits, it was believed, of British imperial power – had flourished and become naturalized in a colonial subject."[173] Some considered the accolade premature: "until Mr. West exhibits some more striking Performances than those he has already done, surely the glorious Title of the *American Raphael* can never be, without Irony, bestowed on him."[174] Still, two years later, another poet hailed West as a "long Expected, wish'd for Stranger" in Britain, who displayed "the mystick Wonders of thy Raphael's School."[175] No artist enjoyed greater fame among West's contemporaries than

Raphael, as indicated by the market for his work. In 1758, a *Holy Family* attributed to him sold for £703.10, the highest price for any picture auctioned during the preceding half century.[176] West's choice of the name Raphael for his first child, born in April 1766, makes plain his admiration for the Renaissance master and the extent of his desire to be linked with the greatest exponent of the Italian school.

"School" in this usage identifies a group of artists less with a master than a place. Eighteenth-century English writers on art were anxious to promote the idea of an English school. "An Essay towards an English-School with the Lives and Characters of above 100 Painters" appeared at the end of the 1706 translation of de Piles's *Art of Painting*, following roughly "300 of the most Eminent Painters" of other continental schools.[177] The title page of the third English edition announced the inclusion of Sir Godfrey Kneller, the German-born portraitist who attained high status in the later seventeenth- and early eighteenth-century English courts. Kneller exemplifies the proven double threat to recognition of English artistic strength: first, the prominence in England of foreign-born painters – the essayist gamely notes that the German and Flemish schools "only excel by the performances of those masters whom we claim as our own" (Holbein and van Dyck, for example) – and, second, the long-standing dominance in England of the maligned genre of portraiture. When the Society of Arts inaugurated a prize for history painting in 1759, Samuel Johnson expressed hope that the honor "may excite an honest emulation, and give beginning to an English School," something the art of portraiture could never do.[178]

West earned his fame as a painter of historical subjects, which the title "American Raphael" also acknowledged, since it was for history painting, not portraiture, that Raphael excited greatest admiration. West's identity as both a history painter and a Briton are evident in the expressed hope, in correspondence to the *Public Advertiser*, that he would prove "the first in his Walk our Country has produced . . . unaffected with the Vanity of excelling his Countrymen" (who, in this context, can only refer to Britons).[179] At once British and American, he represented an American school that might just succeed where the English school had not in making history painting viable and, in so doing, lead British art to full respectability in the international sphere.

The word American in Pratt's title signals affirmative regionalism at a time of North America's expanding economic role in the British empire and of attendant prophecies, on the rise following the French and Indian War, of American cultural greatness. Whig political thought linked economic productivity and artistic creativity as consequences of freedom from excessive governmental restraints. Such restraints had been imposed on colonists by the British Parliament when it passed the Stamp Act, but American opposition led to its repeal. Yet this was not a period of protonationalism; instead, historians have adopted the terms "colonial nationalism" or "emulative patriotism" for the new rhetoric of Britishness among colonists.[180] Pratt's depiction of a self-regulating association of artists who are identified as American metaphorically represents a desired political as well as artistic condition. In its relationship to the mother country, as far as colonists were concerned, America was growing up. Just as America might serve as a political example to its wayward, even corrupt parent, so might it be an example – a school – in the arts.[181]

George Berkeley had anticipated such a glorious New World in his "Verses on the Prospect of Planting Arts and Learning in America," composed in 1726, published in 1752, and widely circulated in the colonial press around 1760, after the Americans had proven their importance to Britain's imperial ambitions. The poem, which contains the famous line "westward the course of empire takes its way," opens:

> The Muse, disgusted at an Age and Clime,
> Barren of every glorious Theme,
> In distant Lands now waits a better Time,
> Producing Subjects worthy Fame.[182]

The Muse – companion to Apollo, the sun god whose daily course is also westward – flees Europe "in her decay" to the site of another golden age, unburdened by "the pedantry of courts and schools," its achievements to be sung by future poets. Smibert, who joined Berkeley in his venture to establish a college in Bermuda and remained in New England when the plan was abandoned, echoed that hope. After receiving a pessimistic report from his friend, fellow artist, and art supplier Arthur Pond concerning the state of painting in London during the early 1740s, Smibert wrote: "If the arts are about to leave Great Britain I wish that they may take their flight into our new world that they may at least remain in some part of the British dominions."[183] The call continued. Philadelphian Nathaniel Evans summoned the muses to America, a land presented as fully worthy to receive them, in his poetic tribute to the "Present Greatness of the English Nation," published in 1762.[184] Evans's friend Francis Hopkinson had with greater particularity already prophesied that a "future Muse" would swell with West's name.[185] But Pratt obviously did not intend that this American school be perceived in terms of West alone as founding

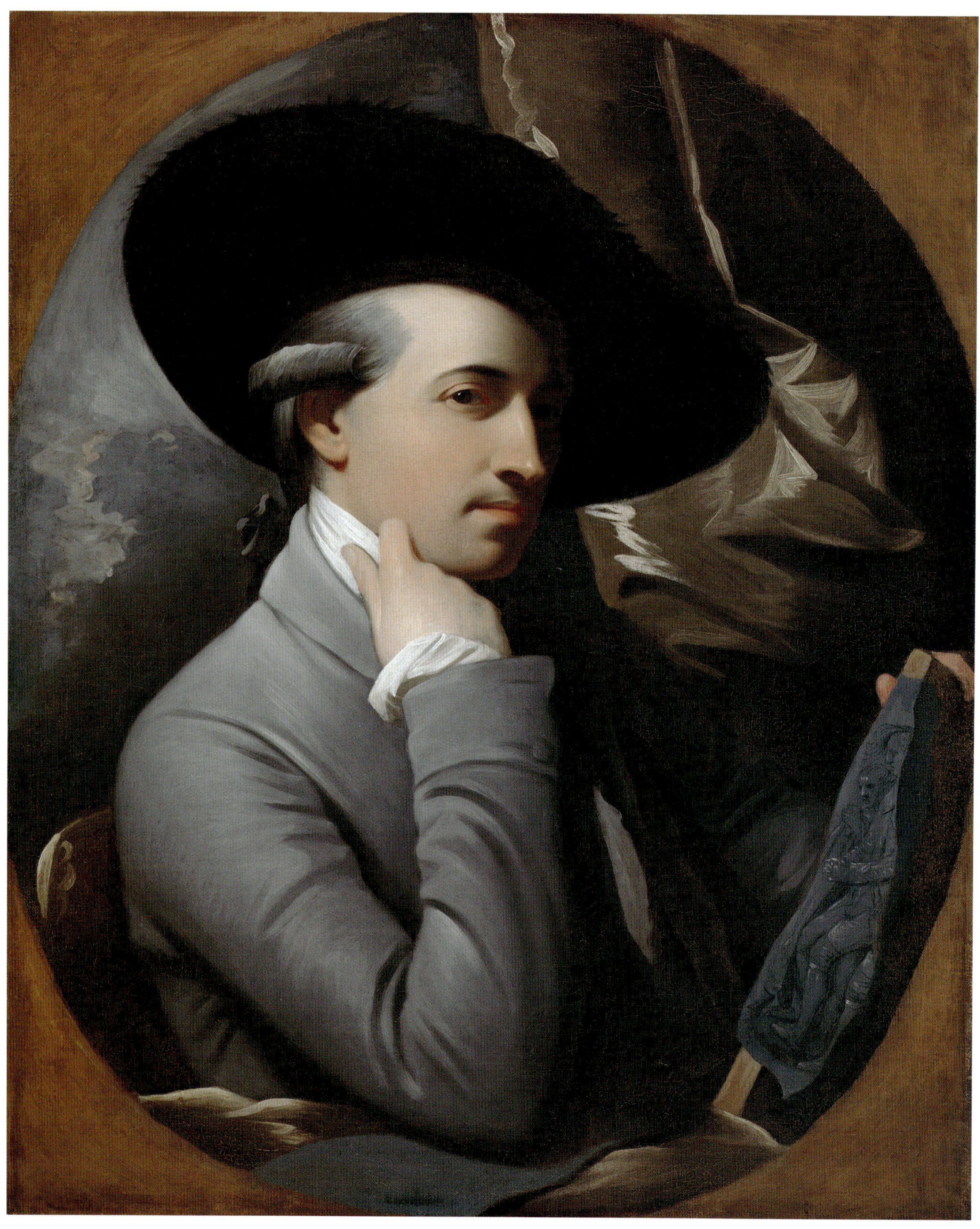

105 Benjamin West. *Self-Portrait*, 1770–76. Oil on canvas, 30¼ × 25⅛ (oval) (76.8 × 63.8 cm). Baltimore Museum of Art, gift of Dr. Morton K. Blaustein, Barbara B. Hirschhorn, and Elizabeth B. Roswell, in memory of Jacob and Hilda K. Blaustein, BMA 1981.73. Photography by Mitro Hood.

father/teacher. He identified the American school with West and himself, fellow Pennsylvanians in London. It is Pratt, not West, who communes with the Muse in *The American School*, and their relationship is symbiotic. She draws aside her veil – a convention by which Nature reveals herself to Art – to whisper in his ear even as he, inspired, creates her.[186]

✦

Pratt gave lasting visual definition to the American school in its infancy, a school in which he reserved a privileged place for himself. Caught up in London's artistic community and buoyed by his countryman West's success, Pratt may have forgotten the sometimes lonely situation of the colonial artist. Or perhaps he remembered it all too well and needed to insist on an American school that seemed to exist more fully on English soil, and even then more strongly in his imagination than in the eyes of others.

Just a decade later, Americans did begin to gain that separate identity, as thirteen British North American colonies united in rebellion against the mother country and emerged victorious as the United States in 1783. That fact did not change the culturally British orientation of most Anglo-Americans, including artists who continued to travel to the London studio of West. He readily welcomed them, though his fortunes were by then much more closely tied to Britain and to the king, whose "Historical Painter" West became in 1772.

In an undated self-portrait of around that time, West represented himself both "as an artist and as a Gentleman" – words that Copley (projecting his own sense of self) used to describe West when the two correspondents finally met in July 1774, as the Bostonian made his way from the turmoil of tea party Boston to Europe.[187] Not so obviously an artist as Pratt showed him, West might be mistaken for a gentleman connoisseur studying a drawing (fig. 105). But the figure just visible on the blue paper where it curls off the board West holds is the man with clasped hands from the right side of *The Death of General Wolfe* (fig. 106). That painting brought West to George III's attention and, in short order, won him the king's patronage and a substantial annual stipend, renewed for more than three decades. In the self-portrait, the drawing refers not only to West's success with a modern historical subject and with the monarch, but also to the high quality engraving then in preparation by William Woollett, a five-year project. Its publication made wealthy men of Woollett, West, and publisher John Boydell, and West

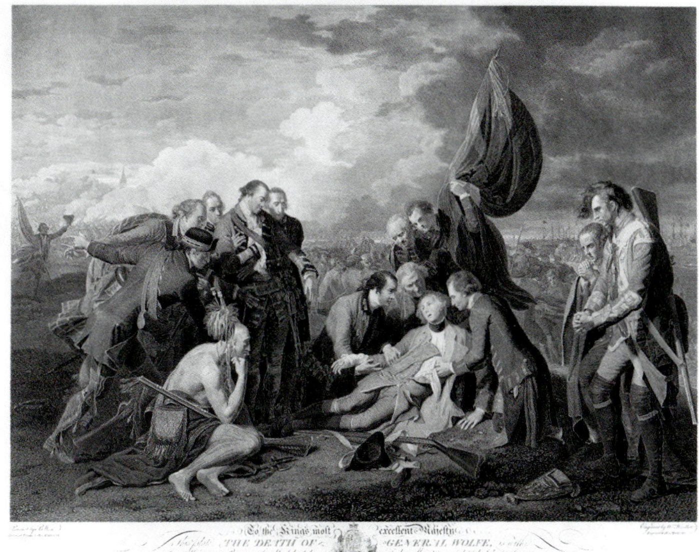

106 William Woollett after Benjamin West, *The Death of General Wolfe*, 1776. Line engraving with etching. Yale Center for British Art, New Haven, Paul Mellon Collection.

107 Peter Paul Rubens, *Self-Portrait*, 1623. Oil on panel. 33¾ × 24½ in. (85.7 × 62.2 cm). Royal Collection Trust, © Her Majesty Queen Elizabeth II, 2014/Bridgeman Images.

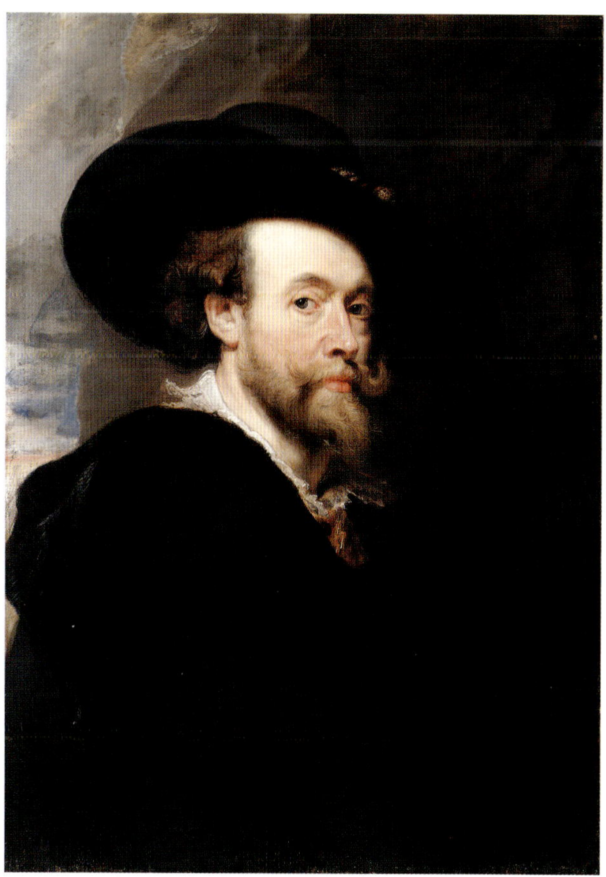

punctuated the moment by copying his self-portrait in 1776 (without bothering to delineate the figure from *Wolfe* on the drawing paper). West's self-portrait further represents him as an artist through its strong visual reference to the self-portrait that Sir Peter Paul Rubens painted for Charles I at that king's request (fig. 107). It was Charles who bestowed the knighthood on the famous Flemish artist and international courtier, as he did on Rubens's younger countryman van Dyck, whose work as court portraitist altered the course of British painting. The honorific manifestly made both artists gentlemen, a prospect that West, then only in his early thirties, must already have anticipated. (When the honor finally came, after West assumed the Royal Academy presidency in 1792, he declined it, hoping in vain for a baronetcy that would convey honor and income on his descendants as well.)

West's large hat in the self-portrait, a key point of reference to Rubens, helped to secure his identification as a gentleman. The material was beaver, as West took care to show in marking the short hairs (called wool) of beaver fur along the brim. Only the finest hats used wool felt (processed beaver skin) made from beaver alone, while less costly versions incorporated fur of other animals, such as rabbits. The high price fetched by beaver pelts contributed to over-trapping and, by 1770, harvests had fallen so precipitously that fur prices jumped.[188] West's hat was an undeniable luxury item. In other ways, too, it contributed to West's image. Beaver came from North America, a key colonial export. In 1752, beaver fur accounted for nearly half the value of all goods shipped from the colony of Pennsylvania to London.[189] The primary agents in the commercial fur trade were Indians, whose intermediaries had been both French and English until France ceded its Canadian territories to Britain, an outcome secured by the battle in which General Wolfe lost his life. So West's beaver hat all at once referred to his native colony, his native continent, its native people, and to British dominion over those lands and people.

By the time of the American Revolution, West had staked his future with the British king and British artists. Born in the colony of Pennsylvania, he had little basis for identifying with the new nation of the United States and had already shown himself open to competing representations, whether in his own self-portraits or in playing to impressions that others had of him. Given the more than four decades remaining in his life and career, it would be surprising if that process were put to rest simply by his residence in England or his maturity as a man in his later thirties. He was who he was, paradoxically. As his fortunes changed, West proved again and again that he was open to new strategies of self-representation. Finally, at nearly eighty and in the last years of his life, West found a compelling reason to promote his identity as an American and a means to do so that would endure long beyond his death, when he collaborated with John Galt on a biography of his years in America. That book, the subject of my final chapter, was the first monograph on an American artist and relatively early among biographies of British artists. In the meantime, other narratives of artists – American, British, and European – had begun to pepper American newspapers and magazines. Whether concerning artists past or present, generally factual or wholly fictional, these accounts reveal that the image of the artist, like so much else in the new nation, was subject to negotiation.

Facing page Detail of fig. 88.

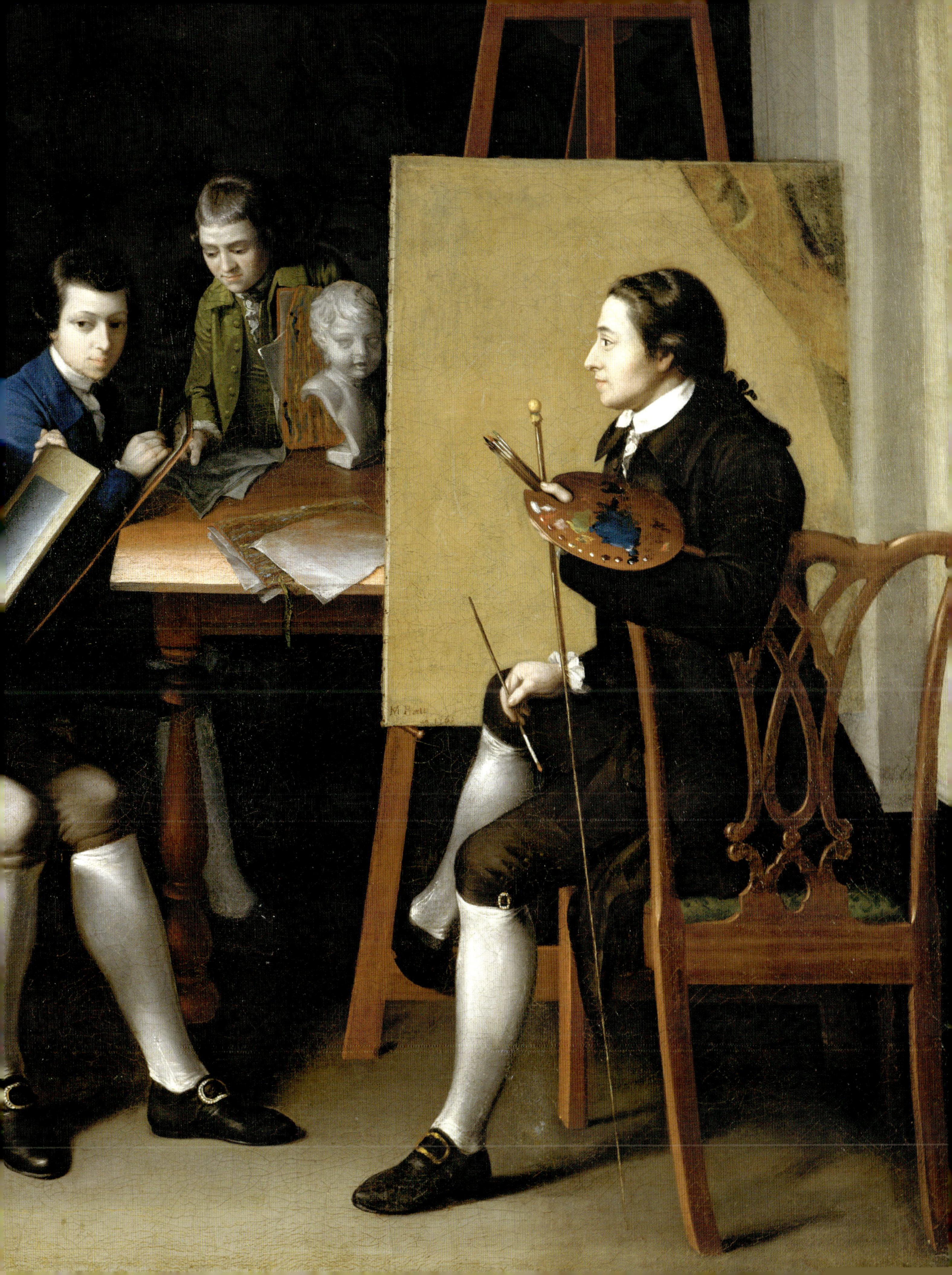

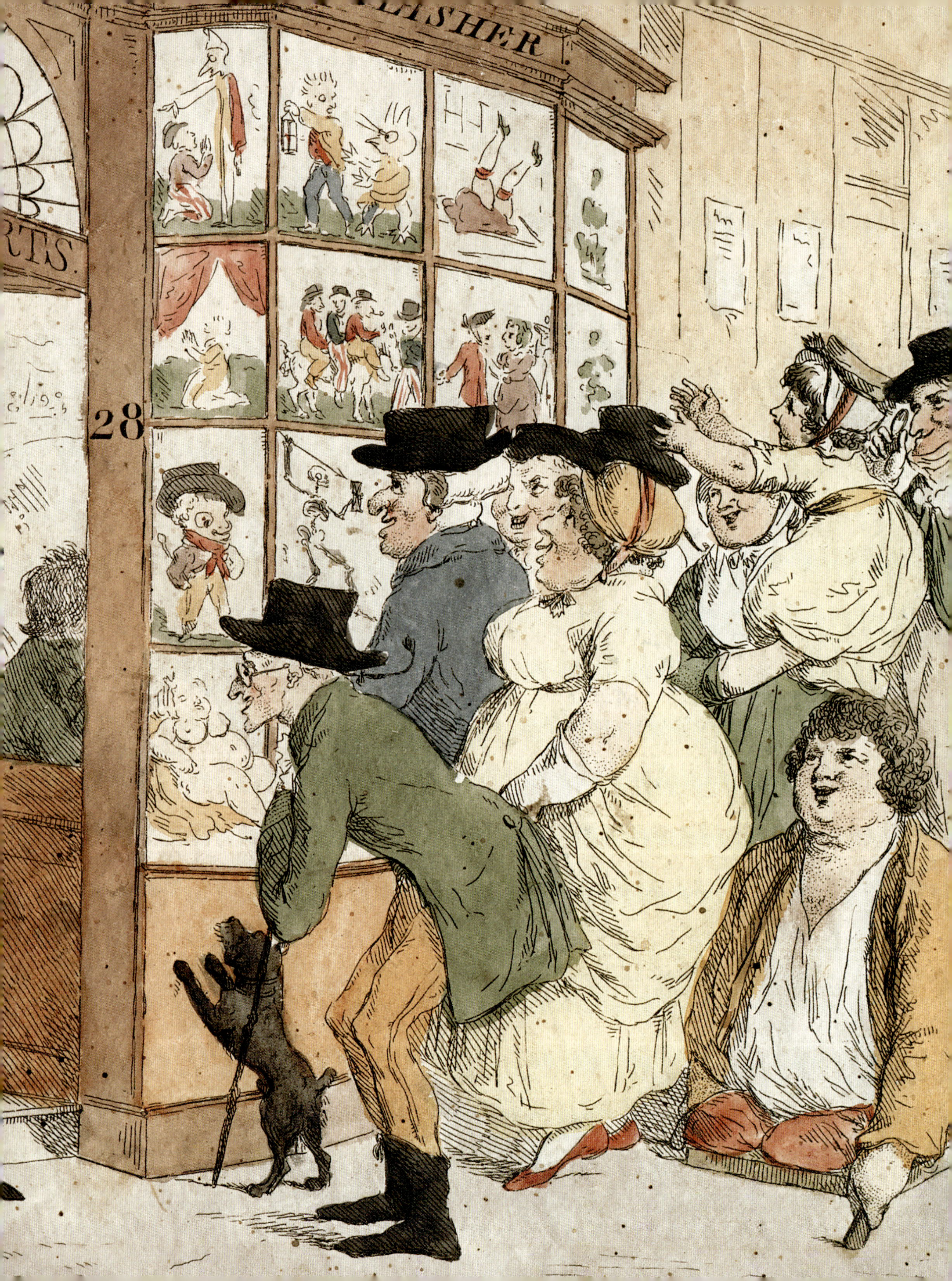
LISHER
RTS.
28

PART 2: THE EARLY REPUBLIC

4

PAINTERS IN PRINT

While most anecdotes of the lives of artists could rightfully claim no more than half truth, some could not claim any truth, as a reviewer for the London *Gentleman's Magazine* observed in 1780: "Those *connoscenti* who expect here a Bellori or a Vasari, a De Piles or a Walpole, will be disappointed. The six 'extraordinary painters' here celebrated never existed but in the author's brain, as the reader may judge by their names . . . Some ridicule on particular characters may perhaps be intended, but the meaning (if any) is much too latent for us to discover."[1]

The author under review was William Beckford, "England's wealthiest son" (in Byron's later words), raised in a Palladian country house so lavish it was known as Splendens, and at the time of the publication in question just twenty years old.[2] Possibly only a young man of such rarefied background – at once arrogant and knowledgeable – could have produced *Biographical Memoirs of Extraordinary Painters* (1780). Variant accounts locate its genesis in Beckford's ploy to provide the housekeeper of his family's Fonthill estate with (mis)information for visitors who were eager to know about the makers of paintings on display there.[3] These "squires and farmers" of Wiltshire, as Beckford recalled them, represented a broad and new non-aristocratic audience for art in Britain. From the elite perspective, they had no basis for arriving at independent judgments of aesthetic merit, relying instead on external information when forming opinions.[4] A work gained interest to the degree that the artist had been documented, just as the value of paintings in a thriving commercial art market – which eighteenth-century England then had – depended (and still does) on attributions to known artists. The more colorful the anecdotes of an artist, the better. Beckford's *Memoirs*, accordingly, parodied biographical accounts of artists' lives of the modern anecdotal type established by Vasari's *Lives of the Artists* (1550) and adapted and extended by many others. Beckford invented ludicrous situations to poke fun at trivialities found in such accounts, the textual equivalent to minutely detailed depictions of quotidian subjects by the Dutch and Flemish painters that so many in the British establishment publicly reviled. He even, as scholars have shown, lifted certain descriptive passages from existing books – the tale of Dutch painter "Watersouchy," for example, derived from a volume at Fonthill on Flemish, Dutch, and German painters – as if to demonstrate (perhaps only for his private amusement) that his fabrications were barely more preposterous than the supposed truths.[5] A recent and proximate entry in the genre of artists' lives, Horace Walpole's *Anecdotes of Painting in England* (its first volume released only in 1780), had played right into Beckford's hands, with a title that betrayed the author's mixed feelings about overstating the importance or coher-

Facing page Detail of fig. 115.

ence of his undertaking, even though the project ran to four volumes. Beckford, with tongue in check, touted the subjects of his slim volume as "extraordinary."

The cognoscenti invoked by the reviewer for *Gentleman's Magazine* would have been disappointed by Beckford's book only if they expected to learn something about real artists. Historical figures enter the narrative at intervals, but as the magazine writer noted, the fantastical names of principal characters immediately betrayed the fiction. Sucrewasser of Vienna, for example, a student of the Italian painter Insignificanti, paints bland and pretty frescos, while Blunderbussiana, a Salvator Rosa type, studies anatomy (informed by an Italian treatise on painting that says artists should do so) by dissecting victims of his banditti-chieftain father in a cavern hideout. The work so engrossed him that, even while walking in the woods in spring, "he never was without a leg or an arm, which he went slicing along, and generally accompanied his operations with a melodious whistling; for he was of a chearful disposition, and, if he had had a different education, would have been an ornament to society."[6] Beckford warped and distorted stories of artists' lives to make a risible account that allowed him to laugh at gullible and unfit judges – though it is hard to imagine that even he thought persons of any station would be truly deceived by his stories. With the ostensibly more informed audience for the book (as opposed to visitors to his house), Beckford called into question how much a reader could actually learn from supposedly authentic accounts of artists in exposing, through the refractions in his book, common biographical formulae. These include showing early signs of promise in art, discovery by a recognized artist, acquisition of noble sponsorship, demonstrations of artistic virtuosity, rivalry/competition with other artists, and establishment of artistic lineage.[7] Though contemporaneous reviewers professed bafflement (one wonders whether they were simply refusing to play along), a second printing, also in 1780, suggests that Beckford and his publisher believed a sufficient number of readers understood the joke.

When Beckford's *Biographical Memoirs of Extraordinary Painters* went into a third edition in 1834 (a second had come out ten years prior), it attracted attention in *New-York Mirror* and *North American Magazine*.[8] These notices appeared because Beckford was already famous for Gothic fiction – his novel *Vathek: An Arabian Tale* (1786), another youthful production, was reissued in 1834 as well – and because Beckford's writings from Italian travels during the 1780s (also newly republished) captured the attention of Americans for whom Italy had by that time supplanted England as cultural Mecca.[9] The nineteenth-century American commentators on Beckford's *Biographical Memoirs of Extraordinary Painters*, unlike eighteenth-century predecessors, recognized (or were willing to acknowledge) the author's satirical intent. Abundant quotations from the book – typical for reviews of the time – make clear, however, that what prompted the reviewers' interest was the "celebrated author" and "fantastic architect of Fonthill Abbey," along with his "vivid and picturesque descriptions of nature," rather than the character of artists or genres of writing about artists. Yet such reflection was newly possible in 1834, the publication year for Dunlap's anecdotally rich *History of the Rise and Progress of the Arts of Design in the United States*. Dunlap's book had been reviewed just two weeks before Beckford's in *New-York Mirror*, a periodical to which Dunlap himself contributed, and in the very same issue of *North American Magazine* that excerpted at length from the Dunlap's colorful life of Stuart, among others.[10] But readers were left to make their own connections and associations, faculties that periodicals were designed to cultivate, in opposition to the grand narratives of history.

Fifty years earlier, inhabitants of the early American republic had far more limited exposure to writing on the subject of art and artists. During the decades after independence, advertisements and short announcements placed by painters remained the most common type of printed matter concerning artists, more useful than ever as an expanded range of techniques and practitioners opened a portrait market formerly dominated by elite patrons and the favored painters who served them. Makers of widely divergent skills both fueled and met the new demand. Fanning across the country, they placed notices that beckoned patrons at almost all economic levels with the promise of inexpensive, quickly produced likenesses.

Only a narrow spectrum of readers had access to British and continental books on art theory, which have been documented in colonial and early national era libraries (most of which were private) and among the offerings of booksellers (usually in major cities).[11] The elevating statements about art and its place in the life of a nation that made their way into print in Britain, with Sir Joshua Reynolds's *Discourses* as the preeminent later eighteenth-century example, had almost no counterparts in the United States before around 1810 and barely even then.[12] Establishment of art organizations – the American Academy of Fine Arts in 1802, the Pennsylvania Academy of the Fine Arts in 1805, and the National Academy of Design in 1825 – eventually provided a platform for such oratory and attendant publications, while the exhibitions these groups staged gave rise to commentary and eventually to a fledgling art criticism. But that had little vigor before the later 1820s, when the often conflicting programs of two organizations in New York City (as had been the case in London during the 1760s) provided real fodder for their spokesmen and critics.

This chapter initially takes up less programmatic types of writing, starting with anecdotes about artists that began to appear in American magazines, publications addressed to a broad readership of women and men. These anecdotal passages have been easy to overlook owing to their sporadic appearance and seemingly inconsequential character. Nevertheless, the fact that they did appear begs for contextualization and explanation. The same holds true for satirical writing that used the personae of artists or artistic practices to carry the message, also relatively rare. Philip Freneau and Hugh Henry Brackenridge – collaborative authors of "A Poem, On the Rising Glory of America" (1771), an exercise in colonial nationalism composed for their Princeton graduation – each employed metaphors of art to make social and political points during the early republic. Leaders of a new generation of American authors, they have attracted as much attention from literary scholars as any writers among their generally neglected eighteenth- and early nineteenth-century cohort, and I will not retrace recent and effective arguments about the place they gave portraiture.[13] My focus for most of chapter four is a less visible writer, newspaper editor Harry Croswell, who – to press a political agenda – used the pseudonym "Peter Pallet," the setting of a portraitist's studio, and the form of letters to the editor. Titled "The Limner" and published between 1804 and 1807 in the *Balance*, a Federalist weekly, Croswell's series of texts present rare sustained engagement with an artist, real or imagined. The fictive portraitist would have had no power as a medium had not anecdotes, advertisements, and the geographical circulation of artists in the United States made them by that time widely familiar.

Anecdotes

Detached anecdotes of artists in magazines reached a far broader spectrum of eighteenth- and early nineteenth-century American readers than did the books on art and art theory found in American libraries or the occasional bookstore. "Urbanus Filter," the editorial persona of Benjamin Mecom (Franklin's nephew), had declared the advantage of periodicals over books in the opening issue of *New-England Magazine*, an early example of the form. Magazines "diffuse Good Sense through the Bulk of a People," he wrote. "Knowledge, instead of being bound up in Books, and kept in Libraries and Retirements, is *thus obtruded* upon the Public; when it is canvassed in every Assembly, and exposed upon very Table," reaching "Persons of all Conditions and of each Sex."[14] Early periodicals fulfilled their broad purpose through miscellany and variety, signaled by the word "museum" in the title of several or the word "magazine" (i.e., storehouse) itself, adopted by the first and unusually enduring such publication, *Gentleman's Magazine* of London, founded in 1731. The "motley and cacophonous" quality was deliberate, as literary scholar Jared Gardner compellingly argued in his study of early magazine culture, at once expressive and constitutive of modern social interactions and Romantic subjectivity: "the fragment, the disjunction, the refusal of totalizing narratives and dominant univocal authorship alone can provide room for the reason and imagination of the individual reader to create new knowledge, to complete the conversation that the periodical seeks to inaugurate."[15] The anecdote and the seemingly haphazard early periodical were in this sense perfectly matched.

Anecdotes of artists had a long history, on which the humor of Beckford's *Biographical Memoirs* had depended. But his parody was also absolutely of his time, part of the wider vogue for anecdotes that took hold during the last third of the eighteenth century in Britain, when some one hundred printed books alone featured the word in their title.[16] Samuel Johnson had initially defined anecdote – derived from the Greek word meaning "things not given out" – as "something yet unpublished; secret history," but he soon acknowledged its newer connotation as "a minute passage of *private life*" within published biography.[17] James Boswell, Johnson's biographer, knew full well that his subject loved anecdotes and declared it his task to record the "innumerable detached particulars" of Johnson's own life, leaving readers, present and future, to determine which were important.[18] In so doing, Boswell helped establish the modern form of anecdotal biography.

Anecdotes acquired an early theorist in Isaac D'Israeli, the English author of *A Dissertation on Anecdotes* (1793), a book composed to elucidate "in what manner any topic may be enforced, or illustrated, by anecdotes."[19] As a contemporaneous reader might have anticipated, he asserted the power of judiciously selected and well-crafted anecdotes to reveal the character of men and their times. With greater originality, D'Israeli argued for anecdote writing as a literary art requiring its own kind of genius (though he does not probe "the manner in which any single anecdote may be given"). "A skilful writer of anecdotes," he proposed, ". . . make[s] something that looks like a discovery of our own; he gives a certain activity to the mind, and the reflections appear to arise from ourselves."

D'Israeli had demonstrated this basic tenet of the anecdote in the two sketches of painters he chose for the first edition of *Curiosities of Literature, Consisting of Anecdotes, Characters, Sketches, and Observations, Literary, Critical, Historical*, published in 1791. The first example highlighted artistic rivalry, skill, and individuated mark making with an account of painterly one-upsmanship in ancient Greece. Visiting the studio of Protogenes in his absence, Apelles marked a line, which Protogenes, knowing full well who had made it, then divided in counterdemonstration of his own skill. After Apelles subdivided that line, once again unobserved, Protogenes conceded his artistic superiority.[20] D'Israeli piqued the reader's curiosity by introducing the ancient anecdote with a reference to modern times: "Imagine that when our Cosways visit each other, if it happens that their friend is not at home, they are incapable, by the perfection of their art, to leave any peculiar beauties behind them, of which a Connoisseur could say – "Certainly *Cosway* has been here to-day; for who but *Cosway* could express this line, or infuse this grace!" The meaning of this remark is not immediately clear. Only when a reader has digested the story of Apelles and Protogenes does the frame come into any focus – and only for the reader who knows that the name Cosway refers to the married painters Richard and Maria Cosway. They presented an easy target; in a farce published in 1786, the satirist Anthony Pasquin lampooned Richard by naming him "Tiny Cosmetic," a play on Cosway's dandified appearance and his engagement in the feminized medium of miniature painting.[21] In D'Israeli's formulation, however, "Our Cosways" stands for all modern British painters. In pairing this preamble with the anecdote from antiquity, D'Israeli implies that British painters let vanity and petty jealousy stand in the way of healthy rivalry, in subtle articulation of a theme that writers like Pasquin and Peter Pindar, whom D'Israeli knew well, used as a bludgeon.[22]

A briefer, second anecdote in *Curiosities of Literature* also engaged the reader, though without contemporary preamble. D'Israeli related that Raphael once portrayed a feverish man with such truth that a doctor was able to diagnose the subject's illness after seeing the likeness. (The anecdote would be revived for Gilbert Stuart, who was said to have detected madness in the face of a man who later went insane.)[23] Readers may question the tale, but anecdotes need not be true to be telling. As D'Israeli stated in *Dissertation on Anecdotes*, "anecdotes are not always facts" but satisfy their purpose if they are revealing of the individual or the type, as in the case of anecdotes about artists.[24] His anecdote of Raphael acknowledged the remarkable powers that great artists may possess, but through an incident that permits identification by a reader – perhaps a woman – who has diagnosed fever in someone oblivious to it himself, such as the man who sat for his portrait when he should have been lying in bed. For D'Israeli, anecdotes crafted by a writer of genius activate the reader, arousing his or her subjectivity. The writer draws the reader into a kind of conversation, as D'Israeli demonstrated with his anecdotes of artists from *Curiosities of Literature*. Anecdotes also bring the reader into company with their object, typically great men (rarely women) who become more accessible when loosed from grand narrative, then being shaken up by a variety of new literary forms, not least the "novel."[25]

In affirming the value of anecdotes to biography in *Dissertation on Anecdotes*, D'Israeli offered an extended example from the life of Milton, as presented in 1734 by Jonathan Richardson and his son, who made thoughtful use of anecdote to show how in Milton's case "genius is not above the little consolations of humanity."[26] When writing about art and artists, as he so often did, Richardson, Sr., had the opposite task. Pressing for the dignity of English painters, as distinguished from artisans, he maintained they must think as gentlemen, meaning that they must show themselves capable of abstracting from experience, a task especially daunting for portraitists for whom particularities of individual sitters grounded the enterprise.[27] For D'Israeli, similarly, the biographer who successfully composes and uses anecdotes must "possess a portion of that genius which he records"; otherwise, he is a "mere antiquary" who cannot rise above triviality. Still, D'Israeli believed that "peculiarities" belonged in life writing. In *Dissertation on Anecdotes*, his sole anecdote concerning a painter makes that important point. Poussin, the famous seventeenth-century French artist (in an anecdote from the painter's friend Marville), collected stones, moss, flowers, and other objects from nature so as to represent them. When asked how he became such a great artist, Poussin replied: "*I have neglected nothing*." The particular undergirds the general, making history come alive and granting points of access to greatness for the reader/observer.

The anecdote of Poussin – a perfect expression of the anecdote writer's charge – was included in a lengthy and uncredited excerpt from D'Israeli's book published in 1806 in *Literary Magazine, and American Register*. Editor Charles

Brockden Brown forthrightly declared his publication to be "an American Review"; still, he found D'Israeli an apt spokesman for his own larger enterprise of providing useful knowledge on a variety of subjects. "The most unconnected anecdote may be advantageously employed," the selection in *Literary Magazine* stated, with regard to the writer's practice. But Brown directed the words at readers of his miscellany: "The works of amusement must relieve those of learning . . . it is therefore as dangerous . . . to read romances as it would be not to read them."[28] Just like the anecdote that destabilizes the authoritative account, Brown, as writer and editor, declined to offer readers the quick or easy judgment. Instead, he recognized writing and reading as a kind of collaboration, in which, at best, the reader is engaged and encouraged to make his or her own meaning – part of the critical exercise of being an independent people and more necessary than ever with the advent by 1800 of divisive party politics in the United States. When reprinting from another of D'Israeli's works, "Remarks on Reading," Brown appended original remarks in the same vein: "One ought not to see everything distinctly, but only certain parts of it; the imagination properly supplies the intermediate links."[29]

Confronted with anecdotes of artists, American periodical readers had a limited supply of "intermediate links" on which to draw. Anecdotes of historical artists lost some of their leveling gratification in a country where such names were less familiar and where artists as a class long held depressed social status. The fact that the subjects of anecdotes in American publications often went unnamed or were quite obscure suggests that they were intended to stand for all artists. Here, D'Israeli offers a useful perspective. In his preface to *Dissertation on Anecdotes*, the British author challenged Johnson's definition of anecdotes in relation to biography as too narrow. Anecdotes ought also to be considered as "interesting particulars. . . . of the art as well as the Artist; of the war as well as the General; of the nation as well as the Monarch."[30] Strikingly, at a late point in his book, D'Israeli included a short section (also reprinted in *Literary Magazine*) on the value that anecdotes of artists might have for artists, in offering "instructions" of value to an artist's own "labours," a more practical and particularized role for anecdotes than he otherwise advanced.[31] The Poussin example belongs to a type that might conceivably serve such a purpose, but it is not representative of anecdotes about artists that appeared in American publications just before and after 1800.

One recurring type of anecdote suggests that interaction with portraitists, a newly common American experience, raised a low level of anxiety among patrons. Historically, the lesser status of makers relative to those who commissioned likenesses had given clients the upper hand. Those positions began to shift in the increasingly democratic United States. Portraiture lost its former class exclusivity, and portrait painters in particular (as opposed to silhouette cutters or other kinds of makers) gained a measure of respect, boosted by the cosmopolitan experience and international success of a select few in the expanding American artistic community. Perceptions of enhanced social authority on both sides of the easel intensified negotiations between sitters and artists. Anecdotes captured that new reality. *New York Weekly Magazine*, in 1796, recounted the threatened retaliation by "William Lilly" against a rich London sitter who disliked his portrait and refused to pay for it. The painter (Sir Peter Lely, court portraitist to Charles II) assured the man that he could find another buyer who would pay double, were he only to paint a tail on the sitter's body, thereby producing "the best piece for a monkey in England."[32] A similar account, concerning an unnamed painter, had appeared four years before in the New Jersey *Christian's, Scholar's and Farmer's Magazine*, its title indicative of the characteristically diverse population that most American magazines editors sought to engage.[33] This kind of story ought not to have had any traction in America, where portraitists' advertisements often assured prospective patrons that those who were dissatisfied need not pay. Yet mere admission of this scenario raised the specter of dispute and reprisal. Strikingly, anecdotes about revenge appeared in American journals even in connection with artists who were not primarily portraitists, as in accounts of Orcagna, the fourteenth-century Florentine fresco painter, and of Michelangelo, both of whom were said to have represented foes among the damned in paintings of the Last Judgment.[34]

Often, anecdotes portrayed artists as a special class of person. Their powers might be presented as innate, recognizable through a specific action on their own parts (as with Apelles and Raphael in D'Israeli's examples) or through the recognition granted by powerful others. According to an anecdote published in *Massachusetts Magazine* in 1794, the Spanish Emperor Charles V lavished so many honors and income on "a celebrated painter" that his courtiers became jealous. The monarch rebuffed them, saying "he had many Nobles in his empire and but one Titiano." Overhearing the compliment, the artist bowed and dropped his pencil, which the emperor picked up, adding "*that, to wait on* Titiano, *was a service for an Emperor.*"[35] In another version, for the Boston magazine *Omnium Gatherum* – a name indicating miscellaneous content – the protagonists are Henry VIII and Holbein. A nobleman who insists on interrupting the artist at work and finds himself pushed down the stairs demands the painter's life, but the king refuses: "I can, whenever I please, make seven lords of seven plowmen, but I cannot make one Holbein of even seven lords."[36]

American-born painter-turned-auctioneer John Greenwood had placed this anecdote in service of modern British artists in a 1787 auction catalogue, where it footnoted introductory remarks touting the "revival of the Arts" in Britain. That introduction was defensive and self-serving, since Greenwood's sale largely comprised Old Master drawings, which the auctioneer presented as collectables that had stimulated and would continue to aid "the rising generation."[37] An anecdote of one member of that rising generation, George Morland (1763–1804) – published in an American magazine after Morland's premature death, by which time he was well known – drew attention to the idea of the struggling English artist and to the notion that even truly humble works might be marked with distinction. The impecunious Morland had arranged to settle his debt at the Black Bull inn by painting a new sign to replace "the disgraceful daub" then in place. A few weeks later, a gentleman passing through the village recognizes it as "the production of that inimitable painter" and pays the landlord £20 for the sign, which subsequently brings one hundred guineas at auction.[38] Nineteenth-century valuation of the artist's hand no matter the work, coupled with belief that genius made itself known in juvenilia (topics for consideration in connection with Stuart and West in chapters five and six) led artists themselves to claim involvement in the humble practice of painting signs. In 1807, West told a Pennsylvania visitor to London that during his youth he had painted a sign of a drove of oxen at Lancaster.[39] A mere twenty years earlier, when fine artists had not long shed the taint of labor, few would have made such an admission. For West, it was more remarkable still, given his role as Royal Academy president and his frequent position at the bull's eye for British satirists.

Satire

If anecdotes gave readers interpretive latitude, satire did not. Widely employed by British and American writers of the eighteenth century for political ends, this sharper form also addressed artists, whose patrons and institutional affiliations necessarily embroiled them in politics, especially in London. There, vigorous satirical writing arose from a context that had no eighteenth-century American counterpart: the annual exhibitions by various art organizations beginning in the 1760s. The Society of Artists had a parodic double in the 1762 "Sign Painter's Exhibition," communicated less through artifacts in the show than by texts about it (newspaper notices and catalogue). Not surprisingly given association with the crown, Royal Academy exhibitions attracted greatest attention, satiric and otherwise. The most prolific satirists were "Peter Pindar" (John Wolcot), who published a series of "Lyric Odes to the Royal Academcians" during the 1780s, and "Anthony Pasquin" (John Williams), whose unsparing "critical guides" to the exhibitions appeared in the following decade. Pasquin's opening salvo was a mock, unfinished play, published in 1786 as "The Royal Academicians: A Farce." Bearing an invocation to St. Luke, "Patron of Painters . . . and Protector of Harp Alley" (center of the sign painting trade), the work opened old wounds by raising the specter of undignified labor against members of the Academy. A long list of dramatis personae included "Sir Varnish Dundizzy" (Reynolds, who over varnished his paintings in pursuit of an Old Master look), "Benjamin East" (a reorientation undercutting West's American distinction), "John Singleton Copperface" (a reference to his exploitation of engraving as a promotional tool, among other interpretive possibilities), and "Charles Coachpannel, Esq." (an ironic use of the gentleman's honorific for Charles Catton, designated "House Painter to the Royal Academy" and, in evident contradiction of the Academy's principles, a member of the organization himself).[40] Most of the characters, including "East" and "Copperface" never appear; the publication ends with the first act, but not before "Tiny Cosmetic" (dandified miniaturist Richard Cosway) flatters "Sir Varnish" that "compared with [his] works, Vandyke was a sign painter, Titian a housedauber, and Sir Godfrey Kneller an old woman."[41] Pasquin showed no such mercy to West. "His best labours," the satirist commented, ". . . appear to me but as the happiest efforts of a Sign Painter of the first order."[42] Such words stung, but elite British painters were so protective of their status that they used even bolder language to describe the artist manqué. In conversation with Samuel Johnson, Reynolds made an unseemly jab at his own niece, Theophila Palmer, an amateur painter: "she might paint signs as the man did who was employd to paint the red Lion. He dip'd his dog in Blood and then dab'd him upon the Board and so got the drawing."[43] The Academy president's willingness to exaggerate the crudity of sign painting suggests the degree to which trade still impinged on the image of the refined artist.

Pindar and Pasquin did not mince words when it came to West, and that may have been enough to inhibit reprints or commentary on their writings on art by American magazines, which otherwise frequently borrowed from British publications and did so for several accounts of West after 1800 (examined in chapter six).[44] But exhibition commentary of any kind – nascent in Britain during the last third of the century – had little resonance in a nation without art exhibitions. Perhaps that helps explain why Pasquin/Williams, a former Royal Academy student and portraitist in Ireland, wrote nothing about art and artists during a residence of seven years (1798–1805) in the United States, to which he moved to avoid legal expenses arising from an unsuccessful libel suit. His silence is striking since he worked as an itinerant portraitist in North America, was acquainted with Dunlap in New York (where both men were involved with theater), and served as editor for several short-lived newspapers.[45] In the latter context, however, he engaged with politics, first in sympathy with Federalists and then with Jeffersonian Republicans.[46]

The opportunity to view political affairs through the scrim of art that Williams declined was taken up by others. In a lightly satirical essay, Francis Hopkinson – lawyer, musician, composer, writer – addressed how the arts and sciences might be extended "beyond the limits of their professed objects, . . . to other purposes than those for which they seem directly intended." While this was not a radical idea, the mutually reinforcing disciplines are here unexpected: portraiture and "Surveying," the publication title in 1792 for a piece likely written eight years earlier.[47] At a time of increasing public concern for truth in likeness, Hopkinson anticipated the satisfaction soon to be widely afforded by mechanically produced physiognotrace portraits when he presented a mock scheme for bringing "a *mathematical* certainty" to the inexact art of portraiture. In the persona of a surveyor, he describes how "a man may, in the division of his estate, so contrive it as to leave his likeness in a tract of land." Hopkinson's target, according to literary scholar Paul Zall, was George Bryan, "political boss of Pennsylvania," whom Hopkinson often opposed, though Bryan appointed him judge of the Admiralty Court for a seven-year term beginning in 1780, a judicial post that also placed him on the state's supreme court and in other offices.[48] Bryan, Zall noted, had designed the state constitution to give his party control of the assembly, essentially "shaping Pennsylvania in his own physiognomy" (or better: his image, since the meaning is metaphorical). That manipulation prompted Hopkinson's comic essay. A man who wishes to secure his legacy, Hopkinson relates, will start by having his profile traced, following a "familiar and well known practice" (which originated in the ancient story of the Corinthian maid). On that basis, "courses and distances" can then be established for marking out his land, allowing an heir, years later, to reverse the process, surveying "his ground and his grandfather at one and the same time." When plotted on paper, descendants would have their ancestor's "whole resemblance," in palpable demonstration of the "the family line in operation," to borrow art historian Margaretta Lovell's characterization of the primary function of eighteenth-century American portraits for families with "inheritable substance."[49] Hopkinson drew the putative portrait that resulted from the undertaking, a caricature of Bryan, with lettered topographical coordinates that refer to the essay, including C for the "foul ditch" (mouth) and D for the "elliptical hollow . . . very moist and unctuous: and fit for the cultivation of Tobacco" (nostril).

If Hopkinson more boldly delineated his political bent in other writings that did not take the frame of art, others more directly linked portraiture and politics. Philip Freneau's "The Picture Gallery," a short tale published with a miscellany of his writings in 1788 (he was by then a well-known poet), drew attention to worrisome civic consequences arising from the commercialization of portraiture. The narrator stops in "a country town," where he visits an artist with his gallery of "half-finished faces" – at once a reference to amateurish execution and a metaphor for the sitters' unpolished characters.[50] An apparently "honest shoemaker" and a "harmless taylor," among others, inquire about having portraits made, on claims of their "great share in accomplishing the American Revolution." After learning that they stole leather and cloth from the army, the painter reconsiders the commission, prompting the tailor to offer "no less than forty guineas as the purchase of immortality." A bystander then proposes "that the picture should be drawn and hung up in the gallery, provided that a naked soldier, perishing with cold, was added to the piece in one corner of the background, and a gallows with a ladder, and a rope suspended from it in the other." Freneau conjures the Renaissance type of the emblematic portrait, with symbolic imagery in the upper corners, a tradition to which Thomas Smith's late seventeenth-century self-portrait (see fig. 4) belongs and which Freneau may have known through prints. Without question, he draws on anecdotes of how painters could retaliate against sitters – with the twist that a conscientious citizen proposes the action and the painter is himself suspect. If gauging a man's virtue had become challenging even in his presence, his static representation in a portrait compounds the difficulty. On the eve of rebellion against Britain, Freneau had extolled the "rising glory of America," but independence opened great possibilities and dangers. As literary scholar Christopher Lukasik has argued in a compelling study, Freneau – a future Jeffersonian Republican committed to democratic principles – worried less about the social mobility of Americans than about the possibility that wealth might overtake virtuous and disinterested conduct as a basis for public distinction.[51]

For Hugh Henry Brackenridge, Freneau's contemporary, physiognomic discernment held the possibility of countering political dissimulation. The practice of reading faces for evidence of character became widely popular by 1800. Brackenridge feared that most gauged character through the face without sufficient regard for conduct, but he considered whether they might be properly schooled by representations of exemplary public characters, the established enterprise of Charles Willson Peale among others. Brackenridge, accordingly, granted portraiture a more positive political role in his five-volume picaresque novel, *Modern Chivalry* (1792–1815). Neither he nor Freneau, however, was prepared to employ a portraitist as his surrogate, an opportunity seized by a Federalist newspaper editor in the new century. Early national newspapers had by then become unrelentingly partisan, and Freneau was among those who helped make them so, as Jefferson's choice for editor of the *Philadelphia National Gazette* in 1791. On the other side stood Harry Croswell of Hudson, New York, a David slinging rocks at the party in power. His decision to foreground a portrait maker and, in sustained fashion, to speak through him on matters of national importance distinguishes the Limner texts among other writings of the period.

"The Limner" and the Portraitist as a Public Figure in the Early Republic

"The Limner" first appeared on October 2, 1804, in the *Balance, and Columbian Repository*, a weekly miscellany published in Hudson, a thriving river port town south of Albany. The series introduced "Peter Pallet," a portraitist who publicized his availability to sitters in a full-page letter to the editor. Portrait makers advertised, but not by addressing editors; the *Balance*, in any case, had a separate advertising supplement. Nor would a real tradesman seeking customers have employed a pseudonym, which "Pallet" clearly is, with its allusion (in the spelling common in English until mid-nineteenth century) to the thin wooden tablet on which a painter lays colors. The painter's palette was a fundamental tool. "The Limner," printed in sixteen issues over two years, proved just as essential to the *Balance* (fig. 108).[52]

"Limner" was a somewhat old-fashioned term for portrait maker, and at the literal level, these essays in the *Balance* parodied a problem as old as the genre of portraiture itself: the potential for disagreement between artist and subject, inherent in the representation of one person by another. Clients expected to prevail, a condition that some American portraitists acknowledged with advertisements that guaranteed satisfaction for work performed. Yet the mere appearance of the Limner letters as a set of contentious statements speaks to the alternate scenario addressed in contemporaneously published anecdotes: under certain circumstances, portraitists were prepared to answer complaints in kind. Such was the case with the fictive Pallet, who publicly vented grievances over transactions that real artists usually kept private.[53]

Yet "The Limner" provided more than amusing literary diversion. Its consistent position as lead item in the *Balance*, generally preceding a political column, indicates centrality to the paper's editorial content. The series pressed issues of national significance and debate: freedom of expression, the right to make a judgment, and the civic importance (and elusiveness) of truth and good character. These had deeply personal resonance for editor Harry Croswell. His overtly political writing, in another context, had already provoked legal action against him. Those proceedings and their aftermath changed American law, and they motivated Croswell to compose "The Limner." His case is central to the remainder of this chapter.

In "The Limner," Croswell framed a partisan argument in terms of portrait methods and terminology, sitter expectations and behavior, and the personae of artists. His employment of the portrait transaction to communicate a political position countermands the idea that artists as a professional class were overlooked in the early United States. That notion arose from an overprivileging of history painting, relative to portraiture, by artists who had absorbed European academic doctrine and found themselves unable to instill those tenets in American patrons. Those painters expressed and acted out their dissatisfaction. Copley's complaint about his fellow Bostonians – their deficient taste, exclusive demand for portraits, and lack of regard for the "noble" profession of painting – long defined the restricted circumstances under which American painters labored,

No. 40. VOL. III.

The Balance,

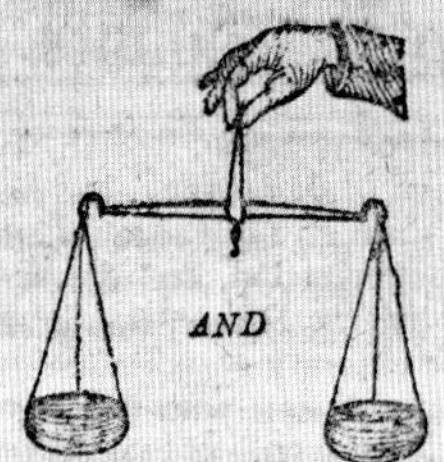

AND

COLUMBIAN REPOSITORY.

" HAIL SACRED POLITY, BY FREEDOM REAR'D !
" HAIL SACRED FREEDOM, WHEN BY LAW RESTRAIN'D !"
BEATTIE.

HUDSON, (NEW-YORK) TUESDAY, OCTOBER 2, 1804.

Original.

Hither the products of your closet-labors bring,
Enrich our columns, and instruct mankind.

FOR THE BALANCE.

THE LIMNER.

MR. EDITOR,

I AM, by profeſſion, a Painter. I am a ſelf-taught artiſt. On this account I claim the peculiar favor of the public. Nor am I the only perſon that has done the ſame thing. No man can offer a higher recommendation at this day. Nor is it confined to painting alone. A *natural genius,*—a ſelf-taught divine, phyſician, or lawyer, is ſure to meet with better ſucceſs in the world, that thoſe who acquire an act or profeſſion by ſtudy and inſtruction. With much ſatisfaction, then, I declare, I took up the painting buſineſs "*of my own head* ;" and after advancing regularly through all the grades of the art, I have at length become a moſt perfect Limner. I paint full length portraits, buſts, or heads, in oil, water colours or crayons ; miniatures, exquiſitely beautiful ; and no *phyſiognotrace* in the country can beat me at a profile ; but I have attained to the greateſt perfection in *tranſparent painting.* This art conſiſts in exhibiting the inſide as well as the outſide of my ſubject. In drawing a face in this way, not only the marks viſible to vulgar eyes are completely pourtrayed, but the furniture *behind the face,* is expoſed to view, particularly that generally called the *brain.* In drawing a full-length or buſt, the heart is wholly uncovered, with all its dark and light ſhades—all its rotten and defective ſpecks, and even all its throbs and vibrations. This kind of painting, I underſtand, was formerly much in vogue ; but I believe the art is now in much danger of being loſt. It is ſaid to be very much diſcountenanced by ſome of our great men, inſomuch that a perſon who keeps the neceſſary implements, (a glaſs called a *Reflector,* and a pencil called *Truth*) is almoſt certain to find an enemy in every upſtart politician in the country. Beſides, the *colours* uſed in this art are very expenſive : Notwithſtanding this, I have obtained an old glaſs, a pencil but little worn, and have laid in a ſmall ſtock of colours, all of which ſhall be at the ſervice of any gentleman or lady, young or old, who is not afraid to ſit for the performance.

Hitherto I have not met with the beſt ſucceſs, becauſe I had not perfectly acquired the art of flattering my cuſtomers. However, I ſhall endeavor to profit by the leſſon contained in the following fable, and do better in future, particularly in *oil.* In my *tranſparencies,* I can uſe no flattery.

" So very like a painter drew,
That ev'ry eye the picture knew ;
He hit complexion, feature, air,
So just, the life itself was there.
No flatt'ry with his colours laid,
To bloom restor'd the faded maid ;
He gave each muscle all its strength ;
The mouth, the chin, the nose's length.
His honest pencil touch'd with truth,
And mark'd the date of age and youth.
He lost his friends, his practice fail'd ;
Truth should not always be reveal'd ;
In dusty piles his pictures lay,
For no one sent the second-pay.
Two bustos fraught with ev'ry grace,
A Venus and Apollo's face,
He plac'd in view ; resolv'd to please
Whoever sat, he drew from these ;
From these corrected every feature,
And spirited each awkward creature.

All things were set ; the hour was come,
His pallet ready o'er his thumb,
My Lord appear'd ; and seated right
In proper attitude and light,
The painter look'd, he sketch'd the piece,
Then dipp'd his pencil, talk'd of Greece,
Of Titian's tints, of Guido's air ;
Those eyes, my Lord, the spirit there,
Might well a Raphael's hand require
To give them all the native fire.
The features fraught with sense and wit,
You'll grant are very hard to hit ;
But yet with patience you shall view
As much as paint and art can do.

Observe the work. My Lord replied,
Till now I thought my mouth was wide ;
Besides, my nose is somewhat long ;
Dear Sir, for me 'tis far too young !

Oh ! pardon me, the artist cried,
In this the painters must decide.
The piece ev'n common eyes must strike ;
I warrant it extremely like.

My Lord examin'd it anew ;
No looking-glass seem'd half so true.

A Lady came : with borrow'd grace
He from his Venus form'd her face.
Her lover prais'd the Painter's art ;
So like the picture in his heart !
To ev'ry age some charm he lent ;
Ev'n beauties were almost content.
Thro' all the town his art was prais'd ;
His custom grew, his price was rais'd.
Had he the real likeness shown,
Would any man the picture own ?
But when thus happily he wrought,
Each found the likeness in his thought.

I have ſet up a little ſhop, which may eaſily be found by thoſe who ſeek it ; and having put my pallet, pencil and paints in order, am now ready to wait on cuſtomers.

PETER PALLET.

108 *Balance, and Columbian Repository* 3 (Oct. 2, 1804). Courtesy American Antiquarian Society, Worcester, Mass.

relative to the opportunities enjoyed by Americans overseas, beginning with West. The experience of others who travelled to Europe and Britain only confirmed the point. Trumbull and, just after 1800, John Vanderlyn and Washington Allston met considerable success abroad as history painters but then found it impossible to support themselves in that genre in the United States. Dunlap, though his project was a comprehensive biographical history of American artists, acknowledged many of the elite painters' grievances (having himself been challenged even to succeed at portraiture) in recounting the "rise and progress" of American art to 1834. Other histories over the ensuing century and a half followed suit in focusing on these same painters and their discontent. Yet as more recent studies have shown, portraitists who were willing to provide what patrons wanted found ready work.[54] They were the most familiar of artists. This common knowledge made the Limner columns possible. That is, Croswell chose to present a political and moral argument using the portrait transaction as metaphor because he was sure contemporaries would understand his message.

The Limner texts prove doubly instructive. They demand to be interrogated for the nuances they add to our general knowledge of the state of American art around 1800. And they demonstrate the extent to which allegories of the professional practice of portraiture could be effective as a political discourse. Where the art historian detects distortions of actual practices, we may suppose the writer's contemporaries did as well. Croswell used that gap to express his grievances. Through it, he could construct his allegories. The Limner articles provide a fresh opportunity to assess attitudes toward artistic practices and practitioners, and they offer an intriguing case study in political representation at the time of Thomas Jefferson's presidency.

THE CROSWELL CASE

Croswell's reasons to compose "The Limner" cannot have been lost on readers of the staunchly Federalist *Balance*, whose editor was by then a figure of notoriety in matters concerning the press. The *Balance* had been established in May 1801, amidst a climate of fierce newspaper politics, at the start of the American party system, as Federalists set out to combat Republican political gains.[55] Jefferson's narrow election as president earlier in the year owed much to effective use of the press to court public opinion. In the process, Jeffersonian Republicans had also discovered the risks of partisan journalism, after the Federalist administration of John Adams passed the Sedition Act in 1798. This legislation made it unlawful "to knowingly and willingly assist or aid in writing, printing, uttering or publishing any false, scandalous and malicious writing or writings against the government of the United States . . . or the President of the United States, with the intent to defame . . . or to bring them . . . into contempt or disrepute."[56] Numerous opposition editors were indicted for libel against the Adams administration, and some were convicted, including, in Connecticut, Charles Holt of the *New London Bee*, whose brief jail term did not silence him. With Jefferson in office and the Sedition Act expired, Holt continued to publish the *Bee*; beginning in August 1802, he did so in Hudson, New York. Holt intended the Republican *Bee* as a counterweight to the Federalist *Balance*, but he met an unexpected and more noisome opponent in the *Wasp*, a satirical paper launched the month before his arrival, in a peremptory "declaration of war" (fig. 109).[57] "Wherever the Bee ranges, the Wasp will follow," announced the pseudonymous editor, Robert Rusticoat, Esquire. He was none other than the young Harry Croswell, acting independently of his senior editorial partners at the *Balance*. The pen name perhaps justified his crude writing in the *Wasp* – a "rusticoat" was a clown as well as a type of potato, both compatible with the idea of the "rustic" unconstrained by any pretense to Federalist decorum (but at odds with the honorific "Esquire," here conferring irony).[58] The *Wasp* ushered in the genre of "Federalist attack papers," which historian Jeffrey Pasley has characterized as concerned less with electioneering – the general aim of Republican newspapers – than with "vengeance and social discipline."[59] Newspapers had none of the subtlety of magazines, whose mostly Federalist editors more idealistically shored up a vision of national unity founded on shared individual interest.[60] By contrast, in his first issue of the *Wasp*, Croswell scurrilously branded opponents "lazy swine . . . wallowing in a puddle" and bluntly stated his purpose: "to displease, vex and torment his enemies" and to deny (in parody of Jefferson's ostensibly conciliatory inaugural address) "the philosophical doctrine, that 'We are all *Wasps* – we are all *Bees*.'"[61]

Croswell helped make First Amendment history. The facts of his case are well known. As editor of the *Wasp*, Croswell published damaging accusations against the president, which were already in general circulation – namely, that Jefferson had previously used covert means to undermine the Constitution. The *Wasp* repeated charges that Jefferson had paid members of the press, including Philip Freneau and James Thomson Callender, to impugn "the private characters of men, who, he knew well were virtuous," chiefly Washington and Adams. Jefferson and his supporters seized this oppor-

[SECOND EDITION.]

THE 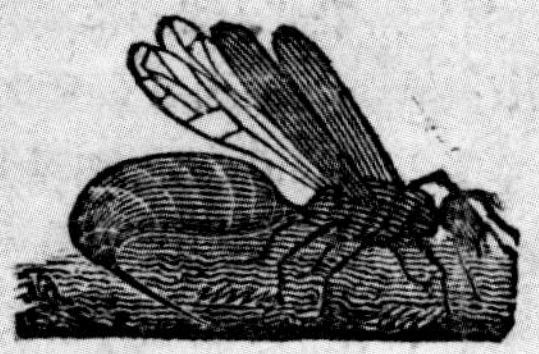 WASP.

By Robert Ruſticoat, Eſquire.

Vol. I.] " *To laſh the Raſcals naked through the world.*" [No. 1.

HUDSON, July 7, 1802.

If there, perchance, ſhould come a Bee,
A Waſp will come as ſoon as he.
Myſelf.

PROPOSALS,

FOR PUBLISHING IN THE CITY OF HUDSON,

A NEW PAPER,

TO BE ENTITLED

THE WASP,

By *ROBERT RUSTICOAT*, Esquire.

This paper will be iſſued occaſionally, as may beſt ſuit the editor, at the moderate price of three cents a number. It will be printed with a legible type, on good paper, and will make its appearance, as ſoon after Holt's Bee is commenced, as poſſible, whether 350 ſubſcribers are obtained or not.

THE editor will make but few promiſes.—Waſps produce but little *honey*: They are chiefly known by their *ſtings*; and the one here propoſed will not materially differ from others.——The Wasp is declared to be at enmity with the Bee.—Wherever the Bee ranges, the Wasp will follow—over the ſame fields, and on the ſame flowers.——Without attempting to pleaſe his *friends*, the Wasp will only ſtrive to diſpleaſe, vex and torment his enemies.—With his ſting always ſharpened for war, he will never accept of peace.—He will never accede to the philoſophical doctrine, that

" We are all *Waſps*—we are all *Bees*."

ADVERTISEMENT.

☞ THE EDITOR did not intend to have commenced the publication of The Wasp, until Charles Holt had iſſued the firſt number of his " Bee," in this city; but a fellow by the name of Mitchell, who is profeſſional blackguard for the Political Barometer, ſeems to demand immediate attention.—This Mitchell ſays, that he *hopes* Mr. Holt will meet with great ſucceſs in this city.—Undoubtedly.—But, pray, Miſter Mitchell, why did you not remember the old ſaying——" Charity begins at home;" and beſtow ſome of your *hopes* upon yourſelf! I know you want them bad enough; and Holt will never *thank ye* for them.—Jacobin printers would cut one another's throats for a morſel of bread—and their *hanging-together* is preciſely like that

109 *Wasp* 1 (July 7, 1802). Courtesy, American Antiquarian Society, Worcester, Mass.

tunity to set a legal precedent away from wider public scrutiny in East Coast cities. Prosecution of Croswell offered a further advantage: Hudson was the home county of New York's Republican attorney general, Ambrose Spencer, who took the case. In early 1803, Croswell found himself indicted for libel, charged as "a malicious and seditious man, of a depraved mind and wicked and diabolical disposition," one who had contrived to "scandalize, traduce and vilify" the president of the United States.[62] *People v. Croswell*, first heard in Claverack, Columbia County, rested on principles rooted in English common law, which protected the press from licensing and prior censorship but did not permit evidence supporting the truth of a publication to be used in defense against libel. (Ironically, the Sedition Act, so reviled by Jefferson, had included such a provision.) A jury found Croswell guilty, and the verdict was narrowly upheld on appeal to the New York Supreme Court, a decision handed down in May 1804. The victors did not move for judgment, however, because the case generated two actions Jefferson's camp failed to anticipate: Alexander Hamilton took on and forcefully argued Croswell's appeal, and the Republican-controlled New York legislature introduced a bill allowing for truth as evidence in cases of libel. This measure, when finally passed, laid the cornerstone for modern freedom of the press.[63]

By January 1804, with the *Wasp* long expired, Croswell had advanced from the position of junior editor and publisher of the *Balance* to become sole proprietor of that newspaper. Unchastened by his legal troubles – the case went before the state's high court that February – Croswell defiantly revived the wasp emblem from the masthead of his former newspaper (see fig. 116). Beginning in March, it appeared over "Editor's Closet," which offered sharp commentary on *People v. Croswell* and its legislative aftermath, among other political concerns.[64] In May, his appeal at an end, Croswell set the stage for "The Limner" with a letter to the editor from the pseudonymous "Uncle Tobey." The name evoked "Uncle Toby" from Laurence Sterne's widely read *Life and Opinions of Tristram Shandy, Gentleman* (1759), a character whose battle wounds leave him impotent and obsessed with military fortifications. "There is a class of citizens among us," Croswell's Tobey began, "who have very much mistaken their own characters"; these "gentry . . . have told the people so often that they are politicians, that they have forgotten they are *only knaves*." If a mirror were held up to these men, Tobey suggested, they might see themselves with greater clarity. "I really wish, Mr. Editor," he continued, "that some ready writer, who is well acquainted with public characters, would employ a little leisure time in sketching a gallery of portraits for the use of the people," to facilitate assessment of governors, judges, justices, legislators, district attorneys, and others.[65] Croswell began to do just that, five months after the second court decision against him, when he introduced "The Limner." A slightly earlier article titled "The Limner," not identified with Croswell, demonstrates that the term had power to signal representation of character without any textual reference to painting or portrait making at all. "Man is a paradox," began the contributor to *Franklin Minerva* in 1799. "His actions and professions are at eternal variance, and exhibit such a complicated system of caprice and inconsistency, as almost to bid defiance to the ridicule of the satirist."[66] In his "Limner," Croswell produced a sustained satire of fellow citizens, though only toward the end of the series would the editor take clear aim at the "knaves" in political power.

INTRODUCING THE LIMNER

"The Limner" presented a man with a confusing set of qualifications for his occupation. "I am, by profession, a Painter," began Peter Pallet, in his first letter to "Mr. Editor": "I am a self-taught artist. On this account I claim the peculiar favor of the public . . . No man can offer a higher recommendation at this day. Nor is it confined to painting alone. A *natural genius*, – a self-taught divine, physician, or lawyer, is sure to meet with better success in the world, that [*sic*, than] those who acquire an act or profession by study and instruction."[67]

The term "profession" originally had the broad meaning of any work by which a person earned a living. Pallet's reference to ministry, medicine, and law acknowledged the privileged status that the most learned branches of these occupations had acquired in eighteenth-century Britain, where they were considered suitable pursuits for gentlemen. In America, where few claimed the independent means that historically defined gentility, the professions had the effect of conferring distinction. Alexander Hamilton and James Madison, in *The Federalist*, granted the same independence of judgment traditionally accorded gentlemen to professionals, whom they envisioned as disinterested and capable of acting unselfishly on behalf of fellow citizens. Such persons could do so because they were considered both learned and rational. In the United States by the later eighteenth century, the professions rested on firmer educational and institutional bases than previously. Yet many doctors, lawyers, and ministers lacked formal professional training and often even bachelors' degrees.[68] Brackenridge, a lawyer and judge as well as writer, comically portrayed the diminishing value of liberal education and gentility to the professions in *Modern Chivalry*. An illiterate, immigrant manservant named Teague O'Regan is a central character, eager to rise in the world and assisted in doing so by an uninformed populace. After seeking positions as a minister and lawyer, among other occupations, Teague wins public office and eventually a federal position. Brackenridge's fictional presentation of direct participation in government by common men acknowledged, from the author's genteel Republican perspective, a coming reality, which posed a radical challenge to the ideals of virtuous, disinterested leadership that many Federalists still endorsed.

When Croswell composed "The Limner," the professional status of American artists was in flux. Through much of the eighteenth century in North America, painters continued to hold the rank of tradesmen. Art theorists continued to tell them otherwise, from Richardson – whose books of 1715 and 1725 were reissued in 1773 and 1792 – to Reynolds – whose first seven *Discourses* were published in 1778, followed by the full series in the posthumous *Works of Sir Joshua Reynolds* (1797).[69] Familiarity with writing that cast artists as men of ideas encouraged American painters, especially those who studied in London and Europe, to conceive of themselves as professionals and to tout their professional connections. Ralph Earl of Connecticut, for example, informed residents of Northampton, Massachusetts, in 1800, that "Mr. EARL, though a native of America, received the last and finishing strokes of his art, from the hands of the immortal *Reynolds*, *West* and *Copeley*," an exaggerated or false statement as concerned Reynolds, if not Copley.[70] Advertisers presented any qualifications that might generate work, and Earl's American customers were in no position to evaluate his claims. On that occasion, Earl announced exhibition of his view of Niagara Falls, not services as a portraitist, his primary employment. Still, his placement of the notice had the whiff of trade.

In counterpoint to elite emphasis on education, a man's claim to be "self-taught" or a "natural genius" – as the Limner advertised himself – resonated with Americans. Copley, decades earlier, had asserted his provincial innocence on matters of art as a strategy for magnifying his "improvement" after he traveled abroad.[71] In the early United States, however, being "one of those artists who started from his own head" might suffice.[72] The example of Baltimore portraitist Joshua Johnson makes clear that Croswell chose the fictional Limner's words based on language employed by real

he will ſell on *moderate terms*.

Portrait Painting.

THE ſubſcriber, grateful for the liberal encouragement which an indulgent public have conferred on him, in his firſt eſſays, in *PORTRAIT PAINTING*, returns his ſincere acknowledgments.

He takes liberty to obſerve, That by dint of induſtrious application, he has ſo far improved and matured his talents, that he can inſure the moſt preciſe and natural likeneſſes.

As a *ſelf-taught genius*, deriving from nature and induſtry his knowledge of the Art; and having experienced many inſuperable obſtacles in the purſuit of his ſtudies, it is highly gratifying to him to make aſſurances of his ability to execute all commands, with an effect, and in a ſtyle, which muſt give ſatisfaction. He therefore reſpectfully ſolicits encouragement. ☞Apply at his Houſe, in the Alley leading from *Charles* to *Hanover Street*, back of *Sears's* Tavern.

JOSHUA JOHNSTON.

110 "Portrait Painting," advertisement of Joshua Johnston (Johnson), *Baltimore Intelligencer* (Dec. 19, 1798). Courtesy American Antiquarian Society, Worcester, Mass.

artists of the early republic. Johnson forthrightly pronounced himself "a *self taught genius*, deriving from nature and industry his knowledge of the Art" of portrait painting (fig. 110). Many artists learned on their own, and the fact that Johnson was biracial probably does not account for his limited access to training. Nor did his race (if even recognized) or self-taught status inhibit patrons. What mattered to Johnson's clients was the visible evidence of his industry. The linearity and, at times, painstaking attention to detail in his portraits were features shared by many self- or minimally trained painters (fig. 111). Those qualities – by contrast with the relative painterliness evident in the work of artists who studied in London, such as Stuart, then the foremost portraitist in the United States – suggested care in execution, consistent practice, and honest work.[73]

Whether proudly self-taught men would respect authority and social hierarchy worried Federalists like Croswell, as it did an essayist for the Federalist-aligned *Monthly Anthology*,

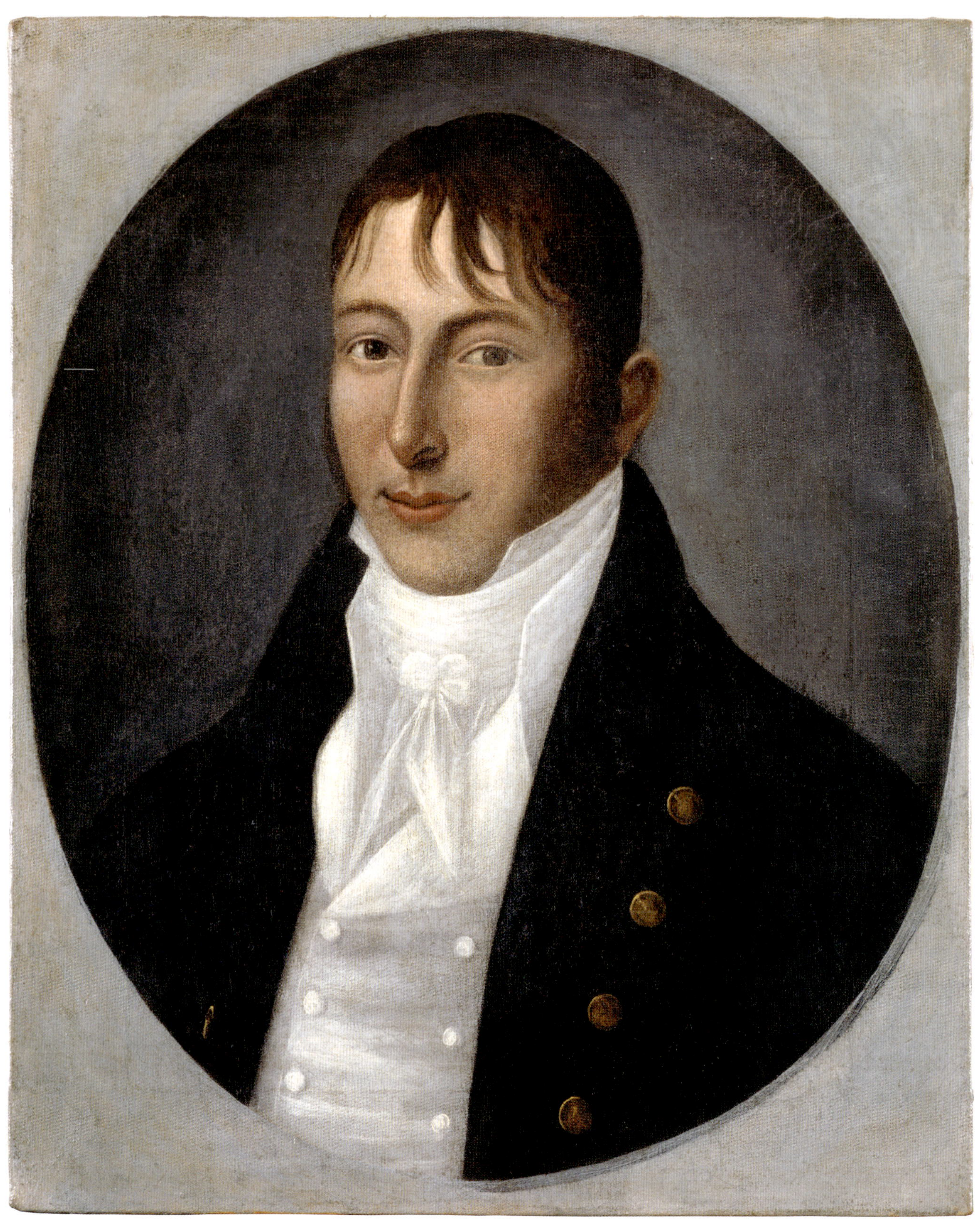

111 Joshua Johnson, *Archibald Dobbin, Jr.*, ca. 1803. Oil on canvas. 22 × 18 in. (55.88 × 45.72 cm). Courtesy of the Maryland Historical Society, Baltimore, 1923.17.2.

and Boston Review (1806). That writer specifically addressed what he perceived as overoptimism about American talent. In his estimation, the international fame of West, Copley, Stuart, and Trumbull had encouraged the idea that "the people of this country have *a natural genius*" for painting, consistent with America's reputation "for the production of self-taught geniuses." But he asserted that the painters he named, however innately gifted, had been "carefully raised to maturity" abroad; "had they continued here," he claimed, "they never would have got beyond the rudiments of their profession."[74] International standards still carried the expectation that genius be molded by education, an assumption soon abandoned in theory, if rarely in practice, by Romantic artists. When American painter Chester Harding, in London around 1823, was asked by Royal Academy president Sir Thomas Lawrence "what school [he] had studied in," Harding replied: "I told him the Stuart School . . . that he need not think that I wished to pass for a prodigy."[75] In view of the fact that Harding was largely self-taught, his reference to Stuart, who honed his skills in West's London studio, acknowledged the continued academic valuation of proper training. Yet rudiments of the profession often sufficed. Few artists had much formal schooling of any kind; Trumbull's Harvard education, begun before he took up painting, made him a rarity in his field. Most learned their art by apprenticing and by teaching themselves. If a bad picture sometimes resulted, the damage seldom exceeded affront to vanity. "Old Squire Worth," of Hudson, complained that his portrait, probably painted around 1801, made him look "'like a one story house with the chimney a fire!'" (presumably because he had red hair).[76] He could have asked for a second version, since portraitists commonly promised satisfaction. A rare (and authentic) painter's ad in the *Balance*, placed by the Dutch-born "G. Schipper, Miniature Painter," assured "Ladies and Gentlemen" of "Correct Likenesses": "if not approved a Likeness, no payment will be requested" (fig. 112).[77] Most bluntly, such ads simply stated, "No likeness, no pay."[78] Emphasis on customer satisfaction reinforced the identification of the painter with the tradesman, as distinct from the professional (a lawyer or a doctor, for example), whose presumed superior judgment obligated him to give clients what he thought best for them and not merely to offer what they wanted.

"Limner," as title for the series in the *Balance*, carried strong connotations of trade, as the case of Williams has made clear. Even after limning became most closely associated with portrait making, client valuation of the mechanical and utilitarian aspects of portraiture inhibited connotations of creative independence associated with fine art. Customers weighed credentials and experience on a scale that seem in certain respects premodern. Philadelphian Bushrod Washington, deliberating between two portraitists in 1783, decided against Peale, whom he considered better at likeness, in favor of Henry Benbridge, based in part on that artist's skill in painting "drapery" (that is, clothing). Since Peale's portraits now appear most "like" in their relationship to one another, Washington's judgment exposes the fluidity of likeness as a concept. He later fretted that his "Countenance" in the portrait by Benbridge had "a degree of ill Nature in it," so perhaps his admiration for Peale arose from that painter's consistency in presenting a well-regulated face. At issue in the commission to either painter, in any case, was the projection of status as a quality of the sitter, not the maker.

The practical connotation of limning seems underscored by the curious conjunction in Raphaelle Peale's listing for a 1799 Philadelphia city directory: "limner and patentee for the preservation of bottoms of vessels from worms."[79] The younger Peale never again employed the term (less relevant once he became a still-life specialist), and it fell from

Correct Likenesses.

G. Schipper,

MINIATURE PAINTER,

GIVES his most respectful thanks to the Ladies and Gentlemen who have favored him in the line of his Art, during his short stay in this place, from whence he intends to depart in the beginning of next week.

Mr. S. takes Likenesses, for which but one sitting of three quarters of an hour is required, set in an elegant frame, with glass, at eight Dollars; and if not approved a Likeness, no payment will be requested. Specimens of his work may be seen at his Lodgings at Mr. NICHOLS' City Hotel, *Hudson*. June 11.

112 "Correct Likenesses," advertisement of Gerrit Schipper, *Balance, or Columbian Repository* 4 (June 11, 1804 [*sic*, 1805]): 24.

common use in the nineteenth century. Artists who continued to call themselves limners must at times have done so in unconscious adherence to tradition, oblivious to elevating arguments about the profession of painting. Conversely, "limner" could be deployed to signal lack of awareness in others. When a self-consciously worldly writer for Philadelphia's *Port Folio* reported (retrospectively) that Lancaster copper and tinsmith Jacob Eichholtz concurrently "professed himself the limner," that phrasing suggested the painter's naïveté.[80] Eichholtz made no distinction between metalwork and painting, as readers of *Port Folio*, the influential political and literary magazine, would have done. Eichholtz, as it happens, appears not to have used the term "limner" in reference to himself. He advertised "Profile and Portrait Painting" in a Lancaster newspaper and called himself "Portrait Painter" on his painted tin shop sign, but those acts reinforced his identification as tradesman.[81] According to *Port Folio*, Eichholtz was set on his way to greater things after a fortuitous encounter with the London-trained portraitist Thomas Sully unleashed his "native genius." Eichholtz abandoned the tight painting manner of his small, early profile portraits and thereafter "progressed with a rapidity scarcely credible." Yet clients outside larger cities favored meticulously finished portraits well into the nineteenth century. Ashbel Stoddard, the first printer in Hudson and a newspaper publisher there from 1785 to 1803, chose Ammi Phillips to portray him in 1812 or 1813 (fig. 113). Phillips, then just twenty-four, had fifty successful years ahead of him as a regional itinerant portraitist, but he strayed little from the precise manner evident in Stoddard's portrait – in which George Washington's Farewell Address, in the proud printer's hand, is fully legible. For makers and consumers of such "correct likenesses," the designation "limner" may have retained positive value.

Why did Croswell choose "Limner" for the title of his series in the *Balance*, when the term appears just once within those texts, less frequently than "artist" and "painter"? While the example of *Port Folio*, commenting on Eichholtz, might indicate that the editor wished to express doubts about the professionalism of openly self-taught painters, historical evidence makes clear that customers for portraits accepted a wide spectrum of skill. Croswell more likely used the old-fashioned "limner" because it implied traditional standards, which seemed to be eroding in modern American society, and because it most directly indicated an artist in the business of representing his fellow men. That was Croswell's metaphorical undertaking over the course of "The Limner." But unlike the customarily ingratiating portraitist, he reflected the weaknesses of fellow citizens back to them, implicitly justifying his harshness as an exercise in patriotism.

The *Balance* was a deeply partisan newspaper. Throughout "The Limner," Croswell tarred the fictional painter's clientele with the same ignoble qualities he identified with democrats: "inconsistency, hypocrisy, shuffling, canting, quibbling, evasion, cheating, falshood [*sic*] and deceit."[82] The Limner himself seems more like Federalists as represented in the pages of the newspaper: men of "private integrity, respectability and worth," "not intoxicated with prosperity," and concerned with truth above all.[83] Yet even though a specific conflict with Jeffersonians gave rise to "The Limner," Croswell's attacks on human folly in his essays potentially targeted not only Republicans but also Federalists, who were presumably his principal readers. With a claimed national subscriber list of 1,800 as of January 1804, about 40 percent of whom lived far enough away to receive the paper by post, the *Balance* addressed a wide audience, including men and women, persons of standing, and farmers.[84] As "the Limner," Croswell employed the genre of satirical moral essay to decry any behavior that threatened the social contract.

TRUTH / TRANSPARENCY

The issue of truth lay at the heart of Croswell's legal defense in *People v. Croswell*, and the editor made truth telling central to his "Limner" series. In the first Limner, Pallet/Croswell dramatized the portraitist's dilemma by quoting verse from John Gay's *Fables* (1727), a collection of moral lessons widely popular during the eighteenth century. "The Painter Who Pleased Nobody and Everybody" (presented in "The Limner" without title, first stanza, or attribution) introduced an artist whose "honest pencil touch'd with truth" drove away friends and destroyed his practice. He reconciles himself to flattering his sitters by any means necessary and thrives: "Thro' all the town his art was prais'd; / His custom grew, his price was rais'd. / Had he the real likeness shown, / Would any man the picture own?" An American response to Gay's poem, attributed to Rembrandt Peale (Croswell's exact contemporary), placed sitter demand for flattery and the difficulty of providing satisfaction squarely before the American readership of *Port Folio* in 1807.[85] Yet the question of truth in portraiture very much concerned Americans, who knew that truth was subject to manipulation by painters, whether intentionally or not, and by sitters who sought an outcome. That was precisely Freneau's concern in "The Picture Gallery," which identified false-

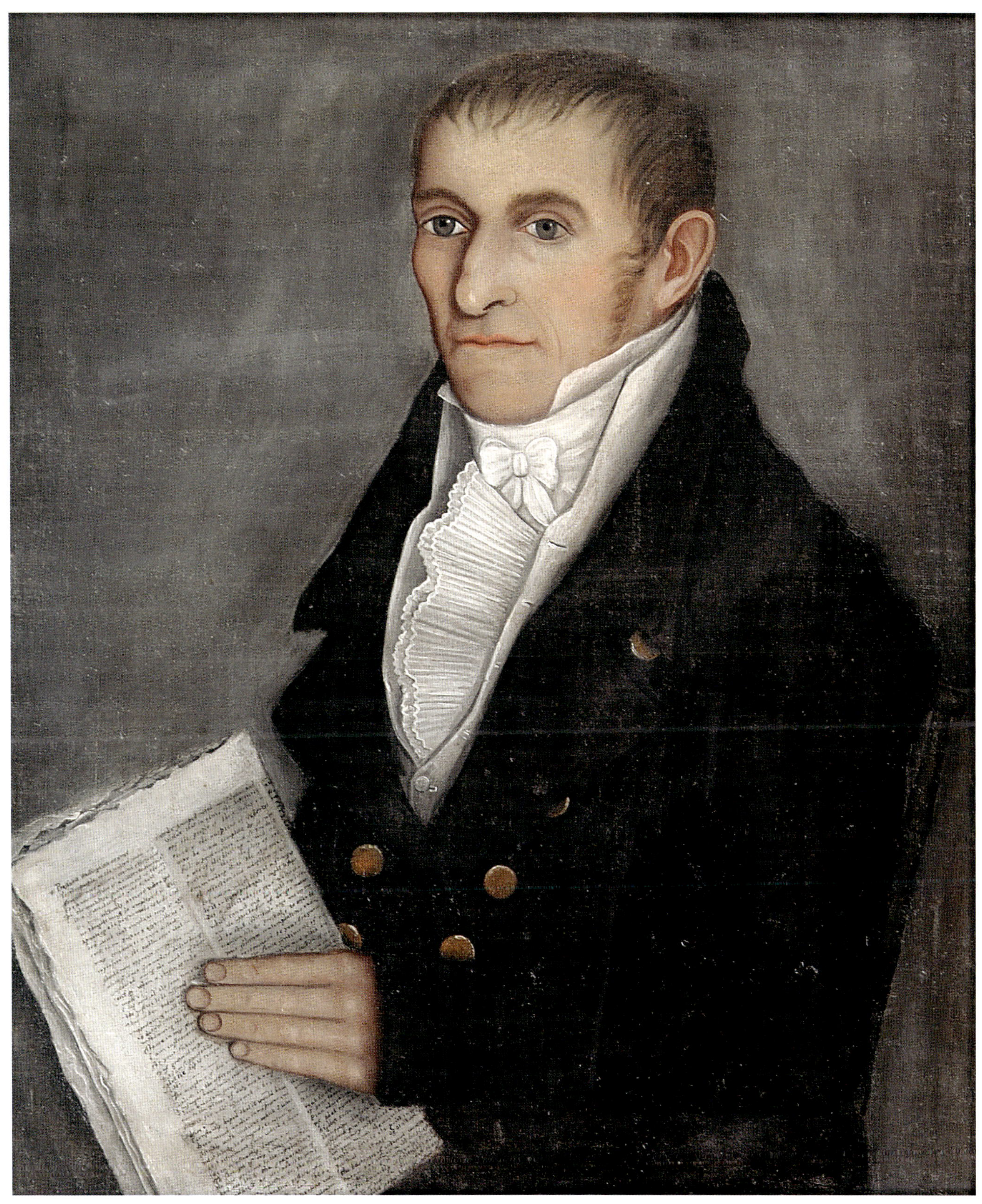

113 Ammi Phillips, *Ashbel Stoddard*, ca. 1812–13. Oil on canvas, 29 × 25 in. (73.7 × 63.5 cm). Stair Galleries, Hudson, N.Y. Photo courtesy Stair Galleries.

hood with the portrayal of unworthy persons as if they were worthy. The portraitist's challenge, which Freneau's fictional painter failed to meet, lay in discerning and projecting character, a quality more or less interchangeable with social identity or public role. Types included gentleman, wise man, brave man, and virtuous woman (among the limited range of "characters" available to women). To "portray" suggests interpretation and judgment – and thus powers of discernment in the portraitist. For Richardson, "to raise the Character . . . is absolutely necessary to a good Face-Painter."[86] According to academic theory, a portraitist should improve on nature, accommodating particular facts of appearance to a more general, or typical, representation.

Physiognomic theory, widely embraced around 1800, found truth in the body. A subject of inquiry dating to antiquity and influentially revived during the 1770s by Johann Caspar Lavater, physiognomy postulated determinate correspondences between certain bodily features, notably fixed portions of the head, and moral condition.[87] Profile portraits enjoyed especial popularity because they most clearly displayed cranial features – and because they were easily and cheaply produced. Profiles made by pantographic machines, called physiognotrace portraits, gained acceptance as one of the truest forms of portraiture available.[88] One type, among several in use, employed a brass gnomon to trace the projected contours of a facial profile, simultaneously activating a stylus that incised these movements in reduced dimension on a folded sheet of white paper. The interior shape would then be cut out and discarded, leaving multiple copies of the likeness, fully revealed only after the negative image had been mounted on dark paper. Such equipment produced accurate profile likenesses with limited human intervention or skill requirements. "Any person without the aid of another, can in less than a minute take their own likeness in profile," asserted an ad for the device in 1803.[89] Wendy Bellion has argued persuasively that the popularity of physiognotrace portraits in an increasingly democratic American society was closely, if not explicitly, tied to the political ideal of actual representation. "Both systems were believed to restore truth to representation," she asserted. "By knowing, seeing, and communicating with their delegates, citizens would keep political representation actual, honest, and transparent. Likewise, the physiognotrace invited sitters to view their profile likenesses as precise, unmediated evidence of their own internal characters."[90]

As a Federalist, Croswell mistrusted unmediated representation, a point he made in "The Limner" by granting authority to a man in the business of representing. Pallet strayed far from the ingratiating language found in real portraitists' announcements by inviting – one might even say, daring – "any gentleman or lady . . . who is not afraid to sit" to have their portraits taken "in transparency." During the eighteenth century, translucent images illuminated from behind, called "transparencies," were a popular spectacle in Britain and America.[91] Pallet described this approach, in which he claimed "greatest perfection," as the ability to penetrate "marks visible to vulgar eyes" and to expose qualities of heart and mind: "the furniture *behind the face*." For this, the Limner employed powerful – but, he claimed, outmoded – tools: "a glass called a *Reflector* and a pencil called *Truth*." A painter's pencil, in eighteenth-century terminology, was his brush, but readers surely recognized "pencil of truth" as an artistic metaphor used by moralists.[92] "Reflector," at a purely functional level, might refer to some kind of optical device, like the "Achromatic Camera Obscura" that assisted miniaturist Gerrit Schipper, lately employed in Hudson, in "imitating Nature correctly."[93] Or, more simply, a mirror. Mirrors remained standard equipment in portrait studios, positioned to reflect sitter to artist, as an aid in pictorial arrangement. The studio mirror did not serve vanity, often personified as a woman who regards herself in a mirror, but truth, allegorized by a woman who turns the mirror's surface away from herself and toward the world. This metaphorical meaning applied to Pallet's "reflector," an emblem of truth allied with his pencil.[94] Reflector, or reflection, also has the double meaning of mirroring and mulling; it suggests intellectual and philosophical agency and, thus, authority on Pallet's part. By contrast, the sitter remains passive, neither reflecting nor viewing. "Transparent painting," in this same context, referred to Pallet's ability to "see through" a person's public posturing. In Jeffersonian America, for Croswell, political duplicity had trumped transparency. Pallet was blunt on the matter: any artist who embraced truth, he wryly suggested in his first letter, "is almost certain to find an enemy in every upstart politician in the country." The adjective "upstart" compounded negative connotations already attached to the word "politician" by Americans of the early republic, and particularly Federalists. A politician acted out of self-interest, threatening the established social hierarchy and the idea that a natural aristocracy of virtuous men made the best leaders.

No politicians ever enter Pallet's shop, but everything that happens there has political implications. Pallet's sitters adopt fashions that interfere with the artist's ability to depict them, like citizens whose ever-changing issues and escalating demands complicate the statesman's efforts to represent them. Clients offer criticism on matters outside their expertise and demand changes to portraits that fail to represent them satisfactorily, like interest groups that lobby government. Finally, dissatisfied patrons withhold payment, as men may do their vote. Pallet finds nothing but folly and self-deception in such actions. Countering the initial mixed message Croswell gave about his "self-taught" professional artist, Pallet emerges as a positive figure, a man defined by civic-mindedness in opposition to the self-interest displayed by his clients.

The cast of characters in "The Limner" include men and women, young and old, patron and passerby. The artist's first clients, described in successive letters, are a fashionable young lady and gentleman whose clothing, coiffure, and demeanor conceal what the painter needs most to see: a face that can be read for character.[95] Physiognomy, in both cases, is disguised by signs of class. Sitters and painters had long considered costume and accessories that defined social position to be critical components of a portrait, as important to likeness as facial representation. The Limner has difficulty even seeing the faces of his fashionable sitters. The man's hair, combed forward, strikes Pallet as a wig worn backward – a buffoonish image – and the sitter's shirt collar, "starched stiff and reached up to his eyes," conceals his jaw. The lady's hair, too, falls into her face, while "a strange inconsistency in female fashion" leaves her bosom exposed. She is more worried about the appearance of her elbow. The Limner "injures the look of the picture," the fictional Fanny Fanciful complains in her own letter to the editor, by making that part too dark; she demonstrates the error by placing her elbow against the painted canvas.

An elbow is not a face. It does not communicate character, though its appearance may suggest lack of refinement and lack of judgment in the person who exposes it. Critics of the fashion for "naked bosoms, bare elbows, and transparent drapery" were particularly harsh on the unattractiveness of elbows.[96] Artists often finessed the angular joint by making it plump or anatomically vague. The Limner describes his sitter's elbow as "rough, high-coloured and uncomely," implying that if the lady knew her own elbow, she would not wear short sleeves. She is less informed than the critical shoemaker in Pliny's account of Apelles, the painter who acknowledged that tradesman's expertise in footwear by revising his pictorial rendering of a sandal but refused further suggestions. Eighteenth-century British writers drew on the tale to support the authority of artists over unqualified critics and to distinguish artists from mere mechanics. In so doing, they refuted arguments originating with Plato that working men were too constrained by their own interests to participate in governance. Though classical republican ideology had a diminishing place in Jeffersonian America, Croswell's parable reinforced the idea of exclusive leadership by casting as the antagonist a person whose sex disqualified her from formal political participation. Only a man of superior judgment – someone capable of appreciating the whole – can represent those who make up its parts. Strikingly, in concluding the Limner's exchange with Fanny Fanciful, Croswell added the initials "A.M." after Pallet's name, distinguishing the artist on that occasion only as the recipient of an advanced degree (Artium Magister) and thus as a person of learning.[97]

Men described in the Limner columns are no less subject to ridicule than women, and more potentially problematic, because they participate in civic life in ways that women cannot. A man "of high standing," who claims to "venerate the truth above all things," may prove a fraud, with enduring negative consequences if his flattery and "countenance disguised in a smile" succeed in deceiving others, as they initially deceive Pallet.[98] In the *Balance*, this is how Croswell described democrats, whose "practice has always been directly at variance with their professions."[99] Pallet is briefly taken in by the prominent and ingratiating man. He feels his spirits raised, despite "degenerate times," by the prospect of a person willing to "appear in *transparency*." At the word, the would-be sitter blanches, then blushes in "shame and confusion," involuntary responses that color his face and give the lie to his composed expression. Fearful of being further exposed, the client decides to have only a profile drawn, to avoid exposing "an ugly scar" on one side of his Janus-like face. The man worries that the mark will "look like a blemish on the picture," oblivious to deeper flaws in himself that the artist cannot – or will not – erase. The patron frowns throughout the sitting and pronounces the finished work a caricature. When Pallet refuses to alter the image, even for extra pay, the man departs without compensating him. Left with the work, Pallet invites curious individuals to see it in his shop. He also reproduces the profile as a silhouette at the head of the newspaper column and encourages readers to identify the sitter among their fellow citizens, that is, to make their own judgment. The face, with its sharply pointed nose, mimics the crudest type of artisan-made silhouettes, while mocking consumers who supported such hack work.[100] Croswell, in text and image, gives full meaning to a term used both for heads cut in the physiognotrace process and for stupid persons: blockhead (fig. 114).[101]

No. 44. VOL. III.

The Balance, AND COLUMBIAN REPOSITORY.

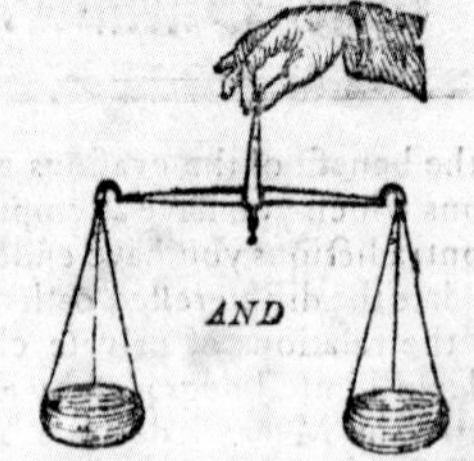

"HAIL SACRED POLITY, BY FREEDOM REAR'D!
"HAIL SACRED FREEDOM, WHEN BY LAW RESTRAIN'D!"
BEATTIE.

HUDSON, (NEW-YORK) TUESDAY, OCTOBER 30, 1804.

Original.

Hither the products of your closet-labors bring,
Enrich our columns, and instruct mankind.

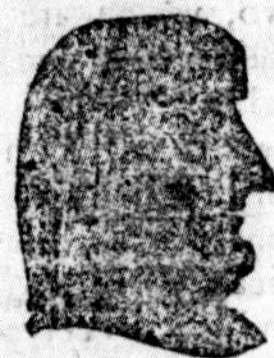

FOR THE BALANCE.

THE LIMNER.

MR. EDITOR,

MY proſpects brighten daily.—My ſhop has attracted the attention of ſome great men, and I have already had a cuſtomer of high ſtanding. But I find you are undoubtedly impatient to know ſomething of my illuſtrious cuſtomer. He entered my ſhop and addreſſed me ſo familiarly, that I confeſs he made a favorable impreſſion. His countenance was diſguiſed in a ſmile, and as he ſhook me by the hand, I thought the graſp beſpoke friendſhip. "I am told, Mr. Pallet," ſaid he, "that you hold the pencil of Truth, and as I venerate the truth above all things, I have come to be your cuſtomer." This declaration taken in connection with his ſmiles and complaiſance, left me no room to doubt that he was a fit ſubject for my *Reflector*. So much goodneſs, thought I, ought to be fully exhibited for the benefit of mankind. "I am extremely happy to find, ſir," ſaid I, "that, in theſe degenerate times, there is at leaſt one man, who is not afraid to appear in *tranſparency*." It was meant as a compliment, Mr. Editor; but what was my aſtoniſhment when I obſerved its when he firſt entered my ſhop, he pretended that his veneration of *Truth* had brought him there. We were unacquainted, and he introduced himſelf by flattering me, and by profeſſing the greateſt regard for the firſt of virtues. But on the firſt intimation that his frail maſk was to be removed, and his real qualities expoſed, how did he tremble! Oh, hypocriſy! diſſimulation! Would to God it were not dangerous for the pencil of Truth to paint thee in thy proper colours.

On returning to my ſhop, my cuſtomer told me he merely wanted his *profile* drawn; and he took his poſition ... floor for the purpoſe. I requeſted him to turn the other ſide of his face towards me, as the light would then ſtrike more favorably. "No, Mr. Pallet," ſaid he, "I have an ugly ſcar, a kind of mark, on that ſide of my face, which will not appear well; indeed, it would look like a blemiſh on the picture." This reaſon was ſatiſ-

114 *Balance, and Columbian Repository* 3 (Oct. 30, 1804).

The Limner's tactic of public ridicule calls on the popular strain of anecdote concerning the power held by portraitists over clients who crossed them. Lely's threat to add a monkey's tail to a likeness was often recast. Hogarth was said to have extracted payment from a dissatisfied nobleman by claiming that he would otherwise exhibit the work "with the addition of a tail, and some other little appendages."[102] His pictorial comic genius, even more appreciated in the early nineteenth century than before, made the anecdote especially believable. Croswell showed his familiarity with such stories in his mock promise two years earlier, in the last issue of the *Wasp* before it was effectively shut down, to "engage some faithful limner" to portray the "Turncoat General" who tried his case, Ambrose Spencer, together with Spencer's assistant, Ebenezer Foote, in the background with "a tail . . . as a caricature of a monkey," phrasing that suggests it is the monkey who is caricatured by association with Foote and not (or not only) the other way around.[103] In the *Balance*, Croswell would limn in even broader strokes.

Croswell expanded on the idea of public ridicule and caricature in "My Shop-Window," a title he used for the two Limner columns that followed Pallet's account of the self-important man.[104] Looking out from his place of work, the artist finds himself struck by the diversity of people in

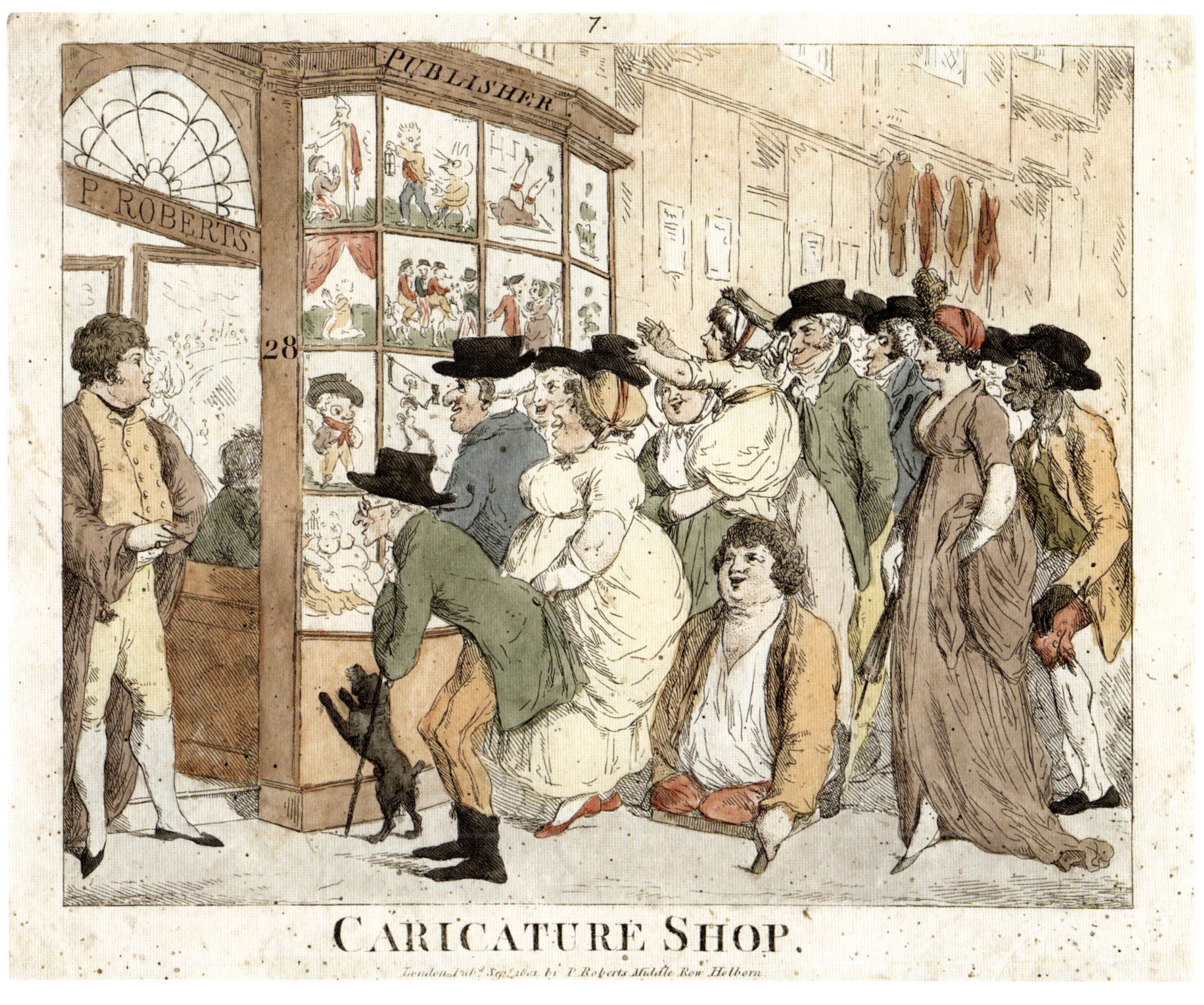

115 Piercy Roberts, *Caricature Shop*, 1801. Hand-colored etching. Courtesy of the Lewis Walpole Library, Yale University, New Haven.

the street, "exceeding, perhaps, the most complicated mixture, ever delineated by Hogarth." He decides to affix "an old caricature" to the window, as a "gull trap" to "catch" passersby, whose heads he can then surreptitiously draw. A gull is "a credulous person . . . a dupe, simpleton, fool," so "gull trap" (a phrase favored by Croswell but otherwise uncommon) is the lure for such an individual.[105] Prints of passersby gawking at displays in print shop windows were popular in Britain from about the 1770s, and Croswell must have known the genre, exemplified close to the time of his writing by Piercy Roberts's *Caricature Shop* of 1801, showing his own print and publishing establishment in Holburn (fig. 115). The joke in this type of image is that the onlookers are also caricatured, as are Pallet's prey. They include "a *knowing, cunning* old fellow" with "such a habit of screwing up his face, blinking, and looking wise, that one could hardly refrain from thinking of a baboon"; "a lump of magisterial dullness"; "a coxcombical chap . . . who passes for more than he is worth"; a rich man "nevertheless delving for more money"; "a man of fortune" yet "selfishness so great, that it is doubtful whether he ever did a benevolent or charitable act"; a fellow with "a pompous strut, and such an air of self-conceit" that he could only be "some troublesome dependent who has been put into a petty office"; "a consequential character" whose "phiz wore every sign of stupidity," while announcing "*I will not be disputed*," an "insufferable" combination were he to be granted any "'little brief authority.'" Though the Limner column had previously targeted women, this crowd (uncharacteristically for the British prints) is exclusively male – greedy, uncouth, ignorant, and unqualified to serve in any other capacity than as subjects for Pallet's tart observations and as negative examples to others. Yet the men occupy positions of authority, or imagine they could, smoothing their way with "smiles, and salutations, and shaking of hands," which, Pallet dismissively notes, "mean nothing."

TOMBOY

The seven Limner letters discussed above – published in sequential issues of the *Balance* during October and November 1804 – explored issues of truth, judgment, and character, which had preoccupied Croswell since at least 1803. He had been indicted for libel against Jefferson in January of that year, convicted in county court in July, petitioned unsuccessfully for a new trial, and appealed to the New York State Supreme Court, which upheld the verdict in May 1804. In his continuing capacity as a journalist, Croswell had every reason to be cautious about criticizing public figures. But prudence was not in his nature. The editor's reports on his own case and other writings appearing throughout those years are filled with contempt for Republicans. In a less direct manner, "The Limner" offered Croswell an imaginative outlet for his anger and frustration, allowing him to address an injustice for which he had no further direct recourse. Croswell's only hope had remained a change in the law, but that too seemed at an end with legislative rejection, on November 6, 1804, of the truth-in-libel bill his case had inspired. He responded in the "Shop Window" columns with an unrelenting vision of a corrupt body politic. Following the second, with its "plotting," "wrong-headed," malicious men, Croswell placed a bitter editorial: "Truth a Libel Still." Under the insignia of his defunct *Wasp*, the paper that started his troubles, Croswell excoriated Jeffersonian democrats for publicly pretending to support a measure that they had so "altered, cut, carved and mangled" that it could not pass (fig. 116). The bill, Croswell predicted, will "*never become a law!*"[106]

He was wrong. In April 1805, the New York legislature finally passed a truth-in-libel bill of genuine conviction. The following month, Croswell resumed "The Limner." The series had disappeared from the *Balance* in the half-year

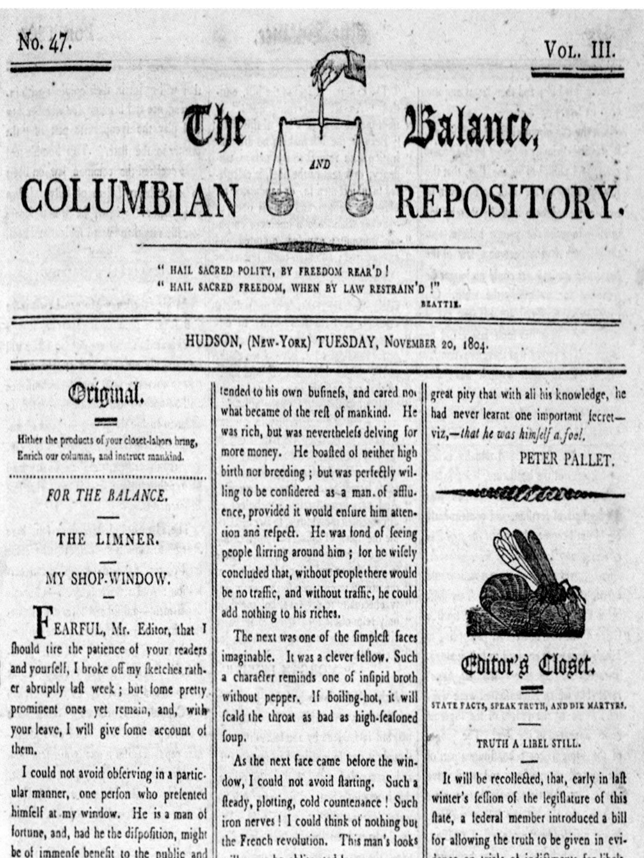
No. 47. VOL. III.

The Balance, and COLUMBIAN REPOSITORY.

" HAIL SACRED POLITY, BY FREEDOM REAR'D!
" HAIL SACRED FREEDOM, WHEN BY LAW RESTRAIN'D!"
BEATTIE.

HUDSON, (NEW-YORK) TUESDAY, NOVEMBER 20, 1804.

Original.

Hither the products of your closet-labors bring,
Enrich our columns, and instruct mankind.

FOR THE BALANCE.

THE LIMNER.

MY SHOP-WINDOW.

FEARFUL, Mr. Editor, that I ſhould tire the patience of your readers and yourſelf, I broke off my ſketches rather abruptly laſt week; but ſome pretty prominent ones yet remain, and, with your leave, I will give ſome account of them.

I could not avoid obſerving in a particular manner, one perſon who preſented himſelf at my window. He is a man of fortune, and, had he the diſpoſition, might be of immenſe benefit to the public and ...

... tended to his own buſineſs, and cared not what became of the reſt of mankind. He was rich, but was nevertheleſs delving for more money. He boaſted of neither high birth nor breeding; but was perfectly willing to be conſidered as a man of affluence, provided it would enſure him attention and reſpect. He was fond of ſeeing people ſtirring around him; for he wiſely concluded that, without people there would be no traffic, and without traffic, he could add nothing to his riches.

The next was one of the ſimpleſt faces imaginable. It was a clever fellow. Such a character reminds one of inſipid broth without pepper. If boiling-hot, it will ſcald the throat as bad as high-ſeaſoned ſoup.

As the next face came before the window, I could not avoid ſtarting. Such a ſteady, plotting, cold countenance! Such iron nerves! I could think of nothing but the French revolution. This man's looks will never be obliterated from my memo-

great pity that with all his knowledge, he had never learnt one important ſecret– viz,–*that he was himſelf a fool.*

PETER PALLET.

Editor's Closet.

STATE FACTS, SPEAK TRUTH, AND DIE MARTYRS.

TRUTH A LIBEL STILL.

It will be recollected, that, early in laſt winter's ſeſſion of the legiſlature of this ſtate, a federal member introduced a bill for allowing the truth to be given in evidence on trials of indictments for libels.

116 *Balance, and Columbian Repository* 3 (Nov. 20, 1804). Courtesy American Antiquarian Society, Worcester, Mass.

since "My Shop Window," its purpose and the writer's creative drive perhaps exhausted. Now, under different conditions, Croswell renewed his objective. As Pallet, he once again addressed the editor: "I am all compliance. When you hinted to me the propriety of withholding my communications during the session of Congress, &c. you heard no more from me. I have waited until all the political obstacles to the admission of my pictures, seem to be removed; and now . . . I once more venture before the public."[107] Croswell had remained before the public as himself, ever-contentious editor of the *Balance*. But having found vindication in the legislative action his case prompted, he faced no "political obstacles" to the presentation of another "portrait." The chronological break in the Limner series corresponds to a conceptual break, as Pallet/Croswell moved his subject into the foreground.

Croswell boldly renewed his offensive against Republicans with a provocative trio of columns, presented as exchanges between Pallet and a female antagonist. When she first approaches the artist about having her picture made, the woman strikes Pallet as "handsome." The word referred not only to fine appearance but also to conduct judged "seemly, courteous, gracious."[108] Handsomeness, in short, carried positive moral connotations. Once again, appearances deceive: the woman quickly reveals her vulgarity by swearing in response to Pallet's discovery that she has hidden his "*pencil* of truth." He exposes her duplicity in the newspaper. She counterattacks in the next issue, insisting that he misplaced the tool. By slandering her in the press, she adds, Pallet has also lost his "*pen* of truth."[109]

Croswell named his outspoken correspondent "Miss Tomboy." The earliest usages of "tomboy" date to the later 1500s, first in reference to "a rude, boisterous, or forward boy," then "a bold or immodest woman," and, finally, "a girl who behaves like a spirited or boisterous boy; a wild romping girl; a hoyden" – the dominant meaning by the eighteenth century.[110] These negative connotations underlay use of the name for the outspoken, independent Miss Priscilla Tomboy in Isaac Bickerstaff's comic opera *Love in the City* (1767). Abridged in 1774 as *The Romp*, a synonym for tomboy, the play became widely popular in Britain and the United States – the third most frequently performed work of musical theater in five major American theatrical centers between 1790 and 1810.[111] The story satirized the ambitions of its upwardly mobile characters, including the physical, swearing Priscilla. Her determination to marry an army officer, a gentleman, ultimately prevails over the wishes of her guardian, a wealthy tradesman with no regard for rank, especially if (as he suspects of the officer) not accompanied by income. Croswell undoubtedly knew that his Miss Letitia Tomboy – whose courtesy title indicates she has not submitted to the authority of a husband – would evoke the comic character in the minds of readers. He used her scheming and social aspirations, together with other characters' obsession with money, to reinforce prior themes of the Limner columns.

Miss Tomboy, in her retort to Pallet, proves assertive and direct. "What have women done, that they must be deprived of the same *liberty of speech* which men enjoy?" she boldly inquires. Croswell's personal experience left him cynical about the possibility of free speech for anyone. Two years earlier, in 1803, he had concluded a mock "Political Catechism" on the subject of liberty with the question "What is liberty of speech?" and the reply, "It is the liberty of speaking well of the present administration, (Mr. Burr excepted) and of all who have obtained, or shall obtain offices under it, in whatever ways and by whatever means."[112] Croswell diminished Miss Tomboy's appeal for free speech by reducing it to a case for the equal freedom to swear, not for the right to say anything of substance. Yet he makes her a player, who does not hesitate to challenge a man, and he no more singled out women for folly, vanity, duplicity, or coarseness than he did men, whether in "The Limner" or the *Balance* more generally. He represents the failings of both as human deficiencies, not those of sex. Interestingly, only female characters defend themselves against what they perceive as Pallet's slander. They respond directly, by writing letters to the editor of their own. "Fanny Fanciful," the fashionable young lady who objected to the representation of her elbow, had done so in advance of Miss Tomboy. She admitted that a naked elbow is not "comely" but defended the fashion for short sleeves and light dresses on the basis of comfort, daring any critic "to swelter through one hot summer, under an ample burthen of muslin, chintz, and dimity."[113] Since muslin, chintz, and dimity are cotton fabrics, often of light weave, Croswell injected irony into Miss Fanciful's complaint. When he created such characters, he acknowledged and engaged a female readership for the *Balance*. Women had not yet been consigned to the separate literary and social sphere of specialized women's magazines, a relatively new genre at the outset of the nineteenth century, and they contributed as writers to such publications as *Port Folio*. Scholars have argued that Federalists, unlike the Jeffersonians, accepted informal participation by women in politics and showed greater concern for female education; still, Federalists were inclined to frame women's rights as "duties," exercised within the constraints of traditional hierarchical society.[114] Croswell's writing is consistent with that view.

Deficient femininity was not Croswell's primary target when he created Miss Tomboy; he plainly also had deficient masculinity in mind. It was not uncommon to impugn political opponents by feminizing them. Alexander Hamilton put down both Jefferson and Madison for displaying "a womanish attachment to France and a womanish resentment against Great Britain," presumably meaning that they were guided by feelings as opposed to reason.[115] The word "tomboy" cut both ways. Some late eighteenth-century English dictionaries, including Johnson's, continued to make the definition "wild coarse girl" secondary to "mean fellow"[116] Croswell unambiguously compared Miss Tomboy to corrupt "great men" and, implicitly, to one man: his real-life nemesis, Tom Jefferson. Miss Tomboy's patently false claim of indifference to "'the daubing of my pencil,' and 'the slander of my pen,'" Pallet charges,

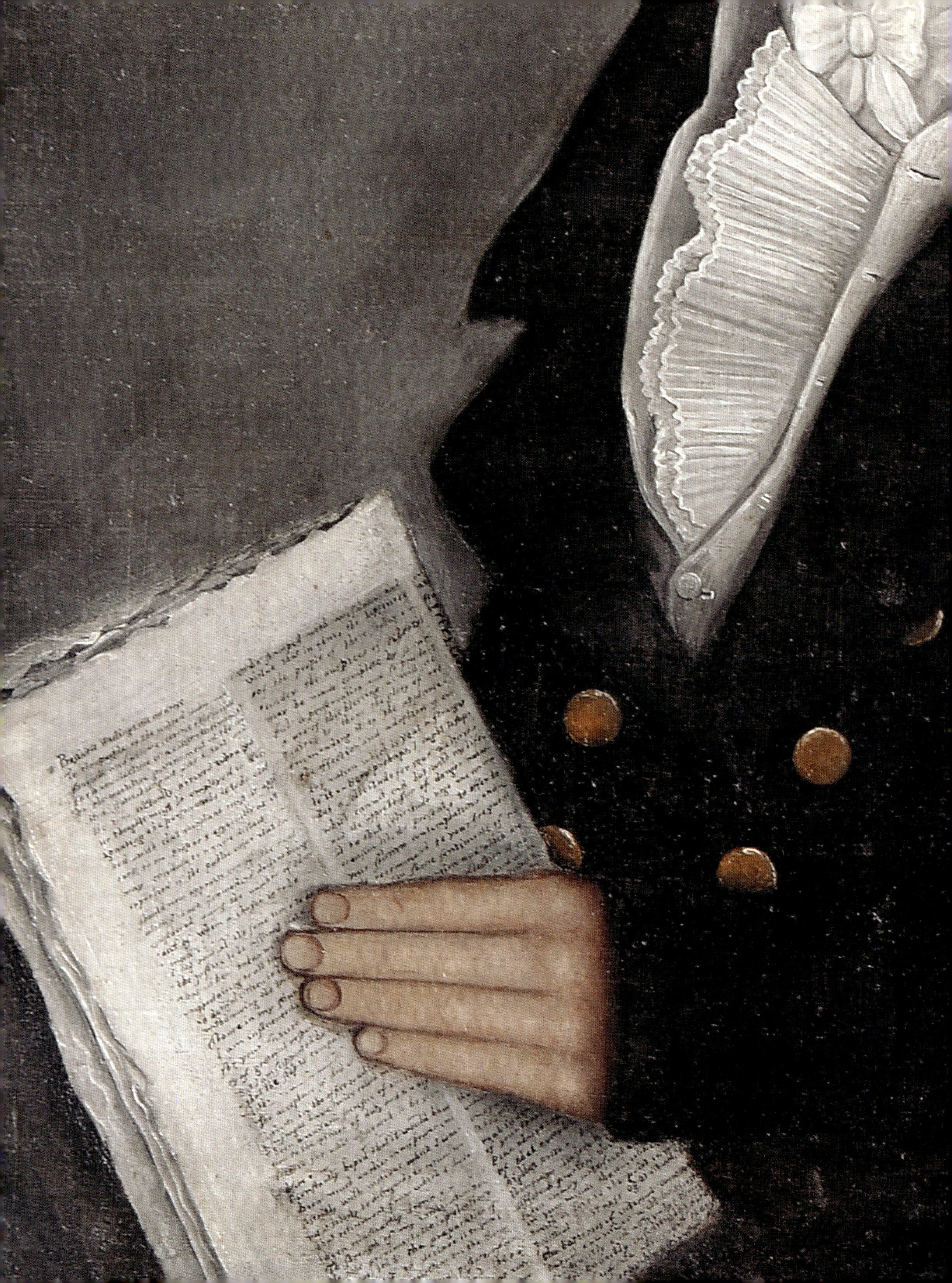

is precisely like certain great men's hypocritical pretension, that they regard not the "lacerations of the press." With these people, plain truth is the worst of slander; and the person who promulgates it, is, of course, a most "vulgar, brutal, low-bred fellow." Miss Tomboy, (still holding her resemblance of our great men) thinks it extremely hard that a person of her "rank and character" should not be exempt from the "slander" of my pen. On this subject, I beg leave to be more than ordinarily serious; for the examples of people of rank, have done more towards corrupting the morals and manner of the community, than any thing whatever. The vices and follies of the great are more contagious than a pestilence. They spread over the country like wild-fire, contaminating everything they touch, and rendering ineffectual every lecture from the pulpit, or lesson from the press.[117]

The linkage of "lesson" and "press" with "lecture" and "pulpit" emphasized the moral seriousness for Croswell of the journalistic enterprise, its vital importance to national politics. As a journalist, Croswell felt obligated at times to cut his fellow citizens – the word "pallet" (in that spelling) could denote a vessel used in bloodletting or the quantity of blood therein.[118] The editor's "lacerations" were like those of the bloodletter, painful actions that might stem "pestilence" and restore the nation to health. He would not spare the president, or the president's men, when they had betrayed truth.

Although Croswell's fierce opposition to Jefferson and his party continued, the corrective legislation prompted by *People v. Croswell*, and the likelihood that the defendant would be vindicated in a retrial authorized by the New York Supreme Court, diminished his motivation to compose "The Limner." The final five letters in the Hudson-based newspaper appear sporadically over the next year. Instead of featuring Pallet's direct exchanges with sitters, these last writings describe events outside the painter's shop in which Pallet is less participant than witness, albeit still wielding his "pencil of truth" against persons who act as if truth were irrelevant. His subjects remain egotism, avarice, selfishness, and duplicity. Perhaps Croswell never cared about art as such. Still, his decision to express himself through the figure of the Limner, a man whom he represented as righteous and empowered, argues for the vital role of portraitists in the early American republic.

In the years immediately following conclusion of his legal case, Croswell's combativeness continued to attract libel suits. At the same time, he began to lose Federalist support, despite relocating the *Balance* to Albany, the state capital, in 1809. Imprisonment in 1811 for minor debt to a leading Federalist left the editor disgusted with the party he had supported for so long and at such personal cost. He promptly abandoned his newspaper and his Congregationalist upbringing to become an Episcopal deacon, then minister. For that position, Croswell received no formal training, making him, in effect, one of those self-taught divines he had lampooned in the first Limner column. By 1816, he was rector of New Haven's increasingly powerful Trinity Church. One of his first acts there holds great irony. Croswell led Connecticut Episcopalians in a decisive break with Congregationalists, their former Federalist cohort, to join with former Republicans and Federalists in a new "Toleration Party." So began the democratization of the state that had always been most resistant to republicanism and, it seems, of Harry Croswell himself.[119]

During a period in which the portrait transaction became common across the American social spectrum, a subject of anecdotes in the press, and a trope in political arguments about equality, Gilbert Stuart's complicated involvement with issues of representation – and the compulsive humor that stands as evidence of his own conflicts – presents a rich field of inquiry. Whereas other leading artists, most notably Peale and Trumbull, were quick to employ public-spirited rhetoric that contributed to their personal and professional advancement, Stuart's strategies of self-promotion were more ingenious and at times even drew cleverly on regressive ideas about the status of artists. Stuart skillfully harnessed contemporary taste for anecdote, telling tales about himself, counting on them to be repeated, and acting in ways that ensured others would relate stories of him. Some of those anecdotes are remarkably close to examples already in circulation about other artists, allowing Stuart to appear of a type with historical lineage. At the same time, he never seemed less than fully individual, entirely himself.

Facing page Detail of fig. 113.

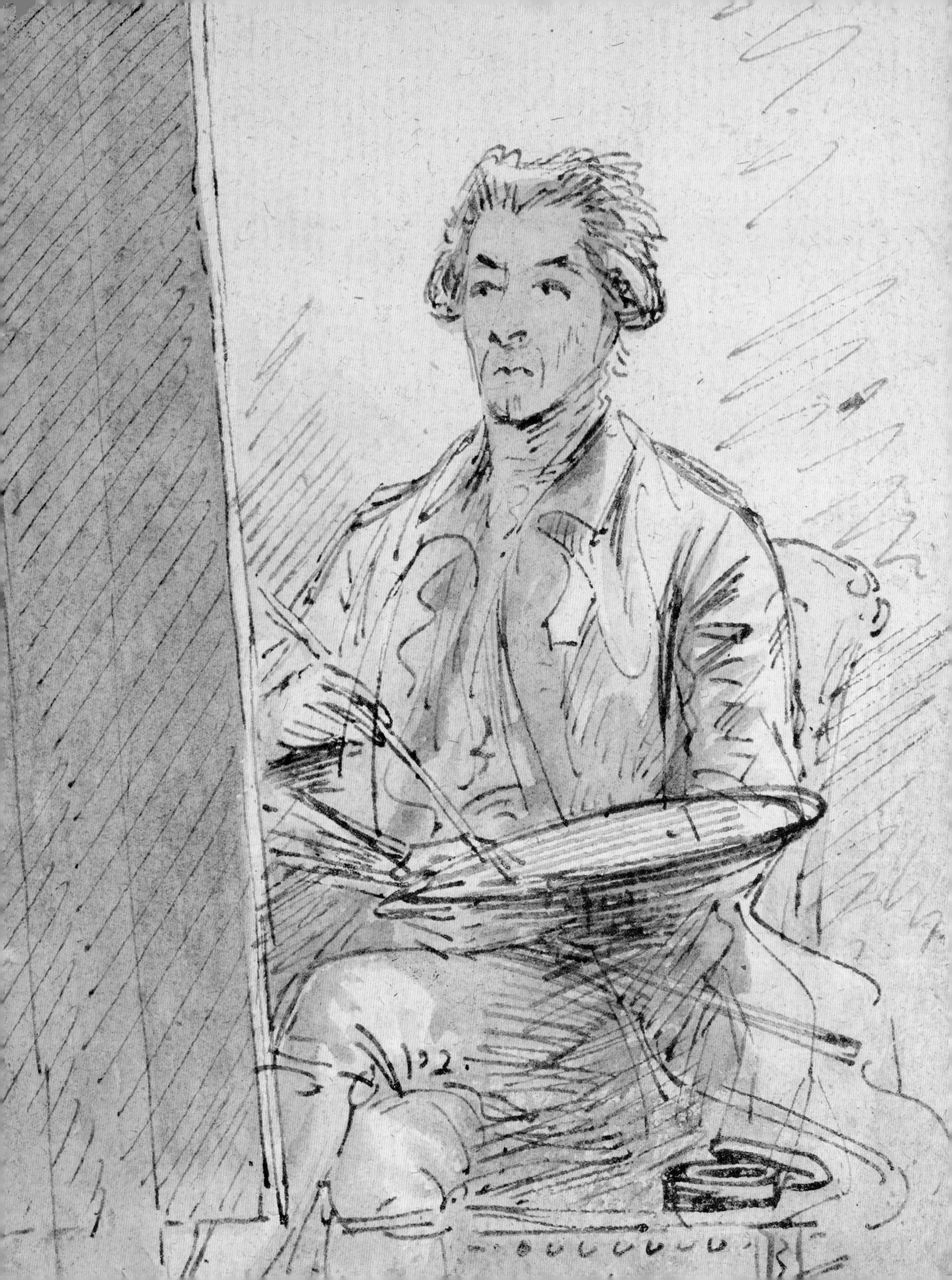
192.

5

CONTRARY STUART

Philadelphia's leading artists had good reason to extol Gilbert Stuart as the "*Father of American Portraiture*" after the painter's death in 1828.[1] Stuart's work had been distinguished, his patrons political and social leaders of the early republic, his style influential on younger American artists. The honorific also tacitly acknowledged Stuart's commanding likenesses of the nation's "father," George Washington. His second portrait of Washington, alone among many representations of the general and president, has proven indelible and indispensable, most enduringly in adaptation for the United States one-dollar bill (fig. 117).

Yet as his contemporaries well knew, Stuart conducted himself in a manner contrary to identities nurtured by other celebrated American artists. International experience and exposure to academic ideals concerning the social value of art – both of which Stuart acquired – raised the sights of many painters active between the 1760s, when Copley and West came to prominence, and 1834, when Dunlap published the first history of American art. They rejected an older association of painters with tradesmen, defining themselves instead as men of ideas whose art could benefit society at large. Peale and Trumbull epitomize the type among artists active in America during the late colonial and early national periods. Peale, having begun his working life as a saddle maker, envisioned painting as a way to improve his position in the world and to instruct his countrymen by making portraits that represented virtue – through the depicted actions or comportment of his sitters as well as the formal and stylistic restraint of his painting manner. Peale established the nation's first public museum, featuring his likenesses of distinguished Americans alongside results of the scientific endeavors that occupied his later career. Trumbull, son of a Connecticut magistrate later elected governor and the beneficiary of a Harvard education, risked downward mobility when he became a painter, so it is not surprising that he actively courted the status of American master with bold historical paintings of Revolutionary War engagements (fig. 118). He also led the American Academy of Fine Arts, one of the first national institutions for the advancement of art.

With posterity in mind, both Peale and Trumbull took other measures to secure their reputations. Peale projected the well-regulated life on which his republican self-image depended in eighteen self-portraits and through prodigious, lifelong self-documentation in diaries, letters, and autobiographical writing. In 1790, the forty-nine-year-old Peale composed his first memoir, to which he returned in his mid-eighties, when he incorporated that work into a longer manuscript (1825–26) meant for publication.[2] Neither foregrounds his achievements as a painter, but Peale tended that legacy in other ways, with a flurry of late self-portraits including the life-size, full-length presentation of the artist

Facing page Detail of fig. 134.

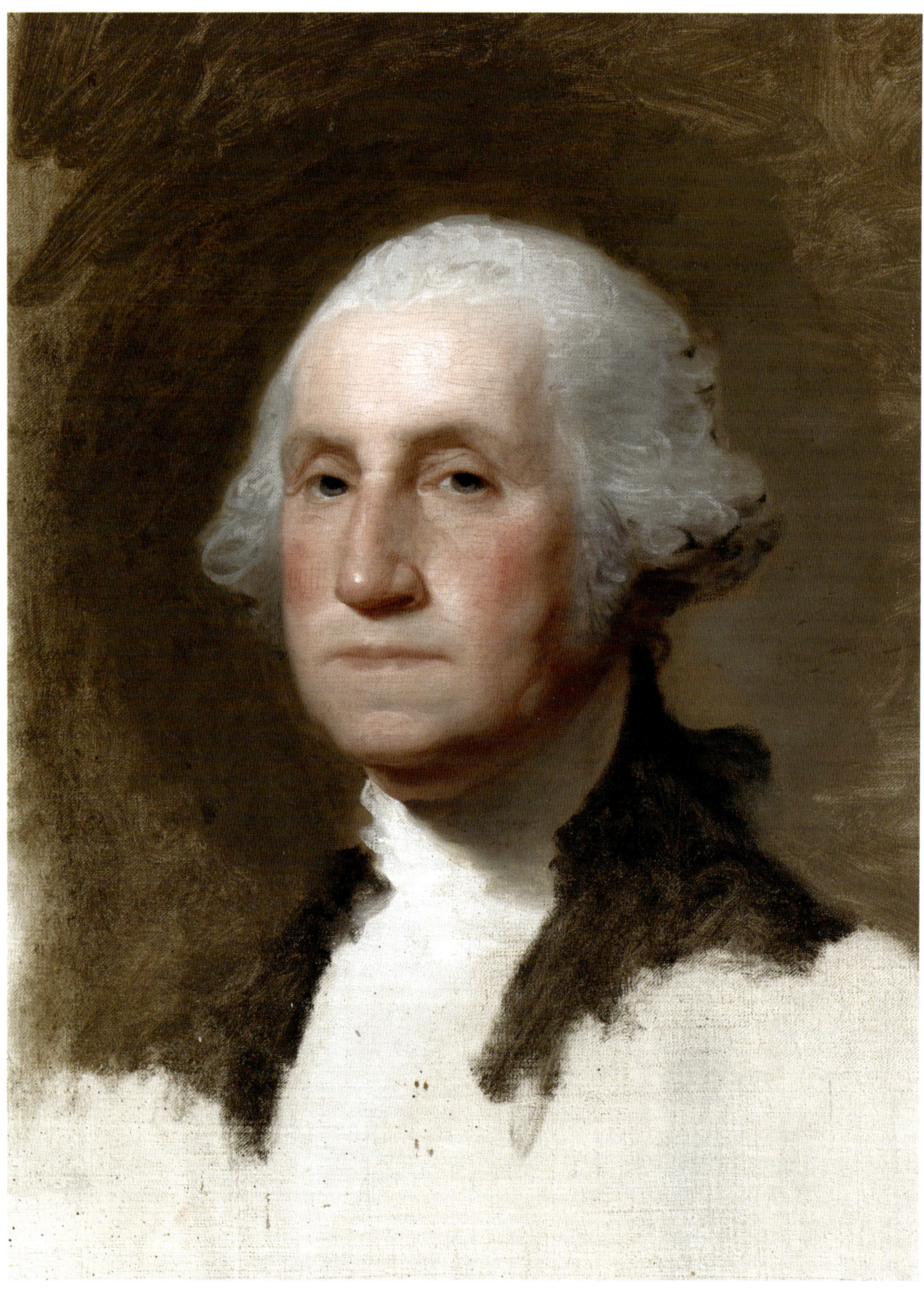

117 Gilbert Stuart, *George Washington (The Athenaeum Portrait)*, 1796. Oil on canvas, 30¼ × 25¼ in. (76.8 × 64.1 cm). Jointly owned by the National Portrait Gallery, Smithsonian Institution, Washington, D.C., and the Museum of Fine Arts, Boston. William Francis Warden Fund, John H. and Ernestine A. Payne Fund, Commonwealth Cultural Preservation Trust.

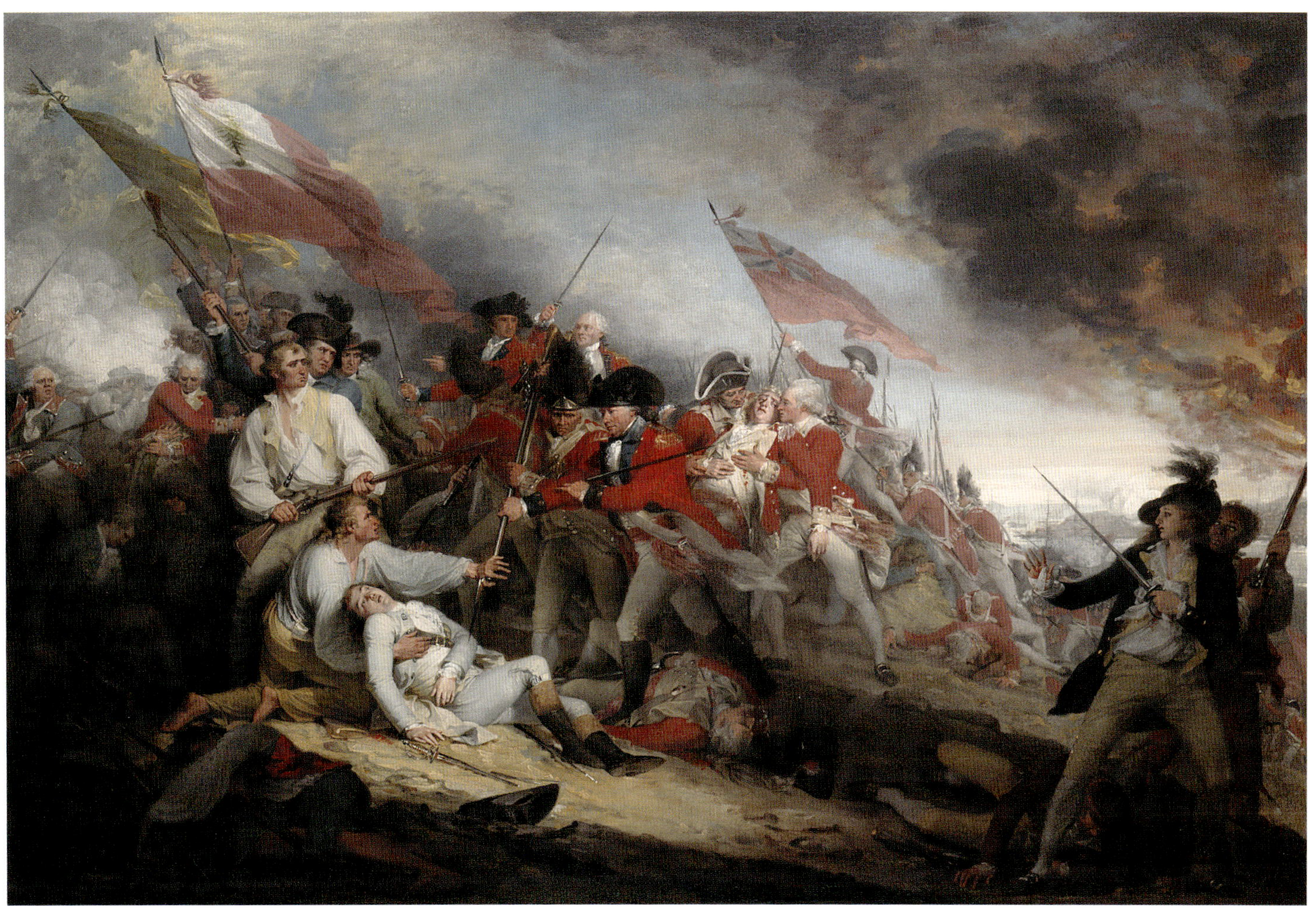

118 John Trumbull, *The Death of General Warren at the Battle of Bunker's Hill, June 17, 1775*, 1786. Oil on canvas, 25⅝ × 37⅝ in. (65.1 × 95.6 cm). Yale University Art Gallery, New Haven, Trumbull Collection, 1832.1.

in his museum, where bust-length portraits of American "worthies" lined the walls (see fig. 153). Had he not died the year before Stuart, Peale would likely have been irritated at the memorial characterization of Stuart, fourteen years his junior, as the father of American portraiture. More injurious, given the broader and more durable context, was Dunlap's prediction in his comparatively short biography of Peale for the *History* that the artist's paintings would be "soon forgotten." Trumbull, still living, received far more attention from Dunlap, a closer contemporary but one he did not personally admire. Desire to represent himself led Trumbull to publish an autobiography in 1841, three years after Dunlap's death.[3] Whether because of generational or class affiliation, both Peale and Trumbull betrayed lingering insecurity over the social status of artists and a concern to prove that they not merely represented but enacted virtue.

Stuart, by contrast, made little effort to convince anyone that he was committed to serving the public good. Although his portraits drew praise for capturing the essential character of sitters – character almost always construed as virtuous – the portraitist perplexed. An "admirable painter & worthless man," the architect Benjamin Henry Latrobe bluntly put it in a letter to Jefferson, a remark at least partly provoked by Stuart's failure to submit any new paintings – as a leader in American art might be expected to do – to an 1811 exhibition at the Pennsylvania Academy of the Fine Arts.[4] Stuart presents the case of an elite painter who nevertheless relished the opportunity to let some of the hot air out of the academic rhetoric surrounding the fine art of painting and to behave in ways that undercut the dignity of his profession. He was a professional who did not always act professional, a man whose own virtue remained open to question.

Stuart's friends, acquaintances, and colleagues sometimes wondered what to make of him. Many thought peculiar his disrespectful attitude toward social and professional superiors, his failure to honor commissions, recurring insolvency, personal slovenliness, and fondness for jokes and pranks. At the same time, they found him fascinating and were quick to relate or record their impressions. Contemporary taste for anecdotal biography encouraged the search for and preservation of telling incidents from a life, and details once considered private (such as personal habits) entered the public domain as valuable indications of character. Accordingly, reviewers condemned Joseph Delaplaine's eulogistic *Repository of the Lives and Portraits of Distinguished American Characters* (1815–18) for failing to include revealing particulars about the subjects, "those little loop-holes through which you might view the furniture and organization of the inner man," as revealed by "inconvenient trifles, a kind of mishaps to which we have given the name of *anecdotes*." Similarly, another reviewer lamented Delaplaine's omission from the biographies of "little foibles and weaknesses," noting that "in the delineation of character, it is of as much importance, to point out the faults, that ought to be shunned, as it is to depict virtues, that ought to be imitated."[5]

Many of the stories about Stuart conform to biographical tropes of artists' lives with roots in antiquity and widely familiar from the modern genre, beginning in the mid-sixteenth century with Vasari. Among the motifs that Ernst Kris and Otto Kurz identified in their classic study of the image of artist, those that resonate with Stuart include the artist's assertion of superiority to contemporaries through witty remarks and jokes; his use of irony to highlight the foolishness of artistic judgments by laypersons; his alteration of paintings in response to conflicts with clients, especially those who were slow to pay; and his insistence that his works of art belonged exclusively to him.[6] Some of the incidents associated with Stuart correspond closely to accounts in the literature. Why then should we believe that he actually did and said what is attributed to him? In some cases, perhaps we should not. But we have to assume that these kinds of stories made sense in connection with Stuart's personality. By contrast, they have no place in the biography of West, to whom an entirely different set of established tropes readily applied, though these were more quickly recognized as such (a matter I consider in the next chapter). Given increasing attention to artists, including anecdotes circulating in the late eighteenth and early nineteenth-century British and American press, it is fair to assume that some of these were adapted to and by Stuart, even knowingly. In that sense, they represent an effort to accommodate Stuart to a historically established artist type, and they became fully constituent of Stuart's public identity.

Often unruly in both personal and professional life, so unlike the almost fanatically self-controlled Peale, Stuart attracted attention.[7] Those who knew him left abundant written testimony, the primary research base for subsequent commentators on the artist, who have not had the benefit of self-generated writings that fueled studies of Copley, West, Peale, and Trumbull. "I doubt if there be in existence a single letter in his remaining family, or any where else, except four of his letters in my possession," Stuart's lifelong friend Benjamin Waterhouse (one of his early portrait subjects) told Dunlap, who was then soliciting such materials for his biographical history of American art (fig. 119).[8] Dunlap published several short articles about Stuart in magazines before composing a much longer account – larded with amusing and critical anecdotes – for his book. His high regard for Stuart's artistic abilities did not prevent Dunlap from calling attention (often by reference to opinions of others) to Stuart's "uncontrollable" "passions and appetites," including multiple references to the artist's fondness for alcohol and snuff and his "extreme negligence and extravagance" in financial matters.[9] Dunlap drew heavily on recollections composed by Waterhouse, who shared Stuart's Newport childhood and studied medicine in Britain while Stuart pursued artistic training. The physician had thought to compose the painter's biography until Charlotte Stuart, his widow, "entreated [him] with tears, not to do it." She knew that Waterhouse had reservations about Stuart's character, which he might all too convincingly represent given his intimate knowledge of the artist.[10] Daughter Jane Stuart, a painter herself, so objected to Dunlap and Waterhouse's representation of her father that she attempted a corrective in three articles published during 1876 and 1877 in *Scribner's Magazine*. But these did little to dispel the image of Stuart as a practical joker and a man who was reckless and "irritable," an unfavorable characterization given prominence by its appearance in the first sentence of her final article.[11] It was Jane Stuart who prompted George C. Mason to compose the first book-length study of the artist (1879), with an anecdotally rich catalogue of Stuart's paintings. In the preface, Mason informed readers that with few exceptions, Stuart "left no papers that could be made available in sketching his career," making it necessary for the author to construct his account on the basis of his own extensive correspondence with individuals who owned portraits by Stuart, often descendants of the sitters.[12] A few related per-

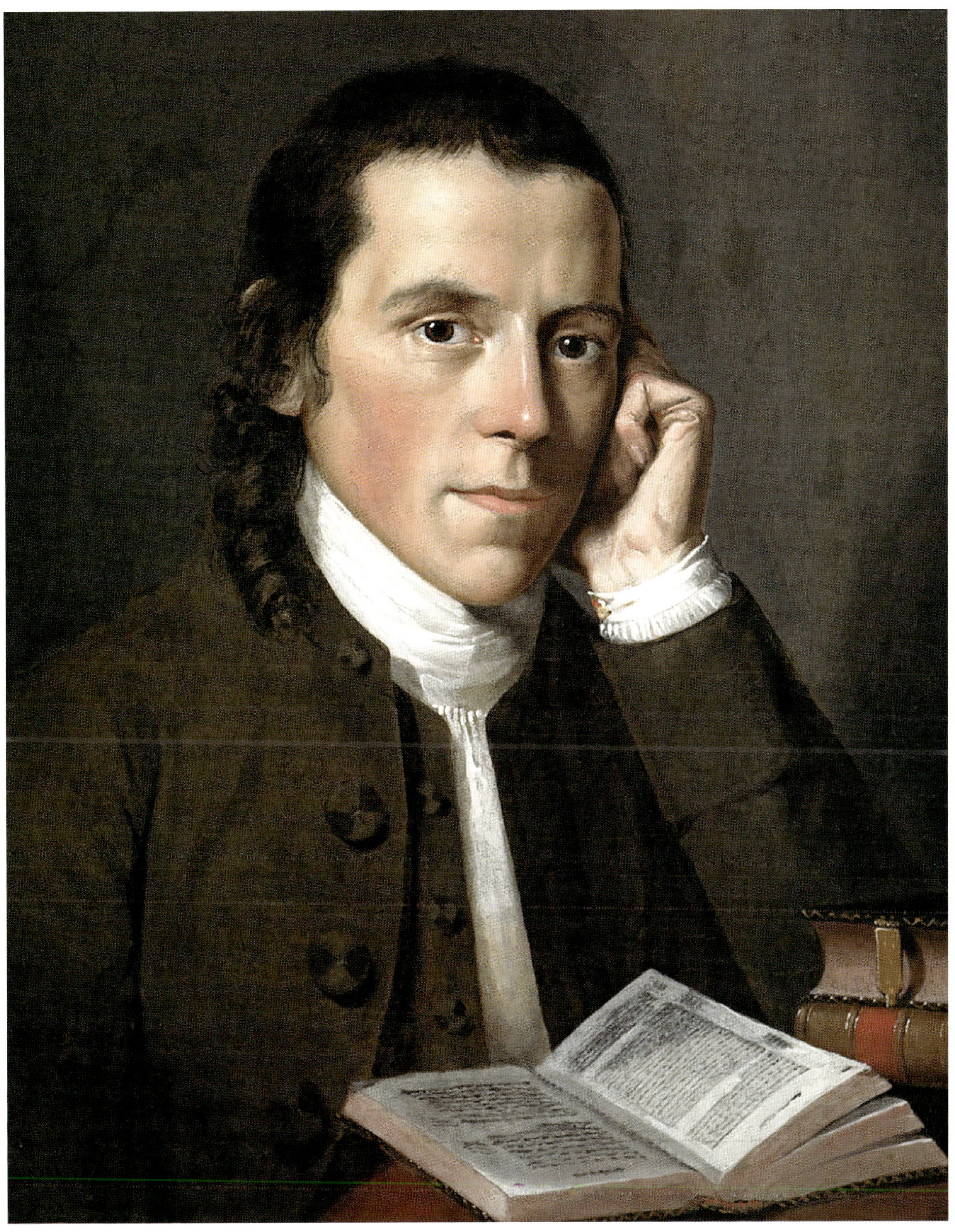

119 Gilbert Stuart, *Benjamin Waterhouse*, 1775. Oil on canvas, 22 × 18 in. (55.9 × 45.7 cm). From the collection of the Redwood Library and Athenaeum, Newport, Rhode Island, bequest of Louisa Lee Waterhouse.

sonal encounters with the painter, and many were able to pass along stories they had heard or to share excerpts from diaries and letters of family members closely connected to the commissions. Over the course of the twentieth century, a sequence of Stuart biographers found additional early published sources that mention him, along with numerous unpublished remarks by colleagues, patrons, and friends or family members of sitters. Dorinda Evans, in particular, recovered several notable first-hand accounts, including Henry Pickering's self-described "interview" with Stuart, his record of visits to the artist's studio in 1810 and 1817, in part recorded as a dialogue.[13]

One of the most striking aspects of these varied texts is their recreation of Stuart's voice, through remarks he supposedly made or conversations he engaged in, frequently recalled many years later. The accounts indicate that Stuart not only talked a lot – people manifestly said he did – but that what he said was memorable. John Quincy Adams was hardly alone in finding Stuart's conversation entertaining, but over the course of several sittings for a portrait, he also recognized it as purposeful: "He considers himself beyond all question the first portrait painter of the age, and tells numbers of anecdotes concerning himself to prove it." Similarly, John Neal recalled a conversation of around 1819 in which the artist told "story after story of himself."[14] Even when contemporaneous sources of information concerning Stuart are filtered, as they usually are to varying degrees, they have a ring of authenticity, a vividness and relative consistency that lend them credibility. Their consistency suggests that Stuart did not attempt to shift course to alter public perception of him, at least not in accordance with ideals of regularity, decorum, and propriety that had been critical to artists prominent during Stuart's formative years in the profession, including his teacher, West. Instead, Stuart shaped his image for posterity in the performance of a self that countered the person and practice of the artist as gentleman and public servant.

Stuart's combativeness, eccentricity, and humor demand to be evaluated as positions the artist cultivated, consistent with his personality and temperament, to distinguish himself from his cohort. One of Stuart's followers in later years, John Neagle (earlier a humble apprentice in coach and sign painting), remembered the great portraitist as "particularly eloquent on the subject of arts and artists." Neatly evoking the mercurial artist's verbal and visual acuity, Neagle added that Stuart "could wield the weapons of satire and ridicule with peculiar force, seize the strong point of character, placing it so dexterously in the light he wished, that the impression was irresistible and not easily effaced."[15] The many stories concerning Stuart's irreverence about painting practice, clients, colleagues, academies, and the status of artists reveal powerful opposition to traditional expectations of and for artists – both the older type of artisan-painter and relatively recent (in Britain and America) conception of the learned and civic-minded artist. Stuart developed a more modern persona as a painter who, for the most part, maintained willful independence of patrons and professional predecessors, who insisted on personal artistic authority, and who resisted social norms. Scholars have recognized that the commercial pressures of bourgeois society in Europe by the late eighteenth century led to the emergence of a modern (and paradoxically normative) artist type: genius as eccentric – an aesthetic model that others could only misuse by following, polluting its essence in the process. A classic genius becomes a collective model and survives in imitation. A modern genius is singular and tolerates no imitation. But, with an irony very often acknowledged by Romantic artists and writers, in a modern culture, modern genius becomes the classic model.[16] It was Stuart who first manifested the type of the artist-genius in the United States.

Genius had long carried connotations of mania, which in Stuart's case may well have had an organic basis. In the context of a short discourse on American artists from 1829, Samuel L. Knapp suggested, with reference to Stuart, that "irritable nerves and delicate fibres" were best omitted from biography and remanded "to the consideration of the physician; for they are mostly diseases of a physical nature."[17] Dr. Waterhouse knew that mental illness ran in the artist's family. Following a condolence call shortly after Stuart's death, which had the added purpose of securing an unfinished portrait of John Quincy Adams, Waterhouse tactlessly wrote the president concerning an adult son in the household who was "insane," though in criticizing Stuart himself Waterhouse referred only to defects in his "character," not to mental illness.[18] Still, he may have suspected it, giving Charlotte Stuart a further reason to oppose Waterhouse's planned biography. Based on such textual evidence concerning Stuart's erratic behavior and on close analysis of his uneven painting manner, Evans, the modern scholar, has made a strong case that Stuart suffered from bipolar disorder, beginning at around age eighteen, most extreme when the artist was in his mid-thirties and painting in Ireland, and easing by the time he reached his mid-fifties, during the first decade of the nineteenth century.[19] While I find the diagnosis plausible and rely for my analysis of Stuart on many of the same accounts that Evans used, I prefer to evaluate Stuart in the terms that his contemporaries did and based on information they had.

Patrons, including those Stuart vexed, showed every inclination to recognize his behavior (without necessarily condoning it) as evidence of genius and artistic temperament. "Genius is always eccentrick, I think," wrote Abigail Adams, in exasperation over fruitless efforts to extract Stuart's first portrait of her husband from the artist; "*Superiour talents* give no security for *propriety of conduct*; there is no knowing how to take hold of this Man."[20] Others, especially women and men of a younger generation, were more forgiving. Sarah Cunningham, daughter of Stuart's three-time sitter Sarah Wentworth Apthorp Morton, found Stuart in 1825 "as eccentric, as dirty, and as entertaining as ever," full of amusing talk, delivered in a "droll & peculiar" manner. She also recognized that the artist gave himself free rein: "He seems to think that his genius gives him a right to follow the entire bent of his temper & spirits, be that what it may."[21] Eliza Susan Quincy, in correspondence with Mason in 1878, worried that her candor about Stuart's comportment impugned the artist. She asked the biographer not to use observations she had shared with him "as rather too familiar & personal for a work like yours." Quincy understood that her contributions would help shape public perception of Stuart, and she was prepared to protect his image – a quaint concern in the expanding culture of celebrity artists, epitomized at that moment by James Abbott McNeill Whistler.[22] Some who had known Stuart believed that he not only made no effort to censor himself but that his behavior was calculated, relieving them of any obligation to mute their impressions. "There is no reason for suppressing the irritable remarks of Mr. Stuart," Marianne Silsbee (daughter of a sitter) advised Mason; ". . . on the contrary I would make the most of it, *as he did* . . . Biographies do not fulfil their design if they are merely eulogistic – and the eccentricities of genius are a relief to the grander passions of the character."[23] Even if not always in control of himself, Stuart both benefited from and exploited modern valuation of individuality and subjectivity.

This chapter considers the formation of Stuart's persona – by himself and others – through an examination of his assertions and actions in relation to four categories of patron, sitter, or associate: more senior artists, the first president, private patrons, and fictional clients and works. Claims in this intriguing last category, concerning paintings he may never actually have made, reveal Stuart's compelling need to shape public perception. He was remarkably successful in doing so. Stuart has come down to us a man who challenged social hierarchy, flouted authority, and could be vigorous (if not consistent) in promoting his interests. While serving social, political, and financial elites, Stuart seems constantly to have renegotiated his relationship to power, alternating between restraint and resistance and inscribing for posterity the image of an artist who succeeded on his own terms.

"An Unruly Subject": West and Reynolds

Stuart's complicated relationship with figures of authority was apparent from the start of his career. He left his native Rhode Island in 1775 seeking artistic opportunity in London. The painter, then just nineteen, was ill-prepared for the venture, without financial backing from patrons or family comparable to that received by West, Peale, and Trumbull during their studies abroad. After a difficult first year, Stuart appealed to West for assistance in a rare surviving autograph document: "Pitty me Good Sir I've just arriv'd at the age of 21 an age when most young men have done something worthy of notice & find myself Ignorant without Business or Freinds, without the necessarys of life so far that for some time I have been reduced to one miserable meal a day & frequently not even that, destitute of the means of acquiring knowledge, my hopes from home Blasted & incapable of returning thither, pitching headlong into misery I have this only hope I pray that it may not be too great, to live & learn without being a Burthen."[24] West responded generously, accepting his abject countryman as a studio assistant. Almost immediately, Stuart sought to contradict that pathetic image, as if he wished to avoid ever again feeling – or appearing – helpless. His effort to take control had both constructive and potentially destructive dimensions: on the one hand, Stuart's rapid artistic progress; on the other, a compulsion to mock West that might have backfired had Stuart been less useful to West or the master, whom Peale remembered as "Extreemely affible and good-natured," less even-tempered.[25]

West proved an irresistible target for a young man driven to oppose superiors. He held exalted rank as historical painter to George III, yet his humble origins as a Pennsylvania innkeeper's son provided a frame of reference for Stuart, whose father had been a snuff miller. Dunlap represented Stuart as "an unruly subject" during his time as West's pupil and assistant, between 1777 and 1782, a phrase that openly refers to the revolutionary era, though the specific choice of words (as opposed to the general charac-

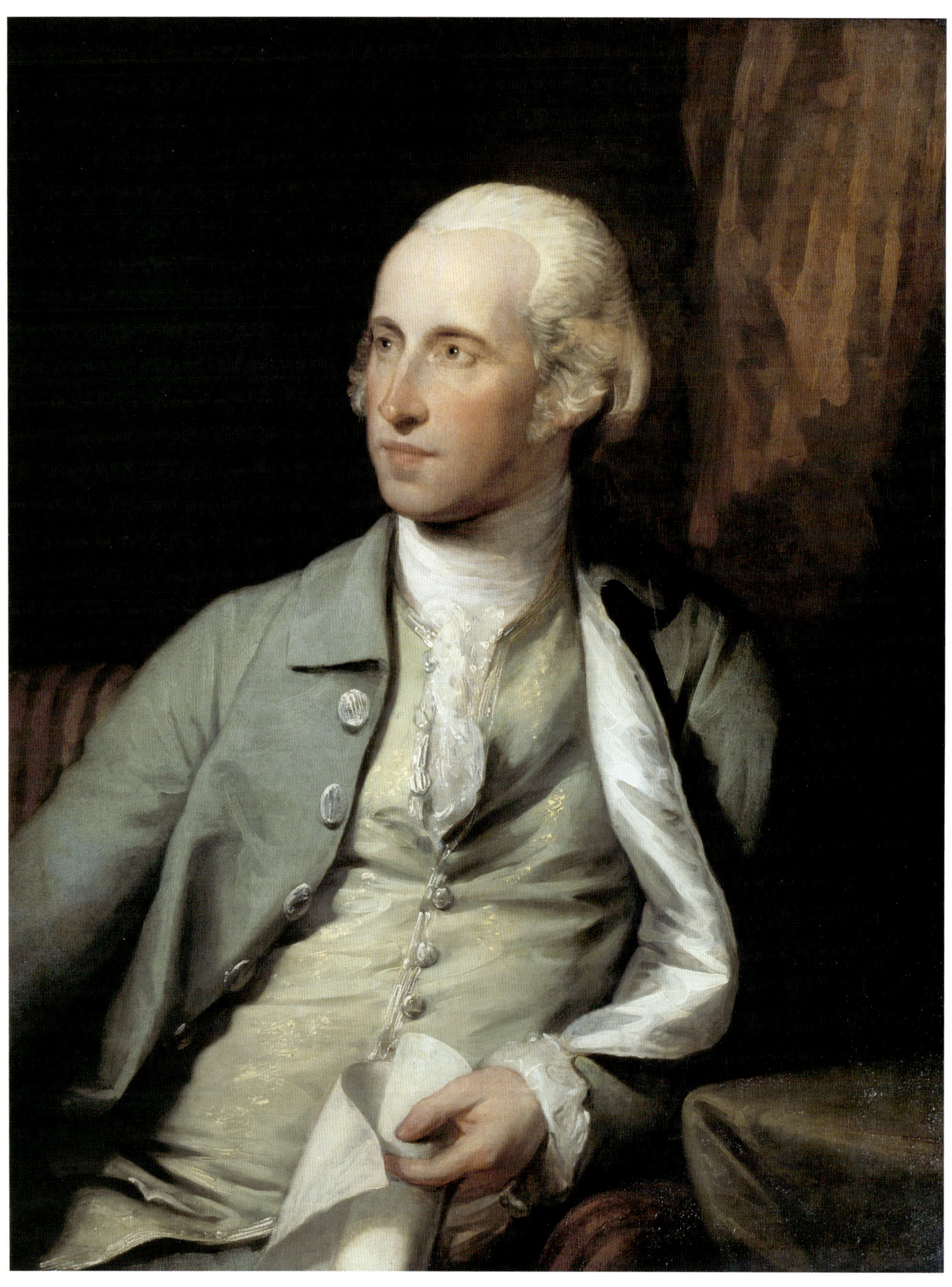

120 Gilbert Stuart, *Benjamin West, P.R.A*, exh. 1781. Oil on canvas, 36 × 28 in. (91.4 × 71.1 cm). Tate Gallery, London.

terization) were Dunlap's in 1834, not Stuart's.[26] Stuart made fun of West's laborious and flawed painting technique and contrastingly impeccable appearance as a man, a graceful ease projected in his portrait of the master of 1781 (fig. 120). Stuart's oppositional self-presentation generally does not inflect his paintings; in this case, for example, the refined appearance he gave West suggests nothing but admiration. An alternative reading emerges only in conjunction with Stuart's remarks from his days in West's studio, as reported by Dunlap. The senior artist, said Stuart, always looked "neat as a lad of wax . . . as if he had stepped out of a bandbox."[27] In *Romeo and Juliet*, Shakespeare assigned the phrase "man of wax" to a comic character, Juliet's nurse, whose words convey approval for the perfection and conventional beauty of Paris, a potential suitor to her mistress; at the same time, comparison with an inanimate object exposes the man's superficiality.[28] In eighteenth-century London, displays of wax figures, colored and clothed in imitation of life, were popular entertainment. The American sculptor Patience Wright, who lived in the metropolis and knew West during the time Stuart worked for him, made the creation of wax portraits a dramatic performance, as reported and provocatively illustrated in the press (fig. 121). She modeled the heads beneath her apron, using the warmth of her body to keep the wax malleable, before producing the herm-like result in a manner that, as Wendy Bellion proposed, suggested both priapic creative urge and maternal birthing process. Professional woman artists, a culturally anomalous conjunction, occasionally endured speculation about their sex, ambiguities alluded to in the portrait of Mrs. Wright. In that context, Stuart's analogy between West and "a lad of wax" may have had feminizing implications for the senior artist, "the celebrated American painter" whose portrait in wax by Mrs. Wright went on display in Philadelphia in 1775.[29] The implication was more up front in Stuart's reference, when describing West's appearance, to a bandbox – typically a container for ladies' millinery and accessories. At a time of unstable British masculinities, Stuart described West in a manner that had the effect of emasculating the courtier-artist, a type that would be especially suspect among Americans of the revolutionary generation and even more so later.[30]

Stuart was prepared to go beyond language to mock West's sartorial refinement and cast himself as the royal painter's antithesis. Counseled by West to discard his outmoded clothes after arrival in London and to adopt fashionable English dress, the impecunious Stuart responded inventively: "I presented myself with my stockings drawn over my shoes, and my waistcoat over my coat." West responded to the disorderly sight with alarm: "'Why, boy, are you mad?'" The underling, playing a clever buffoon, had a coherent explanation and a target larger than West in pointing out the illogical figures of speech. "'Sir,' [Stuart] replied, 'You told me to dress myself as the English do, and I know that they always say "Put on your shoes and stockings," and "Put on your coat and waistcoat," and so I have done.'" The physical humor affirmed Stuart's self-identification as "an uncouth kind of cub" and an unrepentant provincial at the outset of his career, in complete contrast to West's elegant composure and ready adoption of courtly accessories.[31] Notably, West wore a sword when he first met the king and queen in 1768, even though the occasion was

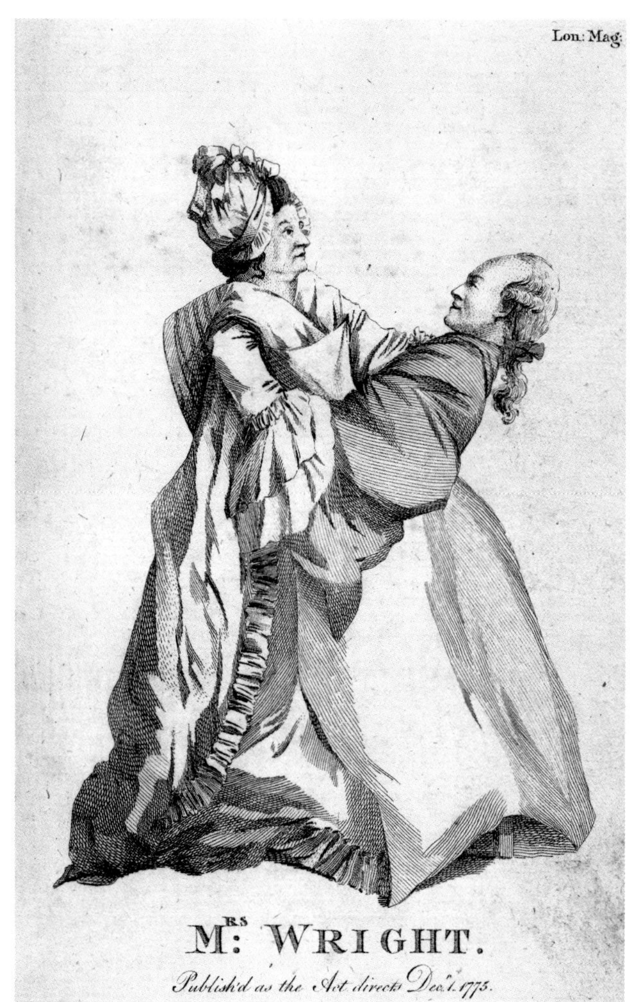

121 Unidentified artist, "Mrs. Wright," from "A Sketch of the Character of Mrs. Wright. (With an exact Likeness of her.)," *London Magazine. Or, Gentleman's Monthly Intelligencer* 44 (Nov. 1775), facing page 556.

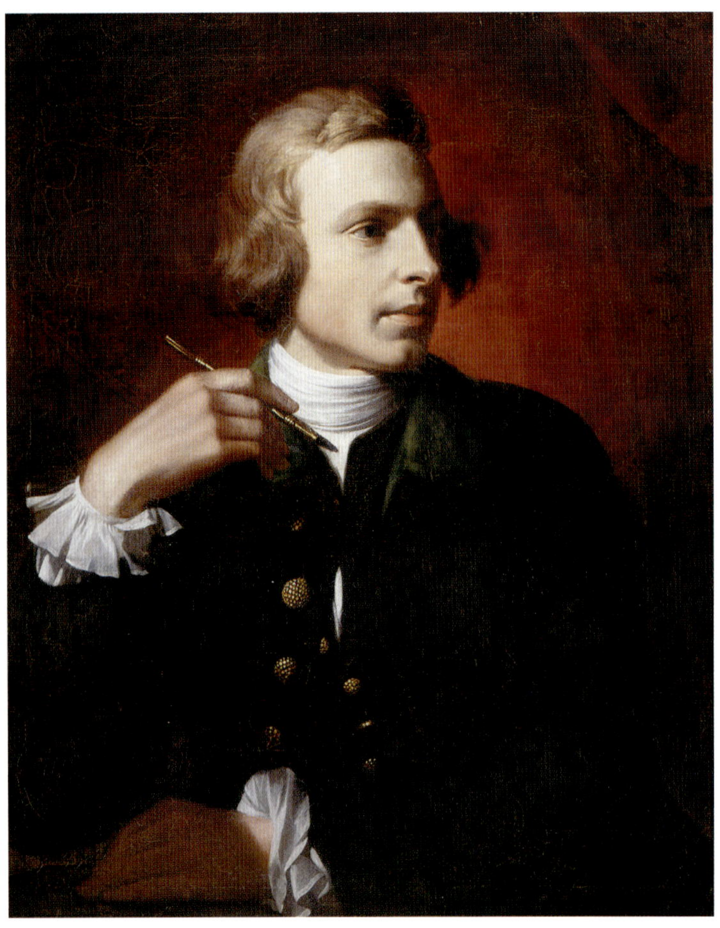

122 Benjamin West, *Charles Willson Peale*, 1767–69. Oil on canvas, 28¼ × 23 in. (72 × 58.5 cm). New-York Historical Society, 1867.293. Photography © New-York Historical Society.

not a formal court appearance. Peale, then working in West's studio, remarked on the importance to West of "appearing to belong to the higher orders of society," even though he was "of a quaker family" (a misconception).[32] Even Peale, despite the sober image of American citizen that he later cultivated, succumbed to the sartorial pressures of cosmopolitan London. Like other newly arrived colonists who made every effort to conform to metropolitan standards of dress, he was reluctant to appear in public until he had new clothes made. Upon arrival in the city for study with West in 1767, Peale spent a considerable portion of his stipend from colonial patrons on fashionable clothing, in order to appear as properly English as possible.[33] Peale's all-around efforts at self-improvement met with West's approbation, evident from his portrayal of Peale in the idealized character of "Artist" (fig. 122), a projection of West himself, as David Ward has plausibly suggested.[34] Stuart, by contrast, resisted West's efforts to mold his image and emphasized his scruffiness in those days. Stuart was not alone in contesting Anglo-American norms of polite society, which some took as evidence of artistic temperament. A titled patron accepted a self-portrait from Scottish painter Alexander Runciman in 1784 in which the artist showed himself sloppily dressed, at work in the company of fellow painter John Brown, whose presumed response to the unseen canvas has left Runciman "irascible, and impatient of reproof . . . making a damnable face."[35] The characterization easily applies to Stuart, both his appearance and demeanor. Once out of West's studio, Stuart freely indulged in the trappings of a much higher standard of living, afforded by his great success in London and Ireland. But he eventually buried that persona. Stuart's anecdote of comically inverted attire indicates that his lack of proper decorum while in West's studio was not later a source of embarrassment to him, but a point – or the invented expression – of perverse pride, consistent with his disregard for refinement during his later American career.

At the outset of his London study, Stuart may have imagined he would take up history painting, following his teacher's example. West's surprising success in mining a vein of patronage for historical subjects, during the years just before and after founding of the Academy, may have made that academically esteemed genre seem viable. In actuality, such works were almost unmarketable as easel paintings, though potentially lucrative when engraved. West's *Death of General Wolfe* (1770) made a fortune for him, engraver William Woollett, and publisher John Boydell once issued as a print in 1775. By that time, West had assumed the rarefied role of historical painter to the king. He capitalized on the position, collecting one thousand guineas from George III for two eighteen-foot-tall religious pictures, *The Ascension of Christ* (ca. 1781–82) and *Moses Receiving the Laws* (1784), made or under way during the time Stuart worked for him.

West's relationships with the monarch, the merchant, and the painter figure in Stuart's second portrait of West (1783–84, fig. 123). Boydell commissioned Stuart to make that picture and fourteen others, all representing engravers and painters whom he promoted (and profited from) as publisher and dealer.[36] West had recently drawn illustrations for Boydell's edition of the Bible, and in Stuart's portrait he grasps one of the volumes, a porte-crayon threaded through his fingers. Behind West, an easel supports a canvas showing Moses receiving the tablets of the law. The work alludes to West's privileged relationship with the king and to the enormous "*ten-acre pictures* . . . with prophets and apostles,"

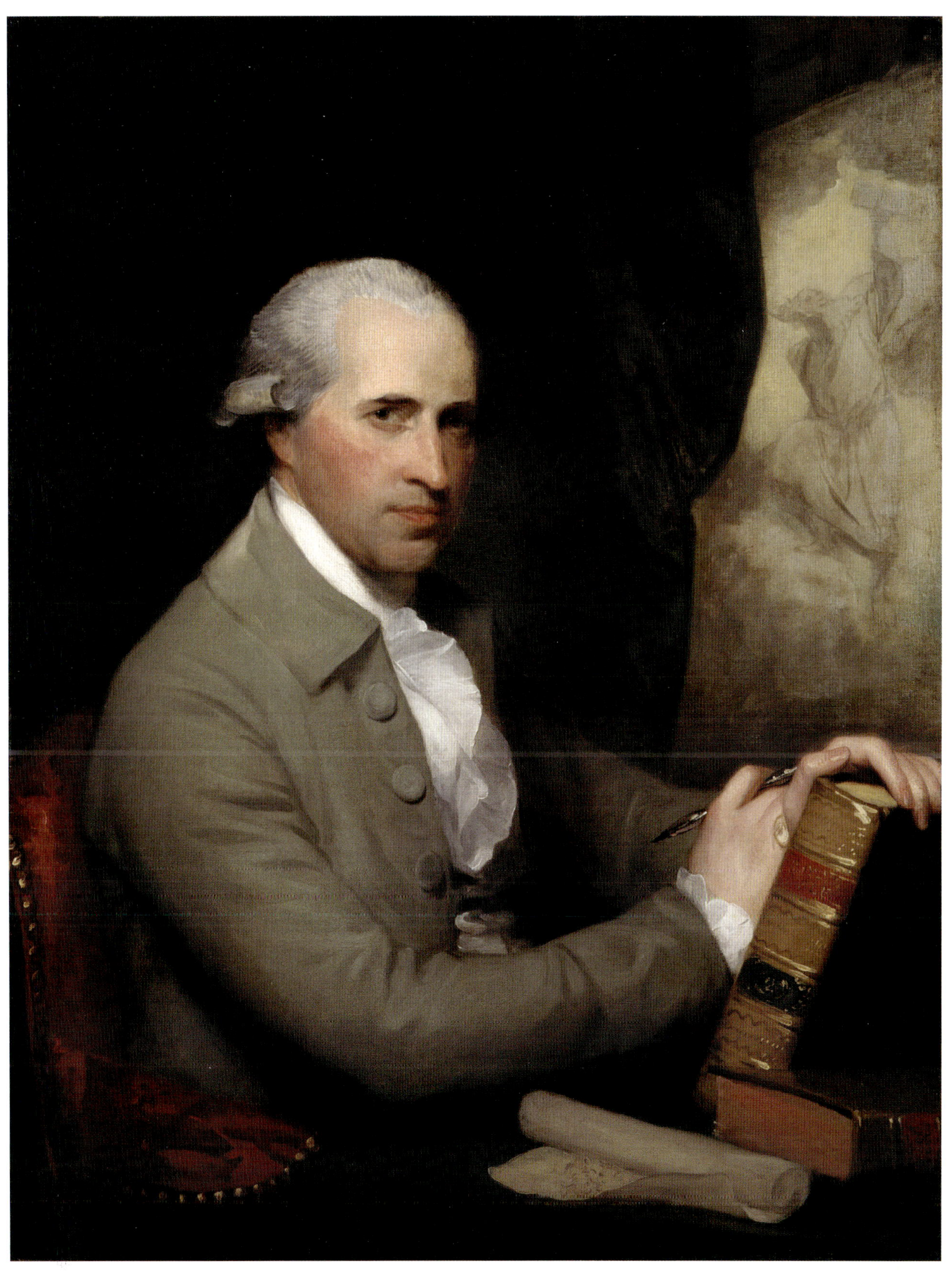

123 Gilbert Stuart, *Benjamin West*, 1783–84. Oil on canvas, 35½ × 27½ in. (90.17 × 68.85 cm). © National Portrait Gallery, London.

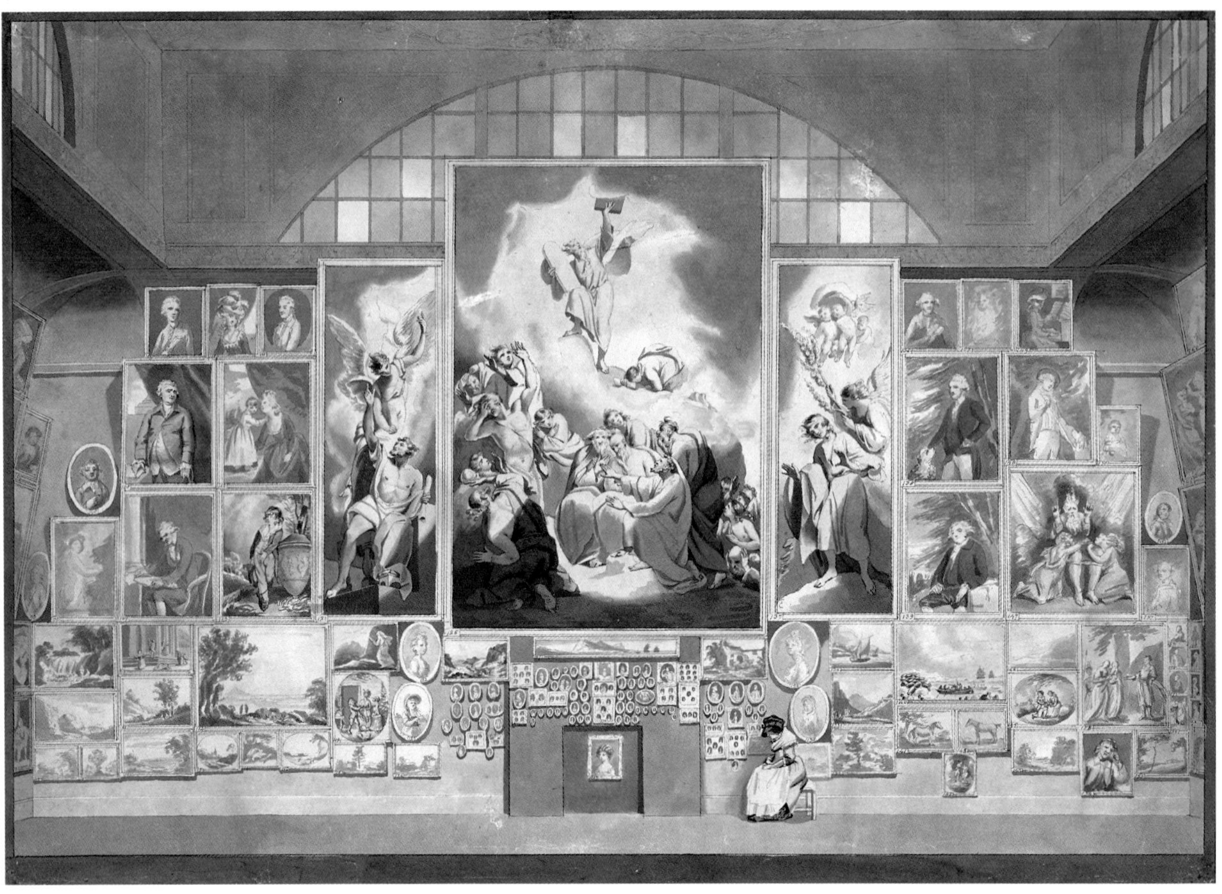

124 Edward Francis Burney, *View of the Royal Academy Exhibition of 1784* (east wall with West's *Moses*). British Museum, London.

as Stuart called them, which made the labor of assistants essential to West's painting practice.[37] At the same time, as Carrie Rebora Barratt reasonably proposed, the relatively compact canvas in the portrait likely refers to an earlier version of the *Moses*, painted from West's design by Stuart soon after joining the studio in 1777. Barratt wondered whether Stuart felt uncomfortable with West's implied authorship of pictures made by his assistants, though the practice had been common to large studio operations for centuries. If so, Stuart's criticism was appropriately muted. In 1784, when he completed the portrait of West for Boydell, the Moses canvas in the public eye was West's monumental work for George III (on which both Stuart and Trumbull assisted).[38] As shown in Edward Francis Burney's rendering of the east wall of the Great Room at Somerset House, West's painting dominated other works around it at the Royal Academy exhibition, reducing the miniature paintings beneath it to mere spots on the wall (fig. 124).

Stuart knew by then that his career lay in portraiture. While correctly assessing his talents, Stuart also accepted market realities. He reflected on those constraints years later, in 1817, during conversations with Henry Pickering. "I paint for bread," Stuart declared, as if portrait painting – "labour I do not like" – had no greater value than that of putting food in the mouths of his family. The remarks more likely communicate exhaustion after thirty years of professional dominance as a portraitist than a long-suppressed desire to paint history. Such expressions of disdain, moreover, were conventional among elite portrait painters. Even as they conceded the academic position that portraits were inferior, they implicitly positioned themselves as superior to makers of likenesses who knew nothing else. During Stuart's years in Britain, Reynolds epitomized the contradiction. Famous for his portraits, Reynolds nevertheless underscored limitations of the genre (while presenting strategies for enhancing it) in his public Discourses as president of the Royal Academy. West's accomplishments as a histori-

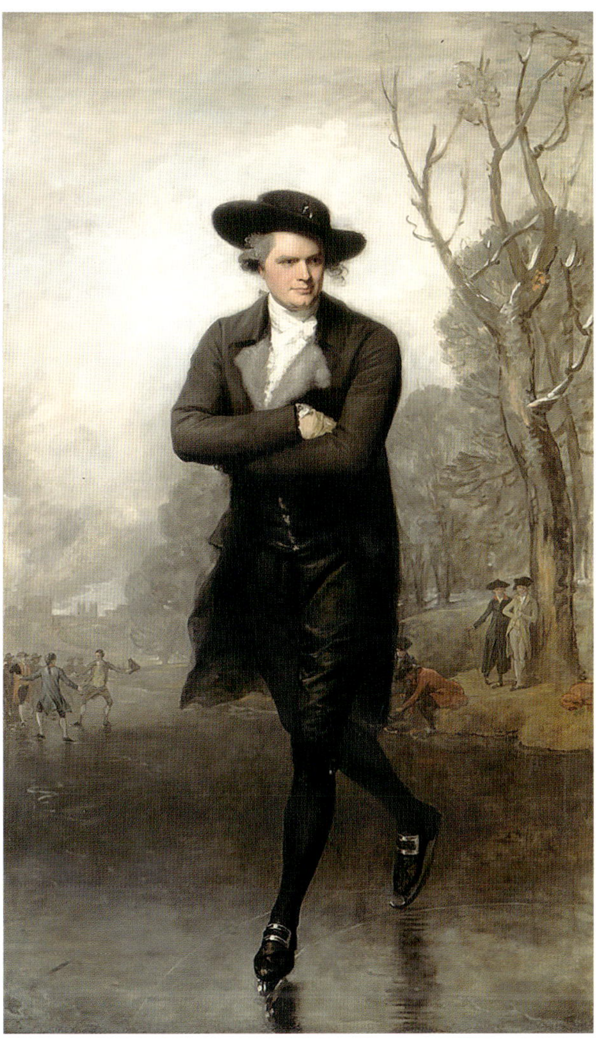

125 Gilbert Stuart, *The Skater (Portrait of William Grant)*, 1782. Oil on canvas, 96⅝ × 58$^{1}/_{16}$ in. (245.5 × 147.4 cm). National Gallery of Art, Washington, D.C., Andrew W. Mellon Collection.

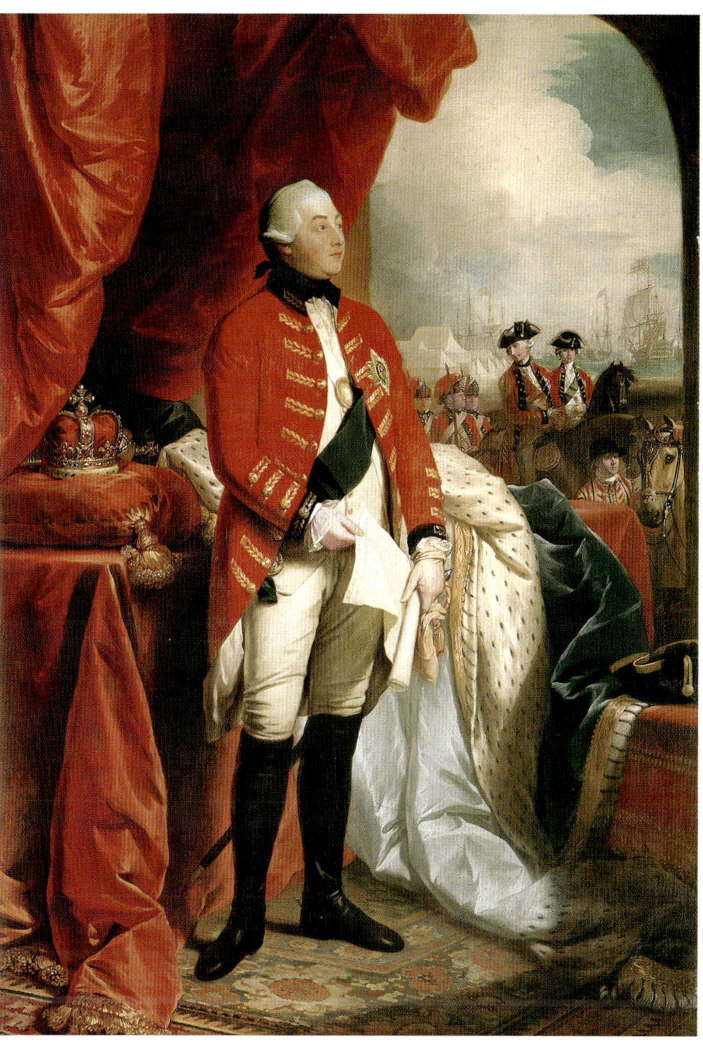

126 Benjamin West, *George III*, 1779. Oil on canvas, 100½ × 72 in. (255.3 × 182.9 cm). Royal Collection Trust, © Her Majesty Queen Elizabeth II, 2014/Bridgeman Images.

cal painter, magnified by Copley's showpieces of modern history after his move to England in 1775, must have colored Stuart's initial expectations. But when Stuart told Pickering that "he thought he should never attempt to paint a subject which required less canvas than would cover the side of a room," the interviewer missed the artist's irreverence. Stuart's strictly materialist definition of grand-scale history painting undercut its weighty moral thematics, of limited interest to patrons even at its Anglophone peak during the last third of the eighteenth century, and virtually exhausted by the time Stuart and Pickering spoke.[39]

Embarking on his fully independent career as a portraitist, Stuart established technical superiority to West and philosophical distance from Reynolds with his first major submission to a Royal Academy exhibition, the full-length *Skater (Portrait of William Grant)* (1782, fig. 125). (In 1783, he put real distance between himself and the two leading Academicians by showing nine canvases with the Society of Artists, an oppositional gesture he could not repeat, since the failing Society did not hold another exhibition until 1790.) West's static portrayals had been mercilessly lampooned. Two portraits of George III exhibited at the Royal Academy were roundly dismissed by critics: "as miserable a failure as any Sun-burnt Sign" and "a stuffed pillow" (fig. 126).[40] The gentleman in Stuart's picture, by contrast, projects graceful animation – as a quality of the subject, who glides in equipoise across the frozen Serpentine (a man-made lake in Hyde Park), and of the artist, his presence registered in the

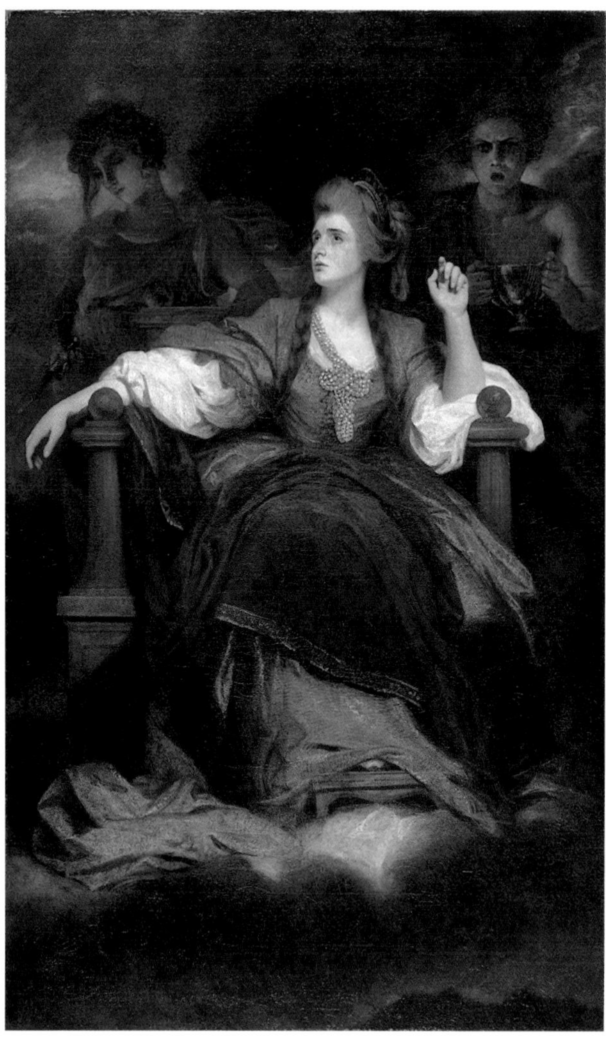

127 Sir Joshua Reynolds, *Mrs. Siddons as the Tragic Muse*, 1784. Oil on canvas, 94¼ × 58½ in. (239.4 × 147.6 cm). Courtesy of the Huntington Art Collections, San Marino, Calif.

lively brushwork. More subtly, *The Skater* posed a wintry, silver-hued challenge to Reynolds's injunction (laid out in his 1778 Discourse) against pictures dominated by cool colors like gray or blue, most famously essayed by Reynolds's rival Thomas Gainsborough in the shimmering portrait known as *The Blue Boy* (RA, 1770). Stuart disagreed with many aspects of the Academy president's teachings, especially his advocacy for the generalized portrait, which suppressed temporal and physical particularities relative to imaginative devices that might bring portraits into closer relationship with history painting, what Reynolds called the "great" or "grand style" (also known as the Grand Manner).[41] That was Reynolds's gambit in *Mrs. Siddons as the Tragic Muse* (1784; fig. 127). Stuart saw the work in progress in the English painter's studio and admired it, but later undiplomatically displayed disappointment with the completed work (or so he told his daughter).[42] Perhaps that response arose from a more painterly quality in the unfinished work; if so, it was at once rooted in history and very much of the present. For Vasari, "many painters . . . achieve in the first sketch of their work, as though guided by a sort of fire of inspiration . . . a certain measure of boldness: but afterwards, in finishing it, the boldness vanishes."[43] By the eighteenth century, artists' sketches, drawn or painted, had become prized collectors' items, while paintings marked by a sketch-like quality attracted increasing admiration – the French theorist de Piles was an early champion and Reynolds himself a later, somewhat grudging one, when he paid tribute to Gainsborough, as discussed later in this chapter. Stuart's objection to Reynolds's completed portrait of Mrs. Siddons just as likely arose from the allegorical figures of Pity and Terror flanking the actress, whose poses Reynolds borrowed from Michelangelo's Isaiah fresco in the Sistine Chapel. No such weighty conceits appear in Stuart's own portrait of Mrs. Siddons (ca. 1785), a naturalistic representation and in that sense much like another contemporaneous image of the actress by Gainsborough.

Stuart staked out difference from Reynolds most fully in his 1784 portrait of the senior artist, a work of ingenious and subversive naturalism (fig. 128). That quality lay less in unflinching depiction of the sitter's rather coarse features – evident in Reynolds's self-portraits – than in its relentless mundanity. A single detail of the portrait speaks to Reynolds's eminence, a painted scroll to one side that may refer to his honorary Doctor of Civil Law degree from Oxford, bestowed in 1773. In a self-portrait of around 1780, Reynolds wears doctoral regalia and holds a scroll, flanked by a bust of Michelangelo, his artistic hero. The elevating details suited a picture commissioned by the Royal Academy. Stuart's portrait was public as well, part of the commission for artist portraits from Boydell, whose patronage helps explain why Reynolds consented to pose for the young American.[44]

The result reportedly displeased Reynolds, whose response, relayed to Dunlap, contradicted testimonials to Stuart's uncanny ability to achieve likeness; "Sir Joshua said, if that was like him, he did not know his own appearance."[45] Yet the artist's self-portraits showed the same distinctive facial features that Stuart captured: puffy eyes with a fleshy lid, broad-bridged nose, coarse mouth, and cleft chin.[46] In further argument for the accuracy of Stuart's portrayal of Reynolds, a posthumous tribute to the Academy president hailed the Boydell portrait (without reference to its maker)

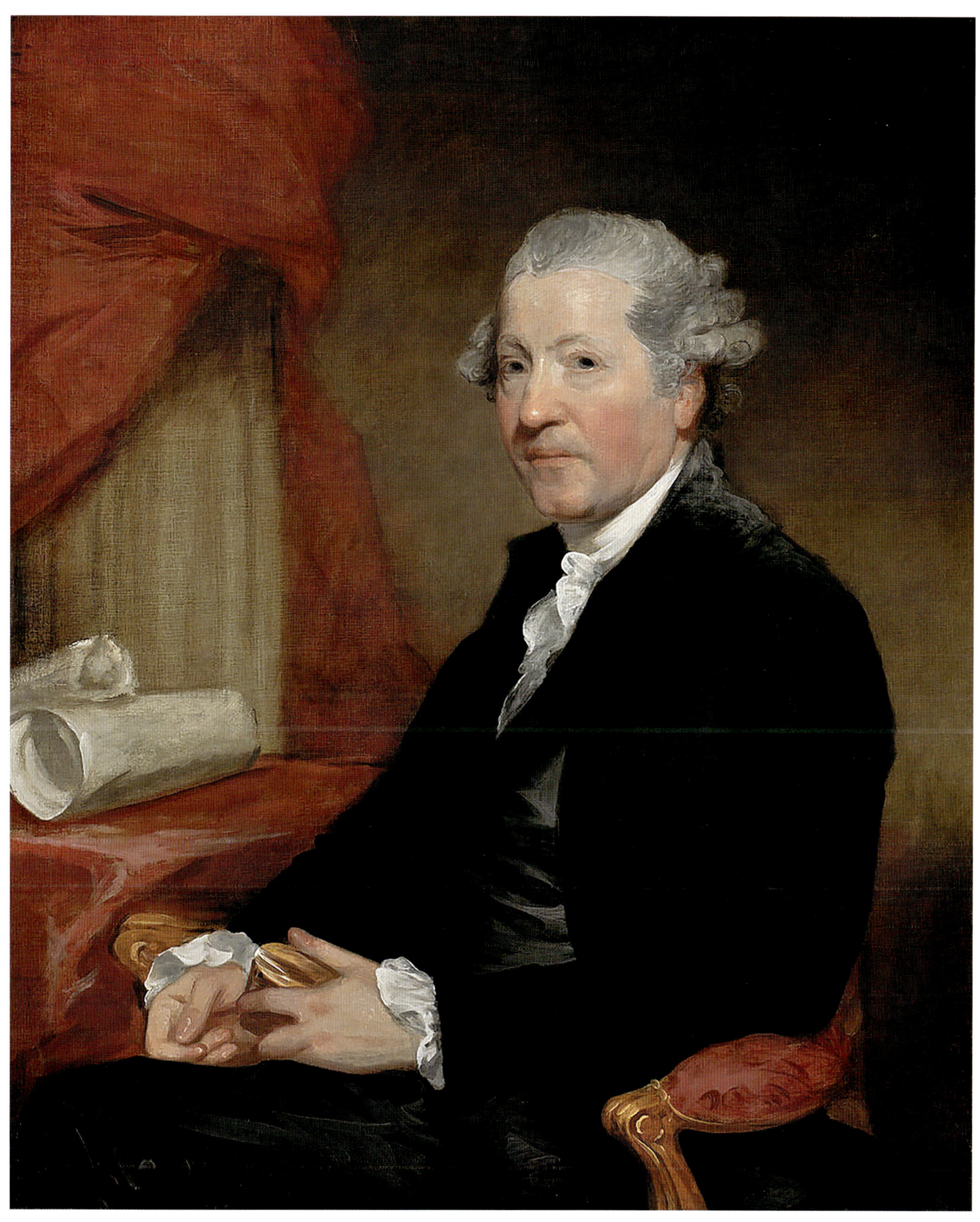

128 Gilbert Stuart, *Sir Joshua Reynolds*, 1784. Oil on canvas, 36 × 30 in. (91.6 × 76.4 cm). National Gallery of Art, Washington, D.C., Andrew W. Mellon Collection.

as "undoubtedly the best painted head of Sir Joshua."[47] All of the Boydell portraits were "strong resemblances," a critic conceded in 1804, with sale impending of the paintings from Boydell's Shakespeare gallery, the most ambitious speculative commercial venture in late eighteenth-century British art. But resemblance did not redeem the affront of their collective ordinariness. "A set of more uninteresting vapid countenances it is not easy to imagine," grumbled the writer; "neither dignity, elevation, or grace appear in any one of them; and had not the catalogue given their names, they might have passed for a company of cheesemongers and grocers . . . smug upon the mart as so many mercers or haberdashers of small wares." He exaggerated, perception colored by context. Among the Boydell portraits, Stuart's Reynolds struck the critic as especially undignified: the "President of the Royal Academy was depicted with a wig that sat as close, and was as tight in curl, as a hackney coachman's caxon, and in the act of taking a pinch of snuff."[48] That remark located the slight in a wig type associated with a lowly profession and in a common, carnal habit, indicated by the snuffbox in Reynolds's left hand and the pinching gesture of his right fingers.

The problem with Stuart's portrait of Reynolds lay in its deviation from the Academy president's idea of what a portrait should do, on which he spoke publicly in his Discourses. In 1771, for example, Reynolds identified a portraitist's adherence to the "defective model" of a particular sitter as wrong-headed: "likeness consists more in taking the general air, than in observing the exact similitude of every feature," he argued. He made almost the same argument in 1782, substituting "the excellence of Portrait-Painting" for "likeness."[49] Only portraits that subjected particularities to a larger purpose were both like and worthy. The idea was hardly new. Jonathan Richardson's defense of portraiture and portraitist, much earlier in the century, rested on that very point. "Tis not enough to make a tame, insipid Resemblance of the Features . . . nor even to make the Picture what is said to be prodigious like . . . A Portrait-Painter must understand Mankind, and enter into their Characters, and express their Minds as well as their Faces." As "a sort of General History of the Life of the Person it represents," he added a few years later, a portrait qualified as a kind of history painting.[50] But the artist must exercise restraint. Reynolds, for his part, inveighed against the "pompous and laboured insolence of grandeur" that he read into Roger de Piles's recommendations to portrait painters; in place of "the tumour of this presumptuous loftiness," Reynolds counseled, the painter should make dignity appear "natural and inherent." Yet Reynolds recognized the portraitist's dilemma: "It is very difficult to ennoble the character of a countenance but at the expense of the likeness, which is what is most generally required by such as sit to the painter."[51]

Stuart evidently did not regard the general and particular as irreconcilable. A story he told about his first effort at portraiture, which misleadingly placed that event soon after his arrival in London, speaks to this issue. He used two facing mirrors, Stuart told a group of artists at a dinner party in Dublin in 1787, positioning his sitter between them to obtain repeated reflections of varying degrees of clarity. He then painted his subject, working from the least distinct, shadowed reflection to "nearer" reflections that allowed him to "discern with more particularizing" the features of the face, until at "his last sitting he faced his sitter, and had all the markings so perfectly distinct, his task was easily accomplished."[52] Stuart described a set-up that allowed him to paint from nature without fear of becoming a slave to detail. With aid of the mirrors, he proceeded from general to particular while assured that the general would remain, since it grounded the entire operation. This satisfied Reynolds's dicta; in fact, Reynolds followed the same practice.[53] Yet Stuart converted what Reynolds presented as an intellectual process – the artist's triumph of mind over matter – into something more mechanistic. The possibility that Stuart intended his story to undermine Reynolds's lofty teaching cannot be discounted, especially since Stuart's remarks reportedly followed those of Christopher Pack, a portraitist who boasted to the assembled company of his intimacy with Reynolds. Despite Stuart's misrepresentation as to when he began making portraits (he had done so in America), the story appears to have a basis in truth. When Thomas Sully sought instruction from Stuart in 1807, the established painter demonstrated his mirroring arrangement, a lesson "so just, and impressive," Sully recalled, that he would always treasure the memory.[54]

Reynolds often disregarded his own official pronouncements when portraying intimate friends. In such works, generally made for private contexts, Reynolds's emphasis on the momentary and singular reveals an approach to likeness entirely different from the one he advocated publicly in the Discourses. Lexicographers Joseph Baretti and Samuel Johnson appear as absorbed readers, each in a private world inaccessible to the viewer – and, Reynolds verges on suggesting, nearly inaccessible to themselves since both portraits emphasize the subjects' extreme myopia (fig. 129). Johnson was blind in the left eye, and Reynolds (in a portrait perhaps made posthumously) showed him holding a book off center

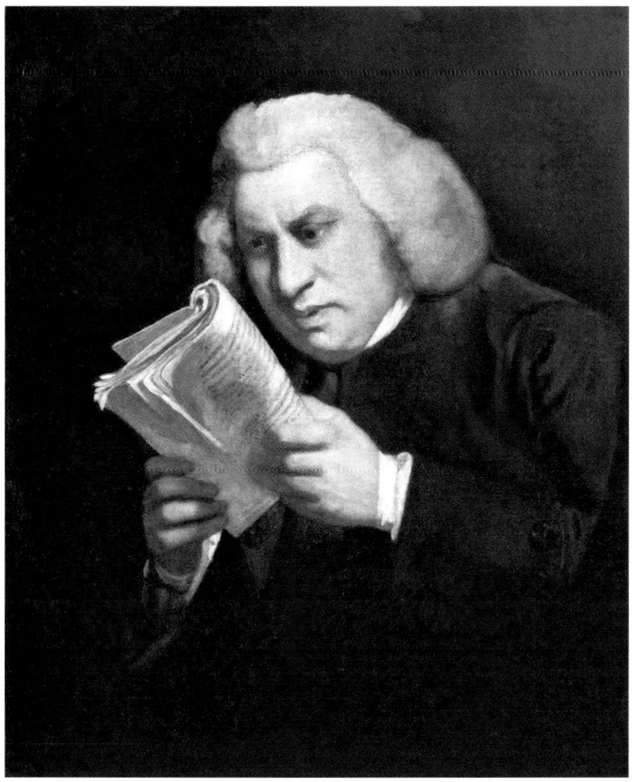

129 Sir Joshua Reynolds, *Samuel Johnson*, ca. 1786. Oil on canvas, 30 × 25 in. (76 × 63 cm). Courtesy of the Huntington Art Collections, San Marino, Calif.

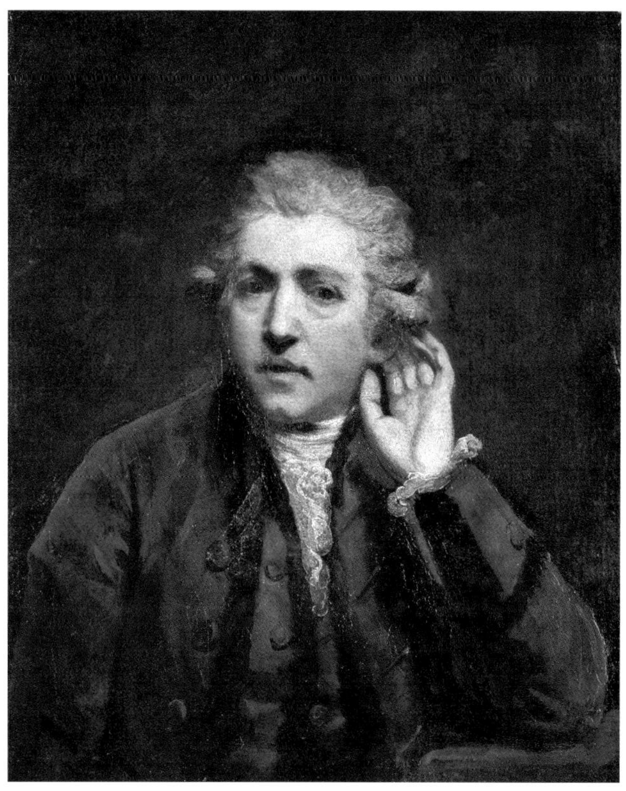

130 Sir Joshua Reynolds, *Self-Portrait (as a Deaf Man)*, 1775. Oil on canvas, 29½ × 24½ in. (74.9 × 62.2 cm). Tate Gallery, London.

to bring it under his good eye. Even when not depicted squinting at a book, Johnson complained about how Reynolds represented him, famously remarking: "It is not friendly to hand down to posterity the imperfections of any man . . . He may paint himself as deaf as he chooses; but I will not be *blinking Sam* in the eyes of posterity."[55] Johnson here referred to Reynolds's contemporaneous self-portrait in which he shows his hand cupped behind ear, acknowledging deafness (fig. 130). But Johnson, who likewise had a hearing impairment, must have recognized an important difference. For Reynolds, showing the effects of his own deafness had milder implications than exposure of difficulties that poor vision imposed on Johnson, a reader and writer. Hearing loss could affect a portraitist, especially one who relied on conversation to put clients at ease (as Stuart did), but its effects did not diminish creative powers exercised primarily through mind, eye, and hand. The gesture that Reynolds makes to concentrate sound also serves the fiction that he converses with a viewer, whom the painting posits as the object of heightened auditory focus; but it is instead his own image – reflected and reversed in a mirror – at which he peers so intently. To paint oneself, an artist must see him (or her) self. That is the point of Reynolds's early self-portrait in which he shades his eyes while looking searchingly out of the picture space (fig. 131). This work has sometimes been compared to Rembrandt's youthful self-portrayals with partially shadowed face, a pictorial sign of melancholic temperament, especially when occurring in the absence of any depicted cause, such as the raised hand.[56] Reynolds greatly admired Rembrandt, to whom he paid homage in other of his self-portraits. But this early example is outwardly directed rather than introspective: Reynolds's gesture emphasizes looking. Significantly, it is one of the few among Reynolds's approximately twenty self-portraits in which he shows himself as an artist. Sight, along with touch, is the painter's privileged sense.[57]

In the rich literature on the senses generated by late seventeenth- and eighteenth-century writers – proceeding above all from Locke's *Essay Concerning Human Understanding* (1690) – vision and touch figure as preeminent sources of information about the world. Without them, Reynolds could not have become an artist nor Stuart have painted

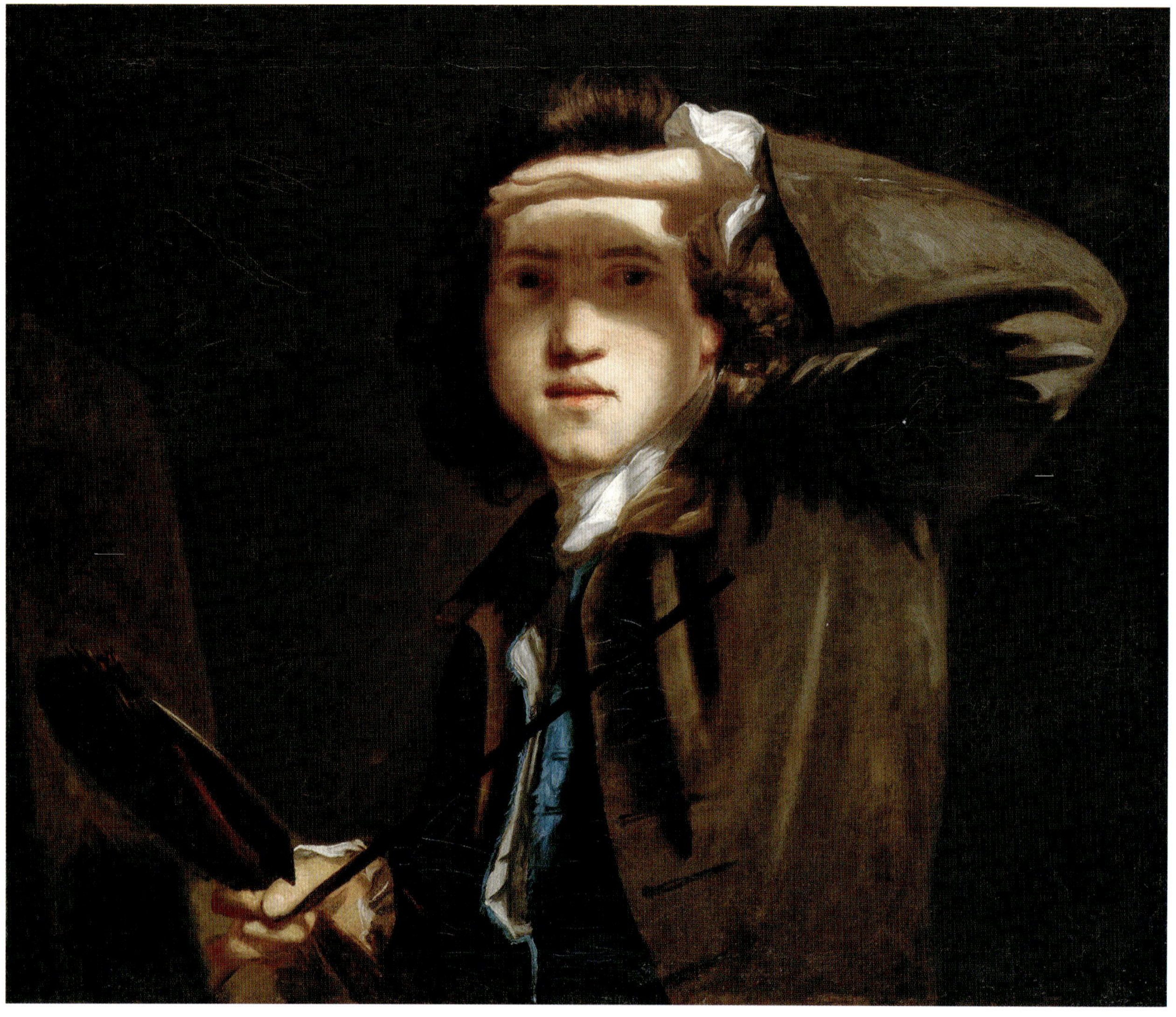

131 Sir Joshua Reynolds, *Self-Portrait Shading his Eyes*, ca. 1747. Oil on canvas, 25 × 29¼ in. (63.5 × 74.3 cm). © National Portrait Gallery, London.

his portrait. In that portrait, Stuart explicitly indicated (and exercised) vision and touch. He also drew attention to taste and smell, both forcefully excited in snuff use. In fact, Stuart's Reynolds engages every sense except hearing, the weakest of Reynolds's faculties. By its suppression, hearing (or lack thereof) acquires a certain presence in the picture.[58]

The history of painting reveals a variety of ways to dramatize hearing and sound. Rembrandt captured both when challenged by the poet Vondel to depict the voice of preacher Cornelis Anslo. In Rembrandt's painting, Anslo makes a gesture that signifies address, while the rapt expression of a listening woman attests to the preacher's rhetorical power, the more so because she does not look directly at him; his voice and words engage her attention – she hears him.[59] In representing deafness, gesture was equally important, as shown in Reynolds's self-portrait and in others' portrayals of him. In 1767, Angelica Kauffmann painted Reynolds with his finger behind his impaired ear (fig. 132). In this case, the gesture has dual signification: Reynolds listens to both the person outside the picture space – presumably Kauffmann herself – and, figuratively, to the voice of genius, embodied in the bust of Michelangelo, positioned as if to speak directly into his ear. No such gentle ambiguity softens a sketch showing Reynolds and Kauffmann in labored conversation (fig. 133). Reynolds strains to hear the young woman, unable to face and hear her at the same time, since he cannot clearly make out her words without turning his head away. With one hand Reynolds cups his ear to capture the sound, while the other hand grips a large snuffbox. Whereas Kauffmann, holding palette and brushes, appears as an artist, Reynolds is identified by his habits and deficiencies.[60]

Snuff excites the nose, stimulating the senses of smell and taste. Pervasive in England among people of fashion (as opposed to habits of smoking or chewing tobacco among the middling and lower sort), snuff use had begun to lose some of the social cachet it enjoyed earlier in the eighteenth century.[61] Once seen as stimulating to conversation and courtship, as well as potentially medicinal, snuff was tolerated more than admired by the 1780s. Shortly before undertaking the portrait of Reynolds, Stuart had portrayed "a Swedish gentleman" dipping his fingers into a snuffbox, a work criticized when shown at the Royal Academy in 1782. Notwithstanding its "strong likeness," the critic suggested that "the original would not like to carry the copy of himself to Stockholm," likely because it showed the subject pinching snuff.[62] Stuart later condemned snuff taking as "a pernicious, vile, dirty habit" – and he did so self-critically, as a chronic user; John Quincy Adams thought he might have taken in as much as half a pound daily.[63] Stuart likened physical deformity and serious addiction, joining the explanation a disabled man gave for his twisted neck – "I was born so" – to autobiographical detail: "I was born in a snuff-mill."[64] Visitors to Stuart's studio commented with distaste on his snuff-covered clothes and the violent sneezing they experienced in his proximity. Stuart's remark that John Adams, in a portrait begun ca. 1800, appeared as if he were "just going to sneeze" expresses humorous reflexiveness. Sitters were never far from Stuart's snuffbox because he was not; it seemed to an acquaintance "almost a part of himself, . . . as necessary for him as the Palette & Pencils – & always . . . on the easel."[65] A large, open snuffbox appears next to Stuart in a drawing that West made of him while sitting for his own portrait by Stuart (fig. 134). In that portrait of West for Boydell and others in the series – excepting the one of Reynolds – Stuart showed his fellow artists in the presence of their work and tools. The decision to put powdered tobacco in the hands of Britain's leading painter was not, in that context, an obvious choice. For the patron, it can only have been a negative. Boydell had vowed to abstain from tobacco use from his days as an apprentice engraver during the early 1740s, when he worked with another artist who "lost much time in taking snuff" from a box that "always lay by him," dipping so often that "one quarter of his time was wasted."[66] Perhaps, for Stuart, the act of taking snuff humanized Reynolds, bringing the great

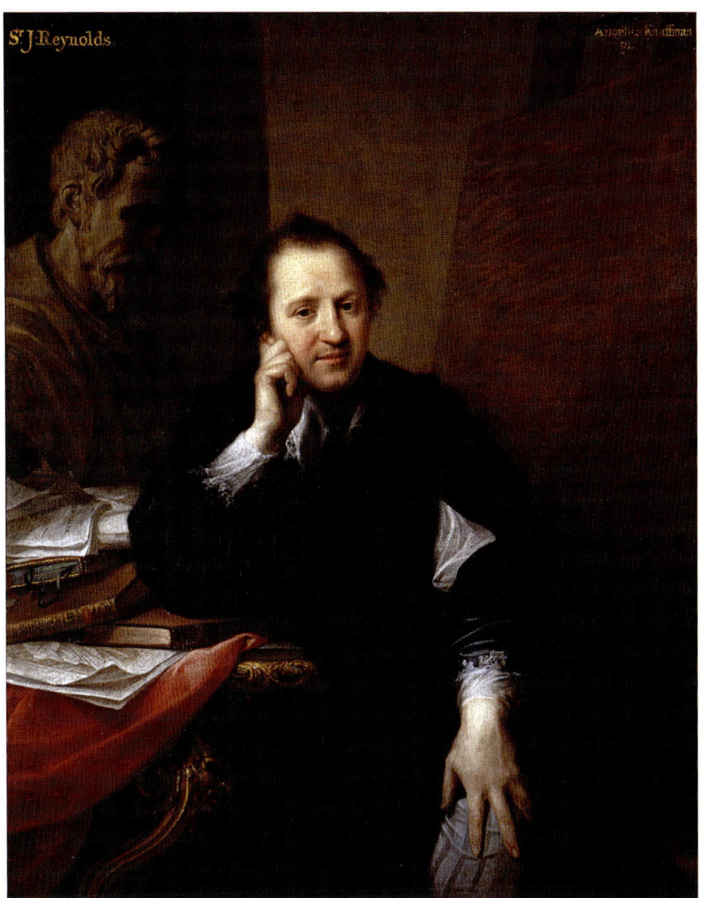

132 Angelica Kauffmann, *Sir Joshua Reynolds*, 1767. Oil on canvas, 50 × 40 in. (127 × 101.6 cm). Saltram Park, Plymouth (Morley Collection), National Trust Images/Rob Matheson.

133 Nathaniel Dance, *Sir Joshua Reynolds and Angelica Kauffmann in Conversation*, ca. 1767. Graphite on paper. Reproduced by the kind permission of the Executors of the 7th Earl of Harewood and the Trustees of the Harewood House Trust.

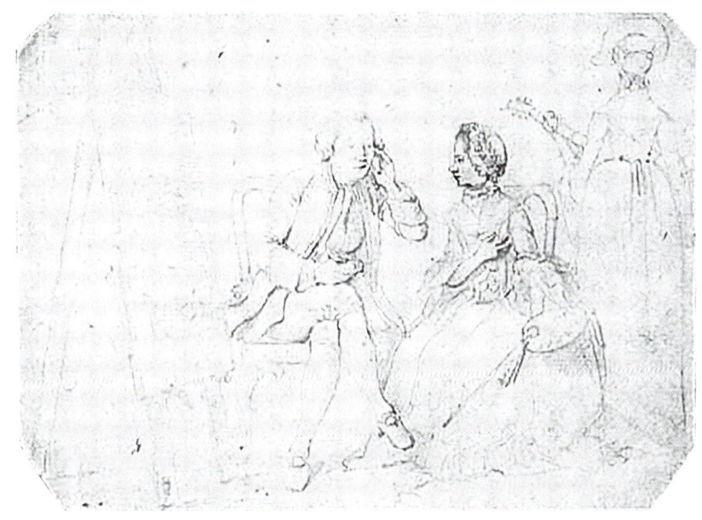

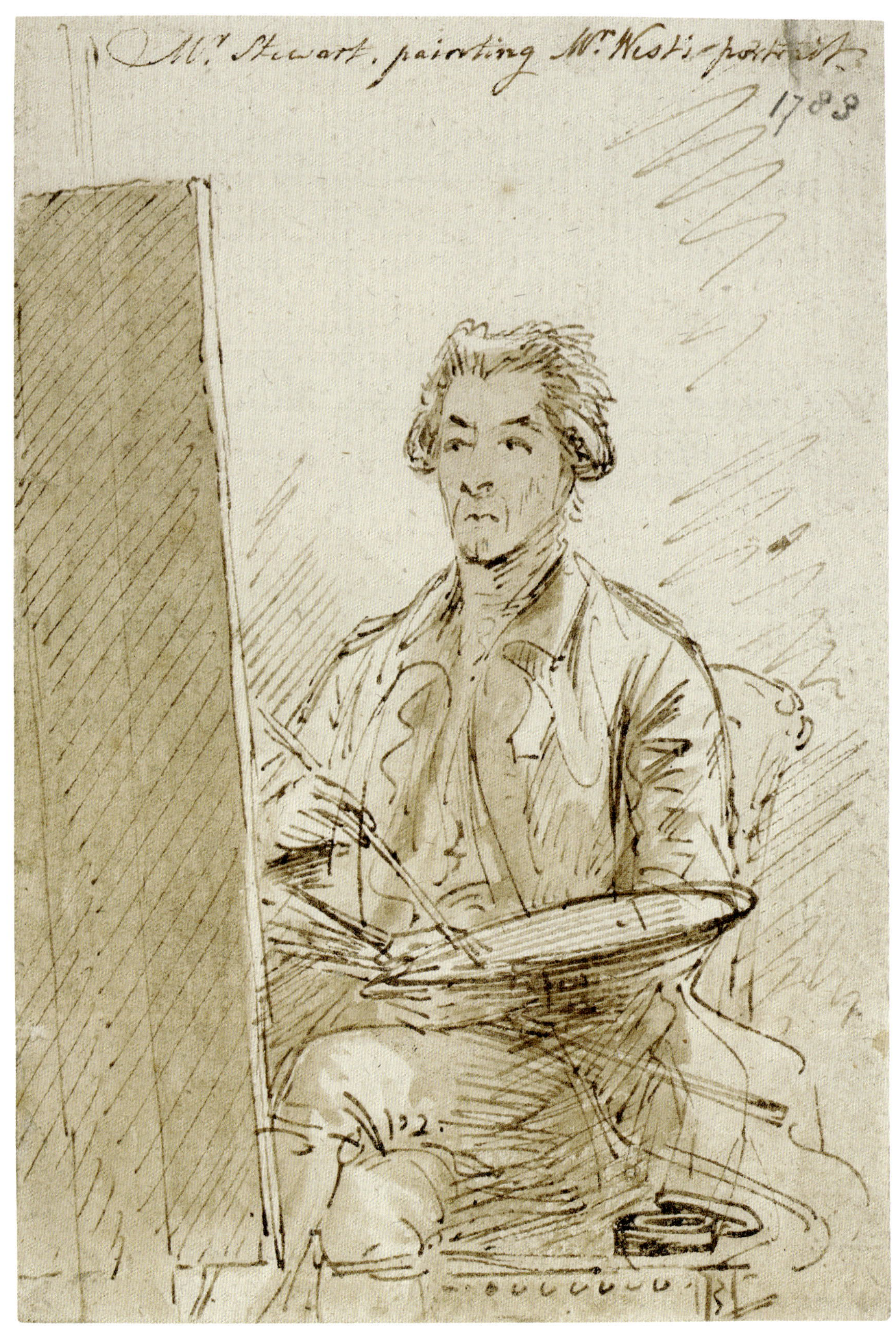

134 Benjamin West, *Mr. Stewart, Painting Mr. West's Portrait*, 1783. Pen and brown ink and brown wash on paper. British Museum, London. © The Trustees of the British Museum.

artist down to Stuart's level and into a realm of conviviality, from which Stuart, then at the start of his career, stood to benefit more than Reynolds.[67] The two men are connected, in terms of the picture, by a personal habit as much as by their public practice as painters.

Some years earlier, Stuart had acquired an object connected to Reynolds: the palette of portraitist Thomas Hudson, Reynolds's first master. It was among the studio effects that Nathaniel Dance (who used the palette himself) made available in 1776, when he retired from painting after receiving an inheritance. In the case of a great artist, so fundamental a tool seemed to have tremendous potency. Satirist Peter Pindar imagined Reynolds's palette – with the painter's head atop, in macabre evocation of the mental–manual duality – floating down the Thames to the Academy's home at Somerset House, where artists vied to retrieve it in hope that "the wood would each inspire to paint like him."[68] Stuart, in later years, "was fond . . . of showing [Hudson's palette] to people and telling them that it had been used by the master of Sir Joshua Reynolds."[69] With a remark that seems initially to signal deference and to establish artistic lineage, Stuart, who claimed to follow only nature, drew attention to Reynolds's former submission to a master – a superior role that Stuart himself metonymically assumed in possessing the palette of Reynolds's master.

If snuff had the potential to represent sociability, it could also do the opposite: the period expression "to take snuff" meant to show resentment.[70] Stuart enacted that connotation during a rare visit to church, where (according to his daughter, Jane) he "stood leaning over the pew when everybody else was sitting, [and] took snuff." After the service, Stuart told his family he would not attend church again, explaining: "I do not like the idea of a man getting up in a box and having all the conversation to himself" – in that instance, presumably, thwarted by the disagreeable and distracting sound effects accompanying Stuart's inhalations.[71] Oliver Goldsmith drew on the figurative meaning of taking snuff for a mock epitaph of Reynolds from "Retaliation," an unfinished sequence of verse epitaphs of various friends, first published after the poet's own death in April 1774 and issued in six more editions before year's end. In the concluding lines concerning Reynolds, Goldsmith invoked the advantages of deafness to the artist, who commonly used an ear trumpet, when in the company of would-be connoisseurs:

> To coxcombs averse, yet most civilly staring,
> When they judged without skill, he was still hard of hearing:
> When they talk'd of their Raphaels, Corregios, and stuff,
> He shifted his trumpet, and only took snuff.[72]

In reference to Reynolds's use of ear trumpet and snuff, an editorial note to the third edition stated: "his manner in both . . . , taken in the point of time described, must be allowed, by those who have been witnesses of such a scene, to be as happily given upon *paper*, as that great Artist himself, perhaps, could have exhibited upon *canvas*."[73] In other words, Goldsmith captured as successfully in verse what Reynolds might have rendered in paint, Reynolds's use of snuff and his deafness – the one figuratively representing his indignation and the other his way to avoid responding to an offense, thereby maintaining his complacence or complaisance. Contemporaries described Reynolds using both words, which in the eighteenth century had the positive connotation of affability; in earlier lines, Goldsmith calls Reynolds "gentle, complying and bland" (that is, soothing). Goldsmith's poem and the contemporaneous editor's note more straightforwardly highlight representative behavior that anyone who knew Reynolds could have observed.[74] Stuart evidently observed it, and in picturing manifest actions and habits specific to Reynolds – the particular – Stuart captured his characteristic expression – the general.[75]

Stuart's unflinching presentation of the mundane in his portrait of Reynolds pierced the carefully developed public facade that some who knew the Academy president thought he put up. Benjamin Haydon, for one, considered Reynolds "naturally irritable" and liable to show it when professionally threatened.[76] Stuart seems not to have aroused such feelings in Reynolds, who in 1784 recommended him to John Parker II (then newly designated 1st Baron Boringdon) for portraits to complement a group that Reynolds painted two decades earlier for the library at Saltram House, Devon.[77] He later agreed with Pickering's assessment of Reynolds as "without envy." Still, when portraying a man who was by almost any account his superior, Stuart declined to flatter, showing the senior artist as an unprepossessing and somewhat grouchy elderly man habituated to snuff – a presentation that undermined Reynolds's public image as leader of the English school of painting. Stuart secured the reality effect by an extremely subtle conceit, a detail that makes his portrait believable in its very inconsequentiality, namely the passing gesture that Reynolds makes as he pinches a bit of snuff between thumb and forefinger before raising it to his nose.[78]

The snuff-pinching gesture functions in still other ways. As a sign for touch, it alludes to a sense as critical to painters as their sight. Gainsborough made the point in correspondence with a portrait client, early in his career: "You please me much by saying that no other fault is found in your picture than the roughness of the surface, for that part being of use in giving force to the effect at a proper distance, and what a judge of painting knows an original from a copy by; in short, being the touch of the pencil."[79] Stuart's contemporaries commented on the physicality of his execution or described other aspects of his work in arrestingly physical terms. West's remark that Stuart "nails the Face to the Canvass" – a reference to his unerring ability to capture likeness – might also be understood as referring to Stuart's sure touch.[80] Using a loaded brush, the painter attacked the canvas directly, as suggested by artist John Sartain's recollection of Stuart's technique: "He deliberated every time before the well-charged brush went down upon the canvas with an action like cutting into it with a knife."[81] Asked why he did not sign "to mark his pictures," Stuart replied by metonymically identifying his brushstroke with himself: "I mark them all over."[82] If the question to Stuart confirms an increasing concern with artistic authorship in late eighteenth-century America, one to which Stuart contributed significantly, then his response reveals a startlingly modern understanding of authorship. Stuart's emphasis on brushwork places him in unexpected sympathy with contemporaneous French ideas of *le faire* (execution).[83]

The elevation of execution in eighteenth-century France contradicted traditional academic reserve regarding the mechanical aspects of painting, which could only be ennobled by a poetic subject generated through intellectual effort and associated adherence to rules. Once painting gained secure status as a liberal art, the rules could be bent, as they were with rising appreciation for execution that appeared natural and impassioned rather than carefully controlled.[84] The process unfolded at a delay in Britain, but by the 1770s a small group of artists began to attract attention for working in highly personal and expressive ways; soon afterwards, official resistance to singularity began to crumble.[85] Reynolds grappled with the matter in his fourteenth Discourse, delivered in 1788 soon after the death of his formidable colleague Gainsborough. In considering the "novelty and peculiarity" of Gainsborough's style (fig. 135), Reynolds composed a famous and memorable passage: "all those odd scratches and marks, which, on close examination, are so observable in Gainsborough's pictures, and which even to experienced painters appear rather the effect of accident than design; this chaos, this uncouth and shapeless appearance, by a kind of magick, at a certain distance assumes form, and all the parts seem to drop into their proper places; so that we can hardly refuse acknowledging the full effect of diligence, under the appearance of chance and hasty negligence." Gainsborough's "unfinished manner," Reynolds concedes, may even enhance "that striking resemblance for which his portraits are so remarkable."[86] The artist captures the general effect but allows the viewer's imagination to supply the rest. In a description of Gainsborough's technique that echoed Reynolds, Sully added that the artist's "manner" struck him "as being, in its results, very similar to Stuart's"; however, as Sully rightly noted, Stuart's handling was firmer.[87] Yet it may be that Stuart's non finito attained a significantly different level in the portrait of Reynolds, an effect arising from Stuart's depiction of and allusion to sensory stimulation. In this case, the painting surface is neither especially spontaneous nor unfinished in appearance. Yet the image itself – once one enters into its thematics – invites the viewer's participation in, and imaginative amplification of, the work.[88]

For Reynolds, Gainsborough's non finito led to happy resolution in portraiture only when the viewer had some knowledge of the subject; otherwise, the painter licensed excessive imaginative liberty. With this qualification, which affirmed imitation as the portraitist's ultimate aim or obligation, Reynolds reasserted the inferior standing of portraiture in the academic hierarchy.[89] He hesitated to judge a portrait according to the strength of its invention, as he routinely would a history painting. With regard to Gainsborough, Reynolds's reluctance arose not only from his insecurity concerning the status of invention in portraiture, but also from doubts as to whether Gainsborough had mindfully arrived at the unfinished quality that was the most striking aspect of his pictures. "The slightness which we see in [Gainsborough's] best works cannot always be imputed to negligence," Reynolds ventured, seemingly in defense of his colleague. But he continued: "His *handling, the manner of leaving the colours*, or in other words, the methods he used for producing the effect, had very much the appearance of the work of an artist who had never learned from others the usual and regular practice belonging to the art; but still, like a man of strong intuitive perception of what was required, he found out a way to accomplish his purpose." Reynolds cannot quite decide whether Gainsborough deliberately calculated his effects or whether they were spontaneously generated. What is certain is that the result seemed effortless and uncontrived – natural. Deciding in favor of nature, Reynolds

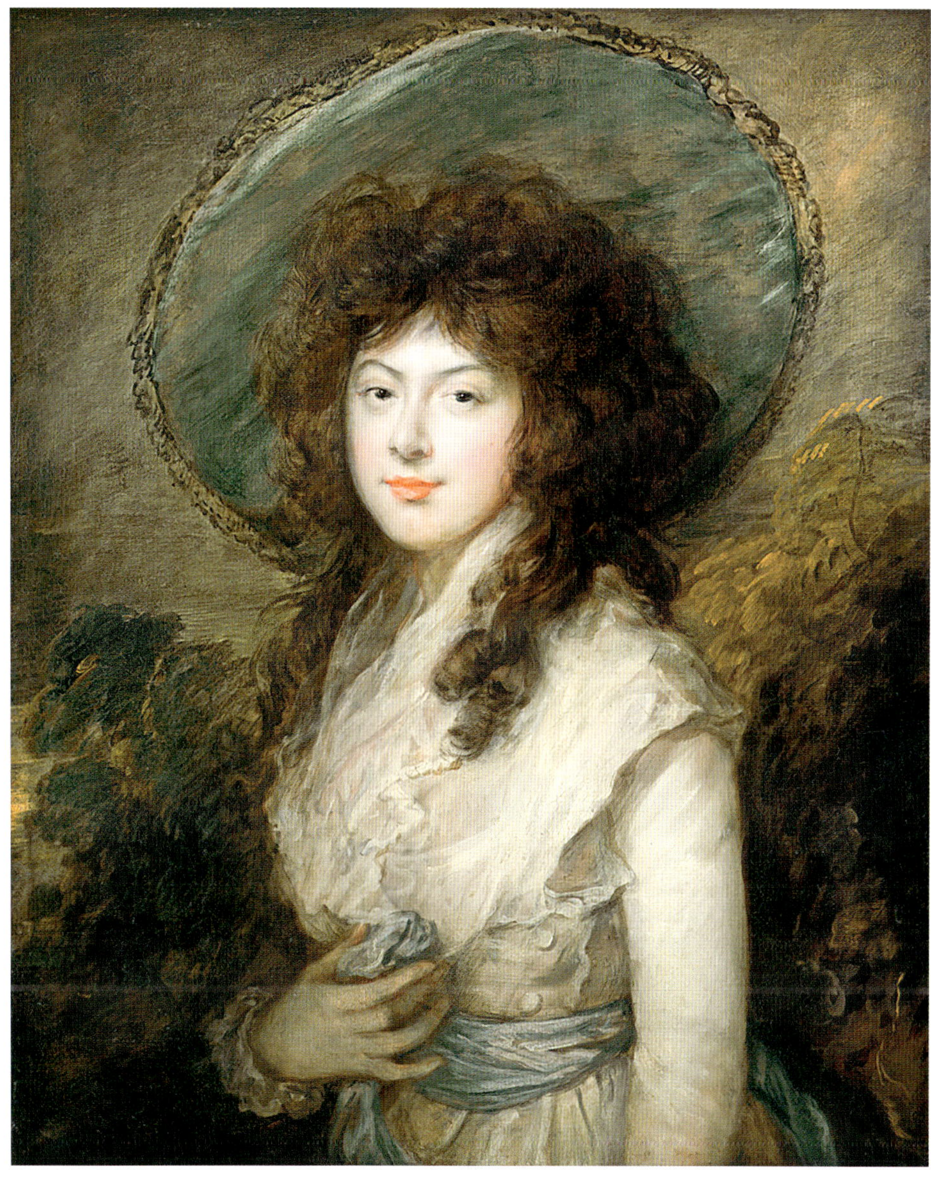

135 Thomas Gainsborough, *Miss Catherine Tatton*, 1786. Oil on canvas, $29^{5}/_{16} \times 25^{3}/_{16}$ in. (76 × 64 cm). National Gallery of Art, Washington, D.C., Andrew W. Mellon Collection.

concludes that Gainsborough's "hatching manner" registers "the lively and forcible impressions of an energetick mind."[90]

Stuart's direct painting manner was also linked to his inner nature or temperament and to his devotion to external nature. In that connection, tellingly, early writers on American art invoked Gainsborough. According to Dunlap (on the authority of John Neagle), Gainsborough overheard Stuart, then still West's student, declare nature to be his only master; he told the young painter that this commitment would make him an artist.[91] Nature had been Stuart's guide from the start, according to Jane Stuart, who related that her father, at the age of five, used a stick to draw the perfect likeness of a neighbor on the ground.[92] As in Vasari's story of the boy Giotto, the anecdote highlights both the artist's precocity and his empiricism. It presents him as a natural, similar as well to the shepherd in Quintilian's account of the origins of pictorial representation.[93]

The oppositional quality of Stuart's portraiture was not lost on contemporaries. The British art critic and satirist Anthony Pasquin recognized it in 1794 when he wrote that "American Stuart was the only disciple of his time who surveyed [Reynolds's] artifices with disdain." Pasquin

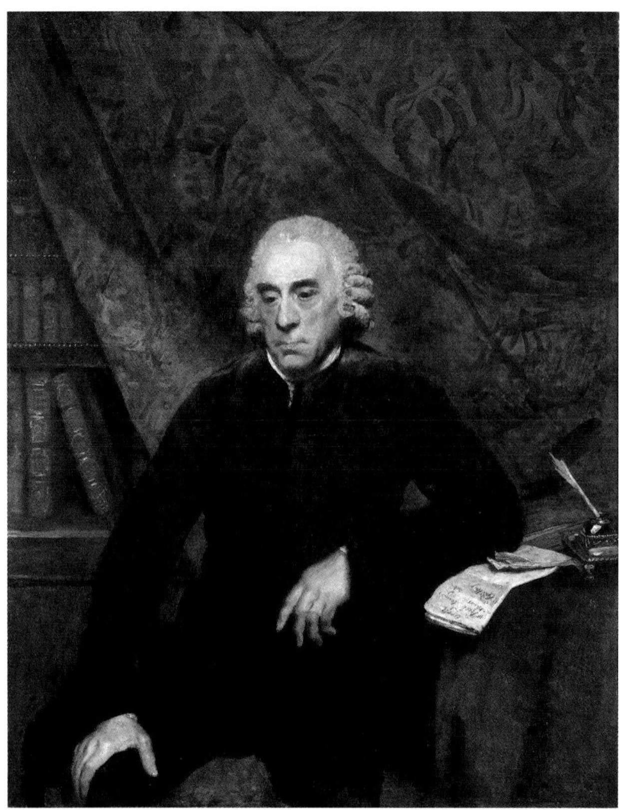

136 Sir Joshua Reynolds, *Joshua Sharpe*, 1785. Oil on canvas, 49⅝ × 39⅜ in. (126 × 100 cm). Private collection. © Tate London 2014.

employed the term artifice in its traditional sense, to target Reynolds's "handling or mechanical parts of the art . . . which even in him was slovenly and bad."[94] But he could just as easily have said that Stuart rejected the poetic "fancy" or imagination that Reynolds brought to portraiture (which Pasquin, unlike Stuart, did not scorn). In the Boydell commission as a whole, Stuart defied Reynolds's directives concerning the elevation of portraits by infusing his works with mundane naturalism. He declined to portray his fellow engravers and painters as conventional characters in a historical drama about the status of artists. Instead, he represented them as contemporaries and colleagues and as enterprising individuals, an approach that suited the group to the commercial context for their display, in Boydell's shop.

The implication that unadorned naturalism might be somehow American is something that Reynolds himself considered. He did so just a year after he made one of his most straightforward portraits, of aging lawyer Joshua Sharpe, a work not so different from Stuart's portrait of him (fig. 136). Portraying Sharpe, Reynolds remarked, was like "copying a ham or any object of still life."[95] But painting "ought to be . . . no imitation at all of external nature," Reynolds asserted in his thirteenth Discourse, also 1786. That "vulgar idea," he added, may appeal to the uncultivated "but these are not the persons to whom a Painter is to look, any more than a judge of morals and manners ought to refer controverted points upon those subjects to the opinions of people taken from the banks of the Ohio, or from New Holland."[96] People from the banks of the Ohio presumably meant Native Americans or traders (while evoking the frontier where British military challenge to the French sparked the Seven Years' War), and those from New Holland signaled descent from the Dutch, whose painting traditions Reynolds identified with copying from nature. Rustics of either type, Reynolds implied, would be as unfit to judge paintings as they would manners and morals.

Stuart, in effect, offered a corrective to such insults. According to Henry Tuckerman, writing about American art in 1867, Stuart appreciated the "unschooled criticism" he received in his native country, where he said that his paintings "were compared with nature, of which they were direct imitations, instead of being estimated, as abroad, by their approach to Titian and Vandyke."[97] The respect that Tuckerman's Stuart accorded his clients collapses under scrutiny, since the artist was quick to talk back to anyone who professed opinions about his paintings contrary to his own. Nor were most of those clients as unschooled as Stuart represented; many recognized and appreciated that he produced portraits in a modern British style. A self-described Briton living in Pennsylvania said that Britons and Europeans identified Stuart's "excellence" with his ability to take a likeness in a "determined and unsophisticated manner," surpassing that of "more prominent artists . . . in London or Paris."[98] Paradoxically, it seems that by outdoing his colleagues abroad, Stuart was all the more American.

Stuart's exclusive concentration on portraiture may have helped to confirm his status as a national artistic hero – not that he was in any way an exception but because, in a blunt dismissal of history painting, he made the rule seem less constraining: "No man ever painted history if he could obtain employment in portraits."[99] Stuart's pronouncement drips with irony. Since few Americans could obtain employment in anything other than portraits, they had little choice. But Stuart's successful career and reputation seemed to validate his decision to paint portraits. True to his words, he never exhibited the least interest in historical subjects or showed embarrassment about specializing in portraiture. What is more, his declaration suggests perverse pleasure taken in opposing the artistic establishment.

Stuart understood his commitment to nature as a difference between himself and Reynolds. "Reynolds was a good painter," he told Washington Allston, an accomplished American artist roughly two decades his junior, "but he has done incalculable mischief to the rising generation by many of his remarks . . . You may elevate your mind as much as you can; but, while you have nature before you as a model, paint what you see, and look with your own eyes."[100] Reynolds agonized over the general and the particular. Stuart, in the portrait of Reynolds, held out the possibility for reconciling the two, and he achieved in that particular painting a radical naturalism that would mark his work in general.

Adrift at the start of his years abroad, Stuart had attained by their conclusion the stature of leading portraitist in Ireland, where he catered to a largely aristocratic clientele. Interactions with Irish clients that bear on Stuart's self-image figure in remaining sections of this chapter. Throughout those nearly two decades, Stuart resisted subservience, notably in connection with senior painters to whom he had every reason to show deference for the concrete help and connections they provided. Stuart was capable of acknowledging kindnesses and merit, evident in comments he made about West and Reynolds later in life, but gratitude on his part did not rule out measured rebellion, whether actual, embellished, or invented for the later effect of affirming his independence as an artist. In the year after Stuart's arrival in London, the same year that thirteen American colonies declared independence, Reynolds, ostensibly speaking of artists, spoke against "resisting the authority of others" and of "submission to others [as] a deference which we owe."[101] Yet he also believed that artists who had acquired a solid foundation of knowledge and understanding should test themselves against the masters, just as those masters had been known to do. Stuart, from the very start of his career, lived out the Grand Manner ideal of artistic challenge.

"Hundred Dollar Bill": Washington

In 1793, after eighteen years in England and Ireland, Stuart recrossed the Atlantic to his homeland, intent on reaping the financial and professional benefits of portraying George Washington. Stuart knew the president's image would be marketable, announcing to his Irish friend and assistant James Dowling Herbert: "I expect to make a fortune by Washington alone."[102] The artist later calculated that each authorized painted copy of his popular second ("Athenaeum") portrait of Washington (see fig. 117) was worth a "hundred dollar bill" to him – a somewhat disrespectful remark, however true. Stuart called that picture "the only legacy I can leave to my family," meaning that it had financial value both as the original and as a source of future copies.[103]

Stuart likewise counted on receiving income from engravings of his various Washington portraits, as potentially lucrative as *Death of Wolfe* had been for West. In believing that he had the right to control and benefit from reproduction of his paintings, Stuart operated under assumptions rooted in his English experience and supported by English jurisprudence but not yet by American law. As is well known, the artist claimed to have been wronged following unauthorized issuance of a print from his third ("Lansdowne") Washington portrait of 1796, a gift to the first Marquis of Lansdowne from merchant and United States senator William Bingham and his wife, Anne Willing Bingham, of Philadelphia.[104] Lord Lansdowne loaned the painting to prominent London engraver James Heath, whose resulting reproduction – opportunistically published in January 1800, the month after Washington's death – added insult to injury by misnaming the painter as "Gabriel Stuart" (fig. 137). When the widely marketed print came to Stuart's attention, the painter composed an uncharacteristically deferential appeal to Lansdowne. It suggests, together with his youthful letter to West, that in direct and private address to persons of position and influence Stuart may have been less confrontational than he let on when speaking about those interactions to others. In this case, so crucial to his reputation and livelihood, he was completely dependent on Lansdowne and had little choice.

Stuart began with an acknowledgment conventionally bestowed on aristocratic patrons, praising the marquis for "the liberality with which you have uniformly patronized the Arts," before raising, in the same sentence, the "injury, to which I have recently been exposed under the apparent sanction of your name." Stuart diplomatically allowed for the possibility of oversight. "I knew of no one in whose hands [the work] could be placed with more propriety and advantage, nor one on whom I could more confidently rely to secure the rights and promote the interest of the artist," he continued. He used the past tense pointedly. Stuart had asserted his rights, he stated, when he "expressly stipulated with [Bingham's] agent in the transaction, that no copy should be taken of the picture, nor should any engraving be allowed but with my consent, and for my benefit."[105] That directive must have been verbal, as the artist made no mention of any written agreement to this effect. Stuart based his claim to Lansdowne – that he had been "despoiled of the fair fruits of an important work" – on his understanding of

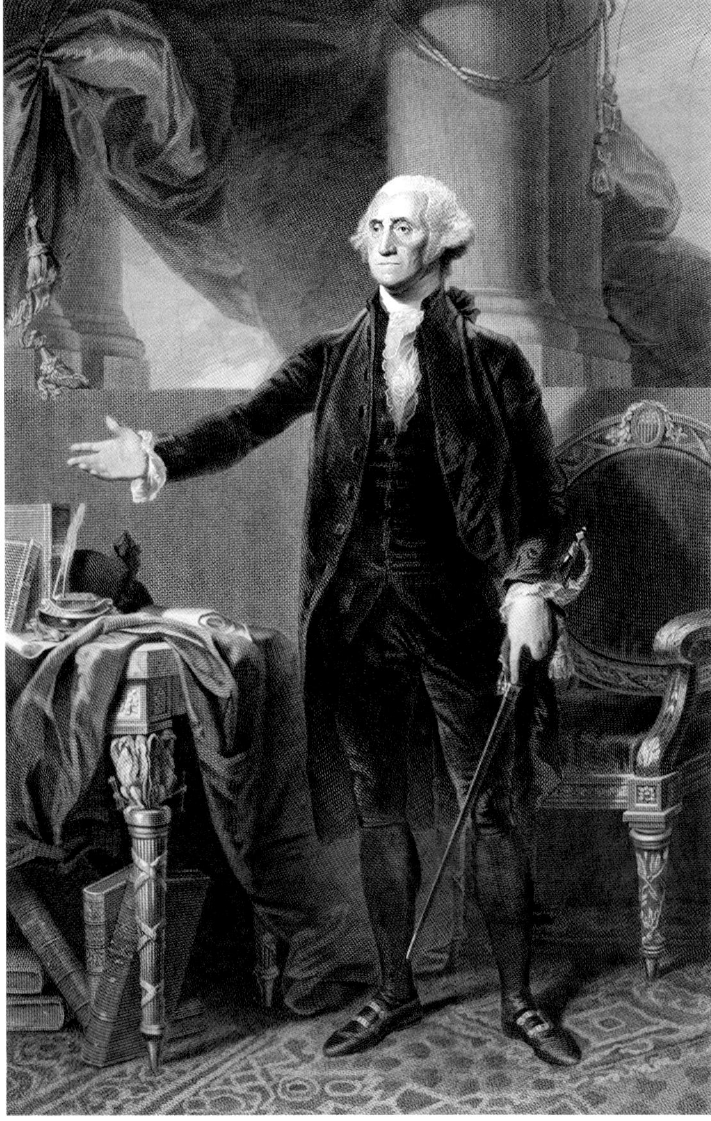

137 James Heath after Gilbert Stuart, *George Washington*, published 1800. Engraving. © National Portrait Gallery, London.

theories relating to the moral and economic rights of English artists and on statutory laws enacted to protect those rights.[106] The first, in 1734, had been prompted by Hogarth's efforts to secure copyright for his engravings, following the precedent of literary copyright laws dating to 1709 (the Statute of Anne). Although the "Hogarth Act" only granted protection to artists who engraved their own work, as Hogarth did, an amendment of 1777 – the year Stuart entered West's studio – prohibited engravers from copying works originating in Great Britain without the written and witnessed "express consent of the proprietor or proprietors" (artists or owners of works of art).[107] Unfortunately for Stuart, as concerned the Lansdowne portrait of Washington, British law provided no legal protections to him, and comparable legal rights had not been codified in the United States.

In 1800, Stuart placed his belief that artists were entitled to certain protections and rights before the people of the United States. Under the heading "Washington," he ran a series of newspaper advertisements in major northern and southern cities that announced his plan to publish engravings of the late president. These notices, together with his letter to Lansdowne, are among the few original documents authored by Stuart and, as such, critically important in conveying his conception of the status of artists. Recognizing that a commercial notice might undercut that status, Stuart assured readers that his resort to the press had become "peculiarly necessary" following the recent "invasion of his Copy-right (a right always held sacred to the Artist, and expressly reserved on this occasion, as a provision for a numerous family)," an offense that had occurred in England, "without any regard to his property, or feelings, as an Artist."[108] Stuart then appealed to "the Public," his American countrymen, to affirm his rights by subscribing to the engraving he proposed to issue. Another year passed before he followed through; meanwhile, both before and after, promotion and sale of Heath's engraving from Stuart's Lansdowne Washington continued unchecked.

Determined not to lose control of his artistic property again, Stuart took more forceful action in an immediately ensuing matter involving yet another unauthorized reproduction. In May 1802, he obtained an injunction against Captain John E. Sword, then actively marketing Cantonese-made copies on glass of an Athenaeum Washington that Sword had purchased from Stuart, ostensibly for a "gentleman in Virginia." Stuart had previously maintained, in a contract negotiation with the State of Connecticut for a Washington portrait (coincident with the Lansdowne affair), that he would insert "in every contract for any of his paintings, that he reserved to himself the entire and exclusive privilege of copyright & publishing prints" from his works.[109] However, he neglected to follow through with Sword, as his sworn petition makes no reference to any written agreement, stating only that Sword did "promise and assure" not to copy the picture.[110] Stuart's lawyers, in presenting his case, asked the court to enjoin Sword from selling copies of the work. The court entered the injunction, with a two-thousand-dollar penalty if Sword did not comply, and Sword was served that same day by federal marshal. Yet no evidence exists that he filed an answer, and no further documents indicate the outcome of this suit.[111]

Perhaps coincidentally, President Jefferson had signed a bill on April 29, 1802, that extended federal copyright protection (previously granted to authors and publishers) to artists, effective January 1, 1803.[112] Stuart responded quickly to the new legalities when he placed an advertisement in April 1803 announcing copyright, shared with engraver David Edwin, of a portrait print of Washington.[113] Notwithstanding his direct reference to the recent Act of Congress, Stuart's claim in this announcement to protection from "injurious piracy" and to his right "to enjoy the fruit of his own labours" invoked the terms of English more than American law. His knowledge of the broad moral reasoning of English statutes, absent from American copyright laws, seems even clearer from other writings – his letter to Lansdowne and advertisements of 1800 – that identify infringement on his rights with harm to his family. Unfortunately for Stuart and his family, written contracts and clarity in business dealings were at best his goal, not a reality. He remained ineffectual in matters of business throughout his life.[114]

Stuart would not have had such valuable property to protect without access to Washington in the first place, contact that allowed him, within a few years of his return to the United States, to paint three portraits of the president from life. These played a major role in solidifying his reputation as the preeminent portraitist of the early republic. Yet however formidable Stuart's command of his art, he was then nothing to Washington. Stuart offered a pictorial comment on the lesser status of portrait painters relative to high ranking patrons a few years earlier, when portraying a young Irish viscount, George Thomas John Nugent (fig. 138). As his surrogate in that work, Stuart included a Newfoundland dog, a breed native to North America. Newfoundlands were known to drool uncontrollably, so owners usually armed themselves with a cloth when interacting with their dogs. Stuart, who himself owned a Newfoundland, did not overlook the telling detail, which he wryly turned back on himself. Though the artist rarely signed his works, in this case he placed his name on the dog's collar, in self-mocking acknowledgment of his dependency. In a dog, slobbering is involuntary; applied to humans, the word slobber connotes effusive display of enthusiasm, a voluntary act – and one Stuart may have felt compelled to affect with certain patrons.[115] Yet Stuart was actually very well positioned among the Anglo-Irish aristocracy, and much had changed since 1715, when Richardson, the portraitist and art theorist, made the case that it took a gentleman to portray one.[116] Sociability and polite conversation had acquired value in gauging gentility, replacing older, more fixed indicators of rank such as titles and land ownership, of little relevance in commercial British culture and no consequence in America. Still, Washington was first president of the United States (as well as a major landholder) and Stuart merely another portraitist to whom he felt bound to submit. Comparing that obligation to the conditioned response of a working animal to its master, Washington showed his sense of humor in correspondence of 1785: "No dray-horse moves more readily to the thill than I to the painter's chair."[117]

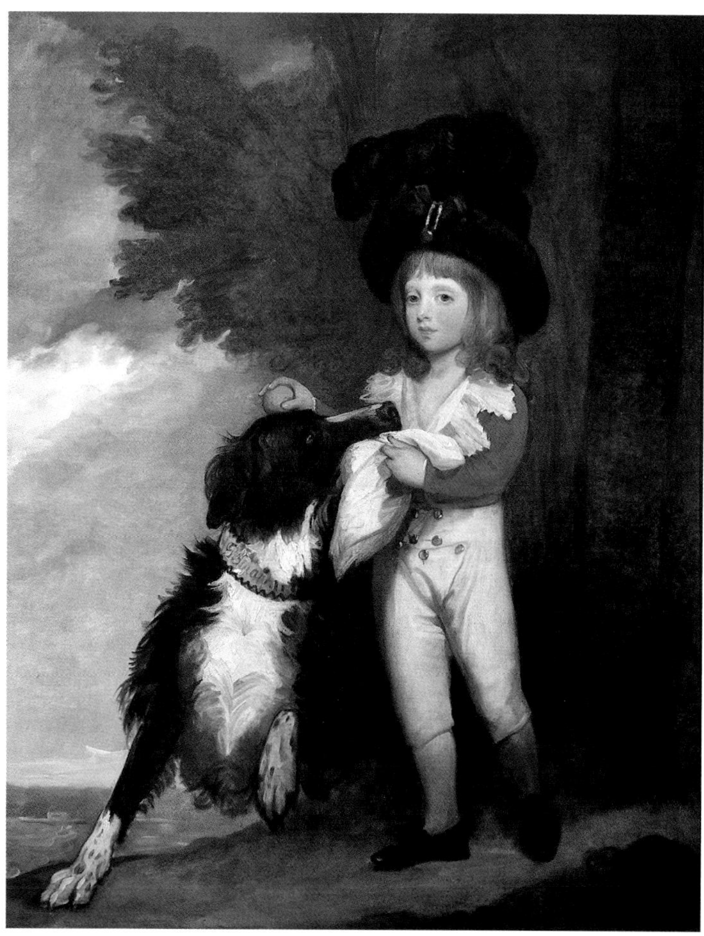

138 Gilbert Stuart, *George Thomas John Nugent*, ca. 1789–90. Oil on canvas, 49¾ × 40 in. (126.5 × 101.5 cm). Courtesy Armand Hammer Foundation.

Peale had been the first artist to portray Washington, in 1772 (fig. 139). By then, having gained early distinction during the French and Indian War, Washington had resumed civilian life as proprietor of a Virginia plantation. To Peale, who grew up on Maryland's agriculturally rich eastern shore and whose early patrons included wealthy and prominent Maryland landowners, that culture was broadly famil-

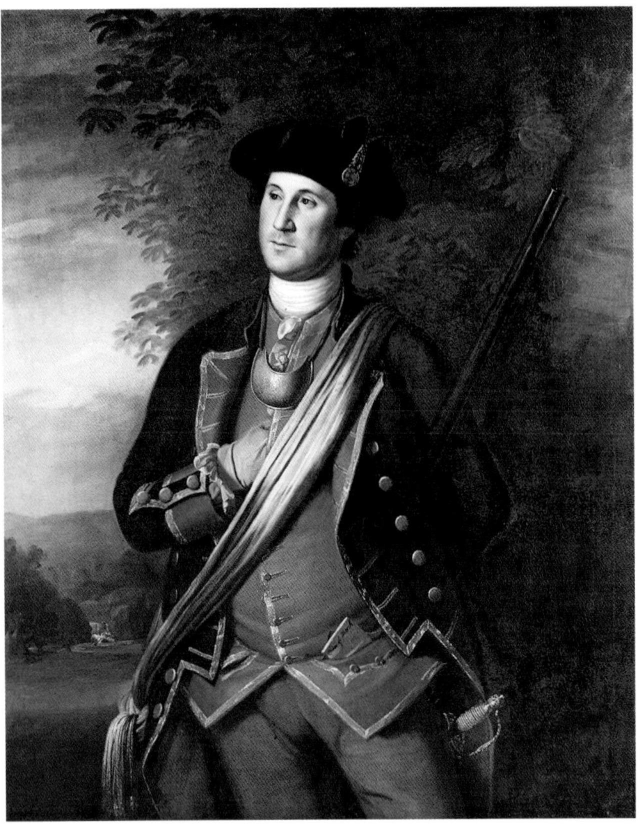

139 Charles Willson Peale, *George Washington as Colonel in the Virginia Regiment*, 1772. Oil on canvas, 50½ × 41½ in. (128.27 × 105.41 cm). Washington-Custis-Lee Collection, Washington and Lee University, Lexington, Va.

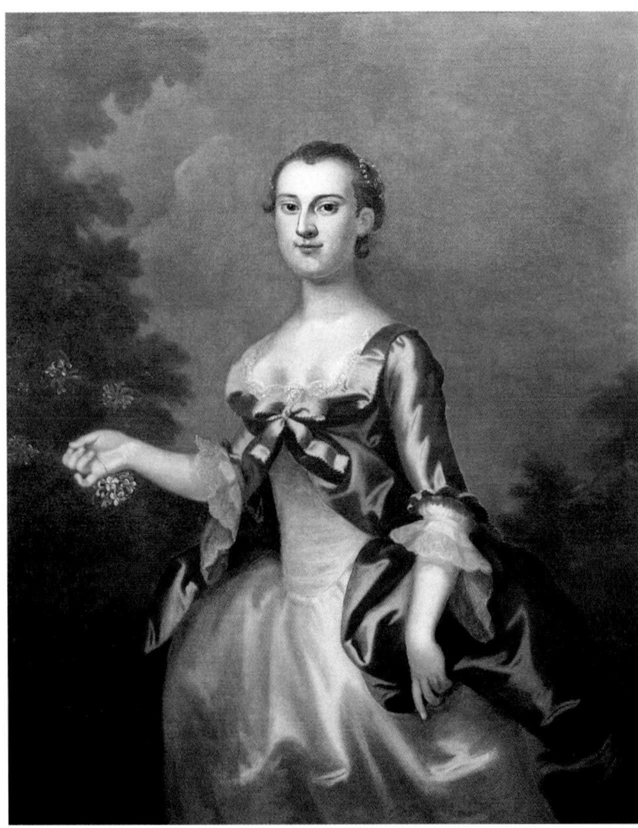

140 John Wollaston, *Martha Dandridge Custis*, 1757. Oil on canvas, 50 × 41 in. (127 × 104 cm). Washington-Custis-Lee Collection, Washington and Lee University, Lexington, Va.

iar. The artist's acquaintance with Martha Custis Washington paved the way to his meeting with her husband. In 1771, Peale painted miniatures of her two children in Williamsburg, Virginia, and the following year traveled to Mount Vernon to accompany her son home from an Annapolis, Maryland, boarding school, by request of headmaster Jonathan Boucher, a mutual friend. Mrs. Washington then prevailed on her husband to pose for his portrait, as a companion piece to hers by John Wollaston, made in 1757 during the prior marriage that, later in the year, left Martha Custis a wealthy widow (and a catch for the socially ambitious Washington, just as Peale's wife was for him) (fig. 140). Peale made a gesture toward closing the fifteen-year time gap between the portraits of husband and wife by showing Washington, then a leader in the Virginia House of Burgesses, in his old uniform as a colonel in the colonial militia. Washington did not enjoy the process of posing but faulted himself, not Peale, whom he recommended to "some Gentlemen at our Court" in Williamsburg.[118] Peale's presence at Mount Vernon during the several weeks it took to fulfill the commission laid the basis for friendship (and intermittent correspondence) between the two men, who were only ten years apart in age, not the generation that separated Stuart and Washington. Peale's later service in the Philadelphia militia during the Revolution afforded him wartime encounters with General Washington, whom he portrayed several more times during the years of the Virginian's rise to international fame. All in all, Peale parlayed seven sittings with Washington into seventy portraits – in turn the basis for popular prints in every conceivable context – as the American leader rose to the dazzling eminence he held when Stuart first encountered him.[119]

Jane Stuart sought to establish her father's feelings of insignificance before the great man. At their initial meeting, she wrote, Stuart was "so intimidated as to lose, for the moment, all self-possession." Even when he took up the brush, for sittings that resulted in Stuart's first ("Vaughan") portrait of the president (1795, fig. 141), the painter did not

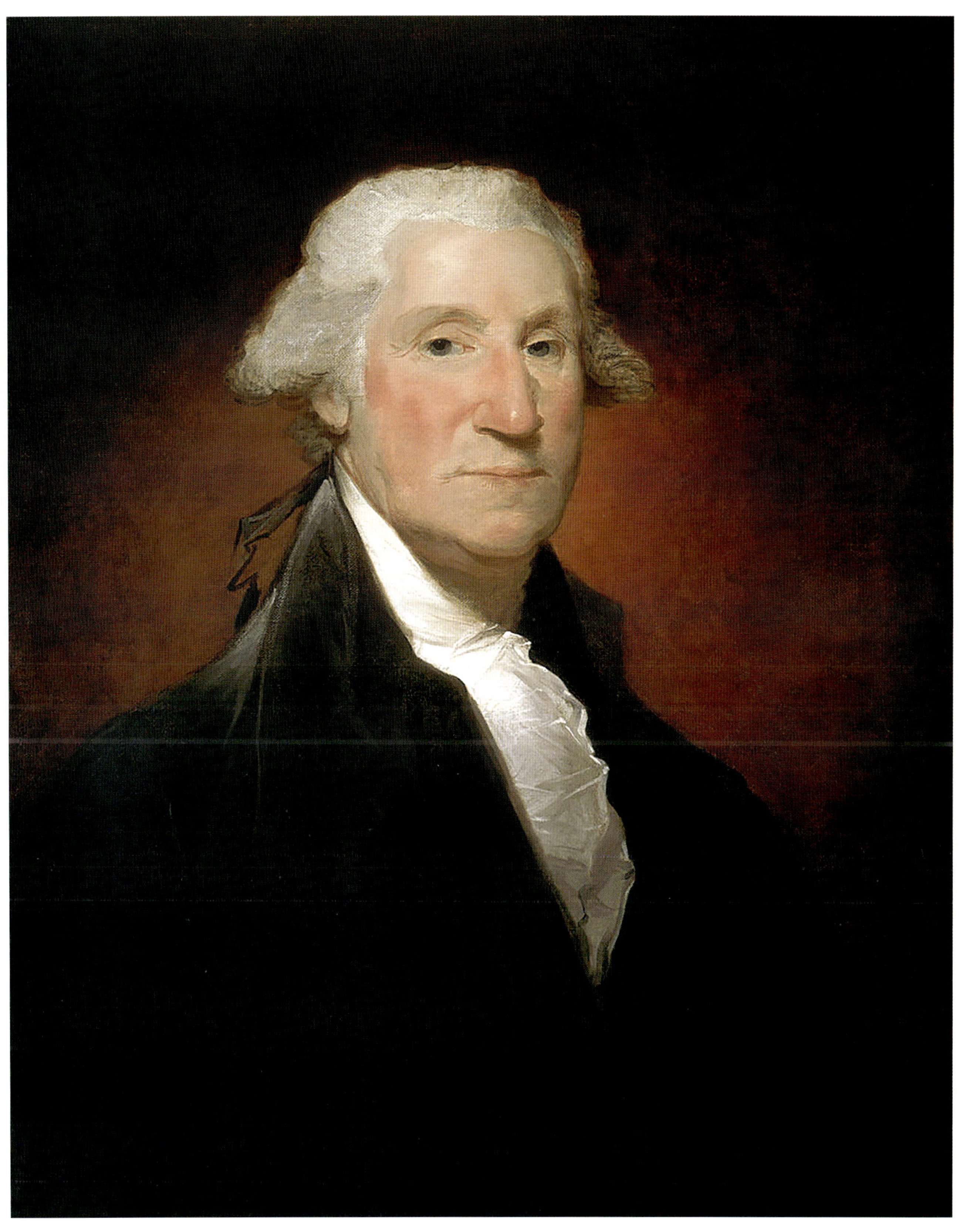

141 Gilbert Stuart, *George Washington (Vaughan Portrait)*, 1795. Oil on canvas, 28¾ × 23^{13}/$_{16}$ in. (73 × 60.5 cm). National Gallery of Art, Washington, D.C., Andrew W. Mellon Collection.

regain his composure; "his admiration and respect were so great," the daughter reported, "that he could not feel at ease."[120] The impression of the nervous painter contradicts abundant testimony concerning Stuart's fluent and witty "eazle-talk." He charmed women and men, young and old. Ann Bartlett Dwight, just sixteen when she posed in 1816, recalled of Stuart: "His anecdotes were always droll, keeping his sitters in a perpetual laugh. I remember hearing him say, it was to catch the exact expression." Henry Bowditch, who found the aged Stuart's portrait of his father, Nathaniel Bowditch (1827–28), "instinct with life," even unfinished, attributed that success "to the stimulus of the conversation, which was uninterruptedly kept up between the two men."[121] In the presence of a uniquely eminent man, it seems plausible that Stuart felt intimidated and told his daughter so years later, when she became a sanctioned copyist of the Washington portraits. At that juncture, Stuart had little reason to invent discomfort never actually experienced; more probably, he remembered it as an encounter with a man whose superiority he acknowledged and had no motivation to deny.

Stuart's interaction with Washington might be understood as deferential, in the sense that historians have tended to define the term, entailing the voluntary acquiescence of inferiors to authority recognized as superior, as well as expectations for conduct by those superiors. Scholarly understanding of deference as a key to eighteenth-century American social relations, at least until independence, has become more nuanced. Gregory Nobles recognized deference as "a performative façade that conceals a more subtle set of responses to power" and which involves a significant measure of role-playing.[122] Stuart demonstrably played various roles with American and British sitters or with potential customers. Toward the beginning of his career, according to Waterhouse, the artist toyed with fellow passengers on an English stagecoach who tried to guess his line of work. As commentators of the time attest, the stagecoach was an anonymous and socially leveling space, a place of potential misunderstanding. Stuart comically exploited those conditions, offering his companions a series of misleading hints as to his occupation. He sometimes dressed gentlemen's and ladies' hair, he related, then acted insulted when they took him for a barber. He punned in saying he brushed gentlemen's hats but was not a valet. Nor, though he made coats and waistcoasts, was he a tailor. "I get my bread," he eventually declared, "by making faces" – which he then proceeded to do by screwing up his features at the men in the coach. From this demonstration, they concluded that he was a comic actor. Finally, Stuart revealed his profession as that of portrait painter, someone who, in his way, performed all the services he had mentioned. He then invited the men to visit his painting room. Fooling his listeners in so engaging a manner captured their interest and possibly thwarted condescension.[123] In what was essentially a business ploy (whether effective or not), Stuart found humor in the unstable status of portraitists in the eighteenth-century Anglophone world and tried to turn it to his advantage. Only when the stakes were exceptionally high, as in the matter of Heath's engraved copy of Stuart's Lansdowne portrait, would Stuart deny himself such humor.

Varying accounts of Stuart's interactions with Washington – arising from the multiple sittings that three portraits required – expose the uncertainties of negotiating a relationship with the distinguished and notably reserved president. Given how many anecdotes of Stuart reprised existing anecdotes of painters, it is interesting to note that those representing great artists as the intimates of kings – Apelles and Alexander, Dürer and Emperor Maximilian, Holbein and Henry VIII, Titian and Charles V, Velazquez and Philip IV – were not adapted to him or by him. Perhaps the republican situation was simply too novel. Nor did Stuart consistently represent himself as knock-kneed. He relieved tension in the painting room, the artist informed an acquaintance, by telling Washington "the old Joe Miller story" about King James II and a tongue-tied mayor, who unwittingly insulted his sovereign. Nudged to "'hold up your head and look like a man,' the blundering Mayor repeated the admonition to the King." In relating the joke, Stuart indirectly let Washington know that he accepted the role of awkward underling; at the same time, he gave the president a cheeky piece of advice directly relevant to the portrait sitting. The tactic worked: "'from that time,' said Mr. Stuart, 'I had him on a pivot and could manage him nicely.'"[124] Portraitists sometimes used a movable sitter's chair on casters, though Stuart's reference to a pivot seems figurative. It placed Washington in an entirely passive role, as if he were no more than a lump of clay to be modeled. Stuart's choice of metaphor suggested that he had gained the upper hand.[125]

In the scenario Dunlap envisioned, Stuart remained Washington's inferior. The writer granted that after the initial encounters Stuart "probably not only had more self-possession, but had inspired his sitter with more confidence in him, and a greater disposition to familiar conversation." One infers that Dunlap still recognized a status differential between the statesman, whose mind he imagined as "busied within" by matters of consequence, and the normally extroverted painter, who had little basis for connecting with such a man. The biographer made his point more directly by quoting Trumbull, also a portraitist of Washington: "Mr. Stuart's conversation could not interest George Washington, – he had no topic fitted for his character – the president did not relish his manner. When he sat to me he was at his ease." The two artists were friends, but Trumbull, unlike Stuart, had an acute, lifelong need to promote his own image as a gentleman. His remarks affirm that he and Washington were social equals (a fair enough claim given Trumbull's family background and education), while insinuating that Stuart was beneath them.[126]

By the nineteenth century, a broadened definition of gentlemen, on the one hand, and a tremendously expanded market for portraits, on the other, narrowed the social gap between painters and sitters – or even, in some cases, reversed it. With presidents other than Washington, Stuart had few difficulties establishing a personal connection. He portrayed Jefferson several times in office and said they were "friends," befitting the head of a party that represented the relationship between leaders and the people as friendship rather than patriarchy. John Adams, who sat for some thirty portraits during his lifetime and compared the tedium of posing to "penance," actually enjoyed his time with Stuart in 1823–24: "I should like to sit to Stuart from the first of January to the last of December, for he lets me do just what I please and keeps me constantly amused by his conversation."[127] As had not been the case with Washington, Adams's presidency lay well in the past (and lacked the distinction of priority), while Stuart had achieved the status of America's preeminent portraitist. They were both old men, too, and in the context of an increasingly democratic United States, more equal than not.

Stuart's portrayal of Federalists and Democratic-Republicans alike indicates that political principle neither constrained him from accepting commissions nor inhibited patrons from seeking him out. In this regard, he was no different from other artists who remained politically circumspect to protect their livelihoods. Copley presents a notable example during the years of mounting American–British hostilities, when it was nearly impossible to avoid taking sides; his patrons, whatever they suspected, were equally willing to look the other way. Peale, though an overt patriot at that same time, declined in public or private to document his post-Revolutionary political convictions, except to observe that it was professionally detrimental to do so. Yet that has not kept later writers from seeing him as one of the most politically conscious artists of the early American republic. Even though his easel paintings did not explicitly engage political circumstances, by contrast (for example) to Trumbull's scenes of Revolutionary War subjects, Peale contributed transparencies for illumination at public events and remained determined, as David Ward has stated, "to build a deep structure of support for the state-making process of early American history," an aim served above all by his museum, a civics lesson in republican virtues and values.[128]

Notwithstanding Stuart's uninterrupted contact with leaders of the early republic during politically volatile times, politics has rarely entered discussion of his life and career. Nearly total silence in the record has left scholars almost nothing to go on. Yet a recently discovered bit of evidence offers the glimpse of a political position. Henry Pickering, from the staunchly Federalist Salem family, wrote that during conversations with the artist in 1817, "Mr. S. mentioned Mr. Jefferson's companionable talents. – They had long been friends, tho they differed in politicks."[129] Those differences would have been relatively fresh in Stuart's mind in the wake of the Hartford Convention of 1814–15, at which resurgent Federalists in New England discussed secession from the Union over opposition to the current war with Britain and to the Republican policies that fueled that conflict. Waterhouse, who once wrote that Stuart "would pass for a Briton on either side of the Atlantic," told Dunlap that he "withdrew" around that time from Stuart and his "hot-headed companions," whose unsuccessful support for such a drastic measure finally broke the Federalist party.[130]

Surprisingly, as of 1802, Stuart remained legally a British subject, a circumstance that has not attracted attention. Stuart's petition in the case against Sword, for unauthorized reproduction of the Athenaeum Washington, and the writ of injunction identified the plaintiff as "an alien and a subject of the King of the united kingdoms of Great Britain and Ireland" and Sword as "a citizen of the United States." This "diversity of citizenship" – meaning that litigants are either citizens of different states or an American citizen and a citizen of another country – may explain why a matter normally handled in state court (an equitable action for an injunction based upon a breach of contract claim) was heard at the federal level, at a time when copyright was not yet a matter of federal law.[131] The terms of citizenship were complicated, variable, and not quickly sorted out in the new United States, to which Stuart had returned ten years after the Treaty of Paris, having departed prior to the Revolution. With confusing looseness of terminology, the architect Benjamin Latrobe, writing to Peale, called Stuart "that greatest of our Artists, and most unprincipled of our Citizens," while adding: "(by the bye he is no American citizen)."[132] As a great artist, it seems, Stuart could be a citizen, though his defects of character required acknowledgment that he was not. Latrobe's phrasing in this letter suggests a sympathetic reader – in fact Peale, for whom virtuous conduct was a prerequisite of citizenship.

The old Federalist ideal of disinterested, genteel, and virtuous leadership – belief in a public authority that would act in behalf of ordinary private citizens, whose commercial interests were thought to disqualify them from behaving selflessly – would never have seemed to hold much appeal for a man of Stuart's temperament. By contrast, in the new era of party politics after 1800, Democratic-Republicans attacked privilege and embraced commerce as a civilizing rather than corrupting force; for them, self-interest was the engine of society. Stuart's actions were not at odds with that view. He was both a product of and a contributor to an increasingly democratic, non-deferential American society. Disposed to make the most of his talents in an emerging free market economy, Stuart set high prices and sought to control circulation of works he created, reaping the financial benefit they offered. He further maintained an unyielding sense of the correctness of his artistic decisions, antagonizing patrons who wanted to direct him in any way. In that sense, there was nothing participatory, or democratic, about Stuart's portrait practice. As the most sought-after portraitist of the early republic, Stuart could and did conduct himself in any manner he chose.

"Not a Man to Flinch": Private Patrons

Stuart asserted an authority of skill not rank, and he was generally disinclined to be complaisant, in the period sense of courteous and yielding. Reynolds had been known for that quality, as was Peale, the most prominent portraitist in America until Stuart's return. Peale occasionally recorded mild annoyance with clients in his diary and other documents never meant to become public, but he kept those judgments to himself, perhaps stung on the one occasion, early in his career, when he did not. In 1774, Peale placed successive notices in the *Maryland Gazette* in which he chided Elie Valette, a portrait client who had not paid promptly enough to satisfy Peale. The patron used the same forum to respond and, as David Steinberg observed, "outflanked" his portraitist by indicating that he would pay only after Peale had learned to be "less insolent."[133] Valette, in other words, held Peale to a place of social inferiority, which the artist dared to think he had escaped. Peale never again aired displeasure with patrons, consistent with an ongoing effort to keep a self-described "colorick disposition" in check.[134] In 1783, he let a prominent early supporter know that he was "labouring hard to give full satisfaction to those who favor [him] with employment"; to West, he offered a glossier but not necessarily less truthful view, noting that he was "so fortunate as to please all that employ" him.[135] Peale's correspondence with patrons or potential patrons exhibits utmost civility and indicates a willingness to do whatever it took to satisfy. He was more like the tradesman or artisan who delivered what customers wanted than a professional who provided clients with what he judged best for them. As late as 1792, two years before Peale turned from painting portraits to more broadly public pursuits (uncharted territory in which he acted more as the professional), the artist offered to repaint a miniature after the subject's wife complained about the likeness. Even Peale acknowledged the failure in his diary, though he asserted that his work ought to have been valued as "a high finished picture."[136] On the defensive, Peale resorted to a traditional artisanal measure of merit, a standard that Stuart rejected.

If Peale remained silent on difficulties with sitters when composing the late-life autobiography, Stuart showed no compunction in opposing clients he felt had crossed him. When sitters tried to tell him how to do his job, he resisted – or so he told third parties, increasing the likelihood that his snappy retorts and reactive measures would be talked about and become a matter of record. After the Archbishop of Dublin complained about the likeness in his daughter's portrait, so Stuart's Irish friend Herbert reported, the artist proceeded to "rub out" the young woman's face, overpainting that part of the canvas with darker pigments. He then lectured his distinguished patron: "A dressmaker may alter a dress, a milliner a cap, a tailor a coat, but a painter may give up his art if he attempts to alter to please."[137] Stuart's defacement of the portrait obliterated the part he most cared about. At the same time, his rebuke obliquely acknowledged what every painter knew: clients judged likeness in portraits as much by costume as by facial depiction. Those portraitists who appeared most ready to oblige made themselves easy targets for colleagues who deployed the still punishing trope of the painter-tailor; "a sort of man-milliner painter" was James Northcote's characterization of Thomas Lawrence, in reference to that artist's attention to fashion.[138] Stuart disdained flashy clothing in portraits; confronted with such work, Sully, his younger colleague, recalled, "he would admire the lace &c & after an interval exclaim: 'Why! there's a face there!'"[139] Stuart must have taken private amusement, then, in making ostentatious portraits of the Spanish diplomat Josef Jaudenes y Nebot and his American wife, representations that bear out contemporaneous descriptions of the couple in person appearing "fine as little dolls" (fig. 142).[140] Often, Stuart butted heads with patrons who wanted him to make alterations in the way he painted their clothing. After a client returned a picture because he thought the cravat painted too coarsely, Stuart responded sarcastically: "I am determined to buy a piece [of cloth] of the finest texture, have it glued on the part that offends their exquisite judgment, and send it back again."[141] Stuart had no intention of satisfying the literal-minded patron, having already transformed the coarse cloth of canvas by his art. Using his brush to produce a more realistic rendering of the necktie, he implied, would violate the integrity of his work as a whole.

Gluing or stitching scraps of fabric and other materials to painted portraits was the actual practice of Connecticut miniature painter Mary Way, her sister Betsey Way Champlain, and niece Eliza Way Champlain, who adapted drawing and needlework accomplishments typically cultivated in genteel young women when they created a group of "dressed miniatures." Mary Way produced dozens of profile portraits, a body of work identified based on the fine, signed portrayal of her cousin Charles Holt (1800), publisher of the New London *Bee* (soon to relocate to Hudson, where he tangled with Harry Croswell). Way charged ten to twenty dollars for her work, traveled in search of clients, and advertised her availability; David Jaffee accordingly credited her as "very likely the first professional woman artist in the post-Revolutionary United States."[142] It would not have helped her case among professional artists like Stuart (or Copley earlier) that Way embodied the "painter tailor," but it hardly mattered, since gender constrained her advancement.

Irritation with clients at times led Stuart to abandon a portrait commission or to warn that he would make unflattering alterations and go public with the result. Portraits of Jerome and Elizabeth Patterson Bonaparte, begun in early 1804, remained incomplete after Jerome spoke to Stuart in a manner the artist found "impertinent," according to Jane Stuart.[143] Her word strikingly captures Stuart's disregard for Jerome's status as brother to Napoleon Bonaparte, First Consul of France and (by May) Emperor, as well as his security in personal accomplishment achieved independently of family connections. In private, Stuart dismissed

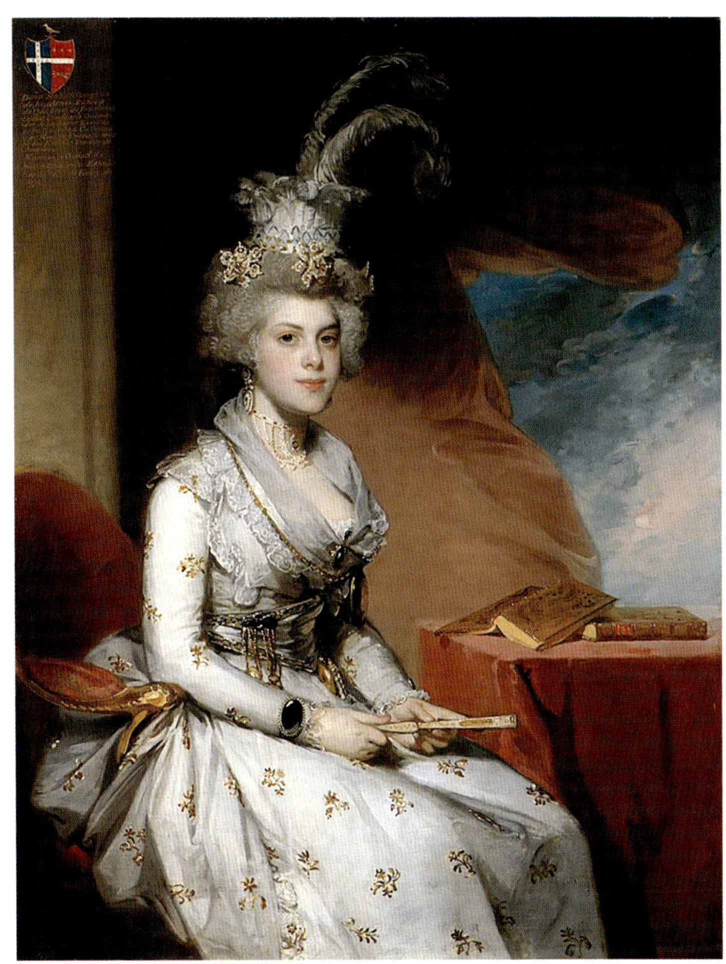

142 Gilbert Stuart, *Mathilda Stoughton de Jaudenes*, 1794. Oil on canvas, 50⅝ × 39½ in. (128.6 × 100.3 cm). Metropolitan Museum of Art, New York, Rogers Fund, 1907 (07.76).

Jerome as "a [damned] French barber" and threatened, if badgered any longer about Elizabeth's picture, to "put rings through the nose, and send it to any tavern-keeper who would hang it up." Sully, to whom Stuart made those remarks in 1807, added: "He would have done it too for he was not a man to flinch from anything of that kind."[144]

Sully had seen an unfinished Stuart portrait with comic alterations, the only such work that survives. John Bill Ricketts, the sitter, was proprietor of a circus and its star equestrian (fig. 143). The artist later claimed to have veered from his original plan of returning to Philadelphia in 1792 so as to avoid sharing a vessel with Ricketts and "all his horses, & dancing devils, & little devils, (company which neither [Stuart] nor his family had been accustomed to associate with)."[145] Stuart's tolerance for antics by others evidently had limits, and it seems that he was also more

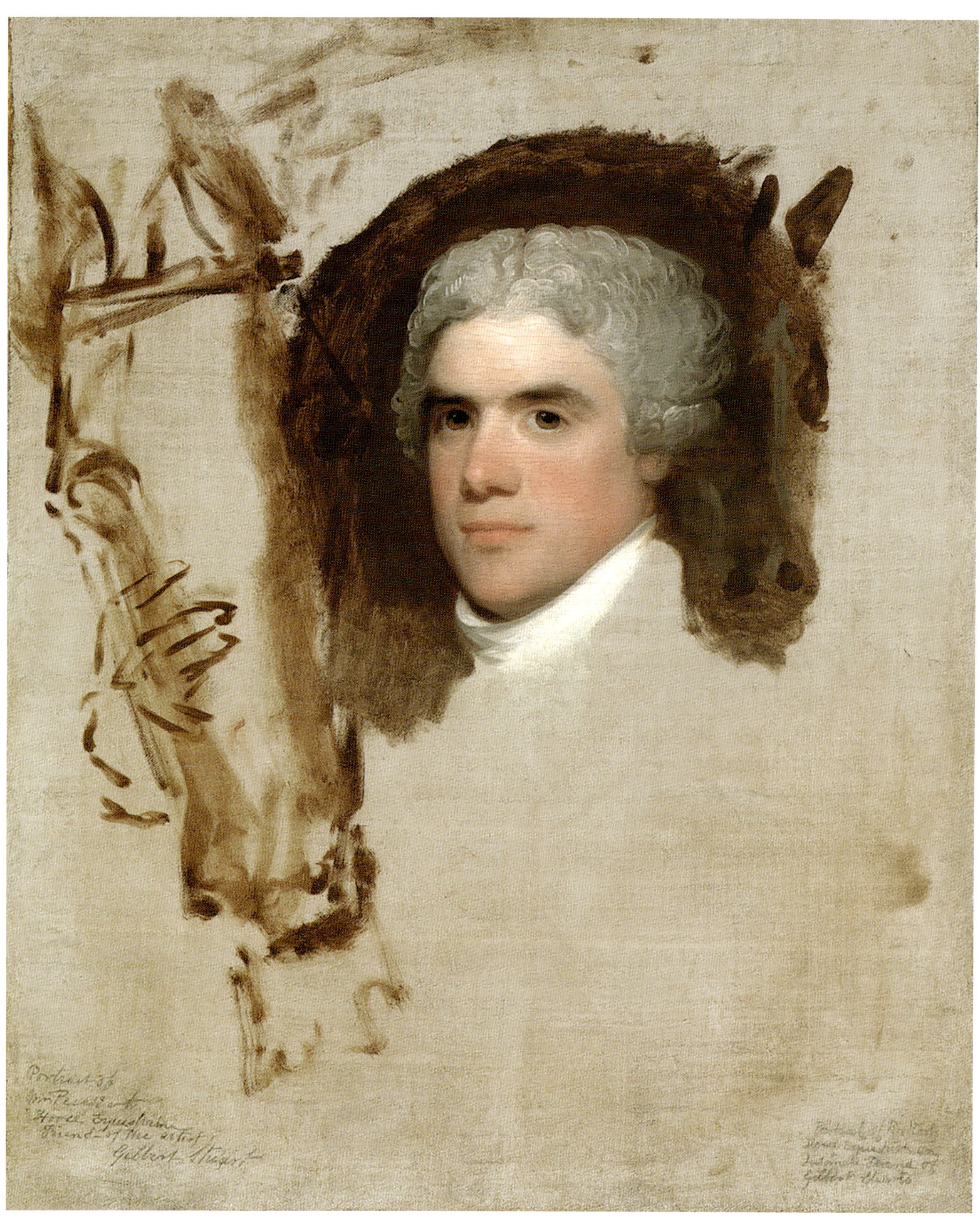

143 Gilbert Stuart, *John Bill Ricketts*, ca. 1795–99. Oil on canvas, $29\frac{3}{8} \times 24\frac{3}{16}$ in. (74.6 × 61.5 cm). National Gallery of Art, Washington, D.C., gift of Mrs. Robert B. Noyes in memory of Elisha Riggs.

interested in bringing down the mighty than in across-the-board social leveling. Why he undertook a portrait of Ricketts remains unclear; possibly he did so because the horseman was a favorite of Washington, Stuart's frequent subject during the years to which the work has been dated (ca. 1795–99). The president attended several circus performances, celebrated his birthday at Ricketts's Philadelphia amphitheater in 1797, and sold Ricketts a horse.[146] But Stuart and Ricketts clashed. The painter reportedly found his subject uncooperative and stopped work after completing only Ricketts's head. To the left, the head of a horse, its muzzle cupped by Ricketts's hand, appears sketched out in paint, a nod to the sitter's occupation that was presumably intended for the finished work. At some point, Stuart fooled around with the unfinished canvas: he transformed the aureole of brown paint that sets off Ricketts's head into another horse, through economical addition of ears, eye sockets, and nostrils. The gesture has the air of a childish prank, Stuart's response in kind to a circus stuntman who put considerable equestrian skills to what some might have considered inglorious display, dancing a hornpipe or juggling oranges while standing in the saddle, among other tricks. The alteration did not detract from the good likeness; some years after Ricketts died prematurely in 1803, his brother acquired the portrait.[147] He could have arranged for someone else to finish the work or, at a minimum, for obliteration of the extra horse head, but perhaps the Ricketts family appreciated Stuart's doodle. The canvas as Stuart left it had the effect of highlighting his dexterous wit and hand, thereby authenticating the portrait as the creation of an artist who had by then become famous – and known for leaving pictures incomplete. Stuart strongly opposed completion of his unfinished paintings by others, perhaps one reason that he did not easily give them up. His widow accordingly attempted to prevent it too, as Waterhouse reported in some detail to John Quincy Adams, with regard to the president's unfinished portrait. Even unfinished, portraits by Stuart were often treasured by sitters as unusually good likenesses.[148]

In his portrait of Anna Payne Cutts (1804), Stuart altered a stock motif of the genre to meaningful and public end, engaging contemporaneous fascination with physiognomy and machine-made portraits only to counter their presumed empirical authority with that of the individual artist (fig. 144). His gesture in this case was considerably bolder than with Ricketts because he completed the picture and his socially prominent young sitter, sister of Dolley Madison, accepted it. While the lady's face is unblemished, Stuart transformed a swag and column base – a generic background feature of his work and of European portraits since the Renaissance – into an outsized, satyr-like profile with hook nose and pointed chin. The features were said to be a "burlesque" of his own, added after Mrs. Cutts lamented that Stuart's friends, among whom she counted herself, had no portrait of him.[149] Stuart's unconventional gesture indulged his pronounced streak of self-parody and, at the same time, parodied – or satyr-ized – the neoclassical profile portrait, at peak fashionability in the United States during the first decade of the nineteenth century.[150] In late 1802, toward the end of Stuart's years in Philadelphia, Peale installed a physiognotrace at his museum in that city, where it generated considerable interest. There Moses Williams, Peale's manumitted slave, performed the work of cutting, typically adding telling details that the machine could not have captured, such as tendrils of hair or eyelashes, evident in a possible self-portrait inscribed with his name and vocation (fig. 145).[151] Machine-assisted profiles, produced by vendors who employed various types of equipment and readily advertised their presence in city and country, appealed to Americans at all social levels. Stuart himself never attempted to capitalize on the "rage for profiles," as Peale termed it. To the contrary, he probably objected to the methods, marketing, and presumed significance of such work.

Stuart's portrait production was efficient in its way – the swag-and-column motif, for example, seems transparently formulaic in his cursory renderings – but his canvases were obviously hand-brushed and highly colored, the antithesis of a mechanically produced, opaque physiognotrace. Not all machine-assisted profiles were so rudimentary or democratic. One of the earliest and most successful physiognotrace operators in America, French émigré Charles Balthazar Julien Févret de Saint-Mémin, created detailed profile portraits in black and white chalk, which he then engraved. Saint-Mémin's sophisticated work attracted clients among the same elite as Stuart, first in Philadelphia and then Washington, where both artists were active between 1803 and 1805. Jefferson sat for Saint-Mémin in 1804, acquiring a more refined profile than the cut physiognotrace that Peale made from a portrait bust and sent the president a year earlier (fig. 146).[152] In 1805, the president found his appetite for profile portraits sufficiently whetted that – as if to cap a hierarchy of artistic production – he requested a painted profile from Stuart, for whom he had posed at least twice before (fig. 147). Stuart had not previously made independent profiles, nor would he again. The resulting portrait is unique in his oeuvre, not least for its

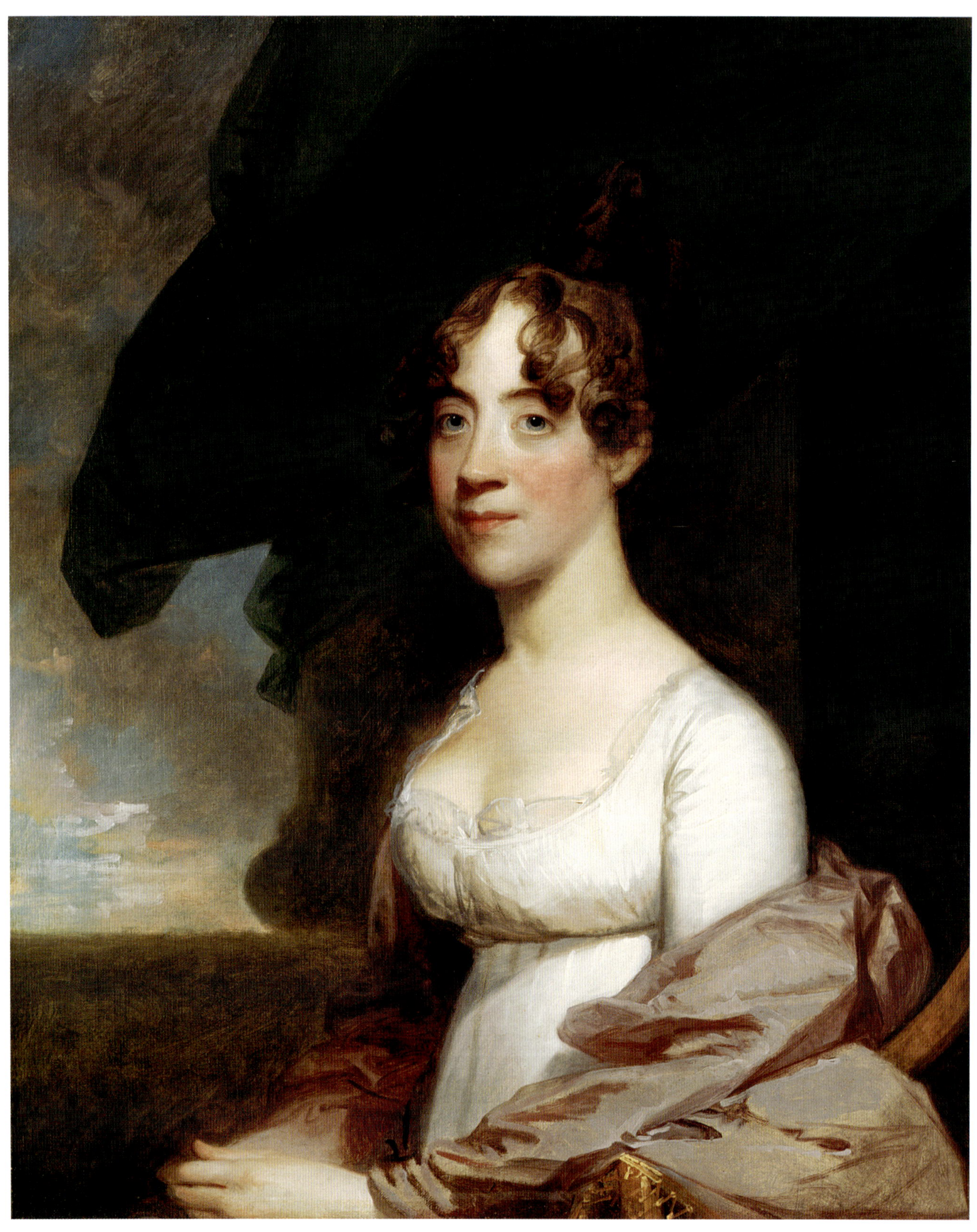

144 Gilbert Stuart, *Anna Payne Cutts*, 1804. Oil on canvas, 29 × 24⅛ in. (73.8 × 61.3 cm). White House Historical Association, Washington, D.C. (White House Collection).

rondel framing and restriction to grisaille (monochromatic paint), both possibly proposed by Jefferson as well. Consistent with Jefferson's taste for classicism, this portrait evokes ancient Roman sculpture and, especially, coins – hence Jefferson's reference to the work as displaying "medallion stile."[153] The profile also communicated political affiliation: Jefferson's short hair, fully evident from the side, called to mind both ancient Roman and modern French fashion, thereby distancing the president from Federalists and reinforcing his republicanism. In almost every respect, the work departs from Stuart's usual practice, a deviation that marked the portrait of Jefferson as a rarefied exception for a particular client, not as a new style, format, or method available to anyone.

The difficulties Stuart's contemporaries and ours have faced in pinning down his views on physiognomy and typological representation of character suggest the artist's success in resisting rules. He knew his works were readily adapted to physiognomic ends – the 1798 English edition of Lavater's *Essays on Physiognomy* included an engraving based on Stuart's Vaughan portrait of Washington. Yet even scholars who believe Stuart purposefully shaped the Vaughan portrait to facilitate physiognomic reading reach opposing conclusions as to how. Did he privilege evidence grounded in physical fact – altering the Vaughan portrait after seeing the sculpted likeness Jean-Antoine Houdon had based on a life mask – or did he adjust his own perceptions to produce a publicly legible type?[154] Accounts of Stuart routinely highlight his powers of discernment, as in the story that he detected and portrayed madness in a sitter shortly before the man committed suicide "from insanity."[155] However, Stuart seems to have regarded that skill as part of his innate gift, not as a power readily available to anyone who perused an edition of Lavater. He delighted in setting up persons who thought otherwise. Jane Stuart told of visitors to Stuart's studio who were "expiating on the wonderful science of physiognomy" and decided to test their "remarkable knowledge" on one of his portraits; they saw "villain written in every line of the face," only to learn the sitter was a clergyman. The daughter

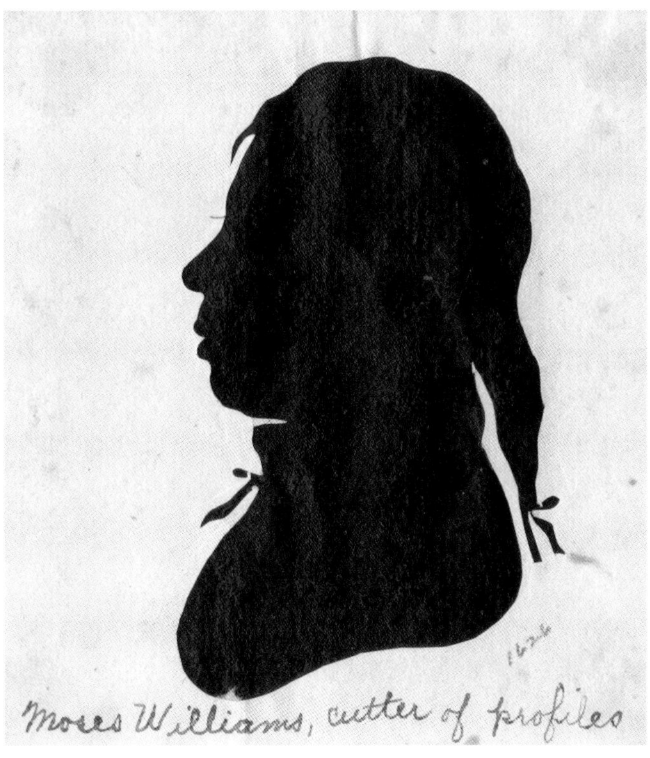

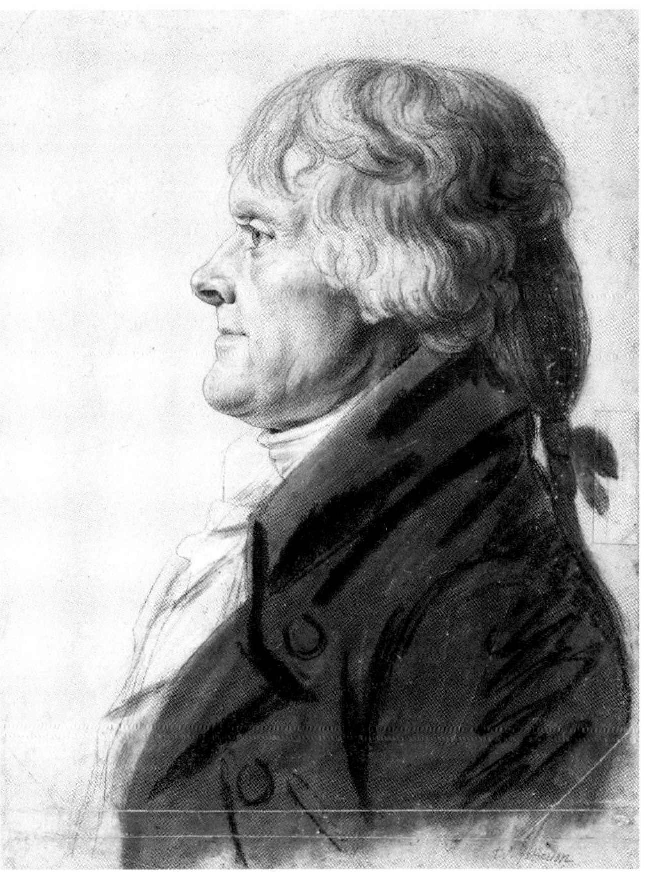

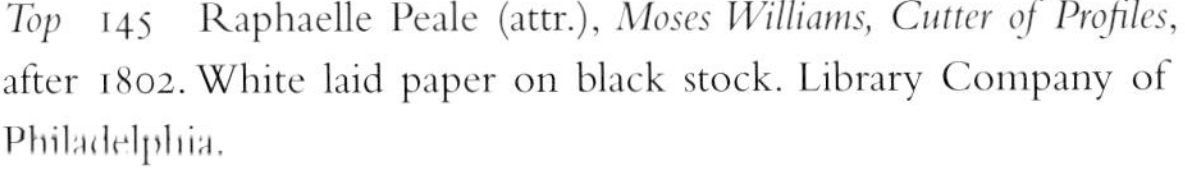

Top 145 Raphaelle Peale (attr.), *Moses Williams, Cutter of Profiles*, after 1802. White laid paper on black stock. Library Company of Philadelphia.

Bottom 146 Charles Balthazar Julien Févret de Saint-Mémin, *Thomas Jefferson*, 1804. Charcoal and black, white, and gray chalk drawing. Worcester Art Museum, Worcester, Mass., museum purchase 1954.82. Image © Worcester Art Museum.

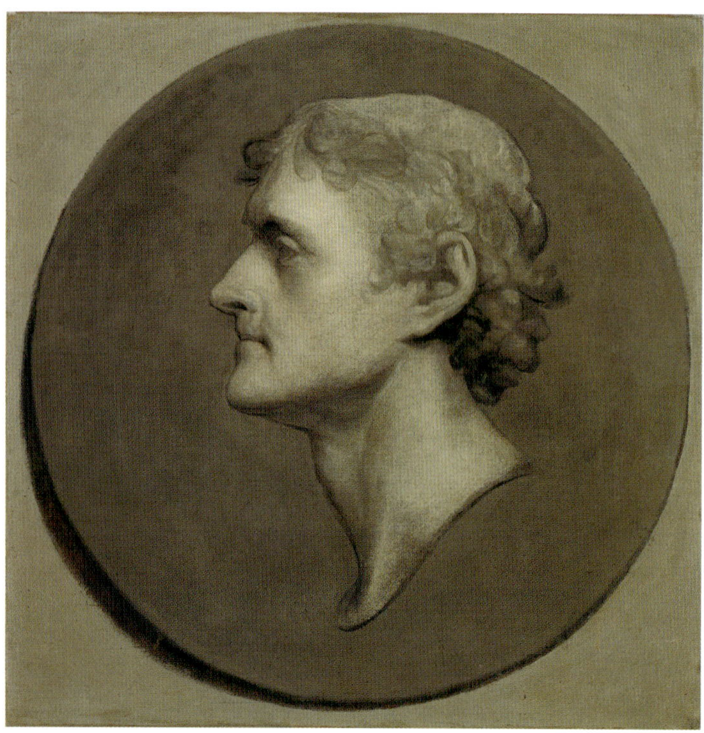

147 Gilbert Stuart, *Thomas Jefferson (The Medallion Portrait)*, 1805. Grisaille, oil and egg mixture on blue laid paper on canvas, 18¾ × 18¾ in. (47.6 × 47.6 cm), framed 26¾ × 27 × 4 in. (68 × 68.6 × 10.2 cm). Harvard Art Museums/Fogg Museum, Cambridge, Mass., gift of Mrs. T. Jefferson Newbold and family, in memory of Thomas Jefferson Newbold, Class of 1910, 1960.156. Imaging Department © President and Fellows of Harvard College.

asserted that her father "had not much confidence in detecting the character of a man by the expression of his face." Though "expression" and physiognomy should be opposed – the one referring to fleeting and the other to fixed characteristics – Jane Stuart uses them interchangeably in this account. In that context, Stuart passed judgment on the average person but exempted himself, as a superior artist.[156]

Art critic John Neal believed that Stuart accepted physiognomic principles while applying them inconsistently. "Stuart's men look as if they were predestined statesmen, or had sat in council, or commanded armies, – their very countenances being a biography, and sometimes a history of their day," Neal stated, implying that the portraits transcended particularities.[157] Stuart's Washington, for example, was indelible but unlike: "If George Washington should appear on earth, just as he sat to Stuart, I am sure that he would be treated as an imposter, when compared with Stuart's likeness of him," declared Neal's fictional alter ego in an early novel; "the painter has infused into it, an amplitude and grandeur, that were never the attributes of Washington's *face*."[158] Restating the point decades later, he added a tribute to Stuart's accomplishment that identifies the work more with him than its subject: "we cling to the magnificent shadow, and let the substance go, willing that Stuart himself should go down to after ages, instead of Washington." For Neal, Stuart's portraits of women did not conform to expectations. They appeared like "creatures of flesh and blood, . . . somewhat too strongly individualized perhaps for female portraiture" and too little like art, deficient in the "grace and tenderness" that Neal saw in Thomas Sully's work. Stuart's transgression in Neal's negative example – a seemingly benign representation of Dolley Madison (appearing very similar to her sister, Anna Cutts) – is not obvious to a modern viewer, and the women who sat to Stuart contemporaneously with Mrs. Madison had no complaints about him. To the contrary. In 1805, Peale reminded his son Rembrandt "how the lady when in our room at Washington, beged [*sic*] Mr. Stewart to commence her picture!" and prodded his son to make the effort to "please the Ladies equally well if not better than Stewart."[159] Stuart may have pleased by, to some degree, ignoring the limiting range of "characters" available to women that Neal's remark exposed. Neal's approving description of Sully's portrayals of women further exposes the constraints: "Their eyes, are the eyes of poetry, deep and melancholy, or patient or timid; but always, whatever be their expression, looking as if copied at the critical moment of their extremest beauty."[160] Sully, not exactly impartial in this matter, agreed that "Stuart rarely excelled in painting the female face. His excellence lay chiefly in delineating strong and vigorous character," which was not, he implied, a feminine quality.[161] When Stuart strayed from type, from conventional and generic femininity, his works became illegible to contemporaries.

Stuart's portrait of Elizabeth Parke Custis Law, George Washington's granddaughter, offers the most obvious case in his oeuvre for intrusion of the "strong and vigorous" arena of male portraiture into female representation (fig. 148). Eliza Law's crossed arm pose – reinforced by her fichu and the bright ribbon on her bonnet – appears relaxed rather than defensive when coupled with a gaze so assertive that the family felt a need to explain her appearance. By tradition, Stuart captured Eliza as she appraised his progress on Washington's second portrait, while the president was posing. That cannot actually have been the case, unless Stuart were working on both pictures at the same time, an unlikely proposition under any circumstance and especially so where the busy statesman was concerned. The rationalization, in

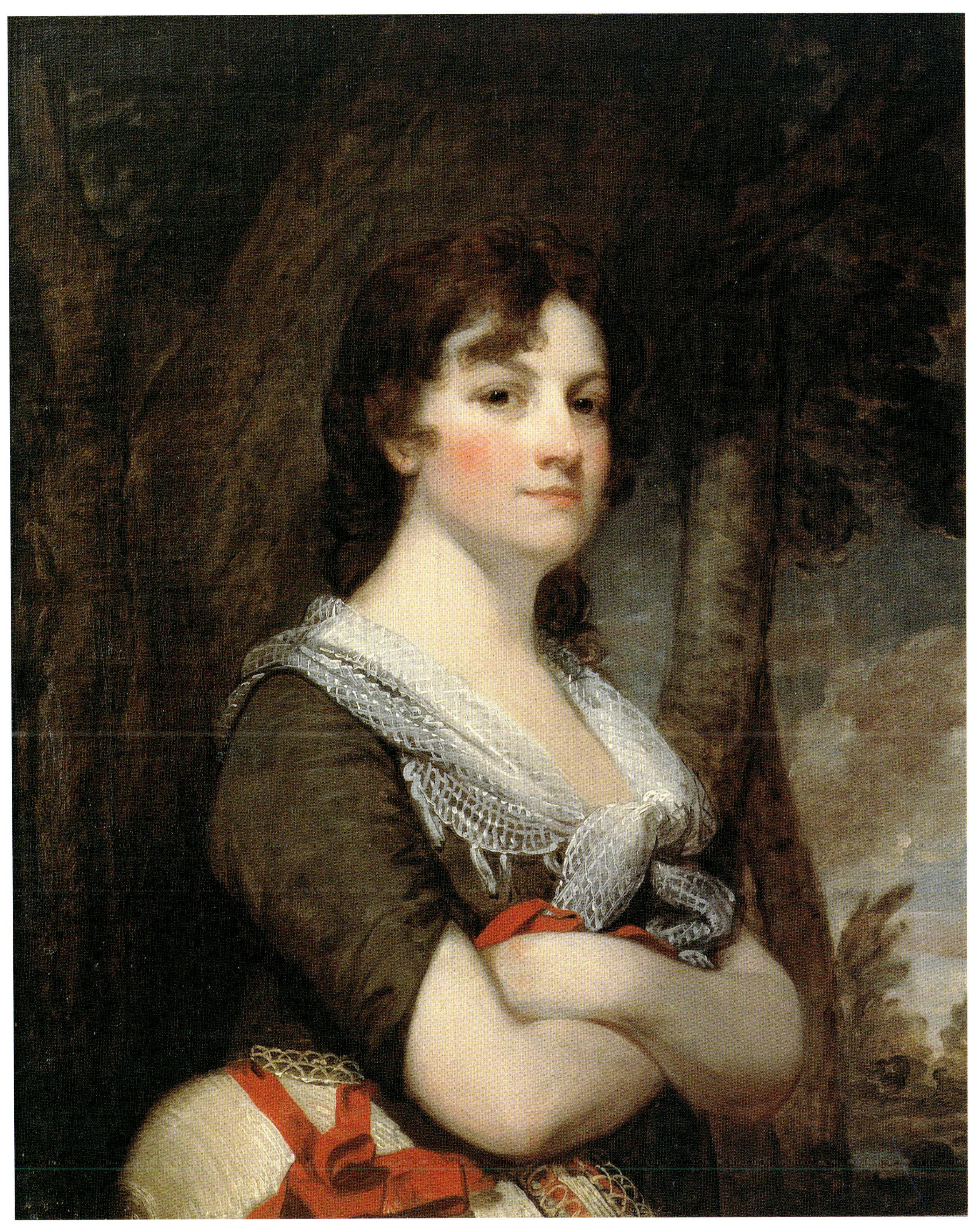

148 Gilbert Stuart, *Elizabeth Parke Custis Law*, 1796. Oil on canvas, 28¼ × 23½ in. (71.8 × 59.7 cm). Private collection.

any event, does nothing to dispel the impression that Eliza was an opinionated young woman. From her aunt's perspective, Eliza "never cared about the compliments she was given on her beauty, but she was always very vain about her mind and knowledge"; "in her tastes and pastimes she is more man than woman and regrets that she can't wear pants."[162] Eliza Law, as this extraordinary remark suggests, did not conform to social expectations of womanly behavior. Stuart made no attempt to neutralize her independence. He responded to qualities particular to the sitter herself.

Stuart reserved the right to make artistic decisions as he saw fit, unconstrained by convention or fashion. Profile portraits held little interest for him, not only because they were ubiquitous, but because the profile view interfered with what Stuart did best and with how he did it. Above all, Stuart sought to endow portraits with persuasive vivacity. His repartee aided the process – only when facing a sitter could the artist fully draw the client into animated engagement – but the effect ultimately resulted from Stuart's dexterous paint handling and skillful coloring. While color especially had been linked to deception in artistic debates dating to the late seventeenth century, no such charges surfaced in connection with Stuart, who was routinely credited for truthful portraits, even when they were faulted as inartistic.[163] "I do not know of any living artist to whom I would so eagerly sit for an immediate and faithful resemblance" as Stuart, Pasquin had stated; "he sees his object, and the infinity of tints constituting that object, with more perspicuity than any other existing portrait painter. But I should add, that he is indebted for this faculty to the paucity of his invention."[164] Stuart copied nature, in other words, and this was at once his greatest virtue and a defect.

The artist gave his portraits the final spark of life with a single, deft finishing touch to the pupil of each eye, a powerful effect that can be gauged from unfinished portraits in which that detail is lacking. "The eyes confer character," Stuart observed emphatically in 1817; "the mouth imparts expression." When he declared the nose the most "characteristic" or "important" feature of a face, Stuart acknowledged its prominence and importance to likeness, not its ability to communicate.[165] The observation was rooted in his own appearance: Stuart had a substantial nose, with capacious nostrils perfectly suited to fueling a snuff habit. He caricatured this feature in the portrait of Anna Cutts. By disfiguring and darkening his own craggy visage in that work, he offered a humorous and purposeful counterpoint to his sitter's smooth and fresh young face, high coloring, and animated eyes. His creative distortion punctures the transparency of the portrait, its seductive promise that the subject is there, just before us. With Mrs. Cutts, manifestly, Stuart compels the viewer to acknowledge that he has conjured her freshness by the power of his artistic skill. Similarly, when Stuart portrayed Ann Penington holding a framed silhouette in a way that makes clear its value to the sitter, his vivid presentation of the young woman's rosy and glistening face denies the possibility that a lumpish black silhouette could ever rival the magic of a great artist (fig. 149).

"His Imagination Approves": Fictional Portraits

An artist, Stuart once asserted, "should never design his picture other than his imagination approves."[166] Stuart's imagination extended to accounts of portraits and patrons that may have been entirely fictitious. Three such cases, upon close examination, disrupt the image of Stuart as a man given to acting impulsively. Instead, consistent with the broader record of his behavior, they provide evidence of Stuart's finely tuned subversiveness and his tactical skill for self-presentation. Tellingly, the stories concern the earlier part of his career, even if they did not originate in that time, underscoring Stuart's determination to be recognized as a man who had achieved success on his own terms.

Much seems odd in Stuart's account to Pickering, in 1817, of the circumstances surrounding his first self-portrait, made in 1778 not long after he entered West's studio (fig. 150). Stuart had borrowed money from a third party to buy a portrait by seventeenth-century English artist William Dobson, which West then became intent on acquiring for his own collection. West offered four times what Stuart had paid for Dobson's picture, but the younger artist set his own terms: when West acknowledged that his pupil could paint a portrait as good as the seventeenth-century master's, Stuart would simply give Dobson's picture to him. Having no one to pose, Stuart used himself as a model, whereupon West "acknowledged the excellency of the work, and obtained what he so much desired."[167]

On the face of it, the story supports the idea that Stuart was exceptionally gifted. Dobson's reputation as a talented contemporary of van Dyck, whom Dobson succeeded as the king's painter, found reinforcement proximate to West's arrival in England. Horace Walpole devoted five pages to Dobson and included an engraved self-portrait in *Anecdotes of Painting in England* (fig. 151), while shorter accounts of the artist appeared in at least three other contemporaneous biographical compendia of the early to mid-1770s. Yet it is

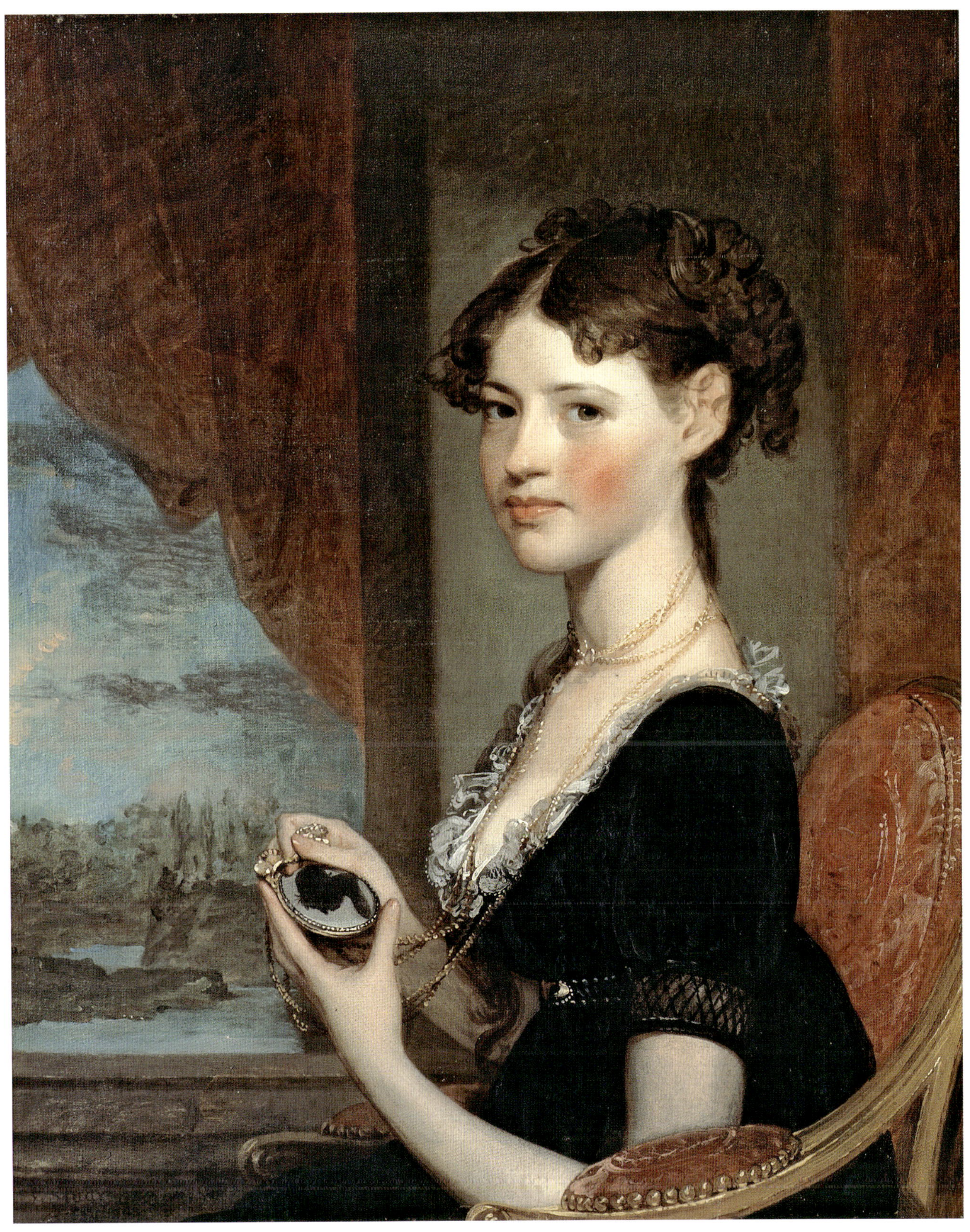

149 Gilbert Stuart, *Ann Penington*, 1805. Oil on canvas, 29 × 23½ in. (73.7 × 59.7 cm). Philadelphia Society for the Preservation of Landmarks, The Powel House, bequest of Miss Frances Wister.

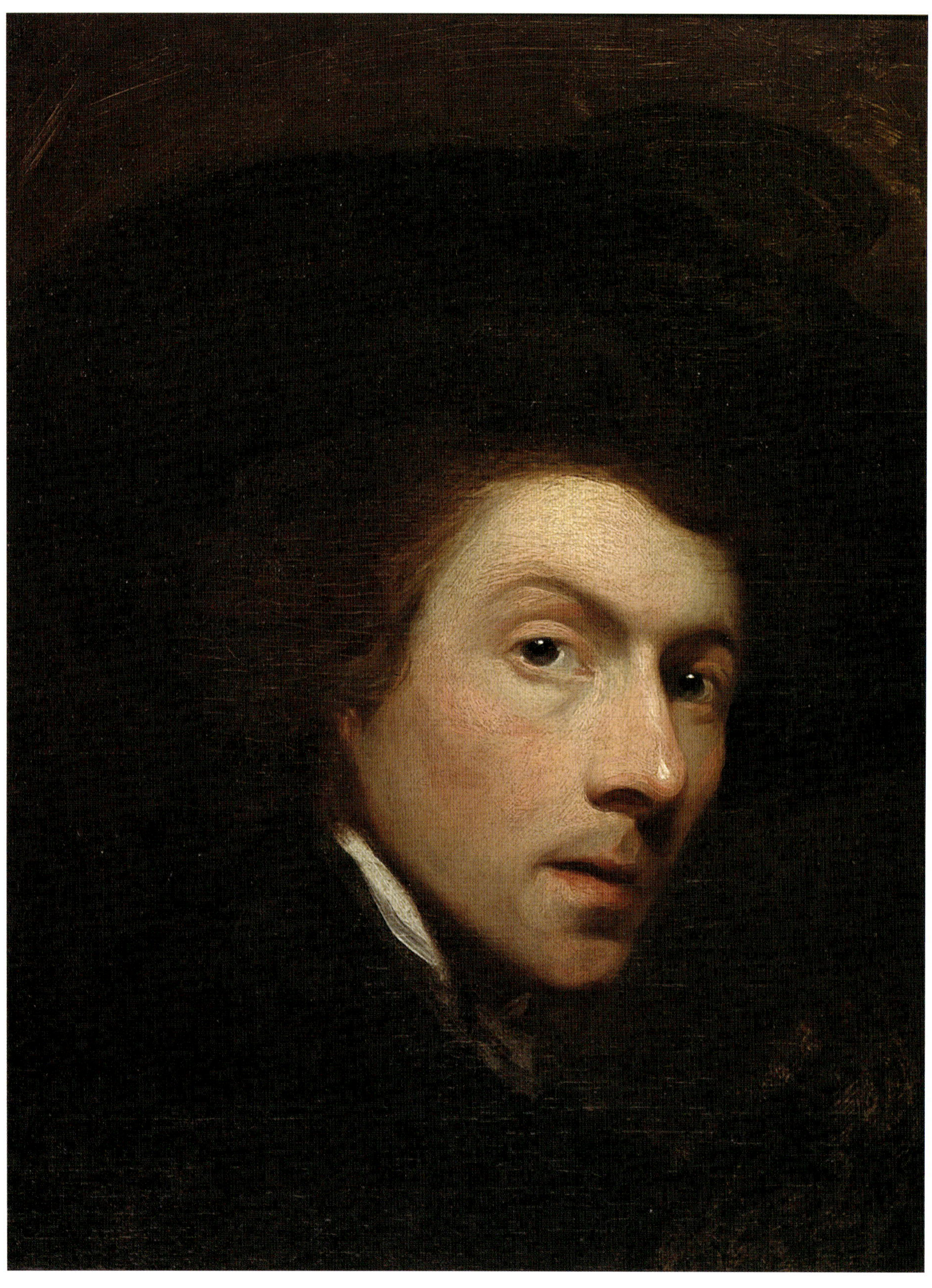

150 Gilbert Stuart, *Self-Portrait at 24*, 1778. Oil on canvas, 16¾ × 12¾ in. (42.5 × 32.4 cm). From the collection of the Redwood Library and Athenaeum, Newport, Rhode Island, bequest of Louisa Lee Waterhouse.

hard to believe that Stuart would have passed up funds he sorely needed (far exceeding any obligation to the lender) by giving Dobson's portrait to West in exchange for a tribute to his skills of questionable sincerity. If what Stuart told Pickering about Dobson had been true, or even an invention dating to his time with West, he surely would have related the events to Waterhouse, to whom he gave the self-portrait around 1780 and who made such copious notes of Stuart's life during those years. Whether Stuart ever owned a painting by Dobson (as opposed to simply admiring one) remains unclear. Nor do records of West's collection after his death mention such a work, which West would likely have retained during his lifetime as a memento of an earlier royal painter.[168]

Given the course of Stuart's life, it is tempting to speculate that when he conversed with Pickering – the only moment at which the story can be fixed – the artist meant to play his own story off Dobson's. Dobson worked in "a poor garret," according to Walpole, until van Dyck saw one the artist's pictures in a shop window and lifted him out of misery (as West did for Stuart). Dobson rose to great success as a portraitist, but he was "idle and dissolute, was involved in debt, and thrown into prison" (as Stuart had been during his time in Ireland). Yet despite his "somewhat loose and irregular . . . way of living," Dobson had "a ready wit, and pleasing conversation."[169] If Stuart were aware of these similarities, he said nothing on the matter that anyone recorded, allowing it to remain a private joke.

With or without Dobson, Stuart's self-portrait, as has long been recognized, resembles a nearly contemporaneous self-portrait by the royal painter who was his mentor, West, who for his part made patent reference to the self-portrait that Rubens painted at the request of the future Charles I (then Prince of Wales) in 1623 (see figs. 105, 107). For Stuart in 1778, the temptation to go head to head with West, even more than with Rubens and Dobson, must have been great.[170] He did so again in 1817, when speaking to Pickering, framing the story of his self-portrait in a way that allowed the impression of his talent to be overpowered by a relatively benign example of West's compromised judgment when he stood to gain something. Far worse, West suffered public humiliation in a transaction of 1796, after falling prey to a swindler who claimed to possess an old manuscript revealing the "Venetian Secret."[171] West's discernment in that case was clouded by his obsession with Old Master techniques, which Stuart had also tried out in the early self-portrait. After encountering the painting again at Waterhouse's residence around 1810, he told the doctor he painted

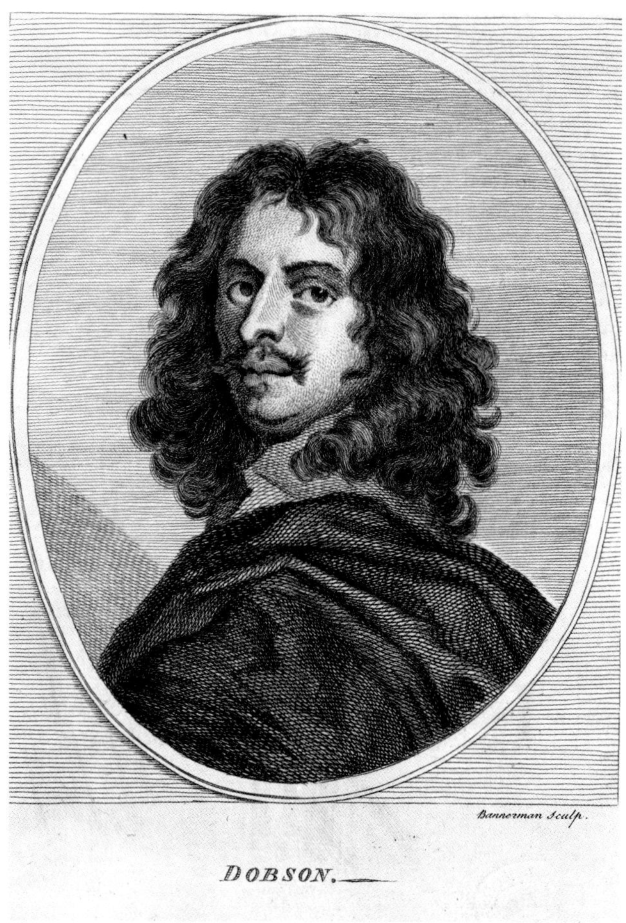

151 Alexander Bannerman after William Dobson, portrait of William Dobson, 1762, illustration to Walpole's *Anecdotes of Painting in England* (London, 1762). Etching and engraving. British Museum, London. © The Trustees of the British Museum.

it to look old (without any mention of Dobson, though that would have been entirely relevant).[172] But Stuart never embraced that vogue of the time; to the contrary, he made every effort to keep his colors looking fresh.[173]

Stuart's fresh palette impressed even West, according to an account in which Stuart reportedly salvaged his master's fumbling attempts to produce an official portrait of George III for the new governor-general of India. Responsibility for the picture fell to West as "the king's painter," Dunlap noted. West decided he would simply retouch an existing likeness of George III by his assistant, rationalizing the shortcut as a convenience to his majesty, who could thereby avoid a sitting. The work proceeded poorly. West then asked Stuart to lend him a palette, which the younger man had already set for his own use, in the hope that Stuart's choice and arrangement of colors would guide him. But West could not adapt Stuart's fresh and sparing approach – involving a small number of pigments and few premixed tints – to his self-consciously Old Masterish idiom. As Stuart put it, West "had got up to the knees in mud," meaning that he overmixed the pigments. In the end, West had to prevail on Stuart to fix the mess he had made of Stuart's original. The story seems highly improbable. Professionally, Stuart was in no position to have made an independent portrait of the king. West, as the king's history painter, did have privileged access, and he occasionally portrayed members of the royal family during the 1770s and early 1780s, when the portraitists Allan Ramsay (the official "Principal Painter in Ordinary to the King") and Johann Zoffany (whom the Queen favored) were unavailable. In 1780 and 1783, West publicly exhibited portraits of the monarch. However, he bore no formal responsibility to manufacture portraits of George III for government functionaries and, in any case, copyists typically produced examples for provincial distribution. So Stuart's story of stepping in to rescue West does not add up. His account, in sum, embellished his superiority to West in a branch of the art that, unlike history painting, was truly competitive.[174]

The strangest and most revealing of Stuart's unprovable stories concerns an unusual commission in Ireland, where the artist had moved in 1787. Many of his patrons there were aristocrats – but not all. Stuart claimed to have met a man whose new fortune, acquired by speculating, allowed him to purchase a castle. Wanting decoration for the walls and a pedigree, the self-made Irishman hired Stuart to paint portraits of "such ancestors as [he] *ought* to have had." The artist said he fulfilled the commission with "a goodly company of knights in armor, judges in bushy wigs, and high-born ladies with nosegays and lambs." The account first surfaced in Mason, who must have heard it from a member of the Quincy family, possibly Eliza Susan Quincy, one of his most obliging correspondents, or her brother Josiah Quincy, to whom Stuart personally related the story – as Quincy reported (with slight variations) in his memoir *Figures of the Past* (1883).[175] William T. Whitley included the narrative as part of his chapter on Stuart's career in Ireland, while expressing doubt as to its veracity; he thought (with good reason) that it would have been related more often if true, and, notably, Herbert made no mention of it in his memoir of Stuart's years in Ireland.[176] Subsequent Stuart scholars have not repeated the story, though they widely quote an anecdote of Stuart and John Adams from Quincy's memoir, always assuming the writer to have been the Josiah Quincy who had portraits made by Stuart in 1806 and 1824, when he was Boston's mayor. Instead, the memoirist was the mayor's son, also named Josiah Quincy (and also later mayor). This fact and a glance at the younger Quincy's fuller description of his interactions with Stuart open a productive way of interpreting the artist's story of the Irish ancestor portraits.

The proper context for the account lies not in Stuart's Irish career, but rather in Boston circa 1824. At the time, as Quincy related in his memoir, he was in the "peculiar" position of posing to Stuart for the likeness of a dead ancestor two generations older than himself. The circumstance and possibly the young man's discomfiture gave Stuart an opportunity to amuse his model, upping the ante by recounting a commission for portraits of dead ancestors who never even existed.

The outlandish tale served serious ends. First, Stuart's claim to have "produced a goodly company of knights in armor, judges in bushy wigs, and high-born ladies with nosegays and lambs" highlighted his own creativity. His job for the Irishman did not involve copying nature, a skill devalued by eighteenth-century academic artists who claimed invention as their domain. He was not even copying art, since he told Quincy the Irishman provided no "miniatures or drawings whose authority he was to follow." Stuart, in short, acted as his own authority, relying on imagination and his knowledge of historical British portrait conventions to fulfill the commission. Stuart may have drawn on more than his knowledge of art for the fabulous story. The inventive and playful Horace Walpole imagined Strawberry Hill, the quasi-medieval architectural confection on which he began construction in the late 1740s, as "the castle (I am building) of my ancestors," the fictional "Barons of Strawberry." In the long gallery, site of ancestral portraits in many an English country house, a group of non-family seventeenth-century portraits outnumbered those of Walpole's own relatives, constituting "a kind of ancestral gallery manqué," according to Alicia Weisbert-Roberts.[177] As she pointed out, Walpole drew on this gallery of fake ancestors for his medieval romance, *The Castle of Otranto* (1764), in which suits of armor and ancestor portraits come alive, including one in which the portrait subject proves not to be grandfather of the main character after all. Walpole's book and house, an instant tourist destination, were famous, and Stuart (or the Irish client, if he ever existed) may have had them in mind.

To nineteenth-century observers, the portrait conventions Stuart claimed to have followed (which he knew at firsthand from his time in England and Ireland) just seemed

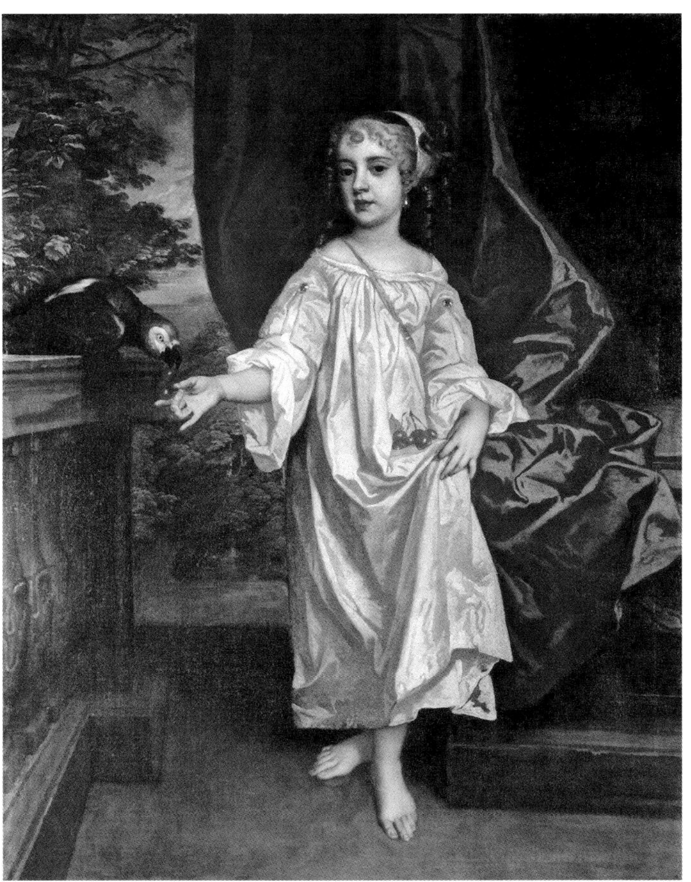

152 Peter Lely, *Girl with a Parrot*, ca. 1670. Oil on canvas, 49 × 40 in. (124.5 × 101.6 cm). Tate Gallery, London.

silly (fig. 152). An essay, "On Affectation in Portraiture," from a Boston magazine in 1821 invoked prominent seventeenth- and eighteenth-century British portraitists to mock "the Lely, or wig-and-armour affectation," along with "the Jervas, or wig, or night-cap and bed-room," "the lady, or cherry-and-parrot," and "the Reynolds, or lamb-and-shepherdess" modes.[178] By invoking his use of such conventions when speaking to Quincy, Stuart highlighted the apparent lack of affectation in his own portraits and reinforced his reputation for naturalism. At the same time, the claim that he could switch between naturalism and obvious stylization acknowledged that all portraits follow conventions. Stuart's were simply more modern.

The second point of Stuart's story was to affirm his disregard for authority. In the (invented) Irish context, he mocked the taste of aristocrats even more than he did the pretensions of an upstart. Stuart, as Herbert recalled from their interactions during the later 1780s, "had all the equalizing spirit of the American, – and he looked contemptuously upon titled rank."[179] With his account of the imaginary ancestor portraits, Stuart also complicated his positive image as an American, by suggesting that he would invent any history required, if the price were right. Young Josiah Quincy was participating in a related scheme, standing in for a deceased man, possibly part of a commission his father, as mayor, gave Stuart to make portraits of "distinguished patriots" from the Revolutionary War for display in city hall.[180] For the Americans, Stuart was prepared to conjure up faces he had never seen; for the Irishman, he was willing to manufacture distinction outright. Stuart's tale of spurious ancestor portraits, given the context in which he related it, subtly subverted his role as leading painter of the American political genealogy, tainting his portraits of American leaders with the idea that they owed their existence as much to his need for money as love of country, no doubt the case.[181]

At around the same time that Stuart undertook the Boston civic commission for portraits of Revolutionary War patriots, Peale painted retrospective portraits of Maryland's six governors – a project he had proposed to civic authorities in exchange for Herman van der Myn's portrait, then in the Maryland State House, of Charles Calvert, fifth Lord of Baltimore (ca. 1730). Peale's labors make clear that the nearly century-old portrait was not for him an object of mockery, however ill-appreciated by authorities prepared to trade it in for newer models. Instead, the work had nostalgic allure, having likely played a part in Peale's decision to take up painting.[182] In his eventual role as a portraitist of American luminaries, Peale had little use for humor and an appetite for self-congratulation that Stuart never shared. Peale's grand self-portrait *The Artist in his Museum* (1822) – a commission from the institution's board (which he led) and the largest painting he ever made – publicly proclaimed Peale's indispensable place among the generation of American leaders enshrined, by his hand, in the carefully ordered world of his museum (fig. 153). In presenting himself as still commanding and vital, Peale made clear his continuing service to the republic and its people.[183] Stuart, by contrast, though in fact the leading portraitist of the early republic, never trumpeted that role, and he certainly did not conceal the tumult of his own life.

Stuart's final self-image, one of only three he made, presents a stark contrast to any of Peale's self-portraits or to the portrait of Stuart that Peale, possibly working together with his son Rembrandt, made in 1805, when the three artists were in the nation's capitol (fig. 154). Charles Stuart, the artist's son, considered the Peale portrait the best like-

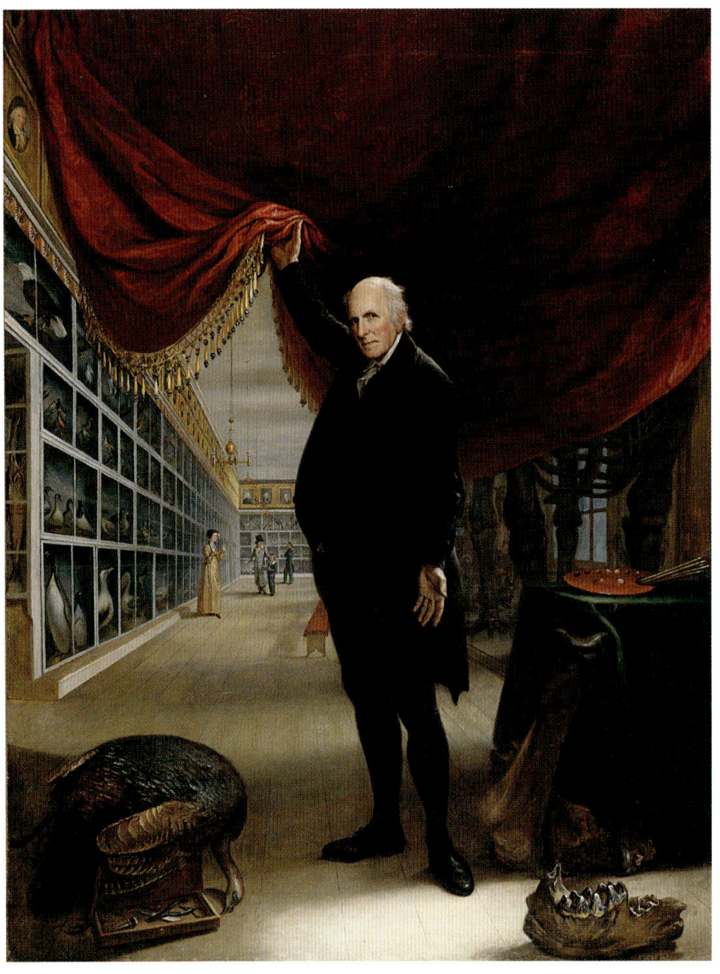

153 Charles Willson Peale, *The Artist in his Museum*, 1822. Oil on canvas, 103¾ × 79⅞ in. (263.5 × 202.9 cm). Courtesy of the Pennsylvania Academy of the Fine Arts, Philadelphia, gift of Mrs. Sarah Harrison (Joseph Harrison, Jr., Collection).

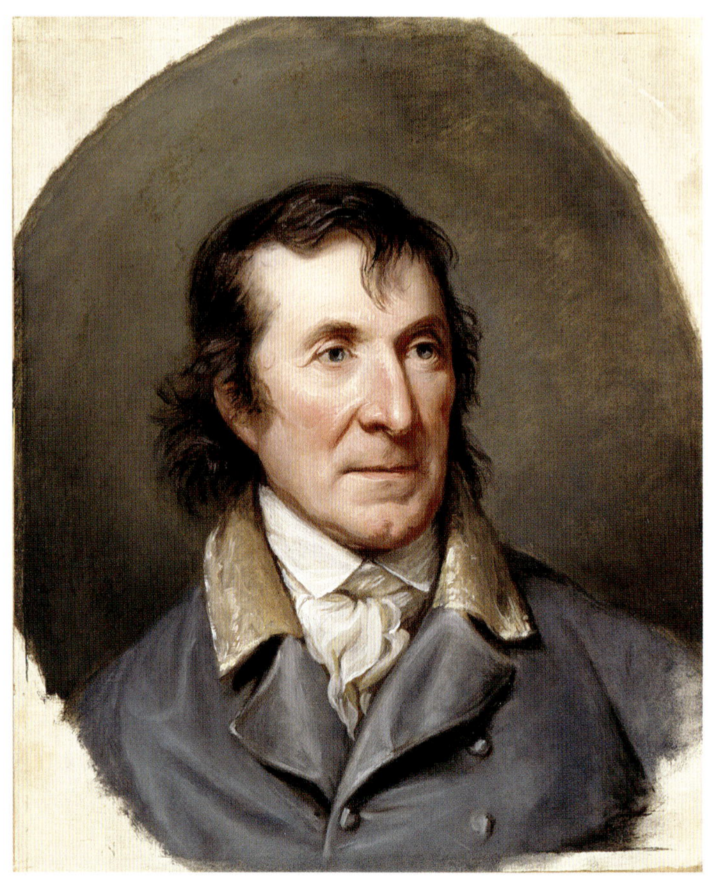

154 Charles Willson Peale and Rembrandt Peale, *Gilbert Stuart*, 1805. Oil on canvas, (oval) 23½ × 19½ in. (59.69 × 49.53 cm). New-York Historical Society, 1867.302. Photography © New-York Historical Society.

ness of his father, though the subject himself reportedly thought it evoked "an awkward clown."[184] This negative judgment has no readily apparent basis, though the portrait is animated relative to Stuart's weary last self-portrait, now known only through the etched copy by James M. Falconer (fig. 155). Falconer acquired a letter from Stuart to a friend that bore this drawing not later than 1867, when Henry Tuckerman saw it and, without clarification, remarked on the "striking device" beneath the portrait bust. Two stick figures engage in a fistfight with a dirty ending, since one has just landed a kick to the groin of the other. Elaborating on Stuart's bipolarity, Dorinda Evans interpreted the vignette as his acknowledgment of internal struggles, a reasonable conjecture given the defeated looking face – all drooping features and downward lines – that Stuart showed his correspondent.[185] A version of this image appeared as the frontispiece to Mason's 1879 biography, but without the fighting figures, as the source image was another engraving of the same original, made by a different artist, who excised the detail (which Mason, or Jane Stuart standing behind his biographical project, would have mandated in any case).[186] The fact that Falconer made his etching in 1879, when he had owned the original drawing for over a decade, begs for explanation. It suggests that the etcher – whom a contemporary described as having "an open eye for the poetry of decay" – disapproved of the sanitized representation Mason published.[187] What exactly he made of the battling stick figures is impossible to know; perhaps whatever Stuart wrote in his letter provided context. Yet a broad conclusion remains: like members of the generation before him and

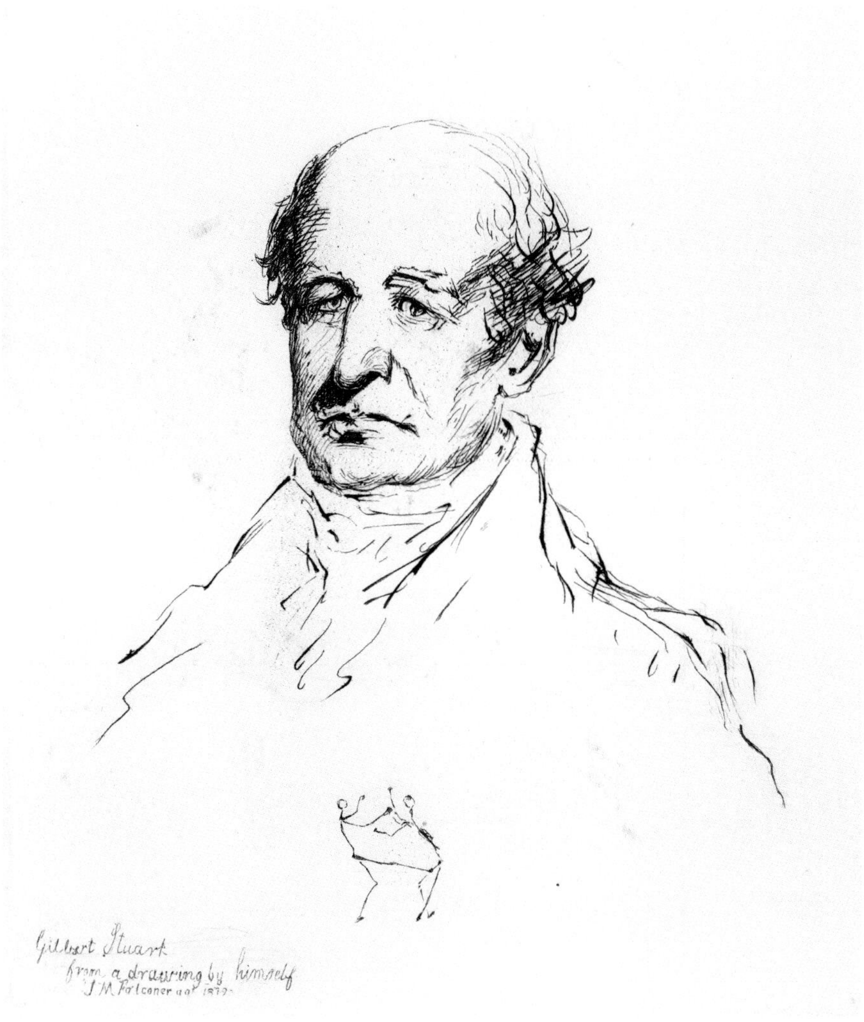

155 James Falconer, *Gilbert Stuart* (copy of a *Self-Portrait*, 1826–28), 1879. Photo: Frick Art Reference Library, New York.

generations afterward, Falconer found Stuart's eccentricity fascinating and integral to his persona.

Stuart made his very life (as would often be said of later modern painters) into a work of art. His masterful portraits secured his artistic reputation, but it was his vivid personality and provocative demeanor that made him stand out among artists of the early republic. He was never complaisant and often contrary. While others took pains to match the gentility of his clients, Stuart was just as likely to mock the manners of patrons. He could be affable, amusing, satirical, and dismissive by turns, according to how patrons treated him. He met the high-handed with disdain, while others found him ready to poke fun at himself rather than at them and to underplay his stature. The only attitude completely alien to Stuart, fortunately for historians, was self-effacement.

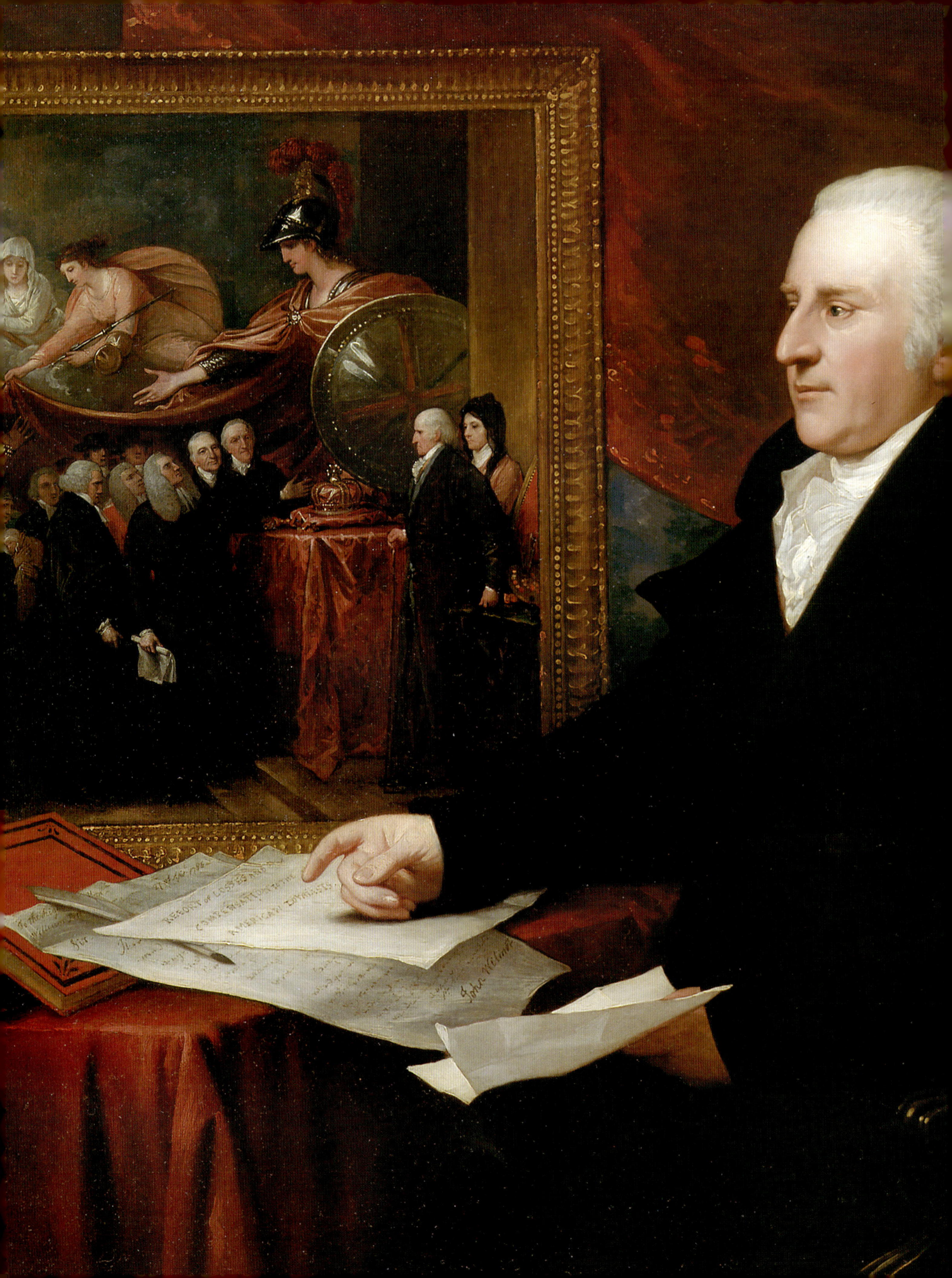
REPORT of LOSSES AND
COMPENSATION TO THE
AMERICAN LOYALISTS

6

THE AMERICAN WEST

"Incalculable": the word expressed William Dunlap's estimation of Benjamin West's effect on American art. In composing his *History of the Rise and Progress of the Arts of Design in the United States* (1834), Dunlap lionized West as the first internationally famous American-born painter and a committed teacher of American artists.[1] A century after that ambitious first chronicle of American fine arts, James Thomas Flexner tried to cement the identification in *America's Old Masters* (1939). West, he proclaimed, was "incontrovertibly the father of American painting."[2] The adverb brooks no challenge and lends Flexner's statement an air of defensiveness, suggesting a complication, one that Dunlap had implicitly confronted in his first sentence on West, a flat declaration that the painter was "indigenous." The trajectory of West's career has always made his distinction as an American problematic. Unlike Copley, the exact contemporary whose twenty-year career in Boston established him as the premier painter in British North America, West came to artistic maturity only after departing the colonies in 1760. Copley eventually moved to England himself – a relocation sometimes judged as abandonment, given its timing on the eve of revolution and the artist's marital alliance with a staunchly loyalist family.[3] Still, Copley left behind a compelling body of work: hundreds of portraits that vividly commemorated Americans at the threshold of independence. West's American portraits, by contrast, offer little more than wan effigies of a few fellow Pennsylvanians. Yet West and his patrons had the audacity to believe he could accomplish something more.

West proved his colonial supporters right. After three years abroad radically altered his prospects, the American became famous and wealthy as a history painter, whose steady employment by the king made his election as second president of the Royal Academy, following Reynolds's death in 1792, a foregone conclusion. In West's self-portrait commemorating this new office, a laurel-crowned bust of the king gazes in imperious profile toward the president, who sits with upright dignity in his official chair (fig. 156). The artist grasps a paper marked with the royal command of 1768, by which the Academy was constituted (suggesting his instrumental role in winning the king's patronage), while books inscribed "Bible" and "History of England" evoke the subject matter of West's paintings for Windsor Castle. The work summarized West's accomplishments: the royal privilege and professional rank that situated him as far as he could have been from his modest American origins.

Throughout fifty-seven productive years in England, West never returned to his homeland, so it is worth asking how he came to be regarded as "father," "dean," or "mentor" of American painting.[4] The words affirm his signal and sustained contribution to the education of American artists, a legacy anticipated in Pratt's *American School*. In addition

Facing page Detail of fig. 158.

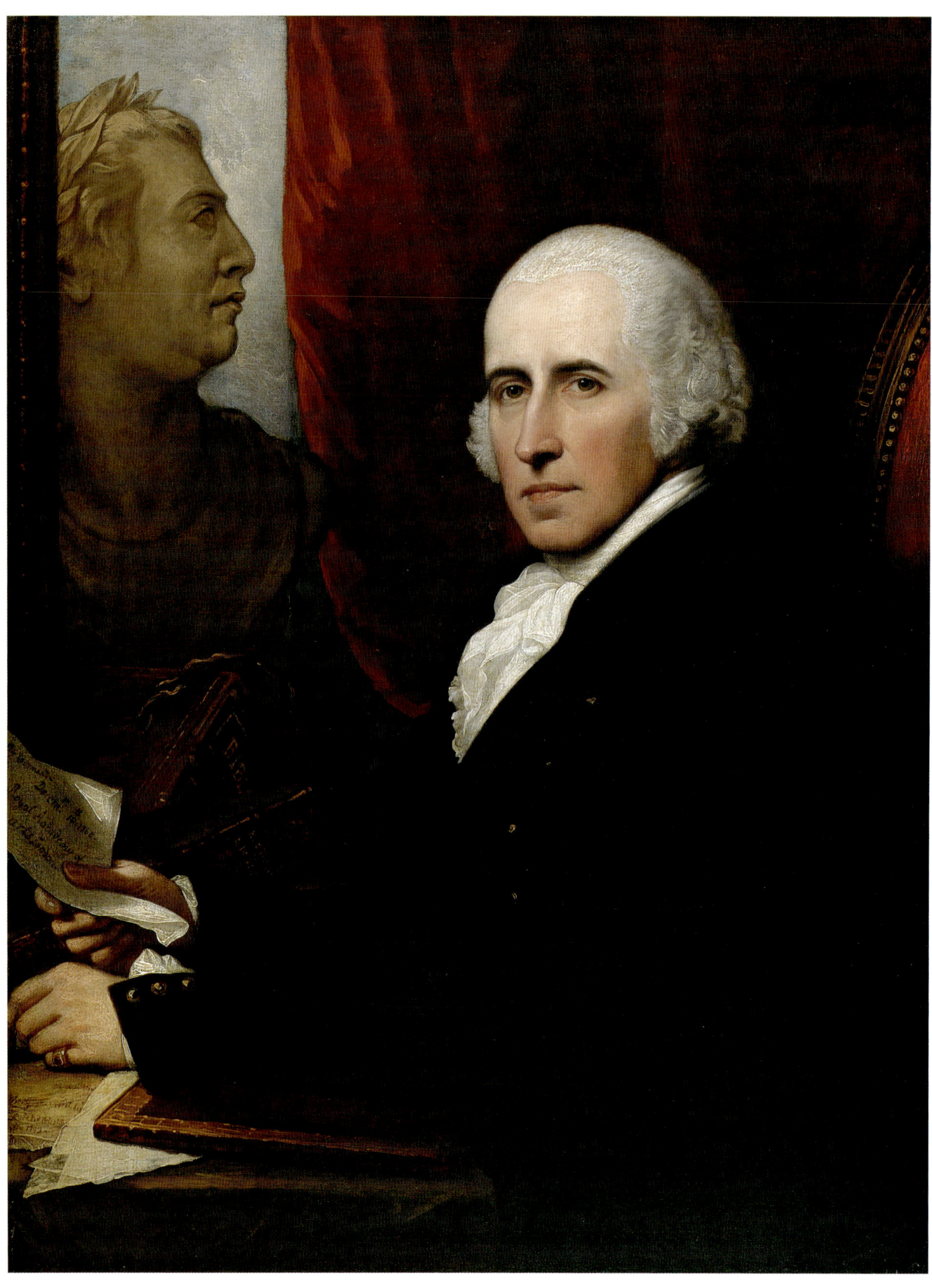

156 Benjamin West, *Self-Portrait*, 1793. Oil on panel, 36 × 27½ in. (91.4 × 69.9 cm). Reproduced by kind permission of the Society of Dilettanti.

to his American students – at least two dozen over five decades – West attracted a less well-documented number of young Britons to his studio, though they never sought to define and never attracted a collective identity. By 1800, West's adherence to rules had come to seem limiting, especially to those whose formal training, paradoxically, afforded them the luxury of developing modes of expression suggestive of unfettered talent.[5] Truly self-taught American artists opportunistically tapped the newly potent trope of the natural genius, as evident in their advertisements, but this is not to say that such artists would have spurned artistic training if granted the opportunity. With few outlets for formal art education at home, many had little choice but to follow the business of art as best they could, using any available strategies to promote themselves. For those able to seize the chance to study in London, West presided over a de facto American academy. In this role, West gave a critical boost to painting in the new republic and earned a place at its head.

Of equal, if not greater, importance to West's identification as American was the very different image summoned by West's youth in Pennsylvania: the artist as unschooled, natural talent. This character was West's to fashion, unconstrained by the public record of his career in London. But he did not do it alone. John Galt – a Scottish professional writer with demonstrated interest in the arts and in biography – served as the painter's collaborator and the author of record for *The Life and Studies of Benjamin West, Esq., President of the Royal Academy in London, prior to his Arrival in England, compiled from materials furnished by himself* (1816). (At the artist's urging, his biographer issued a companion volume in 1820, covering West's long career in England, but Galt had not initially planned to do so.)[6] Both men were obviously familiar with this fundamental trope in artist biographies, rooted in antiquity, revived by Vasari, and carried forward by others, even in parody as by Beckford. West's biography acknowledged the Romantic potency of the unschooled talent, in the artist's remark that "with all his subsequent knowledge and experience, he had not been able to surpass" his "first juvenile essay" as a painter. The type, while in no respect exclusively American, acquired compelling authenticity from a colonial American context that few were inclined to overestimate when it came to the development of the fine arts. The biography had a profound impact on the historical picture of West, as the indispensable source for his youth, notwithstanding its mythicized portrayal.

Galt's narrative cohered around the representation of West as an artist who acquired art artlessly. As a young child, this prodigy sketched his infant niece in the cradle, to the amazement of his family. He resourcefully fashioned brushes using hair snipped from the family cat – and confessed to a father who could not be angry at his son's ingenuity or, presumably, his honesty, like Washington's father when young George admitted to cutting down the cherry tree, in the enduring fable invented by Parson Weems.[7] For his rudimentary palette of primary colors, West had his mother and accommodating Indians. (Textual and archaeological evidence that Indians possessed and valued colonial or European-made pigments adds to the argument made in chapter three against any such interaction.)[8] Galt, while presenting the anecdote as "real," openly acknowledged his purpose: "The mythologies of antiquity furnish no allegory more beautiful; and a Painter who would embody the metaphor of an Artist instructed by Nature, could scarcely imagine any thing more picturesque than the real incident of the Indians instructing West to prepare the prismatic colours."[9] Native Americans could teach the fledgling artist to make paints, the reader understands, but not to paint by European standards. West's charmed path continued. Astonished by the image of cows projected on a wall through his bedroom shutter, he stumbled on the principles of the camera obscura, a tool for reproducing nature, which, in Galt's account, West then managed to "invent." He admired the truthfulness of landscapes painted by an unschooled artist, who became his first teacher. West eventually enlarged his sights with the guidance of fellow provincials: a governess who instructed the boy in ancient history and poetry and a gunsmith who urged West to look beyond portraiture to history painting. Still, the artist arrived in Italy with his American innocence intact. According to Galt, he could be considered "original and self-instructed" "without any other explanation" than "the single fact, that he was born in Pennsylvania, and did not leave America till the year 1760."[10] West confirmed his aesthetic purity before a public that witnessed his first sight of the *Apollo Belvedere*. The complexities of such an encounter at that moment in history faded before the power of Galt's indelible rendition.

Galt's prefatory characterization of the *Life of West* as the artist's "memoirs" relieved him of the obligation to verify his subject's recollections, but he would not have wished to do so in any case. Galt valued the interaction of imagination and memory. In 1813, he proposed that "their united endeavor to supply what has been forgotten, begets reflections with the character of truth about them, such as the offspring of fancy never possesses; and with more beauty, no less interesting than the hard features of veteran and serviceable facts."[11] I, too, am largely unconcerned with establishing the historical veracity of incidents related in West's biography, a project other scholars have undertaken selectively.[12] Nor will I detail the numerous biographical motifs that Galt's *Life of West* shares with other accounts of artists' lives, a list not limited to divine portent in the child's birth (West's mother went into labor during an impassioned sermon on the future greatness of America), the artist's precocity, triumph over potential obstacles to his chosen profession (West's provincial isolation and supposed Quakerism: "In the whole Christian world no spot was apparently so unlikely to produce a Painter as Pennsylvania"), the chance encounter that led him to a teacher, and rise from humble beginnings to social prominence.[13] Even if some of Galt's stories about West had a basis in fact, he drew much of his account from what Ernst Kris and Otto Kurz, in their classic study of these biographical formulae, called the "moveable scenery inserted in the biographer's workshop."[14] Galt's account of West's relationship with Williams analyzed together with antecedent versions of that relationship serve in the present chapter to demonstrate how author and artist bent West's early life experiences to ends that were at once predictable and more complex than they at first appear. Because West's rediscovery of Williams catalyzed his act of American recovery, almost a decade before his initial meeting with Galt, this section precedes fuller exploration of the Scottish writer and of the reasons for his interest in West.

Assessments of West's purpose in relating his story and Galt's in composing it remain fundamental to understanding the scope, form, content, and impact of this influential account. Galt's narrative of the American innocent had a powerful effect on West's reputation, rehabilitating him as an American artist. That may not have been precisely, or at any rate wholeheartedly, West's intent. Over the course of his professional life, his readiness to be considered American proved inconsistent. Publicly, and for good reason, he was capable of nearly complete denial, a posture laid bare in the pre-Galt biographical accounts that West endorsed. This chapter explores his apparent change of heart and the role in that turnabout played by a writer who was, it appears, something more than an amanuensis to the famous artist.

Important as it is to consider West and Galt's motivations, the puzzle of West's evolving identity takes shape only within a broader context. Accordingly, this chapter also addresses the ways West's life and career were framed by writers over whom he had no control: commentators on art/art critics, satirists, friends, enemies. It addresses the fluctuating status of other British painters and of British cultural institutions, along with the shifting political relations between Britain and the United States. Americans acquired during this time an emerging consciousness of their own artistic masters and traditions and the desire to define them. Many of the themes and personae introduced earlier in this book, not least West himself, coalesce in this historiographically oriented chapter to illuminate, in the end, the fits and starts by which West ultimately was absorbed, as founding father, into the history of American art.

An Insistent Englishman

Even as West mined New World subjects during his career in England, especially early on, he disclosed little of his American formation. And perhaps few imagined that anything he might say on the matter could be revealing of how he became an artist or what kind of artist he became. West had moved quickly to secure his identity as a painter of history, a subject matter with deep thematic, stylistic, and institutional roots in continental Europe. Its status in Britain of the 1760s was so new that simply being "one of our first History Painters," a writer for the *London Chronicle* conceded in 1773, qualified West as "one of our first Painters: for History Painting is universally acknowledged to be the noblest branch of the art."[15] West promoted that image vigorously by any means possible, not least through the impressive studio and gallery he built after leasing property at 14 Newman Street in London in 1774.[16]

Although within two decades, few could have denied that West had "dedicated [his] life, to inform future times of the height of the British School of History," his reputation was being undermined.[17] West's privileged relationship with George III and his prominence as the Royal Academy president made him a ready target, especially in opposition newspapers and with the two anti-Tory satirists who frequently wrote about artists, "Peter Pindar" (John Wolcot) and "Anthony Pasquin" (John Williams). In "Ode to the Academic Chair, on the Election of Mr. West to the Presidency," Pindar took aim at both painter and king, whose voice he assumed:

> I like West's works – he beats the Raphael school –
> I never like'd that Reynolds – 'twas a fool –
> Painted too thick – a dauber – 'twon't, 'twon't pass –
> West, West, West's pictures are smooth as glass:
> Besides, I hated Reynolds, from my heart
> He thought that I knew naught about the art.

West tells me that my taste is very pure –
That I'm a connoisseur, a connoisseur:
I like, I like, I like the works of West.[18]

The stammering speech, susceptibility to flattery, and lack of visual sophistication attributed to George III in this characterization only matched the king to his favored painter, whom Pindar – calling West "our Yankey painter" – had often portrayed as a vain bumbler.[19] Even close friends, such as fellow academician Joseph Farington, thought West's opinion of himself immodestly high; he made regular notations in his diary concerning the artist's inflated sense of self, usually citing others but often agreeing with their opinions.[20] After West assumed the president's chair, for example, he declined the knighthood bestowed on his predecessor, because he hoped for a hereditary title and income, a wish never fulfilled.[21] If that decision affected no one but West, other demonstrations of his ample self-regard were more broadly injurious. West openly promoted a book praising himself alone among modern artists, the Rev. Robert Bromley's *Philosophical and Critical History of the Fine Arts* (1793–95), and some believed he stood behind Bromley's cutting characterization of Copley as "a painter from America who, before his arrival in this country, had sent hither a *squirrel* as the harbinger of his fame."[22] West continued to make professional blunders that angered his colleagues and raised grave questions about his competence. Among the group of artists defrauded in 1796 by the "Venetian Secret" hoax, West was the most prominent. Then, in 1803, the Royal Academy president faced charges of attempting to violate a basic rule of his own institution, which prohibited any work previously included in one of the annual exhibitions from being shown again. Though West countered that he had substantially repainted *Hagar and Ishmael*, his submission for that year, his failure to cover over the original signature and date, 1776, suggested otherwise. Copley, at the head of the hanging committee, had a history of opposing West, and he did not hold back in this matter or in the broader, ongoing power struggle within the Academy that often pitted the two Americans against one another.[23]

Five early biographies of West offered few facts and no speculation concerning West's life in America. The first published magazine article about him, in *European Magazine and London Review* in 1794 (fig. 157), noted simply that West (whose portrait appeared on the facing page) was "by birth an American," adding: "we have not learnt under whom he received the rudiments of his Art, nor to whom he was obliged for the direction of his studies."[24] Only West could have provided such information, and he chose not to do so. Privately, West invoked an early lack of training when it suited him, as when declining an American student in 1771. Writing to the boy's father, Shrimpton Hutchinson, West declared the benefit to himself of "having [had] no other Assistance but what I drew from Nature (the Early Part of my Life being quite obscured from Art)," implying that young Hutchinson should take advantage of his provincial isolation. West reinforced his point by reference to Copley, whom West recommended as a possible teacher, pronouncing Copley "better qualified for coming to Europe now than he was seven Years ago." To Copley, however, West had given quite different advice, albeit on the basis of the Bostonian's proven accomplishment: "nothing is wanting to Perfect you now but a Sight of what has been done by the great Masters, as if you Could make a viset to Europe for this Porpase, for three or four years, you would find yourself then in Possession of what will be highly valuable."[25] Since West actively mentored Americans at the time of his letter to Hutchinson, his advice carries little weight as a pedagogical or ideological position.

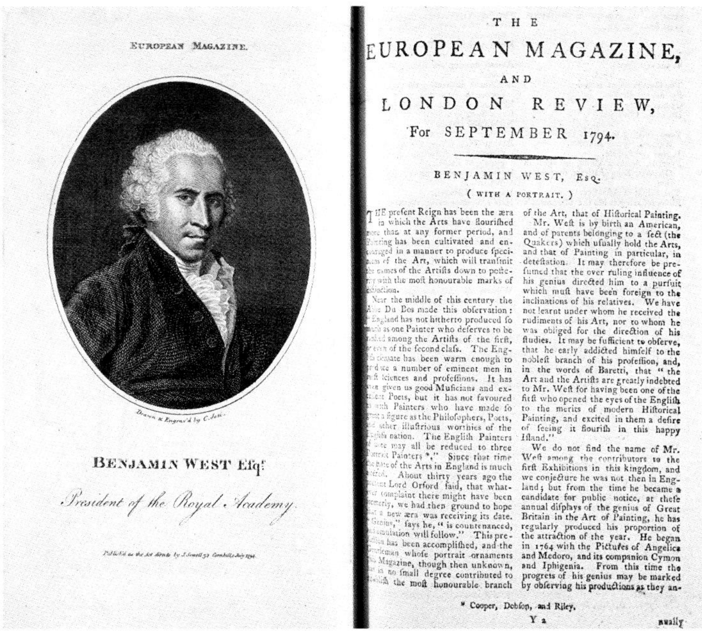

EUROPEAN MAGAZINE.

Drawn & Engrav'd by C. Josi.

BENJAMIN WEST Esq.

President of the Royal Academy.

THE
EUROPEAN MAGAZINE,
AND
LONDON REVIEW,
For SEPTEMBER 1794.

BENJAMIN WEST, Esq.
(WITH A PORTRAIT.)

THE present Reign has been the æra in which the Arts have flourished more than at any former period, and Painting has been cultivated and encouraged in a manner to produce specimens of the Art, which will transmit the names of the Artists down to posterity with the most honourable marks of distinction.

Near the middle of this century the Abbe Du Bos made this observation: "England has not hitherto produced so much as one Painter who deserves to be ranked among the Artists of the first, or even of the second class. The English climate has been warm enough to produce a number of eminent men in most sciences and professions. It has even given us good Musicians and excellent Poets, but it has not favoured us with Painters who have made so great a figure as the Philosophers, Poets, and other illustrious worthies of the English nation. The English Painters of note may all be reduced to three Portrait Painters *." Since that time the state of the Arts in England is much altered. About thirty years ago the present Lord Orford said, that whatever complaint there might have been formerly, we had then ground to hope that a new æra was receiving its date. "Genius," says he, "is countenanced, and emulation will follow." This prediction has been accomplished, and the gentleman whose portrait ornaments this Magazine, though then unknown, has in no small degree contributed to establish the most honourable branch of the Art, that of Historical Painting.

Mr. West is by birth an American, and of parents belonging to a sect (the Quakers) which usually hold the Arts, and that of Painting in particular, in detestation. It may therefore be presumed that the over ruling influence of his genius directed him to a pursuit which must have been foreign to the inclinations of his relatives. We have not learnt under whom he received the rudiments of his Art, nor to whom he was obliged for the direction of his studies. It may be sufficient to observe, that he early addicted himself to the noblest branch of his profession, and, in the words of Baretti, that "the Art and the Artists are greatly indebted to Mr. West for having been one of the first who opened the eyes of the English to the merits of modern Historical Painting, and excited in them a desire of seeing it flourish in this happy Island."

We do not find the name of Mr. West among the contributors to the first Exhibitions in this kingdom, and we conjecture he was not then in England; but from the time he became a candidate for public notice, at these annual displays of the genius of Great Britain in the Art of Painting, he has regularly produced his proportion of the attraction of the year. He began in 1764 with the Pictures of Angelica and Medoro, and its companion Cymon and Iphigenia. From this time the progress of his genius may be marked by observing his productions as they an-

* Cooper, Dobson, and Riley.

Y 2 nually

157 "Benjamin West, Esq.," drawn and engraved by C. Josi after West's 1793 self-portrait, as published in *European Magazine and London Review* 26 (Sept. 1794).

Contemporaneous with the *European Magazine* article, a briefer profile in a book known as *The Windsor Guide* offered specifics as to West's birthplace ("Springfield, Chester

County, Pennsylvania, in America"), but little more information on his training: "Mr. West's love for painting, shewed itself at an early age; at sixteen, with the consent of his parents and friends, he embraced it as a profession. In 1760, he left for Italy."[26] Essentially the same sentence was repeated in two accounts of 1805, in *Universal Magazine* and *Public Characters*, a biographical annual. The latter added that West painted both portraits and historical pictures "with considerable success" in the American colonies, employment that made possible his sojourn abroad. By contrast, these articles, and one further profile of the artist in another London-based journal, *La Belle Assemblée* (1808), paid more attention to West's European study, by then widely accepted as important to a British artist's education.[27] Yet none related the episode that so strikingly evoked West's American origins – his encounter with the *Apollo Belvedere* – although West himself had told the story in a public address at the Royal Academy, in 1794, after which it appeared in several quite different print contexts.[28]

At the same time that they underplayed West's Americanness, these articles amplified his identity as a Briton. All but the first publication attest to West's English bloodline, traced from his father (born in England) and maternal grandparents (who immigrated with other Quakers to Pennsylvania) back to Lord De La Warr, who received the title in the fourteenth century for military service under Edward III.[29] More broadly, these accounts situated West prominently within the generation of artists represented as having overcome commonly identified impediments to the flowering of the arts in Britain, most notably, the nation's commercial preoccupations. If trade fueled selfish desires and suppressed fine art or encouraged the wrong kind of art, its pernicious effects might be tempered by an art promoting public responsibility. Historical subjects best satisfied this criterion, in an argument well rehearsed among eighteenth-century artists and commentators who struggled to negotiate the role of the fine arts in commercial society. For the nineteenth-century author of West's *Public Characters* biography, however, art and trade were not at odds.

> The country which supplied all Europe with many of the luxuries, and most of the conveniences of life, whose merchandize occupied an extent unequalled by any other nation on the globe, was now about to add to her other means of wealth a new source of commerce, and, along with her hardware, her woollens, and broad cloaths, to traffic in pictures and engravings with those countries from which she had so long contented to be supplied. To the politician and the oeconomist, who question the influence and use of the fine arts in society, and who allege that they lock up a great portion of the wealth of the country in mouldering and unproductive canvas, it will be sufficient answer to refer them to the receipts and entries at the custom-house: they will there find what a channel of commerce has been opened to other countries, and what a prodigious saving has accrued to our own.[30]

West, the writer continued, was the outstanding model of artistic productivity, with an oeuvre having "no parallel in the annals of painting, if we consider the number, size, and extent of their composition in figures, and their great diversity in matter." In demonstration of this assertion, the essay concluded with a "correct catalogue" of West's paintings in ten pages of small print, the first published list of his work. (Notably, West excluded his early *Indian Family*, perhaps because it did not fit the image he wished to project to readers of this British publication.)[31] Engravings of West's history paintings, furthermore, "were spread by a commercial intercourse through the civilized world," facilitated by the market in performing the most exalted function of art: to instruct "mankind in honourable and virtuous deeds." Honor, in turn, accrued to both artist and country. As the final paragraph assured, West's wish to be "worthy of the distinction of his Sovereign's notice" and "to fulfill his duty as a faithful subject to the British constitution" motivated his life.

Such expressions of allegiance might be regarded as merely conventional if West were unimpeachably English, but his American birth interfered with that perception. George III made the distinction when, in 1805, he vented his frustration with the quarreling Royal Academicians to William Beechey (an artist the king briefly favored over West): "West is an American, so is Copley, and you are an Englishman, & if you were all at the Devil, I wd. not enquire after you."[32]

Anxiety that Britons, in general, did not hold West in sufficient regard lay close to the surface of the "Biographical Sketch of Benjamin West" that appeared in the May 1805 issue of *Universal Magazine*. On the portentous first page of text, the artist – whose engraved image (based on the 1793 self-portrait) floats within an oval frame on the facing page – goes unmentioned. Instead, the author expounds on the importance of fine art in shaping nations, the need to compete "in arts as much as in arms" with Britain's French "enemy," and on the debt Britain owed its artists "for increasing its wealth, and enhancing its honour and reputation. Among these [we read at the turn of the page], and at the head of them all stands Benjamin West."[33] The customary assertions of his prolific output follow, with assurances that even the works of Michelangelo and Titian, both long-lived artists, hardly "bore any proportion in number" to those of West. The immediate purpose of this strained valuation of quantity over quality, it appears, was to demonstrate that West had little motivation to "disguise" the picture he had reworked and resubmitted for exhibition at the Royal Academy two years earlier. How gravely that miscalculation wounded the artist is fully exposed in the well-rehearsed defense of his actions and heavy-handed condemnation of his critics, which precede any biographical details. That account, once initiated, breaks for a long paragraph lauding West's service and value to king and country, both represented as insufficiently appreciative. An implicit rebuke to such mistreatment follows in a passage touting the professional regard shown West during his trip to Paris in 1802, together with the text, in French, of a celebratory poem addressed to West during an official dinner in France. Any suggestion that West enjoyed a cozy relationship with the French played a dangerous game. Only a decade earlier the artist had come under suspicion as a "democrat" sympathetic to the French revolutionaries and their American allies, temporarily costing him the king's favor.[34] If the article in *Universal Magazine* had the purpose of bolstering West's position in Britain, then it was rife with missteps, which expose West's sense of embattlement and his tone deafness to critics. Nothing could contain his professional slide. In June 1805, West received instructions to discontinue his paintings for the Chapel of Revealed Religion at Windsor Castle, and in December of that year he resigned his presidency of the Royal Academy. Though eventually returned to the chair, West suffered a more grievous loss to his pride and well-being in 1810. No longer protected by the mentally incapacitated George III, West was, finally, stripped of his income and position as the king's history painter.

West's stipend had kept him in England when he might otherwise have returned to the United States – so thought Farington, who added: "West certainly has not an English mind."[35] The conjunction is revealing. A widespread perception that Americans were obsessed with money adhered easily to both West and Copley, whose concern with making money, and success in doing so, was quite undisguised.[36] Soon after his arrival in London, Copley created a remarkable formula for success – if not for good relations with his fellow Academy members – in the single-picture exhibitions to which he charged admission, while soliciting subscriptions for engravings. Satirist Pasquin, the American painters' most relentless and public critic, kept the charges alive in publications spanning two decades. "To talk of any man possessing genius, who is so immoderately fond of money, is preposterous," he wrote of Copley, in *Memoirs of the Royal Academicians* (1796), which also presents a mock academic oath administered to West: "That you shall never take one hundred pounds for a picture, when you can get one hundred guineas."[37] Since persons in gentlemanly professions customarily took payment in guineas (a unit of currency worth one pound and one shilling), Pasquin's mere suggestion that pounds ought to have sufficed for West's compensation undercuts the artist's status, while highlighting West's mercenary bent.[38] Pasquin's perception that Americans loved money was reinforced during the decade he later spent in the United States (to which he was politically sympathetic). In 1811, he imagined the American foreign minister toasting harmony between his country and Britain at the Royal Academy's annual dinner and calling upon "his fellow citizens, Messrs. West and Copley" to sing a duet (to the tune of Yankee Doodle). "From Philadelphia's broad-brimmed race [that is, Quakers] / Who vanity have undone / I took my easel on my back / And crossed the seas to London!" begins West, who is then joined by Copley: "Let David paint for hungry fame / And Wilkie subjects funny / Let Turner sit and study storms / But *we* will paint for money."[39] Against such reminders of his American origins and the background of renewed hostilities between Great Britain and the United States, West continued to assert his ties to the country he had lived in for fifty years. He represented himself with his wife at the side of Britannia in *The Reception of the American Loyalists by Great Britain*, a painting (unlocated) featured prominently in West's 1812 portrait of John Eardley Wilmot, the commissioner who had investigated claims by loyalists for compensation of losses suffered during the American Revolution (fig. 158).[40] West showed Wilmot's portrait at the Royal Academy in 1812, and though he cannot have wished to reinforce opinion about his excessive concern for money, that may have been an unintended effect of the picture.

West's vulnerability on the subject of his nationality increased during the war of 1812–14 between Britain and the United States. Samuel F. B. Morse, who benefited from West's guidance between 1811 and 1815, bluntly assessed "the virulence of national prejudice" among Britons, who, he said "no longer despise, they hate, the Americans."[41] West's long residence in London granted him no immunity,

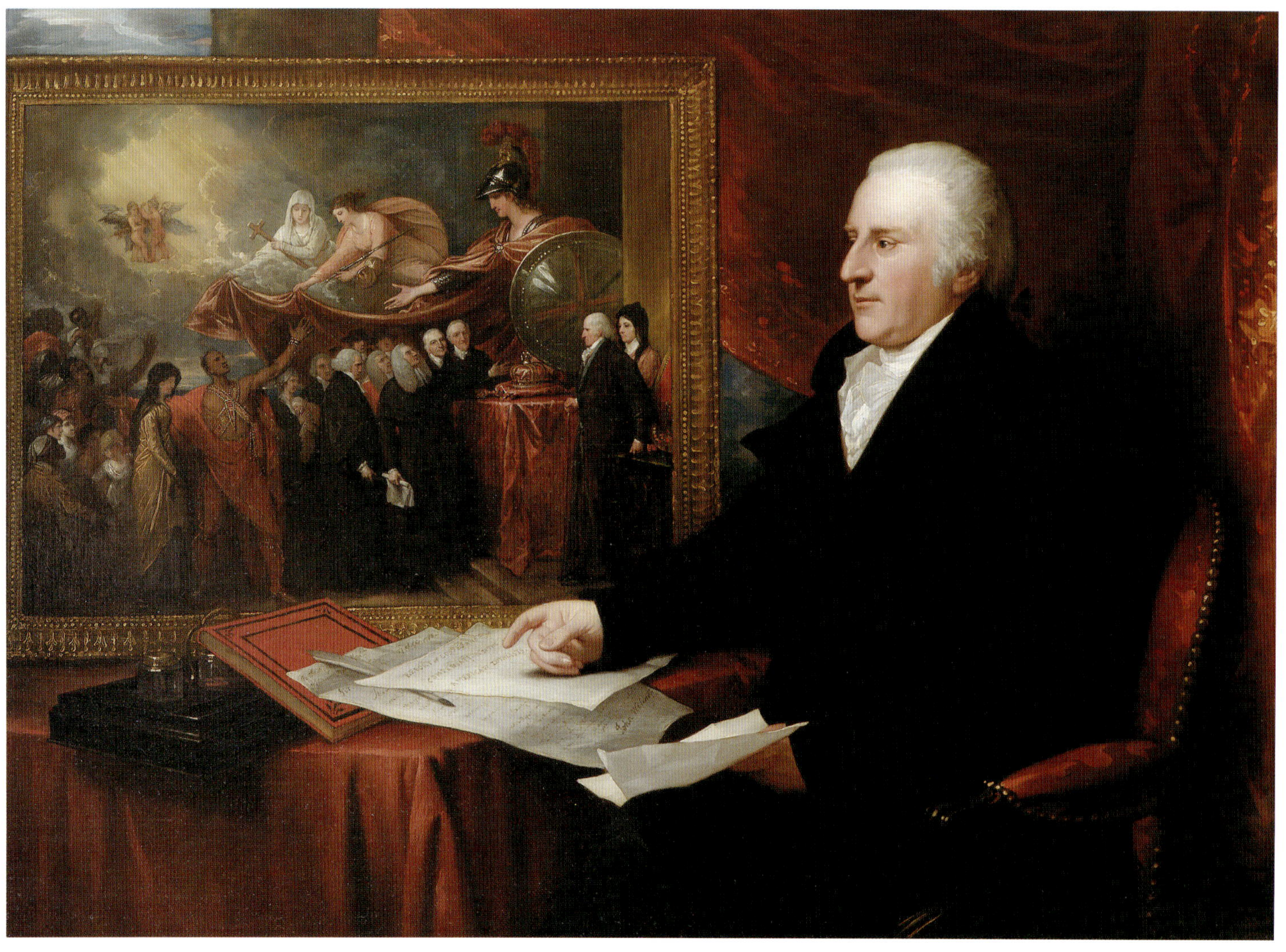

158 Benjamin West, *John Eardley Wilmot* (with West's lost *Reception of the American Loyalists by Great Britain*), 1812. Oil on canvas, 41½ × 58¼ in. (105.4 × 148 cm). Yale Center for British Art, New Haven, Paul Mellon Collection.

as Morse noted (without reference to international politics) in writing of the "slanders," "virulence," and "sneers" directed at the artist by his enemies: "he is one of those geniuses who are doomed in their lifetime to endure the malice, the ridicule, and neglect of the world." His status as a Briton around this time became increasingly vulnerable.

West and his supporters responded with increasing exasperation, painfully evident in a short biography published in 1813 to accompany an engraved portrait of West by Henry Meyer after Thomas Lawrence's painting of 1811 (fig. 159). Exactly fifty years after West's arrival in England, the writer felt compelled to devote a third of the text to tedious demonstration of "the erroneousness of an opinion entertained by many, that the venerable President of the Royal Academy is not an Englishman, nor even a British subject."

> The father of Mr. West, as it has been shewn, was unquestionably English, and he himself born when Pennsylvania was an English province, and both the father and son having quitted America long before the Northern Colonies had ceased to form a part of the British Empire, the allegiance of neither had been dispensed with by the parent State: consequently nothing can be more unjust than to question the validity of Mr. West's title to the honour of being a citizen of this country, only because he was not actually born in these islands. Children of Englishmen are born in every part of the world; these,

nevertheless, the country is bound to receive as its legitimate offspring; and the State cannot withhold from them its protection. It is manifest, therefore, that the above-mentioned opinion respecting the country of Mr. West must have been owing to the ignorance of the true circumstances of the life of that eminent Artist, as communicated in this short memoir.[42]

The uncredited author was Joseph Farington, writing on commission from Thomas Cadell (whose firm would publish Galt's emphatically American *Life of West* three years later). Though intimately acquainted with his subject, Farington sought from West "a Biographical acct. of himself to accompany the print," implying that the artist could control the content. West simply directed Farington to the earlier biographies in *Windsor Guide* and *Public Characters*: "I have seen both of those publications," he added, "and as far as they have gone respecting my families History, and myself – they are accurate."[43] Ten days later, Farington met with Cadell to discuss the project, which came out within two months. After Farington showed it to West, he noted the artist's approval and particular attention to the passage concerning his nationality. "He could be considered only to be an Englishman," observed Farington (who made a distinction between West's legal status and lack of "English mind"); "he did not object to this statement and proof."[44]

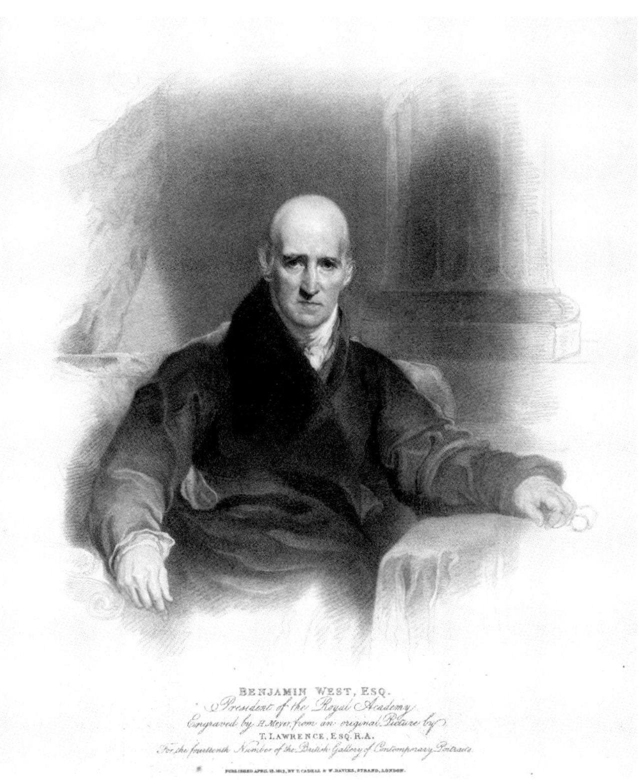

159 Henry Meyer, engraver, after Thomas Lawrence, *Benjamin West*, 1813. © National Portrait Gallery, London.

While the forceful assertion of West's Englishness appears Farington's idea, he was responding to pressure on the artist, if not directly from him. West had been less passive in shaping published accounts of himself than these exchanges over the 1813 biography suggest, as Farington well knew. Twice before, West had hinted at his own involvement. In 1808, for example, after Farington "mentioned to West the good observations" in *La Belle Assemblée*, West responded: "'You know where they come from,' meaning Himself."[45] His controlling hand becomes graphically evident when these early biographies are compared with an autobiographical manuscript in West's handwriting, marked as an original text by his numerous strikeovers and insertions.[46] Thoroughly mined for the various publications on the artist that appeared during his lifetime, the document yields no new biographical details. But it demonstrates that West's determination to shape accounts of his life did not commence with Galt – and that self-consciously autobiographical writing by American artists did not begin with Peale. West's 1816 biography, instead, more openly continued a practice he had engaged in all along, even as it dramatically changed course by featuring the American story West had previously suppressed.

West's repeated efforts to secure his nationality as English served an ambitious goal: to facilitate his identification as head of the English school of painting. To the extent that such leadership was defined in terms of the Royal Academy and its agenda, West had some legitimate claims to the distinction. Though not the institution's founding president (his relative youth in 1768 would have made that unthinkable), West succeeded on terms that Reynolds laid out but could not himself meet: as a specialist in history painting, with royal patronage no less. He might have expected his election to the presidency, following Reynolds's death, to complete his triumph. In that role, however, West fell completely short of Reynolds's authority, inviting immediate and unfavorable comparison to his learned predecessor with his inaugural address, West's only published discourse.[47] By contrast, Reynolds's erudition, demonstrated in frequent publications during his lifetime, was fully displayed in a two-volume edition of his complete writings (1797) by Shakespeare scholar Edmond Malone, an executor of the artist's estate.[48] Malone added his own glowing appraisal of Reynolds's life and character – amplifying the effect of the immediately posthumous *Testimonies to the Genius and*

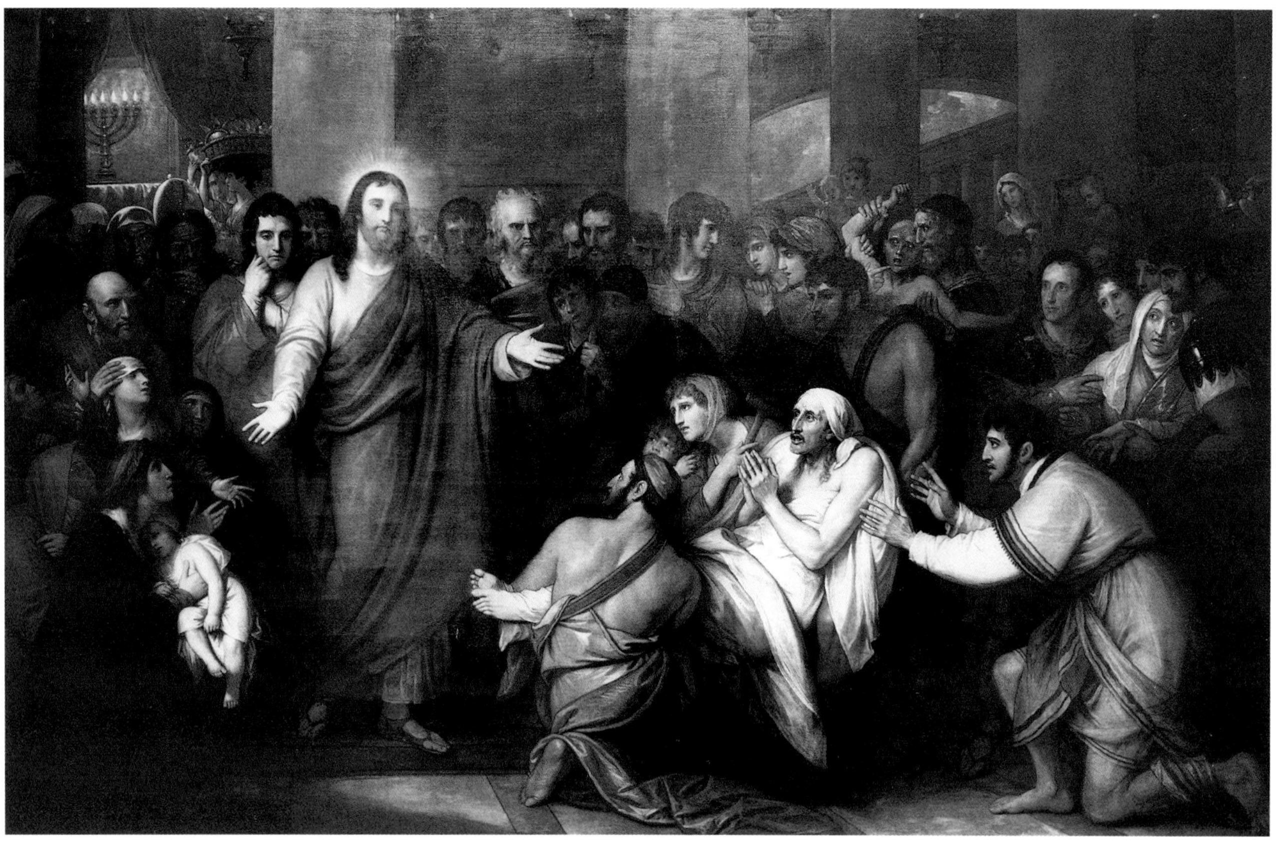

160 Benjamin West, *Christ Healing the Sick in the Temple*, 1815. Oil on canvas, 120 × 180 in. (305 × 457 cm). Courtesy Pennsylvania Hospital Historic Collections, Philadelphia.

Memory of Sir Joshua Reynolds – and he had gathered sufficient new material, including an assessment by Edmund Burke – another close friend and executor – to issue an expanded three-volume edition in 1798.[49] Strikingly, many of Reynolds's supporters chose to remember him as a history painter, a limited aspect of his production relative to portraiture – and from West's perspective a distortion. The accolades continued into the nineteenth century in broader contexts. "The English school of painting must acknowledge Sir Joshua Reynolds as its great founder," proclaimed John Gould in *A Dictionary of Painters, Sculptors, Architects, and Engravers . . . from the Earliest Ages to the Present Time . . . to which is added an Appendix . . . forming a complete English School* (1810).[50] Though Gould praised West warmly in the introduction, his decision to limit proper entries to deceased artists had the effect of highlighting Reynolds. Academy professor J. M. W. Turner, a star among the younger generation of English painters, removed even the barrier of death when, in 1811, he praised Reynolds as "that ever living ornament of the English school."[51]

If West chose to measure success by income from painting or sheer numbers of works, and clearly he did, then he had been among the most successful artists of his generation. In 1811, he broke all records for a living painter, gaining a much-needed boost to his public profile and finances (recently diminished by the loss of his royal sinecure) when the British Institution for Promoting the Fine Arts in the United Kingdom paid the staggering sum of 3,000 guineas to acquire his enormous painting *Christ Healing the Sick in the Temple*. (The artist originally promised the work to the Pennsylvania Hospital in Philadelphia, but later sent that institution a close variant, fig. 160.) West showed his gratitude – and pressing need to keep his image in memory – by having a medal struck with his profile for distribution to British Institution patrons, including the prince regent and other nobility, whose names appear with a tribute on the verso. (A modified version bore a different, even more immodest inscription on the verso: BENJAMIN WEST/AGED SEVENTY SEVEN/IN THE FULL POSSESSION/OF HIS POWERS/AND OF HIS GLORY/

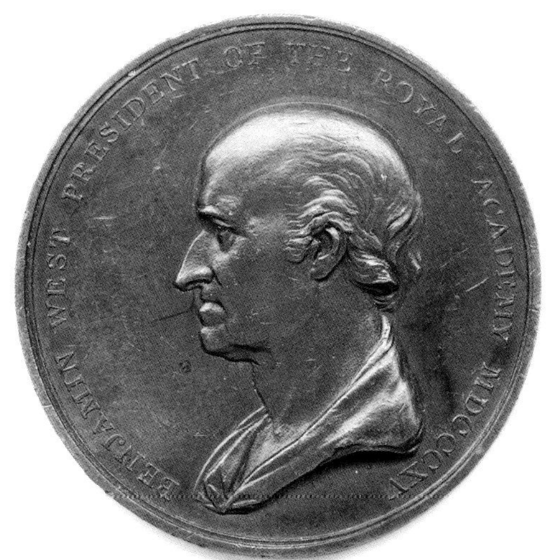

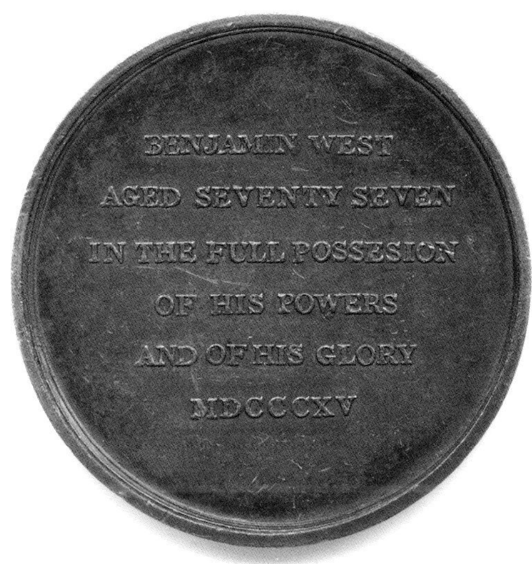

161 George Mills, *Benjamin West, President of the Royal Academy*, 1815, bronze medal. Private collection.

MDCCCXV; fig. 161.)[52] Though West had been one of the organizers of the British Institution in 1805, he gained only honorary membership (as President of the Royal Academy) because George III, wearied of ongoing conflicts in the Academy, made royal patronage conditional on the limited involvement of artists.[53] Even so, the purchase of *Christ Healing the Sick* gave the embattled Academy president good reason to consider the British Institution an ally in preserving his reputation.

West's longevity worked against him when the British Institution, which usually showed contemporary art or continental Old Master paintings, decided to mount retrospective exhibitions of work by several prominent eighteenth-century British painters – in effect, defining them as British Old Masters.[54] The first, in 1813, focused on Reynolds, with a comprehensive display of some two hundred paintings, including 138 portraits, 10 history paintings, and 57 other works.[55] West responded defensively to this sweeping survey of Reynolds's career; in 1814, he announced a plan (never realized) to show "the entire body of his Works, produced in the last half century, which he intends shall appear in Exhibition before the Public in the course of the two subsequent years," implying that his huge catalogue could not be accommodated at once.[56] That same year, the British Institution staged a second, group retrospective: 221 paintings by William Hogarth, Richard Wilson, Thomas Gainsborough, and (in smaller number) Johann Zoffany, nearly excluded on grounds that he was not British.[57] West probably did not regard the latter three artists as a threat, since they specialized in the academically less-exalted genres of landscape and portraiture. Hogarth presented more of a problem, as the only serious contender to Reynolds in contemporaneous debates as to the rightful founder of the British school.

The revival of Hogarth's reputation, already under way in 1814, caught entrenched Academicians off guard and had the potential to further undermine West's position. During his lifetime, Hogarth's combatively anti-elitist stance attracted barbs from Reynolds and his coterie, who sought to dismiss Hogarth as a "sign painter," the sort of artisan from whom they distinguished themselves as professionals. West, in London for only a year when Hogarth died, had considerably less exposure to the rancorous exchanges between Hogarth and his various enemies and did not share their antipathy for him. West may even have styled himself as a teacher following the relatively egalitarian Hogarthian model, a possibility suggested by Pratt's *American School*. West's centrality to the Royal Academy, and his paintings, nevertheless firmly identified him with the continental method of instruction, based on copying and the veneration of European Old Masters, that Hogarth firmly opposed. In the dramatically different political climate of the early nineteenth century, concerns that British art had become corrupted by slavish adherence to European models rekindled interest in Hogarth, whose work was promoted as more natural and more English. Hogarth's canvases of modern moral subjects, once dismissed as frivolous and vulgar (and long familiar only in engraved form), gained new respect as history paintings.[58] This development cannot have escaped West's attention, and it must have alarmed him. If not only Reynolds but also Hogarth might be exalted as founders of modern British painting, how would West be remembered?

In 1805, in the face of compounding professional troubles, an unexpected encounter launched West on the process by which he began to recover and reimagine a simpler time in his life, the days of his youth. West's thoughts had lately turned toward his homeland: "were He 10 years younger He wd. go to America, where He was sure that much might be done as the people had a strong disposition to the Arts," Farington recorded in 1804.[59] Considerations of family and financial security held West in England, but his mind was prepared to drift. A nudge came from the castaway adventure story penned by West's former teacher, William Williams, then in possession of Thomas Eagles, whose solicitude toward the aged Williams had prompted the surprising bequest described at the beginning of chapter two. In his short memorandum of July 10, 1805, Eagles sketched out the circumstances of West's encounter with the manuscript, which took place at Eagles's lodgings, facilitated (for reasons not given) by their mutual friend Sir Francis Annesley, a Member of Parliament for Reading, Master of Downing College, Cambridge, and a noted bibliophile. Surprised to learn of the connection between West and Williams, Eagles immediately recorded what West told him. Then, in 1810, West himself composed detailed recollections of Williams, fully aware that Eagles planned to use what he wrote to persuade publishers as to the authenticity of the Penrose manuscript. Yet both he and Eagles were complicit in a deception: neither man can have fully accepted Williams's story, which takes place over twenty-seven years, coinciding almost exactly with the period during which Williams resided in America.[60]

West's two accounts to Eagles filtered for posterity what he wanted known about Williams. To put it another way, West used Williams to reinforce a particular image of himself as a precocious youth. His promise at only age twelve, for example, had inspired Williams to place a poem about him in a Philadelphia newspaper, which was "much admired, tho' no one knew who was the author."[61] Regarding another poem that Williams composed after seeing a self-portrait his former pupil sent from abroad, West told Eagles: "what is most extraordinary [is that] the lines may be considered as prophetic of my future success in life, which it anticipates in a most extraordinary manner."[62] West's inclination to reflect Williams's poetic "power" (his word in 1810) back on himself is revealing. Galt's 1816 biography of West, having the distinct purpose of promoting its subject, furthered the process, eliminating most of the detail from West's prior accounts of Williams while expanding on parts that enhanced West's image. Galt's narrative reduced Williams to a witness, "a man of observation" who recognized in West "no common boy" but a child with "something extraordinary in his character."[63] As his one significant contribution to West's career, in the biography Williams brought culture, in the form of books on art theory, to West's nature, seeding his instinctive talent and innocent eye. With Galt's assistance, West recast his early interaction with Williams to portray himself as a painter in touch with theory and nature, a British artist who never ceased to be American.

West's accounts of his childhood experience with the camera obscura expose his inclination to dispense with Williams entirely, given the opportunity to assert his own genius. What first impressed West about Williams, he told Eagles in 1805, was the Englishman's accuracy as a painter of landscapes and "cattle pieces." Williams revealed his "secret, . . . a small box which prov'd to be a camera." "He shewed me the construction of it," said West (who would then have been around age nine). "I went home & was not at rest 'til I had made one for myself." West did not mention the incident in his subsequent letter to Eagles, but for the 1816 biography he sanctioned a dramatically altered version, completely detached from the narrative of Williams. According to Galt, West discovered the principles of the camera obscura independently, at about age sixteen. Confined by illness to a darkened bedroom, he saw cows walking upside down on the walls, an effect produced by the projection of light into his room (*camera*, in Italian) through a pinhole in the solid wooden shutters. He figured out how to duplicate the effect using a wooden box and thus "contrived, without ever having heard of the instrument, to invent the *Camera*." Remarkably, the youth's discovery of the camera received more attention in Galt than the boy's relationship with his teacher. The account served an important point of the biography: to argue that West possessed "that peculiarity of intellect which is discriminated from the effects of education, by the name of original talent."[64]

In giving such prominence to the camera – a device prized for its ability to capture the appearance of objects in the natural world – Galt's biography encouraged readers to think of West as an artist with a special relationship to nature. The opposition, in Galt's presentation of the camera, of "innate talent" and the "self-educated man of genius" to "instructed habits" and "the most mechanical disciple of the schools" suggests that West was not hurt by his early isolation from master teachers or masterly paintings. In the estimation of some eighteenth-century writers, the camera offered more than art and artists ever could. In a treatise on optics, Benjamin Martin praised the camera's image as "Nature's Art of Painting . . . infinitely superior . . . to the finest Performance of the Pencil." Even if united, the "Excellencies" of the principal artists (and he was precise on the terms of painterly accomplishment) would amount to little more than "sorry daubing" compared to the image focused through a lens. Thus, Martin reasoned, "the Camera Obscura is the School in which every Designer and Painter ought to learn the first Rudiments of his Art."[65] Other writers, less condescending to artists, were equally persuaded of the camera's value as a tool for painters. The Italian art theorist and critic Francesco Algarotti devoted a chapter to the device in his *Essay on Painting*, a book dedicated to English artists and published in London soon after West's arrival in that city.[66] Yet Algarotti's advocacy of the camera is striking in view of his assertion that the "ideal Painter . . . alone is a true painter." How does the image of "nature herself" made by a camera teach a painter whose art depends on filtering nature's imperfections? Algarotti never explicitly addressed the contradiction, but he suggested an answer in characterizing the camera as an instrument that perfectly "distills" perspective, chiaroscuro, color, and other elements of artistic representation, bringing into focus "that which, viewed directly, would present too confusing a scene for the eye to organize." The Dutch artist and theorist Samuel van Hoogstraten, writing in 1678, had made the point another way: "Besides gaining knowledge of nature, . . . one sees [in the camera's image] what main or general [characteristics] should belong to truly natural painting."[67] The camera, in effect, filters the welter of things and affords a measure of both the particular and the general.

Reynolds – art theory's last great advocate for the general and West's predecessor in the Royal Academy chair – did not concur. In his thirteenth Discourse, he argued that "a view of nature represented with all the truth of the camera obscura" (an accomplishment he granted Dutch painters) would remain "little and mean" by comparison with "the same scene represented by a great Artist . . . [who] has the power of selecting his materials as well as elevating his style."[68] As a portraitist, Reynolds could take fewer liberties with nature than a history painter, but when speaking for the record, he discouraged the imitation of unimproved nature. Reynolds was not above owning cameras, however, including one disguised as a book – not an unusual form, but an amusing choice for an artist who insisted on cloaking raw nature in ideas. Around 1777, both Reynolds and West acquired a newly invented model known as the Royal

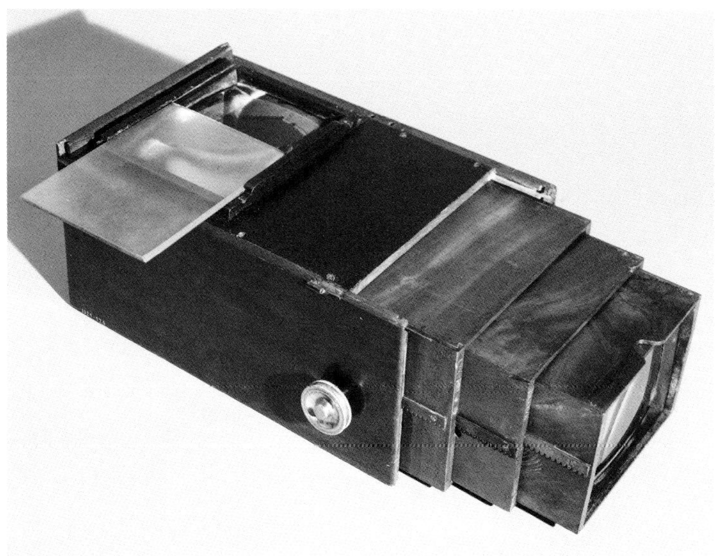

162 William Storer, Royal Accurate Delineator, 1778, camera obscura (model owned by Sir Joshua Reynolds and Benjamin West). Science Museum/Science & Society Picture Library, London.

Accurate Delineator (fig. 162). According to Walpole, the two painters "are gone mad with it, and it will be their own faults if they do not excel Rubens in light and shade, and all the Flemish masters in truth."[69]

As a painter of historical subjects, West could not be accused of imitating nature too closely; invention was a condition of his art. Instead, he and Galt may have invoked the camera precisely to strengthen his association with nature. That purpose evidently underlay a similar account in the 1830 biography of English painter George Romney by his son, John. In that story, Romney "received his first impressions of picturesque representation by contemplating objects . . . exhibited" in a camera, shown to him by a watch-maker (that is, someone of strong mechanical talent). "It is quite as plausible," says the biographer, "as the story of the Corinthian maid; for Mr. Romney being then a pupil of nature knew no more of art than the daughter of Dibutades" (the young woman who, in Pliny's account of the origin of representation, traces the shadow of her lover on the wall).[70] The characterization "*then* a pupil of nature" implied that Romney later acquired the fine artist's ability to select, as West did in becoming a history painter. Representations of the Corinthian maid, highly popular in Britain during the 1770s, may have been intended to serve a negative example; in their intensifying campaign for intellectual stature, painters insisted that they did not simply copy nature.[71] That need for distance – not a concern for

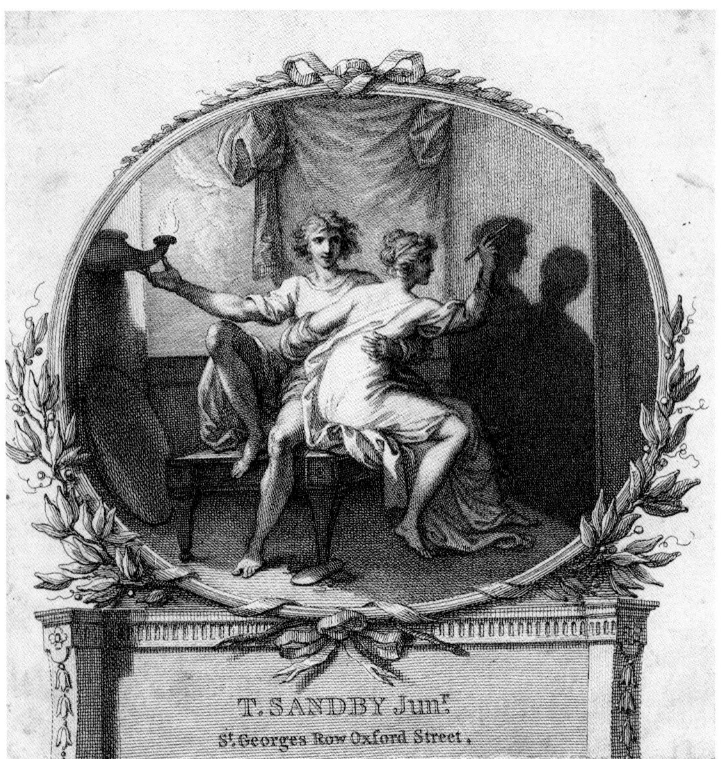

163 Francesco Bartolozzi after Benjamin West, trade card for Thomas Sandby, Jr., 1791. Etching and engraving. Yale Center for British Art, New Haven, gift of William Drummond.

drawing master Thomas Sandby, Jr., for whom West, in an unorthodox move, designed a trade card with the Corinthian maid in 1790 – nearly vanished for most painters during the early nineteenth century (fig. 163). In the biographies of both Romney and West, the parable of the camera obscura, by contrast to that of the Corinthian maid, asserted primary closeness to nature by means of a more scientific and masculine device.

Williams first caught West's innocent eye with his faithful replications of nature, but it was his collection of painters' lives that made the boy want to become a painter, or so West told Eagles in 1805.[72] In 1810, West restated the impact of "lives . . . of the great Masters of painting," implying that he had read accounts of artists in books Williams gave him by Richardson and Du Fresnoy. These, West claimed, were his "companions by day, & under [his] pillow by night." As a substantially unlettered ten-year-old, he could have done little more than hold or sleep on them, yet Galt – whose account of West's formation also overlooks Williams's "lives" – asserts otherwise: "The impression which these books made on the imagination of West finally decided his destination. He was allowed to carry them with him into the country; and his father and mother, soon perceiving a change in his conversation, were referred to the books for an explanation of the cause." After themselves consulting the volumes, West's parents "treasur[ed] in their minds those anecdotes of the indications of the early symptoms of talent with which both works abound" – and which their child had already demonstrated.[73] Yet no tales of artistic precocity figure in either book. West must later have become familiar with such accounts, most famously, Vasari's story of the shepherd boy Giotto. Vasari was on West's mind in 1807, when he declared to Nicholas Biddle: "Vasari was no great painter, but his lives are invaluable treasures."[74] Lives of that kind were the prism through which he and Galt filtered the artist's recollections of genuinely humble beginnings.

By dropping any reference to Williams's collection of artists' lives and emphasizing instead his early encounter with theory – Richardson's in particular – West highlighted an essential point of similarity (or so he must have hoped) with Reynolds. Samuel Johnson attested that his close friend "had the first fondness for his art excited by the perusal of Richardson's Treatise"; the quotation appeared in a biography of Reynolds published in 1813, by which time assertions of Richardson's importance to Reynolds were routine.[75] Richardson, a painter himself, had been the first great champion of English artists – and one who wrote in a vernacular they had a better chance of understanding than the elegant rhetoric of most aesthetic treatises.[76] But it was Reynolds who led the British school to full respectability after the mid-eighteenth century. Reynolds's distinction arose not only from his success in elevating portraiture to the level of high art – West, as a history painter, would have challenged him at the summit – but also from his authority as a theorist. The dedication to the 1773 edition of *Works of Mr. Jonathan Richardson* addressed and lauded Reynolds: "Had Richardson lived to see the inimitable productions of your pencil, he would have congratulated his country on the prospect of a School of Painting likely to contend successfully with those of Italy," wrote Jonathan Richardson, Jr. "At the same time, he would have confessed, that your admirable discourses would have rendered his own writings less necessary."[77] Reynolds's engagement with theory in the "Discourses" was wide-ranging and comprehensive. He applied his talents on a smaller scale as well, annotating Du Fresnoy in the 1783 edition by William Mason, who dedicated the volume to Reynolds in a poetic epistle. West's inability to muster any of Reynolds's intellectualism drove him to increasingly clumsy attempts to assert the power of theory on his imagination. Galt, his collaborative biographer, tried to persuade readers of the decisive impact of Williams's books (that is, Du Fresnoy and Richardson) on West's choice of career by an improbable episode from his childhood: young West's refusal to ride on horseback with another boy who intended to become a tailor and who questioned whether painting could be a livelihood. Dismissing the tailor's trade as "feminine" and lowly, West informs his erstwhile friend that further association between them would not do for a future painter, "a companion for Kings and Emperors" (here we recognize the impact of established artist anecdotes).[78] This jab at the tailor's trade summoned recurring resistance by eighteenth- and early nineteenth-century portrait painters – from Hogarth to Reynolds and Copley to Stuart – to the idea that they served personal vanity and no more. West, as readers of his biography knew, had exercised the more masculine prerogative of addressing public virtue as a history painter.

The inclusion in his biography of this conspicuous, early display of pomposity confirms what West's critics said about him later and seems a high price to pay to demonstrate what Galt explains as the "effect of the enthusiasm inspired by Richardson and Fresnoy." Richardson had asserted that "a painter ought to be a title of dignity" and that even a portrait painter, "as his business is chiefly with people of condition, . . . must think as a gentleman."[79] But he never attempted to deny the mechanical aspect of painting and waged his campaign on behalf of the art not against mechanics (if somewhat at their expense) but against gentlemen who resisted any intrusion into their ranks. Richardson's more nuanced message became a blunt instrument in the report of West's encounter with the would-be tailor, preventing any reader from missing the point: that the eventual historical painter to the king, guided by art theory, transcended his humble beginnings. West became a gentleman artist, distinct from the kind of artisan painter he knew Williams to have been.

West used Williams – and Eagles – to begin a process of strategic reinvention. The preface ("advertisement") to *The Journal of Llewellin Penrose, a Seaman*, issued in 1815 with a dedication to West, extensively excerpted West's testimony from the memo and letter; it offered the first published glimpse of the eminent artist's early training.[80] Yet, as the preceding discussion makes clear, it was Galt who played the decisive role in shaping West's image for posterity. With significant encouragement from the writer, West authorized a complete tactical reversal of his insistent claims of Englishness. The biography of 1816, instead, presented a remarkable, and at the time quite unfamiliar, account of the famous British painter's formative years – the story of the American West.

An Enterprising Scot

John Galt's role in creating *The Life and Studies of Benjamin West, Esq.* has been easy to underestimate, an outcome in which Galt was directly complicit. The phrase "compiled from materials furnished by himself" – that is, by West – appearing after the title and above Galt's name immediately qualified the nominal author's role. So did Galt's prefatory characterization of the book as West's "memoirs." Years later, Galt reaffirmed the point: *The Life of West* was, "as nearly as it possibly can be, an autobiography."[81] We should not believe him. Galt had a lifelong habit of obscuring or creating confusion about his authorship. He made conventional use of pseudonyms (in periodical writing) and anonymity (in novels); he inserted his own perspective into texts purportedly by others without clarifying his contribution; and he was fascinated with autobiography, both real (two distinct accounts of himself take up three volumes) and imaginary (fig. 164).[82] He even melded the two in a fictional autobiography based on an authentic autobiographical manuscript that he purchased from its American author – who then published the original text with an introduction by Galt, a complication the Scot must have delighted in.[83] Although many of those activities postdated *The Life of West*, Galt in 1816 qualified as something more than "an unsuccessful hack writer," once the default position among West scholars, as if there were nothing to learn from his work.[84] Galt might more generously be described as a writer of unfocused talents. He was in that respect the antithesis of his biographical subject, more like the "man of genius, [who] in his first effusions, is so far from revealing his future powers, that . . . no reasonable hope can be formed of his success" – a type that interested D'Israeli, the apologist for anecdotes.[85] Not until the early 1820s would Galt's literary gifts become apparent, in a series of ironic, fictive autobiographies. These genuinely innovative works won him the respect of peers – Samuel Coleridge, among them, judged Galt "in the first rank of contemporary Novelists" – and later attracted the attention of literary scholars.[86] Yet literary historians have been barely more concerned with Galt's nonfiction writing than art historians were with Galt's oeuvre beyond *The Life of West*. Such disciplinary focus has

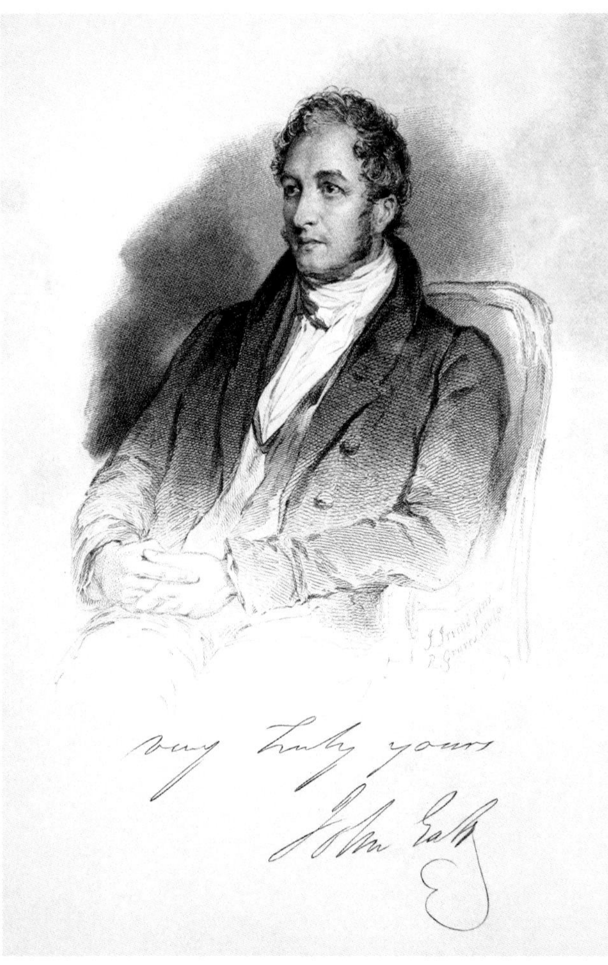

164 John Galt, engraved portrait by R. Graves after painting by I. Irvine, frontispiece to *The Autobiography of John Galt* (1833).

flattened an interesting story, which takes shape when *The Life of West* is considered in light of Galt's early and later work, both fiction and nonfiction: the story of Galt and West's mutually beneficial relationship and their collaborative crafting of a memorable life.[87]

Precisely when biographer and subject first became acquainted remains unclear. Galt was forty-one years younger, born in 1779 in western Scotland and raised in Greenock, the port city of Glasgow. He became a customs house clerk at sixteen and soon after joined a merchant firm; business engaged him intermittently throughout his life, with consistently poor results. Galt's interest in writing emerged early, marked from the first by experimentation with diverse genres – poetry, plays, biography, essays, novels – and by an "ominous facility of output," in biographer Ian Gordon's apt phrase.[88] Encouraged by the publication of a few works in Scottish newspapers and journals and hoping to expand his business prospects, Galt moved to London in 1804, the same age then as West had been when he settled in the city. A decade later, Galt was still floundering, with one commercial bankruptcy behind him and no better than marginal success as a writer. At the same point in life, by contrast, West had become famous.

Galt's earliest published remarks on the subject of art appear in two books of essays and an article based on his travels in the Mediterranean. In each case, a business venture in Gibraltar gave way to an extended tour, the first intermittently in the company of Lord Byron, whom Galt met en route (and later made the subject of a biography). Each tour resulted in a volume printed at the author's expense by the London firm of Cadell and Davies. Galt's few pages on painting in *Voyages and Travels in the Years 1809, 1810, and 1811* (1812) express a conventional belief in the primacy of nature. The Old Masters in the royal collection at Palermo, Sicily, attracted him because they did not try to surpass nature, unlike "the artists of the English Academy" (unspecified), who "have much to unlearn." Next, admitting a "shocking disregard of keeping" (proper subordination of parts in a painting but in this context a reference to discrete classes of painting), Galt makes a conceptual leap from "master-pieces of the Italian artists to the Barbers' signs of Palermo," an association he defends as "natural" because the latter were also "pictures."[89] Galt did not invoke signboards to subvert the Old Masters, as had Hogarth and the Sign Painters' Exhibition of fifty years before. Instead, as a writer whose works were strongly colored by Scottish Enlightenment concern for social evolution and for whom progress would be a constant theme, he may have regarded the signboards as representing a relatively primitive stage in the development of painting that in Sicily coexisted with more mature manifestations. Artists of humble beginnings might, under such circumstances, make accelerated individual progress. Galt offers the example of a shoemaker's son from Trapani, Sicily, who was "permitted to indulge the invincible propensity of his genius" only after he had "spoiled a great deal of leather by scratching figures on it with an awl." By the time of Galt's writing, the distracted apprentice had become one of "the most eminent" living painters, creating works in Rome deemed "little inferior to Raphael."[90] The story of irrepressible genius, a well-established convention, anticipates Galt's more sustained engagement with artistic beginnings in *The Life of West*.

During the visit to Sicily, the writer acquired material for his first publication expressly concerned with art, which appeared in *Philosophical Magazine* (a journal edited by his new father-in-law, Alexander Tilloch) in 1813: "On the Fine Arts: An Essay founded on a Discourse delivered by the Cavaliere Ferro e Ferro, President of the Accademia del Decernimento of Trapani.* By Mr. John Galt."[91] Galt's contribution is unclear, as would often be the case with publications in which he had a hand. The note to the title (marked by the asterisk) stated that the "original Italian work, consisting of two volumes quarto, containing four discourses by Sig. Ferro, was not printed for sale, but was circulated gratuitously among the Author's friends"; however, passages on English architecture, the Parthenon sculptures brought to England by Lord Elgin, and poet Robert Southey dispel the impression that the essay is merely a translation. Galt was franker about his hand in the work when he expanded on the same putative base in *Letters from the Levant* (1813), his second collection of travel essays. Letter 26 (dated in Athens) presents, he writes, a distillation of the same discourses interspersed with his own ideas, including the remarks on English poetry, "something complimentary and national, in case your [the reader's] patience has been worn out."[92]

Letters from the Levant offers the earliest evidence for Galt's acquaintance with West. To justify including his own opinions on fine art in that volume, he announced in its preface: "they have been printed in consequence of the approbation with which Mr. West, unquestionably the greatest artist of the age, was pleased to notice a few observations on the same subject, which the Author has elsewhere published" (presumably the *Philosophical Magazine* essay).[93] If this marked the beginning of a dialogue between the two men, it was an opportune moment for both. After terrible reviews for a volume of blank-verse tragedy, published in 1812, Galt's *Life and Administration of Cardinal Wolsey*, also 1812, had been more favorably received, with good sales of the biography adding a concrete boost to his perennially shaky finances.[94] Galt conceived the biography of Wolsey in 1805, soon after moving to England, but did not begin that work in earnest until 1809, at the cost of a "considerable sum" for an assistant who transcribed original documents for publication in an appendix.[95] He must have been casting about for another biographical subject, and he soon found one who would spare him the time and expense of research (no longer feasible after his marriage in April 1813) and whose connections might do him good. In April 1814, *New Monthly Magazine* announced that Galt was "engaged upon a life of the venerable President of the Royal Academy . . . under the immediate superintendance of Mr. West himself."[96] West had biography in mind as well, following the publication in 1813 of painter James Northcote's *Memoirs of Sir Joshua Reynolds*. Rushed into print to coincide with the British Institution retrospective, this book intensified the spotlight on Reynolds, but few considered the rambling memoir by Reynolds's former pupil a success. West and his friends pronounced the volume "vulgar" and full of inappropriate and undigested material; irked reviewers saw a momentous life – whose history was, "so far as it extends, the history of the modern English school of painting" – reduced by an undiscerning author to a "trifling," "dull," "hackneyed" "bundle of bon mots."[97] "We shall have to lament that Sir Joshua Reynolds was not also his own biographer," ventured one critic, who concluded that "a life self-written, and commented upon afterwards by an impartial acquaintance, would be the most perfect piece of biography."[98]

West's collaboration with Galt came as close to meeting those parameters as the artist could have managed. He was not known for facility with language, spoken or written. Even during a time of loose orthographic standards, West's deficiencies appear pronounced, as in 1767, when he explained his delay in responding to a letter on grounds of "having been so much ingaged in the Study of my Bussiness, particularly that of History painting which demands the greates cear & intelegance amaginable."[99] Such problems were exposed after West became a public figure, if often exaggerated: "Most young gentleman that I am acquainted with can read and write," declared a commentator for *Middlesex Journal*, who made clear that he did not see West as qualified for the title of gentleman on any account: "Mr. W**t lies under a violent suspicion of ignorance in both these vulgar accomplishments; for I am well informed that Mr. W**t, in the subscription of his name, is guided by his wife."[100] Elizabeth West made diplomatic apologies for her husband – "He was so devoted to drawing while a Child, and a Youth, that every other part of his education was neglected" – but her grandnephew, the English poet Leigh Hunt, put it more bluntly: West "had received so careless, or so homely an education when a boy, that he could hardly read."[101] Nor did the artist's verbal skills redeem him. His pronunciation seemed at best odd – Hunt termed it "puritanical barbarism" – and, at worst, laughably wrong. He spoke in a way that even his friend Sir George Beaumont deemed "crude."[102] West, in short, had every reason to desire professional assistance in relating the story of his life. If the language in *The Life of West* is rather plain and flat, unlike Galt's descriptive writing in the biography of Cardinal Wolsey (or the ornate prose in parts of his *George III* of 1820), an explanation may lie in Galt's wish to represent,

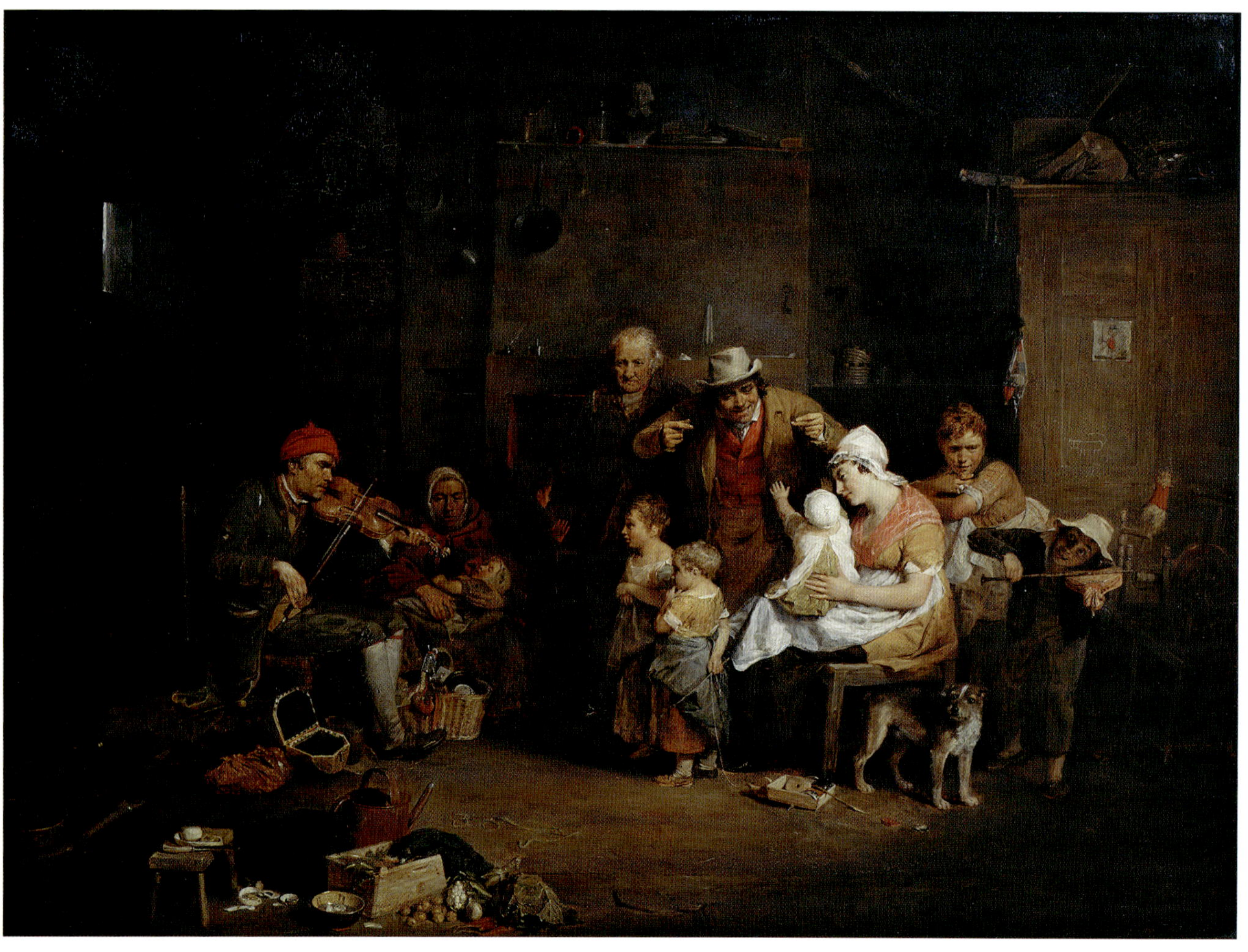

165 Sir David Wilkie, *The Blind Fiddler*, 1806. Oil on mahogany, 22¾ × 31¼₁₆ in. (57.8 × 79.4 cm). Tate Gallery, London

albeit indirectly, a speaking style that might charitably be called unadorned. Galt also knew that "understatement appears to denote modesty," as Nick Whistler wrote of Galt's own autobiography, in which the writer "chose a plain clear style and adopted an anti-heroic stance to give the impression that his protagonist was a modest but true hero."[103] Galt applied this principle to *The Life of West*. At least one reader made a connection between West's youth in Pennsylvania and the prose in his biography, "told in a style of stiffness not ill-suited to the outlines of a life commenced among the Quakers of America."[104]

West's narration of his own story played right into the biographer's hands, to a degree that could only have been appreciated in retrospect but simply went unnoticed. Galt's major literary works of the 1820s can be described as imaginary autobiographies, featuring provincial characters whose lives the reader pieces together from idiomatic correspondence, reminiscences, or self-consciously constructed memoirs. Galt rejected the classification of these works as "novels," citing his lack of concern for plot; in many of his stories, he insisted, "the only link of cohesion . . . is the mere remembrance of the supposed author."[105] To create the appearance of truth through realistic representation of the ordinary and particular was Galt's aim – a literary parallel, in his view, to the genre paintings of his slightly younger countryman, David Wilkie. Wilkie's wildly successful first submission to a Royal Academy exhibition, *The Village Politicians* in 1806, impressed Galt deeply; *The Blind Fiddler*, shown in 1807, moved him to write the artist. Galt invoked a shared interest in "the peculiarities of conduct, opinion and notions among the peasantry" and enclosed a literary "scetch of two pieces," which he compared to Wilkie's "visible representation of a portion of the same class of ideas" (fig. 165).[106] West, despite his contradictory pictorial insistence on generality, also admired Wilkie and can hardly have avoided discussing the Scottish painter with the Scottish writer (who could not escape that characterization even when his subject was not Scottish).[107]

Galt's engagement with Scottish subjects had intensified by 1813, when he contacted Edinburgh publisher Archibald Constable with a book proposal, the chronicle of fifty years in a country parish (1760–1810), composed by a fictive lowland Scots minister at the end of his life and career.[108] He met with no encouragement, advised that Scottish novels would not succeed.[109] (It cannot have helped that Galt's story offered none of the Highlands exoticism celebrated in the poetry of Walter Scott, whose first novel, *Waverley*, was still a year away from publication.) Galt then drew on his extensive travels in the Mediterranean to produce his first published work of fiction in 1816, *The Majolo*, another experiment with the self-told narrative. Cast as the recollected observations of a Sardinian who had long ago traveled across Europe and Great Britain, as told to an Englishman, it is, in effect, a disquisition on national character. Galt termed it "a species of moral portraiture."[110] Issued a few months after *The Life of West*, *The Majolo* was poorly received. In 1820, taking advantage of his good acceptance rate for essays by the recently established *Blackwood's Edinburgh Magazine*, Galt returned to Scottish subjects with "The Ayrshire Legatees," a story serialized in *Blackwood's*.[111] Expanding on his own experience and on the type of the epistolary novel, Galt threw his Scottish characters into relief by setting them against the background of metropolitan London. On the one hand are four family members who travel to the city to collect an inheritance and who relate their adventures in letters home; each has a distinct voice, with varying mixtures of Scots and English suggesting age, gender, education, and aspirations. On the other, presented directly, are a sharply drawn cast of small-town, Scottish characters, who read and comment on the letters in passages combining narration and dialogue. The "provisional, extemporaneous, wandering character" of these anecdotal tales, as Martha Bohrer noted, opposed "sweeping, privileged, canonical and nationalistic genres" in their emphasis on particulars over universals.[112] Hugely popular, the series accomplished a resurrection of the fictive minister's chronicle, issued as *Annals of the Parish* in 1821, followed closely by *The Ayrshire Legatees* in book form. At forty-one, Galt had become an important novelist.[113]

Galt's subjects during the five years before and after publication of *The Life of West* reveal how neatly the artist's story dovetailed with the writer's own interests and aspirations, both literary and entrepreneurial. West was a provincial unknown who became an international success; an observer in Mediterranean lands and an exotic curiosity to be observed; an American who, like the Scottish writer, could never be English; a shaper of his own life story; a supremely well-connected public figure; and a man like any other, aging and concerned for his legacy. At the time he met Galt, West was ripe for biography. After a conversation with West in 1807, Nicholas Biddle observed: "He really is a good old man, fond of talking about himself & like all distinguished men I have ever seen equally fond of flattery."[114] He must have responded readily to the attentions of Galt (who, in Rembrandt Peale's biased later recollection, appeared to "prey" on the elderly artist).[115] Given West's previous reticence about his life in the American colonies and his endorsement of repeated characterizations of himself as English, it seems highly unlikely that he would have decided to produce a full public account of his American experience without Galt's intervention. That point, at least, Galt acknowledged. In his own autobiography, he noted that during his visits to West's studio, the painter "mentioned anecdotes of his early youth"; "these seemed to me interesting," Galt continued, "and ultimately I proposed to write the first part of [West's] Life, to which he assented." At what point in their acquaintance West made this decision remains unknown; however, he may partly have felt freed by the death in August 1815 of his American colleague Copley, a constant professional irritant and rival in London and the one man who could and would have challenged West's American story.[116]

Galt had a long-standing interest in the Americas. His father owned a West Indian trading ship, and his brother and other relatives had emigrated to Honduras, Virginia, Vermont, and Canada.[117] While writing West's biography, Galt worked (unsuccessfully) as a parliamentary lobbyist on behalf of Canadians who had suffered losses in the most recent war between Britain and the United States. (Galt himself later moved to Canada in 1825, a business venture that ended in another bankruptcy and a stay in debtor's prison after his return to London in 1828.) His early publications included "A Statistical Account of Upper Canada" (1807), an anecdotal hodgepodge of secondhand information on Canadian climate, diseases, lakes, hemp cultivation, and religion, among other topics. Under the heading "miscellaneous considerations," Galt broadly introduced one of his enduring subjects: "the plain tales of those who, by virtue of their designs alone, have improved the conditions of mankind." Despite his nominal focus on Canada, Galt singled out "the high moral character of the Pennsylvanians even at this day . . . [as] the fairest monument that wisdom and enterprise can hope to obtain."[118] As West's biographer, he gained the opportunity to focus on one exemplary and resourceful Pennsylvanian, a great man of humble beginnings whose story neatly accommodated Galt's conception of progress as the result of providential design and human action in the everyday world.[119]

Galt's focus on West's formation and West's voice allowed him to substantially avoid critical consideration of West's art, which might have opened the writer to charges that he lacked qualifications as an artist or theorist.[120] A few years earlier, the artist John Hoppner had cited those very reasons in stating publicly that William Hayley was unqualified to write *The Life of George Romney, Esq.* (London, 1809). Galt appears also to have been sensitive to perceptions that West himself had difficulty articulating theory, as opposed to method, on which the artist found it easy to be precise. The limitation hardly mattered: in his preface to the 1816 volume, Galt contended that West's decision to relate "the circumstances by which he was led to approximate, without the aid of an instructor, to those principles and rules of art, which it is the object of schools and academies to disseminate, has conferred a greater benefit on young Artists than he could possibly have done by the most ingenious and eloquent lectures on the theories of his profession."[121] The compiler's role (even if only that) was hardly trifling. By serving as West's sounding board and providing structure to the old artist's recollections, Galt too had made a contribution to art and its history.

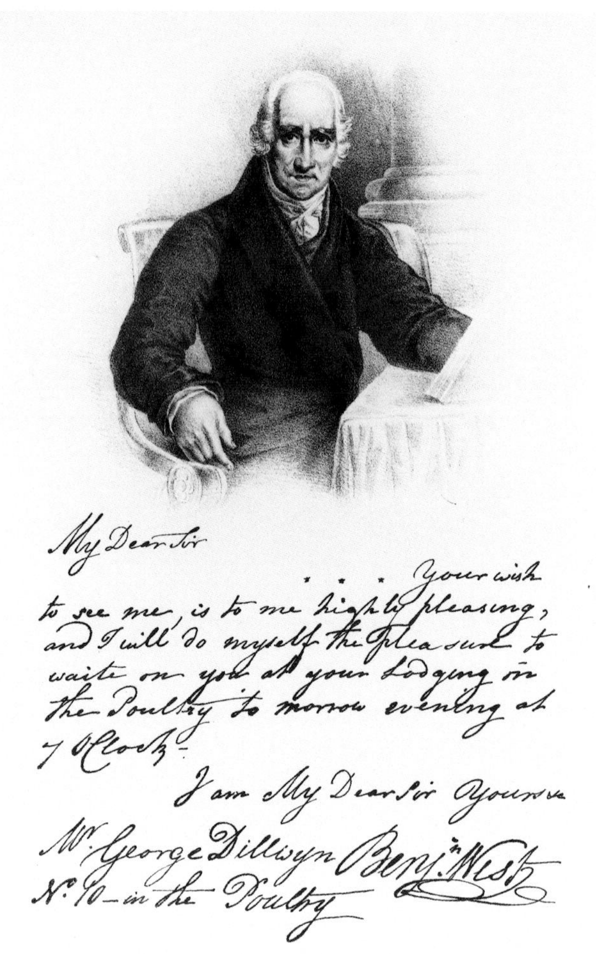
My Dear Sir

. . . Your wish to see me, is to me highly pleasing, and I will do myself the pleasure to waite on you at your Lodging in the Poultry to morrow evening at 7 OClock.

I am My Dear Sir Yours &c

Mr George Dillwyn
N° 10 – in the Poultry

Benj.n West

166 Benjamin West, undated letter (1810s) to George Dillwyn, on stationery engraved with West's portrait. Historical Society of Pennsylvania, Philadelphia, Gratz Collection.

"Sir Benjamin": West and "Port Folio"

In hindsight, it is clear that the stakes in the collaboration between West and Galt, whose subsequent reputation in no way depended on this work, were all West's. He had legitimate reasons to fear continued decline of his reputation in England and went to remarkable lengths to keep his name, work, and image in circulation – astonishingly, even using stationery engraved with his portrait (fig. 166). With the biography, West may have hoped to persuade the British art world to read his American origins as closer to nature, a quality in the ascendant relative to academic credentials in 1816. He stood to gain even more in the United States. Fifty-six years away from his native land had limited his negative exposure there, while more than two dozen American students augmented the positive. In the role of mentor, West had done as much as anyone to nurture the development of American art.

It appeared that this contribution might not be enough, judging from items on West published regularly in *Port Folio*, the influential American literary and political magazine. Founded in Philadelphia in 1801 and issued weekly until 1809, *Port Folio* served up a miscellany of original and reprinted essays under the direction of Joseph Dennie. Whether as "Oliver Oldschool, Esq." – the journal's imaginary editorial persona – or in other guises, Dennie and his fellow contributors conveyed a Federalist dismay over the democratic and commercial course of American society under Jefferson's presidency. *Port Folio* may have been elitist and Anglophilic, but its perspective remained manifestly American, as the many items on West demonstrate.[122]

The magazine signaled ambivalence about the famous artist in its first volume, which announced "Sir Benjamin West's" plan to donate a major painting to the Pennsylvania Hospital. West never was knighted, yet the honorific recurred in *Port Folio* for a decade, always in commentary that, on one level, seems disparaging. Why "this *American* artist, after experiencing the good fortune to be born and educated in Pennsylvania, should sullenly retreat to England" is a mystery. "It is perfectly inexplicable, that he should barter *citizenship* for knighthood, that he should receive a king's money, and, more provoking still, be soothed by regal praise. What are titles, honors and gold, to an independent republican, who, remaining at home, might have had the noblest and *amplest* opportunities of – *giving away* as many pictures as he pleased!"[123] *Port Folio*'s humor about the American alternative to West's illustrious English career exposes the editorial irony, apparent again in 1804: "SIR BENJAMIN WEST, an American genius, who, most unaccountably, prefers the banks of the Thames to the banks of the Delaware, and chooses to tint historic canvas, under the patronage of his KING, rather than to paint sign boards for some republican major in the militia, or cover with Spanish brown the dead flat of some Quaker, out of pure brotherly love and affection."[124] West, in other words, could hardly be faulted for staying away from a country with such restricted opportunities for painters. But he seemed open to insinuation on the matter of the presumed title, which he did not actually hold though it was persistently identified with him. Even Peale, writing to West in 1800, addressed his letter to "Sir" Benjamin West.[125] The editor of *Port Folio*, if once honestly confused himself, should not have been in 1805, when he reprinted the entire West biography from *Universal Magazine*, titled, as in the original, "Biographical Sketch of Benjamin West, Esq., President of the Royal Academy." The English text criticized the crown for failing to honor West sufficiently, not least by reward of a title, but the Philadelphia editor composed an introduction that kept up the pressure on "Sir Benjamin," in "voluntary exile from his natal land" but "perhaps sigh[ing] to return to a country, *free* to discern and *sovereign* to reward merit."[126] In *Port Folio*'s American view, as a courtier, West was a knight whether or not he had actually been granted a title.

After three years without further mention, West resurfaced in *Port Folio* with a second biographical account in 1809. The magazine had been losing money and the new owner, Philadelphia publisher Samuel Bradford, was determined to broaden its appeal. (Dennie remained as editor, though intermittently sidelined by poor health.) Illustrations formed part of the popularizing strategy; however, none of West's pictures was reproduced until 1811, when line engravings of *The Death of General Wolfe* and other works accompanied the reprinted *Belle Assemblée* biography. The 1809 account – adapted from *Universal Magazine* and *Public Characters* – made a clear pitch to readers in the United States, beginning with the title: "Anecdotes of American Painters: West." Although the first sentence introduces him (somewhat anomalously) as "the head of the English school of painters," the biography pruned West's English family tree and early association with important Britons, while condensing details of his career in London. A new paragraph on the undeveloped state of painting in "our country" during West's youth and a passage injecting some tension into his decision to stay in England provide an American perspective. But the allure of "princely favor" proved too great, culminating (again, only on paper) in West's knighthood.[127]

West made a number of indirect attempts to assuage American feelings about his British alliances. With equal indirectness, contributors to *Port Folio* rebuffed those efforts, in a manner suggesting that West was out of touch with the United States. In 1810, the magazine published a long letter from West to the painter Charles Willson Peale, his former student, then most prominent as a Philadelphia museum proprietor. Citing his own feelings "as a native of the state of Pennsylvania," West applauded state support of Peale's museum and the establishment of an academy in Philadelphia (the Pennsylvania Academy of the Fine Arts, founded in 1805, with West as an honorary member). Without originality, he predicted that the city would eventually become "the Athens of the Western empire" – a distinction he professed to believe no longer possible for Great Britain. In response, "a citizen of Philadelphia" tersely undercut West's flattery. Nations in which nature retained "dominion over manners and character" – namely, Britain and the United States – had little need of art, he wrote: "we are still in a state of nature . . . we stand in no need of copies of it."[128] Whether this pronouncement expresses a serious position remains open to question; it seems more a tongue-in-cheek response, so characteristic of this magazine, to the famous painter. Even though West's international profile brought him sustained attention from *Port Folio*, those notices betray considerable ambivalence about the artist.

West's most transparent efforts to promote himself nearly always worked against him. The January 1812 issue of *Port Folio*, the last edited by Dennie, contains a long response to the "pompous and pedantic panegyric" on West's *Christ*

Healing the Sick published several months earlier in *Poulson's American Daily Advertiser*, a Philadelphia newspaper.[129] *Poulson's Advertiser* in fact published two items: a letter from West to Philadelphian Joseph Wharton, explaining his decision to allow *Christ Healing the Sick* – which he had originally promised the Pennsylvania Hospital – to remain in Britain, and the offending "Description of the Picture," which West had enclosed with his letter. West endorsed that text as the product of "one of the ablest Pens in this country" (England) and immodestly added: "The judges of literature with us, say, the inspired pencil [of the artist], has created an inspired pen, in that written account of the picture."[130] *Port Folio*'s criticism of the gloss on West's picture thus implicitly targeted the artist himself.

The essay in *Port Folio*, entitled "Some Remarks on Mr. West's Picture," opens with a string of unattributed quotations, apparently the first level of the offending remarks: "the *Corregiescity* of Corregio," "the airs of Guido," "draperies . . . flowing and '*moelleux*,'" "handling . . . like Tintoret, the very thunderbolt of the pencil." The disconnected prose in the article fully exposes the trite affectation of these passages – only some of which derive from the published description of *Christ Healing the Sick* (the two last cited here are a quotation and a paraphrase). The opening phrases (including the first two here) are instead quotations from Laurence Sterne's masterpiece of literary invention, *Tristram Shandy*. *Port Folio*'s highly literate readers might have been expected to make the connection themselves, but the writer did not leave the matter to chance: "'Grant me patience just heaven!,' I exclaimed in the words of Sterne," the writer interjected; "'. . . of all the cants that are canted in this canting world . . . the cant of criticism is the most tormenting.'"[131] Sterne's book, however eccentric, made a case for common sense, and that was the point of *Port Folio*'s essay. The author denounced all pretension and "jargon" in art criticism and offered a constructive alternative, taking as his reference point the line engraving of *Christ Healing the Sick* published in *Port Folio* two months earlier.[132] He conceded limitations to evaluating a painting from a simple engraving and systematically assessed which parts of a picture might fairly be judged on such a basis. He then carefully defended the ability of any man with "pretensions to little more than plain sense, and common observation" to make reasonable judgments and the right of such a person to do so in plain terms. If a hypothetical painting were sufficiently absurd to show "Abraham about to blow out the brains of Isaac with a pistol," it would be merely "the criticism of common sense" to describe the work as such (laughter permissible). Finally, though relatively briefly, the writer demonstrated the process for readers with remarks on West's picture, mostly unfavorable. The essayist's broad purpose had been to demystify art criticism and to encourage a plain American alternative to the inflated language of English connoisseurship. The immediate effect, however, was deeply unflattering to West.[133]

The sequence of articles on West that appeared in *Port Folio* between 1801 and 1812 makes clear that, for all its attentions to a painter who had done much to advance American art, the magazine's editors and contributors did not stand in awe of him. On the one hand, West remained an American from whom the nation gained no "profit," whose "overgrown daubing," moreover, served the wrong kind of example. On the other, he was the "illustrious countryman" whose opinion of talented young Americans carried weight.[134] Brief notices of other American painters had appeared in *Port Folio* but never as proper biographies, whereas West had been the subject of three such profiles in six years. Those accounts acquired a broader context when the journal's second editor, Nicholas Biddle – who had heard West say that Americans "have a genius for the arts" – inaugurated a year-long series of twenty-two biographies of European artists.[135] Ranging from Michelangelo and Raphael through five painters of the French or "Flemish" school (including Rembrandt), these constituted "a complete history of the modern [sixteenth- and seventeenth-century] arts."[136] In 1814, West explicitly gained a place in a distinguished sequence of painters: "Raphael, Titian, Corregio, Rubens, or West."[137] He was on his way to becoming an American Old Master.

The year 1814 marked an abrupt turnabout in *Port Folio*'s sniping over West's abandonment of America, precipitated by the *British Gallery of Contemporary Portraits* biography published in London in 1813. I have argued that the insistence on West's Englishness in that account, with its corresponding suppression of his Americanness, originated with the artist, in a desperate effort to promote himself as head of the British school. If identified with him, that effort might have unleashed tremendous scorn in the pages of *Port Folio*. Instead, led by new editor Charles Caldwell, the magazine hastened to the artist's defense over the attempt, "which we have reason to believe is sanctioned by the concurring voice of the [British] nation, to wrest from his native country and appropriate to themselves, the glory conferred on the present age by the resplendent talents of our countryman, Mr. West" – now pointedly not "Sir Benjamin."[138]

The magazine made its case for West in an article headed "American and British claims," which opens by reassuring readers that "state affairs" are not at issue, though they lay in the near background with renewed hostilities between the two countries. Invoking "the painter's well known admonitory rebuke, *ne, sutor, ultra crepidam*," the journalist grants that he, like the cobbler who sought to challenge Apelles, should refrain from judging beyond his expertise. But – and the reader senses a qualification coming – a writer provoked will express his opinion (just as may a shoemaker or any other artisan in the American republic). Politics is not simply a matter of statecraft. In four adamant pages, matching the insistent tone of the London biography, *Port Folio* laid out the American position.

> Mr. West was born and reared to manhood in the province of Pennsylvania. Here, of course, the natural foundation of all his subsequent greatness was conclusively laid: here were received and brought to their unusual strength and perfection, those excellent stamina of body, which have sustained, unbroken, the toils and challenges of more than seventy years of exertion. The texture of his mind, too, is altogether American. Here he imbibed that noble and enterprising spirit, and here were formed those habits of industry, perseverance and virtue, which, under Providence, were the proximate means of his elevation and fame. To complete the picture, here did our great countryman manifest his taste, and commence his career in the use of the pencil.
>
> . . . what was left for Great Britain to perform? . . . From America did this great artist derive his talents and all his good qualities both physical and moral, and only found in Great Britain a suitable field for the exercise and display of them.

In the context of the ongoing war between Britain and the United States, nothing less than the honor of the young nation was at stake: "as well might the people of England assert their claim to the glory attached to the names of Washington . . . and the whole host of our revolutionary worthies, because they were born in a British province before the acknowledgment of our independance [*sic*] as a nation." West, in this account, attained the status of a national hero, "as much a native of the United States, as any one born in Pennsylvania within the last twenty years, who has never breathed the air of a transatlantic region."[139]

Here was a vacuum waiting to be filled with all the unreported details of West's life in America. Whether Galt or West was aware of *Port Folio*'s claim on him as American is unknown. But it would be hard to find two more opportunistic men than they, and by almost any reckoning, the right moment had come for a full public account of West's early years.

Galt's "West": Critical Reception and Legacy

Not surprisingly, Galt's biography of 1816 did little to shore up West's reputation in Britain, where its excesses and shortcomings were readily attributed to the artist himself. *Critical Review*, which published the first of four contemporaneous British assessments, accepted the book "as a specimen of auto-biography" in all respects, including the "observations accompanying the facts." Whether ascribed to West or not, "they bear internal evidence that they could have flowed from no other source." The "arrogance" of so insistently representing West as "an instrument chosen by Providence to disseminate the arts of peace in the world" is, by implication, West's arrogance; the "uncultivated" mind that sees an Indian in the Apollo, exposed in that moment as "little susceptible of grand and beautiful impressions," is West's mind; and the "cautious abstinence from the slightest mention of errors in conduct or opinion" by himself or anyone else represents West's failure of authority, symptomatic of a "habitual and somewhat overstrained anxiety . . . to displease nobody."[140] The *British Critic* openly set West up. The four pages on Galt's biography follow twelve that conclude the journal's previously initiated review of a life of Michelangelo, a coupling for which the reviewer apologized, noting "the luster even of the brightest planet is extinguished as it approaches the sun." Compounding the insult, just before introducing the biography of West, the writer added that "of the modern English school Sir Joshua Reynolds was the founder, and his works still remain its greatest glory."[141] *Eclectic Review* proposed that Galt had been "meditating a history of the Arts in England," in which he could not figure out how to accommodate the "singularly remarkable" American portion of West's life. Accordingly, this writer assigned Galt more control and responsibility than did most reviewers, but that response was unusual among Britons.[142] Galt simply reported what West told him, asserted Allan Cunningham, whose popular six-volume *Lives of the Most Eminent British Painters, Sculptors, and Architects* (1829–32) – reissued five times by 1908 – proved the most enduring British context for anecdotes from the 1816 biography. The collaborators, moreover, were "intimate friends," inhibiting Galt's ability to place West's recollections in perspective.

Cunningham (like Galt a lowland Scot) took that role on himself, turning a number of reported incidents against a subject he viewed as blinded, albeit "amiably," by extravagant vanity. An Italian *improvisatore* who extolled the promise of the young American and his destined leadership in the arts is, in Cunningham's reimagining, in cahoots with a "wily Scot" (painter Gavin Hamilton, a period-appropriate substitute for Galt), who proposed West as the subject for a song: "West, who never in his life conceived what a joke meant, sat grave and steady like one of his own sitters, while the minstrel unslung his guitar, and, with a glance that told Hamilton he knew what to do, burst into song. At first he was something mystical, till he saw that his subject had a reasonable gift of credulity, and then he tried plainer words . . . On the raving of this wily mendicant, West bestowed both money and tears; and even in riper years he was willing to consider this as another prophecy." Cunningham added: "West cannot be born, nor choose his profession, nor enjoy himself in a coffee-house, nor travel through France without the influence or the accompaniment of prediction," though he granted that West's belief in predestination "did no one any harm, and himself some good."[143] The basic story of West's encounter with the bard had originated with the artist, according to William Dunlap, who published the anecdote three years before Galt did. Dunlap neither cloaked the event in solemnity (as Galt would do) nor used it to ridicule West (Cunningham's approach). Instead, he expressed irritation with "a vagabond Italian rhymster treating us as savages," "one among the many thousand instances of the profound ignorance in which Europeans generally remain respecting this country."[144] Galt's *Life of West* did little to set the record straight.

In the United States, reviewers were more divided about the relative responsibilities of subject and author but showed no greater inclination than their British counterparts to endorse the fabulous passages in Galt. *Analectic Magazine, and Naval Chronicle* issued the first assessment in September 1816, just two months after printing a biographical article based on earlier British accounts of West. The journal title had been expanded that year, after editor Thomas Isaac Wharton began a history of the United States Navy. For Wharton, the military and artistic conjunction made sense, since he believed American skill in both gunnery and fine arts arose from a particularly American acuity of sight. *Analectic* publisher Moses Thomas, for his part, had every reason to draw attention to Galt's *Life of West*, since he was in the process of bringing out an American edition. Characteristically for the period, the review either described or quoted Galt's text, with minimal evaluation. In general, the writer found Galt's narration "plain and simple . . . without any ambitious metaphors or affected antitheses," if somewhat too much "reverence" on the part of the author, who appeared too readily "inclined to make miracles of ordinary occurrences."[145]

North American Review saw the matter a bit differently, objecting to the "style" of narration in the biography, its "appearance of inflated vanity." Expressions that the writer would have considered "only justice" if West were deceased seemed "misplaced" during the artist's lifetime, "apt to implicate him in Mr. Galt's want of taste."[146] Similarly, *Portico* found "abundant evidence, to say nothing of the compiler's avowal, that the anecdotes have all been taken from the lips, or from the pen, of Mr. West." "We are proud of him *as our countryman*," the writer granted, "but we cannot consent to believe that the fruit appeared before the blossom," as if West sprung from nothing but his own special destiny, as Galt's *Life of West* represents. The review implicated West in authorship of his exceptionalist history.[147]

So did *Port Folio*, in a somewhat more forgiving vein. An epigraph on the subject of puffery opened the journal's review of January 1817, dialogue drawn from Richard Brinsley Sheridan's 1779 play *The Critic*: "And do you think there are any who are influenced by this? Oh lud! Yes, sir; – the number of those, who undergo the fatigue of judging for themselves, is very small indeed."[148] Judging, the American reviewer continued, is nearly impossible – "There is something in the fortunes of Mr. West so peculiar, that credulity readily seizes the sceptre, because reason is almost unable to accompany his rapid career to wealth and fame."[149] Galt's book, in short, would have certain impact on how people remembered West – or came to know him in the first place. With a sense of humor and only a little impatience, the reviewer dismissed a few episodes from the biography. The story of a minister who predicted West's fame at his birth was "really too ridiculous to claim our attention." A minor detail about provisions left for nocturnal wayfarers by the boy's innkeeper father betrayed the author's unfamiliarity with Quaker customs (they never did practice "such prodigal benevolence") as well as the subject's "fond and romantic enthusiasm" for days of his youth. *Port Folio* teased West lightly on other points. The artist's negative opinion of New York, formed during a painting trip during his youth, showed that he "is still a Philadelphian." His effort to capture the nocturnal effect of a Flemish picture by placing his model in a dark closet with candle in hand demonstrated that "genius, though often baffled, is never overcome." If Galt's book "drops the curtain" at the point of West's departure for England, the reviewer does not. He concludes by relating how West, years earlier during the Revolution, expressed regret for an American battle loss while in the presence of George III. West was on his way to being reclaimed as an American.

In the years immediately following West's death in 1820, some Americans continued to revisit the matter of the artist's nationality and to question his importance, though in contexts somewhat less readily available to compatriots than *Port Folio*. *Randolph: A Novel* (1823) offered extended commentary on West, among other American painters, framed in letters from an American gentleman to a British correspondent. Author John Neal emerged during that decade as an independent-minded critic and an influential proponent of literary and artistic nationalism. But he was no fan of West. Acknowledging near "blasphemy," his alter-ego in *Randolph* lambasted *Christ Healing the Sick* as "a miserable failure" and mocked the laudatory pamphlet on that work that had also been severely criticized in *Port Folio*, a magazine Neal well knew as founder of the Baltimore literary magazine *Portico* (1816–18). Neal poked fun as well at the competing claims to "Sir Benjamin," having his American character remind the Briton that "Mr. West" is American," though he adds: "I am not boasting of this."[150] In essays published in 1824 and 1825, during a residence in London, Neal went further, pronouncing West's "reputation much greater than he deserved" and predicting that "his fame will not increase; it will diminish."[151] The utter collapse of West's reputation in England is evident in a history of British art of 1861 that both acknowledged and stingingly dismissed the artist's self-conception: West "looked on himself as a sacred being, and the founder of English Art."[152]

Nearly two decades after Galt's life of West first appeared, the book and its decisive presentation of West as American were absorbed into the history of American art, through the long biography devoted to West in *History of the Rise and Progress of the Arts of Design in the United States*. Author William Dunlap, already a noted playwright and historian of the American theater, had been a student of West's during the 1780s and, intermittently, a painter himself. When Dunlap began writing his account of American art in 1832 – framed as a sequence of biographies – he was deeply involved in art world politics. As a founder (1825) and vice-president (1831–38) of the National Academy of Design, Dunlap squarely opposed a more elitist organization in which he had once been active, the American Academy of the Fine Arts (established 1802). The National Academy positioned itself as the champion of working artists, with a primary goal of providing instruction that the American Academy effectively denied. In his *History*, Dunlap reserved harsh words for artists who did not offer assistance when they could, while he honored others whose active mentoring helped nurture American art.[153] As a teacher, West had no peers, and Dunlap could with good reason pronounce his effect on American art "incalculable."

Dunlap composed West's biography at the very start of his writing process, making it the foundation and touchstone of his subsequent efforts in composing his history of "the rise and progress" of American art.[154] Though profiles of eight painters precede West's, Dunlap's opening assertion that West was "indigenous" immediately set him apart. The distinction meant something more than "born here," since the author had already indicated that Nathaniel Smibert had been "born and died in America."[155] For Dunlap, West exemplified qualities of virtue, industry, and talent, which the first pages of his book emphatically defined as the only criteria of personal superiority in the United States. Never mind that West was a British courtier and never lived in the independent United States; he lived by American principles, absorbed from American soil, where "from the very first settlement of this country, the germs of republican equality were planted."[156] Without Galt's *Life of West*, Dunlap would have been challenged to develop a credible profile of West as an "indigenous" artist. He collected much of his information for the book by querying persons who knew his subjects and the subjects themselves if still alive. But West had died over a decade before the project began. The many students who contributed recollections of their mentor apparently did so without commenting on Galt's version of West's American life – perhaps as much from reluctance to challenge the authorized biographer as from lack of information. Dunlap, however, had no qualms about doing so and, unlike most English and some American reviewers, blamed the more "absurd tales" in Galt's volume not on West himself but on the "most injudicious biographer." Expressing "hope" that he could "separate the poetry from the facts," Dunlap mined the biography for both, thereby perpetuating even those incidents he was inclined to deny.[157]

Dunlap concluded his narrative of West's life on a curiously defensive note, as if a credible case for the artist's superiority depended on acknowledgment of the contrary position. But he let others state the problem. In Britain, according to Sir Martin Archer Shee, the Royal Academy president in 1834, West "is unsparingly censured where he fails, and is allowed little credit where he has succeeded. He is tried, not by his merits, but by his defects, and judged before a tribunal which admits only evidence against him . . . few artists have been less favoured by fortune, or more ungenerously defrauded of their fame." Shee's defense of West takes up the last four, uninterrupted pages of Dunlap's profile of the artist. "Who will hesitate to acknowledge," Shee asked finally, that West ". . . well merits to be considered, in his peculiar department [history], the most distinguished artist of the age in which he lived?" The question completes the body of Dunlap's text on West. Rather than allowing it to resonate with the reader, Dunlap added a curious footnote, in which he gave Sir George Beaumont, West's longtime patron and supporter, the last, dispiriting words: "'*I am ashamed of the recent ungrateful neglect of my countrymen, – it surprised and grieved me.*'"[158] By highlighting British negativity at the conclusion of West's biography, Dunlap implicitly challenged Americans to do the right thing by honoring West, following his own example in *History of the Arts of Design*, as founding father of the American painting tradition.[159]

The course of painting in the United States attenuated that connection in ways that Dunlap, nearly seventy when his book appeared, glimpsed but could not fully anticipate. Landscape and genre gained a popularity never enjoyed by historical subjects, and by the mid-nineteenth century, American artists of the colonial and early national periods seemed to many irrelevant. Writers who continued to pay tribute to West felt obliged to confront the instability of his reputation. C. Edwards Lester excavated Beaumont's lament from the footnote at the end of Dunlap's West biography and made it the epigraph to his own chapter on the painter in *The Artists of America* (1846). "It has been the fashion in this country to speak slightingly of West," Lester acknowledged, but this was simply wrong; West, he declared, was "the pioneer and father of American Artists."[160] In a much broader and intellectually more ambitious context, James Jackson Jarves was equally emphatic about West's importance: "Americans owe him a statue . . . for asserting to the world the aesthetic capacity of a newly fledged race . . . He quickened our blood into aesthetic life."[161] Jarves could and did speak of the world – he had been living in Italy for more than a decade, and *The Art-Idea* (1864) advanced his idiosyncratic theory and history of western art – but he spoke to Americans (the book was published in New York and Boston) and devoted half the text to American painting, sculpture, architecture, cityscapes, and art institutions. Jarves, like Dunlap, granted West a privileged indigenousness. He dismissed Copley as "American only by birth," and "in every other respect . . . thoroughly English." West (whom Jarves thought would have been "more original in invention and national in motives" by remaining on American soil) had, on the other hand, made his mark as the country's "first-born artist, fresh from the wilderness of the New World." Jarves introduced no details of West's life in his brief discussion, but there can be little doubt that his image of the artist had been shaped by Galt's tale of the charmed American boy.

More than a century after Galt helped West reinvent himself as an American, James Flexner built on that foundation to perform the same task in *America's Old Masters*, a book designed for general readers. When he began his research in the late 1930s, Flexner recalled, "the English dismissed [West] as an American, and the Americans . . . denounced him as an unpatriotic English artist."[162] Some authors of American art survey texts published during the first half of the twentieth century would gladly have excluded West, who had "nothing at all in common with the development of American art," in the opinion of Sadakichi Hartmann, an early twentieth-century advocate for a distinctly native vision. Suzanne LaFollette, in a pioneering social history of American art, echoed the opinion but pointed up the conundrum: "West's whole career, although it began in this country, really belongs to the history of English rather than American painting, and would have no place in a discussion of American art if it were not for his peculiar relation to the American painters of the late eighteenth and early nineteenth centuries." Oskar Hagen characterized that influence as "fatal."[163] West's undeniable role as mentor, for better or worse, prevented historians from ignoring him. Nor could they deny the durability of the West myth. As Samuel Isham noted in 1905, the artist's life had been "worked into a sort of tradition . . . known to thousands who never saw one of his pictures." "The story is a remarkable one," he added, "but it has been aided greatly in popularity by telling."[164] Isham, one of the first writers since Dunlap to give serious consideration to earlier American artists, recognized the degree to which Galt's "style [was] in harmony with his subject," and he granted the Scottish author the same awareness. He drew on the biography as freely as other writers, yet maintained a critical perspective that was quite unusual. Flexner, for his part, later decided he had been taken in by West's "senile reminiscences" and "desire to be considered an incarnation of the 'Noble Savage.'"[165] Still, even the 1967 revised edition of his book continued the tradition of preserving colorful stories from Galt's biography. In the rapid expansion of American art history as a scholarly discipline, beginning in the later 1960s, the literature on West increased dramatically. Americanists came to accept him, without apology or censure, as an important figure in the history of the nation's art. Observing the situation from outside the specialized field in addressing the hoary question of "what is American in American art?," Robert Rosenblum stated in 1990 that West "is worshipped as an American ancestral figure." This suggests a reverence not actually representative of recent scholarship but does reflect the sustained commitment by Americanists to the study of West – even though, in Rosenblum's opinion, "it would be hard to be more British" than he.[166] This was West's position, too, until his collaboration with Galt decisively altered that course.

Instrumental in stirring the old artist's memories, open to the lapses, ready to imagine, and, above all, interested (in both senses of the word), John Galt helped West secure his place in history. West provided the details, while Galt persuaded him of their importance and imposed a chronological terminus on the narrative, arguing in favor of confining the biography to West's formation as an artist. West himself had been uneasy about ending the story there; he pressed Galt to compose a sequel and examined the last proof "on his death bed," according to the biographer.[167] Galt's account of West's English career, with the exception of a few incidents, has proven less indelible; on that subject, other contemporaries, especially Farington, are more provocative and interesting. But no historical reconstructions of West's years in America and study in Italy, no matter how many emendations to Galt they may provide, have banished the picture of the artist that Galt drew in 1816. West earned his prominent place in American art history as a mentor, but he also created it, working together with John Galt in a public relations effort of enormous consequence for the history of American – and, arguably, also of British – art.

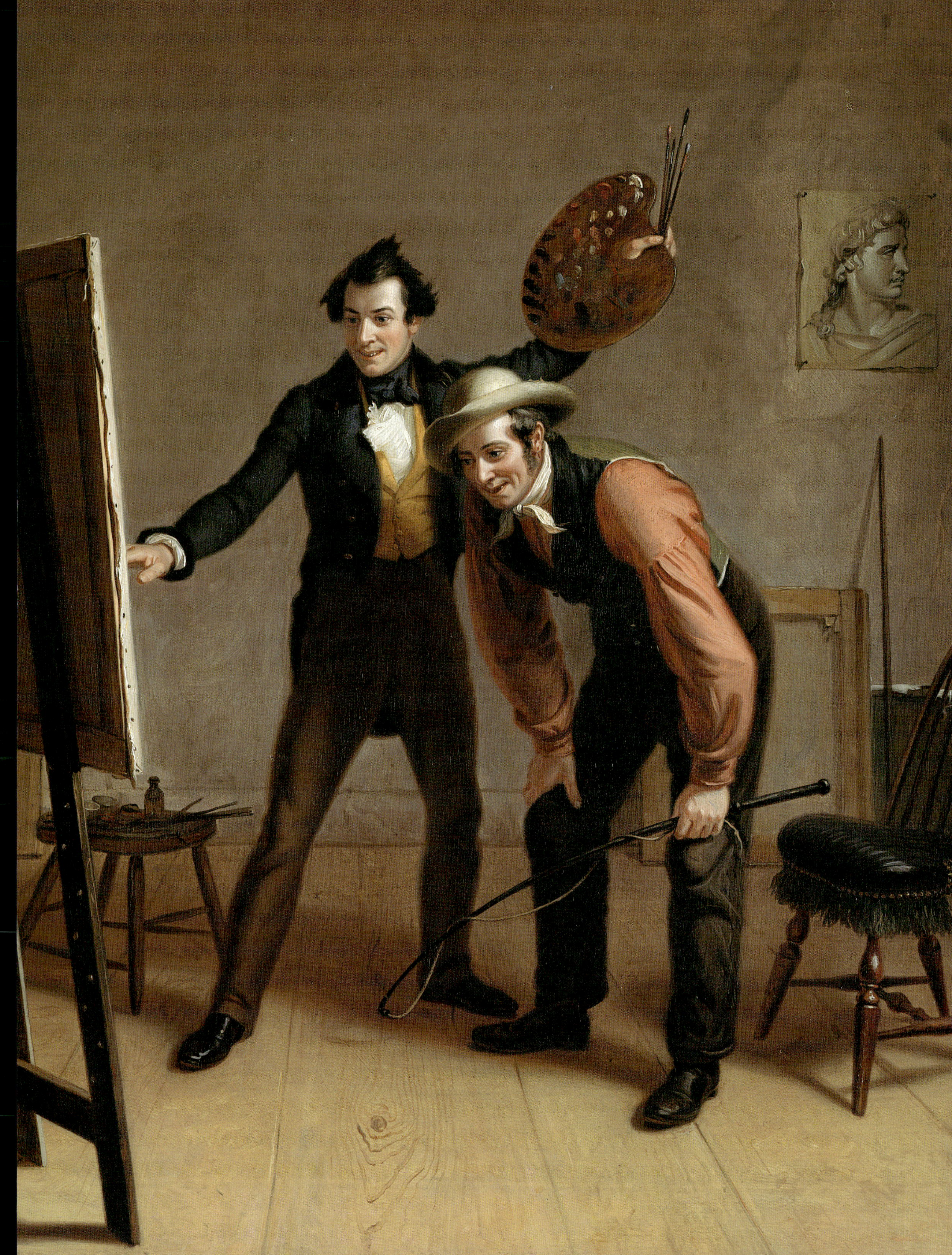

CONCLUSION

What was American in American art – or, more to the point of this book, what was American about American artists – remained elusive even to would-be boosters for fully half a century after independence. Americans came from everywhere. "In the commencement of our history as colonies, every painter was from beyond the sea," Dunlap wrote in the introduction to his *History of the Rise and Progress of the Arts of Design in the United States*, "but no sooner did native artists appear than their works exceeded in value immeasurably, [those of] the visitors who preceded them."[1] With some inconsistency, Dunlap most celebrated the early "native artists" who eventually steeped themselves in continental traditions on the way to becoming professionals, as if their American birth had prophylactic value. He was less inclined to praise those who had more artisanal careers. Yet he made a serious effort to include every artist for whom he had even a name.[2] Nearly a century after Dr. Alexander Hamilton remarked on Robert Feke's "extraordinary genius" and painter's "Phizz," Feke's name (gleaned from an old canvas) was all that remained, garnering the artist a sentence in Dunlap's account. Another century and a half later, in a history of American colonial painting as thumpingly nationalistic as Dunlap's, Feke was still being identified as the first native-born American genius, a predecessor to Dunlap's "indigenous" West.[3] By that time in the mid-1980s, however, a long-cherished essentialist view of American art had become an anachronism. Scholars looking across the centuries at a much broader spectrum of artists, including women and African-Americans, went beyond mere identification of borrowed motifs to consider not only what American artists took from Britain, Europe, and elsewhere but what and how they gave back. During the late colonial and early national periods, the dominant cultural point of reference for American artists was Britain, but with professional artistic practices there still in formation, American artists had the possibility of affecting those outcomes, or believed they did. If that objective no longer seemed attainable by the 1820s, American artists and their supporters were ready to move on.

Dunlap boldly asserted that independence from British rule brought independence to American artists, too. Under new political and social conditions, they gained the freedom to succeed by virtue and talent, unconstrained by the whims of aristocratic patrons to whom the artist had been little more than a servant, "an appendage to my lord's tailor."[4] Dunlap's phrase reprised complaints by Copley and many another eighteenth-century artist on both sides of the Atlantic. His rosy retrospection was not entirely founded. A rise in status for American artists did not arrive at once, nor did painting acquire the important position in the United States many believed it warranted. In 1800, John Trumbull, decrying indifference to the arts that even educated Americans displayed, turned the tables on Copley's lament. Remonstrating a young man who wanted to abandon study

Facing page Detail of fig. 170.

of law for art, he made his point by referencing not law or even high status occupations like silversmithing but low and dirty trades: "I would sooner make a Son of mine a Butcher or a shoemaker, than a Painter."[5] Roughly a decade later, Rembrandt Peale used bitter words and irony to ward off a mother who sought him as a teacher for her son: "This is not the road to wealth. Let him apply himself industriously at carpentering or shoemaking and he will become rich, but never by painting."[6]

Unfortunately for painters, the association of their work with hand labor, and especially with the work of tailors, proved remarkably durable. The opening epigraph to my study highlighted the prominence of both in Peter Manigault's report of his decision-making process when choosing a portraitist in 1751. In 1783, another young lawyer, also writing to his mother, had similar concerns. Bushrod Washington, nephew of the future president, believed that Charles Peale would provide "the most striking likenesses," while Henry Benbridge offered the advantage of "elegant and superior Drapery." Giving the lie to his professed belief that likeness mattered most, Washington chose Benbridge. Americans still shared those priorities as late as 1832, according to Frances Trollope, the caustic English chronicler of American ways: "From all the conversations on painting, which I listened to in America, I found the finish of drapery was considered as the highest excellence, and next to this, the resemblance in a portrait."[7] Bushrod Washington had been swayed in his decision by a socially prominent Philadelphian, who argued further for the value of Benbridge's continental experience. That artist, the young man reported in turn, had "every improvement . . . study, and travelling could procure – He has seen all the finest paintings . . . and his taste could not fail of being highly improved – Besides he has paints brought with him from Italy, which Peale cannot procure –."[8] The last point in Benbridge's favor, tellingly, concerned materials valued independently of whatever skill the artist might have in using them, an artisanal rather than artistic measure of value.

In 1811, Yale graduate Samuel F. B. Morse remarked that, among Americans, painting was "only thought to be an employment suited to a lower class of people."[9] His decision to pursue painting as a career was thus far from an obvious choice, and he wasted no time in traveling to London where art and artists commanded considerably greater respect. Some forty-seven years after Pratt, Morse became one of the last students mentored by West. Predictably, he gravitated to history painting. West's artistic powers still seemed formidable to Morse, who had younger American role models

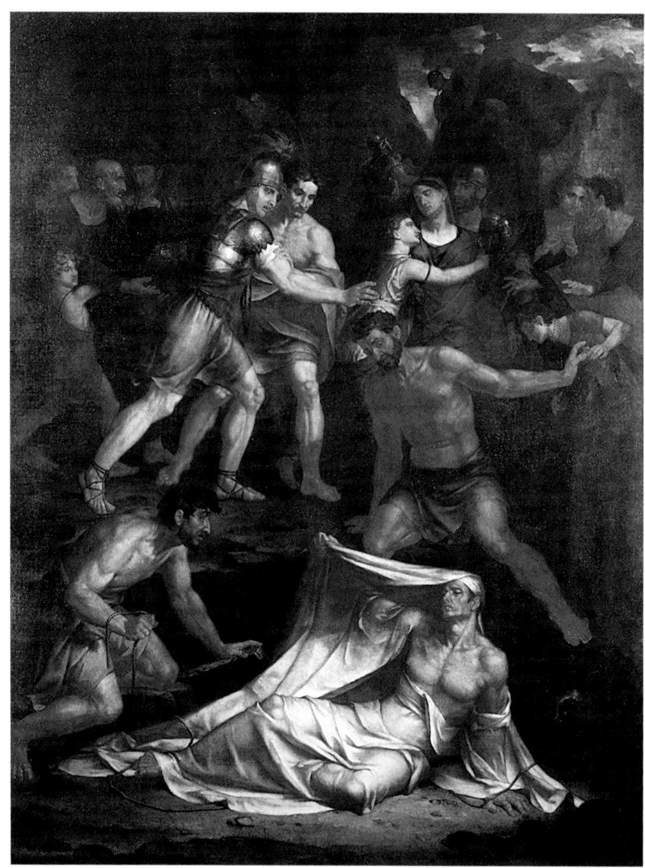

167 Washington Allston, *The Dead Man Restored to Life by Touching the Bones of the Prophet Elisha*, 1811–13. Oil on canvas, 156 × 122 in. (396.2 × 309.9 cm). Courtesy of the Pennsylvania Academy of the Fine Arts, Philadelphia. Pennsylvania Academy Purchase, by subscription.

as well, especially Washington Allston, whose *Dead Man Restored to Life by Touching the Bones of the Prophet Elisha* (1811–13) garnered considerable praise when shown at the British Institution in 1814 (fig. 167). Allston, another West pupil whom Morse (slightly more than ten years younger) considered his teacher, had graduated from Harvard, so Morse would be justified in thinking things were looking up. After his return to the United States in 1815, however, Morse found employment for little other than portraits. Just like Copley so many years before, he considered portrait making to be "throwing away the talents which Heaven has given me for the higher branches of art."[10]

Yet unlike Copley and others in the first half century following independence, Morse gained an unprecedented opportunity to change the direction of American art, when he became first president of the new National Academy of Design in 1825. The organization was to be of, by, and for artists, in opposition to the older American Academy of the Fine Arts, also based in New York. Trumbull, its president at that same time, stated his opposition to allowing young artists to sketch from plaster casts at the American Academy on grounds that "*the gentlemen* have gone to a great expense in importing casts" and students "have no property in them . . . They must remember that beggars are not to be choosers." A more contemptuous characterization could hardly be imagined. Dunlap (who reported overhearing the remark) may be an unreliable narrator, since in the interim he had become professor of historical composition at the National Academy.[11] The impediment Trumbull threw up seems almost inexplicable, irreconcilable with his valorization of history painting – to which study of ancient statuary remained fundamental – and his view that portraiture was no better than cabinet-making, potentially "exquisite" but fundamentally unintellectual.[12] Almost inexplicable but not quite, since Trumbull had by then more stake in being a gentleman, a status more readily shored up by his military career and intermittent diplomatic service than by painting, especially as he had of necessity made many portraits. In his 1841 autobiography, the eighty-six-year-old "Colonel" John Trumbull accordingly placed proportionately greater weight on non-artistic pursuits. No one could deny the momentousness of the American Revolution and the republican experiment in the early United States, whereas the social status of artists had remained unstable for much of Trumbull's working career.

Morse and his academy – not merely American but "national" – aimed to change that. Among its ambitious goals: provide a place for the instruction, exhibition, and professional cultivation of American artists; promote the relevance and even necessity of art and artists to society at large; encourage the creation of a national art worthy of international respect and freed from invidious comparisons with European art. Exhibitions were to feature "Original Works by Living Artists, never before Exhibited by the Academy," in challenge to the American Academy, hyperbolically condemned in 1828 for showing "the *huge* copies, and the *little* copies, the *whole* copies and *half* copies, and *good* copies and *bad* copies."[13] While portraits still dominated at early exhibitions of the National Academy, newspaper commentators openly questioned the status quo. One wondered whether it was bad taste or egotism that led so many Americans to prefer "the daily contemplation of their own physiognomy, to the sublime and beautiful scenery of their native country, fresh from the true and vivid pencils of Doughty and Cole."[14]

Like William Williams more than fifty years earlier, the largely self-taught, English-born-and-raised Thomas Cole had been an itinerant portraitist, experimented with historical and genre subjects, painted stage scenery and transparencies, and executed some decorative work. But his career took off after three novel wilderness landscapes displayed in a New York book and print shop were acquired by Trumbull, Dunlap, and the prominent engraver Asher B. Durand. Dunlap related the circumstances in the *New-York Evening Post* (November 22, 1825), for which he used the fitting pseudonym "American" to present a New World discovery story.[15] Promoted especially by Trumbull, Cole, then only in his mid-twenties, quickly rose to eminence among the old Federalist aristocracy with a genre poised for popularity in the United States.[16] Most patrons wanted American scenes from Cole; however, in acknowledgment of his genius, some acceded to his own strong preference for imaginative landscapes that fulfilled the didactic aims of history painting, the academically admired genre that excited few, whether in either the United States or Britain. Cole received greatest latitude from self-made men like Luman Reed, who built his fortune in wholesale dry goods and gave Cole free rein in the ambitious five-canvas series *The Course of Empire*, intended for the gallery he added to his impressive home. Reed's modest beginnings likely inhibited him from imposing judgment on an artist already favored among the elite. Instead, Reed's commission to Cole in 1833 conferred prestige on him, as if (though he could not have known this example) he might be liberated from the sneering characterization of grocers by the critic who thought Stuart made Reynolds look like one of them, "uninteresting, vapid." Another retired dry goods merchant, Rufus Lord, commissioned a picture to hang over the parlor mantel in his new house in New York, so he was particular about the size but not the subject. The two men met in Florence in 1831, where Cole was two years into a three-year stay abroad, at just the time when travel to Italy had decisively eclipsed more formalized study in Britain. Accordingly, Cole tendered an Italianate landscape with ruined tower, a work of imagination that may have been acceptable to the patron given the long history of fanciful overmantels. But when later commissioning a companion scene, Lord made clear that he wanted American scenery. Cole, in choosing Crawford Notch in New Hampshire as that subject, still managed to satisfy the demands of history painting (fig. 168). Only two years before his first visit there, a massive landslide had killed a family living at the Notch when they fled their home, which was left untouched – "a

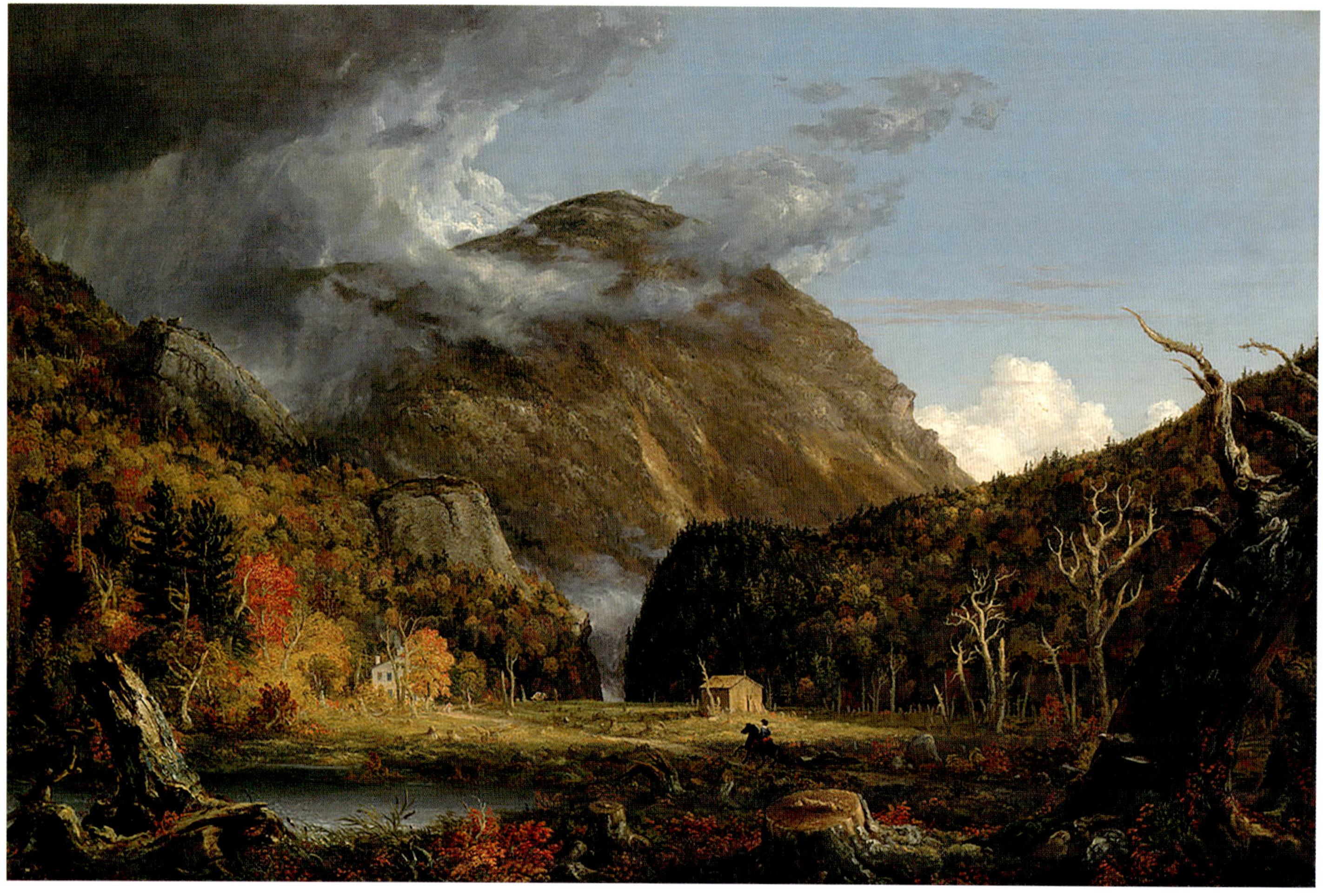

168 Thomas Cole, *A View of the Mountain Pass Called the Notch of the White Mountains (Crawford Notch)*, 1839. Oil on canvas, 40 3/16 × 61 5/16 in. (102 × 155.8 cm). National Gallery of Art, Washington, D.C., Andrew W. Mellon Fund.

dreadful mystery," Cole wrote in his journal, and a reminder that men were "as worms" before nature's power.[17] In a single canvas, Cole lacked the ability for narrative expansion available to Nathaniel Hawthorne when he composed "The Ambitious Guest," a morality tale inspired by the same event.[18] But in *A View of the Mountain Pass Called the Notch of the White Mountains (Crawford Notch)* the artist nevertheless employed various pictorial strategies to stimulate meditations on human frailty. Yet Cole was frustrated, echoing (as so many had) Copley's words of eight decades earlier, when he wrote in the mid-1840s: "I am not the artist I should have been, had taste been higher. For instead of indulging myself in the production of works such as my feelings & fancy would have chosen – in order *to exist* I have painted to please others."[19]

For American artists during the second quarter of the nineteenth century, far more than previously, new opportunities to market their work offered freedom from individual patrons, but not freedom from pleasing if they wanted to sell their works. For Morse, sale of his most ambitious painting was the unhappy outcome of not attracting the public he hoped to educate with *Gallery of the Louvre* (1832–33), an art history lesson for Americans with nationalist intent (fig. 169).[20] The enormous space Morse depicted (in fact, the Salon Carré) had been transformed into a gallery of French art shortly before he revisited it in 1832, but the artist, who disliked modern French art, repopulated the room with established Old Masters. He meant them to inspire but not to limit what modern American artists might do. Morse made that point, born out in his other works and writings on art as Academy president, with some subtlety in *Gallery of the Louvre*: the man painting a landscape in the left foreground, the only visible work among several in progress, appears not to be copying anything on

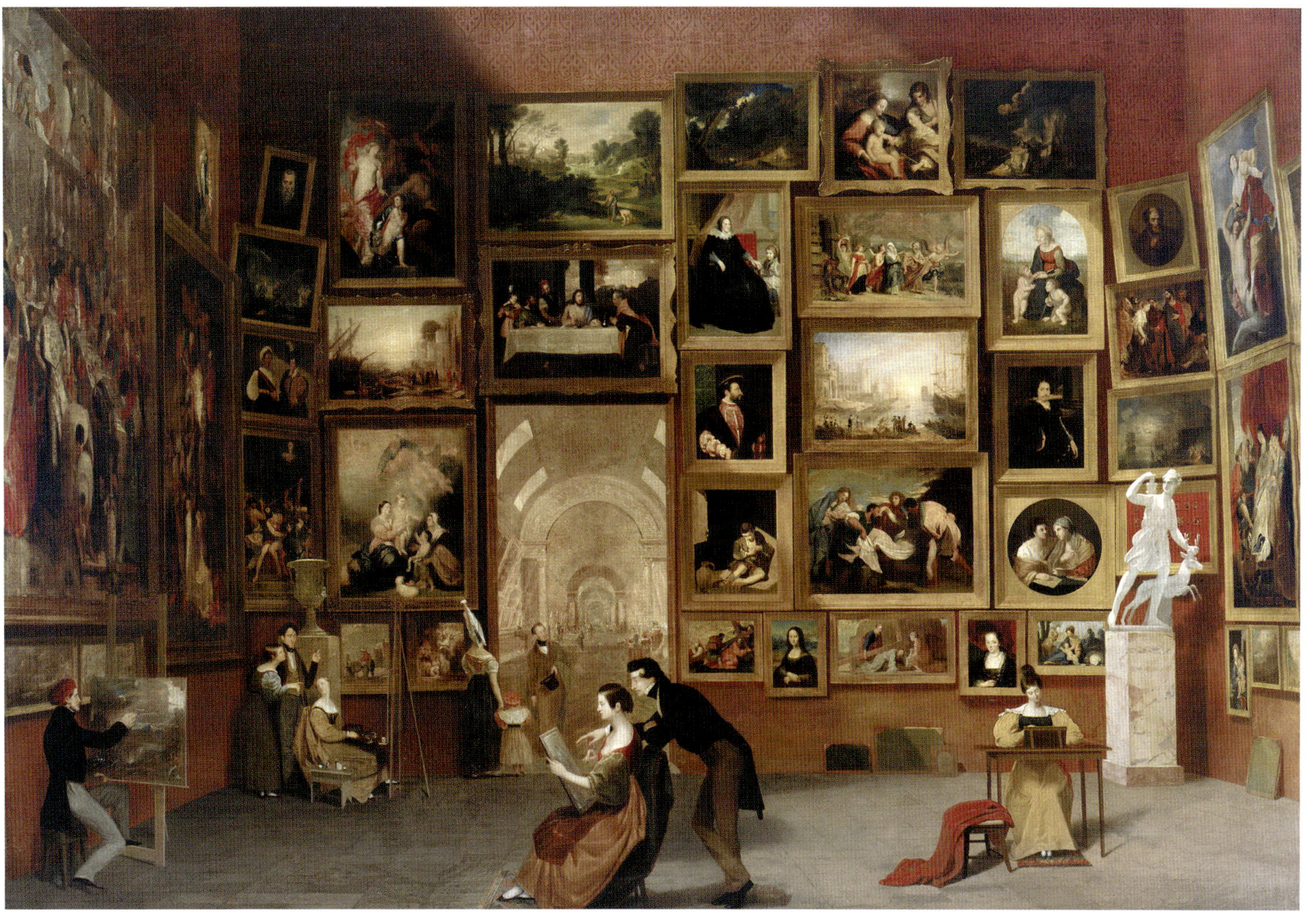

169 Samuel F. B. Morse, *Gallery of the Louvre*, 1832–33. Oil on canvas, 73¾ × 108 in. (187.32 × 155.73 cm). Terra Foundation for American Art, Chicago/Art Resource, N.Y.

the walls, while the woman at right sits at a miniaturist's work table. Although pictorial records of later eighteenth-century Royal Academy exhibitions show miniatures on the walls beneath huge historical canvases and other works (as in fig. 124), Morse included none among his imagined exempla. The miniaturist, working in a traditionally acceptable genre for women, is among three women artists in the scene – a proportional misrepresentation of the number of American women artists then, but a herald of their exponential increase during the last third of the century. That growth was aided, though Morse could not have predicted it, by the many opportunities American women found for study and advancement in Paris, art capital of the western world by 1870. Morse's own recent pupil from Paris, Susan Cooper, appears at an easel in *Gallery of the Louvre*, in company with her mother and her father, James Fenimore Cooper, Morse's frequent companion in Europe. At the picture's center, Morse leans over the shoulder of another young woman, critiquing her drawing, as the (by then) American Old Master West had done with a young man in Pratt's *American School*. If the point of Pratt's picture, like the fugitive figure on his depicted canvas, faded by comparison to Morse's, it is worth recalling that the colonial artist had a purpose just as ambitious at the time: to present Americans as leaders in a nascent British school. Yet that meaning had been lost at its second known exhibition in 1811 in Philadelphia six years after Pratt's death; as "School of West," shortly before publication of Galt's biography, the title projected little that was particularly American. In Dunlap's *History*, despite his grandly national objectives, it became the "London School of Artists."[21] Morse, who showed *Gallery of the Louvre* at his New York studio with a descriptive catalogue and key (and the further plan of taking it on tour), took care to let audiences know his painting

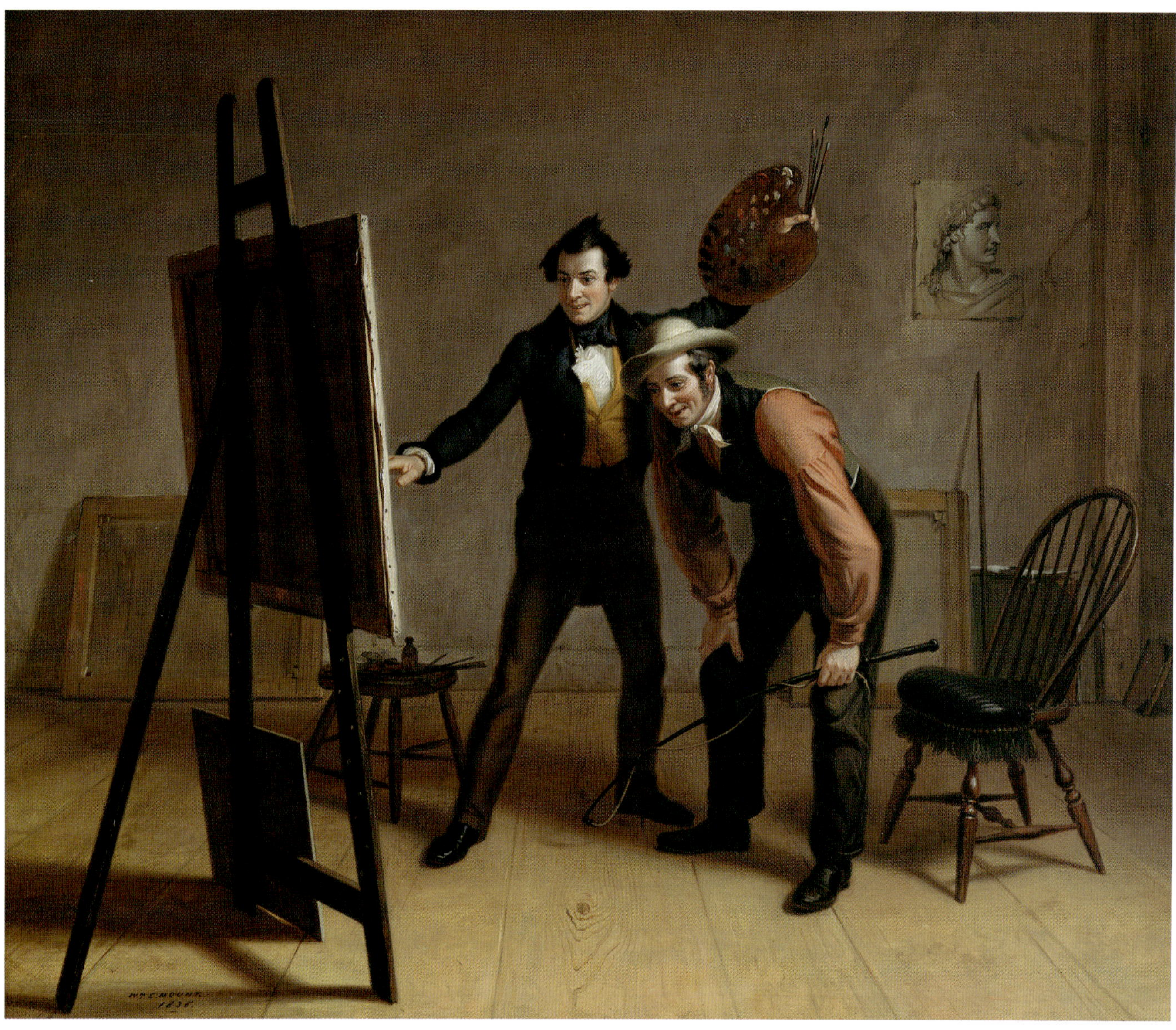

170 William Sidney Mount, *The Painter's Triumph*, 1838. Oil on wood, 23 9/16 × 19½ in. (59.85 × 49.53 cm). Courtesy of the Pennsylvania Academy of the Fine Arts, Philadelphia. Bequest of Henry C. Carey (The Carey Collection).

had meaning for them as citizens of the United States. But few came to see it or comprehended his message, and Morse sold the picture in 1834 to George Hyde Clark, an Englishman who had moved to New York State to oversee vast inherited lands in the Hudson and Mohawk valleys, a legacy of British colonial America.

William Sidney Mount envisioned the American painter's ability to please a new kind of consumer in a picture he prosaically called "Artist showing his own work," now known as *The Painter's Triumph* (1838; fig. 170).[22] Mount's surrogate in this genre scene gestures dramatically toward a canvas on the easel, arms open to a fencer's *en garde* (though the back-weighted stance does not correspond). The upraised left hand brandishes brushes and a palette, turned fully and unapologetically to the picture plane, while the extended right hand points out a detail low on the canvas for the benefit of delighted visitor. His clothing identifies him as a farmer, one who has just stopped by the artist's studio, judging from the whip he still holds. The picture as a whole has been read as a wink to city audiences by Mount, whose Long Island clients – "mugs" in his words, "muffin-faces" to a newspaper critic – preferred the portraits that still then made his living.[23] Yet the painting forthrightly presents the farmer's enthusiasm for a canvas that, even turned away from the viewer, does not readily suggest a portrait. The participants focus on an area below the point at which a portrait subject's face would appear. Notwithstanding Mrs. Trollope's recent disparagement of American fixation with drapery in portraits, it seems implausible that a detail of clothing would arouse such excitement. A small board propped against the easel, as if for comparison, also tends to rule out a portrait, for which few painters made studies. Mount declared that "a painter's studio should be every where, wherever he finds a scene," whether "in doors or out . . . in the black smith's shop, the shoe maker's, the tailor's"; above all, he liked to work under "the canopy of heaven . . . the most perfect paint room for an *artist*."[24] In sum, the large canvas must be the type of subject that Mount showed at exhibition: rural genre scenes. His country neighbors may not have appreciated such works if, conservatively, they wanted what they had always had (portraits); but they no more desired classical and historical subjects than did metropolitan patrons, which is to say very little.

In the mostly bare studio Mount depicted, with two other canvases turned to the wall (Mount's usual practice when not actively working on a picture), a drawing pinned to the wall at the upper right is conspicuously exposed.[25] Above an arrow-like mahlstick, it is the head of *Apollo Belvedere*. West, in the early Italian self-portrait drawing, used this most honored ancient sculpture to identify himself with history. The sight of West's historical canvases on exhibition in 1825 in New York – where Mount was then apprenticed to his brother in the trade of sign and ornamental painting – had initially given the young artisan aspirations to paint history. He began his studies by sketching and painting from the antique at the National Academy (since he could not do so at Trumbull's American Academy). Some early efforts attracted favorable notice, but an even more positive reception of several genre subjects a few years later prompted Mount to change course in his submissions to public exhibition. Mount's painting of the artist showing his work might suggest his own lack of interest in European art, except that he is known to have been extremely well informed about historical painters and painting practices. Yet unlike predecessors going all the way back to West and Peale, Mount declined offers from patrons to fund his travel abroad. He showed no greater inclination to do so on his own, perhaps wishing to retain independence in every respect possible. In *The Painter's Triumph*, conceivably a rebuke to Morse, Mount intimates that the European past had limited relevance for the American present. He (and his proxy) could summon the ancients and Old Masters; he just chose not to.

Mount's painting was commissioned by publisher Edward L. Carey, who had the work engraved and reproduced as "The Painter's Study" in *The Gift* for 1840, a type of popular special edition annual, issued, in this case, in a run of 7,500. A short story accompanied the engraving, which in that context illustrated one segment of a narrative that had been composed in response to the image, following customary practice.[26] As it opens, the newly betrothed Herbert Shockley learns that he and an English cousin must marry as a condition of receiving an inheritance, which either party forfeits in not acquiescing. To break the ties of affection, his parents send him to New York, where "the modest sign of R. Sketchly, artist" beckons the youthful amateur. In the studio, he comes upon "Mr. Raphael Sketchly" rhapsodizing to a visiting farmer about the artful naturalism in his painting of a scene near the farmer's home, including "the variety of mellow tints upon that broken plaster on the gable of the house!" (Good painting here makes bad plastering, reversing Manigault's equation of bad painting with good plastering.) "Nat'ral as life," the farmer responds, "but you might have made the gable a bit smarter, for we're a going to mend and whitewash it in the fall." The comment is absurd and makes most sense in the light of criticisms that portraitists endured from clients who objected to some aspect of their pictures and who could withhold payment if not satisfied. The young man intervenes by commissioning a portrait of himself for the English fiancée he has not yet met, and the farmer decides to do likewise for his wife. Although the resulting works please both parties, Sketchly's Irish assistant "O'Blurr" mistakenly sends the farmer's portrait to England. The recipient is horrified by the "vulgar-looking portrait" that seemed to show "an animal" of "unforgivable" American habits of the type "recorded in the veracious pages of Mrs. Trollope." To "escape . . . a matrimonial alliance with a savage!" the young woman marries an English suitor, freeing Shockley to wed his beloved and receive the entire inheritance. But he does the right thing as the story ends, crossing the Atlantic "both to undeceive that lady as to the utter barbarism of her American relations [just as West undeceived the Europeans in 1760], and to enable Herbert to put her in possession of an equal share of the estate . . This act of justice was also one of patriotism, as it prevented an Irish blunder from being mistaken for a Yankee trick." Although the cunning but virtuous Yankee farmer was a stock character on the New York stage, the word Yankee in this instance refers more broadly to an American, here a man full of integrity and "patriotism."[27]

Among those stereotyped in "The Artist's Study" is, of course, the artist, by then a fixture in American popular culture. The writer describes him as belonging to the *genus irritable*, meaning (though the traits barely figure in the story) that he is excessively sensitive, prickly, moody, and so on – qualities that Stuart had helped bind to the persona of "artist" in the United States. The Romantic type of the genius-eccentric found vivid evocation a few years later in Hawthorne's short story "The Artist of the Beautiful," which starkly contrasts a no-nonsense blacksmith and a visionary watchmaker. The watchmaker is a man of refinement, with a "sensitive brain in a mist of indefinite musings," who fashions an animated golden butterfly as evanescent as a dream. Hawthorne found inspiration for the character in his friend Allston, an anxious perfectionist whose inability to complete an ambitious historical work left "half his conception on the canvas to sadden us with its imperfect beauty," a poignant characterization inserted into the fictional work.[28] Allston's death the year before resonated with Hawthorne's tale, and his personal delicacy seems paradoxically fixed in an unfinished portrait of around 1818 by Stuart, a case in which that artist's own habit of leaving work undone perfectly matched its subject.

A younger generation of American artists, those who matured fifty years after independence, may have continued to navigate between varying professional identities, but their sense of American identity was not by then one of the shoals.[29] Abroad and at home, they felt their nationality and saw it emphasized. John Neal, the pioneering American art critic, did it in the flattest possible way for British readers of *Blackwood's Edinburgh Magazine* in 1824 and 1825. Copley "was an American"; "Mr. Trumbull is an American"; and the same for Stuart, Rembrandt Peale, Allston, Morse, and Chester Harding, who began his career in sign painting and by the time of Neal's writing had made his way to London. Neal's discussion of Harding preceded the conclusion in which he put a finer point on the matter: they were all "truly American, in that property which I have chosen to call a serious versatility."[30] Such versatility was born of necessity and, while not unique to the American situation, may have seemed so in London, where Neal was then living. Institutional support for the arts there had a solid, nearly sixty-year history, by contrast to the United States where Neal found fine arts "neglected." He could not know then that the United States was like Britain in the 1760s, poised for dramatic change. Yet by 1829, Neal found reason to brag. "There are more distinguished American painters than are to be found in any one of what are called the modern schools of Europe," he wrote in *The Yankee and Boston Literary Gazette*; "they are better than we deserve; and more than we know what to do with . . . The whole country is on their side now."[31]

American artists were on the side of their country too. Writing from Europe in the early 1840s, veteran engraver Asher Durand confessed a degree of sensory overload by no means uncommon among American travelers abroad. "I can look with admiration and wonder on the beauty and sublimity of the scenes now before me. I can look with gratification and advantage on the great works of art . . . yet when all this looking and studying and admiring shall have an end, I am free to confess that I shall enjoy a sight of the signboards in the streets of New York more than all the pictures in Europe."[32] By the second quarter of the nineteenth century Americans more usually relieved their art exhaustion with thoughts of American nature, but Durand (soon to become a leading landscape painter) identified a homely antidote in signboards. At the time, lettered signs cluttered New York City building facades, pictorial signboards having mostly disappeared. Yet in juxtaposition to the "pictures of Europe," those cannot have been far from Durand's mind. In the simple, direct, artisan-made signboard, Durand glimpsed American artistic beginnings as he chose to imagine them, implicitly non-hierarchical and democratic. He shared in the cultural nationalism of that moment, most famously expressed by Ralph Waldo Emerson in his "American Scholar" address of 1837: "I embrace the common, I explore and sit at the feet of the familiar, the low. Give me insight into to-day, and you may have the antique and future worlds."[33]

Dunlap took the long view, having himself once been (as retrospectively characterized in 1830) "one of those artists who started from his own head," meaning that, at the outset of his career, he was self-taught.[34] So much had changed for artists since his birth in the 1760s, the decade in which Copley, Williams, Pratt, West, and others revealed the many dimensions of artistic practice and status for colonial Britons. In the United States by the 1830s, American artists profited from new institutions, patrons, and marketplaces, while receiving more attention than ever from writers. They could afford to be optimistic. Dunlap's *History* took stock of the paths they followed and, on firmer grounds than Pratt in his hopeful painting, projected a great future for the American school.

NOTES

INTRODUCTION

1 Peter Manigault to Ann Manigault, Apr. 15, 1751, in "Peter Manigault's Letters," Mabel L. Webber, ed., *South Carolina Historical and Genealogical Magazine* 31 (Oct. 1930): 277–78. The painting is now known only through an old black-and-white photograph (Gibbes Museum of Art/Carolina Art Association). Throughout this book, I have retained eighteenth-century spelling, punctuation, and capitalization.

2 Denis Diderot, "My Feeble Ideas About Color," 1765, in *Diderot on Art*, 2 vols., trans. John Goodman (New Haven and London: Yale University Press, 1995), 2: 199. Earlier, in 1708, his compatriot Roger de Piles had placed ability to capture a sitter's coloring at the very heart of the portraitist's enterprise; *Principles of Painting* (London, 1743), 165 (first English translation of *Cours de Peinture par Principes*). Among English artists, see William Hogarth, *The Analysis of Beauty*, ed. Ronald Paulson (New Haven and London: Yale University Press for the Paul Mellon Centre for Studies in British Art, 1997), 87–93, 132–34 (the latter rejected from the original published version), and Sir Joshua Reynolds, *Discourses on Art*, ed. Robert R. Wark (New Haven and London: Yale University Press for the Paul Mellon Centre for Studies in British Art, 1975), 152 (Discourse VIII, 1778).

3 Oliver Millar, *Sir Peter Lely, 1618–80* (London: National Portrait Gallery, 1978), 17. For this reference and other citations to Vertue's notebooks in this paragraph, I have drawn on Robin Simon's discussion of seventeenth- and eighteenth-century studio practices in *The Portrait in Britain and America, with a Biographical Dictionary of Portrait Painters, 1680–1914* (Boston: G. K. Hall; Oxford: Phaidon, 1987), 16, 98–99. Half and whole length referred to standard canvas sizes, which corresponded with three-quarter and full-length representations of sitters.

4 George Vertue, "Vertue Note Books," *Walpole Society* 22 (1933–34): 91.

5 William Hogarth, from Michael Kitson, "Hogarth's Apology for Painters," *Walpole Society* 41 (1966–68), 98, 100; see also 83.

6 Vertue, "Notebooks," 123.

7 Gotthold Ephraim Lessing, *Emilia Galotti* (1772), Act 1, Scene 4. The speaker, an artist, addresses the limitations of painting and the ultimate inability of the hand to do the bidding of the eyes (or mind).

8 Neil Harris, *The Artist in American Society: The Formative Years, 1790–1860* (Chicago: University of Chicago Press, 1966); Lillian B. Miller, *Patrons and Patriotism: The Encouragement of the Fine Arts in the United States, 1790–1860* (Chicago: University of Chicago Press, 1966); Jules Prown, *John Singleton Copley*, 2 vols. (Cambridge, Mass.: Harvard University Press for the National Gallery of Art, 1966). Although sustained study by scholars with university training in art history began in earnest in the 1960s, the literature has deeper roots. See, e.g., Elizabeth Johns, "Histories of American Art: The Changing Quest," *Art Journal* 44 (Winter 1984): 338–44; and Wanda Corn, "Coming of Age: Historical Scholarship in American Art," *Art Bulletin* 70 (June 1988): 188–207. Andrea L. Volpe assessed Harris's scholarly legacy in "The Neil Harris Effect," *Reviews in American History* 38 (Dec. 2010): 636–43.

9 John Davis, "The End of the American Century: Current Scholarship on the Art of the United States," *Art Bulletin* 85 (Sept. 2003): 544–80 (quotation 561). Notable, non-biographical interventions over the ensuing decade include Margaretta M. Lovell, *Art in a Season of Revolution: Painters, Artisans, and Patrons in Early America* (Philadelphia: University of Pennsylvania Press, 2005), and Wendy Bellion, *Citizen Spectator: Art, Illusion and Visual Perception in Early National America* (Chapel Hill: University of North Carolina Press for the Omohundro Institute of Early American History and Culture, 2011).

10 Citations to my prior publications appear in the chapters to which they most closely relate.

11 David Peters Corbett and Sarah Monks, "Anglo-American: Artistic Exchange between Britain and the USA," introduction to a special issue of *Art History* 34 (September 2011): 630–51 (quote at 633). While

contributions to that volume (all but one originating in a 2009 conference) stretched across the nineteenth and deep into the twentieth centuries, the first two essays plumbed transatlantic visual culture at the time of the American Revolution: Sarah Monks, "The Wolfe Man: Benjamin West's Anglo-American Accent," 652–73, and Jennifer L. Roberts, "Failure to Deliver: *Watson and the Shark* and the Boston Tea Party," 674–95. For analytical juxtaposition of two key figures, see Emily Neff with Kaylin H. Weber, *American Adversaries: West and Copley in a Transatlantic World* (Houston: Museum of Fine Arts, Houston, 2013). Wendy Bellion and Mónica Dominguez Torres address continental transmission in "Teaching Across the Borders of North American History," in *A Companion to American Art*, ed. John Davis, Jennifer Greenhill, and Jason LaFountain (London: Wiley-Blackwell, 2015), 193–210. My own essay for that volume, "Painters and Status in Colony and Early Nation," 359–77, offers a brief survey of themes I engage in this book.

12 The identification of empiricism as a distinctively American artistic quality, beginning with Copley, was most influentially presented by Barbara Novak in *American Painting of the Nineteenth Century: Realism, Idealism, and the American Experience* (New York: Praeger, 1969), and had its last major statement in Wayne Craven, *Colonial American Portraiture: The Economic, Religious, Social, Cultural, Philosophical, Scientific, and Aesthetic Foundations* (Cambridge: Cambridge University Press, 1986). Roberts breathed new life into the idea of Copley's empiricism, shaking it free from American essentialism and restoring it to a broader, more complex Enlightenment and transatlantic nexus, as ultimately realized in Jennifer L. Roberts, *Transporting Visions: The Movement of Images in Early America* (Berkeley: University of California Press, 2014). For probing theorization of the case for American exceptionalism beginning in the 1930s and its unacknowledged persistence in even recent scholarship of transnational perspective, see Winfried Fluck, "Transatlantic Narratives about American Art: A Chapter in the History of Art History's Hegelian Unconscious," *Art History* 35 (June 2012): 554–73.

13 David Solkin, *Painting for Money: The Visual Arts and the Public Sphere in Eighteenth-Century England* (New Haven and London: Yale University Press for the Paul Mellon Centre for Studies in British Art, 1993). Pioneering scholarship on West by Edgar Wind, a German émigré to England, did not lead to the artist's resurrection in Britain but certainly contributed to his later elevation among Americanist art historians; "The Revolution of History Painting," *Journal of the Warburg Institute* 2 (Oct. 1938): 116–27.

14 In a study of southern painting that far exceeded anything previously available, Carolyn J. Weekley renounced any aim of "identifying distinctive 'southern' characteristics or a regional aesthetic," and she made clear how much southern artists shared with their northern counterparts; *Painters and Paintings in the Early American South* (Colonial Williamsburg Foundation, Virginia, in association with Yale University Press, 2013), 1–33 (quote at 2). The book is broadly useful for the wealth of information Weekley marshals about painters' practices, amidst details of particular paintings and sitters, in the southern colonies (where, as elsewhere, most surviving works are portraits). In characterizing eighteenth-century American buyers of paintings, Weekley elects not to use the terms "patron" or "patronage" on grounds that those words then connoted more general benefaction or aid as well as "an air of entitlement, privilege, or superiority" (8). Since American clients so often did have those attitudes, even in one-time transactions, I see no reason to discard customary modern usage in referring to those who commissioned paintings interchangeably as customers, clients, or patrons.

15 On Kauffmann, see especially *Angelica Kauffmann: A Continental Artist in Georgian England*, ed. Wendy Wassyng Roworth (London: Reaktion Books, 1992), and Angela Rosenthal, *Angelica Kauffman: Art and Sensibility* (New Haven and London: Yale University Press for the Paul Mellon Centre for Studies in British Art, 2006). With regard to the French eighteenth-century context, Mary D. Sheriff offered exemplary analysis of the problem of the woman artist in *The Exceptional Woman: Elisabeth Vigée-Lebrun and the Cultural Politics of Art* (Chicago: University of Chicago Press, 1996).

16 Memorandum of Johnson, Apr. 18, 1775, in James Boswell, *Boswell: The Ominous Years, 1774–1776*, ed. Charles Ryskamp and Frederick A. Pottle, Yale Editions of the Private Papers of James Boswell (New York: McGraw Hill, 1963), 149. William Hazlitt provided a later male perspective in "On Sitting for One's Picture," in *The Complete Works*, ed. P. Howe, 21 vols. (London and Toronto: J. M. Dent and Sons, 1930–34), 12: 107–16 (essay II).

17 *The Belfield Farm Years, 1810–1820*, vol. 3 of *The Selected Papers of Charles Willson Peale and his Family*, ed. Lillian B. Miller et al., 5 vols. (New Haven and London: Yale University Press for the National Portrait Gallery, 1983–2000), 176. I give full titles when first citing the other volumes – all named in this introduction – but otherwise refer to them only as *Peale Papers* with volume number. For broader art historical consideration, see Angela Rosenthal, "She's Got the Look! Eighteenth-Century Female Portrait Painters and the Psychology of a Potential 'Dangerous Employment,'" in *Portraiture: Facing the Subject*, ed. Joanna Woodall (Manchester and New York: Manchester University Press, 1997), 147–66.

18 At a time of rising interest in women artists and of feminist scholarship, Wright was the subject of a conservative but still remarkable study by Charles Coleman Sellers, *Patience Wright: American Artist and Spy in George III's London* (Middletown, Conn.: Wesleyan University Press, 1976). Wendy Bellion has brought more up-to-date disciplinary perspective to the artist in "Patience Wright's Transatlantic Bodies," in *Shaping the Body Politic: Art and Political Formation in Early America*, ed. Maurie D. McInnis and Louis P. Nelson (Charlottesville: University of Virginia Press, 2011), 15–46.

19 Frederick Douglass, "Negro Portraits," *Liberator* 19 (Apr. 20, 1849), excerpted from Douglass, review of "A Tribute for the Negro," *North Star* (Apr. 7, 1849). Elsewhere in the passage, Douglass more clearly faults white artists, but that does not foreclose on other readings for the quoted sentence, whether intended or not. He preferred photographic portraits, for the presumed impartiality of the camera. See Laura Wexler, "A More Perfect Likeness: Frederick Douglass and the Image of the Nation," *Yale Review* 99 (Oct. 2011): 145–69.

20 *Massachusetts Gazette: and the Boston Weekly News-Letter*, Jan. 7, 1773.

21 Ellen G. Miles suggested the artist may have been Scipio Moorhead, an enslaved man in Rev. John Moorhead's Boston household, and the presumed subject of a poem "To S.M. A Young African Painter, on Seeing his Works," by Phillis Wheatley, another enslaved Bostonian educated and aided in literary pursuits by the Wheatley family; Ellen G. Miles and Richard H. Saunders, *American Colonial Portraits, 1700–1776* (Washington, D.C.: Smithsonian Institution Press for the National Portrait Gallery, 1987), 309–10. A long line of scholars committed to African-American art history have proposed, on thin evidence, that Moorhead drew or painted the portrait of Wheatley engraved for the frontispiece to her celebrated 1773 volume of poetry. This "origin story" of African-American art has been dispatched by Gwendolyn DuBois Shaw, who provides Wheatley's por-

trait (possibly made in London) with a much more thoughtful, iconographically rich context in *Portraits of a People: Picturing African Americans in the Nineteenth Century* (Andover, Mass.: Addison Gallery of American Art, Phillips Academy, 2006), 27–41. No extant paintings can be identified with Scipio Moorhead, but if, as sometimes suggested, he received instruction from Rev. Moorhead's wife Sarah – who advertised that she taught drawing, japanning, and painting on glass (*Boston Evening Post*, Apr. 18, 1748) – then he is not likely to have been the painter who advertised London connections in the same year (perhaps not coincidentally) that Wheatley gained celebrity in London. Eric Slauter reckoned that Scipio Moorhead was then not more than about thirteen years old, in his "experimental portrait" of a man whose historical invisibility arose largely from his enslavement; "Looking for Scipio Moorhead: An 'African Painter' in Revolutionary North America," in *Slave Portraiture in the Atlantic World*, ed. Agnes Lugo-Ortiz and Angela Rosenthal (New York: Cambridge University Press, 2013), 89–116.

22 "Anecdote of Gilbert Stuart," *Boston Musical Gazette* 1:24 (Mar. 20, 1839): 187–88, reprinted from the newspaper *Newport Herald of the Times*. After an iteration in Edward Peterson's *History of Rhode Island* (1853), the story – though resurrected by twentieth-century writers on African-American art – did not again appear in the literature on Stuart until 1999, when Dorinda Evans used it in the introductory paragraph of her monograph on Stuart, as evidence that the artist's preference for portraits had been set very early; *The Genius of Gilbert Stuart* (Princeton: Princeton University Press, 1999), 3. In a society that placed high value on portraits, gravitation to representing faces seems unremarkable – for Stuart or Thurston. It is more interesting to consider the intervening suppression of an account that identified Stuart's formation as a portraitist with a black man.

23 *Baltimore Intelligencer*, Dec. 19, 1798. Despite spelling of the name in this ad, other period documents omit the t.

24 In their chapter "The Question of Joshua Johnston," Romare Bearden and Harry Henderson provided a useful historiographic perspective on efforts to fix the artist's race, which they considered still unverifiable; *A History of African-American Artists from 1792 to the Present* (New York: Pantheon Books, 1993), 3–17. The authors regarded as problematic Carolyn Weekley's well-intentioned presumption of Johnson's African ancestry, in Weekley et al., *Joshua Johnson: Freeman and Early American Portrait Painter* (Williamsburg, Va.: Abby Aldrich Rockefeller Folk Art Center, Colonial Williamsburg Foundation, 1987). Her book nevertheless remains the major presentation of Johnson's work, with as many as eighty portraits attributed to a recognizable hand (including just two of African-American men). Subsequent to these studies, Jennifer Bryan and Robert Torchia discovered chattel records attesting to Johnson's birth to an enslaved black woman and a white man (whose name is spelled both Johnston and, more often, Johnson in the same document), who acknowledged paternity and freed his son at age nineteen; "The Mysterious Portraitist Joshua Johnson," *Archives of American Art Journal* 36:2 (1996): 2–7.

25 William Dunlap, *A History of the Rise and Progress of the Arts of Design in the United States* (1834), 3 vols., ed. Rita Weiss (New York: Dover, 1969), 1: 138, 141, 142 (quotations in this paragraph).

26 James Thomas Flexner, *America's Old Masters: First Artists of the New World* (1939; rev. ed., New York: Dover, 1967).

27 James Thomas Flexner, *Maverick's Progress: An Autobiography* (New York: Fordham University Press, 1996), 245–46. Charles Coleman Sellers, *The Artist of the Revolution: The Early Life of Charles Willson Peale* (Hebron, Conn.: Feather and Good, 1939), followed by the more extensive two-volume edition in *Memoirs of the American Philosophical Society* 23 (1947).

28 David Steinberg, "Review: The Work of Autobiography and the Workings of Conscience," *William and Mary Quarterly*, 3rd ser., 58 (April 2001): 498. Steinberg's review addressed *The Autobiography of Charles Willson Peale*, vol. 5 of *Peale Papers*.

29 *Peale Papers*, 5: 14–17.

30 Charles Carroll to Peale, Oct. 29, 1767; *Charles Willson Peale: Artist in Revolutionary America, 1735–1791*, vol. 1 of *Peale Papers*, 70–71. Peale had earlier announced to another benefactor his plan to study miniature painting, noting that West offered to borrow examples for him to copy; John Beale Bordley, March 1767; ibid., 1: 47–48.

31 John Singleton Copley to Peale, Dec. 17, 1770; ibid., 1: 85–86.

32 For the idea that Peale developed an American aesthetic for American political circumstances, see Brandon Brame Fortune, "Charles Willson Peale's Portrait Gallery: Persuasion and the Plain Style," *Word and Image* 6 (Oct.–Dec. 1990): 308–24; David C. Ward, *Charles Willson Peale: Art and Selfhood in the Early Republic* (Berkeley: University of California Press, 2004), 39–43. The "American Pitt": "Extract of a letter from a gentleman in Newport, to his friend in Philadelphia," *Pennsylvania Gazette*, Apr. 7, 1768.

33 Peale to John Beale Bordley [1770–71], *Peale Papers*, 1: 86. During the eighteenth century, Antonio da Correggio ranked among the most esteemed historical Italian painters.

34 For a contextually rich study of itinerant artists, see David Jaffee, *A New Nation of Goods: The Material Culture of Early America* (Philadelphia: University of Pennsylvania Press, 2010), esp. 1–45, 219–73.

35 *Dunlap and Claypoole's American Daily Advertiser*, Apr. 23, 1794, as cited in *Charles Willson Peale: The Artist as Museum Keeper, 1791–1810*, vol. 2, pt. 1 of *Peale Papers*, 91. On Peale's museum, see David R. Brigham, *Public Culture in the Early Republic: Peale's Museum and Its Audience* (Washington, D.C.: Smithsonian Institution Press, 1995).

36 C. W. Peale, diary entry, July 1804, and Peale to Mrs. Nathaniel Ramsay, Sept. 7, 1804, *Peale Papers*, 2, pt. 2: 728, 752.

37 In his earliest years as a painter, Peale saw the self-portrait of a "Mr. Steele," but even though such works were rare, he was not impressed: "a ½ length Canvas; a full face very like, but of too purple red colour, his right leg across his knee, therefore it was in part a whole length picture"; C. W. Peale to Rembrandt Peale, Oct. 28, 1812, *The Belfield Farm Years, 1810–1820*, vol. 3 of *Peale Papers*, 174.

38 *Peale Papers*, 2, pt. 2: 698.

39 Peale to Rembrandt and Rubens Peale, Mar. 20, 1824, in *Charles Willson Peale: His Last Years*, vol. 4 of *Peale Papers*, 389. Peale's remark encompasses himself as both subject and as maker.

40 *Peale Papers*, 5: xxii–xxiii.

41 Although Ward, *Peale: Art and Selfhood*, asserted the exceptional status of Peale's autobiographical manuscript, he was mistaken in claiming that, even in the mid-1820s, "the genre was almost nonexistent." See, e.g., the rich body of writing mined by Joyce Appleby, *Inheriting the Revolution: The First Generation of Americans* (Cambridge: Belknap Press of Harvard University Press, 2000), and Stephen Carl Arch, *After Franklin: The Emergence of Autobiography in Post-Revolutionary America, 1780–1830* (Hanover, N.H.: University Press of New England, 2001).

42 Whether the documented painter Thomas Smith and the portrait subject are the same man remains an open question, but it is usually accepted on circumstantial evidence. The Worcester Art Museum website provides excellent online entries for paintings in its collection, including thorough and thoughtful discussion of this work.

43 Roger Stein, "Thomas Smith's Self-Portrait," *Art Journal* 44 (Dec. 1984): 316–27.

44 The sensuality and materiality of Smith's self-portrait and of Puritan traditions have been stimulatingly restored by Max Cavitch, "Interiority and Artifact: Death and Self-Inscription in Thomas Smith's *Self-Portrait*," *Early American Literature* 37:1 (2002): 89–117.

45 The point opens a probing analysis of Smibert's work presented by Lovell, who expanded on limiting considerations of the painting as a commemorative group portrait, teasing out its dynamic relationship to Berkeley's venture and its testament to Smibert's sophistication; *Art in a Season of Revolution*, 184–224. For a comprehensive study, see Richard H. Saunders, *John Smibert: Colonial America's First Portrait Painter* (New Haven and London: Yale University Press/Barra Foundation, 1995).

46 "To Mr. Smibert on the Sight of his own Picture," *American Weekly Mercury*, Feb. 19, 1730; "To Mr. Smibert on the Sight of his Pictures," *London Daily Courant*, Apr. 14, 1730. Byles, a nephew of Cotton Mather, was twenty-two when he wrote the poem and on his way to becoming one of the best known writers in colonial New England. His royalist attitudes damned him late in his life, while his literary style perpetuated the scorn afterwards. Paul Giles thoughtfully historicized that marginalization in a brief but probing examination of Byles's art in *Transatlantic Insurrections: British Culture and the Formation of American Literature, 1730–1860* (Philadelphia: University of Pennsylvania Press, 2001), 28–39.

47 Smibert's notebook – maintained from the conclusion of his apprenticeship in 1709 until almost the end of his life and used to record possessions, expenses, and travels as well as commissions – is one of the most important surviving documents for any painter active in colonial America; *The Notebook of John Smibert*, with essays by Sir David Evans, John Kerslake, and Andrew Oliver (Boston: Massachusetts Historical Society, 1969).

48 Among colonial artists, Feke was the relatively early object of study by Henry Wilder Foote, *Robert Feke: Colonial Portrait Painter* (Cambridge, Mass.: Harvard University Press, 1930).

49 Varying dates have been proposed for the self-portrait reproduced here, but it is most likely from the 1740s and not earlier, as Foote believed. In a later self-portrait (Rhode Island Historical Society), Feke probably painted only the head and upper body, with the rest of the composition – including palette and brushes in hand to identify him as an artist – added ca. 1880; see Foote, *Feke*, 140–41.

50 Carl Bridenbaugh, ed., *Gentleman's Progress: The Itinerarium of Dr. Alexander Hamilton, 1744* (Chapel Hill: University of North Carolina Press for the Institute of Early American History and Culture at Williamsburg, Virginia, 1948), 102.

51 "genius, n. and adj". *Oxford English Dictionary* online.

52 *Boston News-Letter*, May 22–29, 1740. Strikingly, the writer acknowledged the transformative power of genius: "some of his Imitations . . . are so exquisite, that tho' we know they are only Paints, yet they deceive the sharpest Shight [*sic*]."

53 Anthony Ashley Cooper, 3rd Earl of Shaftesbury, *Characteristicks of Men, Manners, Opinions, Times*, 3 vols. 2nd ed. (London, 1714), 3:346–91 (quotes at 347, 349).

54 Shaftesbury characterized de Matteis in a letter to Sir John Cropley, Feb. 16, 1712; *The Life, Unpublished Letters, and Philosophical Regimen of Anthony, Earl of Shaftesbury*, ed. Benjamin Rand (London: S. Sonnenschein; New York: Macmillan, 1900), 468–69. Livio Pestilli devoted a chapter to negotiations between Shaftesbury and de Matteis and to versions of *The Judgment of Hercules* in *Paolo de Matteis: Neapolitan Painting and Cultural History in Baroque Europe* (Farnham, Surrey, and Burlington, Vt.: Ashgate, 2013), 115–44 (quote at 128–29; Pestilli's translation). This first monograph on the artist makes clear that, however overlooked by posterity, de Matteis had considerable standing during his lifetime and ample self-esteem.

1 PORTRAIT PAINTING AND STATUS IN BOSTON AND LONDON

1 [William Duff], *An Essay on Original Genius* (London, 1767), 190. Copley [to Benjamin West or Captain R. G. Bruce, 1767?], in *The Letters and Papers of John Singleton Copley and Henry Pelham, 1739–1776* ([Boston]: Massachusetts Historical Society, 1914), 65–66 (hereafter Copley–Pelham Letters). The present chapter updates and expands but does not alter the argument first presented in Susan Rather, "Carpenter, Tailor, Shoemaker, Artist: Copley and Portrait Painting around 1770," *Art Bulletin* 79 (June 1997): 269–90.

2 Jules Prown's foundational study of Copley's career, admirable in its breadth and detail at a time when Copley's British work had barely been studied, nevertheless had the effect of authorizing the division in committing one volume to America and one to England; Jules Prown, *John Singleton Copley*, 2 vols. (Cambridge, Mass.: Harvard University Press for the National Gallery of Art, 1966). Though not conceived to fortify that divide, the chronological coincidence of Carrie Rebora and Paul Staiti et al., *John Singleton Copley in America* (New York: Metropolitan Museum of Art, 1995), and Emily Ballew Neff et al., *John Singleton Copley in England* (Houston: Museum of Fine Arts, 1995), did exactly that in the minds of exhibition reviewers.

3 In a rare departure from the prevailing iconographic reading of Copley's works, Sarah Monks detected compositional continuity across the whole career of an artist whom she provocatively proposed as "estranged" or "alienated" from his own work; "Out of Time, Out of Place: Copley's Last Pictures," in the symposium "In Circulation: John Singleton Copley and Benjamin West in England, France and America," Paul Mellon Centre for Studies in British Art, London, March 28, 2014.

4 Pierre Eugène Du Simitière's list of paintings seen in various Boston homes, ca. 1768, included: "a landskip by Berghem & . . . the deluge having a great number of figures & a very good Madona with the child asleep done by Demina an Italian painter in England about 40 [?] years ago"; "a ceres [?] head an Italian piece by Batista a small head in oyl of Oliver Cromwell, some little battle piece done in a ruff manner . . . , a still life of game"; "pictures done by Sir Peter Lely." At Harvard Hall, Du Simitière took note of three portraits "painted by John Singleton Copley of Boston." Pierre Eugène du Simitière Collection 1492–1784, Papers relating to New England and New York, circa 1774, Library Company of Philadelphia. Regarding Copley's stake in his own provinciality, see Emily Ballew Neff, "Copley's 'Native' Realism and his English 'Improvement,'" in Neff et al., *John Singleton Copley in England*, 12–22.

5 Samuel Johnson, *A Dictionary of the English Language*, 3rd ed., 2 vols. (London, 1765), s.v., "artisan," "craftsman," "liberal," "mechanick." "Artist" and "manufacturer" appear as synonyms in Daniel Defoe, *The Complete English Tradesman* (London, 1745; repr. New York: Burt Franklin, 1970), 2. Alfred F. Young found the terms "artisan" and "craftsman" less frequent than "tradesman" during the colonial period, while "mechanic" was a term of derision and not of pride, as it became during the 1790s; "How Radical Was the American Revolution?," in

Beyond the American Revolution: Explorations in the History of Radicalism, ed. Alfred F. Young (DeKalb: Northern Illinois University Press, 1993), 330–31. See also Thomas J. Schlereth, "Artisans and Craftsmen: A Historical Perspective," in *The Craftsman in Early America*, ed. Ian M. G. Quimby (New York and London: W. W. Norton for the Henry Francis du Pont Winterthur Museum, 1984), 34–61.

6 Anthony Ashley Cooper, 3rd Earl of Shaftesbury, *Second Characters or the Language of Forms*, ed. Benjamin Rand (Cambridge: Cambridge University Press, 1914), 135–36; this work, composed around 1712, remained unpublished until the twentieth-century edition. But see also Shaftesbury, *Characteristicks of Men, Manners, Opinions, Times*, 3 vols. (London, 1732), 1: 144–45.

7 Jonathan Richardson, *An Essay on the Theory of Painting* (London, 1715), 19–38 (quote at 76). Mark A. Cheetham addressed nationalistic purpose in Richardson's writing on art, which he sees as suffused with the example of John Locke, in *Artwriting, Nation, and Cosmopolitanism in Britain: The "Englishness" of English Art Theory since the Eighteenth Century* (Farnham, Surrey, and Burlington, Vt.: Ashgate, 2012), 19–22.

8 For example, Daniel Webb, *An Inquiry into the Beauties of Painting* (London, 1765), 4–5, 35–36. In a letter from Italy in 1775 (*Copley–Pelham Letters*, 303), Copley casually referred his half brother, Henry Pelham, to a passage in Webb, in a manner suggesting their common familiarity with the book prior to Copley's departure from the colonies. For Copley's early exposure to art theory, see Prown, *Copley*, 1: 16–19, and my n. 52.

9 For extended discussion of gentility in late colonial British America, from which I have much benefited, see Gordon Wood, *The Radicalism of the American Revolution* (New York: Alfred A. Knopf, 1992), esp. 21–42. A concise history of the meanings for the word "gentleman" can be found in K. D. Bülbring, introduction to [Daniel Defoe], *The Compleat English Gentleman* (London, 1890), xxxii–xlv (the first publication of this treatise, composed ca. 1728–29).

10 On different ranks, see, e.g., John Adams, "A Defence of the Constitutions of Government of the United States of America," in *The Works of John Adams*, vol. 6, ed. Charles Francis Adams (Boston: Little Brown, 1851), 185. I have avoided references to any social groups under the rubric of "class," the modern understanding of which does not adequately represent the structure of colonial society. On this matter, see Wood, *Radicalism*, 21–24; also Gary B. Nash, *The Urban Crucible: Social Change, Political Consciousness, and the Origins of the American Revolution* (Cambridge, Mass., and London: Harvard University Press, 1979), 243.

11 Gary B. Nash, "Artisans and Politics in Eighteenth-Century Philadelphia" (1984), repr. in Nash, *Race, Class, and Politics: Essays on American Colonial and Revolutionary Society* (Urbana: University of Illinois Press, 1986), 246. For an older, opposing view, see Carl Bridenbaugh, *The Colonial Craftsman* (1950; New York: Dover, 1990), 165.

12 John Styles, *Dress of the People: Everyday Fashion in Eighteenth-Century England* (New Haven and London: Yale University Press, 2007), 74–75 (with other observations on the lowly status of tailors and shoemakers).

13 On the Boston guild, see John R. Commons, "American Shoemakers, 1648–1895: A Sketch of Industrial Evolution," *Quarterly Journal of Economics* 24 (Nov. 1909): 40–41. In Philadelphia, apprenticeship records for Oct. 1771–Oct. 1773 document 100 boys bound to master cordwainers, the largest number of any craft; tailors followed, with 78 new apprentices for the same period; Ian M. G. Quimby, "The Cordwainers Protest: A Crisis in Labor Relations," *Winterthur Portfolio* 3 (1967): 85. Billy G. Smith paid especial attention to shoemakers and tailors in *The "Lower Sort": Philadelphia's Laboring People, 1750–1800* (Ithaca, N.Y.: Cornell University Press, 1990). His grim account of the laborer's lot countered an older belief among historians in colonial social fluidity. The term cordwainer for a maker of new shoes, somewhat old-fashioned by the eighteenth century, derives from association with the Spanish leather-producing city of Cordova; a cobbler, by contrast, worked in old leather as a shoe repairman.

14 Nash, *Urban Crucible*, 313–15.

15 [William Henry Drayton], *The Letters of Freeman, Etc.: Essays on the Nonimportation Movement in South Carolina Collected by William Henry Drayton* (1771), ed. Robert M. Weir (Columbia: University of South Carolina, 1977), 31.

16 Sir James Wright to the Earl of Dartmouth, Dec. 19, 1775, in *Collections of the Georgia Historical Society* 3 (1873), 228.

17 For a definition of this tradition, also known as the discourse of civic humanism, that strongly influenced later twentieth-century scholars, see J. G. A. Pocock, *The Machiavellian Moment: Florentine Political Thought and the Atlantic Republican Tradition* (Princeton: Princeton University Press, 1975). For the Anglo-American context, see Wood, *Radicalism*, 95–124.

18 Quoted in *Gentleman's Progress: The Itinerarium of Dr. Alexander Hamilton, 1744*, ed. Carl Bridenbaugh (Chapel Hill: University of North Carolina Press for the Institute of Early American History and Culture at Williamsburg, Virginia, 1948), 27 (Hamilton's entry for June 12, [1744]).

19 On MacIntosh, see Nash, *Urban Crucible*, 293–300. More generally, E. J. Hobsbawm and Joan Wallach Scott, "Political Shoemakers," *Past and Present* 89 (Nov. 1980), 86–114.

20 William Shakespeare, *King John*, 4.2.193–200.

21 John Wilkes attracted political notoriety and a host of legal troubles with his attacks on George III and the king's ministers in the periodical *North Briton* 45 (1762). He found passionate supporters among the politically weak urban middle and lower classes, who rallied to the cry "Wilkes and Liberty." Declared an outlaw after his flight to France (1764–68), then tried for seditious libel, imprisoned, and expelled from Parliament, Wilkes was nevertheless returned to the House of Commons in spring 1769 by defiant voters, who saw him as a champion of the common people. Parliament unseated him once again, and the controversy continued into the following year. David Solkin speculated that Joseph Wright of Derby's two relatively dignified blacksmith scenes shown with the Society of Artists in 1771 constituted a rebuke to Penny and to the exclusiveness of the Royal Academy, in *Painting for Money: The Visual Arts and the Public Sphere in Eighteenth-Century England* (New Haven and London: Yale University Press for the Paul Mellon Centre for Studies in British Art, 1993), 300 n.46; see 262–66 regarding the implications of the Wilkes affair for contemporary disputes in the London art world. Historian Annabel Patterson reevaluated the politics of Academy president Reynolds, in connection with his portrait practice and *Discourses* (a "formal screen for that practice"), in insightful juxtaposition to the politics of art and literary historians writing about Reynolds during the 1980s and 1990s; "The Two Snuffboxes: Recovering the Whig in Reynolds," in *Nobody's Perfect: A New Whig Interpretation of History* (New Haven and London: Yale University Press, 2002), 163–200 (quote at 195).

22 Soldiering, under command of gentleman superiors, presented an exception when it came to public service. Among Boston artisans who substantially filled the muster rolls for the Crown Point expedition in 1756, the greatest numbers came from the ranks of carpenters, tailors, and shoemakers; Nash, *Urban Crucible*, 244.

23 John Adams, diary entries for June 17, 1760 and [Jan. 1761], in *Diary and Autobiography of John Adams*, 4 vols., ed. L. H. Butterfield et al. (Cambridge, Mass.: Belknap Press of Harvard University Press, 1961), 1: 135–36, 197–98. On Adams's shifting conception of the "natural aristocracy," see John R. Howe, Jr., *The Changing Political Thought of John Adams* (Princeton: Princeton University Press, 1966), 136–42, 164–74.

24 Pliny, *Natural History*, trans. H. Rackham (Cambridge, Mass.: Harvard University Press; London: W. Heinemann, 1961), 9: 323–25 (35.36.85). Shaftesbury used the tailor to make a similar point about the mechanic's inability to judge the whole; *Second Characters*, 115.

25 Plato, *Republic*, trans. Tom Griffith (Cambridge: Cambridge University Press, 2000), 317 (X.598b).

26 Sir Joshua Reynolds, *Discourses on Art*, ed. Robert R. Wark (New Haven and London: Yale University Press for the Paul Mellon Centre for Studies in British Art, 1975), 233 (Discourse XIII, 1786). See also Roger de Piles, *The Art of Painting* (London, [1754]), 80–81; de Piles, *Principles of Painting* (London, 1743) 183; and (for a variation on Pliny) Edmund Burke, *A Philosophical Enquiry into the Origin of our Ideas of the Sublime and the Beautiful* (1757), ed. James T. Boulton (Notre Dame, Ind., and London: University of Notre Dame Press, 1968), 19. The malleability of Pliny's story about Apelles and the shoemaker is evident from *An Essay on Perfecting the Fine Arts in Great Britain and in Ireland* (Dublin and London, 1767). To make a point about the public benefits of publicly available art and the absence of those conditions in Great Britain, the anonymous author misreads Plato; in ancient Greece, he stated, "the most ordinary mechanick could *judge*. Because his eye was familiarized to the best models. He imperceivably caught the standard of taste and rule of beauty: the least deviation from which became offensive" (39).

27 My thinking in this paragraph owes much to John Barrell, *The Political Theory of Painting from Reynolds to Hazlitt* (New Haven and London: Yale University Press for the Paul Mellon Centre for Studies in British Art, 1986), 1–68, esp. 13–23. Barrell's elaboration of a civic humanist theory of painting and his reading of Pocock were seriously challenged by Andrew Hemingway in a book review, "The Political Theory of Painting without the Politics," *Art History* 10 (Sept. 1987): 381–95. Stephen Copley modified some of Barrell's conclusions in "The Fine Arts in Eighteenth-Century Polite Culture," in *Painting and the Politics of Culture: New Essays on British Art, 1700–1850*, ed. John Barrell (Oxford and New York: Oxford University Press, 1992), 13–38.

28 William Hogarth, quoted in Michael Kitson, "Hogarth's Apology for Painters," *Walpole Society* 41 (1966–68), 100.

29 Robert Campbell, *The London Tradesman* (1747; Newton Abbot: David & Charles, 1969), 197. In a general guide to business practices and personal conduct, Defoe made a negative example of mercers, using the trade to condemn the "fatal national folly" of preferring foreign, especially French, manufactures; *Complete English Tradesman*, 199–205. For the relationship between mercers, tailors, and their clients, see Aileen Ribeiro, *Dress in Eighteenth-Century Europe, 1715–1789* (London: Batsford, 1984), 49.

30 John Galt, *The Life and Studies of Benjamin West, Esq.* (London: T. Cadell and W. Davies, 1816), 29–30. In 1674, a Virginia tailor who bet on a horse he had entered into a race was fined for participating in a sport reserved for gentlemen; P. A. Bruce, *Economic History of Virginia in the Seventeenth Century*, 2 vols. (New York: Macmillan, 1896), 2: 473 (p. 84 of York County Deeds, Orders, Wills, Etc. 1672–1694, The Library of Virginia, Richmond).

31 *The Ear-Wig; or An Old Woman's Remarks on the Present Exhibition of Pictures of the Royal Academy* (London, 1781), 12. William T. Whitley suggested that the author was Mauritius Lowe, an unsuccessful history painter; *Thomas Gainsborough* (New York and London: Smith, Elder, 1915), 175–76.

32 William Dunlap, *A History of the Rise and Progress of the Arts of Design in the United States* (1834), 3 vols., ed. Rita Weiss (New York: Dover, 1969), 1: 189.

33 J. D. Herbert, *Irish Varieties for the Last Fifty Years* (London: William Joy, 1836), 232–34. By the time Stuart made his remark, conceptions of artists had changed sufficiently to permit his frequent challenges to patrons, which he was in any case temperamentally disposed to make, as I discuss in chapter five. Charles Coypel offers an earlier French parallel for these British complaints, writing in 1739: "I pity the plight of those . . . who are obliged to produce something every day, and who find themselves in the sad necessity of promising to furnish the beautiful on a given day as one might promise a suit of clothes"; quoted and trans. in Candace Clements, "Noble Liberality and Speculative Industry in Early Eighteenth-Century Paris: Charles Coypel," *Eighteenth-Century Studies* 29:2 (1995–96): 213.

34 Although persons who could afford portraits probably had their clothing custom made, ready-made clothing became increasingly available during the later eighteenth century. See Beverly Lemire, "Developing Consumerism and the Ready-made Clothing Trade in Britain, 1750–1800," *Textile History* 15:1 (1984): 21–44.

35 *The Miraculous Power of Clothes . . .*, trans. from the German (Philadelphia, 1772), 8. Similarly, see Campbell, *London Tradesman*, 191. On clothes and the blurring of class divisions in eighteenth-century England, see Neil McKendrick, "The Commercialization of Fashion," in McKendrick, John Brewer, and J. H. Plumb, *The Birth of a Consumer Society: The Commercialization of Eighteenth-Century England* (Bloomington: Indiana University Press, 1982), 34–99. For America, see Karin Calvert, "The Function of Fashion in Eighteenth-Century America," in *Of Consuming Interests: The Style of Life in the Eighteenth Century*, ed. Cary Carson, Ronald Hoffman, and Peter J. Albert (Charlottesville: University Press of Virginia for the United States Capitol Historical Society, 1994), 252–83.

36 Campbell, *London Tradesman*, 100.

37 On the importance of material goods in eighteenth-century portraiture, see T. H. Breen, "The Meaning of 'Likeness': American Portrait Painting in an Eighteenth-Century Consumer Society," *Word & Image* 6 (Oct.–Dec. 1990): 325–50; and Rebora and Staiti, *Copley*, esp. Staiti, "Character and Class," 53–77.

38 Gainsborough to William Jackson, undated letter, as quoted in *The Letters of Thomas Gainsborough*, ed. John Hayes (New Haven and London: Yale University Press for the Paul Mellon Centre for Studies in British Art, 2001), 74. On the widespread use of drapery painters, see William T. Whitley, *Artists and their Friends in England, 1700–1799*, 2 vols. (1928; New York and London: B. Blom, 1968), 1: 53–55, 219, 278–80. For Reynolds in particular: M. Kirby Talley, Jr., "'All Good Pictures Crack' – Sir Joshua Reynolds's Practice and Studio," in *Reynolds*, ed. Nicholas Penny (New York: Abrams, 1986), 57–58.

39 Campbell, *London Tradesman*, 101.

40 Kitson, "Hogarth's Apology," 98, 100; see also 83. Hogarth's ratio may derive from the old saying that "Nine Taylors make a Man," although opinions vary on the meaning of that phrase.

41 For other criticisms of tradesman-like portrait practices, see Celina Fox in *The Arts of Industry in the Age of Enlightenment* (New Haven and London: Yale University Press for the Paul Mellon Centre

for Studies in British Art, 2009), 294–95. Fox's book meticulously explores the status of useful arts and their overlap with polite arts, so it is not surprising that her chapter "Empirical Portraits" (293–355) mines many of the same sources, to the same end, that do I here and in my antecedent article on Copley. Fox argues for the development of "a hybrid type of portraiture which managed to achieve an empirical likeness but which also did justice to the sitter's ingenuity and indicated the means whereby he had contributed to the public good," for which, she asserts, "artists dissolved commonplace distinctions between mechanical and liberal arts and science, repudiating traditional hierarchies in the affirmation of their own skills" (302). She makes a novel and persuasive case, suggestive in connection with the type of empirical portrait associated with Copley (whose *Revere* she discusses on 319, 321) but not necessarily illuminating of Copley's artistic aims, as he seems to have understood and articulated them, my principal focus here.

42 Reynolds, *Discourses*, 62 (Discourse IV, 1771).

43 W. Hayley, "To Mr. Mason, On his sending the Author his Translation of DuFresnoy, with Notes by Sir Joshua Reynolds, 1783," *Poems and Plays*, 6 vols. (London, 1788), 1: 191. Grogram was a stiffened material of silk and wool. Drapery was a standard subject in academic treatises; see, e.g., C. A. Du Fresnoy, *The Art of Painting* (London, 1716), 27–31, 141–49; Richardson, *Theory*, 182–89; Francesco Algarotti, *An Essay on Painting* (London, 1764), 66–70.

44 Reynolds, *Discourses*, 140 (Discourse VII, 1776) and 48 (Discourse III, 1770).

45 Gainsborough to William, 2nd Earl of Dartmouth, Apr. 8, 1771, and Apr. 13, 1771; as quoted in *The Letters of Thomas Gainsborough*, ed. Hayes, 87–90. In the end, he did make a new portrait, in which Lady Dartmouth wears an interpretation of the styles of dress seen in portraits by Sir Anthony van Dyck but in which Gainsborough particularized the face.

46 Hester Thrale Piozzi, as quoted in an editorial footnote to [Hester Lynch Piozzi], *Autobiography, Letters and Literary Remains of Mrs. Piozzi (Thrale)*, ed. A. Hayward, 2 vols., (London, 1861), 2: 12n.

47 Algarotti, *Essay on Painting*, 113–14.

48 Ibid., 174–75.

49 Copley to West, Jan. 17, 1768, *Copley–Pelham Letters*, 67–68.

50 Charles Robert Leslie and Tom Taylor, *Life and Times of Sir Joshua Reynolds*, 2 vols. (London: John Murray, 1865), 1: 248.

51 For example, Copley based *Mrs. Jerethmial Bowers* (1763) on the mezzotint after Reynolds's *Lady Caroline Russell*. Less frequently, he asked sitters to lend him their clothes for use in portraits. A notoriously slow worker, Copley retained the academic robes in which he painted Myles Cooper (1768–69) for so long that the exasperated client begged him to return the garment; Cooper to Copley, Aug. 5, 1768, and Jan. 9 1769, *Copley–Pelham Letters*, 70–71, 74.

52 "Fresnoy and Depile" are mentioned in a letter to Copley from his half brother, Henry Pelham, Oct. 22, 1771 (*Copley–Pelham Letters*, 160–61). The book(s) in question could simply be Du Fresnoy's *The Art of Painting*, translated from Latin into French by Roger de Piles (who added his own remarks) and then into English by John Dryden (1695), an edition later revised by portraitist Charles Jervas (1716). However, the distinct mention of de Piles may indicate Copley's awareness of that author's *Principles of Painting* (1708), translated into English in 1743. De Piles's "Balance of Painters," a system for assessing the work of master artists, had, in its apparent simplicity, considerable appeal for English advocates for the arts, beginning with Richardson. In the same letter to Copley, Pelham mentions Walpole, who had published three volumes of *The Anecdotes of Painting in England* by 1764. Copley referred to Algarotti (*Essay on Painting*) in a letter to West of Nov. 12, 1766, and to Webb (*An Inquiry into the Beauties of Painting*) in a letter to Pelham from Italy; *Copley–Pelham Letters*, 51–52, 303.

53 Algarotti, *Essay on Painting*, 82.

54 Copley to John Greenwood, Jan. 25, 1771, *Copley–Pelham Letters*, 105–6.

55 The quoted words are Shaftesbury's from his plan for a painting of the Choice of Hercules; *Characteristicks*, 365. For Shaftesbury's essay and the civic humanist theory of painting, see Barrell, *Political Theory of Painting*, 27–33.

56 R. G. Bruce (relaying Reynolds's opinion) to Copley, Aug. 4, 1766, *Copley–Pelham Letters*, 41.

57 Copley anguished over money and fame in three fragmentary letters to either R. G. Bruce or West, all probably from 1767; *Copley–Pelham Letters*, 64–66, and Allan Cunningham, *The Lives of the Most Eminent British Painters, Sculptors, and Architects*, 6 vols. (London, 1829–32), 5: 164–65. They are the sources for his words in this paragraph. Copley's undisguised self-interest places him firmly in the camp of the social theorist Bernard Mandeville, who regarded commerce as the engine of society. Not surprisingly, Mandeville (who immigrated to England from the Netherlands) favored Dutch painting, faithful to nature, highly finished, and commercially viable – qualities that elicited disdain from English commentators and that, similarly, made Reynolds uneasy about Copley's art. On the inferiority of Dutch painting, see, e.g., Richard Steele, *Tatler* 129 (Feb. 4, 1710); Joseph Addison, *Spectator* 83 (June 5, 1711); Reynolds, letter to *Idler* 79 (Oct. 20, 1759). For stimulating discussion of Mandeville's *Fable of the Bees*, the Shaftesburian position it opposes, and eighteenth-century painting, see Solkin, *Painting for Money*, 1–26.

58 Copley to West, Jan. 17, 1768, *Copley–Pelham Letters*, 68.

59 J. Ralph, *The Case of Authors by Profession or Trade* (1758; Gainesville, Fla.: Scholars' Facsimiles & Reprints, 1966), 18.

60 The engraving appeared as the frontispiece to Sir Nicholas Nipclose [Francis Gentleman], *The Theatres: A Poetical Dissection* (London, 1772), a work that presented Garrick as in thrall to fashion.

61 The prologue was published in *St. James's Chronicle*, Aug. 27–29, 1767, and subsequently with the play *The Tailors: A Tragedy for Warm Weather, in Three Acts* (London, 1773).

62 For the most illuminating articulation of the ways in which Copley's portraits enhanced sitter prestige, see Staiti, "Character and Class," 53–77, in Rebora and Staiti, *Copley*.

63 "To the Proprietors of the Universal Magazine," *Universal Magazine of Knowledge and Pleasure* 3 (Nov. 1748): 230.

64 Bruce to Copley, Aug. 4, 1766, *Copley–Pelham Letters*, 42.

65 For Jennifer Roberts, the glass of water and other details of the painting (most notably the flying squirrel) refer to the transatlantic exchange in which the work participated; "Copley's Cargo: Boy with a Squirrel and the Dilemma of Transit," *American Art* 21 (Summer 2007): 20–41. The representation of human subjects with pet squirrels was not just a conceit. Paul Revere charged a Mr. John Welsh for making "a silver squirrel chain" on Nov. 21, 1772 (Revere Account Books, Massachusetts Historical Society, Boston). On the social significance of keeping pet squirrels, see Staiti, "Character and Class," 64, in Rebora and Staiti, *Copley*.

66 Reynolds's opinion in R. G. Bruce to Copley, Aug. 4, 1766, and West's in West to Copley, Aug. 4, 1766; *Copley–Pelham Letters*, 42, 44.

67 [Fanny Burney], *Diary and Letters of Madame d'Arbley*, 4 vols., [ed. Charlotte Barrett], (London: Henry Colburn, 1842–46), 1: 279 (diary entry for 1779).

68 Reynolds, *Discourses*, 191, 192, 200 (Discourse XI, 1782).

69 *New-York Mercury*, May 19, 1755.

70 Peter Manigault to Ann Manigault, Feb. 20, 1750, in "Peter Manigault's Letters," ed. Mabel L. Webber, *The South Carolina Historical and Genealogical Magazine* 31 (Oct. 1930): 272.

71 According to Margaret H. Swain, "banyan was the word for a Hindu trader and became in the West the name of the gown it was erroneously supposed they wore." She finds the name banyan more often used in America than England; "The Nightgown of Governor Jonathan Trumbull," *Bulletin of the Wadsworth Atheneum*, 6th ser., no. 3 (Winter 1970): 28. For this reason, and to avoid confusion with women's nightgowns (i.e., bedclothes) of a later period, I will use the term banyan. A more restricted description of banyans as a "more formal sort of nightgown," fitted to the torso and closed with decorative frogged fastenings, appears in Ribeiro, *Dress in Eighteenth-Century Europe*, 26–27. For the different terms and variations in the cut of these gowns, see also Patricia A. Cunnington, "Eighteenth Century Nightgowns: The Gentleman's Robe in Art and Fashion," *Dress* 10 (1984): 2–11.

72 *Spectator* 49 (Apr. 26, 1711). Oliver Goldsmith, *Collected Works of Oliver Goldsmith*, 5 vols., ed. Arthur Friedman (Oxford: Clarendon Press, 1966), II: *The Citizen of the World* (1762), 319.

73 William Paterson, "On Personal Appearance" and "On the Effeminacy and Dissoluteness of Modern Manners," quoted in J. E. O'Connor, *William Paterson: Lawyer and Statesman, 1745–1806* (New Brunswick, N.J.: Rutgers University Press, 1979), 10, 16.

74 As quoted in Alice Morse Earle, *Costume of Colonial Times* (New York: Empire Book Co., 1924), 172–73.

75 Jonathan Prude found that "no occupational group consistently lacked or possessed particular garments" and that the clothing of servants was marked as ungenteel more by fit, style, color, and material than by type of garment (which remain distinctions of elite attire): "To Look upon the 'Lower Sort': Runaway Ads and the Appearance of Unfree Laborers in America, 1750–1800," *Journal of American History* 78 (June 1991): 145. In Perth Amboy, New Jersey, during his travels in America, Dr. Alexander Hamilton observed "an antick figure pass by having an old plaid banyan, a pair of thick worsted stockings, ungartered, a greasy nightcap and no hat"; *Itinerarium of Dr. Alexander Hamilton*, 38 (entry for June 15, [1744]). He did not revise his unfavorable opinion of the man after learning he was wealthy.

76 I have borrowed T. H. Breen's phrase from "An Empire of Goods: The Anglicization of Colonial America, 1690–1776," *Journal of British Studies* 25 (Oct. 1986): 467–99.

77 Benjamin Franklin, "The Examination of Doctor Benjamin Franklin, . . . relating to the Repeal of the Stamp Act," in *The Papers of Benjamin Franklin*, ed. Leonard W. Labaree, 40 vols. (New Haven: Yale University Press, 1959–2011), 13: 135.

78 Dunlap, *History*, 1: 340; John Trumbull, *The Autobiography of Colonel John Trumbull*, ed. Theodore Sizer (New Haven: Yale University Press, 1953), 11. Trumbull must have seen Copley's self-portrait during his visit to the artist's house in 1772, possibly inspiring his 1778 portrayal of his father, Jonathan, in a banyan (a portrait that seems as well to owe a compositional debt to Copley's double portrait of Mr. and Mrs. Thomas Mifflin of 1773). A wool damask nightgown owned by Jonathan Trumbull, though not the one shown in the portrait by his son, is among the collections of the Wadsworth Atheneum in Hartford; see Swain, "Nightgown."

79 Prown, *Copley*, 1: figs. 182–85, 215, 218, 228, 230, 234, 236, 240, 251, 252.

80 Margaretta Lovell offered extended analysis of strategic sharing of an outfit by portrait sitters in her chapter "The Empirical Eye: Copley's Women and the Case of the Blue Dress," in *Art in a Season of Revolution: Painters, Artisans, and Patrons in Early America* (Philadelphia: University of Pennsylvania Press, 2005), 49–93.

81 Hogarth, in an early self-portrait dated ca. 1735, overpainted the cap in which he originally showed himself with a wig. He abandoned this indication of gentility for later self-portraits, in which his cap and banyan represent both the down-to-earth working artist and the man of intellect.

82 Marjorie Shelley notes that infrared reflectography reveals underdrawing in Copley's self-portrait, including "a line describing the juncture between the forehead and the hair," suggesting that he intended a wig, although the detail is elided in the finished work; "Painting in Crayon: The Pastels of John Singleton Copley," in Rebora and Staiti, *Copley*, 133.

83 "The Autobiography of the Reverend Devereux Jarratt, 1732–1763," ed. Douglass Adair, *William and Mary Quarterly*, 3rd ser., 9 (July 1952): 361, 367. General information on wigs can be found in Earle, *Costume of Colonial Times*, 257–64, and Calvert, "Function of Fashion," 263–70, in *Of Consuming Interests*, ed. Carson et al. For a provocative account of wigs in male portraiture, see Marcia Pointon, "Dangerous Excrescences: Wigs, Hair and Masculinity," in Pointon, *Hanging the Head: Portraiture and Social Formation in Eighteenth-Century England* (New Haven and London: Yale University Press for the Paul Mellon Centre for Studies in British Art, 1993), 107–39.

84 Amelia Rauser probed issues of class, gender, and nationality raised by macaroni fashion and caricature prints of macaroni during the 1770s in "Hair, Authenticity, and the Self-Made Macaroni," *Eighteenth-Century Studies* 38 (Fall 2004): 101–17, in a special issue of the journal devoted to "Hair."

85 Rauser observed that "the accidental exposure of a man's bald head [in public] was an acutely embarrassing, quasi-sexualized action, akin to a man dropping his pants and decidedly impolite in mixed company" (ibid., 103).

86 John Hancock had been groomed to take over his uncle's shipping business after the death of his father, a minister. But he showed poor stewardship when it came to money and lived extravagantly. In 1760, while in England on his uncle's business and purse, John Hancock spent at least five hundred pounds sterling, more than five times what a successful London artisan could expect to earn in that period. He had no worries, inheriting two-thirds of an estate valued at one hundred thousand pounds. W. M. Fowler, Jr., *The Baron of Beacon Hill: A Biography of John Hancock* (Boston: Houghton Mifflin, 1980), 41.

87 Remick's advertisement, *Boston-Gazette and Country Journal*, Oct. 16, 1769. The only book on the artist remains Henry Winchester Cunningham, *Christian Remick: An Early Boston Artist* (Boston: The Club of Odd Volumes, 1904).

88 *Idler* 79 (Oct. 20, 1759).

89 Ann Bermingham, *Learning to Draw: Studies in the Cultural History of a Polite and Useful Art* (New Haven and London: Yale University Press for the Paul Mellon Centre for Studies in British Art, 2000), 77–91.

90 Lovell is surely correct to argue that Remick's watercolor, despite its "calmly factual" appearance, "points to turmoil and extraordinary public enmity" in "a face-off of hemispheric proportions"; *Art in a Season of Revolution*, 199–200.

91 Mary Farwell Ayer, *Early Days on Boston Common* (Boston: n.p., 1910), 15–16. Two early buildings on the Common were the watch

house and the powder house, shown on the 1769 map. See also David Hackett Fischer, "Boston Common," in *American Places: Encounters with History*, ed. William E. Leuchtenburg (New York and Oxford: Oxford University Press, 2000), 125–43.

92 Some of the land Thomas Hancock began acquiring in 1735 bordered the Common, which had ill-defined boundaries; in 1752, questions were raised about the legitimacy of his claim to a recently purchased parcel, ultimately resolved in Hancock's favor by the Boston selectmen (of whom he was himself one); W. T. Baxter, *The House of Hancock: Business in Boston, 1724–1775* (Cambridge, Mass.: Harvard University Press, 1945), 76. If John Hancock planted his trees as early as 1764, they would have been no larger than twelve feet high in 1768, based on information Henry Pelham gave Copley on Sept. 10, 1771, about the size of four-year-old saplings Hancock's gardener, Mr. Spriggs, was prepared to sell to Copley for his property; *Copley–Pelham Letters*, 158. Hancock's music stand: Ayer, *Early Days*, 22.

93 The idea that Remick's work might be a metaphorical portrait is implicit in Lovell's discussion on 199–200 and explicit in her consideration of hatchments in relationship to portraits on 43–44, 118–19, in *Art in a Season of Revolution*. Lovell also suggested that the hatchment could be self-referential, if understood as made by Remick, who advertised "Coats of Arms."

94 Hewes's words from "A Bostonian" [B. B. Thatcher], *Traits of the Tea Party; Being a Memoir of George R. T. Hewes* (New York, 1835), 52–55. See also Alfred E. Young, "George Robert Twelves Hewes (1742–1840): A Boston Shoemaker and the Memory of the American Revolution," *William and Mary Quarterly*, 3rd ser., 38 (Oct. 1981): 561–623. For a brief overview of the concept of deference, see J. G. A. Pocock, "The Classical Theory of Deference,"*American Historical Review* 81 (June 1976): 516–23. For thoughtful reconsideration of the idea that colonial American society was fundamentally deferential, see the eight essays in "Deference in Early America: The Life and/or Death of an Historiographical Concept," ed. Billy G. Smith and Simon Middleton, a special issue of *Early American Studies* 3 (Fall 2005). Gregory Nobles, in his contribution "A Class Act: Redefining Deference in Early American History" (286–302), cites the example of Hewes in arguing against overemphasis on polarities of deference or defiance and in favor of recognizing deference as "a performative façade that conceals a more subtle set of responses to power" (287).

95 The remodeling effort, supervised by Henry Pelham during Copley's six-month working visit to New York in 1771, is the subject of extensive correspondence between the two; *Copley–Pelham Letters*, 116–79. Interestingly, Copley decided that a row of locust trees in front of his house would be superior in effect – less likely to obscure the house – to the lime trees he could have had from Hancock's gardener, in continuation of Hancock's allée; Copley to Pelham, *Copley–Pelham Letters*, 160 (Sept. 20, 1771). See also Prown, *Copley*, 1: 63–65; Lovell, *Art in a Season of Revolution*, 220–23; and Allen Chamberlain, *Beacon Hill: Its Ancient Pastures and Early Mansions* (Boston and New York: Houghton Mifflin, 1925), 42–65, 117–18.

96 Louise Lippincott, *Selling Art in Georgian London: The Rise of Arthur Pond* (New Haven and London: Yale University Press, 1983), 42.

97 For Johnston, see Alexander Forsyth, ed., *Henrietta Johnston: "Who Greatly Helped . . . by Drawing Pictures"* (Winston Salem, N.C.: Museum of Early Southern Decorative Arts; Charleston, S.C.: Gibbes Museum of Art, 1991).

98 Copley's work in pastel receives a good overview, including detailed technical information, in Marjorie Shelley, "Paintings in Crayon," in Rebora and Staiti, *Copley*; for his copy of Johnston's pastel, see 127. For a broader accounts of the medium with strong technical focus, see Marjorie Shelley, "Painting in the Dry Manner: The Flourishing of Pastel in 18th-Century Europe," in Marjorie Shelley and Katherine Baetjer, *Pastel Portraits: Images of 18th-Century Europe* (New York: Metropolitan Museum of Art, 2011), and Thea Burns, *The Invention of Pastel Painting* (London: Archetype, 2007). Among the first publications with substantial discussion of crayons – known to have circulated in the colonies – was Robert Dossie, *Handmaid to the Arts* (London, 1758), 181–201. As for all topics in that book, the author placed greatest emphasis on materials and processes. Dossie was not an artist but an eminent agriculturalist and a promoter of useful as well as fine arts. On pastel in mid-eighteenth-century England, see Lippincott, *Selling Art in Georgian London*, 76–81, 85, 88. The versatile Pond supplied materials to fellow British artist John Smibert after Smibert moved to Boston in 1730, where he and Pelham must have been acquainted. Smibert's studio remained intact long after his death in 1751 (the same year as Pelham), affording Copley a proximate source of materials and inspiration.

99 Draft of letter, Copley to Jean-Etienne Liotard, Sept. 30, 1762, *Copley–Pelham Letters*, 26.

100 Receipt from J. Powell, London, Oct. 18, 1765, ibid., 37.

101 R. G. Bruce to Copley, Aug. 4, 1766, and West to Copley, Aug. 4, 1766, ibid., 41–42, 45.

102 *An Essay on Perfecting the Fine Arts*, 42–43.

103 Copley to West, Nov. 12, 1766, *Copley-Pelham Letters*, 51.

104 R. G. Bruce to Copley, June 11, 1767, ibid., 53.

105 *Imperial Magazine, or Complete Monthly Intelligencer* (May 1760): 245.

106 Whitley, *Artists and their Friends in England*, 1: 268. The entry on Liotard in vol. 4 of Walpole's *Anecdotes*, not printed until 1771 or released until 1780, criticizes Liotard for lack of imagination and slavishness to truth.

107 Copley to West, Jan. 17, 1768, *Copley-Pelham Letters*, 66–68.

108 David Hackett Fischer, *Paul Revere's Ride* (New York and Oxford: Oxford University Press, 1994), 3–4. Revere's father, Apollos Rivoire, was a French Huguenot who emigrated to America at age thirteen; his mother, Deborah Hitchborn, belonged to an old and respectable Boston family of modest means.

109 Dunlap, *History*, 1: 148–54.

110 The date, in tiny characters discovered under microscopic examination, appears in the worn and abraded lower right-hand corner of the painting (under the frame), and next to it apparently the initials JC. According to Jean Woodward, a conservator at the Museum of Fine Arts, Boston, the marking is unquestionably old, though whether placed there by Copley remains unclear (conversation with author). This date was published in the entry on Revere in Rebora and Staiti, *Copley*, 248. Prown, *Copley*, 1: 74–75, located the work stylistically with a group of paintings Copley produced between 1769 and 1772 while suggesting that it would not have been painted after March 29, 1770, when Henry Pelham accused Revere of having pirated his engraving of the Boston Massacre. In a checklist of Copley's American paintings (1: 226), Prown suggested a date range of 1768–70.

111 Richard Avedon, *In the American West, 1979–1984* (New York: Abrams, 1985), foreward (n.p.).

112 Prown, *Copley*, 1: 122.

113 Campbell, *London Tradesman*, 141–42. Apprenticeship: Barbara M. Ward, "Boston Goldsmiths, 1690–1730," in *Craftsman in Early America*, ed. Quimby, 140.

114 Revere Family Papers, 1746–1964, in the collection of the Massachusetts Historical Society, Boston, include extensive business records and family correspondence. All citations of prices given in this chapter, unless otherwise noted, are from this source. Useful accounts of Revere's business may be found in Deborah A. Federhen, "Paul Revere, Silversmith: A Study of his Shop Operation and his Objects," master's thesis, University of Delaware, 1988, and Federhen, "From Artisan to Entrepreneur: Paul Revere's Silver Shop Operation," in *Paul Revere – Artisan, Businessman, and Patriot* (Boston: Paul Revere Memorial Association, 1988), 65–93.

115 Revere's account books banish a widely repeated notion, perhaps originating with Esther Forbes, that Copley painted Revere in exchange for the goldsmith's services; Forbes, *Paul Revere and the World He Lived In* (Boston: Houghton Mifflin, 1942), 107. The most recent monograph on Revere opens with the same assumption, even more fancifully expressed, of "an irresistible offer" to Revere, "who knew an incredible deal when he heard one," "posed for Copley in his silversmith shop" and eventually gathered with his family in their living room "for the great unveiling"; Robert Martello, *Midnight Ride, Industrial Dawn: Paul Revere and the Growth of American Enterprise* (Baltimore: Johns Hopkins University Press, 2010), 11–13. On the intricacies of eighteenth-century exchange, see John J. McCusker, *Money and Exchange in Europe and America, 1600–1775* (Chapel Hill: University of North Carolina Press for the Institute of Early American History and Culture, Williamsburg, Va., 1977), and William T. Baxter, *The House of Hancock: Business in Boston, 1724–1755* (Cambridge, Mass.: Harvard University Press, 1945), 11–38. McCusker (119) describes four modes of exchange used in pre-Revolutionary America, including "bookkeeping barter," a term he borrows from Baxter to describe transactions "in which two [or more] individuals kept running accounts of the money value of goods traded – in terms of the money of account," that is, in terms of imaginary moneys (such as the pound). Where Revere's account books state "by cash received," he presumably was paid in real money.

116 In the most recent study of the iconic *Revere*, Ethan W. Lasser presents the portrait as a promotional tool for the silversmith; "Selling Silver: The Business of Copley's *Paul Revere*," *American Art* 26 (Fall 2012): 27–43.

117 Information on Revere's neighbors is from Carol Ely, "North Square: A Boston Neighborhood in the Revolutionary War," unpublished paper, Brandeis University, 1983, which I consulted in the files of the Paul Revere Memorial Association at the Paul Revere House in Boston.

118 The Boston tax list of 1771 has been widely used by historians to analyze the extent of political, economic, and social inequality in eighteenth-century Boston; see, e.g., James Henretta, "Economic Development and Social Structure in Colonial Boston," *William and Mary Quarterly,* 3rd ser., 22 (1965), 75–92. Gregory B. Warden challenged its reliability in "Inequality and Instability in Eighteenth-Century Boston: A Reappraisal," *Journal of Interdisciplinary History* 6 (Spring 1976): 585–620, esp. 604–11.

119 Fischer, *Paul Revere's Ride*, 5, 16–17, 20.

120 Revere was commissioned a major in the Massachusetts Militia in April 1776 and a lieutenant colonel in the Massachusetts State Train of Artillery in November 1776, though his military career ended in 1779; Patrick M. Leehey, "Reconstructing Paul Revere," 29, in Paul Revere Memorial Association. For opening the files at the Paul Revere Memorial Association, Boston, and for helping to clarify Revere's social standing, I am grateful to the institution's coordinator of research, Patrick M. Leehey.

121 Forbes, *Paul Revere*, 122–24.

122 Revere to Mathias Rivoire, Oct. 6, 1781, Revere Family Papers.

123 Defoe, *Complete English Tradesman*, 241–53, quote at 246. Defoe argued at greater length for the gentleman "bred" rather than "born" in *Compleat English Gentleman.*

124 Fischer, *Paul Revere's Ride*, 19 (unfortunately, Fischer does not provide a citation for Revere's definition of a gentleman).

125 The proportion of Philadelphia taxpayers designated as "gentleman" or "esquire" tripled between 1756 and 1772, an "obvious sign of their growing prosperity and pretentiousness"; Smith, *The "Lower Sort,"* 89. On the liberalization of gentility in America, see Wood, *Radicalism*, 195–96; in England, Peter Borsay, *The English Urban Renaissance: Culture and Society in the Provincial Town, 1660–1770* (Oxford: Clarendon Press, 1989), 226–32. Johnson's *Dictionary* offers five quite varied definitions for the term "gentleman," including "the servant that waits about the person of a man of rank." It was used in that sense by the moralist Jonas Hanway, commenting on the blurring of class divisions in mid-eighteenth-century England: "It is the curse of this nation, that the laborer and mechanic will ape the lord"; "the different ranks of people are too much confounded: the lower classes . . . press so hard on the heels of the higher, if some remedy is not speedily found the lord will be in danger of becoming the valet of his gentleman"; [J.] H[anway], *A Journal of Eight Days Journey . . . to which is added an Essay on Tea*, 2 vols. (London, 1757), 2: 272, 263.

126 J. T. Smith, *Nollekens and his Times*, 2 vols. (London, 1828), 2: 56. No date is given for the remark but since Wilkie was born in 1785, it must not have been earlier than around 1805.

127 Novelty appears to have been a selling point for painters, judging from the advertised claims of eighteenth-century artists. See, for example, the ads placed in New York newspapers by painter Lawrence Kilburn and engraver Michael De Gruls in 1754 and 1763, respectively, in William Kelby, *Notes on American Artists, 1754–1820, Compiled from Advertisements appearing in the Newspapers of the Day* (New York: New-York Historical Society, 1922), 1, 4.

128 John Guillim's *Display of Heraldry*, first published in 1611, was substantially revised for a sixth edition of 1724. K. C. Buhler has tentatively identified the other volume as Samuel Sympson's *Book of Cyphers* (London, 1726), in "Three Teapots with Some Accessories," *Bulletin of the Boston Museum of Fine Arts* 56:324 (1963): 53.

129 Federhen, "Paul Revere, Silversmith," 80–92.

130 Styles, *Dress of the People*, 78–79.

131 In an unpublished paper that she kindly shared with me, Rebecca Zurier analyzed You's advertisement, which features a Masonic emblem, in connection with Copley's portrait of Revere, also a mason – both in light of the revolutionary implications of the organization.

132 Paulette Marie Kaskinen also reached this conclusion in her master's thesis, "Artists, Craftsmen and Patriots: Social Pretensions and Propaganda in John Singleton Copley's Portraiture," University of Virginia, 1992. In a refinement of my argument from my 1997 article on Copley, Jonathan L. Fairbanks proposed the teapot as "more suggestive of Copley's [Tory] affinities at this time than Revere's" Whig sympathies, which he found manifest in the voluminous linen sleeve, at a time when Americans turned to domestic manufacture of that fabric in political protest; "Paul Revere and 1768: His Portrait and the Liberty Bowl," in *New England Silver & Silversmithing, 1620–1815*, ed. Jeannine Falino and Gerald W. R. Ward (Boston: University Press of Virginia for the Colonial Society of Massachusetts, 2001), 135–51.

133 On tea drinking as an identifiably British and feminine activity, see Beth Kowalski-Wallace, "Tea, Gender, and Domesticity in Eighteenth-Century England," *Studies in Eighteenth-Century Culture* 23 (1994): 131–45. See also Solkin, *Painting for Money*, 67–72.

134 Among the more extended publications condemning tea, see Hanway, *A Journal of Eight Days*, and Simon Mason, *The Good and Bad Effects of Tea Considered* (London, 1745).

135 Josiah Wedgwood perfected creamware manufacture in 1762; little refined ceramic tableware was produced in the colonies. The phrases "No Stamp Act" and "America Liberty Restored" on other such teapots support the conclusion that they were made after repeal of the Stamp Act, in March 1766, and probably for the American market. Although no evidence supports American ownership of the Williamsburg teapot during the eighteenth century, the inventory of a Maryland tobacco factor and merchant, James Brown, listed a variety of vessels as "Enamel'd No Stamp Act." My information on the Williamsburg teapot comes from Janine Skerry, when she was curator of ceramics at Colonial Williamsburg, and from the Colonial Williamsburg website.

136 *A Report of the Record Commissioners of the City of Boston Containing the Boston Town Records, 1758 to 1769* (Boston, 1886), 220–21; *Boston Evening-Post*, Nov. 2, 1767.

137 For accounts of the non-importation movement, see Charles M. Andrews, "Boston Merchants and the Non-Importation Movement," *Transactions* (Colonial Society of Massachusetts) 19 (1916–17): 159–259, and John W. Tyler, *Smugglers & Patriots: Boston Merchants and the Advent of the American Revolution* (Boston: Northeastern University Press, 1986). The broadest and most compelling study of "how consumer politics shaped American independence," to use the book's subtitle, is T. H. Breen, *The Marketplace of Revolution* (Oxford and New York: Oxford University Press, 2004).

138 Henry Pelham to Paul Revere, draft of letter (perhaps never sent), Mar. 29, 1770, *Copley–Pelham Letters*, 83.

139 On Jan. 31, 1770, some three hundred women of Boston entered an agreement to forswear tea drinking both in the privacy of their homes and in company; *Boston Evening Post*, Feb. 12, 1770. Non-participants felt tremendous pressure, and some resorted to brewing tea in coffee pots; [Thatcher], *Traits of the Tea Party*, 148–49. Tellingly, before 1769 Revere had made only two coffee pots, but in that year he manufactured six, followed by four more in 1772–73. On the politicization of tea during the period 1767–70, see Andrews, "Boston Merchants," 194–95, 205–7; see also T. H. Breen, "'Baubles of Britain': The American and Consumer Revolutions of the Eighteenth Century," *Past and Present* 119 (1988): 93, 97–102, 103, and Breen, *Marketplace of Revolution*.

140 *Massachusetts Gazette, and Boston Post-Boy*, June 27, 1774.

141 Unlike Copley, Revere provided goods to clients across the social spectrum, a circumstance made possible by the much wider variation in cost of items he produced, the fact that he performed repairs, and the quotidian function of such goods as buttons and buckles. On Revere's patrons, see Jeannine Falino, "'The Pride Which Pervades thro every Class': The Customers of Paul Revere," in *New England Silver & Silversmithing*, 152–82.

142 Copley to [West], Nov. 24, 1770, and John Wilkes to Nathaniel Barber, Sept. 21, 1770 (acknowledging receipt of the portrait of Wilkes Barber); *Copley–Pelham Letters*, 98, 95.

143 Robert Dubuque proposed that Copley made the Revere portrait with the intention of submitting it for exhibition in London and believes the artist changed his mind after the Boston Massacre made this politically inflammatory; he duly cites Copley's concerns about taking sides, expressed in the letter to West of 1770; *Revere House Gazette* 17 (Autumn 1989): 5. The suggestion is provocative; however, to my mind, the acuteness of Copley's sensitivity to partisanship and the fact of the tea tax throughout this entire period argue against the idea.

144 Andrews, "Boston Merchants," 191–98, 204–6, 224–26.

145 On the linen sleeve as emblematic of Revere's politics: Fairbanks, "Revere and 1768," 140. At the height of the protest against the Townshend Acts, John Gore of Boston advertised a wide array of goods "just imported from London," most subject to duty; *Boston News-Letter*, Oct. 13, 1768. In 1771, Pelham, acting on Copley's behalf, bought 100 pounds of white lead from Gore to be used in painting Copley's newly remodeled Boston house; Pelham to Copley, Oct. 22, 1771, *Copley–Pelham Letters*, 173. For duties on painting materials, see Sir Lewis Namier and John Brooke, *Charles Townshend* (London: Macmillan; New York: St. Martin's Press, 1964), 189–91 (Appendix B: Preliminary Draft of the Townshend Duties). That tax could only have amounted to much if it targeted pigments used in house painting, though these overlapped with materials employed in painting pictures.

146 The transcriber of Revere's account books, 1761–83, for the Massachusetts Historical Society, noted that Revere miscalculated the cost of the teapot he made for Samuel Treat in 1762 as £11.4.5; the sum should be £12.4.5 (the cost of each component is given in my text on p. 40). On Copley's prices, see Prown, *Copley*, 1: 97–99. My references are to Copley's oil portraits of Mr. and Mrs. Alexander McWhorter (1769, Yale University Art Gallery, New Haven) and his pastel of Thomas Amory (1770, Museum of Fine Arts, Boston), for which the price appears in ibid., 1: 206.

147 In 1771, Copley received a shipment from London containing 30 canvases of varying sizes, 12 unspecified tools, 5 brushes, paints, and oils, and 185 squares of glass measuring 14½ by 10½ in.; the price (including shipping, packing materials, and other miscellaneous charges) was £18.8.5; invoice from Henry and Thomas Bromfield, Aug. 17, 1771, *Copley–Pelham Letters*, 140–41. For a smaller order, less carefully detailed, see J. Powell to Copley, Oct. 18, 1765, ibid., 37.

148 Richardson, *Two Discourses: I. An Essay on the whole Art of Criticism as it relates to Painting . . . II. An Argument in behalf of the Science of a Connoisseur . . .* (London, 1719), II: 49–50.

149 Campbell, *London Tradesman*, 97.

150 Boston shoemaker William Scott presents an exception. He not only commissioned a portrait from Joseph Badger – a painter-in-general who died in 1765 – but published doggerel on the subject in the *New Hampshire Gazette and Historical Chronicle* (Portsmouth) of Feb. 3, 1764. One of four women who responded in kind wrote: "The women are now out of Shoes/and sorely they Complain/They view Scott's Face, and gratify/a curious Taste though vain." For poetry on paintings, see Jessie Poesch, " 'In Just Lines to Trace' – The Colonial Artist, 1700–1776," in *The Portrait in Eighteenth-Century America*, ed. Ellen G. Miles (Newark: University of Delaware Press; London: Associated University Presses, 1993), 61–83.

151 *Book of Trades; or, Library of the Useful Arts*, 3 vols. (London, 1805), 2: 138; first American ed., Philadelphia, 1807.

152 R. G. Bruce to Copley, June 11, 1767, *Copley–Pelham Letters*, 53–54. Copley may well have raised his prices, given the complaint registered in a letter of Sept. 14, 1767, from George Livis to Copley, ibid., 61.

153 Calipers were used to measure and transfer outside dimensions of objects, especially round or curved. But Revere's right hand could

also be likened to a compass, employed for drawing circles and making geometric calculations. In illustrated emblem books dating to the early seventeenth century, the compass is a prominent and earthbound attribute of the stooped personification of "Practice" and a crown atop the head of her counterpart "Theory"; see, e.g., Marco Fascari, "Maidens 'Theory' and 'Practice' at the Sides of Lady Architecture," *Assemblage* 7 (Oct. 1988): 14–27. With specific reference to an English emblem book of 1779, Wendy Bellion compellingly argued that Charles Willson Peale represented his sons in the guise of theory and practice in *The Staircase Group (Portrait of Raphaelle and Titian Ramsay Peale)*, 1795; see her "Illusion and Allusion: Charles Willson Peale's *Staircase Group* at the Columbian Exhibition," *American Art* 17 (Summer 2003): 18–39, and Bellion, *Citizen Spectator: Art, Illusion, and Visual Perception in Early National America* (Chapel Hill: University of North Carolina Press for the Omohundro Institute of Early American History and Culture, 2011), 102–8. The compass had an even closer relationship with freemasonry and thus applicability for Revere, as argued by Edith J. Steblecki, *Paul Revere and Freemasonry* (Boston: Paul Revere Memorial Association, 1985).

154 An exception had been made for the salaried engraver to the king, Francesco Bartolozzi, an Italian active in London from 1764; otherwise, the Royal Academy did not admit engravers to full membership until the 1850s, on grounds that their work was essentially imitative.

155 "To the Proprietors of the Universal Magazine," *Universal Magazine of Knowledge and Pleasure* 3 (Oct. 1748): 178–83. The magazine's November issue addressed the art of painting and limning (225–33), with a plate in which both portraitist working at his easel and sitter appear as gentlemen.

156 De Piles, *Principles of Painting*, 169–70; in the original 1708 French text, the word is also "artisan." "Depile" mentioned by Pelham to Copley, Oct. 22, 1771, *Copley–Pelham Letters*, 160–61, without indication of which book by or associated with Roger de Piles.

157 Campbell, *London Tradesman*, 102.

158 On invention, see, e.g., Richardson, *Theory of Painting*, 43–84, and Algarotti, *Essay on Painting*, 81–103.

159 George Vertue, "Vertue Note Books," *Walpole Society* 22 (1933–34): 40–41, entry for 1729.

160 Revere's descendants, one infers, did object to the artisan portrayal (preferring the later portrait by Gilbert Stuart), as the Copley portrait lay neglected in an attic until 1875; Elbridge Henry Goss, *The Life of Colonel Paul Revere*, 2 vols. (1891; Freeport, N.Y.: Books for Libraries Press, [1971]), 2: 597–98. Its recovery presumably owes something to a surge of interest in the colonial period on the eve of the United States centennial.

161 In his family portrait of 1776–77, painted in celebration of Copley's reunion in London with his wife, children and father-in-law, Copley shows himself holding papers, on which no marks are evident. A critic for the *Morning Chronicle*, writing of this work, described the figure of Copley simply as "the gentleman . . . with some plans in his hand"; review of the Royal Academy exhibition, Apr. 26, 1777.

162 On this matter, see Wood, *Radicalism*, 34–35.

163 Rembrandt Peale, "Reminiscences, Exhibitions and Academies," *Crayon* 1:19 (1855): 290.

164 Baldassare Castiglione introduced the term *sprezzatura* in *The Book of the Courtier* (1528), trans. and intro. Charles S. Singleton (Garden City, N.Y.: Doubleday, 1959), 43 (I.26). See also Wayne A. Rebhorn, *Courtly Performances: Masking and Festivity in Castiglione's Book of the Courtier* (Detroit: Wayne State University Press, 1978), 33–40, and – for *sprezzatura* in the context of eighteenth-century painting – Mary Sheriff, *Fragonard: Art and Eroticism* (Chicago: University of Chicago Press, 1990), 122–24. Reynolds did not use the term; however, he expressed its essence, by negative example, in stating that "an inferior artist is unwilling that any part of his industry should be lost upon the spectator" and in associating "laborious finishing of the parts" with mechanics; *Discourses*, 59 (Discourse IV, 1771) and 201 (Discourse XI, 1782).

165 Joseph Wright to Ozias Humphry, July 24, 1775, as quoted in William Bemrose, *The Life and Works of Joseph Wright, A.R.A., Commonly Called "Wright of Derby"* (London: Bemrose and Sons, 1885), 36.

166 Neal's alter ego in John Neal, *Randolph, A Novel*, 2 vols. (n.p., 1823), 2: 67.

2 THE TRADE OF ART IN PHILADELPHIA AND NEW YORK

1 Neatly written, without strikeovers, the manuscript was – according to a fiction introduced at its conclusion – "copied . . . out" by a man who received it thirdhand; William Williams Manuscripts, Manuscripts Department, Lilly Library, Indiana University, Bloomington (hereafter Williams MSS). J. Eagles surmised that the document "may have been considered a mere sailor's journal, and not read" by his father, at least initially; "The Beggar's Legacy," *Blackwood's Edinburgh Magazine* 77 (Mar. 1855): 251–72; reprinted in John Eagles, *Essays Contributed to Blackwood's Magazine* (Edinburgh, 1857), 457–502 (quote at 494). In due course, T. Eagles edited the Penrose story, which first appeared as [Williams Williams], *The Journal of Llewellin Penrose, a Seaman*, 4 vols. (London and Edinburgh: John Murray, 1815). The manuscript as prepared by Thomas and John Eagles for submission to publishers, bearing reader annotations, and bound with thirty-seven watercolors by Nicholas Pocock and others, sold at Christie's, London, Sept. 27, 2006; the sale included Williams's 1791 will naming Eagles as his executor and legatee, an autograph letter from West to Thomas Eagles of Oct. 10, 1810, and a letter to Eagles (transmitting West's) from Francis Annesley. These materials are now in the collections of the National Maritime Museum, Greenwich, England.

2 David Howard Dickason argued that Williams had firsthand knowledge of the Mosquito coast of present-day Nicaragua. He speculated on the choice of the Penrose pseudonym, on when Williams wrote the manuscript, and when and why he gave it to T. Eagles in *William Williams: Novelist and Painter of Colonial America, 1727–1791* (Bloomington: Indiana University Press, 1970), 76–99, 32–34, 70–75. Dickason also published Williams's book in unexpurgated form, with notes and commentary, as *Mr. Penrose: The Journal of Penrose, Seaman*, ed. David Howard Dickason (Bloomington: Indiana University Press, 1969). Working with the original manuscript as Dickason did, Terry Breverton "marginally updated" (his phrase) and reformatted Dickason's literal transcription for the sake of modern readability in *The First American Novel* (Y Bontfaen, Wales: Glyndwr Publishing, 2007). The most recent edition, a reissue of Dickason's, includes a compelling argument for "Penrose in the Twenty-First Century," by Sarah Wadsworth. A literary scholar, Wadsworth makes a strong case for the thematic modernity and relevance of Williams's novel, and she faults "the nationalist, exceptionalist model of [American] literary history" for its omission from "the canon of American literature"; Wadsworth, "Afterword: Penrose in the Twenty-First Century," for Williams, *The Journal of Penrose, Seaman*, ed. Dickason (Bloomington: Indiana University Press, 2013), 387. Wads-

worth interestingly frames her essay in terms of painting genres that Williams engaged – history, portraiture, landscape – though without need or, presumably, space to develop them in terms of his practice.

3 Thomas Eagles, memorandum of a conversation with Benjamin West, July 10, 1805, Williams MSS (hereafter cited as Eagles, 1805 memo). Eagles recorded that their mutual friend Mr. Annesley brought the Academy president to Eagles's lodgings to see the manuscript, but why this occurred is unclear. According to Dickason, the encounter took place at Eagles's "London quarters at No. 4 Pall Mall"; "Benjamin West on William Williams: A Previously Unpublished Letter," *Winterthur Portfolio* 6 (1970): 129. West's fame set the terms for modern rediscovery of Williams, as revealed by the title of the first article written about him in the twentieth century: William Sawitzky, "William Williams, First Instructor of Benjamin West," *Antiques* 31 (May 1937): 240–42. Portions of this chapter draw on my article "Benjamin West's Professional Endgame and the Historical Conundrum of William Williams," *William and Mary Quarterly*, 3rd ser., 59 (October 2002): 821–64.

4 West to Thomas Eagles, Oct. 10, 1810, as transcribed by T. Eagles, Williams MSS (hereafter cited as West, 1810 letter); the original letter (which I have not seen) was privately owned until its acquisition by the National Maritime Museum, Greenwich, together with the illustrated Penrose manuscript. Dickason published the letter in "Benjamin West on William Williams," 127–33.

5 Some of Dickason's attributions were promptly challenged by the art historian E. P. Richardson, who identified four later eighteenth-century artists by that name; "William Williams – A Dissenting Opinion," *American Art Journal* 4 (Spring 1972): 5–23. In his opinion, Williams No. 1 (as he labeled the artist who taught West) was not the William Williams "mariner" who in 1757 wed a sister of New York artist John Mare, an idea initially proposed by a researcher on Mare, Helen Burr Smith, in "The Two William Williamses," *The New-York Historical Society Quarterly* 35 (1951): 375–85. Nor then – if Richardson was correct – did Williams No. 1 father the William Williams to whom Mary Mare give birth in 1759 and who became an artist (Richardson's No. 3) – although that lineage is accepted by some Williams family genealogists. Williams No. 1 may have had an artist-son, Richardson's No. 2, whom he distinguished from 1 and 3 on the basis of connoisseurship. No. 4 was an English painter.

6 Breverton, *The First American Novel*, 215. Breverton revived basic questions about Williams (209–56), but, in the process, sowed unnecessary confusion. For example, his speculation that Williams was Welsh, not English, introduced a host of other candidates for the artist, some born long before 1727, a birth date Breverton questioned on multiple grounds, not always well reasoned. Yet he ignores the evidence of Williams's first will of 1788 (even though he reprints it), in which the testator gave his age as sixty-one. Breverton complicates a reader's efforts to make independent judgments, introducing and reproducing a host of errors in an account that consists largely of paraphrase and extended quotation (or misquotation) from primary and secondary sources, strung together without discrimination or reliable citation.

7 West, 1810 letter.

8 Gary B. Nash, "Up from the Bottom in Franklin's Philadelphia," *Past and Present* 77:1 (1977): 62, table 1 and note.

9 C. W. Peale to Rembrandt Peale, Oct. 28, 1812, *Peale Papers*, 3: 174. Peale's sketch in this letter of artistic activity in and around Philadelphia during the late colonial period did not include Williams, who painted in the West Indies during Peale's initial visit to the city as a fledgling painter in Dec. 1762. A dated but still engaging and notably early attempt to envision Philadelphia's artistic community is Carl and Jessica Bridenbaugh, *Rebels and Gentlemen: Philadelphia in the Age of Franklin* (1942; New York: Oxford University Press, 1965), 162–78. See also Ellen G. Miles, "The Portrait in America, 1750–1775," in Ellen G. Miles and Richard H. Saunders, *American Colonial Portraits, 1700–1776* (Washington, D.C.: Smithsonian Institution Press for the National Portrait Gallery, 1987), 32–35 and all relevant catalogue entries.

10 Hannah Benner Roach, "Taxables in the City of Philadelphia, 1756," *Pennsylvania Genealogical Magazine* 22:1 (1961): 27.

11 *Pennsylvania Journal and Weekly Advertiser*, January 13, 1763.

12 Williams's "talent for fiction" extended to exaggeration of his output, in E. P. Richardson's view, though Richardson aimed more broadly to challenge Eagles's and West's credulity on other matters and to correct what he quite reasonably regarded as modern misattributions by Dickason and others; "Williams," 10–11.

13 Benjamin Franklin to his wife, Deborah Franklin, June 10, 1758, *The Papers of Benjamin Franklin*, ed. Leonard W. Labaree et al., 40 vols. (New Haven: Yale University Press, 1959–2011), 8: 92. E. P. Richardson believed this to be a reference only to the print, not the painting, of Lay; "William Williams," 12–13. Franklin withheld his printer's imprimatur when he published Benjamin Lay, *All Slave-keepers That Keep the Innocent in Bondage, Apostates Pretending to Lay Claim to the Pure and Holy Christian Religion* (Philadelphia: Printed for the Author, 1737). For the previously overlooked history of his own changing involvement with slavery, see David Waldstreicher, *Runaway America: Benjamin Franklin, Slavery, and the American Revolution* (New York: Hill and Wang, 2004); also Gary B. Nash, "Franklin and Slavery," *Proceedings of the American Philosophical Society* 150 (Dec. 2006): 618–35.

14 Williams, *Penrose*, ed. Dickason, 117, 358–59.

15 [Tryon], *The Way to Health, Long Life and Happiness . . .* (London, 1683). For concise accounts of the painting and the print of Lay, see Miles and Saunders, *American Colonial Portraits*, 207–8, 227. Wilford P. Cole offered a detailed history of the print in "Henry Dawkins and the Quaker Comet," *Winterthur Portfolio* 4 (1968): 34–46.

16 Robert D. Harlan, "A Colonial Printer as Bookseller in Eighteenth-Century Philadelphia: The Case of David Hall," *Studies in Eighteenth-Century Culture* 5 (1976): 355–70.

17 Robert Hurd Kany established Hall's indispensability to Franklin and to Philadelphia book and print culture in "David Hall: Printing Partner of Benjamin Franklin" (Ph.D. dissertation, Pennsylvania State University, 1963). Franklin owed Hall almost £1,000 at the dissolution of the partnership, an account Franklin disputed and never settled; "James Parker: Final Report on the Franklin and Hall Account," *Papers of Benjamin Franklin*, 13: 87–99. See also Waldstreicher, *Runaway America*, 67–68.

18 Edwin Wolf, II, touched on Smollett in the Philadelphia context in his focused study, *The Book Culture of a Colonial American City: Philadelphia Books, Bookmen, and Booksellers* (Oxford: Clarendon Press, 1988), 103–5. Smollett's history sold exceptionally well – and benefited booksellers – following strategic distribution of the revised 1758 edition as weekly sixpenny pamphlets, one hundred in all, from which the author earned £500; Kenneth Simpson, "Smollett, Tobias George (1721–1771)," *Oxford Dictionary of National Biography* online.

19 "Ezra Stiles in Philadelphia," *Pennsylvania Magazine of History and Biography* 16 (1892): 375; "Extracts from the Diary of Hannah Callender," *Pennsylvania Magazine of History and Biography* 12 (1888): 454–55. See, more broadly, my source for these citations: Elizabeth McLean, "Town and Country Gardens in Eighteenth-Century Philadelphia," *Eighteenth Century Life*, n.s., 8 (Jan. 1983): 136–47, part of a

special issue on "British and American Gardens," edited by Robert R. Maccubbin and Peter Martin.

20 For interpretation of select details in Williams's *Deborah Hall*, see Roland E. Fleischer, "Emblems and Colonial American Painting," *American Art Journal* 20:3 (1988): 3–9. Judging only from a fair black-and-white reproduction, a plausible attribution to Williams can be made for a similar painting loaned by Hirschl & Adler Gallery to the exhibition *Childhood Long Ago*, catalogue by Richard McLanathan (New York: I.B.M. Corporation, Gallery of Arts and Sciences, 1965). That work showed a somewhat younger girl, holding a peach and flowers, in front of a large urn and extensive, manicured garden; if by Williams, a 1760s date seems more likely than ca. 1750 suggested in the catalogue.

21 Petition of June 2, 1759, Society Collection, Historical Society of Pennsylvania (HSP), Philadelphia. The theater opened on June 25, 1759, so Williams presumably was paid. On the theater controversy, see Dickason, *Williams*, 28–30.

22 For costs of portraits during the third quarter of the eighteenth century, see Miles and Saunders, *American Colonial Portraits*, 64. For costs of scenery, see Mary C. Henderson, "Scenography, Stagecraft, and Architecture in the American Theatre: Beginnings to 1870," among the informative essays on all aspects of early American theatrical practice in *Cambridge History of American Theatre, Vol. One: Beginnings to 1870*, ed. Don B. Wilmeth and Christopher Bigsby (Cambridge: Cambridge University Press, 1998), 373–423.

23 Regarding compensation, see Sybil Rosenfeld, *Georgian Scene Painters and Scene Painting* (Cambridge and New York: Cambridge University Press, 1981), 8–10.

24 An amateur playhouse in Williamsburg, built around 1716–18 and known only from its foundation, was probably not much more than a large barn. Charleston's amateur players had a more traditional English pit-box-and-gallery structure in the original Dock Street Theatre, built 1735 and destroyed by fire in 1740. Henderson, "Scenography," 373–77.

25 *Virginia Gazette*, June 12, 1752.

26 Brooks McNamara, "David Douglass and the Beginnings of American Theater Architecture," *Winterthur Portfolio* 3 (1969): 131–32; also Rosenfeld, *Georgian Scene Painters*, 23–29.

27 Rosenfeld, *Georgian Scene Painters*, 24. John R. Wolcott proposed that in understanding eighteenth-century American scene painting "the most promising source other than printed descriptions, barren at best, are non-theatrical landscape and topographical (view) painting of America's early scenic artists"; "Scene Painters and their Work in America before 1800," *Theatre Survey* 18 (May 1977): 57. In the case of Williams, whom Wolcott discusses (62–64, 66), I would say the opposite is true: that is, Williams's exposure to and involvement in theatrical scene painting, little as we know about it, more likely informed his approach to landscape in the portraits of his Philadelphia years.

28 *Imaginary Landscape*, in the Newark Museum, is signed and dated to the right of the tower base, though it is difficult to discern, owing to the painting's poor condition. It was such a wreck when received by the museum in 1956 (with attribution to one "Samuel Stibbs," a relative of a previous owner) that the panel-mounted canvas was given for treatment to conservation apprentices. Roger B. Stein downplayed Williams's architectural inventiveness in this work, suggesting that the tower had real-life models in European and Spanish-American harbors and artistic precedents in paintings and engravings by seventeenth-century Dutch marine painters (several of whom specialized in imaginary harbor scenes), as well as Claude Lorrain; *Seascape and the American Imagination* (New York: Clarkson N. Potter in association with the Whitney Museum of American Art, 1975), 16. I cannot substantiate either at the level of invention found in Williams's landscape.

29 The classic study is Nina Fletcher Little, *American Decorative Wall Painting 1700–1850*, new enlarged ed. (New York: E. P. Dutton, 1972).

30 Peale to Cadwalader, Sept. 7, 1770, and Mar. 22, 1771, *Peale Papers*, 1: 82–85, 92. The patron acquired decorative paintings from London instead. Highly artificial landscapes had been popular subjects since the seventeenth century among English amateur draftsmen as well; Kim Sloan, *"A Noble Art": Amateur Artists and Drawing Masters, c. 1600–1800* (London: British Museum Press, 2000), 78–84.

31 "By Permission," *Pennsylvania Gazette*, Aug. 9, 1759.

32 All three plays were colonial premieres, judging from the evidence gathered by Odai Johnson and William J. Burling for their useful book *The Colonial American Stage, 1665–1774: A Documentary Calendar* (Madison and Teaneck, N.J.: Fairleigh Dickinson University Press; London: Associated University Presses, 2001), 162–98.

33 As cited ibid., 38. Dickason (*Williams*, 30) believed Williams painted scenery for use at the new Southwark Theatre in 1766, citing two early histories of Philadelphia, though a check of his sources does not support that contention, since the authors made obvious errors, confusing the first Philadelphia theater for the second. Henderson ("Scenography," 384–86) repeated the claim, without citation.

34 Apart from the list I have reproduced here, Eagles mentioned a "small whole length of William Williams Junr. Painter," presumably a son of the painter and possible creator of certain signed but questionable works attributed by Dickason to the senior Williams but assigned by Richardson to "Williams No. 2"; "Williams," 8–9, 22–23.

35 Alexander Garden to David Colden, Feb. 1, 1764, *The Letters and Papers of Cadwallader Colden*, 9 vols. (New York: New-York Historical Society, 1918–37), 6: 281–82.

36 "To the Printers of the Pennsylvania Gazette," *Pennsylvania Gazette*, Jan. 22, 1767.

37 National Archives of Scotland, Edinburgh Commissary Court, Case 127, as cited in L. Leneman, *Marriage Litigation in Scotland, 1694–1830* [computer file] (Colchester, Essex: UK Data Archive, Oct. 1999), SN: 3970. According to UKDA, "the data comprise a transcription of the gist" of cases included but are not a direct transcription. The fact that Lord Rosehill's marriage was common knowledge can be found in a contemporaneous review of *The Peerage of Scotland . . . from the Union to 1767*: "In the title we are told this book is corrected to the 20th of April 1767. Let us examine: No mention is made of Lord Rosehill's late marriage . . ."; *Political Register; and Impartial Review of New Books* 1 (May 1767): 41. Peerage records do not agree on the identity of Lady Rosehill, and only one, which names Margaret Cheer, contained a footnoted clue to the contested first marriage: G[eorge] E. C[okayne], *The Complete Peerage of England, Scotland, Ireland, Great Britain and the United Kingdom*, rev. ed. Vicary Gibbs, 13 vols. (London: St. Catherine Press, 1910–59), vol. 9 (ed. H. A. Doubleday and Lord Howard de Walden, 1936), 696. For a fuller account of the Rosehill saga and of Miss Cheer's career, see Susan Rather, "Miss Cheer as Lady Rosehill: A Real-Life Drama in Late-Colonial British America," *Theatre Notebook* 64:2 (2010): 82–95.

38 Macrabie provided colorful characterizations of life in the colonies between 1768 and 1770 in letters to his brother-in-law, this one dated Feb. 18, 1768; Joseph Parkes and Herman Merivale, eds.,

Memoirs of Sir Philip Francis, K.C.B., with Correspondence and Journals, 2 vols. (London, 1867), 1: 418, 414.

39 In a letter to her sister, Rosehill's mother related the "mournful tale" of her son's "vice and wickedness," culminating in his marriage to "a bastard girl . . . with a long list of misdemeanors" and disinheritance by his father. Interestingly, the Countess Northesk's understanding of how the couple came to be wed disagrees with the more sanitized version Rosehill's abandoned wife gave in her lawsuit. Anne Leslie Carnegie, Countess Northesk, to Lady Mary Hamilton, Mar. 14, 1767, Lady Mary Hamilton Papers, James Marshall and Marie-Louise Osborne Collection, Beinecke Rare Book and Manuscript Library, Yale University. The sender noted that she enclosed copies of Rosehill's appeal to his father and her own reply to their son, but these documents are not among the papers at Yale. I am grateful to Douglas Cushing for reviewing the collection on my behalf.

40 *New-York Gazette, or the Weekly Post-Boy*, Apr. 24, 1769, where the play is erroneously announced as for "Monday next, the 24th of April"; the same performance date also appears in *New-York Gazette, and the Weekly Mercury*, Apr. 24, 1769.

41 *New-York Gazette, and the Weekly Mercury*, May 8, 1769.

42 Perhaps Douglass had even turned to Williams again in New York; his company's *Othello* at the John Street Theater in April 1769 featured "a new Set of Scenes which were painted at a great Expence"; *New-York Gazette, and the Weekly Mercury*, Apr. 10, 1769.

43 Inventory of the Household . . . of Ethie [Castle] – Belonging to the Right Honourable Earl of North Esk – Taken . . . 23 July 1822," GD 130/Ethie inventories, Northesk Papers, Dundee City Archives. Like many young aristocrats, Rosehill received drawing instruction in Edinburgh while under a tutor's care; "to Lord Rosehill for the Teaching of Drawing by Mr. Laimé," 1761, GD 130/Box 9/ Bundle VI. "Mr. Laimé, Limner (lately returned from England)" advertised in the *Edinburgh Evening Courant* (Dec. 1, 1762) that he painted miniatures, for which a new vogue had been ignited by the royal bride, Queen Charlotte; for this information and what little is known of that artist, probably Francis Lainé, a Berlin-born French Huguenot, see Stephen Lloyd and Kim Sloan, *The Intimate Portrait: Drawings, Miniatures and Pastels from Ramsay to Lawrence* (Edinburgh: National Galleries of Scotland; London: British Museum, 2008), 17, 36 n.17.

44 One of only two paintings by Williams with a secure provenance (the other is the artist's self-portrait), the Denning portrait descended in that family until 1982, when it was bought by Hirschl & Adler Galleries, New York, and then sold in 1986 to the Martin and Gracia Andersen Foundation of Orlando, Florida.

45 Karol Ann Lawson argued persuasively that the landscape in Smibert's *Bermuda Group* manifested a "spiritual vision" central to the meaning of the work; "A New World of Gladness and Exertion: Images of the North American Landscape in Maps, Portraits, and Serial Prints Before 1820" (Ph.D. dissertation, University of Virginia, 1988), 147–80. Among artists in colonial America, with the exception of Williams (as I will argue), Smibert presents the best evidence of investment in landscape representation. See Lawson, ibid., and Richard H. Saunders, *John Smibert: Colonial America's First Portrait Painter* (New Haven and London: Yale University Press/Barra Foundation, 1995), 102–3, 109–10.

46 The argument that the English outdoor conversation piece helped landowners mask and justify enclosure of common lands was made by Ann Bermingham, *Landscape and Ideology: The English Rustic Tradition, 1740–1860* (Berkeley: University of California Press, 1986), 9–33. For the concept of unsettled land as empty and therefore subject to possession – the basis for seventeenth-century English claims of ownership to land formerly occupied by Native Americans – see David Grayson Allen, "Vacuum Domicilium: The Social and Cultural Landscape of Seventeenth-Century New England," in *New England Begins*, 3 vols., ed. Jonathan Fairbanks (Boston: Museum of Fine Arts, 1982), 1: 1–10.

47 See Bruce Robertson, "Venit, Vidit, Depinxit: The Military Artist in America," in Edward J. Nygren et al., *Views and Visions: American Landscape before 1830* (Washington, D.C.: Corcoran Gallery of Art, 1986), 83–103.

48 *Copley–Pelham Letters*, 120 (June 20, 1771) and 174 (Nov. 6, 1771). Copley's sense that New Yorkers were discerning about painting contradicts the judgment attributed to West, who made a painting trip to New York in 1759 at age twenty-one. He found New Yorkers "wholly devoted to mercantile pursuits" and thought "mercantile men . . . habituated by the nature of their transactions to overlook the intrinsic qualities of the very commodities in which they deal" and, one infers, also the commodities they consumed, such as paintings; Galt, *West* (1816), 81–82. West's recollections fifty-five years later of a visit lasting only a few months raises suspicions that the judgment came from his biographer Galt, who unsuccessfully engaged in mercantile activities while also pursuing a career as a writer; see chapter six for a fuller discussion of Galt and his stake in West's biography.

49 Peale to John Beale Bordley, Nov. 1772, *Peale Papers*, 1: 127. Copley to Pelham, *Copley–Pelham Letters*, 173 (Nov. 6, 1771).

50 William Carson to Copley, Aug. 16, 1772; *Copley–Pelham Letters*, 187–89.

51 See Ellen G. D'Oench, *The Conversation Piece: Arthur Devis & his Contemporaries* (New Haven: Yale Center for British Art, 1980), 14–18. Perhaps Williams drew on prints of Dutch seventeenth-century genre paintings and French *fêtes galantes*, sources English portraitists adapted. The closest contemporaneous New World parallel to Williams's conversation pieces is the portrait of the Anglo-Jamaican Edward East family (ca. 1775, National Gallery of Jamaica, Kingston), attributed to the English painter Philip Wickstead, who arrived at the island colony in 1773; see Miles and Saunders, *American Colonial Portraits*, 323–24. Henry Benbridge, as the leading painter in Charleston, S.C., made similar works beginning around 1775; in his case, knowledge came at firsthand from the time he spent in London, 1769–ca. 1772. See Maurie D. McInnis et al., *Henry Benbridge: Charleston Portrait Painter (1743–1812)* (Charleston, S.C.: Gibbes Museum of Art, 2000), esp. cat. 2, 15, 29.

52 Copley to Henry Pelham, June 16, 1771; *Copley–Pelham Letters*, 116–17.

53 Bermingham analyzes the ideological implications of the English outdoor conversation piece – and the "breakdown of the sign system" in the artificial naturalism of Devis's work in particular – in *Landscape and Ideology*, 14–33.

54 New-York Historical Society, Misc. MSS, William Hawxhurst, fifteen letters and receipts. Rodney MacDonough, "William Denning," *New York Genealogical and Biographical Record* 30 (July 1899): 133–41.

55 Henry Reed Stiles, *A History of the City of Brooklyn*, 2 vols. (Brooklyn, 1867), 1: 308.

56 In *Mannahatta* (New York: Abrams, 2009), Eric Sanderson and Markley Boyer ingeniously reconstructed the appearance and character of the island in 1609, most of which remained unchanged at the time of the Revolution, as evidenced by one of the authors' key sources, the astonishingly detailed British Headquarters Map, in the Public Records Office, London. That map and many others are reproduced

and analyzed in Robert T. Augustyn and Paul E. Cohen, *Manhattan in Maps, 1527–1995* (New York: Rizzoli, 1997).

57 *Boston News-Letter*, May 22–May 29, 1740. Smibert's inventory (with very low valuation of the landscapes relative to other paintings) published in Saunders, *Smibert*, 263–64.

58 The most comprehensive study of early American landscape is Nygren et al., *Views and Visions: American Landscape before 1830*. Essays in that volume on landscapes produced by military artists, on natural history illustration, and landscape gardening would seem promising in connection with Williams; however, very few works, projects or period texts discussed by the authors (Bruce Robertson, Amy R. W. Meyers, and Therese O'Malley, respectively) date as early as Williams's 1772 landscape (which was not in the exhibition). For a more recent and broadly contextual account, see John E. Crowley, *Imperial Landscapes: Britain's Global Visual Culture, 1745–1820* (New Haven and London: Yale University Press for the Paul Mellon Centre for Studies in British Art, 2011), esp. 141–67 (on the United States). John Taylor (1735–1806), a wealthy and well-connected Philadelphian who knew many of West's supporters, became, in his own day, a notable landscape painter after moving to Bath to pursue art in 1762. Taylor's age and purposefulness when he left argue for prior activity as a gentleman amateur in late 1750s Philadelphia, though no landscapes from that period survive. See Arthur S. Marks, "An Eighteenth-Century American Landscape Painter Rediscovered: John Taylor of Bath," *American Art Journal* 10 (Nov. 1978): 81–96. Among Peale's patrons, John Beale Bordley – Maryland planter and agronomist – was an avid amateur landscapist, as affirmed by correspondence between himself and Peale during the early 1770s; his only surviving landscape, however, is a 1776 copy from a print by Claude Lorrain. *Peale Papers*, 1: 82–83, 86–87, 118. Peale later stated that his own earliest works included a landscape; *Peale Papers*, 5: 15.

59 Eagles, 1805 memo, recorded that West met Williams on his own, but West, 1810 letter, named Edward Pennington, his cousin, and Samuel Shoemaker, the neighbor, as facilitators of the introduction.

60 The author of a popular manual on art observed that a "prospect" could be taken most simply by boring a hole through a window shutter; [Robert Dossie], *The Handmaid to the Arts*, 2 vols., 2nd ed. (London, 1764), 1: 394. Philadelphians could have seen a camera obscura on display in 1745; J. Thomas Scharf and Thompson Westcott, *History of Philadelphia, 1609–1844*, 3 vols. (Philadelphia, 1884), 2: 864.

61 On overmantels, see Little, *American Decorative Wall Painting*, 25–64, and cf. esp. figs. 41, 42, by the Neopolitan artist Michel Felice Cornè – even though these greatly postdate West's presumed overmantels.

62 Helmut von Erffa and Allen Staley, *The Paintings of Benjamin West* (New Haven and London: Yale University Press, 1986), 434–35 (cats. 480, 481). The works survived through West's intervention from across the Atlantic and late in his life at a time when he had begun to reflect on his legacy. Long before then, however, West's attachment to his own early efforts – or, to be less cynical, to their subject matter – can be gauged by his ownership of a *Landscape with Cow* by George Barret and Sawrey Gilpin, and a *Storm at Sea* by Francis Swaine, both of which Peale copied during his time in West's London studio 1767–69. Peale mentioned his versions ("piece of Cows & a Sea piece") in his diary, 1778, with identifications provided by the editor in a note; *Peale Papers*, 1: 263–64.

63 "New York, October 9," *Pennsylvania Gazette* (Oct. 12, 1758).

64 Stein speculated that in New York of 1772, *Imaginary Landscape* made "an appeal to the commercial and political interests of the Court party against the claims of the protesting American Whigs." He also considered it a possibly "remembered" image of Havana harbor, based on Williams's time in the West Indies earlier in the preceding decade, and he noted the similarity of the ships to those in an engraving by Peter Canot published in 1764, soon after the British took Havana in the Seven Years' War. Stein, *Seascape and the American Imagination*, 16 and 132 n.20, which credits research undertaken by Melanie Schwarzer.

65 On the "social and political work" that topographical landscapes were meant to perform, see Ann Bermingham, *Learning to Draw: Studies in the Cultural History of a Polite and Useful Art* (New Haven and London: Yale University Press for the Paul Mellon Centre for Studies in British Art, 2000), 78–91.

66 Ralph Hyde, *A Prospect of Britain: The Town Panoramas of Samuel and Nathaniel Buck* (London: Pavilion Books, 1994).

67 See, e.g., the overview offered by Edward J. Nygren, "From View to Vision," in Nygren et al., *Views and Visions: American Landscape before 1830*, 3–81.

68 Only one work beyond those I discuss in this chapter has been generally accepted as by this Williams, a small whole length portrait of Jacob Fox (1774) at Colonial Williamsburg. Other attributed works presented by Dickason (*Williams*, 138–80, 207–17), but not knowledgeably discussed, were reasonably disputed by Richardson ("Williams"), who assigned them to three other painters of the same name. Reconstructing Williams's corpus is not my aim.

69 Reynolds's critique, as relayed by Captain R. G. Bruce; *Copley–Pelham Letters*, 41–44.

70 The date in which newspaper advertisements overtook editorial content is from T. H. Breen, *The Marketplace of Revolution* (Oxford: Oxford University Press, 2004), 55 (analysis of merchant advertisements, 53–59).

71 Online resources such as America's Historical Newspapers now offer ready access to the full original contexts; however, print advertisements for eighteenth-century American artists and artisans can be conveniently surveyed in several still useful compendia: William Kelby, *Notes on American Artists, 1754–1820, Compiled from Advertisements Appearing in the Newspapers of the Day* (New York: New-York Historical Society, 1922); George Francis Dow, *The Arts & Crafts in New England, 1704–1775: Gleanings from Boston Newspapers* (Topsfield, Mass.: Wayside Press, 1927); Alfred Coxe Prime, *The Arts & Crafts in Philadelphia, Maryland, and South Carolina, 1721–1785: Gleanings from Newspapers*, 2 vols. ([Topsfield, Mass.]: The Walpole Society, 1929); and Rita Susswein Gottesman, *The Arts and Crafts in New York, 1726–1776: Advertisements and News Items from New York City Newspapers* (New York: New-York Historical Society, 1938). Williams's ads of 1763 and 1769 appeared over several weeks each, a common practice.

72 William Sawitzky, *Matthew Pratt, 1734–1805: A Study of his Work* (New York: New-York Historical Society in cooperation with the Carnegie Corporation of New York, 1942), 15.

73 "To the Proprietors of the Universal Magazine," *Universal Magazine of Knowledge and Pleasure* 3 (Nov. 1748): 230. By the mid-seventeenth century in England, "limner" meant a miniature painter, a usage arising from similarities in scale and medium (watercolor) between that art and techniques of late medieval manuscript illumination, called "limning." Since most miniatures were portraits, "limner" soon became synonymous with "portrait painter," regardless of medium. For terminology, see Edward Norgate, *Miniature or the Art of Limning*, ed. Jeffrey M. Muller and Jim Murrell (New Haven and London: Yale University Press for the Paul Mellon Centre for Studies in British Art, 1997), 113–14 n.6; and Carol Aiken, "The Emergence of the Portrait Miniature in New England," *Painting and Portrait Making in the American Northeast*,

Dublin Seminar for New England Folklife: Annual Proceedings, 1994, ed. Peter Benes (Boston: Boston University Press, 1995), 34–40.

74 Arthur Pond presents a well-documented metropolitan model of artistic enterprise and adaptability, as detailed by Louise Lippincott, *Selling Art in Georgian London: The Rise of Arthur Pond* (New Haven and London: Yale University Press for the Paul Mellon Centre for Studies in British Art, 1983).

75 West (1810 letter) said that Williams undertook the painting and ornamentation of ships for a Philadelphia shipbuilder named Penrose, whose name he borrowed for his fictional alter ego; however, no further evidence supports or disproves Williams's involvement in the decoration of ships.

76 The Benjamin Loxley that Williams mentioned in his Philadelphia ads was a carpenter and real estate investor who lived on Arch Street, between Third and Fourth; from there he opened a court running north, on which he built houses. Williams occupied one of those by 1763, if not earlier. Present-day Loxley's Court is in this same location, and in the eighteenth century there was a second Loxley's Court, developed by the same man, on the south side of Spruce Street, between Front and Second Streets. See Thompson Westcott, *The Historic Mansions and Buildings of Philadelphia* (Philadelphia: Porter & Coates, 1877), 190–91. For an overview of early American music, see Kate Van Winkle Keller, with John Koegel, "Secular Music to 1800," in *The Cambridge History of American Music*, ed. David Nicholls (Cambridge: Cambridge University Press, 1998), 49–77.

77 On drawing as a polite activity, see Kim Sloan, *"A Noble Art": Amateur Artists and Drawing Masters*, and Bermingham, *Learning to Draw*.

78 On the language of early American advertisements, see "Shopping and Advertising in Colonial America," in *Of Consuming Interests: The Style of Life in the Eighteenth Century*, ed. Cary Carson, Ronald Hoffman, and Peter J. Albert (Charlottesville and London: University of Virginia Press for the United States Capitol Historical Society, 1994), 233–51 (esp. 247–51).

79 Jefferson's frustration over proposed revisions to the Declaration of Independence prompted Franklin's tale of the hat maker and his sign; for the story and an analysis of its meaning, see Robert A. Ferguson, *The American Enlightenment, 1750–1820* (Cambridge, Mass., and London: Harvard University Press, 1997), 14–19. See also Bryan J. Wolf, "Signs of the Times: A Brief Cultural History of Sign Painting," in *Lions & Eagles & Bulls: Early American Tavern & Inn Signs from the Connecticut Historical Society*, ed. Susan P. Schoelwer (Princeton: Princeton University Press in association with the Connecticut Historical Society, 2000), 14. Schoelwer and her co-authors in that catalogue brought a multifaceted scholarly treatment to inn and tavern signs, in much later general use than shop signs and consequently the largest surviving class of American signs.

80 Williams, the teacher of West, did not, however, make the statement concerning signs attributed to him by Susan P. Schoelwer ("Introduction: Rediscovering the Public Art of Early American Inn Signs," in *Early American Tavern & Inn Signs*, ed. Schoelwer, 9), which appeared in William Williams, *An Essay on the Mechanic of Oil Colours* (Bath, 1787). That author gave his Bath street address on the title page of the pamphlet, whereas the Williams under consideration here was by then an established resident of a Bristol almshouse.

81 On sign-painting technique, see Sandra L. Webber, "'Faithfully and Promptly Executed': A Conservator's View of Sign Painting," in *Early American Tavern & Inn Signs*, ed. Schoelwer, 66–79.

82 Ambrose Heal catalogued signs displayed by tradesmen in a wide range of occupations, with illustrations based on imagery found on trade cards then in the author's collection and now in the British Museum; *The Signboards of Old London Shops* (1947; New York: B. Blom, 1971). See also Ambrose Heal, *London Tradesmen's Cards of the XVIII Century* (1925; New York: Dover, 1968). The most extensive cultural analysis of trade cards can be found in a history department thesis by Patricia Constance Kidd, "Aspects of Eighteenth Century Advertising in Britain – London Trade Cards 1660–1770" (M.A. thesis, University of Victoria, British Columbia 2005).

83 Hicks's account books, 1806–33, analyzed by Carolyn Weekley, *The Kingdoms of Edward Hicks* (Williamsburg, Va.: Colonial Williamsburg Foundation, 1999), 65–89. Weekley noted that painted texts bordering eight versions of *The Peaceable Kingdom* offer strong links to Hicks's work as a sign painter.

84 Reynolds, quoted in James Northcote, *The Life of Sir Joshua Reynolds*, 2 vols. (2nd ed., rev., London: Henry Colburn, 1819), 1: 55.

85 Ronald Paulson, *Hogarth*, 3 vols. (New Brunswick, N.J., and London: Rutgers University Press, 1991), 3: 357. Samuel Wale, the first Professor of Perspective at the Royal Academy of Arts, also painted signs during his career.

86 Chester Harding, *My Egotistigraphy* (Cambridge, Mass., 1866), 26. Harding used the name "Infant Artists," but the 1783 stipple engraving by Francis Hayward bore the title "The Infant Academy"; at the Royal Academy exhibition in 1782, Reynolds's painting was simply titled "Children."

87 Japanning was ornamental painting, often on furniture, in imitation of Japanese lacquerwork. Gore's sign, carved in wood, survives at Gore Place, home of Christopher Gore, a tradesman's son who became governor of Massachusetts. The oldest surviving sign in colonial use, also carved, hung by 1701 at the Boston shop of painter-in-general Thomas Child, who emigrated to Massachusetts during the 1680s; the sign bore the coat of arms of the London Painter-Stainers Company, as well as the initials of Child and his wife, Katherine. Jonathan Fairbanks et al., *New England Begins: The Seventeenth Century*, 3 vols. (Boston: Museum of Fine Arts, 1982), 3: 477–78.

88 On the gradual dispersal of contents of Smibert's studio, see Saunders, *Smibert*, 122–25.

89 Paulson, *Hogarth*, 2: 77–87.

90 The unidentified maker of Israel Putnam's tavern sign based its design on a mezzotint by Richard Houston after Hervey Smith; Nancy Finlay, "Lions and Eagles and Other Images on Early Inn Signs," in *Early American Tavern & Inn Signs*, ed. Schoelwer, 59.

91 *Boston Gazette, and Country Journal*, July 9, 1764.

92 Robert Campbell, *The London Tradesman* (1747; Newton Abbot, Devon, 1969), 103–4, 100 (quotations this paragraph).

93 William Salmon attributed the strategy of selling prepared paints with instructions for use to Alexander Emerton, Joseph Emerton's brother; *Palladio Londinensis* (London, 1755), 63.

94 Lawrence, quoted in D. E. Williams, *The Life and Correspondence of Sir Thomas Lawrence*, 2 vols. (London, 1831), 1: 221.

95 For Calfe's trade card, see James Ayres, *The Artist's Craft: A History of Tools, Techniques and Materials* (Oxford: Phaidon, 1985), 130, fig. 183.

96 Gottesman, *Arts and Crafts in New York*, 1–7, also 438: list of signs mentioned in collected ads.

97 *Spectator* 28 (Apr. 2, 1711). Ad for John Winters, *Pennsylvania Gazette*, Mar. 20, 1740.

98 Inventories and advertisements document the presence of Hogarth's prints in colonial British America. See E. McSherry Fowble, *Two Centuries of Prints in America, 1680–1880: A Selective Cata-*

logue of the Winterthur Museum Collection (Charlottesville: Published for the Henry Francis du Pont Winterthur Museum by the University Press of Virginia, 1987), 19, 179, 258, 260; Joan Dolmetsch, "Prints in Colonial America: Supply and Demand in the Mid-Eighteenth Century," in *Prints in and of America to 1850*, ed. John D. Morse (Charlottesville: University of Virginia Press, 1970), 54–55; Dow, *Arts & Crafts*, 25, 32, 36.

99 John Adams thought Hogarth's text sufficiently practical and accessible to recommend the author's discussion of the "line of beauty," as applied to dress, to his young nieces; Adams's draft of an unpublished essay of 1761 addressed "Dear Nieces," from *Diary and Autobiography of John Adams*, 4 vols., ed. L. H. Butterfield et al. (Cambridge, Mass.: Belknap Press of Harvard University Press, 1961), 1: 194. Peale, newly returned from West's London studio in 1769, made the line of beauty the subject of a drawing lesson in the late 1760s; *Peale Papers*, 5: 41.

100 Papers relating to New England and New York circa 1774, Pierre Eugène du Simitière Collection 1492–1784, Library Company of Philadelphia.

101 "Warren Johnson's Journal 1760–1761," in *The Papers of Sir William Johnson*, 14 vols. (Albany: University of the State of New York, 1921–65), 13: 185; Andrew Burnaby, *Travel through the Middle Settlements in North-America in the Years 1759 and 1760* (London, 1775), 65. A traveling Scot offered a contrasting view, finding that in 1744 Dutch "language and customs begin pritty much to wear out" in New York; *Gentleman's Progress: The Itinerarium of Dr. Alexander Hamilton, 1744*, ed. Carl Bridenbaugh (Chapel Hill: University of North Carolina Press for the Institute of Early American History and Culture, Williamsburg, 1948), 89.

102 Simon Middleton, *From Privileges to Rights: Work and Politics in Colonial New York City* (Philadelphia: University of Pennsylvania Press, 2006), 189. The Federal Census of 1790 counted 80,000 Dutch immigrants and descendants of Dutch settlers within fifty miles of New York City; *The Encyclopedia of New York City*, ed. Kenneth T. Jackson (New Haven and London: Yale University Press; New York: New-York Historical Society, 1995), 351–52 (s.v., "Dutch"). Nan A. Rothschild charted the city's ethnic diversity and Dutch and English convergence, from the perspective of urban anthropology, in *New York City Neighborhoods: The 18th Century* (San Diego: Academic Press, 1990), esp. chs. 3, 4. As of 1730, however, third-generation men of Dutch ancestry in New York City still overwhelmingly married Dutch-descended women; Joyce D. Goodfriend, *Before the Melting Pot: Society and Culture in Colonial New York City, 1664–1730* (Princeton: Princeton University Press, 1992), 178–86.

103 The name Dey (pronounced "Dye," judging from that common spelling on some maps and documents) was neither Dutch in origin nor the family's true name. Dirck Janszen Siecken, the landowner as of the 1670s, used Dey as a surname for the first time in his will of 1683; Paul Cushman, *Soldiers, Civil Servants, and a Silversmith: William Gilbert, Theunis Dey and their Dutch-American Families Participate in the Development of 18th Century America* (Hackensack, N.J.: Long Dash Publishing, [2007]), 11–12. The Dey family property had been carved from one of the earliest Dutch land grants (ca. 1638), the Jan Jansen Damen farm. I. N. Phelps Stokes, *The Iconography of Manhattan Island, 1498–1909*, 6 vols. (New York: R. H. Dodd, 1915–28), 6: 86 and Pl. 84B-a, at 80–81; "Operations in Real Estate in the City of New York, in the Olden Time," in D. T. Valentine, *Manual of the Corporation of the City of New York for 1860* (New York, 1860), 527–30. See also Carl Abbott, "The Neighborhoods of New York, 1760–1775," *New York History* 55 (Jan. 1974): 35–54.

104 Theophilus Pell's ropewalk noted in connection with his will of Oct. 27, 1724, in Stokes, *Iconography*, 6: 502. Evert Pels (or Pells, in Stokes) owned it by the early 1740s but advertised its sale in *Weyman's New-York Gazette*, beginning July 16, 1759. David Grim purportedly drew his detailed plan from memory in 1813, looking back to a date when he was at most seven. Even so, his drawing has been judged remarkably accurate to the precise period he claimed to represent (suggesting that he must have availed himself of other maps). New York had at least three other ropewalks, including one established along Broadway near "the Fields" (or Common) in 1719, shown on city plans of ca. 1730, 1735, and 1742–44; see Augustyn and Cohen, *Manhattan in Maps*, 54–55, 60–65.

105 On "battoes," see Peter Kalm, *Travels into North America*, 3 vols., trans. John Reinhold Forster (London, 1771), 2: 242. For the boom in shipbuilding, see Middleton, *Privileges to Rights*, 212, 220; for dock construction, George William Edwards, *New York as an Eighteenth Century Municipality, 1731–1776*, Studies in History, Economics, and Public Law no. 178 (New York: Columbia University Press, 1917), 151–57. The arsenal near "Dyes" Street appears on the "Ratzen Plan" of New York.

106 A list of common names for New York streets compiled by Du Simitière included "Batteaux" (spelled differently by others) for "Dyes Street"; Papers relating to New England and New York, Du Simitière Collection, Library Company.

107 Stokes, *Iconography*, 4: 733–34 (Mar. 15, 1763). One block of Dey Street still runs west from Broadway below Fulton, its extent truncated after 1965 for development of the World Trade Center.

108 John C. Hamilton described his father's walks in *Life of Alexander Hamilton*, 2 vols. (New York: Halsted & Voorhies, 1834–40), 1: 22.

109 As quoted in Stokes, *Iconography*, 4: 769 (his various entries for Oct. 30, [1766]).

110 Patrick M'Robert, *A Tour through Part of the North Provinces of America, being a Series of Letters Wrote on the Spot, in the Years 1774 & 1775* (Edinburgh, 1776), 13. The area became "the first spatially discrete, economically homogenous sector of the city," foreshadowing developments in nineteenth-century New York; Rothschild, *Neighborhoods*, 128–29.

111 Occupations are named in leases ("indentures") granted by Dirck Dey – who divided the properties among his four children at his death in 1764 – and lists of bonds, among the Dey Family Estate Papers, Richard Varick Papers, New-York Historical Society. Trade advertisements provide more detailed descriptions but for a narrower spectrum of trades; e.g., *New York-Mercury*, Feb. 28, 1763; *New-York Journal; or, the General Advertiser*, Oct. 12, 1769.

112 William Dunlap, *A History of the American Theatre from its Origins to 1832*, intro. Tice L. Milles (1832; Urbana and Chicago: University of Illinois Press, 2005), 44.

113 Sale of the house "in Battoe street, in occupation of William Williams painter" appears in *New-York Journal*, Oct. 18, 1770, 174; the other citations are from *New-York Gazette, and the Weekly Mercury*, Feb. 27, 1769, and Jan. 29, 1770.

114 In 1769, Du Simitière catalogued 178 "Names of the families of Dutch Extract remaining in New York in 1769"; Papers relating to New York, 1644–1770, Box 1, folder 65–67, Du Simitière Collection, Library Company.

115 For the importance of Dutch artistic traditions in eighteenth-century British North America, see Ruth Piwonka and Roderic H. Blackburn, *A Remnant in the Wilderness: New York Dutch Scripture History Paintings of the Early Eighteenth Century* (New York: Bard College

Center for the Albany Institute of History and Art, 1980), and Louisa Wood Ruby, "Dutch Art and the Hudson Valley Patroon Painters," in *Going Dutch: The Dutch Presence in America, 1609–2009*, ed. Joyce D. Goodfriend, Benjamin Schmidt, and Annette Stott (Leiden and Boston: Brill, 2008), 27–57. Esther Singleton cites inventories that included pictures likely made in the Netherlands, e.g., a seapiece, a "small winter," a "sea strand," "ye city of Amsterdam"; *Social New York under the Georges, 1714–1776* (New York: D. Appleton, 1902), 90, also 87 for a 1771 sale of art works that included pictures by several named seventeenth-century Dutch painters.

116 Kalm, *Travels into North America*, 1: 250.

117 Papers relating to New England and New York, Du Simitière Collection, Library Company.

118 Sloan, *"A Noble Art": Amateur Artists and Drawing Masters*, 78–79.

119 William Smith, Jr., *The History of the Province of New-York*, 2 vols., ed. Michael Kammen (Cambridge, Mass.: Belknap Press of Harvard University Press, 1972), 226.

120 John Durand, ad in *New-York Gazette, or the Weekly Post-Boy*, Apr. 11, 1768, and in three successive issues; also April 21 and May 5 in the *New-York Journal; or, the General Advertiser*.

121 "John Durand, Portrait Painter," *Connecticut Journal*, May 13, 1768, 30. Carolyn Weekley constructed a plausible history for this relatively little known artist, who was probably born in London to parents of Huguenot descent, his father a pewterer. Durand's sophisticated ideas about art, evident in his advertisement, and his appealing but unsophisticated (flat and linear) painting manner may, paradoxically, have come from the same source: an apprenticeship in London 1760–ca. 1767 with Charles Catton, a coach and heraldic painter who became a founding member of the Royal Academy of Arts in 1768, roughly the time of Durand's presumed emigration. Weekley, *Painters and Paintings in the Early American South* (Colonial Williamsburg Foundation, Va., in association with Yale University Press, 2013), 279–91.

122 Peale to John Beale Bordley, Nov. 1772, *Peale Papers*, 1: 127.

123 "R. G. Esq" [Richard Graham], life of Rembrandt, in C. A. Du Fresnoy, *Art of Painting* (London, 1716), 371. West said Williams loaned him a copy of Du Fresnoy, though it is impossible to determine the exact edition. Graham's perspective on Rembrandt, like that of other writers, had been shaped by Roger de Piles, *Abrégé de la vie des peintres* (1699), first trans. into English as *The Art of Painting, and The Lives of the Painters* (London, 1706; reissued 1744, 1754), 316–20.

124 Jonathan Richardson, *An Essay on the Theory of Painting*, 2nd ed. (London, 1725), 66–69, 117, 141, 252–53.

125 David Alexander, "Rembrandt and the Reproductive Print in Eighteenth Century England," 49, in the broadly useful book by Christopher White, David Alexander, and Ellen D'Oench, *Rembrandt in Eighteenth Century England* (New Haven: Yale Center for British Art, 1983).

126 Du Simitière's sale of 1779, as cited in John A. Kouwenhoven, *The Columbia Historical Portrait of New York: An Essay in Graphic History* (New York: Harper and Row, 1972), 64; I have not been able to locate this document. Among the thirty-eight pictures inventoried Dec. 1774 for third-generation New York City resident Elbert Haring, eight had been consigned to "the garret"; reprinted in full in Ruth Piwonka, "New York Colonial Inventories: Dutch Interiors as a Measure of Cultural Change," in *New World Dutch Studies: Dutch Arts and Culture in Colonial America, 1609–1776: Proceedings of the Symposium Organized by the Albany Institute of History and Art*, ed. Roderic H. Blackburn and N. A. Kelley (Albany, N.Y: Albany Institute of History and Art, 1987), 76–79. Du Simitière, "Miniature Painter," advertised his intended departure from New York in the *New-York Gazette, and the Weekly Mercury*, July 31, 1769.

127 Harding, *My Egotistigraphy*, 26–27, 33.

128 *Witness* (Litchfield, Conn.), Feb. 5, 12, 18, 26, 1806. Bissell's inn sign attribution to Wales by Schoelwer, *Early American Tavern & Inn Signs*, 9.

129 Walter Blair and Hamlin Hill, *America's Humor: From Poor Richard to Doonesbury* (New York: Oxford University Press, 1978), 93.

130 "The Convention of 1787," *Port Folio* 264 (Apr. 1824): 310–11.

131 William Dunlap, *A History of the Rise and Progress of the Arts of Design in the United States* (1834), 3 vols., ed. Rita Weiss (New York: Dover, 1969), 1: 102.

132 Julie Ann Plax, "Gersaint's Biography of Antoine Watteau: Reading Between and Beyond the Lines," *Eighteenth-Century Studies* 25 (Summer 1992): 545–60.

133 John Romney, *Memoirs of the Life and Works of George Romney* (London, 1830), 18–19; see also David A. Cross, *A Striking Likeness: The Life of George Romney* (London: Ashgate, 2000), 12.

134 Dunlap, *History*, 1: 191–92. Delanoy invoked West in his ad in the *New-York Gazette, and Weekly Mercury*, Jan. 7, 1771. He announced his sale of goods in the *New-York Journal*, June 20, 1771, and his diversified painting practice (including carriages, houses, ships, and signs) in the *Connecticut Journal* in 1784 and 1785.

135 On this artist, see Joseph Jackson, "John A. Woodside, Philadelphia's Glorified Sign-Painter," *Pennsylvania Magazine of History and Biography* 57:1 (1933): 58–65, and Lee Ellen Griffith, "John Archibald Woodside, Sr.," *Antiques* 140 (Nov. 1991): 816–20. Griffith and others have proposed that Woodside's *Still Life – Rabbits* (1827; Philadelphia Museum of Art) was a study for a Philadelphia restaurant sign, but this cannot be substantiated and seems improbable. A sign for the Rising Sun Inn in the Chester County (Pa.) Historical Society has been attributed to Woodside.

136 *Public Ledger* (Philadelphia), Feb. 28, 1852, as quoted in Jackson, "Woodside," 63.

137 Jacob Larwood [H. D. J. van Schevichaven] and John Camden Hotten, *The History of Signboards from the Earliest Times to the Present Day* (London, 1867), 82; Bryant Lillywhite, *London Signs: A Reference Book of London Signs from the Earliest Times to about the Mid-Nineteenth Century* (London: Allen & Unwin, 1972), 283–84, 447; Heal, *London Tradesmen's Cards of the XVIII Century*, 21; and Heal, *Signboards of Old London Shops*, 148–50. "Hogarth's Head & Dial" was the Fleet Street shop sign of Ryall and Withy, whose trade card from the Heal Collection, British Museum (37.16) is illustrated by Kidd, "Aspects of Eighteenth Century Advertising," 194.

138 Ronald Paulson, *Hogarth's Graphic Works*, 3rd rev. ed. (London: Print Room, 1989), no. 180.

139 For an overview of the market for Rembrandt's etchings, of which artists were among the most avid collectors, see White et al., *Rembrandt in Eighteenth Century England*.

140 West, 1810 letter.

141 Timothy Clayton discusses the increasingly active trade between London printsellers and provincial markets during the period 1730–70 (though with minimal reference to the colonies) in *The English Print, 1688–1802* (New Haven and London: Yale University Press for the Paul Mellon Centre for Studies in British Art, 1997), 105–28.

142 Kennedy print shop advertisement from *Pennsylvania Chronicle*, Dec. 5, 1768, 399. A bill from Robert Kennedy to John Cadwalader,

Mar. 23, 1770, documents the sale of a range of prints, including West's *Angelica and Medoro* and *Pyrrhus*; Cadwalader Collection, HSP. Du Simitière, while living in Philadelphia, purchased a remarkably diverse selection of some three hundred items during a mere five month period in 1765, according to Paul Ginsberg Sifton, *Pierre du Simitière (1737–1784): A Collector in Revolutionary America* (Ph.D. dissertation, University of Pennsylvania, 1960), 375–77.

143 Dutch and Flemish artists, for example, receive the most attention in *Portraits of the Most Eminent Painters and Other Famous Artists, that have flourished in Europe* (London, 1739).

144 Quotation in Williams's unsigned first will, dated Apr. 6, 1788. A second will, witnessed and signed by Williams on his deathbed, made Thomas Eagles his sole beneficiary. The full text of both wills appears in Dickason, *Williams*, 185–87.

145 Eagles referred to the "Lives" in a note on his copy of West's 1810 letter. In 1855, the manuscript was evidently still in the possession of John Eagles, who mentioned it in "The Beggar's Legacy." Dickason, who died in 1974, gave no indication that he had found the manuscript of artists' lives, and my own efforts to discover its whereabouts have proved unproductive.

146 Du Fresnoy's *Art of Painting* had been translated from Latin into French by Roger de Piles (who added his own remarks) and then into English by John Dryden (1695), an edition later revised by the portraitist Charles Jervas (1716). The first edition of Richardson's *Theory* appeared in 1715, a much revised edition in 1725. Vasari's inclusion of artist portraits appears in Richardson, *Theory* (1715), 99, and *Theory* (1725), 102; and Du Fresnoy, *Art of Painting* (1716), 317 (life of Vasari by R. Graham).

147 William Aglionby, *Choice Observations upon the Art of Painting. Together with Vasari's Lives of the Most Eminent Painters, from Cimabue to the Time of Raphael and Michel Angelo. With an Explanation of the Difficult Terms* (London, 1719).

148 [Bainbrigg Buckeridge], "An Essay toward an English School of Painting," in de Piles, *The Art of Painting, and The Lives of the Painters* (1706), 397.

149 Horace Walpole, *Anecdotes of Painting in England*, 4 vols. (Strawberry Hill, 1765–71); vol. 4, printed in 1771, was not released until nine years later. On the *Anecdotes*, in general, and the pronounced differences between Walpole's enterprise and that of Vasari, in particular, see Lawrence Lipking, *The Ordering of the Arts in Eighteenth-Century England* (Princeton: Princeton University Press, 1970), 127–63. Nigel Llewellyn paid especial attention to the post-Vasarian literature in "The *Anecdotes of Painting* and Continental European Art History," in *Horace Walpole's Strawberry Hill*, ed. Michael Snodin (New Haven and London: Yale University Press, 2009), 137–53.

150 T. Eagles, 1810 letter, in which the list of paintings is merely summarized.

151 I am here adapting, in more circumscribed fashion, Benedict Anderson's highly influential definition of modern nations as imagined communities enabled by print culture, which encouraged shared identity among members even when not personally connected (a formulation that later scholars challenged as too unitary); Benedict R. O'G. Anderson, *Imagined Communities: Reflections on the Origin and Spread of Nationalism* (London: Verso, 1983).

152 J. Eagles, "Beggar's Legacy," 492–93.

153 Richardson, "William Williams," 17. Richardson estimated a date in the 1760s based on the artist's apparent age and vigor and on the popularity of banyans in America during that decade (though they did not "disappear" thereafter, as Richardson asserted).

154 For those connotations of the outfit, see Brandon Brame Fortune, with Deborah J. Warner, "Banyans and the Scholarly Image," in *Franklin & his Friends: Portraying the Man of Science in Eighteenth-Century America* (Washington, D.C.: Smithsonian Institution; London: National Portrait Gallery in association with University of Pennsylvania Press, 1999), 51–65.

155 Edgar P. Richardson interpreted the x-rays as showing the subject writing, but that is not apparent to me; *American Paintings and Related Pictures in the Henry Francis du Pont Winterthur Museum* (Charlottesville: Published for the Henry Francis du Pont Winterthur Museum by the University Press of Virginia, 1986), 74. Curiously, given Richardson's own earlier surmise that the *Self-Portrait* had been made in the 1760s, the Winterthur *American Paintings* catalogue entry dates the work (as Dickason did) ca. 1788–90. But Richardson, a former Winterthur director who died in 1985, may not be responsible for the date; on the other hand, his opinion might have changed after the x-ray revealed a book and (to his eye) writing activities, if the depicted volume is presumed to refer to Penrose (though that is not expressly stated in the entry).

156 A similarly represented and placed palette appears in the oval-framed portrait of drapery painter Alexander Van Haecken (who wears banyan and cap) by his frequent employer, portraitist Thomas Hudson. J. Faber made a mezzotint engraving of that work in 1748, reproduced in Iveagh Bequest, Kenwood, *Thomas Hudson, 1701–1779: Portrait Painter and Collector* (London: Greater London Council, 1979), no. 38, n.p.

157 J. Eagles, "Beggar's Legacy," 492–94.

158 Pastor Shewkirk, diary entry for Aug. 28, 1775, from Johnson's *The Campaign of 1776*, part 2, 103, as cited in Stokes, *Iconography*, 4: 901. Shewkirk's observation came early in the process; by mid-1776, New York City's civilian population had fallen from 22,000 to 5,000. In Sept. 1776, after the British seized control, fire in the South and West Wards destroyed about a third of the city; Abbott, "Neighborhoods," 40.

159 J. T. Smith (1766–1833) became a notable chronicler of the London art scene, the author of *Nollekens and his Times*, 2 vols. (London, 1828), an account of the sculptor Joseph Nollekens – for whom both he and his father had worked – and his cohort during the period 1750–1800. Smith recorded (2: 369–88) that he was frequently present in West's studio while the artist was working on the painting and print for *The Battle of La Hogue*. Williams makes no appearance in Nollekens, however, and Smith's memorandum for West remains undetected.

160 As quoted in Mary Beth Norton, *The British-Americans: The Loyalist Exiles in England, 1774–1789* (Boston and Toronto: Little, Brown, 1972), 102.

3 THE AMERICAN SCHOOL, ITALY AND LONDON

1 Almost three decades later, West detailed such a program in a letter advising the young German painter Johann Heinrich Ramberg, a protégé of George III's who was West's student during the 1780s. See Franziska Forster-Hahn, "The Sources of True Taste: Benjamin West's Instructions to a Young Painter for his Studies in Italy," *Journal of the Warburg and Courtauld Institutes* 30 (1967): 367–82.

2 Scott Paul Gordon, "Martial Art: Benjamin West's *The Death of Socrates*, Colonial Politics, and the Puzzles of Patronage," *William and Mary Quarterly*, 3rd ser., 65 (Jan. 2008): 65–100 (97–98, regarding the unusual signature and its implications).

3 Sarah Monks has argued rather ingeniously that "the equivocal quality of [West's] oeuvre – its position on the verge of statements it

never quite makes and between genres, manners and formal vocabularies with which it never truly affiliates" – was part of a strategic effort to make himself unobjectionable in a politically fraught climate; "The Wolfe Man: Benjamin West's Anglo-American Accent," *Art History* 34 (Sept. 2011): 652–73 (quote at 671). The literature on West's early career as a history painter is extensive. For book-length studies, see Ann Uhry Abrams, *The Valiant Hero: Benjamin West and Grand-Style History Painting* (Washington, D.C.: Smithsonian Institution Press, 195), and Stephen Mark Caffey, "An Heroics of Empire: Benjamin West and Anglophone History Painting 1764–1774" (Ph.D. dissertation: University of Texas, Austin, 2008). For a broader but conceptually focused consideration of British history painting and of West's distinctive contribution, see Martin Myrone, *Bodybuilding: Reforming Masculinities in British Art, 1750–1810* (New Haven and London: Yale University Press for the Paul Mellon Centre for Studies in British Art, 2005).

4 Copley's *Watson* has been the subject of much scholarly attention. Most recently, Jennifer L. Roberts offered a compelling political reading in "Failure to Deliver: *Watson and the Shark* and the Boston Tea Party," *Art History* 34 (Sept. 2011): 674–95. Prior interpretations have addressed that painting's religious resonance, its relationship to early American salvation narratives, to contemporary political prints, and to debates over the slave trade; respectively: Irma B. Jaffe, "John Singleton Copley's Watson and the Shark," *American Art Journal* 9 (May 1977): 15–25; Roger Stein, "Copley's Watson and the Shark and Aesthetics in the 1770s," in *Discoveries and Considerations: Essays on Early American Literature & Aesthetics*, ed. Calvin Israel (Albany: State University of New York, 1976), 85–130; Ann Uhry Abrams, "Politics, Prints, and John Singleton Copley's Watson and the Shark," *Art Bulletin* 61 (June 1979): 265–76; Albert Boime, "Blacks in Shark-Infested Waters: Visual Encodings of Racism in Copley and Homer," *Smithsonian Studies in American Art* 3 (Winter 1989), 19–47. For a concise overview, see Ellen Miles's entry on *Watson and the Shark*, in *American Paintings of the Eighteenth Century*, ed. Ellen Miles (Washington, D.C.: National Gallery of Art, 1995), 54–71.

5 Evidence for Robert Kennedy's print shop "at West's head" comes from the proprietor's elaborate trade card (on which those words, but no portrait, fill the upper cartouche), datable by his business address to not earlier than 1769.

6 Only one other American painter preceded West abroad, Boston-born John Greenwood (1727 1792), who began in the trade of painting as apprentice to Thomas Johnston before turning to portraiture, in which he was self taught. He made many portraits in the Dutch West Indian colony of Surinam before traveling to Amsterdam, Paris, and London, his permanent home from 1763, the same year West arrived. Greenwood admired West and did not attempt to compete with him or others, making his living instead as an art dealer and auctioneer. See his letter to Copley, Mar. 23, 1770, in *Copley-Pelham Letters*, 82.

7 West's early days in Rome as related in John Galt, *The Life and Studies of Benjamin West* (London: T. Cadell and W. Davies, 1816), 101–3.

8 Thomas Jefferson, *Notes of the State of Virginia* ([Paris], [1782, 1784]), 106.

9 For changing terminology of color, see Alden T. Vaughan, "From White Man to Redskin: Changing Anglo-American Perceptions of the American Indian," *American Historical Review* 87 (Oct. 1982): 917–53.

10 "Autobiography of the Rev. John Barnard," *Collections of the Massachusetts Historical Society*, 3rd ser., 5 (1836): 200; cited by T. H. Breen, *The Marketplace of Revolution* (Oxford: Oxford University Press, 2004), 83.

11 An anonymous reviewer of Galt's *Life of West* recognized the story of West and Apollo as "one of the few anecdotes [of West's youth] that have been made public by Mr. West himself in his lectures at the Royal Academy, almost in the same words"; *Critical Review*, 5th ser., 3 (June 1816): 585–86. The portions of West's 1794 discourse concerning the Apollo that Galt reprinted in a second volume on West make no reference to Indians, perhaps because Galt had already related the story in his first book on West's life; the latter was republished with the story of West's English career as John Galt, *The Life, Studies, and Works of Benjamin West, Esq.*, 2 vols. (London: T. Cadell and W. Davies; Edinburgh: W. Blackwood, 1820), 2: 99–101.

12 English appraisals of the *Apollo Belvedere* prior to 1760 include Jonathan Richardson, Sr., and Jr., *An Account of Some of the Statues, Bas-Reliefs, Drawings, and Pictures in Italy* (London, 1722), 275–76 ("an Air, particularly in the Head, Exquisitely Great, and Awful, as well as Beautiful"); Joseph Spence, *Polymetis; or, an Enquiry concerning the Agreement between the Works of the Roman Poets, and the Remains of the Antient Artists* (London, [1747]), 83–84; and William Hogarth, *The Analysis of Beauty*, ed. Ronald Paulson (New Haven and London: Yale University Press for the Paul Mellon Centre for Studies in British Art, 1997), 71–74 (in the chapter "Of Proportion"). Reynolds discussed the Apollo and responded to Hogarth's characterization of it in 1780; Sir Joshua Reynolds, *Discourses on Art*, ed. Robert R. Wark (New Haven and London: Yale University Press for the Paul Mellon Centre for Studies in British Art, 1975), 179–80, 184 (Discourse X, 1780).

13 Daniel Defoe, *A Review of the State of the British Nation*, 8: 153 (Mar. 15, 1712), as quoted in Alden T. Vaughan, *Transatlantic Encounters: American Indians in Britain, 1500–1776* (Cambridge: Cambridge University Press, 2006), 129. The Mohawk reputation for cruelty, however pervasive, was a myth, according to Francis Jennings, *Ambiguous Iroquois Empire: The Covenant Chain Confederation of Indian Tribes with English Colonies from its Beginnings to the Lancaster Treaty of 1744* (New York: Norton, 1983), 43. On Anglo-American rabble rousers, see Roger D. Abrahams, "Mohawks, Mohocks, Hawkubites, Whatever: Down and Dirty in Eighteenth-Century London and Boston," www.common-place.org.vol.08/no-04/tales.

14 Galt, *West* (1816), 105–6.

15 Ibid., 94.

16 Horatio Greenough, *Letters of Horatio Greenough, American Sculptor*, ed. Nathalia Wright (Madison: University of Wisconsin Press, 1972), 401.

17 Robert C. Alberts assumed West's exposure to Conestoga and Delaware Indians based on notes of 1789 by Benjamin Smith Barton, a young American naturalist, concerning the reported prevalence of settlements near Lancaster and below Philadelphia, respectively, ca. 1726; *Benjamin West: A Biography* (Boston: Houghton Mifflin, 1978), 10. That was two long decades away, in terms of Indian resettlement, from West's boyhood. See Benjamin Smith Barton, "Historical Notes," *Pennsylvania Magazine of History and Biography* 9:23 (1885): 334–38. For dispersal of Native Americans from eastern Pennsylvania, see C. A. Weslager, *The Delaware Indians: A History* (Brunswick, N.J.: Rutgers University Press, 1972), and Francis Jennings, "'Pennsylvania Indians' and the Iroquois," in *Beyond the Covenant Chain: The Iroquois and their Neighbors in Indian North America, 1600–1800*, ed. Daniel K. Richter and James H. Merrill (Syracuse, N.Y.: Syracuse University Press, 1897), 75–92. For Conestoga, specifically, see Barry Kent, *Susquehanna's Indians*, Anthropological Series No. 6 (Harrisburg: Pennsylvania Historical and Museum Commission, 1993), esp. 24–108. Jane T. Merritt mined an unusually rich array of primary sources to reconstruct the

variety and complexity of Native American and white interaction in eighteenth-century Pennsylvania for *At the Crossroads: Indians and Empires on a Mid-Atlantic Frontier, 1700–1763* (Chapel Hill: University of North Carolina Press, 2003); nothing in her book, however, lends credibility to the stories associated with West.

18 Peter Kalm, *Travels into North America*, 3 vols. (Warrington and London, 1770–71), 1: 225.

19 James Hart Merrell, *Into the American Woods: Negotiators on the Pennsylvania Frontier* (New York: W. W. Norton, 1999), 88–91 (quote at 91). Kent reported that most of the materials excavated at Conestoga were of European or colonial manufacture; *Susquehanna's Indians*, 379–91. See also Merritt, *Crossroads*, 283.

20 Indians entered into or confirmed existing treaties with British authorities in Lancaster in 1756 and 1757, possibly overlapping with West's time in the town; Jerome H. Wood, "Conestoga Crossroads: The Rise of Lancaster, Pennsylvania, 1730–1789" (Ph.D. dissertation, Brown University, 1969), 84–85. See also the chapter "Demonizing Delawares" in Merritt, *Crossroads*, 169–97.

21 William H. Truettner further noted that "no self-respecting Mohawk warrior had hunted with anything but a musket or rifle since the beginning of the eighteenth century, when trade with the British and French kept them well supplied with firearms"; *Painting Indians and Building Empires in North America, 1710–1840* (Berkeley: University of California Press, 2010), 10. Julia A. Sienkewicz, without discounting the possibility that West made some kind of connection between the Apollo and an Indian, argued that the specific link to Mohawk arose later; "Beyond the Mohawk Warrior: Reinterpreting Benjamin West's Evocations of American Indians," *19: Interdisciplinary Studies in the Long Nineteenth Century* 9 (2009), www.19.bbk.ac.uk. The most thorough account of West's informed investment in representation of Native Americans is Emily Ballew Neff's essay "At the Wood's Edge: Benjamin West's *The Death of Wolfe* and the Middle Ground," in Emily Ballew Neff with Kaylin H. Weber, *American Adversaries: West and Copley in a Transatlantic World* (Houston: Museum of Fine Arts, Houston, 2013), 64–103.

22 [John Shebbeare], *Lydia, or Filial Piety: A Novel* (1755), 2 vols., repr. ed. (New York and London: Garland, 1974), quotation in this paragraph in vol. 1 at 7, 3–4, 15, 41–43. On the author, see M. John Cardwell, "Shebbeare, John (1709–1788)," *Oxford Dictionary of National Biography* online.

23 Cadwallader Colden, *History of the Five Indian Nations Depending on the Province of New-York in America* (New York, 1727), iii. The retitled and expanded 2nd (1750) and 3rd (1755) London editions of this book brought it to wider attention. The type of the virtuous Indian gained importance in the wake of the Seven Years' War, in part as a model for American heroism; see, e.g. *Historical Account of the Expedition Against the Ohio Indians* (1765) by William Smith, the minister and classical scholar who instructed West in Philadelphia during the late 1750s. Secondary literature concerning white perspectives of Native Americans is extensive. For the period 1700–85, broadly, see, e.g., Richard Slotkin, *Regeneration through Violence: The Mythology of the American Frontier, 1600–1860* (Middletown, Conn.: Wesleyan University Press, 1973), 180–267, and, with particular reference to the southern colonies, Gary Nash, *Race, Class, and Politics: Essays on American Colonial and Revolutionary Society* (Urbana and Chicago: University of Illinois Press, 1986), 35–64. For a recent argument that West was familiar with British tropes of noble savagery and that those ideas outweighed negative perceptions so long as the Iroquois were considered useful to British imperial aims, see Truettner, *Painting Indians*, 7–11 and 18–48.

24 For the first art historical exploration of the motif, see Robert Rosenblum, "The Origin of Painting: A Problem in the Iconography of Romantic Classicism," *Art Bulletin* 39 (Dec. 1957): 279–90, George Levitine, "Addenda to R. Rosenblum's 'The Origin of Painting,'" *Art Bulletin* 40 (Dec. 1958): 329–31. As Rosenblum pointed out, the story has ancient western and non-western roots but did not find visual expression until the seventeenth century or become widely popular until the 1770s in Britain and then specifically in the version with the Corinthian maid.

25 West was one of those "Americans on the make in Europe," in Richard Slotkin's phrase, who used romanticized conceptions of Indians to their advantage. Slotkin cites the example of Major Robert Rogers, a New Englander who sought privilege in London by presenting himself, in books published there in 1765, as a key player in the French and Indian War. In his persona of a frontier hero skilled in guerilla-style fighting tactics, Roberts "violated English convention just enough to create a sense that his knowledge and experience were deeper than any Englishman's, but not enough to confuse his audience or strain their credulity" (*Regeneration*, 235). Major Robert Rogers, *A Concise Account of North America* (London, 1765) and *Journals of Major Robert Rogers* (London, 1765).

26 Joseph Shippen outlined the commission to West in a letter of Sept. 17, 1760, Pennsylvania Academy of the Fine Arts, Philadelphia (AAA roll P50/779–81). Letter quoted in Hugh Honour, "Benjamin West's *Indian Family*," *Burlington Magazine* 125 (Dec. 1983): 727 (full article, 726–33). Honour offered the first detailed account of West's *Indian Family*, crediting the work with much greater anthropological correctness than have later writers. See also Helmut von Erffa and Allen Staley, *The Paintings of Benjamin West* (New Haven and London: Yale University Press, 1986), 420–21.

27 For the judgment that the painting in the Royal College of Surgeons, London, is a copy and not by West, I rely on Neff and Weber, cited in Neff, "At the Wood's Edge," in *American Adversaries*, 77, 100 n.2 – in which Neff states that Allen Staley (an author of the West catalogue raisonné) concurred in this opinion via correspondence.

28 The original Italian text accompanying Francesco Bartolozzi's engraving after West and an English translation appear in von Erffa and Staley, *West*, Appendix 2, 582–83. Most scholars assume West wrote the text (in English) that was used in the Italian edition.

29 On British familiarity and fascination with Native American material culture, see Troy O. Bickham, "'A Conviction of the Reality of Things': Material Culture, North American Indians and Empire in Eighteenth-Century Britain," *Eighteenth-Century Studies* 39 (Fall 2005): 29–47, and, more broadly, Bickham's *Savages within the Empire: Representations of American Indians in Eighteenth-Century Britain* (Oxford: Clarendon Press, 2005). West's immediately ensuing works featuring Native Americans received attention from Jules D. Prown, "The Expedition Against the Ohio Indians in 1764 under Colonel Bouquet: Two Early Drawings by Benjamin West," in *British Art, 1740–1820: Essays in Honor of Robert Wark*, ed. Guilland Sutherland (San Marino, Calif: Huntington Library, 1992), 205–33.

30 Accounts of West's life in Italy include E. P. Richardson, "West's Voyage to Italy, 1760, and William Allen," *Pennsylvania Magazine of History and Biography* (Jan. 1978), 3–27; Abrams, *Valiant Hero*, 73–93; and Jules David Prown, "Benjamin West and the Use of Antiquity," *American Art* 9 (Summer 1996): 29–49. See also Jules David Prown, "A Course of Antiquities at Rome, 1764," *Eighteenth-Century Studies* 31 (Fall 1997): 90–100.

31 Henry Benbridge to his stepfather, Thomas Gordon, London, Jan. 23, 1770, reprinted in appendix to Maurie D. McInnis et al., *Henry Benbridge: Charleston Portrait Painter (1743–1812)* (Charleston, S.C.: Gibbes Museum of Art, 2000), 125, from transcribed photocopies at Winterthur Museum, Garden and Library, Winterthur, Delaware (originals in Carolina Art Association/Gibbes Museum of Art).

32 West's Italian portraits: von Erffa and Staley, *West*, 486, 529, 538, 573 (cats. 582, 658, 676, 730). Staley later accepted another work as by West, a portrait of Baron Rutherford (ca. 1760) offered for sale by Sotheby's, London, in 1999; Staley/von Erffa, Series 12: Other Working Notes re: West, Box 48, Folder 6, Historical Society of Pennsylvania, Philadelphia.

33 Von Erffa and Staley, *West*, 450 (cat. 524); also Robin Jaffee Frank, *Love and Loss: American Portrait and Mourning Miniatures* (New Haven and London: Yale University Press, 2000), 37–46. Von Erffa and Staley include as cat. 525 (450–51) a self-portrait West supposedly gave to his early Lancaster patron William Henry before departing America in 1760, but the work is unidentified. West made his earliest reported (likewise unidentified) self-portrait at about age twelve, a drawing in which he showed his hair "hanging loosely about his shoulders"; as quoted in Dunlap, *History*, 1: 38. The Mr. Lewis to whom Dunlap attributes this information was Enoch Lewis, who composed the biographical entry on West for *Encyclopaedia Americana*, 13 vols. (Philadelphia: Lea & Carey, 1829–33), 13: 125–28. No reference to the boyhood self-portrait appears in that volume; it may have come from a letter Dunlap received from Lewis's son, Joseph J. Lewis, while gathering materials for his *History*; William Dunlap, *The Diary of William Dunlap, 1766–1839: The Memoirs of a Dramatist, Theatrical Manager, Painter, Critic, Novelist, and Historian*, 3 vols. in 1, ed. Dorothy C. Barck (1930; repr., New York: Benjamin Blom, 1969), 2: 685 (entry [May] 31, 1833).

34 Prior to publication of Susan Rather, "Painters and Status in Colony and Early Nation," in *A Companion to American Art*, ed. John Davis, Jennifer Greenhill, and Jason LaFountain (London: Wiley-Blackwell, 2015), 359–77, West's self-portrait drawing had only ever been reproduced by Abrams, who gave it four sentences in the context of a cursory overview of West's self-portraits (*Valiant Hero*, 18–27). From Thomas Eagles's 1805 memo concerning West's recollections of Williams, it appears there may have been yet another early self-portrait: "on my return from Italy, I sent to my friends in America my picture, as a remembrance of me, I had painted whilst abroad. I receiv'd a letter from Williams . . . with a complimentary copy of verses, in which he was pleas'd to flatter me very highly." West said he still had these "somewhere" but neither the documents nor self-portrait are known. Tempting as it is to speculate that the self-portrait drawing, usually dated ca. 1762–63, was a study for the lost painting, there is no real basis for doing so.

35 For van Dyck's liberties with actual styles of dress, see Emilie E. S. Gordenker, *Anthony Van Dyck (1599–1641) and the Representation of Dress in Seventeenth-Century Portraiture* (Turnhout: Brepols, 2001).

36 Horace Walpole to Horace Mann, Feb. 18, 1742, in *Horace Walpole's Correspondence with Sir Horace Mann*, ed. W. S. Lewis, Warren Hunting Smith, and George L. Lam, *The Yale Edition of Horace Walpole's Correspondence*, vol. 17 (New Haven: Yale University Press, 1954), 339. Walpole's famous van Dyck would later be reattributed to Rubens and may represent his sister-in-law Susanna Fourment. For its impact on British artists, see *Van Dyck & Britain*, ed. Karen Hearn (London: Tate, 2009), 217–19. Susanna Fourment was Rubens's subject in another much admired and emulated portrait that was similarly misattributed to van Dyck, known as the *Chapeau de Paille* or "straw hat," a misnomer (the hat is beaver) resulting from corruption of the French word for (animal) hair, *poils*. Aileen Ribeiro assessed the English tradition of depicting men and women in masquerade-inspired dress in "The Dress Worn at Masquerades in England, 1730 to 1790, and its Relation to Fancy Dress in Portraiture" (Ph.D. dissertation, Courtauld Institute, University of London, 1977; New York: Garland Publishing, 1984). On colonial use of these conventions, especially in portraits of Charleston women made by English-trained artist John Wollaston, see Jennifer Van Horn, "The Mask of Civility: Portraits of Colonial Women and the Transatlantic Masquerade," *American Art* 23 (Fall 2009): 8–35.

37 *Mr. and Mrs. John Sawrey Morritt* (ca. 1765) and *Mr. and Mrs. John Williams* (1766), in von Erffa and Staley, *West*, 536 (cats. 669, 671) and 564 (cats. 715, 716). A family portrait by Angelica Kauffmann (which leaves the child nude) exhibits the same gender distinction in costuming: *Edward Stanley, 12th Earl of Derby, with his First Wife, Elizabeth Hamilton and their Son, Edward Stanley Smith* (ca. 1776), Metropolitan Museum of Art, New York.

38 Von Erffa and Staley, *West*, 486 (cat. 582, *John Allen*, ca. 1760) and 548 (cat. 689, *Thomas Robinson*, 1760; not illustrated/location unknown). After publication of the catalogue, Staley concluded that their cat. 730 – *Unidentified Man*, ca. 1760–61 (p. 573) – was the lost portrait of Robinson: Staley/von Erffa, HSP.

39 About a half-dozen of Batoni's 175 British sitters wear Vandyke dress, among the several ways in which he shaped portraits to British taste; see Edgar Peters Bowron, *Pompeo Batoni: Prince of Painters in Eighteenth-Century Rome* (New Haven and London: Yale University Press in association with Museum of Fine Arts, Houston, 2007), 37–87. For Mengs, see Steffi Roettgen, *Anton Raphael Mengs 1728–1779 and his British Patrons* (London: A. Zwemmer, 1993), figs. 11, 14, 17; also cat. 3 (formerly attributed to both Mengs and Batoni).

40 Kauffmann's more dynamic draftsmanship in other contemporaneous drawings led Anthony Clark to propose her portrait of West as an exercise in the manner of Mengs and L. G. Blanchet; Clark, as cited in Angela Rosenthal, "Kauffmann and Portraiture" in *Angelica Kauffmann: A Continental Artist in Georgian England*, ed. Wendy Wassyng Roworth (London: Reaktion Books, 1992), 101.

41 Jonathan Richardson, *An Essay on the Theory of Painting* (London, 1715), 9. From a French perspective, the value the English accorded portraits by van Dyck had more to do with his own fame than the noble status of his sitters; M. Grosley, *A Tour to London: or, New Observations on England and its Inhabitants*, 3 vols., trans. Thomas Nugent (Dublin, 1772), 2: 217–18. For van Dyck's impact on later artists and their patrons, see [Susan Sloman], "Van Dyck's Continuing Influence," in *Van Dyck & Britain*, 205–9.

42 *Iconographie, ou vies des hommes illustres du XVII. siècle écrites Par M. V** avec les portraits peints par le fameux Antoine Van Dyck, et gravées sous sa direction*, 2 vols. (Amsterdam and Leipzig, 1759). Ger Luitjen traced the history of this project in "The *Iconography*: Van Dyck's Portraits in Print," in Carl Depauw and Ger Luitjen, *Anthony van Dyck as a Printmaker* (New York: Rizzoli, 1999), 73–91 (cats. 92–217). Van Dyck's portrait of engraver Paulus Pontius appeared prominently among a raft of engravings in Nathaniel Hone's painting *The Conjuror* (1775), a thinly veiled attack on Joshua Reynolds as, among other things, a plagiarist, though there was nothing covert about his debt to van Dyck in the 1765 portrait of David Stewart, Lord Cardross.

43 Xanthe Brook, *Face to Face: Three Centuries of Artists' Self-Portraiture* (Liverpool: Walker Art Gallery, 1994), 24, 27.

44 Francesco Moücke, *Serie di ritratti degli eccellenti pittori dipinti di propria mano che esistana nell' Imperial galleria di Firenze*, *Museum Florentinum*, vols. 7–10 (Florence: Nella Stamperioa Moukiana, 1752–62); and Orazio Marrini and Pietro Antonio Pazzi, *Serie di ritratti di celebri pittori dipinti di propria mano in seguita a quello gia' pubblicata nel Museo fiorentino*, *Museum Florentinum*, vols. 11–12 (Florence: Nella Stamperia Moukiana, 1765–66).

45 Edward Gibbon, *Gibbon's Journey from Geneva to Rome: His Journal from 20 April to 2 October 1764*, ed. Georges A. Bonnard (London: Thomas Nelson & Sons, 1961), 130–59, 165–87 (artist portraits, 130–32; quote at 131).

46 Vasari 1550, II (Part 3), 656, and Vasari 1568, II (Part 3), 77; as cited in a critical "biography" of the portrait, which retained the identification as Raphael's self-portrait into the nineteenth century: David Alan Brown and Jane Van Nimmen, *Raphael and the Beautiful Banker: The Story of the Bindo Altoviti Portrait* (New Haven and London: Yale University Press, 2005), 9; see esp. ch. 2, "Raphael's Face Value," 31–45 (quote at p. 31).

47 Giorgio Vasari, *Le vite de' più eccellenti pittori scultori e architetti . . .*, 3 vols., ed. Giovanni Gaetano Bottari (Rome: Niccolò & Marco Pagliarini, 1759–60), 2: 88, n.1; translated in Brown and Van Nimmen, *Raphael*, 38.

48 For surgeon Angelo Nannoni's account of his treatment plan, see Adrian W. Zorniotti, "Benjamin West's Osteomyelitis: A Translation," *Bulletin of the New York Academy of Medicine* 49 (Aug. 1973): 702–7.

49 The basic study of Ignazio and his brother Enrico, a Benedictine monk and master scagliola artist, is John Fleming, "The Hugfords of Florence," *Connoisseur* (Oct. 1955): 106–10, and (Nov. 1955): 197–206. Hugford's father was an English Catholic watchmaker who moved to Italy to work for the Medici.

50 The evidence in this paragraph simplifies the complicated personae and chain of events presented by Brown and Van Nimmen, *Raphael*, 36–44.

51 Giovan Domenico Campiglia made the drawing that served as the basis for Frey's engraving; he was also a close friend of Bottari and his collaborator on the 1759–60 edition of Vasari.

52 The compiler of an "extra-illustrated" edition of Galt's *Life of West* (a folio in which pages from Galt's text were interleaved with documents and visual material) included a British engraving of the Altoviti portrait, labeled as Raphael, though publication of that print in 1825 rules out West as the owner; "The Life, Studies, and Works of Benjamin West, Esq. by John Galt, in extra-illustrated form" (Collection 3239), box 1, folder 4, Historical Society of Pennsylvania. West must have known another presumed Raphael self-portrait, showing a very young man, which the 3rd Earl Cowper presented to George III in 1781 (Royal Collection, now as "follower of Raphael").

53 According to Brown and Van Nimmen (*Raphael*, 191 n.44), Hugford's portrait drawings for the series – among 3,150 drawings purchased from his estate in 1779 by Pietro Leopoldo, Grand Duke of Tuscany – are catalogued under the name of the engraver, Giovanni Battista Cecchi, in the Gabinetto Disegni e Stampe degli Uffizi, Florence (Inv. 3947 F–4246 F). In the case of the Altoviti Raphael, Hugford's connections to the family facilitated copying from the original.

54 *Peale Papers*, 5: 98. West's drawing frame is mentioned in "Benjamin West, Esq.," *Public Characters of 1805* (London, 1805), 528. West characterized his work of the time in Benjamin West, "Original Manuscript Autobiography," Charles Allen Munn Collection, Fordham University Library, New York.

55 Angela Rosenthal, *Angelica Kauffman: Art and Sensibility* (New Haven and London: Yale University Press for the Paul Mellon Centre for Studies in British Art, 2006), 223–83 ("The Image of Angelica").

56 Oscar Sandner proposed the identification of artist and sitter in *Angelika Kauffmann und ihre Zeitgenossen* (Bregenz: [Vorarlberger Landesmuseum], 1968), 75, cat. 76. The work was subsequently reproduced as a portrait of West in *Firenze e l'Inghilterra: Rapporti artistici e culturali dal XVI al XX secolo* (Florence: Centro Di, 1971), cat. 66 (n.p.). The entry for Kauffmann's portrait drawing of West in Vandyke dress on the website of National Portrait Gallery, London, suggests that drawing as a study for the Uffizi painting. Peter Walch found it "improbable" that Kauffmann's Uffizi portrait represents West, but he did not say why; "An Early Neoclassical Sketchbook by Angelica Kauffmann," *Burlington Magazine* 119 (Feb. 1977): 98, 101–2, 104–11.

57 John Peacock, *The Look of Van Dyck: The "Self-Portrait with a Sunflower" and the Vision of the Painter* (London: Ashgate, 2006), 245–50, where he credits the initial connection with Ripa's Pittura to J. Bruyn and J. A. Emmens, "The Sunflower Again," *Burlington Magazine* 99 (Mar. 1957): 97.

58 The identification "John Green (Painter)" comes from a key in the front of the notebook, in the Historical Society of Pennsylvania. Nothing is known about Green's life before the mid-1760s, when he went to Bermuda. In 1774, he traveled to London for study with West.

59 West, *Apollo Belvedere*, ca. 1760–62, crayon on paper, Friends Library, Swarthmore College, Pennsylvania.

60 Edward Wright, *Some Observations Made in Travelling through France, Italy, etc., in the Years 1720, 1721, and 1722*, 2 vols. (London, 1730), 1: 302–3. The first and often reissued English translation of *Geschichte der Kunst des Altertums* (1764), by G. Henry Lodge, included Winckelmann's characterization of Apollo's hair as styled in a manner shared by young men and women; e.g., *History of Ancient Art*, 2 vols. (New York: Frederick Ungar, 1968), 1: 216. However, Lodge used some material judged extraneous to the author's original text, and that passage is absent from a recent, more faithful edition: Winckelmann, *History of the Art of Antiquity*, intro. Alex Potts, trans. Harry Francis Mallgrave (Los Angeles: Getty Research Institute, 2006).

61 Batoni's *Edward Dering* (1758–59) presents the rare example; the same artist showed the full sculpture in *Thomas Dundas* (1763–64).

62 As quoted in Alastair Smart, *Allan Ramsay: Painter, Essayist and Man of the Enlightenment* (New Haven and London: Yale University Press for the Paul Mellon Centre for Studies in British Art, 1992), 150–52.

63 Mark Hallett, "Reynolds, Celebrity and the Exhibition Space," in Martin Postle et al., *Joshua Reynolds: The Creation of Celebrity* (London: Tate Publishing, 2005), 38.

64 Walpole to David Dalrymple, Feb. 25, 1759, in *Horace Walpole's Correspondence with Sir David Dalrymple*, ed. W. S. Lewis, Charles H. Bennett, and Andrew G. Hoover, *The Yale Edition of Horace Walpole's Correspondence*, vol. 15 (New Haven: Yale University Press, 1951), 47.

65 Samuel Sharp, *Letters from Italy, describing the Customs and Manners of that Country, in the Years 1765 and 1766* (London, 1766), 218 (Apr. 14, 1766).

66 André Rouquet, *The Present State of the Arts in England* (London, 1755), 16.

67 The uneasy relationships between painters, luxury, and money received full scholarly due in David Solkin's influential *Painting for Money: The Visual Arts and the Public Sphere in Eighteenth-Century England* (New Haven and London: Yale University Press for the Paul Mellon Centre for Studies in British Art, 1993).

68 For the broad context in which the Society for the Encouragement of Arts, Manufactures, and Commerce was conceived as well as for detailed information about its operations, see Celina Fox, *The Arts of Industry in the Age of Enlightenment* (New Haven and London: Yale University Press for the Paul Mellon Centre for Studies in British Art, 2009), esp. 179–229.

69 Histories of these organizations date to the eighteenth century. Recent studies include Matthew Hargraves, *Candidates for Fame: The Society of Artists of Great Britain, 1760–1791* (New Haven and London: Yale University Press for the Paul Mellon Centre for Studies in British Art, 2005), and Holger Hoock, *The King's Artists: The Royal Academy of Arts and the Politics of British Culture, 1760–1840* (Oxford: Clarendon Press; New York, Oxford University Press, 2003). In some cases, loyalty to the Society resulted from being passed over by the Royal Academy, as had been all engravers except Francesco Bartolozzi, who was admitted as a painter; see the useful short account, "Painters and Engravers: Stubbs, the Society of Artists and the Royal Academy," in Tim Clayton, Rob Dixon, and Christopher Lennox-Boyd, *George Stubbs: The Complete Engraved Works* (Culham, London, and New York: Stipple Publishing, 1989), 9–19.

70 [John Nichols], *Biographical Anecdotes of William Hogarth*, 3rd ed. (London, 1785), 102. John Thomas Smith recalled Hogarth's sign in *Nollekens and his Times*, 2 vols. (London, 1828), 2: 209. Samuel Ireland indicated that Charles Catton, a friend of Hogarth's and later RA member who began his career in the painting trade, told him that Hogarth had early on made signs, of which Catton owned an example, later acquired by Ireland and reproduced in *Graphic Illustrations of Hogarth: From Pictures and Drawings, in the Possession of Samuel Ireland*, 2 vols. (London, 1799): 2: 43–44, 46–47. In this purported pavior's sign (ca. 1725, Yale Center for British Art, New Haven), the artist deviated from emblematic representation to show a contemporary genre scene of paviors at work, their effort as part of a civic initiative in Georgian London that extended by 1742 to St. Martin's Lane, near Hogarth's residence and drawing academy. That circumstance might support a 1740s date and even a non-utilitarian purpose, though the wood support is consistent with a sign and the square format unusual for an independent painting. On the paving of London, see Ronald Paulson, *Hogarth*, 3 vols. (New Brunswick, N.J., and London: Rutgers University Press, 1991), 3: 515 n.40.

71 William T. Whitley lists three other artists who employed the Golden Head, including an engraver, a miniature painter, and the painter Sir Robert Strange; *Artists and their Friends in England, 1700–1799*, 2 vols. (1928; New York and London: B. Blom, 1968), 1: 123.

72 *Adventurer* 9 (Dec. 5, 1752). Ronald Paulson suggested that Thornton composed his letter in response to Henry Fielding's statement that bad translations "can give the Reader no more Idea of the Spirit of Lucien, than the vilest Imitation by a Sign-post Painter can convey the spirit of the excellent Hogarth"; Henry Fielding, *Covent-Garden Journal* 52 (June 30, 1752), cited in Paulson, *Hogarth*, 3: 344.

73 On the Sign Painter's Exhibition, see Paulson, *Hogarth*, 3: 336–61; Ronald Paulson, *Popular and Polite Art in the Age of Hogarth and Fielding* (Notre Dame and London: University of Notre Dame Press, 1979), 31–48; Lance Bertelsen, *The Nonesense Club: Literature and Popular Culture, 1749–1764* (Oxford: Clarendon Press, 1986), 138–50; and Jonathan Conlin, "'At the Expense of the Public': The Sign Painters' Exhibition of 1762 and the Public Sphere," *Eighteenth-Century Studies* 36 (Fall 2002): 1–21.

74 *St. James's Chronicle* (Mar. 25–27, 1762).

75 For Hogarth's royal appointment, see Paulson, *Hogarth*, 3: 209–16; also 2: 250–51, for the 1758 self-portrait.

76 Hoock, *King's Artists*, 30–31.

77 *A Catalogue of the Pictures, Sculptures, Designs . . . Exhibited by the Society of Artists of Great-Britain, at the Great Room, Spring-Garden, Charing-Cross, April the Twenty-first, 1766* (London, 1766).

78 Condition can complicate identification; the figure in *The American School* always presumed to be West was "savaged by a previous restorer," according to a 1978–79 Record of Painting Examination and Treatment in the Curatorial Files, Department of American Paintings and Sculpture, Metropolitan Museum of Art, New York.

79 Robert G. Stewart proposed that Benbridge stopped in London on his way to Italy in 1765 and that he may be the third figure from the left in *The American School*; *Henry Benbridge (1743–1812): American Portrait Painter* (Washington, D.C.: National Portrait Gallery, Smithsonian Institution Press, 1971), 16. However, nothing in Benbridge's correspondence concerning West's kind reception of him in 1769, following four years in Italy, suggests they had met before; McInnis et al., *Benbridge*, 123, 126. C. W. Peale referred to Pratt's painting as "a family picture in which he introduced Mr. West and some of his Pupils" – whose identities even he could not propose despite his 1767 incorporation into West's studio, his long proximity to Pratt in Philadelphia, and his interest in the history of early American art; *Peale Papers*, 5: 105. Peale's reference to family, not literal in this case, loosely acknowledges that most conversation pieces depicted persons who were related.

80 I first proposed an alternative identification of Pratt and a different reading of his painting during an internal seminar at the National Museum of American Art (now Smithsonian American Art Museum), in March 1983, and published those ideas as part of a more extensive analysis in "Painter's Progress: Matthew Pratt and *The American School*," *Metropolitan Museum Journal* 28 (1993): 169–83. A selective list of those who had named Pratt as the man drawing includes: Pennsylvania Academy of the Fine Arts, *Loan Exhibition of Historical Portraits* (Philadelphia, 1887), 105–6; Charles Henry Hart, "A Limner of Colonial Days," *Harper's Weekly* 40 (July 4, 1896), 665; Theodore Bolton and Harry Lorin Binsse, "Pratt, Painter of Colonial Portraits and Signboards," *Antiquarian* 17 (Sept. 1931), 24, 48; William Sawitzky, *Matthew Pratt, 1734–1805: A Study of his Work* (New York: New-York Historical Society, 1942), 35–38; John Wilmerding, *American Art* (Harmondsworth: Penguin, 1976); Dorinda Evans, *Benjamin West and his American Students* (Washington, D.C.: Smithsonian Institution Press for the National Portrait Gallery, 1980), 27–28. For exceptions to that identification, see Jules David Prown, *American Painting from its Beginnings to the Armory Show* (Geneva: Skira, 1986), 34, and Miles in Ellen G. Miles and Richard H. Saunders, *American Colonial Portraits, 1700–1776* (Washington, D.C.: Smithsonian Institution Press for the National Portrait Gallery, 1987), 265–68. The Metropolitan Museum of Art followed the majority opinion in *American Paintings in the Metropolitan Museum of Art*, ed. Kathleen Luhrs, vol. 1: *A Catalogue of Works by Artists Born by 1815* (New York: Metropolitan Museum of Art in association with Princeton University Press, 1994), 57, but thereafter accepted the reading I proposed in the 1993 article. See, e.g., *American Stories: Paintings of Everyday Life, 1765–1915*, ed. H. Barbara Weinberg and Carrie Rebora Barratt (New York: Metropolitan Museum of Art; New Haven and London: Yale University Press, 2009), 3.

81 Ruthann McNamara, "The Theme of the Learned Painter in Eighteenth-Century British Self-Portraiture" (Ph.D. dissertation, Bryn Mawr College, 1983), Appendix III, 195–97.

82 "Pratt's Autobiographical Notes," as reprinted in Sawitzky, *Matthew Pratt*, 15–16. These notes, believed to have been written in 1770, may exist only in Charles Henry Hart's transcription of 1892, published in *Pennsylvania Magazine of History and Biography* 20 (1895), 460–66, and now in the Historical Society of Pennsylvania. The circumstances and length of Pratt's apprenticeship were altogether traditional; on that subject in general, see Ian M. G. Quimby, *Apprenticeship in Colonial Philadelphia* (New York and London: Garland, 1985).

83 *Peale Papers*, 5: 100.

84 Pratt, "Autobiographical Notes," 18. Pratt noted that he set up in trade with one Francis Foster in 1755 and so continued until late 1757, when he left on a trading voyage to Jamaica. I have not been able to identify Foster or his line of work; however, Pratt's advertisement for his painting business in 1756 makes no mention of Foster as partner, while "trading voyage" would be odd terminology for a painting trip.

85 Sawitzky (*Matthew Pratt*, 9) overestimated West's impact on Pratt at this early point, considering him the source of an English mannerism – the distinctly almond-shaped eye – that Wollaston had introduced to the colonies.

86 Pratt's autobiographical notes record a July 1764 landing whereas Elizabeth Shewell in her Pocket Almanack (Princeton University Library) documented the party's arrival on Aug. 6 and her marriage at St. Martin-in-the-Fields on Sept. 2; cited in Helmut von Erffa, "Benjamin West: The Early Years in London," *American Art Journal* 5 (1973), 9. The spring 1764 catalogue of the Society of Artists gave West's address as Castle Street.

87 As quoted in Sawitzky, *Matthew Pratt*, 19.

88 Letter from Elizabeth Shewell West to "Kitty," ca. 1770; transcript from the E. P. Richardson Collection, in a file on Matthew Pratt, housed during the 1980s at the (since relocated) Smithsonian American Art Museum/National Portrait Gallery Library. Rembrandt Peale likewise noted that Pratt "was considered but an indifferent painter, incapable of profiting by the opportunities he had in England," although he offered the mitigating opinion of his father, Charles Peale, that Pratt was "a mild and friendly man, not ambitious to distinguish himself," perhaps a fair representation of Pratt in later years but not, I argue here, of his posture around 1765; Rembrandt Peale, "Reminiscences," *Crayon* 3 (Jan. 1856), 5; also *Peale Papers*, 5: 105.

89 Rosenthal, *Kauffman*, 235–36.

90 Changes to *The American School* were discovered by Metropolitan Museum of Art conservator Dorothy Mahon during summer 1991, using X-radiography, ultraviolet illumination, and infrared scanning.

91 In *Traité des sensations* (Paris, 1754), the Abbé de Condillac explored the development of mind using the conceit of a statue, or a human being with a marble exterior, brought to life through its successive endowment with the five senses; see Étienne Bonnot de Condillac, *Condillac's Treatise on the Sensations*, trans. Geraldine Carr (Los Angeles: School of Philosophy, University of Southern California, 1930). In observations on Du Fresnoy's *Art of Painting*, Roger de Piles counseled the young artist to study antique busts representing persons of various ages, including children, "for example . . . the little *Nero*"; trans. John Dryden (London, 1716), 218.

92 The entry on *The American School* in the Metropolitan Museum's *Catalogue of Works by Artists Born by 1815* refers to this detail as a "chalk underdrawing," which somewhat confusingly identifies what Pratt intended to represent – a drawing sketched on the depicted canvas as a guide – with his means of representation. In conversation with me in 1991, Metropolitan Museum conservator Dorothy Mahon suggested that Pratt might have used oil mixed with chalk, which would have been almost immediately fugitive, rather than any of the pigments that later proved fugitive, as those would not have had the right color to match the appearance of chalk; Barratt, however, mentions lead white paint (*American Stories*, 3). Abrasion of the paint surface and a change in the refractive index eventually rendered this drawing nearly invisible to the naked eye; no evidence exists that anyone deliberately obliterated the image. Discovery of the "underdrawing" was published by Trudy E. Bell, "Technology: Ultraviolet Detection," *Connoisseur* 210 (May 1982), 140–41.

93 Stewart (*Benbridge*, 16) reassigned the portrait of the veiled woman to Benbridge, dating it ca. 1775, not long after his establishment in Charleston. The sitter has been identified as either Sarah Boyer or Mary Boyer, the first or second wives of Robert Shewell, Jr., a nephew of Elizabeth West, to whom Benbridge was loosely related by marriage; see McInnis et al., *Benbridge*, 85–86. Margaretta Lovell, who reproduced the portrait in support of her argument that Pratt's *American School* is not allegory, stood by the older attribution to Pratt in *Art in a Season of Revolution: Painters, Artisans, and Patrons in Early America* (Philadelphia: University of Pennsylvania Press, 2005), 38. My reading does not depend on one conclusion or the other, and for that matter, in my opinion, neither does Lovell's.

94 E.g., Richardson, *Theory of Painting*, 29–30.

95 References to de Piles in this paragraph are from the section "On the order which ought to be observed in the study of painting," in *Principles of Painting* (London, 1743), 234–52; this was the first English translation of *Cours de peinture par principes* (Paris, 1708).

96 *The Compleat Drawing-master* (London, 1763). See also Thomas Bardwell, *The Practice of Painting and Perspective Made Easy* (London, 1756) and [Robert Dossie], *The Handmaid to the Arts*, 2 vols., (London, 1758; 2nd ed. 1764).

97 See Janice G. Schimmelman, "Books on Drawing and Painting Techniques Available in Eighteenth-Century American Libraries and Bookstores," *Winterthur Portfolio* 19 (Summer–Autumn 1984): 193–205. She found Robert Dossie's *Handmaid to the Arts* – which Charles Peale purchased on a visit to Philadelphia in 1762 – the most popular of these publications.

98 Du Fresnoy, *Art of Painting* (1716), 71.

99 John Kenworthy-Browne, "The Duke of Richmond's Gallery in Whitehall," *British Art Journal* 10 (Spring–Summer 2009): 40–49. Advertisement, *London Chronicle*, Feb. 25, 1758, as quoted in James Northcote, *The Life of Sir Joshua Reynolds*, intro. R. W. Lightbown, 2 vols. bound as 1 (2nd ed., rev., London, 1819; repr., London: Cornmarket Press, 1971), 1: 84–85.

100 Society of Arts, *A Register of the Premiums by the Society, Established at London, for the Encouragement of Arts, Manufactures, and Commerce, London*, published annually from April 1758. For the history of this organization, see Derek Hudson and Kenneth W. Luckhurst, *The Royal Society of Arts 1754–1954* (London: John Murray, 1954), and D. G. C. Allan, *William Shipley: Founder of the Royal Society of Arts*, rev. ed. (London: Scolar Press, 1979).

101 For Mortimer's distinctive path in history painting before his early death in 1779, see Myrone's assessment of his "outlaw masculinity" in *Bodybuilding*, 121–44. By contrast, West took a more "bourgeois" perspective in presenting the type of the refined masculine hero (ibid., 105–20), a reading for which Myrone acknowledged a debt to David Solkin's analysis of West and others in his chapter "Exhibitions of Sympathy," in *Painting for Money*, 157–213.

102 In 1771, Mortimer showed a life class, to some degree imaginary, in "An Academy," a work designed to bolster the standing of the

Society of Artists, to which Mortimer remained loyal after many others left to found the Royal Academy. Simon Ravenet engraved the work for the frontispiece to vol. 2 of John Boydell, *Sculptura Britannica: A Collection of Prints, Engraved from the Most Capital Paintings in England* (London, 1771).

103 Even though Romney later signed the rolls of the Society of Artists, to which Reynolds, Mortimer, and West belonged, he did not cease to exhibit with the less prestigious Free Society; David A. Cross, *A Striking Likeness: The Life of George Romney* (London: Ashgate, 2000), 33, 38–40. He continued to show with both societies after being excluded from the Academy in 1768 and served as a director of the Society of Artists in 1770–72, years of relative strength – owing to membership by Mortimer, George Stubbs, as well as many prominent engravers – before the organization declined.

104 Peale offered his recollections of painters in late colonial America to Rembrandt Peale, Oct. 28, 1812, *Peale Papers*, 3: 174–75. He noted that Steele belonged to "a respectable and wea[l]thy family on the easter[n] shore of Maryland," where he himself was from, although Steele may have been their British relative, as proposed by Miles, in Miles and Saunders, *American Colonial Portraits*, 31–32, 33–34. In late 1762, the peripatetic Steele departed England for the West Indies; Adam Walker to George Romney, Dec. 12, 1762, quoted in John Romney, *Memoirs of the Life and Works of George Romney* (London, 1830), 42–44.

105 William Hayley, *The Life of George Romney, Esq.* (Chichester, 1809), 39–40. See also J. Romney, *Memoirs of Romney*, 45–51. For the unlikelihood that Reynolds had any involvement in reassignment of the prize, see Whitley, *Artists and their Friends in England*, 1: 191–92. Romney's finished painting of Wolfe remains unlocated, but studies survive in one of the artist's sketchbooks as does a painted fragment. Myrone offers a useful analysis of the prize retraction in *Bodybuilding*, 34–38.

106 Whitley, *Artists and their Friends in England*, 1: 191.

107 Leonardo da Vinci, *A Treatise of Painting* (London, 1721), 29, 36. Romney mentioned his father's interest in Leonardo's book in *Memoirs of George Romney*, 11. On the "ambiguous position" of Leonardo's treatise relative to British discourses on art, see Geoff Quilley, "The *Trattato della Pittura* and Leonardo's Reputation in Eighteenth-Century British Art and Aesthetics," in *Re-Reading Leonardo: The "Treatise on Painting" across Europe, 1550–1900*, ed. Claire Farago (London: Ashgate, 2009), 495–507.

108 [Jean Dubreuil], *The Practice of Perspective*, trans. E. Chambers (London, 1726), iii.

109 C. K., *Art's Masterpiece*, 5th ed. (London, [1710?]), 8. For Romney's use of the manual, see J. Romney, *Memoirs of George Romney*, 11. This geometrical method was not unusual in English art manuals, and perhaps Romney was familiar with a more proximate exemplum in Benjamin Ralph's impressively illustrated (102 copper plates) *The School of Raphael; or, The Student's Guide to Expression in Historical Painting* (London, 1759). For his "strange fusion" of academic and Hogarthian approaches, Ralph has been proposed as a model for the self-styled "Connoisseur" parodied by Reynolds in his *Idler* essays of 1759; see Bernd Krysmanski, "Benjamin Ralph's *School of Raphael* (1759): Praise for Hogarth and a Direct Source for Reynolds," *British Journal for Eighteenth-Century Studies* 24 (Spring 2001): 15–32.

110 See, e.g., *The Artist's Vade Mecum* (London, 1762) [pl. 5], *The Compleat Drawing-master*, 2.

111 John Northall, *Travels through Italy, Containing New & Curious Observations on that Country* (London, 1766), 309. For the history and reception of the *Farnese Hercules*, I have relied on the concise presentation in Francis Haskell and Nicholas Penny, *Taste and the Antique: The Lure of Classical Sculpture, 1500–1900* (New Haven and London: Yale University Press, 1981), 229–32.

112 Giovanni Baglione, *Le vite de' pittori scultori et architetti dal pontificato di Gregorio XXXI del 1572* (Rome, 1642), 151; as quoted in Haskell and Penny, *Taste and the Antique*, 230. According to these modern authors, the French took a more conservative approach and had casts of the ancient legs made for display with the cast of the rest of the statue, available in Paris by the mid-seventeenth century. The originals were reunited with the classical body after the Hercules was moved to Naples in 1787.

113 Hogarth, *Analysis of Beauty*, ed. Paulson, 26.

114 Drawing from casts, not from drawings and outlines, became the foundational stage in artistic training at the Royal Academy schools, beginning in 1769; Hooch, *King's Artists*, 55. Artists drawing from a cast are the subject of one of the most notable paintings in the British debate about the course and character of artistic training: Joseph Wright of Derby's *An Academy by Lamplight*. Wright, however, was not an RA member and intended his work, shown at the Society of Artists in 1769, in criticism of the newer institution's strict hierarchy and rules. See Solkin, *Painting for Money*, 239–46.

115 The painting was titled "School of West" on the occasion of its second recorded exhibition, with the Society of Artists, Philadelphia, in 1811, six years after Pratt's death. "London School of Artists" is from Dunlap, *History*, 1: 101; "West's School of Painters in London" in PAFA, *Loan Exhibition of Historical Portraits*, 105.

116 For the compelling argument that consumption made Americans British and then American in their revolt against Britain, see Breen, *Marketplace of Revolution*.

117 For an overview of the Scottish as both central to and marginalized within the British empire, see Eric Richards, "Scotland and the Uses of the Atlantic Empire," in *Strangers within the Realm: Cultural Margins of the First British Empire*, ed. Bernard Bailyn and Philip D. Morgan (Chapel Hill and London: University of North Carolina Press for the Institute of Early American History and Culture, Williamsburg, Va., 1991), 67–114; on "Scotophobia," 98–101.

118 Lord Adam Gordon, as quoted in *Narratives of Colonial America, 1704–1765*, ed. Henry H. Peckham (Chicago: R. R. Donnelley, 1971), 261.

119 Julie Flavell, *When London Was Capital of America* (New Haven and London: Yale University Press, 2010), 69–70 (for quote and Americans vs. Scots), "Appendix" for a concise statement of methodology and a list of sources used to arrive at the estimated number of Americans in London. Covering a somewhat broader span of years, Susan Lindsey Lively arrived at similar numbers, drawing on a database of 1,057 colonists who traveled to Britain, for her 1997 Harvard Ph.D. dissertation, "Going Home: Americans in Britain, 1740–1776." However, she reached different conclusions. For all that colonists thought of themselves as "going home," Lively contends, once they got there, they did not so easily integrate, experienced difficulties in accomplishing business and educational objectives, and began to identify more strongly as Americans. The sources support both perspectives, and the differences in the two accounts seem largely a matter of what the authors chose to emphasize.

120 *Maryland Gazette*, Aug. 8, 1765 (reprinted from *Boston Gazette*, July 15, 1765); as quoted in Breen, *Marketplace of Revolution*, 202.

121 The foundational study of emerging British identity is Linda Colley, *Britons: Forging the Nation 1707–1837* (New Haven and London: Yale University Press, 1992).

122 As quoted in Ned C. Landsman, "The Provinces and the Empire: Scotland, the American Colonies and the Development of British Provincial Identity," in *An Imperial State at War: Britain from 1689 to 1815*, ed. Lawrence Stone (London: Routledge, 1993), 266. The idea of America as a place of unlimited potential, unique and exceptional, Landsman proposed, was "in origin, British, liberal and provincial" (278).

123 Stephen Conway explored changing British attitudes toward Americans in "From Fellow-Nationals to Foreigners: British Perceptions of the Americans, circa 1739–1783," *William and Mary Quarterly*, 3rd ser., 59 (Jan. 2002): 65–100 (quote at 83). He argues for the Franco-American alliance of 1778 as the critically alienating factor for Britons, much more so than the Declaration of Independence.

124 I have relied on T. H. Breen, "Ideology and Nationalism on the Eve of the American Revolution: Revisions Once More in Need of Revising," *Journal of American History* 84 (June 1997): 13–39. Celebrating "America" as a place may have been another matter. A news item from *New-York Gazette, or the Weekly Post-Boy*, Aug. 30, 1764, took note of stockings made in that city that bore stitching spelling out "AMERICA" at the ankles in place of the decorative vertical stitching (called clocking) usually found there.

125 West to Joseph Shippen, Sept. 1, 1763, as quoted in Thomas Balch, ed., *Letters and Papers Relating Chiefly to the Provincial History of Pennsylvania* (Philadelphia: Crissy and Markley, 1855), lxxi.

126 Ilaria Bignamini's lists of subscribers to the St. Martin's Lane Academy, compiled from several sources, do not include West, though she found "good reasons to believe that the Academy had a larger membership, especially in the years 1755–68"; "The Second St. Martin's Lane Academy, 1735–68," 95–124 (explanation of lists at 114), in "George Vertue, Art Historian, and Art Institutions in London, 1689–1768," *Walpole Society* 54 (1988): 1–148.

127 Northcote as quoted in Charles Robert Leslie and Tom Taylor, *Life and Times of Sir Joshua Reynolds with Notices of Some of his Contemporaries*, 2 vols. (London: John Murray, 1865), 1: 418; see also 2: 159–60.

128 Stephen Gwynn, *Memorials of an Eighteenth Century Painter (James Northcote)* (London: T. Fisher Unwin, 1898), 49; also 46–49, 58–59, 110–11, 225–26. For the number of assistants in 1763, see Northcote, *Life of Sir Joshua Reynolds*, intro. Lightbown, 1: 120. For an overview, see M. Kirby Talley, Jr., "'All Good Pictures Crack' – Sir Joshua Reynolds's Practice and Studio," in *Reynolds*, ed. Nicholas Penny (London: Royal Academy of Arts, 1986), 55–70.

129 James Northcote, in *Conversations of James Northcote R.A. with James Ward on Art and Artists*, ed. Ernest Fletcher (London: Methuen, 1901), 153–54.

130 "Northcote hated West, and acknowledges it now; . . . West couldn't tell the truth, he says"; [John Neal], "American Painters Abroad," *Yankee and Boston Literary Gazette* (1829): 184–85. The source of the statement was a Mrs. Brigden, landlady to several American painters in London. Neal can be identified as author of that article by comparison with his much later account, "Our Painters," *Atlantic Monthly* 23 (Mar. 1869): 337–47.

131 As cited in G. C. Williamson, *John Downman, A.R.A.: His Life and Works* (London: Otto Ltd., 1907), xix.

132 Smith, *Nollekens and his Times*, 2: 369.

133 Dunlap, *History*, 1: 99. For an overview of West's mentoring, focused on the twenty-four Americans whom Dunlap identified as pupils in his *History* or *Diary* (2: 543n), see Evans, *West and his American Students*.

134 For a defining study of these changing social relations, see Jay Fliegelman, *Prodigals and Pilgrims: The American Revolution Against Patriarchal Authority, 1750–1800* (Cambridge: Cambridge University Press, 1982).

135 Benjamin West, *A Discourse Delivered to the Students of the Royal Academy on the Distribution of the Prizes, December 10, 1792* (London, 1793), 11–12.

136 Matthew Harris Jouett, "Notes on Painting," in John Hill Morgan, *Gilbert Stuart and his Pupils* (New York: New-York Historical Society, 1939), 84.

137 C. Willet Cunnington and Phillis Cunnington, *Handbook of English Costume in the Eighteenth Century* (London: Faber and Faber, 1957), 241. In 1765, peruke makers petitioned George III, concerned over the decline in their business; Marcia Pointon, *Hanging the Head: Portraiture and Social Formation in Eighteenth-Century England* (New Haven and London: Yale University Press for the Paul Mellon Centre for Studies in British Art, 1993), 122.

138 In "Benjamin West's Family Picture: A Nativity in Hammersmith," Jules D. Prown explained the somewhat fixed stare of the two Quakers as evidence that they are focused inwardly, in prayer; *Essays in Honor of Paul Mellon, Collector and Benefactor*, ed. John Wilmerding (Washington, D.C.: National Gallery of Art, 1986), 277. However, Quaker doctrine stipulated that the head be uncovered during prayer; see, e.g., Robert Barclay, *An Apology for the True Christian Divinity* (7th ed., Dublin, 1737), 15, 529–30 (Fifteenth Proposition), and *Canons and Institutions Drawn Up and Agreed Upon by the General Assembly or Meeting of the Heads of the Quakers* (London, 1669), 7. Charles Robert Leslie, writing of West's family portrait, more plausibly described the Quakers as sitting "for a few minutes in silent meditation which will soon be ended by the old man's taking off his hat and offering up a prayer for the mother and infant"; *Autobiographical Reflections* (London, 1860), 41. For a general account of hat-wearing among Quakers, see Amelia Gummere, *The Quaker: A Study in Costume* (Philadelphia, 1901; repr., New York and London: Benjamin Blom, 1968), 57–90.

139 John Styles, *The Dress of the People: Everyday Fashion in Eighteenth-Century England* (New Haven and London: Yale University Press, 2007), 202–5.

140 Leigh Hunt, *The Autobiography of Leigh Hunt* (Oxford: Humphrey Milford, Oxford University Press, 1928), 114, 111.

141 Susanna Morikawa, Archival Specialist at Friends Historical Library, Swarthmore, reported the cause of disownment as "disunity" in a letter to Laura K. Mills, Curatorial Assistant, Worcester Art Museum, May 6, 1998. Abrams says the cause was "fornication"; she discusses West's investment in his Quaker heritage in *Valiant Hero*, 36–38. According to one contemporaneous source, West, Sr., had attended monthly meetings and guided his family according to Quaker principles; John Pemberton's recollection, as reported by Benjamin Smith Barton, Journal [Commonplace Book], "Mr. West," 1789, B. S. Barton Papers, Historical Society of Pennsylvania, Philadelphia.

142 Galt, *West* (1816), 145. After becoming president of the Royal Academy, West wore a hat at meetings of that organization – as depicted by Henry Singleton in *The Royal Academicians in General Assembly* (1795) – to honor the office, as he announced in his acceptance speech to the Academy; Whitley, *Artists and their Friends in England*, 2: 161–62.

143 Robert Barclay, *An Apology for the True Christian Divinity* (London, 1678), 516. Styles noted that Quaker customs of dress made members "highly distinct and targets for hostility"; *Dress of the People*, 205.

144 Rousseau's books enjoyed wide circulation beginning in the early 1760s and were available in English in Philadelphia by 1763.

According to Paul Merrill Spurlin, no book by that author was advertised more often by American booksellers than *Émile*; *Rousseau in America, 1760–1809* (Tuscaloosa: University of Alabama Press, 1969), 74.

145 De Piles, *Principles of Painting*, 237. In the opening sentence of *An Essay on Painting* (London, 1764) Francesco Algarotti identified lack of parental encouragement as a factor inhibiting excellence in the sciences and liberal arts. He envisioned a corrective in carefully directed education and spelled out its course with regard to artists in his book, dedicated to English artists of "The Society Instituted in London for Promoting Arts Manufactures Commerce" (i.e., the Society for the Encouragement of Arts, Manufactures, and Commerce) and known to Americans like Copley by 1766.

146 Painting ca. 1761, Royal Academy of Arts; attribution in Martin Postle, "The St. Martin's Lane Academy: True and False Records," *Apollo* 134 (July 1991): 33–38.

147 Rouquet, *Present State of the Arts in England*, 23–24.

148 Reynolds, *Discourses*, 16 (Discourse I, 1769).

149 J. T. Smith described the street building by building in his colorful "Recollections of Public Characters, Sometime Inhabitants of St. Martin's Lane," in *Nollekens and his Times*, 2: 221–44. West associated the St. Martin's Lane Academy with the Society of Artists, as evident from his manuscript autobiography at Fordham, the basis for the account published in *Public Characters of 1805* (London, 1805), 533.

150 *The Charter, Laws, and Catalogue of the Library Company of Philadelphia* (Philadelphia, 1764), 43.

151 Hogarth, *Analysis of Beauty*, ed. Paulson, 18.

152 West on the *Analysis*, to J. T. Smith in his youth, from Smith, *Nollekens and his Times*, 2: 343.

153 *Peale Papers*, 5: 41. Benjamin Ralph included a lesson on drawing the line of beauty, because he thought Hogarth – whom he much admired – remiss in not providing one; *School of Raphael*, 4.

154 As originally published, the *Analysis* alluded only to a method by which an artist could "gradually arrive at the knack of recalling [objects] into his mind when the objects themselves are not before him"; Hogarth, *Analysis of Beauty*, ed. Paulson, 22, see also xxxvi–xxxvii (from editor's introduction), 121–22 (textual fragment from Hogarth's "Autobiographical Notes"). Joseph Burke recognized the centrality to Hogarth's practice of visual mnemonics in the first modern scholarly edition of Hogarth's *Analysis* (Oxford: Clarendon Press, 1955), xxxvii–xli.

155 Michael Kitson, "Hogarth's Apology for Painters," *Walpole Society* 41 (1968): 69 (lines 678–81).

156 Du Fresnoy, *Art of Painting*, 13. De Piles expanded on those words in his "Observations" to the text: "The Attributes of the *Muses* are often taken for the *Muses* themselves; and it is in this Sense, that *Invention* is here call'd a *Muse*" (109). Cf. the later, more graceful translation in Charles Du Fresnoy, *Art of Painting*, trans. William Mason, with commentary by Sir Joshua Reynolds (Dublin, 1783), verses 106–9. De Piles offered extended discussion "Of Invention" as the painter's highest accomplishment and of Raphael's invention in *The School of Athens*; *Principles of Painting*, 24–45, 46–47.

157 I thank David Steinberg for first suggesting to me that this figure might represent a muse, which he framed as a question following my talk on *The American School* at the February 1991 College Art Association annual conference. Lovell disagreed with my formulation. Identification of the work as a portrait and Pratt (among other Americans) as portraitist is central to her reading of the painting and her general thesis in *Art in a Season of Revolution*, 36–40, as in her prior "Bodies of Illusion: Portraits, People, and the Construction of Memory," in *Possible Pasts: Becoming Colonial in Early America*, ed. Robert Blair St. George (Ithaca: Cornell University Press, 2000), 270–301. I see no reason to insist that one of us is right. Competing arguments need not always be mutually exclusive, if both rest on well-argued foundations.

158 Abrams, *Valiant Hero*, 98–105. Angelica Kauffmann adapted the subject of the choice of Hercules for an allegorical self-portrait in the 1790s; Rosenthal, *Kauffman*, 272–81.

159 Solkin tracked rising concern over the predominance of portraits at the newly instituted exhibitions in 1760s London, in *Painting for Money*, 180ff. He points out that West initially became known for history paintings that exhibited "a feminine (and feminised) beauty," high in both color and sentiment (181–86), not, however, a characteristic of his *Choice of Hercules*. See also Myrone, *Bodybuilding*, 17–22. By contrast to these authors, Stephen Caffey, in a compelling and nuanced reading of West's early history paintings, argues that the artist "formulated a visual mythopoetics of imperial martial virtue" that performed serious and "manly" cultural work in the service of empire; Caffey, symposium paper "*Exempla Virtutis Imperialis*: The Paintings of Benjamin West, 1764–1774," for "1763 and All That: Temptations of Empire in the British World in the Decade after the Seven Years' War," Institute for Historical Studies, University of Texas, Austin, Feb. 25–26, 2010. See also Caffey, "Heroics of Empire."

160 Benjamin West to John Green, Sept. 10, 1771, in "Letter from Benjamin West," *Archives of American Art Journal* 4 (Jan. 1964): 12.

161 On West's painting of Johnson, see Caffey, "Heroics of Empire," 33–77. Caffey argues convincingly for thematic linkage between these two history paintings of 1764; in the subject from the recent war in North America, he asserts, West cast the viewer in the role of Hercules, "witnessing the powers of virtue" embodied in Johnson. See also Jonathan Conlin, "Benjamin West's *General Johnson* and Representations of British Imperial Identity, 1759–1770: An Empire of Mercy?" *Eighteenth-Century Studies* 27 (Mar. 2004): 37–59.

162 Galt, *West* (1816), 119–22.

163 Batoni made some 130 history paintings between 1730 and 1750 but only a half-dozen portraits (Bowron, *Pompeo Batoni*, 1–35). Even after his portrait production surged dramatically, starting around mid century, he continued to make subject pictures.

164 Thomas Robinson to his father, William Robinson, 1st Baron Grantham, Aug. 9, 1760; quoted ibid., 115.

165 Northcote, *Conversations of James Northcote*, 175.

166 West to Joseph Shippen, Sept. 1, 1763, as quoted in Balch, *Letters and Papers Relating Chiefly to the Provincial History of Pennsylvania*, lxix. West had lately made a copy of a *Holy Family* by Mengs, the only living artist whose work he copied while abroad; see von Erffa and Staley, *West*, 444–46 (cat. 510, 511). Galt reports contact between West and Mengs, but the relationship was probably not one of formal tutelage; *West* (1816), 118–230. For the idea that Mengs's theory of art continued to resonate with West in the 1780s, see Forster-Hahn, "Benjamin West's Instructions to a Young Painter for his Studies in Italy," 375–76, and for West's praise of Mengs as late as 1807, Nicholas Biddle, "Conversations with Benjamin West," *Pennsylvania Magazine of History and Biography* 102 (Jan. 1978): 112 (1807).

167 This interpretation is from Steffi Röttgen, "Mengs, Alessandro Albani und Winckelmann – Idee und Gestalt des Parnass in der Villa Albani," *Storia dell'arte* 30–31 (May–Dec. 1977), 100–22, esp. 101. For a classic art historical explication, see W. Rensselaer Lee, "*Ut Pictura Poesis*: The Humanistic Theory of Painting," *Art Bulletin* 22 (Dec. 1940): 197–269.

168 J. J. Winckelmann to J. J. Volkmann, Mar. 27, 1761, *Briefe*, 4 vols., ed. Hans Diepolder and Walther Rehn (Berlin: Walter de Gruyter, 1952–56), 2: 130, no. 397.

169 Winckelmann, *History of the Art of Antiquity*, ed. Potts, 213.

170 Mengs, *Gedanken über die Schönneit und über den Geschmack in der Malerei* (1762), as translated in *Neoclassicism and Romanticism, 1750–1850*, I: *Enlightenment/Revolution*, ed. Lorenz Eitner (Englewood Cliffs, N.J.: Prentice-Hall, 1970), 32. Mengs's book did not appear in English translation until 1796.

171 Thomas Pelzel, *Anton Raphael Mengs and Neoclassicism* (New York: Garland, 1979), 111–14.

172 "A Monsieur West, Peintre celebre . . . connu en Italie sous le Nom du Raphaël Americain," *Public Advertiser*, Apr. 20, 1764; W.G., "To Mr. West, a celebrated painter . . . ," *Public Advertiser*, Apr. 23, 1764. Whitley (*Artists and their Friends in England*, 1: 197) long ago recognized that the poem was from another context altogether, though he did not cite it: *Les Tetons, ouvrage curieux, galant, et badin, composé pour le divertissement d'une dame de qualité* (Amsterdam, 1760), 22–23. Cf. the Abbé Peter Grant's reference to West as "your young American Raphael" in a letter from Rome to Dr. John Morgan, Aug. 31, 1765, quoted in Arthur S. Marks, "Angelica Kauffmann and Some Americans on the Grand Tour," *American Art Journal* 12 (Spring 1980): 23.

173 Monks, "Wolfe Man," 657.

174 "To the Printer of the Public Advertiser" [on the exhibition at Spring Garden], *Public Advertiser*, May 2, 1764.

175 *The Exhibition: or, A Candid Display of the Genius and Merits of the Several Masters, Whose Works are Now Offered to the Public, at Spring Gardens* [London? 1766?], 9. A young American Quaker from a prominent Philadelphia mercantile family took the characterization for granted when he visited West in 1776: "the Raphael of the present Age, whose views [i.e., paintings] are too well known to need any comment"; *An American Quaker in the British Isles: The Travel Journals of Jabez Maud Fisher, 1775–1779*, ed. Kenneth Morgan (Oxford: Oxford University Press for the British Academy, 1992), 198.

176 Iain Pears, *The Discovery of Painting: The Growth of Interest in the Arts in England, 1680–1768* (New Haven and London: Yale University Press for the Paul Mellon Centre for Studies in British Art, 1988), 166–68. Between 1711 and 1759, only 545 paintings brought more than £40 at auction.

177 "An Essay Towards an English School of Painters," in de Piles, *Art of Painting* (1706), 398–480. The third edition (1754) identified the principal original author of the English lives as B[ainbrigg] Buckeridge. See also T. B., *A Call to the Connoisseurs, or Decisions of Sense with Respect to the Present State of Painting and Sculpture, and their Several Professions in these Kingdoms* (London, 1761), 37–43.

178 Samuel Johnson, *Idler* 45 (Feb. 24, 1759). See John Sunderland, "Samuel Johnson and History Painting," in *The Virtuoso Tribe of Arts & Sciences: Studies in the Eighteenth-Century Work and Membership of the London Society of Arts*, ed. D. G. C. Allan and John L. Abbott (Athens and London: University of Georgia Press, 1992), 183–94, and Morris R. Brownell, *Samuel Johnson's Attitude to the Arts* (Oxford: Clarendon Press, 1989), 72–78.

179 "To the Printer of the Public Advertiser" [on the exhibition at Spring Garden], *Public Advertiser*, May 1, 1767.

180 Breen, "Ideology and Nationalism," 13–39. For the idea of provincialism as a stimulus to originality and creative vigor, see Bernard Bailyn and John Clive, "England's Cultural Provinces: Scotland and America," *William and Mary Quarterly*, 3rd ser., 11 (1954): 200–13. Theirs was a novel argument, and later scholars have gone further in charting the transatlantic flow of ideas and positive valuation of provincial identity; see, e.g., Landsman, "The Provinces and the Empire," 258–87.

181 The sense of the term *school* as "example" figures in William Aglionby's *Choice Observations upon the Art of Painting* (London, 1719), 26–27 (first published in 1685): the "first Rank of Painters," he writes, are those "whom all must look upon as the Great Originals that Heaven hath given to Mankind to Imitate; and whose Works will not only be the School, but the Delight and Admiration of all the Ages." A more down-to-earth and practical application of the term appeared in a proximate English book title: Ralph, *School of Raphael* (1759).

182 For the entire six-quatrain poem and editorial commentary, see George Berkeley, *The Works of George Berkeley, Bishop of Cloyne*, 9 vols., ed. A. A. Luce and T. E. Jessop (London: Nelson, 1967), 7: 369–73. See also Rexmond C. Cochrane, "Bishop Berkeley and the Progress of Arts and Learning: Notes on a Literary Convention," *Huntington Library Quarterly* 17 (May 1954): 229–49, and Joseph J. Ellis, *After the Revolution: Profiles of Early American Culture* (New York: Norton, 1979), 3–21.

183 Smibert, letter [to Arthur Pond], July 1, 1743, Charles Henry Hart autograph collection, Archives of American Art, Smithsonian Institution, Washington, D.C.; reprinted in Richard H. Saunders, *John Smibert: Colonial America's First Portrait Painter* (New Haven and London: Yale University Press/Barra Foundation, 1995), 257.

184 Nathaniel Evans, *Ode, on the Late Glorious Success of His Majesty's Arms, and Present Greatness of the English Nation* (Philadelphia, 1762).

185 *American Magazine* (Sept. 1758): 607. See also Hopkinson's invocation of the Muse in *Science: A Poem* (Philadelphia, 1762). As Monks observed, once it became clear that West would not likely return to America and that "American subject pictures were a dead end in Britain, West sublimated his colonial identity, shifting the weight within the name 'the American Raphael' so that it implied less the westward flow of the arts toward the American destiny envisaged by Bishop Berkeley, than the incorporation of an American into the ranks of the European tradition"; "Wolfe Man," 657.

186 For an example of this convention, see the frontispiece and explanatory verse in G. Smith, *The Laboratory, or School of the Arts* (London, 1739).

187 Copley to Henry Pelham, July 11, 1774, *Copley–Pelham Letters*, 226. West's confidence had limits. In a letter of 1772, he identified with (Aztec) "natives" of "South America in the time of that conquest," sharing with them (he presumed) better ability to express himself through painting than writing; West to Peter Thompson, Historical Society of Pennsylvania Collection, Philadelphia, Archives of American Art, Microfilm Reel P23, as cited by Sienkewicz, for whom the metaphor powerfully captured West's "cultural misfit within this transatlantic situation"; "Beyond the Mohawk Warrior," 10.

188 Ann Carlos and Frank Lewis, "Fur Trade (1670 to 1870)," ed. Robert Whaples, March 16, 2008. http://eh.net.encyclopedia/the-economic-history-of-the-fur-trade-1670-to-1870/.

189 Merritt, *Crossroads*, 77.

4 PAINTERS IN PRINT

1 *Gentleman's Magazine* 50 (June 1780): 290 (these three sentences constitute almost the entire notice). Other early reviews appeared in *Critical Review* 49 (June 1780): 478–79, and *Monthly Review* 63 (Nov. 1780): 469.

2 Byron used the phrase in *Childe Harold's Pilgrimage* (canto 1, stanza 22), referring to Beckford as "Vathek," the title of Beckford's best known literary work, a Gothic novel published in 1786.

3 Robert J. Gemmett, introduction to William Beckford, *Biographical Memoirs of Extraordinary Painters* (London, 1780; Rutherford, Madison, and Teaneck, N.J.: Fairleigh Dickinson University Press, 1989). For Beckford's account of the circumstances under which he composed his tales of fictional painters, in an article published a month after his death, see Cyrus Redding, "Recollections of the Author of *Vathek*," *New Monthly Magazine* 71 (June 1844): 151–52.

4 Redding, "Recollections, 152.

5 M. J. B. Descamps, *La Vie des peintres flamands, allemands et hollandois, avec . . . une indication de leurs prinicipaux ouvrages, & des réflexions sur leurs différentes manieres*, 4 vols. (Paris, 1753–54). The relationship to this text was first noted by André Parreaux, "Les *Peintres extraordinaires* de Beckford sont-ils une satire des écoles flamande et hollandaise?" *Revue du Nord* 169 (Jan.–Mar. 1961), 15–42 (Watersouchy, as he pointed out, corrupts the Dutch word for "boiled fish"). See also Frans De Bruyn, "William Beckford," in *Dictionary of Literary Biography, Volume 39: British Novelists, 1660–1800*, ed. Martin C. Battestin (The Gale Group, 1985), 31–48 (Gale Literary Databases).

6 Beckford, *Biographical Memoirs*, 85–86.

7 The classic study is Ernst Kris and Otto Kurz, *Legend, Myth, and Magic in the Image of the Artist: A Historical Experiment* (1934), rev. ed., trans. Alastair Laing and Lottie M. Newman (New Haven and London: Yale University Press, 1979).

8 "Memoirs of Extraordinary Painters," *New-York Mirror*, Nov. 15, 1834, 158–59; "Beckford's Memoirs of Painters," *North American Magazine* 5 (Dec. 1834): 113–19 (for quotations in this paragraph).

9 Beckford, *Italy; with Sketches of Spain and Portugal, by the Author of Vathek* (London; Philadelphia, 1834). For early examples of a Gothic visual sensibility – brooding, mysterious, exotic – in American art, see Sarah Burns in *Painting the Dark Side: Art and the Gothic Imagination in Nineteenth-Century America* (Berkeley: University of California Press, 2004).

10 "Literary Notices. A *History of the Rise and Progress of the Arts of Design in the United States*. By William Dunlap," *New-York Mirror*, Nov. 1, 1834, 139; and "Dunlap's *History of the Arts of Design*," *North American Magazine* 5 (Dec. 1834): 130–40.

11 Janice Gayle Schimmelman documented 183 titles in *Books on Art in Early America: Books on Art, Aesthetics and Instruction Available in American Libraries and Bookstores through 1815* (New Castle, Del.: Oak Knoll Press, 2007).

12 William H. Gerdts's preliminary attempt to identify earlier American statements on the arts yielded only one, a commencement address at Yale College by John Trumbull (cousin to the painter of that name); "The American 'Discourses': A Survey of Lectures and Writings on American Art, 1770–1858," *American Art Journal* 15 (Summer 1983): 61–79. Annie V. F. Storr identified and analyzed other early orations, most also delivered in collegiate contexts, in "Ut Pictura Rhetorica: The Oratory of the Visual Arts in the Early Republic and the Formation of American Cultural Values, 1790–1840," Ph.D. dissertation, University of Delaware, 1992.

13 In particular, Christopher J. Lukasik, "The Face of the Public," *Early American Literature* 39:3 (2004): 414, and his *Discerning Characters: The Culture of Appearance in Early America* (Philadelphia: University of Pennsylvania Press, 2011), 121–52. Even scholars who specialized in eighteenth-century American literature once routinely took apologetic approaches to the subject, exemplified in the title Lewis Leary gave to his book *That Rascal Freneau: A Study in Literary Failure* (New Brunswick, N.J.: Rutgers University Press, 1941). William C. Spengemann offered a useful historiographic perspective in *A New World of Words: Redefining American Literature* (New Haven and London: Yale University Press, 1994).

14 "The Design &c," *New-England Magazine* 1 (1758): 7, 10.

15 Jared Gardner, *The Rise and Fall of Early Magazine Culture* (Urbana, Chicago, and Springfield: University of Illinois Press, 2012), 64. Gardner makes the case that magazines in the early United States – though frustratingly indecipherable to scholars and partly for that reason long overlooked – were as central to contemporaneous readers as novels, which had their fitful start at the same time but have nevertheless enjoyed privileged status among literary historians, including (previously) himself. Michael Cody made similar arguments somewhat earlier, in a more circumscribed study: *Charles Brockden Brown and the Literary Magazine: Cultural Journalism in the Early American Republic* (Jefferson, N.C.: McFarland, 2004). In a chapter on periodical writing concerning the visual arts during the early nineteenth century, Maura Lyons found little of substance for the first two decades, when coverage was especially spotty and insubstantial; *William Dunlap and the Construction of an American Art History* (Amherst and Boston: University of Massachusetts Press, 2005), 39–47.

16 James M. Osborn, ed., introduction to Joseph Spence, *Observations, Anecdotes, and Characters of Books and Men, Collected from Conversation*, 2 vols. (Oxford: Clarendon Press, 1966), 1: xxi.

17 Samuel Johnson, *A Dictionary of the English Language*, 3rd. ed., 2 vols. (London, 1765), and 4th ed., rev., 2 vols. (London, 1773), s.v., "anecdote." Anecdotes had a central place in the New Historicism pioneered by literary scholar Stephen Greenblatt and have received consideration in and of themselves from others, including Joel Fineman, "The History of the Anecdote: Fact and Fiction," in *The New Historicism*, ed. H. Aram Vesser (New York: Routledge, 1989), 49–76; Annabel Patterson, *Early Modern Liberalism* (Cambridge: Cambridge University Press, 1997), 153–82; and Lionel Gossman, "Anecdote and History," *History and Theory* 42 (May 2003): 143–68. Patterson's chapter on the historiographical function of anecdotes in English historical writing from the late sixteenth through the eighteenth centuries stands alone in attributing intentionality to the anecdote writers and in its thoughtful analysis of selected examples.

18 James Boswell, *Life of Johnson*, ed. R. W. Chapman, corrected by J. D. Fleeman (London: Oxford University Press, 1970), 4. On Johnson's fondness for anecdotes: *Boswell's Life of Samuel Johnson, Including a Journal of his Tour to the Hebrides, etc.*, ed. Wilson Croker (London: John Murray, 1839), 4: 31.

19 Isaac D'Israeli, *A Dissertation on Anecdotes* (1793; New York: Garland, 1972), 74, 30, 80–82, for quotes in this paragraph. On D'Israeli and anecdote, see April London, "Isaac D'Israeli and Literary History: Opinion, Anecdote, and Secret History in the Early Nineteenth Century," *Poetics Today* 26 (Fall 2005): 351–86.

20 Isaac D'Israeli, *Curiosities of Literature, Consisting of Anecdotes, Characters, Sketches, and Observations, Literary, Critical, Historical* (London, 1791), 469–71.

21 Anthony Pasquin [John Williams], *The Royal Academicians: A Farce* (London, 1786), 40.

22 In an anonymously published poem "On the Abuse of Satire," *Gentleman's Magazine* 59 (July 1789): 648–49, the very young D'Israeli attacked "Pindar" and then acknowledged authorship after John Wolcot, who wrote as Pindar, lashed out at the wrong man; D'Israeli's honorable admission won Wolcot's admiration and kindled a friend-

ship. On this episode, see James Ogden, *Isaac D'Israeli* (Oxford: Clarendon Press, 1969), 18–19; 21–39 for a straightforward account of D'Israeli's investment in anecdotes.

23 William Dunlap, *A History of the Rise and Progress of the Arts of Design in the United States* (1834), 3 vols., ed. Rita Weiss (New York: Dover, 1969), 1: 187.

24 D'Israeli, *Dissertation on Anecdotes*, 30.

25 Modern theorists of the anecdote have located its popularity in emerging middle-class ideology, which demands "a sense of difference in sameness." "If one of the major tasks of eighteenth-century Britain was to come to terms with the continued existence of residual and emergent elites," David Simpson proposed, ". . . then one can perhaps regard the anecdote, along with the literary mode of which it was a part, as playing a significant role in this coming to terms, in its work of making everyone seem ordinary and open to sympathetic identification, without diminishing the claim that we would all like to make to potential exceptionality"; David Simpson, *The Academic Postmodern and the Rule of Literature: A Report on Half-Knowledge* (Chicago and London: University of Chicago Press, 1995), 57.

26 D'Israeli, *Dissertation on Anecdotes*, quotations in this paragraph from 59, 82, 8, 81, 62–63. Jonathan Richardson, Sr., and Jr., *Explanatory Notes and Remarks on Milton's Paradise Lost* (London, 1734).

27 [Jonathan Richardson, Jr., ed.], *The Works of Mr. Jonathan Richardson* (London, 1792), 11, 13, the edition proximate to D'Israeli's time of Jonathan Richardson, *An Essay on the Theory of Painting* (London, 1715).

28 "For the Literary Magazine: The Use of Anecdotes," *Literary Magazine, and American Register* 5 (Jan. 1806): 53–57 (quotes at 54, 53). Brown stated his aims for the journal in "The Editors' Address to the Public," *Literary Magazine* 1 (Oct. 1803): 5. Brown, best known to Americanist literary scholars as a novelist, began his magazine career in 1799, around the time of his least successful and most interpretively porous novels. Gardner has resurrected both not as signs of failure but as "a bold attempt to define an authorial role to which readers will not risk being made 'prisoner'"; *Rise and Fall of Early Magazine Culture*, 23.

29 "Remarks on Reading," *Literary Magazine* 5 (Mar. 1806): 163–68; from D'Israeli, "On Reading," *Miscellanies* (London: Cadell and Davies, 1796), 189–207. For the connection to D'Israeli, see Gardner, *Rise and Fall of Easly Magazine Culture*, 183 n.43.

30 D'Israeli, *Dissertation on Anecdotes*, vi.

31 Ibid., 64–65. The great number of available artist anecdotes can be judged by the hundreds included in James Elmes, *The Art and Artists, or Anecdotes & Relics of the Schools of Painting, Sculpture & Architecture*, 3 vols. (London, 1825). The volume one frontispiece featured Raphael's portrait of Bindo Altoviti as the artist's self-portrait, a routine error in which West had shared, as a young man in Italy, as I discuss in chapter three.

32 "Anecdote," *New York Weekly Magazine; or, Miscellaneous Repository* 2 (Oct. 12, 1796): 119 (with errors in identification of both painter and king).

33 "Anecdotes," *Christian's, Scholar's and Farmer's Magazine* 2 (June–July 1790): 230.

34 "Anecdote" (Michelangelo), *Literary Magazine, and American Register* 3 (Apr. 1805): 294–95; and "Painting" (Orcagna), *Emerald, or, Miscellany of Literature, Containing Sketches of the Manners, Principles and Amusements of the Age* 1 (Dec. 27, 1806): 416.

35 "Anecdote," *Massachusetts Magazine, or Monthly Museum* 6 (Aug. 1794): 456. The later nineteenth-century collection *Art and Artists: Curious Facts and Characteristic Sketches*, issued by different publishers in New York, Philadelphia, and Edinburgh around 1870, offered facing vignettes on the title page and frontispiece, showing, respectively, Charles V retrieving Titian's brush and West drawing his infant niece in the cradle.

36 "Hans Holbein, the Celebrated Painter," *Omnium Gatherum* 1 (Nov. 1809): 32–33.

37 *A Catalogue of that Superb and Well Known Cabinet of Drawings of John Barnard, Esq., . . . Which Will be Sold by Auction by Mr. Greenwood, on Friday Feb. 16, 1787*, 3–6.

38 "Selected for the Emerald: Singular Anecdote of Morland the Painter," *Emerald* 2 (Aug. 8, 1807): 377–78.

39 Nicholas Biddle, "Conversations with Benjamin West," *Pennsylvania Magazine of History and Biography* 102 (Jan. 1978): 111. In 1832, "an English gentleman" purchased "a Bull's Head [sign], [as] one of the earliest productions of West"; *Literary Gazette*, cited in William T. Whitley, *Artists and their Friends in England, 1700–1799*, 2 vols. (1928; New York and London: Benjamin Blom, 1968), 1: 195. A (possibly different) sign of a bull's head, long attributed to West because of its "superior execution," was instead by Bernard Wilton, an English artist working in Philadelphia in 1760, according to J. Thomas Scharf and Thompson Westcott, *History of Philadelphia, 1609–1844*, 3 vols. (Philadelphia: L. H. Everts & Co., 1884), 2: 1035.

40 As Pasquin likely knew from his time in Ireland, John Scott, the humbly born Lord Chief Justice of the King's Bench for Ireland, was known as "Copper-face Jack" for "the coarse effrontery of his address" or, perhaps, for having an alcohol-inflamed red face; Sir Jonah Barrington, *Historic Memoirs of Ireland, Comprising Secret Records of the National Convention, the Rebellion, and the Union*, 2 vols. (London, 1835), 2: 5. While neither is documented for Copley, he was of Irish descent and a certain nervous provincialism crept into his speech, as lampooned by his mid-1770s European traveling companion, George Carter; see Emily Ballew Neff, "Italy: Copley and West on the Grand Tour," in Emily Ballew Neff with Kaylin H. Weber, *American Adversaries: West and Copley in a Transatlantic World* (Houston: Museum of Fine Arts, Houston, 2013), 121–28.

41 Pasquin, *The Royal Academicians*, 40.

42 Anthony Pasquin, *Memoirs of the Royal Academicians*, ed. R. W. Lightbown (1796; repr., London: Cornmarket Press, 1970), 77.

43 Conversation between Reynolds and Johnson, recorded by James Northcote, as cited in Richard Wendorf, *Sir Joshua Reynolds: The Painter in Society* (Cambridge, Mass.: Harvard University Press, 1996), 67.

44 Other of Pindar's writings were popular in America, and he himself was the subject of articles; see "Memoirs of John Wolcot, M.D.," *Lady's Monitor* 1 (Mar. 27, 1802): 250–51, and "Living Satirist," *Monthly Anthology, and Boston Review* 5 (Apr. 1808): 197–201.

45 Dunlap's diary includes six separate entries mentioning Williams, often with distaste, but none indicate that they ever discussed art; William Dunlap, *The Diary of William Dunlap, 1766–1839: The Memoirs of a Dramatist, Theatrical Manager, Painter, Critic, Novelist, and Historian*, 3 vols. in 1, ed. Dorothy C. Barck (1930; repr., New York: Benjamin Blom, 1969), 1: 262, 304, 316, 320, 342, 352.

46 For an overview of Williams's life, see R. W. Lightbown, introduction to Pasquin, *Memoirs of the Royal Academicians*, 1–72; also James Sambrook, "Williams, John (1754–1818)," *Oxford Dictionary of National Biography* online.

47 Francis Hopkinson, *Miscellaneous Essays and Occasional Writings of Francis Hopkinson, Esq.*, 3 vols. (Philadelphia, 1792), 2: 127–37 and illustration facing 377 (the author gives the date 1784 in the essay on 137).

48 Paul M. Zall, *Comical Spirit of Seventy-Six: The Humor of Francis Hopkinson* (San Marino, Calif.: Huntington Library, 1976), 12–14 (this and next sentence). Zall reproduced the drawing said to represent Bryan, but he did not explicitly mention the "Surveying" essay.

49 Margaretta M. Lovell, *Art in a Season of Revolution: Painters, Artisans, and Patrons in Early America* (Philadelphia: University of Pennsylvania Press, 2005), 10.

50 Freneau's "Picture Gallery," in *The Miscellaneous Works of Mr. Philip Freneau* (1788), ed. Lewis Leary (Delmar, N.Y.: Scholars' Facsimiles and Reprints, 1975), 49–53.

51 Lukasik, *Discerning Characters*, 121–52. For discussion of metaphors based on pictorial ideas about likeness in the constitutional debates of 1787 and 1788, see Eric Slauter, "The State as a Work of Art: Politics and the Cultural Origins of the Constitution" (Ph.D. dissertation, Stanford University, 2000), ch. 4.

52 This section of the chapter was previously published as "'The Limner': Harry Croswell, Newspaper Politics, and the Portraitist as a Public Figure in the Early Republic," in *Shaping the Body Politic: Art and Political Formation in Early America*, ed. Maurie D. McInnis and Louis P. Nelson (Charlottesville: University of Virginia Press, 2011): 231–67. "The Limner" appeared in *Balance*, 1804: Oct. 2, 9, 16, 30, Nov. 6, 13, 20; 1805: May 21, 28, June 4, 11 [misdated 1804], 18, July 9, Aug. 6; 1806: Oct. 28, Nov. 25. After editor Harry Croswell moved the paper to Albany, he published two more, chronologically isolated Limner columns: July 7, 1808, and July 19, 1808. Curiously, the June 18, 1805, "Limner" column had been previously printed, under that same heading, in *Spirit of the Public Journals; or Beauties of the American Newspapers* 1 (Jan. 1, 1805): 54–57.

53 Modern writer Julian Barnes made tension between portraitists and sitters of ca. 1800 the subject of a short fictional piece titled "The Limner," which appeared in *New Yorker* 84 (Jan. 5, 2009): 60–65. In adopting the artist's point of view, Barnes composed a tale that could easily take its place among the Limner letters; almost nothing in his story would have surprised readers of the *Balance* in 1804 or should surprise readers now.

54 Neil Harris's *Artist in American Society: The Formative Years, 1790–1860* (Chicago: University of Chicago Press, 1966), unusual for the time in its divergence from biography as well as for its diverse cast of characters, nevertheless underscored the frustrations of American artists; see, e.g., "The Burden of Portraiture," 56–88. David Jaffee, among recent scholars, has been especially alert to the employability of portraitists who adapted; *A New Nation of Goods: The Material Culture of Early America* (Philadelphia: University of Pennsylvania Press, 2010), esp. 1–45, 219–73.

55 The *Balance* was first published May 21, 1801 (renumbered as vol. 1:1 on Jan. 5, 1802), by founding editors Ezra Sampson, a retired Congregational minister, and George Chittendon, bookseller, with Harry Croswell as junior editor and publisher. Croswell became sole proprietor of the newspaper on Jan. 3, 1804.

56 "An Act in Addition to the Act, Entitled 'An Act for the Punishment of Certain Crimes Against the United States,'" July 14, 1798, Sec. 2. The Sedition Act expired March 3, 1801.

57 The *Bee* ran from June 14, 1797, to June 23, 1802, in New London, Conn., and Aug. 17, 1802, to 1821 in Hudson, N.Y. (Holt ended his term as editor in 1810.) The *Wasp* lasted for only twelve intermittent issues, July 7, 1802, to Jan. 26, 1803.

58 Thomas Wright, *Dictionary of Obsolete and Provincial English*, 2 vols. (London, 1857), 2: 816; Amelia Simmons, *American Cookery* (Hartford, Conn., 1798), 10.

59 Jeffrey L. Pasley, *"The Tyranny of Printers": Newspaper Politics in the Early American Republic* (Charlottesville: University Press of Virginia, 2001), 254, and generally ch. 6: "Charles Holt's Generation: From Commercial Printers to Political Professionals," 132–75, and ch. 10: "The Federalists Strike Back," 229–57. Pasley does not sufficiently acknowledge Croswell's social distance from relatively more genteel Federalist editors, such as Joseph Dennie, the Harvard-educated attorney behind Philadelphia's *Port Folio*. "The sometime printer and clergyman," as Pasley calls Croswell, began his working life without formal higher education (though he did serve as an assistant to Noah Webster in 1798), before becoming a printer and, soon after, editor; he did not enter the ministry until 1812. John L. Brooke subsequently considered Croswell, Holt, and the partisan newspapers and culture of Hudson in the more geographically focused context of *Columbia Rising: Civil Life on the Upper Hudson from the Revolution to the Age of Jackson* (Chapel Hill: University of North Carolina Press for the Omohundro Institute for Early American History and Culture, 2010), 295–309. The book, in press at the same time as my Limner essay for *Shaping the Body Politic*, does not engage the Limner columns.

60 Gardner, *Rise and Fall of Early Magazine Culture*, 71–78. Gardner (125–33) identifies *Port Folio* as a partisan exception among magazines of the early republic, unusual also for the firm authorial voice of its editor Joseph Dennie, whose features on Benjamin West I analyze in chapter six.

61 *Wasp*, July 7, 1802. "We are all republicans: we are all federalists" is how Jefferson penned the text of his first inaugural address; Mar. 4, 1801, Thomas Jefferson, *The Writings of Thomas Jefferson*, 10 vols., ed. Paul Leicester Ford (New York: G. P. Putnam's Sons, 1892–99), 8: 2. He used the terms in reference to governing principles of the nation, but capitalization of the words in newspaper reprints of the speech (parodied by "Wasps" and "Bees" in *Wasp*) suggested Jefferson's endorsement of parties – not yet accepted by any faction as an American political reality.

62 Quotations from the indictment against Croswell, Jan. 10, 1803, for items in *Wasp*, Aug. 12, 1802, and Sept. 9, 1802. The editor was tried only for the second item, which repeated Callender's claim that he had been paid by Jefferson to denounce Washington and Adams.

63 In the appellate court, the four seated justices upheld the verdict by split decision, preventing further appeal. By that time, the legislative act had already been proposed, though it did not pass until Apr. 6, 1805. Croswell was subsequently awarded a new trial. *Reports of Cases Adjudged in the Supreme Court of Judicature of the State of New York, from January Term, 1799, to January Term, 1803*, 3 vols., 2nd ed. (New York: Banks, Gould, 1849), vol. 3: *People v. Croswell*, 336–413. The most thorough modern overview of the case appears in Julius Goebel, ed., *The Law Practice of Alexander Hamilton: Documents and Commentary*, 4 vols. (New York: Columbia University Press for the William Nelson Cromwell Foundation, 1964), 1: 775–848.

64 The wasp emblem preceded intermittent editorials, beginning Mar. 13, 1804. Croswell reported on his indictment and trials under other headings as well throughout 1803–4. When the contents of the *Balance* were not overtly political, they were often implicitly so, a circumstance not fully revealed by the paper's section titles. In 1804, those included "Original Communications – Political and Miscellaneous," "Editorial and Closet Articles," "Political Selections," "Agricultural," "Monotorial" (moral and religious essays), "Wreath" (verse), "Improvements, Discoveries, Inventions, Recipes, &c.," and "Diversity, Miscellaneous Selections, &c."

65 "Uncle Tobey," Letter to Mr. Editor, *Balance*, May 22, 1804.

66 Anon., "The Limner," *Franklin Minerva* 1 (Aug. 1799): 54–55. George Kenton Harper published that paper in Chambersburg, Franklin County, Pa., during 1799 and 1800.

67 "The Limner," *Balance*, Oct. 2, 1804. A pretentious and ignorant English painter named Pallet was a significant character in Tobias Smollett's novel *The Adventures of Peregrine Pickle* (London, 1751), chs. 46–70. Only in ch. 68 is his first name revealed: "Layman" – an artist's dummy. Croswell was presumably familiar with Smollett's moralizing novel, though his Limner does not prove a dolt.

68 Samuel Haber traced professionalization in ministry, medicine, and law during the second half of the eighteenth century, with particular attention to regional variations, in *The Quest for Authority and Honor in the American Professions, 1750–1900* (Chicago: University of Chicago Press, 1991), chs. 1–3; his discussion of Hamilton and Madison appears on pp. 7–8. Haber pointed out that in 1800 three-quarters of states set educational requirements for the practice of law, and almost all had medical licensing laws; in 1860 those proportions had shrunk to one-quarter and "almost none" (104–5).

69 Joshua Reynolds, *Seven Discourses delivered in the Royal Academy* (London, 1778); Edmond Malone, *The Works of Sir Joshua Reynolds . . . containing his Discourses, Idlers, A Journey to Flanders and Holland, (now first published,) and his commentary on Du Fresnoy's Art of Painting; printed from his revised copies, (with his last corrections and additions,) . . . To which is prefixed an account of the life and writings of the author . . .*, 2 vols. (London, 1797).

70 Earl's repeated claim – in this case from the *Daily Hampshire Gazette*, Mar. 5, 1800 – could not be substantiated by Elizabeth Mankin Kornhauser; see Kornhauser et al., *Ralph Earl: The Face of the Young Republic* (New Haven and London: Yale University Press; Hartford, Conn.: Wadsworth Atheneum, 1991), 16–30.

71 On Copley's "improvement," see Emily Ballew Neff's opening essay in Neff et al., *John Singleton Copley in England* (Houston: Museum of Fine Arts, Houston, 1995), 12–22.

72 A "Yankee phrase," according to Ignatius Loyola Robertson, *Sketches of Public Characters . . .* (New York: E. Bliss, 1830), 186–87, who used it in reference to William Dunlap at the outset of his career.

73 Ellen Hickey Grayson proposed the term "artisan aesthetic" to characterize the look of "painstaking labor" in paintings popular especially, but not exclusively, with nonmetropolitan clients; "Toward a New Understanding of the Aesthetics of 'Folk' Portraits," in *Painting and Portrait Making in the American Northeast*, Dublin Seminar for New England Folklife: Annual Proceedings, 1994, ed. Peter Benes (Boston: Boston University Press, 1995), 217–34. That end was not necessarily achieved by painstaking means. Efficiency of production – achieved by use of stock poses, bold lines, and broadly colorful design – was critical to the work of "artisan entrepreneurs," in David Jaffee's estimation. Such artists, he concluded, catered to rural patrons who were "attracted to, rather than alienated by, the standardized and homogenous products that were becoming increasingly available in the countryside"; "One of the Primitive Sort: Portrait Makers of the Rural North, 1760–1860," in *The Countryside in the Age of Capitalist Transformation: Essays in the Social History of Rural America*, ed. Steven Hahn and Jonathan Prude (Chapel Hill: University of North Carolina Press, 1985), 118.

74 E. E., "An Essay on the Liberal Arts," *Monthly Anthology, and Boston Review* 3 (June 1806): 300–2. Copley is the exception in the group named, having attained a high level of artistic sophistication while still in Boston, although Trumbull's elite background would seem to disqualify him as "the child of nature," as he was called in *Literary Magazine, and American Register* 6 (July 1806): 35.

75 Chester Harding, *My Egotistigraphy* (Cambridge, Mass., 1866), 62.

76 [Gorham A. Worth], *Recollections of Hudson* (Albany, N.Y.: printed by Charles Van Benthuysen, 1850), 49. The writer, born in 1783, presented the anecdote while discussing the political clubs formed in Hudson around the time of Jefferson's election, hence my approximated date for the (now unknown) portrait.

77 Curiously, Gerrit Schipper's notice appeared in the main part of the paper, even though it had a separate advertising section; *Balance*, June 11, 1804 [*sic*, 1805]. Perhaps editor Croswell chose the placement so the ad could be read against the "Limner" in the same issue. Schipper traveled and worked in the northeastern United States between 1802 and 1808, as a specialist in small-scale profile portraits in pastel; about sixty American portraits are attributed to him. Jeanne Riger, "New Light on Gerrit Schipper, the Painter," *Clarion* 15 (Winter 1990): 65–70. Schipper was not included in the checklist of painters "related to Columbia County" published in Ruth Piwonka and Roderic H. Blackburn, *A Visible Heritage: Columbia County, New York: A History in Art and Architecture* (New York: Columbia Historical Society, 1977), 157–58. No extant portraits of Hudson citizens have been firmly linked to any artists working locally, from the time of the city's incorporation in 1785 through at least 1810, according to Helen M. McLallen, curator at the Columbia County Historical Society, in correspondence with the author.

78 "No likeness, no pay": e.g., ads placed by Raphaelle Peale, *Philadelphia Federal Gazette*, June 16, 1800; and John Wesley Jarvis and Joseph Wood, *New York Chronicle Express*, June 23, 1803, as cited in Rita Susswein Gottesman, *The Arts and Crafts in New York, 1800–1804: Advertisements and News Items from New York City Newspapers* (New York: New-York Historical Society, 1965), 7.

79 Raphaelle Peale's directory listing, as quoted in David C. Ward and Sidney Hart, "Subversion and Illusion in the Life and Art of Raphaelle Peale," *American Art* 8 (Summer/Autumn 1994), 121 n.44. Charles Bird King, a prominent painter of diverse talents, was called "limner" as late as 1820 in a Rhode Island probate document, a context in which such archaic usage is not surprising; cited in Andrew Cosentino, *The Paintings of Charles Bird King (1785–1862)* (Washington, D.C.: Smithsonian Institution Press, 1977), 107 n.62. For a study of King's diverse undertakings, see Rowena Houghton Dasch, "'Now Exhibiting': Charles Bird King's Picture Gallery, Fashioning American Taste and Nation, 1824–1861," (Ph.D. dissertation, University of Texas, Austin, 2013).

80 "Russel," "Mr. Editor," *Port Folio*, 3rd ser., 5:4 (Apr. 1811): 340–42. Thomas R. Ryan and David Jaffee plausibly identified the writer as Nicholas Biddle, a frequent contributor to *Port Folio* and its editor by 1812; Thomas R. Ryan, "Defining Jacob Eichholtz," and David Jaffee, "Accounting for Jacob Eichholtz," *The Worlds of Jacob Eichholtz: Portrait Painter of the Early Republic*, ed. Thomas R. Ryan (Lancaster, Pa.: Lancaster County Historical Society, 2003), 9–10, 43–44.

81 *Lancaster Intelligencer and Weekly Advertiser*, Feb. 26, 1808. Eichholtz's shop sign, Lancaster County Historical Society.

82 "Editorial. Freedom of the Press," *Balance*, May 14, 1805.

83 "Original" (on differences between Federalists and Democrats), *Balance*, June 25, 1804 [*sic*, 1805]; "Editorial. Federalism," *Balance*, Jan. 8, 1805.

84 The first issue of a revised *Balance* announced a section devoted to agriculture, in the hope that "the farmer, and particularly any one of that useful calling, who has not had the advantages of general reading," will find useful content and feel "compensated for the

expense of the paper"; *Balance*, Jan. 5, 1802. Subscriptions quadrupled over the next two years. Croswell announced subscriber figures in his first issue as sole editor, *Balance*, Jan. 3, 1804; 1,800 was a "very respectable" figure for this period, according to Pasley, *"Tyranny of Printers,"* 324.

85 R. P., "On Reading Gay's 'Painter, Who Pleased Nobody and Every Body,'" *Port Folio*, 2nd ser., 3:26 (June 27, 1807): 416. Attribution to Peale proposed by Carol Eaton Hevner, *Rembrandt Peale, 1778–1860: A Life in the Arts* (Philadelphia: Historical Society of Pennsylvania, 1985), 113.

86 Richardson, *Theory of Painting*, 175, 24.

87 Lavater first published his theories in German in 1772 and 1775–78 (illustrated), but many translations and editions followed. The major ones in English, titled *Essays on Physiognomy*, were issued in London, 1789–98, and Boston, 1794. The secondary literature on physiognomy is extensive; for a recent discussion, see, e.g., Lukasik, "Face of the Public," 419–38.

88 Ellen G. Miles considered diffusion of the technology in "1803 – The Year of the Physiognotrace" in *Painting and Portrait Making*, ed. Benes, 118–37; in that volume, see also Peter Benes, "Machine-Assisted Portrait and Profile Imaging in New England after 1803," 138–50. Benes's Appendix 1, "Documented Physiognotrace Makers and Operators in New England and New York, 1803–11" (149–50) lists a D. H. Cromwell as active during 1808 in Hudson, N.Y., and Montreal.

89 *New-York Evening Post*, Jan. 4, 1803.

90 Wendy Bellion, "The Mechanization of Likeness in Jeffersonian America," *MIT Communications Forum* (http://web.mit.edu/comm-forum/papers/bellion.html); revised as "Heads of State: Profiles and Politics in Jeffersonian America," in *New Media, 1750–1914*, ed. Lisa Gitelman and Geoffrey B. Pingree (Cambridge, Mass.: MIT Press, 2003), 31–59.

91 Gottesman found several examples advertised in American newspapers; *Arts and Crafts*, 83, 473, 1197, 1213.

92 E.g., "Art. XI, [Review of Sarah Morton], *The Virtues of Society*," *Monthly Magazine, and American Review* 3:2 (Aug. 1800): 129; "Messrs. Gilbert & Dean," *Boston Weekly Magazine* 2 (Dec. 10, 1803): 25; "Indiscretion," *Weekly Visitor, or Ladies' Miscellany* 3 (Nov. 3, 1804): 36.

93 Schipper's *Balance* ad made no mention of the optical device, but he had previously touted it in *Columbian Centinel*, Oct. 19, 1803, and *New England Palladium*, Jan. 6, 1804.

94 That sense of the word was invoked in [Peter Shaw], *The Reflector: Representing Human Affairs, as they are; and may be improved* (London, 1750), a moral treatise republished in 1762 under a new title that also resonates with "The Limner": *The Tablet, or Picture of Real Life: Justly representing, as in a Looking-Glass, the Virtues and Vices, Fopperies and Fooleries, Masks and Mummeries of the Age.*

95 "Limner," *Balance*, Oct. 9, 1804; Oct. 16, 1804; Nov. 6, 1804.

96 "Samuel Saunter, Esq." and several fictitious correspondents squared off on the subject of elbows in the "American Lounger" columns in *Port Folio*, ser. 1, 3:5 (Jan. 29, 1803): 33 (source of the quotation) and 3:6 (Feb. 5, 1803): 41–42. "Bare Elbows" was the title for comic items in *Philadelphia Repository and Weekly Register* 2:51 (Dec. 18, 1802): 402, and in *Weekly Museum* 15:36 (Nov. 18, 1803): 2. "Song for the Ladies. The Maid with Elbows Bare," a poem by "Simper," appeared in *Balance*, Apr. 26, 1803.

97 "Limner," *Balance*, Nov. 6, 1804.

98 Ibid., Oct. 30, 1804.

99 "Editorial," *Balance*, May 14, 1805.

100 In a later "Limner," Pallet complains that profile cutters have undermined his business, with cheap work for which "no other recommendation is wanted"; *Balance*, May 21, 1805.

101 Moses Williams, who operated C. W. Peale's physiognotrace machine, called the discarded interior shapes of cut profiles "his blockheads," according to Rembrandt Peale (the negative image, laid atop a dark background, produced the likeness); Rembrandt Peale, "Notes and Queries – The Physiognotrace," *Crayon* 4 (Oct. 1857): 308. Originally, "blockhead" meant "a wooden head, a wooden block for hats and wigs; *hence*, a head with no more intelligence in it than one of these" or "an utterly stupid fellow"; "blockhead, n. and adj." *Oxford English Dictionary* online. A man deemed a "blockhead" in the latter sense offers overenthusiastic praise of a portrait, already judged deficient by a "Connoisseur," in a humorous anecdote titled "The Painter," *Philadelphia Repository and Weekly Register* 4 (Apr. 7, 1804): 107. Croswell used the same anecdote, and painting as metaphor, in his editorial mocking a new Hudson newspaper dedicated to "*pure* republicanism"; "Editor's Closet," *Balance*, Nov. 11, 1806.

102 *Wit's Magazine; or, New Convivial Jester* (London, 1782), 36–37; also *Comick Magazine* (London, 1797), 38–39. Croswell published a different anecdote of Hogarth, pitting him against a nobleman who wanted to pay less than Hogarth thought he deserved, in *Balance*, July 9, 1805.

103 "A Card," *Wasp*, Jan. 26, 1803. In the 1740s, American colonist Nathaniel Ames hung a sign at his tavern that mocked two members of the Massachusetts Superior Court of Judicature for dissenting in a case that Ames had already won. A sketch of the design, in which those judges were shown with their backs to the court, along with a court order that Ames's sign be removed constitute the surviving evidence of this pictorial insult; see Martha J. McNamara, "Object Lessons: Nearest Kin to a Fisher," www.common-place.org.vol-02/no-02/lessons.

104 "Limner," *Balance*, Nov. 13, 1804, and Nov. 20, 1804, for quotations in this paragraph.

105 "Gull, n.3." *OED* online. March 2015. Oxford University Press. http://www.oed.com. The dictionary has an entry for "gull catcher" (from Shakespeare, *Twelfth Night*) but none for "gull trap." An APS (American Periodical Series) Online search of American periodicals beginning in 1741 found a first use in 1796, followed by seven instances in the *Balance*, between 1803 and 1809, and then no other until 1827.

106 "Limner," *Balance*, Nov. 20, 1804.

107 Ibid., May 21, 1805. The second session of the New York 8th Congress ran from Nov. 5, 1804, to Mar. 3, 1805.

108 "handsome, adj., adv., and n.". *OED* online.

109 "Limner," *Balance*, May 28, 1805; June 4, 1804 [*sic*, 1805]; June 11, 1804 [*sic*, 1805].

110 *OED* online cites no examples of the first two meanings after 1700, though a few late eighteenth-century dictionaries preserve the application to men.

111 Susan L. Porter, "English-American Interaction in American Musical Theater at the Turn of the Nineteenth Century," *American Music* 4 (Spring 1986): 11.

112 *Balance*, July 26, 1803.

113 Ibid., Nov. 6, 1804.

114 For example, Rosemarie Zagarri, "The Rights of Man and Women in Post-Revolutionary America," *William and Mary Quarterly*, 3rd ser., 55 (Apr. 1998): 203–30 (quotation 215 n.56), and Rosemarie Zagarri, "Gender and the First Party System," in *Federalists Reconsidered*, ed. Doron Ben-Atar and Barbara B. Oberg (Charlottesville: University

of Virginia Press, 1998): 118–34. The *Balance* acknowledged female intellect and rights in an article "On Education" but identified women's fulfillment and happiness in domesticity; Nov. 16, 1802, 361–62. Brooke took up the subject of women in the Hudson press in *Columbia Rising*, 342–51; he drew on pioneering scholarship on women and the public sphere in the early republic, usefully listed in his 567 n.5.

115 Hamilton to Edward Carrington, May 26, 1792, as quoted in Andrew Trees, *The Founding Fathers and the Politics of Character* (Princeton: Princeton University Press, 2004), 68.

116 Samuel Johnson, *A Dictionary of the English Language*, 9th ed. (abridged) (London, 1790), s.v., "tomboy" (citing Shakespeare).

117 "Limner," *Balance*, June 11, 1804 [*sic*, 1805]. The internal quotations may refer to Republican charges against Croswell in publications, legal documents, or testimony against him.

118 The word "pallet" fell from use during the nineteenth century, presumably as bloodletting lost favor in medical practice; *OED* online.

119 On Croswell's role in forming the "Toleration Party," see Pasley, *"Tyranny of Printers,"* 376–77. Franklin B. Dexter sketched Croswell's grievances against Federalists in *The Rev. Harry Croswell, D.D., and his Diary*, a reprint from *Papers of the New Haven Colony Historical Society* (New Haven, 1918), 48. According to Dexter, Croswell "never again attended a political meeting (unless as a clerical duty) or exercised his rights as a voter" during his long ministerial career (forty-three years at Trinity); he nevertheless exhibited "tacit sympathy" with the Democratic Party (48). Croswell, though not an active abolitionist, proved a sympathetic advocate for black parishioners and for African-Americans seeking to form independent Episcopal congregations; Randall K. Burkett, "The Reverend Harry Croswell and Black Episcopalians in New Haven, 1820–1860," *North Star: A Journal of African American Religious History* 7 (Fall 2003): 1–20.

5 CONTRARY STUART

1 From a memorial resolution drawn up by artists of Philadelphia, as quoted in William T. Whitley, *Gilbert Stuart* (Cambridge, Mass.: Harvard University Press, 1932), 214–15; Whitley did not include citations, and I have been unable to locate the source text. This chapter expands on my article "Contrary Stuart," *American Art* 24 (Spring 2010): 66–93.

2 In reviewing the modern publication of Peale's late-life autobiographical manuscript (*Peale Papers*, vol. 5), David Steinberg made a case for the integrity of the artist's 1790 memoir, which he felt the modern editors overlooked; "Review: The Work of Autobiography and the Workings of Conscience," *William and Mary Quarterly*, 3rd ser., 58 (Apr. 2001): 498–505.

3 John Trumbull, *The Autobiography of Colonel John Trumbull, Patriot-Artist, 1756–1843*, ed. Theodore Sizer (1841; New Haven: Yale University Press, 1953). William Dunlap, *A History of the Rise and Progress of the Arts of Design in the United States* (1834), 3 vols., ed. Rita Weiss (New York: Dover, 1969), 1: 136–42 (Peale), 340–93 (Trumbull).

4 Benjamin Henry Latrobe to Thomas Jefferson, May 18, 1811, excerpt included in *Peale Papers*, 3: 92.

5 *Analectic Magazine, and Naval Chronicle* 8 (Sept. 1816): 197; *Portico* 2:4 (Oct. 1816): 286. Delaplaine responded to the criticism in a thirty-four-page pamphlet, a defense out of all proportion to the criticism; *The Author Turned Critic; or, The Reviewer Reviewed; Being a Reply to a Feeble and Unfounded Attack on Delaplaine's Repository, in the Analectic and Naval Chronicle for the Month of September 1816* [Philadelphia, 1816].

6 Ernst Kris and Otto Kurz, *Legend, Myth, and Magic in the Image of the Artist: A Historical Experiment* (1934), rev. ed., trans. Alastair Laing and Lottie M. Newman (New Haven and London: Yale University Press, 1979), 91–114.

7 David Ward persuasively argued that his subject's concern with self-regulation exceeded anything strictly necessary for the maintenance of a public image; *Charles Willson Peale: Art and Selfhood in the Early Republic* (Berkeley: University of California Press, 2004).

8 As quoted in Dunlap, *History*, 1: 175.

9 Dunlap, *History*, 1: 161–223 (quotations 195, 193, 219). Dunlap had even harsher words for Stuart in his diary: "eccentric & immoral Artist," "an imprudent man, a bad Husband & father"; Dunlap, *The Diary of William Dunlap* (New York and London: Benjamin Blom, 1969), 386, 674 (entries for Feb. 17, 1806, [Apr.] 11, 1833).

10 Benjamin Waterhouse to John Quincy Adams, July 21, 1828, as quoted in Andrew Oliver, *Portraits of John Quincy Adams and his Wife* (Cambridge, Mass.: Belknap Press of Harvard University Press, 1970), 125–26. Indeed, in that same letter, Waterhouse referred to Stuart as "heteroclite," "about as (*strange*) selfish a man as ever lived. An obstinate, ungovernable, self sufficiency marked and marred his character through life" (the word strange was cancelled in Waterhouse's letter but restored in the published document). As early as 1808, Waterhouse had "a copious journal" that contained "many anecdotes" of Stuart, according to a writer who consulted the journal for a "Sketch of the Life of Benjamin Waterhouse, M.D.," *Polyanthos* 12 (May 1, 1806): 75. In all likelihood, that document was the same as Waterhouse's "Memoirs," with extensive recollections of Stuart, in the Francis A. Countway Library of Medicine, Harvard University, until it became lost in the late 1990s. The library still has a much shorter (82 pp.) "Biography of Benjamin Waterhouse," with mention of Stuart.

11 Jane Stuart, "The Stuart Portraits of Washington," *Scribner's Monthly* 12 (July 1876): 367–74; "The Youth of Gilbert Stuart," *Scribner's Monthly* 13 (Mar. 1877): 640–46 (quotations 643, 644); "Anecdotes of Gilbert Stuart," *Scribner's Monthly* 14 (July 1877): 376–82.

12 George C. Mason, *The Life and Work of Gilbert Stuart* (New York: Charles Scribner's Sons, 1879), v. The author's correspondence survives in the George C. Mason Papers, MSS 742, Rhode Island Historical Society, Providence (hereafter RIHS). A critical review of Mason's "pretentious" book objected to the "padding" of catalogue entries with unnecessary details of sitters relative to space given to the artist's life; Eugene L. Didier, "Recent Biography," *North American Review* 130 (Jan.–June 1880): 300–2.

13 Henry Pickering, "Conversations with Mr. Stuart, the Painter," 1810, 1817, Manuscript, Henry Pickering Papers, Pickering Foundation, Salem, Mass., on deposit at Phillips Library, Peabody Essex Museum, Salem, Mass. (MSS 0.608/Pickering). Dorinda Evans, *The Genius of Gilbert Stuart* (Princeton: Princeton University Press, 1999).

14 John Quincy Adams, Sept. 19, 1818; Diary 30, The Diaries of John Quincy Adams: A Digital Collection, Massachusetts Historical Society, Boston; John Neal, "Our Painters," *Atlantic Monthly* 22 (Dec. 1868): 642.

15 As quoted in Dunlap, *History*, 1: 215–16.

16 Richard Shiff explored the paradox of the modern classic – already an issue for Delacroix in the 1830s – in *Cézanne and the End of Impressionism* (Chicago and London: University of Chicago Press, 1984), 175–84. On the emergence in Britain of the artist-genius – "rebellious and defiant . . . outsiders who reject conventional artistic standards as well as conventional standards of personal conduct" (16) – see William L. Pressly, *The Artist as Original Genius: Shakespeare's "Fine

Frenzy" in Late-Eighteenth-Century British Art (Newark: University of Delaware Press, 2007). The artists on whom he focused – John Hamilton Mortimer, John and Alexander Runciman, Henry Fuseli, James Jeffreys, James Barry, and George Romney – painted unconventional historical scenes and highly inventive self-portraits inspired by Michelangelo, Salvator Rosa, and Shakespeare; artistically, they were not Stuart's brethren.

17 Samuel L. Knapp, *Lectures on American Literature* (1829), reprinted as *American Cultural History, 1607–1829*, ed. Richard Beale Davis and Ben Harris McClary (Gainesville, Fla.: Scholars' Facsimiles & Reprints, 1961), 197–98 (from Lecture XI, concerning American artists).

18 Waterhouse to Adams, as quoted in Oliver, *Portraits of John Quincy Adams*, 125–26.

19 Evans first proposed the diagnosis in the last pages of *Stuart*, 118–20. She elaborated on the matter, with especial reference to Stuart's paintings, in Dorinda Evans, "Gilbert Stuart and Manic Depression: Redefining his Artistic Range," *American Art* 18 (Spring 2004): 10–31, and then at length in *Gilbert Stuart and the Impact of Manic Depression* (Farnham, Surrey, and Burlington, Vt.: Ashgate, 2013). Evans's evidence for the institutionalization of several of Stuart's children, previously suppressed, and his nephew, the painter Gilbert Stuart Newton, aids her case for hereditary mental illness in the Stuart family.

20 Abigail Adams, letter to John Quincy Adams, Dec. 30, 1804, Adams Papers, quoted in Andrew Oliver, *Portraits of John and Abigail Adams*, in *The Adams Papers*, ed. L. H. Butterfield, ser. 4: Portraits (Cambridge, Mass.: Belknap Press of Harvard University Press, 1967), 134.

21 Sarah A. Cunningham to her daughter Griselda Clinch, Aug. 5, 1825, Morton-Cunningham-Clinch Family Papers, 1754–1903, Massachusetts Historical Society, Boston.

22 Eliza Susan Quincy, letter to Mason of Sept. 25, 1878, Mason Papers, RIHS. Quincy was insistent on Mason's compliance: "To make my meaning clear, I have recopied the extract as I am willing it should be inserted. – & request you to return to me, the first copy I sent you." On cultural construction of the late nineteenth- and early twentieth-century American artist, see Sarah Burns, *Inventing the Modern Artist: Art and Culture in Gilded Age America* (New Haven and London: Yale University Press, 1996); for Whistler, esp., 221–46.

23 M[arianne] C. D. Silsbee to Mason, Oct. 9, 187[8?]; Mason Papers, RIHS; my emphasis.

24 The approximate date of Stuart's letter can be established by his early December birthday – he turned twenty-one in 1776, by which time he had been in London for just over a year. Notwithstanding alternate and less pitiful accounts of how Stuart came under West's protection (Dunlap, *History*, 1: 173, 174), the seal and stamp marks on the letter confirm that Stuart mailed it. I am grateful to Tammy Kiter of the New-York Historical Society for replying thoughtfully to my several queries about this document.

25 Peale to Launcelot Jacques, [1767], *Peale Papers* 1: 49 n.3.

26 Dunlap, citing Stuart, "Biographical Sketch of the late Gilbert Stuart," *Knickerbocker; or the New York Monthly Magazine* 1:4 (Apr. 1833): 196 (until July 1833, the title appeared as *Knickerbacker*).

27 Ibid., 198. Stuart's characterization of West as looking "as if he had stepped out of a bandbox" appears as the second cited use – from Dunlap's *Knickerbocker* essay – for a phrase meaning "to look extremely smart and neat"; "bandbox, n." *Oxford English Dictionary* online.

28 William Shakespeare, *Romeo and Juliet*, 1.1.460.

29 Wendy Bellion analyzed Wright's "erotically suggestive techniques," especially as presented in an illustration of Wright for *London Magazine*, in "Patience Wright's Transatlantic Bodies," in *Shaping the Body Politic: Art and Political Formation in Early America*, ed. Maurie D. McInnis and Louis P. Nelson (Charlottesville: University of Virginia Press, 2011), 15–46. Wright's portrait of West: *New-York Journal; or The General Advertiser* (Apr. 13, 1775). "Lad of wax" as applied to West may also have diminished him by reference to low tradesmen, given the characterization of a shoemaker as a "lad of wax" in 1794; "lad, n. 2." www.oed.com.

30 On this topic generally, see Martin Myrone, *Bodybuilding: Reforming Masculinities in British Art 1750–1810* (New Haven and London: Yale University Press for the Paul Mellon Centre for Studies in British Art, 2005).

31 [Dunlap], "Stewart," *Euterpeiad: An Album of Music, Poetry & Prose* (Apr. 1, 1831): 232; repeated in Dunlap, *History*, 1: 193. Evans assumes that when Stuart wore stockings over his shoes, he was in a manic state and at his most "socially maladroit" (*Stuart and the Impact of Manic Depression*, 27). However, she does not take into account that he was the likely source of this story, possibly much later. If the incident occurred as he related, Stuart was not only sufficiently self-possessed to remember it but – more importantly – found reason to repeat it, indicating that he was not ashamed of himself. In concluding her chapter on Stuart's unevenness as a painter and his alteration of, failure to finish, or destruction of some works, Evans observed that "manic depression did not somehow enslave [Stuart] or prevent self-censorship. He remained, by various degrees, subject to or in control of his ever-changing disorder . . . Knowing where his weaknesses lay and habitually pruning his work contributed to his success. Given his degree of control, in retrospect, the impact of his hereditary illness has to be understood as having both positive and negative qualities" (85–86). If at times similarly unable to regulate his behavior, Stuart evidently found ways to later reframe those episodes, creating a paradoxically consistent image of himself as an artist who went his own way.

32 *Peale Papers*, 5: 100.

33 Ibid., 1: 57–58 (Diary 1, Part 2: Memoranda and Accounts While in England). For the pressures to dress well in general, see Susan Lindsey Lively, "Going Home: Americans in Britain, 1740–1776" (Ph.D. dissertation, Harvard University, 1997), 152–58.

34 Ward, *Peale: Art and Selfhood*, 30–31.

35 John Brown to the Earl of Buchan, Aug. 1784, as quoted in Duncan Macmillan, *Painting in Scotland: The Golden Age* (Oxford: Phaidon, 1986), 61. Myrone introduced this example in *Bodybuilding*, 155, observing that "within the larger panorama of late eighteenth-century cultural politics, a studied neglect of personal hygiene or being short-tempered" represented a form of resistance to English models of correctness and to "Anglo-British cultural imperialism."

36 On Boydell, art and commerce in late eighteenth-century Britain, see Morris Eaves, *The Counter-Arts Conspiracy: Art and Industry in the Age of Blake* (Ithaca, N.Y., and London: Cornell University Press, 1992), esp. 33–55.

37 Dunlap, *History*, 1:178.

38 Von Erffa and Staley included a smaller Moses canvas (77½ × 29 in.) in their catalogue of West's paintings; Helmut von Erffa and Allen Staley, *The Paintings of Benjamin West* (New Haven and London: Yale University Press), 202–3. Barratt cited Mason's characterization (*Stuart*, 277) of a version of Moses as "designed by West, and painted by Stuart," information she assumed came from Jane Stuart, in Carrie Rebora Barratt and Ellen G. Miles, *Gilbert Stuart* (New York: Metropolitan Museum of Art; New Haven and London: Yale University Press, 2004), 55–57 (hereafter, when citing from this text, my notes name only Barratt or Miles, according to their contributions). Barratt

and Miles's comprehensive catalogue is a trove for Stuart scholars, valuable especially for its careful attention, in lengthy entries on individual paintings, to Stuart's patrons. Barratt assessed Stuart's connection with Boydell and his entrepreneurial ventures, as well as discussing five of the commissioned portraits, on pp. 48–62.

39 Pickering, "Conversations with Stuart," Oct. 4, 1817. Sir Joshua Reynolds, *Discourses on Art*, ed. Robert R. Wark (New Haven and London: Yale University Press for the Paul Mellon Centre for Studies in British Art, 1975), e.g., 52, 70, 72.

40 "For the Public Advertiser: Royal Academy Exhibition," *Public Advertiser*, May 7, 1783, and *The Ear-Wig; or An Old Woman's Remarks on the Present Exhibition of Pictures of the Royal Academy* (London, 1781), 12, regarding the portrait of George III that West showed in 1780. That work, with its companion showing Queen Charlotte and her children, was a centerpiece of the Great Room at the Academy's first exhibition in its imposing new quarters in Somerset House, a state project. For this momentous occasion, Reynolds, no favorite of the king, obtained sittings with the royal couple and exhibited those portraits, less effective even than West's. West, moreover, had a "winning formula" in the context of French entry into the American war, since his full-length military portrait of George III resonated with West's monumental historical canvases at the same exhibition, which showcased past British military victories: *Destruction of the French Fleet at La Hogue, 1692* and *Battle of the Boyne* (William III's defeat of James II in 1690). See Holger Hoock, *The King's Artists: The Royal Academy of Arts and the Politics of British Culture, 1760–1840* (Oxford: Clarendon Press; New York, Oxford University Press, 2003), 153–55.

41 Reynolds, *Discourses on Art*: on portraiture, e.g., 59, 70 (Discourse IV, 1771), 200 (Discourse XI, 1782); against overuse of cool colors, 158 (Discourse VIII, 1778); great style (Discourse III, 43–45; IV, 59–60, V, 80–84).

42 J. Stuart, "Youth," 643.

43 Giorgio Vasari, *Lives of the Most Eminent Painters, Sculptors and Architects*, 10 vols., trans. Gaston du C. de Vere (London: Macmillan and the Medici Society, 1912–15), 5: 260–61 (entry on Jacopo Palma [Vecchio]).

44 Reynolds had four sittings with Stuart, at a time of year when bookings from his own clients were slow; Sir Joshua Reynolds's pocket ledger, July 23, 28, 30, Aug. 27, Royal Academy of Arts, London. I first presented arguments about the portrait in "Stuart and Reynolds: A Portrait of Challenge," *Eighteenth-Century Studies* 27 (Fall 1993): 61–84.

45 Charles Fraser's recollection, quoted in Dunlap, *History*, 1: 184.

46 Reynolds may have been born with a relatively thick upper lip, but his mouth suffered some disfigurement from a youthful riding accident; he flirtatiously assessed its effect in correspondence of 1749, recounting to a Miss Weston "a fall from a horse down a precipice which cut my face in such a manner [that] my lips are spoiled for kissing"; Frederick Whiley Hilles, ed., *Letters of Sir Joshua Reynolds* (Cambridge: Cambridge University Press, 1929), 5.

47 *Testimonies to the Genius and Memory of Sir Joshua Reynolds* (London, 1792), 67.

48 Anon., "Monthly Retrospect of the Fine Arts," *Monthly Magazine* 17 (July 1, 1804): 595.

49 Reynolds, *Discourses*, 59, 70 (Discourse IV, 1771), 200 (Discourse XI, 1782).

50 Jonathan Richardson, *An Essay on the Theory of Painting* (London, 1715), 24; Jonathan Richardson, *Two Discourses: I. An Essay on the whole Art of Criticism as it relates to Painting . . . II. An Argument in behalf of the Science of a Connoisseur . . .* (London, 1719), II: 45.

51 Reynolds, *Discourses*, 149–50 (Discourse VIII, 1778) and 72 (Discourse IV, 1771).

52 James Dowling Herbert, *Irish Varieties for the Last Fifty Years* (London: William Joy, 1836), 230–31. Herbert first met Stuart at that dinner and saw him frequently thereafter during the American's stay in Ireland between 1787 and 1793, the basis for Herbert's lively chapter, "Memoir of Stuart, Portrait-Painter," 226–48.

53 Richard Wendorf, *Sir Joshua Reynolds: The Painter in Society* (Cambridge, Mass.: Harvard University Press, 1996), 116–17. Leonardo da Vinci influentially advised that a painter should "take the mirror as [his] master," while also presenting it as a figure for the painter's mind; *Leonardo on Painting*, ed. Martin Kemp (New Haven and London: Yale University Press, 1989), 202, 205. For mirrors in the metalanguages of media since antiquity, see *Theories of Media*, University of Chicago, http://csmt.uchicago.edu/glossary2004/mirror.htm. See also M. H. Abrams, *The Mirror and the Lamp: Romantic Theory and the Critical Tradition* (New York: Norton, 1953), 30–46.

54 Thomas Sully, "Memoirs of the Professional Life of Thomas Sully Dedicated to his Brother Artists," November 1851, Joseph Downs Collection of Manuscripts and Printed Ephemera, Henry Francis du Pont Winterthur Museum, Del.

55 James Northcote, *The Life of Sir Joshua Reynolds*, intro. R. W. Lightbown 2 vols. bound as 1. (2nd ed. rev., London, 1819; repr., London: Cornmarket Press, 1971), 2: 3–4. David Mannings, countering previous writers, argues that the portrait to which Johnson objected was the one that Reynolds made among a series (1770s) representing intellectuals and artists – including himself and the portrait of Baretti as a reader – for the newly built library at Streatham Park, home of Henry and Hester Thrale; *Sir Joshua Reynolds: A Complete Catalogue of his Paintings* (New Haven and London: Yale University Press for the Paul Mellon Centre for Studies in British Art, 2000), 280–82 (text vol., cats. 1014 and 1016). On that group, see Nadia Tscherney, "Reynolds's Streatham Portraits and the Art of Intimate Biography," *Burlington Magazine* 128 (Jan. 1986): 4–10. For Reynolds's portraits of Johnson, see Richard Wendorf, *The Elements of Life: Biography and Portrait-Painting in Stuart and Georgian England* (Oxford: Clarendon Press, 1990), 250–60; and for portraits of Johnson more generally, Morris R. Brownell, *Samuel Johnson's Attitude to the Arts* (Oxford: Clarendon Press, 1989), 79–90. An unfinished portrait of Johnson reading (Donald and Mary Hyde Collection of Dr. Samuel Johnson, Harvard College Library, Cambridge, Mass.) has been attributed to Stuart, who supposedly made it for his friend William Bowles, Sheriff of Wiltshire, during Johnson's visit with Bowles in Sept. 1783; Mary Hyde, *The Impossible Friendship: Boswell and Mrs. Thrale* (Cambridge: Harvard University Press, 1972), 84. Stuart and Johnson had become acquainted by the 1780s (Dunlap, *History*, 1: 181–82) but the life-portrait scenario seems improbable given the similarity to the portrait by Reynolds and the unlikelihood that Reynolds simply copied a portrait by Stuart (or anyone else).

56 On the shaded face as an indication of a troubled or melancholic mind, see H. Perry Chapman, *Rembrandt's Self Portraits: A Study in Seventeenth-Century Identity* (Princeton: Princeton University Press, 1990), 24–32.

57 Reynolds had a temporary but severe eye problem in 1783 (Hilles, *Letters of Sir Joshua Reynolds*, 97), and in 1789, the year of his last self-portrait – in which he wears spectacles – Reynolds lost sight in his left eye.

58 Reynolds's hearing loss would not be foremost in a viewer's mind when looking at his portrait, but deafness in Stuart's portrayal

of an unidentified woman comes up twice, without detail, in "Notes on Painting by Matthew Harris Jouett, from Conversations with Gilbert Stuart in 1816," in John Hill Morgan, *Gilbert Stuart and his Pupils* (New York: New-York Historical Society, 1939), 85, 87.

59 Rembrandt van Rijn, *The Mennonite Preacher Cornelis Claeszoon Anslo and a Woman*, 1641, Gemäldegalerie, Staatliche Museen, Berlin-Dahlem.

60 The draughtsman – likely Nathaniel Dance, a suitor Kauffmann purportedly spurned for a passing flirtation with Reynolds – does not spare Kauffmann. Her gesture of sincerity, hand pressed to heart, seems undermined by the visible ring (from her imprudent marriage to a spurious Swedish count in November 1767), while the profile view accentuates the weakest features of Kauffmann's face. The drawing (coll. The Earl of Harewood, Harewood House, Leeds) is now simply classed as "English school," according to Wendy Roworth, "Angelica in Love: Gossip, Rumor, Romance, and Scandal," in *Angelica Kauffman: A Woman of Immense Talent*, ed. Tobias G. Natter (Ostfildern, Germany: Hatje Cantz, 2007), 51 n.22; however Dance seems the likely artist, in view of a nearly identical sketch of Kauffmann alone from an album once owned by Dance's brother and now in the British Museum, attributed to Dance; see Stephen Lloyd, *The Intimate Portrait: Drawings, Miniatures, and Pastels from Ramsay to Lawrence* (Edinburgh: National Galleries of Scotland; London: British Museum, 2008), 131, cat. 80.

61 Three figures using different forms of tobacco, along with associated text, represent a social spectrum on the lid of a tobacco box of 1772 at the Winterthur Museum. Madeline Siefke Estill discusses and illustrates that object in a concise discussion of the social value of snuff use: "Colonial New England Silver Snuff, Tobacco, and Patch Boxes: Indices of Gentility," in *New England Silver & Silversmithing, 1620–1815*, ed. Jeannine Falino and Gerald W. R. Ward (Boston: University Press of Virginia for the Colonial Society of Massachusetts, 2001), 48.

62 *London Courant*, as cited by Whitley, *Stuart*, 31. Evans (*Stuart*, 27) identified the subject as diplomat Christopher Springer. In a commissioned work, Gainsborough portrayed Ralph Bell (ca. 1772–74, North Carolina Museum of Art, Raleigh) at full-length in a landscape, dipping his fingers into a snuffbox.

63 John Quincy Adams, Sept. 19, 1818; Diaries of John Quincy Adams: A Digital Collection, MHS.

64 Dunlap, *History*, 1: 162–63, 215.

65 I. P. Davis to Thomas Sully, Apr. 26, 1830, as quoted in Mason, *Stuart*, 76. Adams, relaying a conversation that Horace Binney had with Stuart in the presence of Adams's portrait, as reported to him by Horace Binney Wallace; ibid., 142.

66 John Boydell, "An Autobiography of John Boydell, the Engraver," intro. by W. Bell Jones, *Flintshire Historical Society Publications* 9 (1925): 79–87.

67 Stuart told John Neagle that he carried two snuffboxes, one (holding a lower grade of tobacco) for common people and one for particular friends; as reported in Dunlap, *History*, 1: 215.

68 Quoted in *Monthly Review* 74 (June 1786): 463–64, as from [Peter Pindar], *More Lyric Odes to the Royal Academicians* (1786), though I cannot find the passage in any of Pindar's volumes. Hogarth's mahlstick was retained by Sir George Beaumont until "a painter should appear who was worthy to receive it," that recipient being the Scottish genre painter David Wilkie; John Timbs, *Anecdote Lives of William Hogarth, Sir Joshua Reynolds, Thomas Gainsborough, Henry Fuseli, Sir Thomas Lawrence, and J.M.W. Turner* (London: Richard Bentley, 1865), 77.

69 Dunlap (*History*, 1: 192) presented the basic fact, related to him by Charles Fraser, but my quotation is from Whitley (*Stuart*, 41), whose source I am unable to identify. An artifact more directly associated with Reynolds, his sitters' chair, was imagined as a "relic" to be cut to pieces; [Samuel Felton], *Testimonies to the Genius and Memory of Sir Joshua Reynolds* (London, 1792), 87n. Intact, it entered a baronet's gallery as a "relic of the founder of the British school of painting"; "Varieties," *Literary Gazette; or, Journal of Criticism, Science, and the Arts* 1 (Aug. 18, 1821): 525.

70 Samuel Johnson, *A Dictionary of the English Language*, 2 vols., 6th ed. (London, 1785), s.v., "snuff."

71 J. Stuart, "Anecdotes," 377.

72 For an introduction and complete reprint of "Retaliation," see Arthur Friedman, ed., *Collected Works of Oliver Goldsmith*, 5 vols. (Oxford: Clarendon Press, 1966), 4: 343–59. On Reynolds's selective exploitation of his hearing loss, see Stephen Lucius Gwynn, *Memorials of an Eighteenth-Century Painter (James Northcote)* (London: T. Fisher Unwin, 1898), 234; notably, the anecdote concerns Reynolds's disinclination to hear a complaint that a portrait he painted was unlike. Snuff also worked to soothe irritability, according to a humorous essay that used Goldsmith's last two lines as an epigraph; "Snuff-Taking," *New Monthly Magazine and Literary Journal* (American ed.) 2 (Jan. 1, 1821): 364.

73 Friedman, *Collected Works of Oliver Goldsmith*, 4: 359.

74 Richard Wendorf contested this point (which I first made in my 1993 article on Stuart's *Reynolds*) in the context of a compelling argument that affability was Reynolds's defining social characteristic. Yet in that 1996 biography of the artist, Wendorf acknowledged that Reynolds had a "relatively unknown" side to his character – cool and reserved – and he proposed that Reynolds presented this more resistant face to Stuart, imposing on the younger artist difficulties that Reynolds, as a portraitist, excelled in overcoming; *Reynolds*, 40–41, 12–18. In that case, Reynolds played right into Stuart's hand, allowing Stuart to show the great man without his customary social mask. Despite his position at the pinnacle of the art establishment and in high society, even Reynolds flouted social niceties as a way of distinguishing himself, as Martin Postle argued in "'The Modern Apelles': Joshua Reynolds and the Creation of Celebrity," in *Joshua Reynolds: The Creation of Celebrity*, ed. Martin Postle (London: Tate, 2005), 26.

75 The point was made by a nineteenth-century champion of snuff, who sweepingly claimed that "the mode of taking a pinch of snuff at once depicts the man – his character – habits. Lavater's Science of Physiognomy is . . . beaten by the science of snuff-taking"; [William Delamotte], *Snuff and Snuff-Takers* (London: Joseph Baker, 1846), 42–43.

76 *Life of Benjamin Robert Haydon, Historical Painter, from his Autobiography and Journals*, ed. Tom Taylor, 3 vols. (London: Longman, Brown, Green, and Longmans, 1853), 2: 135.

77 Pickering, "Conversations with Stuart," Nov. 4, 1817; Barratt, *Stuart*, 29. Saltram, a National Trust property, presently has thirteen portraits by Reynolds (listed by Mannings in the Reynolds catalogue raisonné) and some half-dozen by Stuart.

78 See Roland Barthes, "The Reality Effect," reprinted in Barthes, *The Rustle of Language*, trans. Richard Howard (New York: Hill and Wang, 1986), 141–48. Similarly, Stuart chose to indicate wig powder on Reynolds's coat, a common sight not usually rendered by portraitists. A Prussian clergyman noted that English gentlemen wore curled and dressed hair that left "half their backs . . . covered with powder"; Karl Philipp Moritz, *Travels in England in 1782* (Bremen: Salzwasser-Verlag, 2010), 45.

79 Thomas Gainsborough, letter to William Mayhew, Mar. 13, 1758, as quoted in *The Letters of Thomas Gainsborough*, ed. John Hayes (New Haven: Yale University Press for the Paul Mellon Centre for Studies in British Art, 2001), 10–11.

80 William Temple Franklin set West's comment in quotation marks, in a letter to his grandfather Benjamin Franklin, Nov. 9, 1784; Benjamin Franklin Papers, American Philosophical Society, Philadelphia. Franklin believed, as well, that West's comment acknowledged the stability of Stuart's coloring, by contrast to that of Reynolds, among others.

81 John Sartain, *Reminiscences of a Very Old Man* (New York: D. Appleton, 1899), 194.

82 Dunlap, *History*, 1: 218.

83 For extended discussion of *le faire*, see Mary D. Sheriff, *Fragonard: Art and Eroticism* (Chicago: University of Chicago Press, 1990), 117–52.

84 John Barrell suggested that singularity in eighteenth-century French painting ought to be understood in political terms, "as if the republic of the fine arts offered a substitute for the freedom which could not be exercised by participation in the civil state – a freedom which is therefore experienced and valued as singularity, as private freedom, in that it must be construed in opposition to one's political identity"; *The Political Theory of Painting from Reynolds to Hazlitt* (New Haven and London: Yale University Press for the Paul Mellon Centre for Studies in British Art, 1986), 130.

85 See Pressly, *Artist as Original Genius*.

86 Reynolds, *Discourses*, 257–59 (Discourse XIV, 1788).

87 Sully, "Memoirs."

88 Eric Rothstein identified continual effort by both painters and poets to excite sensory participation in the viewer or reader as an eighteenth-century tendency; "'Ideal Presence' and the 'Non Finito' in Eighteenth-Century Aesthetics," *Eighteenth-Century Studies* 9 (Spring 1976): 307–32.

89 Cf. Sheriff's succinct review of the French debate over the characteristics of successful portraits; *Fragonard*, 172–76. Reynolds likely knew that conventional standards for portraiture had been relaxed in France, judging from his contacts with French artists, as sketched by Robert Rosenblum, "Reynolds in an International Milieu," in *Reynolds*, ed. Nicholas Penny (London: Royal Academy of Arts, 1986), 43–54.

90 Reynolds, *Discourses*, 257–59 (Discourse XIV, 1788, emphasis in original).

91 Dunlap, *History*, 1: 181.

92 J. Stuart, "Youth of Gilbert Stuart," 641.

93 Quintilian, *Institutio Oratoria*, trans. H. E. Butler (London: William Heinemann; New York: G. P. Putnam's Sons, 1921), X.ii.7. See also the story of the Corinthian maid: Pliny, *Natural History*, 35.5.15, trans. H. Rackham (Cambridge, Mass.: Harvard University Press; London: W. Heineman, 1961), 9. 271.

94 Anthony Pasquin [John Williams], *A Liberal Critique on the Present Exhibition of the Royal Academy* (London, 1794), 17; see also 22 regarding a Reynolds portrait that had aged with its sitter to become "brown, exactly in proportion as the peer became bilious from malady," a "miracle . . . effected though the medium of flying varnishes!"

95 Charles Robert Leslie and Tom Taylor, *Life and Times of Sir Joshua Reynolds*, 2 vols. (London: John Murray, 1865), 2: 476 (with ham erroneously printed as barn), as quoted in Nicholas Penny, *Reynolds*, 17; see also the catalogue entry on 310–11.

96 Reynolds, *Discourses*, 232–33 (Discourse XIII, 1786).

97 Henry T. Tuckerman, *Book of the Artists: American Artist Life* (New York: G. P. Putnam; London: Sampson Low, 1867), 115.

98 "Remarks on the Fine Arts," *Monthly Anthology* 1 (Dec. 1803): 52. This writer considered Stuart and the fine arts more broadly to be insufficiently appreciated in the United States.

99 Dunlap, *History*, 1: 185.

100 Ibid., 1: 217.

101 Reynolds, *Discourses*, 132–33 (Discourse VII, 1776). Barrell finds Reynolds's seventh Discourse the most complex and most revealing "about the degree to which Reynolds's theory of art is, at base, a theory of society"; *Political Theory of Painting*, 141–58 (quote at 145).

102 Herbert, *Irish Varieties*, 248.

103 "Hundred dollar bill": Horace Binney Wallace, diary entry, June 31, 1852, as cited by Mason, *Stuart*, 141. "Legacy": Stuart's words, as related by John Neagle in Dunlap, *History*, 1: 198–99. For painstaking reconstruction of the history of Stuart's various Washington portraits, see Miles, *Stuart*, 133–90. Like Stuart, Washington's early biographer Mason Locke Weems aimed to profit by his *Life of Washington*, of which the first among many editions appeared in 1799. On Jan. 13, 1809, Weems pressed publisher Mathew Carey for a new edition, noting: "You have a great deal of money lying in the bones of old George if you will but exert yourself to extract it"; as quoted in Paul Ford Lancaster, *Mason Locke Weems: His Works and his Ways*, ed. Emily E. F. Skeel, 3 vols. (New York: n.p., 1929), 1: 47. Steven Watts, "Masks, Morals, and the Market: American Literature and Early Capitalist Culture, 1790–1820" (which led me to the Weems quotation) offers a cogent analysis of the tension between republican ideals of virtue and the "market creed of individual opportunity and ambition," as expressed in the writings of Weems, Philip Freneau, Hugh Henry Brackenridge, and Charles Brockden Brown, in *New Perspectives on the Early Republic: Essays from the Journal of the Early Republic*, ed. Ralph D. Gray and Michael A. Morrison (Urbana and Chicago: University of Illinois Press, 1994), 244–66 (on Weems and money: 250, 256).

104 For useful accounts of contrasting style, see the popularizing and entertaining essays – in a short book occasioned by acquisition of the Lansdowne portrait for the National Portrait Gallery – by Richard Brookhiser, Margaret C. S. Christman, and Ellen G. Miles, *George Washington: A National Treasure* (Washington, D.C.: National Portrait Gallery, Smithsonian Institution, 2002); Miles's punctilious catalogue entry in *Stuart*, 166–75; and Paul Staiti's clever spin in "Gilbert Stuart's Presidential Imagery," in *Shaping the Body Politic*, 162–93.

105 Mason, *Stuart*, 95–96, quoting "the draft" of Stuart's letter to Lord Lansdowne, i.e., a copy that he presumably kept for himself as a record (present location unknown; Mason's access probably through Jane Stuart). Possibly Stuart never sent the letter; in any case, no reply is known.

106 See Charles Palmer Phillips, *The Law of Copyright in Works of Literature and Art* (London: V&R Stevens, Sons, & Haynes, 1863); B. A. Cohen, *The Law of Copyright* (London: Jordan & Sons, 1896); and Simon Stokes, *Art and Copyright* (Oxford: Hart, 2001), 10–18. Stuart's various copyright disputes have been widely discussed in literature on the artist, but I owe my understanding of the fine points to research undertaken on my behalf by attorney Lynn Bradshaw, in the course of her graduate studies in art history at the University of Texas, Austin.

107 Phillips, *Law of Copyright*, Appendix, v–ix, xiii–xiv, reprints the successive Acts protecting reproductive prints: 8 Geo. II. c. 13 (The Engraving Copyright Act, 1734); 7 Geo. III. c. 38 (The Engraving

Copyright Act, 1766); 17 Geo. III. c. 57 (The Prints Copyright Act, 1777).

108 *Aurora General Advertiser* (Philadelphia), June 12, 1800; as quoted in Alfred Coxe Prime, *The Arts and Crafts in Philadelphia, Maryland, and South Carolina, 1786–1800, Series Two: Gleanings from Newspapers* (Topsfield, Mass.: Walpole Society, Hartford, 1932), 34–35; *Independent Chronicle*, Boston, June 23, 1800; *Federal Gazette and Daily Advertiser*, Baltimore, July 1, 1800; *City Gazette and Daily Advertiser*, Charleston, S.C., July 16, 1800; *South-Carolina State Gazette*, Oct. 8, 1800 (citation of first appearance only for advertisements that ran on multiple dates).

109 Israel Whelen, agent in the transactions with Stuart, to Oliver Wolcott, Jr., for the State of Connecticut, Aug. 6, 1800, Papers of Oliver Wolcott Jr., vol. 15, no. 108, Connecticut Historical Society, Hartford; as cited by Miles, *Stuart*, 189.

110 National Archives Microfilm Publications, M985, Equity Records of the United States Circuit Court for the Eastern District of Pennsylvania, 1790–1847: Roll #20, Equity Case Files (Stewart [*sic*] v. Swords [*sic*]), Roll #1 Dockets (Injunction). These court filings include the original bill or petition, the court's injunction, and the return of service by the federal marshal. The first two documents are reprinted in E. P. Richardson, "China Trade Portraits of Washington after Stuart," *Pennsylvania Magazine of History and Biography* 94 (Jan. 1970): 95–100.

111 It remains unclear whether Stuart's case was the first for artistic copyright in the United States, as sometimes asserted. Evans (*Stuart*, 148 n.20) believed it "the first of its kind" since his attorneys cited no prior legal precedent in their petition, but this may not be correct. When lawyers requested immediate, preliminary action by a court, reference to existing legal precedent would not have been required, especially in a case for emergency injunctive relief, which is an equitable action as opposed to a pleading under common law. Earlier filings by artists requesting copyright protections could have been filed and gone unrecorded or unreported. But Stuart's case, whether or not the first, lays claim to noteworthy status owing to his importance as a portraitist at the time and its place in the early formation of copyright law protection for artists in America.

112 The Federal Copyright Act of 1790 granted protection of any "map, chart, or book" to authors or their executors, administrators, or assigns for fourteen years, renewable under certain conditions; see *Copyright Enactments of the United States, 1783–1906* (Washington, D.C.: Government Printing Office, 1906). For the first case to uphold and interpret the statute, in which Alexander Hamilton served as the plaintiff's counsel, see John D. Gordan, III, "Morse v. Reid: The First Reported Federal Copyright Case," *Law and History Review* 11 (Spring 1993): 21–42. The congressional history indicates no petitions by individual artists as instrumental in passing the Act of 1802, and none of the congressmen who introduced the bill appear to have had a relationship to Stuart.

113 "Gilbert Stuart," advertisement in *Gazette of the United States*, Apr. 12, 1803.

114 Cf. Wendorf's account of Reynolds's industry and discipline and his accomplishments as an eighteenth-century "man of business," in *Reynolds*, 87–128 (ch. 3: "The Marketplace and the Studio").

115 Barratt outlined characteristics of the breed in *Stuart*, 90–93, noting as well that Newfoundland dogs were "famous for an even temperament" and for "steadfast reliability . . . and skill." She proposed these as attributes Stuart might have wanted to claim, but the artist was neither even-tempered nor steadfast and he made little effort to cultivate those virtues, so the association could only be ironic. Although the figurative meaning of slobber does not appear in dictionaries until the nineteenth century, little stretch is required to link the faithful slavering dog in Stuart's portrait of young Nugent with the artist himself.

116 Richardson, *Theory of Painting*, 23–25.

117 Washington to Francis Hopkinson, May 16, 1785; George Washington Papers: Series 2 Letterbooks, Library of Congress, Manuscript Division, Washington, D.C. "Thill" refers to the shafts of a wagon or carriage that are used to harness the animal pulling it.

118 Two documents relating to Peale's interactions with Washington in 1772 include an excerpt from a letter from George Washington to Jonathan Boucher, May 21, 1772, in which he mentions sitting to Peale "in so grave – so sullen a Mood – and now and then under the influence of Morpheus . . . that I fancy the skill of this Gentleman's Pencil, will be put to it, in describing to the World what manner of Man I am," and Peale's receipt to Washington, May 30, 1772, for a miniature of his wife; *Peale Papers*, 1: 120–22. Even more than the portrait, Peale's later recollection of an encounter with Washington that spring captured his regard for Washington as a man of superior powers; see Rembrandt Peale, "Reminiscences: The Person and Mien of Washington," *Crayon* 2 (April 1856): 388, and the analysis by Ward, *Peale: Art and Selfhood*, 45–47.

119 On the ubiquity of Washington's image, see Wendy C. Wick, *George Washington, an American Icon: The Eighteenth-Century Graphic Portraits* (Washington, D.C.: Smithsonian Institution; Barra Foundation, 1982), esp. 3–33.

120 J. Stuart, "Washington," 369. Isaac Weld, in a digressive footnote that reports Stuart's remarks to him concerning Washington's character and comportment, noted (without direct reference to Stuart) that "veneration and awe" were customary responses by those who found themselves in Washington's presence; Isaac Weld, *Travels through the States of North America . . . during the Years 1795, 1796, and 1797* (1799; reprint of 1807 ed., 2 vols., New York and London: Johnson Reprint Corp., 1968): 1: 105–7.

121 "Eazle-talk": Dunlap, "Stuart," *Knickerbocker*, 198. Ann Bartlett Dwight, quoted by her nephew Thomas B. Hall in a letter to Thomas Amory, Oct. 13, 1878 (intended for use by Mason), and Henry Bowditch to Mason, Sept. 2, 1878; Mason Papers, RIHS.

122 Gregory Nobles, "A Class Act: Redefining Deference in Early American History," *Early American Studies* 3 (Fall 2005): 286–302 – one of eight essays on deference that appeared in that issue.

123 Stuart's story of the stagecoach: Dunlap, *History*, 1: 189–90. Jonathan Mason, an American artist in England (ca. 1823), was chagrined to learn that the fellow stagecoach passenger whom he feared he had wronged was a titled Member of Parliament (though silent as to that identity); "Recollections of a Septuagenarian," [1866?]–1881, 3 vols., Joseph Downs Collection of Manuscripts and Printed Ephemera, Winterthur Museum and Library, Del., vol. 3. John Neal called "delightful" conversations overheard on stage coaches "*live* stories"; "Story-Telling," *New England Magazine* 8 (1835): 9.

124 Stuart himself offered this account of "embarrassment" in Washington's presence, according to Margaret Hall Hunter, letter of Oct. 14, 1827, as quoted in *The Aristocratic Journey; Being the Outspoken Letters of Mrs. Basil Hall Written during a Fourteen Months' Sojourn in America, 1827–1828*, ed. Una Pope-Hennessy (New York: G. P. Putnam's Sons, 1931), 93–94.

125 The president's submission to portraitists gave rise to one of Stuart's famous puns. Upon hearing from Mrs. Washington about the

occasion in 1795 when four members of the Peale family – Charles, Rembrandt, Rubens, and James – surrounded the president, each painting his portrait, Stuart joked that Washington had been "*Pealed all round*"; C. W. Peale to Rubens Peale, Jan. 18, 1824, *Peale Papers*, 4: 365. Peale, who described Stuart as "a man of wit & humour," wrote elsewhere that he had "never loved the characters of witty Persons . . . [who] do not always consider whether a witty saying may not hurt the feeling of another"; C. W. Peale to Rembrandt Peale, Oct. 28, 1812, and to Angelica Peale Robinson, Dec. 23, 1813, *The Belfield Farm Years, 1810–1820*, vol. 3 of *Peale Papers*, 176, 222.

126 Dunlap, *History*, 1: 197–98, 205. In print, Dunlap attributed Trumbull's remark only to "the president of an academy," without identifying the institution; however, informed readers would easily have recognized the source, since Trumbull was then president of the American Academy of Fine Arts and a portraitist of Washington. Dunlap plainly named Trumbull in his *Diary*, 728 (entry for Aug. 12, 1833). Trumbull reversed his position on Stuart's status out of consideration for the artist's family: "Your father was a gentleman," he told Anne Stuart, "not the tavern jester, he [Dunlap] has represented"; as quoted in Evans, *Stuart*, xvii. Trumbull's objections to Dunlap's portrayal of him gave him motivation to discredit Dunlap's biographies in the *History*, not least by publishing an autobiography.

127 Adams's remarks to Josiah Quincy, as quoted in Josiah Quincy, *Figures of the Past from the Leaves of Old Journals* (Boston: Roberts Brothers, 1883), 83. Alan Taylor, "From Fathers to Friends of the People: Political Personas in the Early Republic," in *New Perspectives on the Early Republic*, 1–20.

128 On his decision to step back from active political engagement, see *Peale Papers*, 5: 83. For the political dimension of Peale's art and endeavors, see Ward, *Peale: Art and Selfhood*, 81–94 (quote at 82). Ward characterizes Peale as a "nonactivist Democratic-Republican," sympathetic to the Jeffersonian party (180, 101).

129 Pickering, "Conversations with Stuart," Nov. 4, 1817. Evans merely alludes to this particular notation, without quoting or analyzing it; *Stuart*, 138 n.16. In her catalogue entry on the Jefferson portraits, Miles quotes Stuart's remarks on Jefferson from Pickering as evidence of Jefferson's charm; *Stuart*, 280.

130 Dunlap, *History*, 1: 219. Waterhouse, notation of Sept. 5, 1842 from Waterhouse's "Memoranda of Things and Events," as quoted in Mabel Munson Swan, "'Scraps' – The Missing Waterhouse Biography of Gilbert Stuart," *Art in America* 41 (Spring 1953): 91. In this case, the "missing" biography, which had been used by Dunlap in writing his account of Stuart, was pages torn from a longer document written by Waterhouse, probably the manuscript now missing from Harvard's Countway Library, which had been catalogued as "partially mutilated, pages missing."

131 United States Courts, Jurisdiction of the Federal Courts, http://www.uscourts.gov/about-federal-courts/types-cases.

132 Benjamin Latrobe, letter to C. W. Peale, July 17, 1808, in *Peale Papers*, 2, pt. 2: 866 and n.4, in which the editors state that Latrobe's bitterness stemmed from Stuart's failure to pay rent on a studio that Latrobe had constructed specifically for him. On citizenship, see James H. Kettner, *The Development of American Citizenship, 1608–1870* (Chapel Hill: University of North Carolina Press, 1978), and William J. Novak, "The Legal Transformation of Citizenship in Nineteenth-Century America," in *The Democratic Experiment: New Directions in American Political History* (Princeton: Princeton University Press, 2003): 85–119.

133 David Steinberg, "The Characters of Charles Willson Peale: Portraiture and Social Identity, 1769–1776." (Ph.D. dissertation, University of Pennsylvania, 1993), 52–59. Peale's first notice in *Maryland Gazette*, Sept. 8, 1774, referred to Valette only as "E.V.," but on Sept. 15 and 22, he openly named the patron, whose response was published on the latter date. In 1784, having not been paid for a posthumous portrait of Captain Moultrie's child, Peale approached the matter more diplomatically, though still with strategic indirectness, in this case via a third party, David Ramsay, a friend to both artist and patron. As it turned out, Moultrie had paid Peale's fee to Ramsay, so the error was in fact Ramsay's. Peale to David Ramsay, Aug. 17, 1784, and Ramsay to Peale, Sept. 27, 1784; *Peale Papers*, 1: 414–15, 418–19.

134 C. W. Peale to his daughter Angelica Peale Robinson, Dec. 23, 24, 25, 27, 1813; *Peale Papers*, 3: 222.

135 Peale to John Beale Bordley, June 14, 1783, and Peale to Benjamin West, Nov. 17, 1788; ibid., 1: 389–90, 544.

136 Ward, *Peale: Art and Selfhood*, 50–53 (on the Valette case, the disputed miniature, and Peale's hesitation to write about patrons). Peale left out particulars when relating the events in his autobiographical manuscript, noting that, although he had "memorandums made on this occasion, he forbears to transcribe them, because he believes it is better to let it be obliterated rather than any one shall be offended with his remarks"; *Peale Papers*, 5: 199.

137 Herbert, *Irish Varieties*, 232–35.

138 Northcote, as quoted in David Piper, *The English Face* (London: National Portrait Gallery, 1978), 20.

139 Sully, as quoted in an undated letter (by a correspondent I could not identify) to George Mason; Mason Papers, RIHS. For testaments to Stuart's focus on heads, see Mason, *Stuart*, 38, 134.

140 Margaret Manigault, as quoted (without citation) in Barratt, *Stuart*, 126.

141 Dunlap, *History*, 1: 218.

142 David Jaffee, *A New Nation of Goods: The Material Culture of Early America* (Philadelphia and Oxford: University of Pennsylvania Press, 2010), 85–88 (quote at 87). The term "dressed miniatures" is from William Lamson Warren, "Mary Way's Dressed Miniatures," *Antiques* 142 (Oct. 1992): 540–49, which features high quality color illustrations that readily demonstrate Way's techniques.

143 Jane Stuart, as quoted in Mason, *Stuart*, 144.

144 Sully, quoted in Whitley, *Stuart*, 125. In a novel thesis focused on Elizabeth (Betsy) Patterson Bonaparte and Stuart's portrait, Lynn Bradshaw has argued for the deliberateness of its non-finito, with the notably absent body designed to conjure the body of the sitter herself, on scandalous display in Washington society beneath the lady's sheer muslin dresses; "Patterson v. Bonaparte and the Interesting Case of a Marriage . . . ," M.A. thesis, University of Texas, Austin, 2012.

145 Pickering, "Conversations with Stuart," Oct. 29, 1817.

146 I have relied on Miles (*Stuart*, 210–12) for information about Washington's interest in Ricketts and for her suggested dating of the portrait. Regarding Stuart's annoyance with Ricketts, Miles cites J. Thomas Scharf and Thompson Westcott, *History of Philadelphia, 1609–1884*, 3 vols. (Philadelphia: L. H. Everts and Co., 1884), 2: 1044.

147 The canvas remained in Stuart's studio as of 1807, when Sully was there and noted in his register making two portraits of "Mr. Ricketts," a small one "copied from a painting" and a larger bust-length portrait six months later; Ellen G. Miles et al., *American Paintings of the Eighteenth Century* (Washington, D.C.: National Gallery of Art, 1995), 208–10. When and how Francis Ricketts came to possess the picture is unknown, but Bill Ricketts evidently never owned it. Sully's father and brother had been performers in Ricketts's circus, so perhaps

the young painter interceded with Stuart in the transfer of Bill Ricketts's portrait to his family.

148 Oliver, *Portraits of John Quincy Adams*, 122–33. The testimony of sitters whose portraits Stuart failed to complete indicates the satisfaction those works provided. In a letter of 1822, Betsy Bonaparte declared the unusual triple portrait her family had finally extracted from Stuart, "the only likeness that has ever been made of me. My other pictures are quite as like any one else as me"; as quoted in Miles, *Stuart*, 255. Despite the "imperfections" Henry Bowditch found "everywhere" in his father's unfinished portrait, he still thought it looked less like a painting than like "a really living head . . . coming out of the canvas": "the *effect* is *perfect*"; Henry Bowditch to George Mason, Sept. 2, 1878, Mason Papers, RIHS. Even so, Sully was employed to finish the painting, an action that must have left him uncomfortable, knowing Stuart as he did. Pliny valued unfinished paintings because they revealed "the artists' actual thoughts"; *Natural History*, trans. Rackham, 9: 367 (35.40.146).

149 Harriet Taylor Upton, *Our Early Presidents, their Wives and Children* (Boston: D. Lothrop Co., 1890), 202; as quoted by Miles, *Stuart*, 262.

150 For a concise history of profile portraiture in Europe and the United States to ca. 1800, see Ellen G. Miles, *Saint-Mémin and the Neoclassical Profile Portrait in America* (Washington, D.C.: National Portrait Gallery and Smithsonian Institution Press, 1994), 27–59.

151 On C. W. Peale's physiognotrace, David Brigham, *Public Culture in the Early Republic: Peale's Museum and Its Audience* (Washington, D.C.: Smithsonian Institution Press, 1995), 68–82. Gwendolyn DuBois Shaw has argued that a profile of Williams in the Library Company of Philadelphia, attributed to Raphaelle Peale, was by Williams himself; "'Moses Williams, Cutter of Profiles': Silhouettes and African American Identity in the Early Republic," *Proceedings of the American Philosophical Society* 149 (Mar. 2005): 22–39; republished in Shaw, *Portraits of a People: Picturing African Americans in the Nineteenth Century* (Andover, Mass.: Addison Gallery of American Art, Phillips Academy, 2006), 44–55.

152 Peale himself recognized the limitations of that profile and asked the president to give a mere minute of time to the tracing of a better one, though he was no more satisfied with that result, executed by Jefferson's private secretary; C. W. Peale to Thomas Jefferson, June 15, 1804 and Peale to Raphaelle and Rembrandt Peale, June 23, 1804, *Peale Papers*, 2, pt. 2: 711–12, 720–21.

153 Jefferson, letter to Joseph Delaplaine, May 30, 1813, polygraph copy, Jefferson Papers, Library of Congress, as cited by Miles, *Stuart*, 284.

154 Miles (ibid., 136–40) believed that Stuart used Houdon's bust to rework his original conception of the portrait, whereas Evans (*Stuart*, 66) argued that Stuart made his work less like the existing life mask of Washington in order to reinforce an existing "interpretation" of the president's character; see also her rebuttal of Miles, in Evans, *Stuart and the Impact of Manic Depression*, 62–63 and 88 n.29. Evans (*Stuart*, 136 n.6) found evidence for Stuart's acceptance of typology in Jouett's notes of his conversations with the artist; in Morgan, *Gilbert Stuart and his Pupils*, 82. Remarks on that page mostly concern technical matters, but Evans presumably had in mind Stuart's condemnation of "mincing painters who paint all the features correctly but so detachd that . . . theres no chain of inter[e]st to connect them" as well as his admonition that everything should "be of a piece: Let not your Pharoahs be beef eating Aldermen nor your buff jerkins who unbutton after dinner lean Cassius." This last remark, however, addressed unity in history painting, to which types are relevant, whereas likeness is not.

155 Dunlap recorded the story of Stuart and the future suicide victim (*Diary*, 693, entry for June 20, 1833), editorializing on the matter for publication: "the real portrait-painter dives into the recesses of his sitters' mind, and displays strength or weakness upon the surface of his canvas. The mechanic makes a map of a man" (*History*, 1: 187).

156 J. Stuart, "Anecdotes," 378.

157 John Neal, "Our Painters," *Atlantic Monthly* 22 (Dec. 1868): 641. Stuart "believed in Lavater, or at least in the leading principles of physiognomy," Neal asserted (644).

158 John Neal, *Randolph: A Novel*, 2 vols. (Baltimore, 1823), 2: 64, 63. Neal, "Our Painters," 645, 641 (succeeding quotation).

159 C. W. Peale, letter to Rembrandt Peale, May 8, 1805, *Peale Papers*, 2, pt. 2: 829–30. Though later and not commissioned, Rembrandt Peale's luminous portrait of his daughter Rosalba (ca. 1820, Smithsonian American Art Museum, Washington, D.C.) indicates his ability as a portraitist of women.

160 Neal, *Randolph*, 2: 68.

161 Thomas Sully, "Memoirs of the Professional Life of Thomas Sully Dedicated to his Brother Artists," November 1851, Joseph Downs Collection of Manuscripts and Printed Ephemera, Winterthur Museum, Del.

162 Rosalie Stier Calvert, letter to Isabelle van Havre, Feb. 18, 1805, in *Mistress of Riversdale: The Plantation Letters of Rosalie Stier Calvert, 1795–1821*, ed. and trans. Margaret Law Callcott (Baltimore and London: Johns Hopkins University Press, 1991), 111; citation from Miles, *Stuart*, 191–94.

163 Vigorous debate over the relative merits of color and drawing arose in the French Academy during the late seventeenth century; see Jacqueline Lichtenstein, *The Eloquence of Color: Rhetoric and Painting in the French Classical Age*, trans. Emily McVarish (Berkeley: University of California Press, 1993). Those ideas were completely familiar to British artists and theorists; more proximate to Stuart's time, William Gilpin called color "the great vehicle of deception"; *Three Essays: On Picturesque Beauty; on Picturesque Travel; and On Sketching Landscape* (London, 1794), 73.

164 Pasquin, *Memoirs of the Royal Academicians* (1796; repr., London: Cornmarket Press, 1970), 134–35.

165 Pickering, "Conversations with Stuart," Nov. 10, 1817. For the nose as "important," Pickering, ibid., and as "characteristic," Mason, *Stuart*, 141, citing Horace Binney Wallace's diary entry of June 31, 1852 (which recorded conversation with his uncle, Horace Binney). Dunlap wrote that Stuart considered likeness dependent on the nose; *History*, 1: 212, 218. Careless word choice must account for the later report that Stuart considered the nose the most "expressive" feature of a face; Anne Hollingsworth Wharton, *Social Life in the Early Republic* (1902; repr., Williamstown, Mass.: Corner House Publishers, 1970), 143–44.

166 Stuart as quoted by Jouett, "Notes on Painting," in Morgan, *Stuart and his Pupils*, 92.

167 Pickering, "Conversations with Stuart," Oct. 29, 1817.

168 Evans (*Stuart*, 16) and Barratt (*Stuart*, 31) do not give citations for the inventories of West's collection they mention. Both authors accept that Stuart owned a Dobson, based on the remarks to Pickering, though they have differing interpretations of the interviewer's notation of the price paid. "12/!!" must indicate twelve pounds (or guineas, Barratt's conclusion), not shillings, given Dobson's stature and reputation at that time.

169 Horace Walpole, *Anecdotes of Painting in England*, 4 vols. ([Twickenham], 1765–71), 2: 120–24; Matthew Pilkington, *The Gentle-*

man's and Connoisseur's Dictionary of Painters (London, 1770), 177–78; James Granger, *A Biographical History of England . . .*, 2nd ed., 4 vols. (London, 1775), 2: 347; Thomas Mortimer, *The British Plutarch*, 6 vols. (London, 1776), 3: 285–87.

170 Stuart's relatively intense expression and parted lips in the self-portrait even more strikingly resemble John Hamilton Mortimer in his *Self-Portrait in Character* of ca. 1775–78. Though Stuart does not invoke any other of the elements of that "character," interpreted as a Salvator Rosian banditto, it is tempting to consider Mortimer – whom contemporaries called the "English Salvator" for his fierce independence and wild genius – as an artistic exemplum for Stuart, if not one with whom he could have had much contact, since Mortimer died prematurely in 1779. On Mortimer, see Pressly, *Artist as Original Genius*, 39–83. An engraving of Stuart's self-portrait, after a copy of that work by Jane Stuart (J. Stuart, "Youth," 639), shows the artist's hat much more clearly than does the painting, in particular its rather high and slightly askew crown and strong dip in the broad brim. Even considering that the copyist and (less likely) the engraver embellished something they had difficulty making out, the hat looks less like West's in his self-portrait than at first appears.

171 For an account of the Venetian Secret, see Angus Trumble, Mark N. Aronson, and Helen Cooper, *Benjamin West and the Venetian Secret* (New Haven: Yale Center for British Art, 2008).

172 Dunlap, *History*, 1: 207–8.

173 Lance Mayer and Gay Myers, the conservators who cleaned Stuart's self-portrait, confirm that the materials he used would have made it look like an older painting, in complete contrast to Stuart's later practices, as detailed in *American Painters on Technique: The Colonial Period to 1860* (Los Angeles: J. Paul Getty Trust, 2011), 43–58; also 11–24 for West's interest in Old Master techniques. For a key primary text regarding Stuart's technique, see Jouett's "Notes on Painting," in Morgan, *Stuart and his Pupils*, 81–93.

174 Dunlap first related the story of West's struggles to portray George III in "Stuart," *Knickerbocker*, and afterward in *History*, 1: 178–80. The portrait of George III that West showed at the Royal Academy in 1783 has not been conclusively identified. Von Erffa and Staley tentatively identified it as their cat. 551, a work without provenance before 1910, and which they describe as having "freer handling" than West's prior portraits of the king; *West*, 466.

175 Mason, *Stuart*, 53; J. Quincy, *Figures of the Past*, 84–85.

176 Whitley, *Stuart*, 75–76.

177 Walpole, as quoted by Michael Snodin, in Michael Snodin, ed., *Horace Walpole's Strawberry Hill* (New Haven and London: Yale University Press, 2009), 15; and Alicia Weisbert-Roberts, "Singular Objects and Multiple Meanings," ibid., 90.

178 C.B., "On Affectation in Portraiture," *The New Monthly Magazine and Literary Journal* 2:12 (1821): 636 (the American edition of a British publication).

179 Herbert, *Irish Varieties*, 232.

180 On the commission for the portraits of "distinguished patriots," never started, see Barratt, *Stuart*, 291–92.

181 Stuart manifested the cultural ambivalence so characteristic of Americans during the early republic, as probed in consideration of objects, commodities, and practices by Kariann Akemi Yakota in *Unbecoming British: How Revolutionary America Became a Postcolonial Nation* (New York: Oxford University Press, 2011).

182 The editors of *Peale Papers* (5: 446) suggested that Peale was "attempting both literally and figuratively to recapture his artistic beginnings" by acquiring the portrait by van der Myn.

183 In an original and controversial interpretation of *The Artist in his Museum*, Ward identifies Peale's vitality with masculine power and sexuality; *Peale: Art and Selfhood*, 184–89.

184 Dunlap, *History*, 1:216. In his diary for Jan. 11, 1805, Peale wrote that he painted a portrait of Stuart, although the timing remains unclear, given his letter to Raphaelle, Rubens, and Sophonisba Peale of Jan. 30, 1805, in which he noted the work as "beg[u]n today" with a postscript of Feb. 1 that he hoped to "finish" it then. Neither reference indicates Rembrandt's involvement, though the editors of the Peale papers offer evidence to support it. *Peale Papers*, 2, pt. 2: 786 and n.16, 797.

185 Evans brought Falconer's etching to modern attention in "Gilbert Stuart and Manic Depression," 28 and n.24. As she pointed out, Tuckerman (in *Book of the Artists*, 111) wrote that that he saw the drawing in Falconer's possession.

186 James Duthie made the engraving of Stuart's self-portrait drawing used for Mason's book, according to Charles Henry Hart, review of Mason, *Stuart*, in *American Art Review* 1 (Mar. 1880), 221; cited by Evans, *Stuart and the Impact of Manic Depression*, 33, n.42. Evans (25–26) believes Falconer made a second etching after Stuart's self-portrait, in which, "possibly inspired by Duthie's commission," Falconer represented the artist as "more dignified and distant" than in either his prior version or Duthie's – a possibility that is inconsistent with the motivation I have proposed here for making the etching in the first place.

187 Frank Weitenkampf, *American Graphic Art* (New York: H. Holt, 1912), 7, quoting S[ylvester] R[osa] Koehler. Though no citation is given, the source text was S. R. Koehler, "The Works of the American Etchers. VI. – J.M. Falconer," *American Art Review* 1 (Mar. 1880): 190.

6 THE AMERICAN WEST

1 William Dunlap, *A History of the Rise and Progress of the Arts of Design in the United States* (1834), 3 vols., ed. Rita Weiss (New York: Dover, 1969), 1: 34. This chapter expands on my "Benjamin West, John Galt, and the Biography of 1816," *Art Bulletin* 86 (June 2004): 323–45.

2 James Thomas Flexner, *America's Old Masters*, rev. ed. (1939; New York: Dover, 1967), 74.

3 See the historiographic essay by Carrie Rebora, "Copley and Art History: The Study of America's First Old Master," in Carrie Rebora and Paul Staiti et al., *John Singleton Copley in America* (New York: Metropolitan Museum of Art, 1995), 3–23.

4 An early reference to West as "the father of the American school" came from an Englishman traveling in the United States: E[manuel] Howitt, *Selections from Letters Written during a Tour through the United States, in the Summer and Autumn of 1819* (Nottingham, 1820), 63. References to West as "father" were once common; "dean" and "mentor": *Art in America*, ed. Holger Cahill and Alfred H. Barr, Jr. (New York: Reynal and Hitchcock, 1934), 20, 22.

5 For a damning characterization of West's adherence to rules, see William Hazlitt, "On the Old Age of Artists," Essay IX from *The Plain Speaker: Opinions on Books, Men and Things* (1826), in *The Complete Works of William Hazlitt*, ed. P. P. Howe, 21 vols. (London and Toronto: J. M. Dent, 1930–34), 12: 94–5.

6 In the text of this chapter, *Life of West* refers to the 1816 volume, published in London by Cadell and Davies, cited as simply *West* (1816); the quotation in this paragraph is from p. 24. The later volume, titled *The Life and Works of Benjamin West*, was bound with

the first and published as *The Life, Studies, and Works of Benjamin West, Esq.* (London: T. Cadell and W. Davies; Edinburgh: W. Blackwood, 1820), 189–90; in notes, references to Galt, *West* (1820) refer only to the part concerning West's life in England. A facsimile reprint of the 1820 edition, with an introduction by Nathalia Wright, appeared as *The Life of Benjamin West* (Gainesville, Fla.: Scholars' Facsimiles & Reprints, 1960).

7 In a collection of biographical vignettes and anecdotes for juvenile readers, Galt highlighted West's inability to dissemble in another encounter with a potentially angry "father," King George III, who then valued his honesty when the American expressed support for the colonies in their rebellion; John Galt, *Pictures, Historical and Biographical: Drawn from English, Scottish, and Irish History*, 2 vols. (London: Phillips, 1824), 2: 254 (the word father is not in Galt's text but it does characterize the relationship of sovereign to subject).

8 A Delaware chieftain accepted a gift of red pigment for use as face paint, ca. 1720s, and excavations at the Indian settlement at Conestoga found the majority of goods to be European or colonial manufactures, including paint pigments. See, respectively, C. A. Weslager, *The Delaware Indians: A History* (Brunswick, N.J.: Rutgers University Press, 1972), 198, and Barry Kent, *Susquehanna's Indians*, Anthropological Series No. 6 (Harrisburg: Pennsylvania Historical and Museum Commission, 1993), 389.

9 Galt, *West* (1816), 18.

10 Ibid., 70. John Trumbull, by contrast, dismissed the idea of natural genius both generally and in regard to himself. Countering the grandiosity of West's story, he characterized his artistic beginnings in terms of "mere imitation," exercised in copying paintings by his older sister Faith, who had learned drawing at school; *Autobiography of Colonel John Trumbull, Patriot-Artist, 1756–1843*, ed. Theodore Sizer (1841; New Haven: Yale University Press, 1953), 5.

11 John Galt, *Letters from the Levant; Containing Views of the State of Society, Manners, Opinions, and Commerce, in Greece, and Several of the Principal Islands of the Archipelago* (London: T. Cadell and W. Davies, 1813), 181, 218.

12 Ann Uhry Abrams unraveled some of the more improbable yarns in Galt, while considering their importance to the narrative of West's career, in *The Valiant Hero: Benjamin West and Grand-Style History Painting* (Washington, D.C.: Smithsonian Institution Press, 1995), ch. 2: "John Galt and the Legendary Origins of Benjamin West," 31–43. See also Robert C. Alberts, *Benjamin West: A Biography* (Boston: Houghton Mifflin, 1978), app. I: "John Galt's Biography of West as a Source," 409–12. Alberts suggested that Galt bore primary responsibility for inflating West's story, whereas Abrams assigned West a more active role in the mythmaking.

13 Galt, *West* (1816), 6–24, 49–56 (quote at 16).

14 Ernst Kris and Otto Kurz, *Legend, Myth, and Magic in the Image of the Artist: A Historical Experiment* (1934), rev. ed., trans. Alastair Laing and Lottie M. Newman (New Haven and London: Yale University Press, 1979), 33.

15 *London Chronicle*, May 18–20, 1773.

16 See Kaylin H. Weber, "A Temple of History Painting: West's Newman Street Studio and Art Collection," in Emily Ballew Neff with Kaylin H. Weber, *American Adversaries: West and Copley in a Transatlantic World* (Houston: Museum of Fine Arts, Houston, 2013), 14–49.

17 *London Courant*, May 10, 1788, quoted in Martin Postle, *Sir Joshua Reynolds: The Subject Pictures* (New York: Cambridge University Press, 1995), 56–7.

18 Peter Pindar [John Wolcot], *The Works of Peter Pindar, Esq.*, 4 vols., new ed. (London: Printed for J. Walker, 1816), 2: 297–98. For a concise biography, see William R. Jones, "Wolcot, John (bap. 1738, d. 1819)," in *Oxford Dictionary of National Biography* online. In his mid-twentieth-century survey text, Ellis Waterhouse concurred: West "was lucky in that the very mediocrity of his mind found a kindred spirit in the mind of George III"; *Painting in Britain, 1530–1790* (1953), Pelican History of Art (Harmondsworth: Penguin Books, 1978), 276. Politics, which neither the king nor West let stand between them, did contribute to George III's dislike of Reynolds, who openly allied with the king's political opponents, including the Prince of Wales; see Martin Postle, in Postle et al., *Joshua Reynolds: The Creation of Celebrity* (London: Tate Publishing, 2005), 22–23.

19 In 1783, Pindar (*Works*, 1: 40–42) offered a mock apology for previous insults to West, "our Yankey painter," whose thirst for praise could barely be quenched: "Don't be cast down – instead of gall/ Molasses from my pen shall fall:/And yet, I fear thy gullet it is such,/ That could I pour Niagara down,/Were Niagara praise, thou wouldst not frown./Nor think the thund'ring gulf one drop too much."

20 E.g., Joseph Farington, *The Diary of Joseph Farington*, ed. Kenneth Garlick, Angus Macintyre, and Kathryn Cave, 16 vols. (New Haven and London: Yale University Press, 1978–84), 4: 1127 (Jan. 4, 1799); 8: 3143–54, 3157 (Dec. 1 and 4, 1807); and 9: 3143 (Mar. 2, 1809). Farington's hundreds of entries concerning West, ranging from 1793 to 1820, are the richest primary source for West's later career. Historians have been somewhat reluctant to rehearse or fully interrogate the struggles of West's later career, but Alberts provided a comprehensive and detailed overview, beginning with chapter 16 ("Fall from Favor") through the end of the book (*West*, 210–402).

21 According to Galt, *West* (1820), West believed he had "already earned by his pencil more eminence than could be conferred on him by that rank" of knighthood (189–90).

22 Rev. Robert Anthony Bromley first levied his charge against Copley in correspondence of Sept. 10, 1794, but he published the same in the *Morning Herald* and in the preface to the second volume of his book, *A Philosophical and Critical History of the Fine Arts, Painting, Sculpture, and Architecture*, 2 vols. (London, 1793–95), 2: xxvii–xlii, at xxxv. According to Farington, Copley "says West is at the bottom, and that the allusion . . . to the picture of the Squirrel cd. only originate with West"; *Farington Diary*, 1: 235 (Sept. 18, 1794).

23 The rivalry between the two men was the subject of an exhibition and catalogue by Neff with Weber, *American Adversaries*.

24 "Benjamin West, Esq.," *European Magazine and London Review* 26 (Sept. 1794): 163. Each issue opened with a biographical profile of a noted individual and an engraved portrait on the facing page; artists figured regularly as subjects.

25 West to Hutchinson, June 18, 1771, and West to Copley, Aug. 4, 1766, *Copley-Pelham Letters*, 118–19, 43–45. West reiterated the point in subsequent letters to Copley (ibid., 58, 72).

26 *The Beauties of the Royal Palaces, or A Pocket Companion to Windsor, Kensington, Kew, and Hampton Court . . . to Which Are Added Short Sketches of the Lives of the Most Eminent Painters, Whose Works are Exhibited in the Royal Palaces* (Windsor, [1794]).

27 "Biographical Sketch of Benjamin West, Esq. President of the Royal Academy," *Universal Magazine*, n.s., 3 (May 1805): 388–96, 525–32; "Benjamin West, Esq. President of the Royal Academy," *Public Characters of 1805* (1805): 523–69, at 525; and "Benjamin West, Esq., President of the Royal Academy," *La Belle Assemblée* 4 (Jan. 1808), 5–10, 52–55, 109–11, 149–51, 197–98.

28 West's Apollo story first appeared in print with a next-day report on West's discourse: "Royal Academy," *True Briton*, no. 610 (Dec.

11, 1794). Others put it to their own uses, including Anthony Pasquin [John Williams] in his stinging *Memoirs of the Royal Academicians*, ed. R.W. Lightbown (1796; repr., London: Cornmarket Press, 1970), 74–75; and Richard Payne Knight, to whom West related the story at some point earlier, since it appeared in Knight, *The Landscape: A Didactic Poem in Three Books* (London, 1794), 3, n. to line 53.

29 Galt specified the "Delawarre" lineage (*West* [1816], 2; *West* [1820], 72–73), unlike prior sources (*Public Characters*, *Belle Assemblée*) that point to, but do not name, the supposed ancestor, whose family name was West. Abrams (*Valiant Hero*, 32–35) identified "concealed" indications in West's art for his identification with "Delawarre" but no support for that genealogy.

30 *Public Characters*, 531–32; succeeding quotations in this paragraph, 534, 537–38, 539, 559. For period arguments and efforts supporting the relationship of art and commerce in late eighteenth-century Britain and for the ensuing politics of anti-commercialism, see Morris Eaves, *The Counter-Arts Conspiracy: Art and Industry in the Age of Blake* (Ithaca, N.Y., and London: Cornell University Press, 1992), which borrows its title phrase from William Blake (the focus of Eaves's study), in reference to the commercial and political interests that he considered so detrimental to creative artists.

31 West had not forgotten the work, however; *Savage Warrior Taking Leave of his Family* appeared among West's "finished paintings" in the celebratory American context of Joel Barlow's *The Columbiad: A Poem* (London, 1809), 399. John Dillenberger correlated the lists of West's work that were published during the artist's lifetime in *Benjamin West: The Context of his Life's Work with Particular Attention to Paintings with Religious Subject Matter* (San Antonio, Tx.: Trinity University Press, 1977), 129–90.

32 *Farington Diary*, 7: 2492 (Jan. 5, 1805). Linda Colley noted the emergence of "England" as a synonym for "Britain" (and of "English" for "British") by the start of the nineteenth century, though she added that the Welsh, Scots, and Irish tended to think of themselves as dual nationals because it benefited them to do so; *Britons: Forging the Nation 1707–1837* (New Haven and London: Yale University Press, 1992), 162–64. In the wake of the American War of Independence, such a perception would not extend to an American, at least not from the British, or English, perspective.

33 *Universal Magazine*, 389–90.

34 See, e.g., Holger Hoock's chapter "French Revolutions in the Royal Academy?" in *The King's Artists: The Royal Academy of Arts and the Politics of British Culture, 1760–1840* (Oxford: Clarendon Press; New York, Oxford University Press, 2003), 180–202 (esp. 192). Hoock overstated West's agency in observing that the artist "coordinated a minor intelligence system among Americans arriving in London" during the time of the American Revolution (ibid., 152).

35 *Farington Diary*, 8: 2908 (Nov. 16, 1806).

36 See, e.g., Emily Ballew Neff et al., *John Singleton Copley in England* (Houston: Museum of Fine Arts, Houston, 1995), 64–74 ("The Problem of Money").

37 Pasquin, *Memoirs of the Royal Academicians*, 138, 53.

38 Payment to artists in guineas was standard, even in the provinces; see, e.g., Trevor Fawcett, *The Rise of English Provincial Art: Artists, Patrons, and Institutions Outside London* (Oxford: Clarendon Press, 1974), 21–24.

39 Pasquin, *Morning Herald*, as quoted in William T. Whitley, *Art in England, 1800–1820* (New York: Macmillan; Cambridge University Press, 1928), 168–69.

40 West's *Reception of the American Loyalists* is known only from the representation in his portrait of Wilmot and an outline engraving of 1815, published as the frontispiece to Wilmot's *Historical View of the Commission for Enquiring into the Losses, Services, and Claims of the American Loyalists* (London, 1815). Helmut von Erffa and Allen Staley speculated that it may never have existed as an independent painting; *The Paintings of Benjamin West* (New Haven and London: Yale University Press, 1986), 219–20, cat. 106.

41 Samuel F. B. Morse, letter to his parents, Dec. 22, 1814 and to his father, Mar. 12, 1812, in *Samuel F. B. Morse: His Letters and Journals*, ed. Edward Lind Morse, 2 vols. (1914; repr., New York: Da Capo Press for Kennedy Galleries, Inc., 1973), 163, 68–69.

42 The biography and engraving first appeared in April 1813 as no. 14 in *The British Gallery of Contemporary Portraits*, later collected as *The British Gallery of Contemporary Portraits, Being a Series of Engravings of the Most Eminent Persons Now Living or Lately Deceased, in Great Britain and Ireland: From Drawings Accurately Made from Life or from the Most Approved Original Pictures, Accompanied by Short Biographical Notices*, 2 vols. (London: T. Cadell and W. Davies, 1822), vol. 2, s.v. "Benjamin West, R.A."

43 West to Joseph Farington, Feb. 3, 1813, Benjamin West Selected Papers, Historical Society of Pennsylvania, Philadelphia. Farington's receipt of same, *Farington Diary*, 12: 4293 (Feb. 3, 1813).

44 *Farington Diary*, 12: 4374 (June 17, 1813). Farington's meeting with Cadell is in 12: 4298 (Feb. 13, 1813).

45 Ibid., 9: 3230 (Feb. 27, 1808). The admission was more oblique in the case of the profile for *Public Characters*, which West said was written by "one of His . . . Sons, & another person"; ibid., 6: 2443 (Nov. 17, 1804).

46 West, "Original Manuscript Autobiography," Charles Allen Munn Collection, Fordham University Library, New York.

47 See, e.g., criticism of West's deficiencies as a writer and his lack of intellect in a review of his first discourse, which Cadell had published in 1793: "Art. XVII: A Discourse delivered to the Students of the Royal Academy . . . Dec. 10, 1792, by the President," *Monthly Review; or, Literary Journal, Enlarged* 13 (Jan.–Apr. 1794), 53–55. Galt excerpted West's discourses in the 1820 volume of the biography. West's utter failure to gain consideration as leader of the English school (which I am not trying to amend) is evident in the absence of his name from scholarly considerations of the matter. I have nevertheless benefited from such accounts, especially Martin Postle's evaluation of the case for Reynolds: "In Search of the 'True Briton': Reynolds, Hogarth, and the British School," in *Towards a Modern Art World*, ed. Brian Allen (New Haven and London: Yale University Press for the Paul Mellon Centre for Studies in British Art and Yale Center for British Art, 1995), 121–43; and Postle, *Sir Joshua Reynolds*, 273–311. A different perspective on the question of the English school, focused on its relationship to commerce – and then not surprisingly including West – is offered by Eaves, *Counter-Arts Conspiracy*. William Vaughan tracked the increasingly exclusive definition of "Englishness" by the mid-nineteenth century, as measured against other traditions in the British Isles and the British empire. Early in the century, he found, the terms English and British were used more or less interchangeably; "The Englishness of British Art," *Oxford Art Journal* 13: 2 (1989): 11–23.

48 Edmond Malone, *The Works of Sir Joshua Reynolds . . . containing his Discourses, Idlers, A Journey to Flanders and Holland, (now first published,) and his commentary on Du Fresnoy's Art of Painting; printed from his revised copies, (with his last corrections and additions,) . . . To which is prefixed an account of the life and writings of the author*, 2 vols. (London: T. Cadell and W. Davies, 1797).

49 [Samuel Felton], *Testimonies to the Genius and Memory of Sir Joshua Reynolds* (London, 1792). The title page identifies Felton only as "the author of imperfect hints towards a new edition of Shakespeare." Regarding early efforts to write Reynolds's biography, some never executed, see Richard Wendorf, *After Sir Joshua: Essays on British Art and Cultural History* (New Haven and London: Yale University Press, 2005), 1–11.

50 [John Gould], *A Dictionary of Painters, Sculptors, Architects, and Engravers* (London, 1810), xxvii; although in this instance, Gould went on to connect Reynolds's role as "founder" to the Academy, he repeats the characterization without qualification two pages later. Gould drew on various sources for this dictionary; his introductory characterization of Reynolds, West, and the English school closely paraphrases James Dallaway, *Anecdotes of the Arts in England, or Comparative Observations on Architecture, Sculpture, & Painting* (London, 1800), 521–26.

51 From Turner's lecture as professor of perspective at the Royal Academy in 1811; quoted in Postle, *Sir Joshua Reynolds*, 291. William Hazlitt offered strong dissent from the admiration for Reynolds's art, theory, or character in six essays for the liberal newspaper *The Champion* that were published between Oct. 1814 and Jan. 1815.

52 The inscriptions on the British Institution medal read on the obverse: BENJAMIN WEST PRESIDENT OF THE ROYAL ACADEMY MDCCCXV; and on the reverse: UNDER THE REGENCY [within wreath surrounded by forty names in five circles] RESPECTFULLY TO PERPETUATE THE NAMES OF THOSE WHO IN MDCCCXI SUBSCRIBED TO PURCHASE THE PICTURE OF CHRIST IN THE TEMPLE FOR THE GALLERY OF THE BRITISH INSTITUTE. In a work satirizing submissions to British Institution exhibitions for 1815 and 1816, the author, relentlessly critical of West, questioned the artist's decision to have the medal struck, asking "To what order of moral action must this be referred?"; [Robert Smirke, attrib.], *A Catalogue Raisonné of the Pictures Now Exhibiting in Pall Mall*, 2 vols. ([London], 1816), 2: 31.

53 For a concise overview, see Peter Fullerton, "Patronage and Pedagogy: The British Institution in the Early Nineteenth Century," *Art History* 5 (March 1982): 59–70; Ann Pullan offered a Marxist reading in "Public Goods or Private Interests? The British Institution in the Early Nineteenth Century," in *Art in Bourgeois Society, 1790–1850*, ed. Andrew Hemingway and William Vaughan (Cambridge: Cambridge University Press, 1998), 27–44.

54 A broader, more eccentric range of deceased British artists received showings organized by a short-lived society calling itself "The British School" (1802–4). See John Gage, "*The British School* and the British School," in *Towards a Modern Art World*, 109–20.

55 In a brief introduction to the catalogue, noted connoisseur (and British Institution founding member) R. P. Knight praised his subject in terms evidently designed to rebuke someone else: Reynolds made "*gradual* progress to excellence, not by any premature pretensions to a capacity for it"; he "was not one of those aspiring geniuses, those self-selected favourites of nature, who imagine that professional eminence is a spontaneous gift of heaven, or an indefeasible inheritance of right, and will not therefore degrade the native dignity of their talents by undertaking any but important subjects, upon a large scale and at a high price"; [Richard Payne Knight], "Preface to the Exhibition in the Year 1813," in *An Account of all the Pictures Exhibited in the Rooms of the British Institution from 1813 to 1823 . . .* , by the British Institution for Promoting the Fine Arts in the United Kingdom (London, 1824), 5. Knight's primary target seems to have been Benjamin Robert Haydon, but he was not an admirer of West, to whom those remarks might equally have applied. Knight and West, at this moment, were the most prominent opponent and proponent of British acquisition of the Parthenon marbles, offered for sale by Lord Elgin. West, characteristically, had used his admiration for the sculptures to enhance his own image, in a letter that appalled West's friends, but which Elgin printed in a pamphlet designed to stir up support for the purchase. Alberts summarized West's involvement with the marbles, in *West*, 349–52.

56 [Benjamin West], *Christ Rejected: Catalogue of the Picture Representing the Above Subject; Together with Sketches of other Scriptural Subjects; Painted by Benjamin West, Esq. . . .* (London, 1814), 15.

57 Sir Thomas Bernard and R. P. Knight objected to inclusion of the Swiss-born Zoffany on grounds of nationality; *Farington Diary*, 13: 4495–96 (Apr. 23, 1814).

58 On the revival of Hogarth's reputation, see David Bindman, *Hogarth and his Times: Serious Comedy* (Berkeley: University of California Press, 1997), 11–28. For the opposition of the "naturalist tradition" associated with Hogarth, Wilson, and Gainsborough to "the historical painting of Reynolds and his followers," see also Vaughan, "The Englishness of British Art," 14.

59 *Farington Diary*, 6: 2339 (May 31, 1804).

60 In his 1810 letter, West attested that "the voluminous manuscript under the signature of Penrose which I saw in your possession . . . appears to me on the investigation of it to have been written by a Wm Williams of Philadelphia & founded on his adventures amongst the uncivilized aborigines in the West India Islands"; West to Thomas Eagles, Oct. 10, 1810, as transcribed by T. Eagles, Williams MSS. "Mr. Annesley of Reading," so-named by West, transmitted West's 1810 letter with a letter of his own, the source for his first name; entry of that correspondence into the public domain in 2006 (National Maritime Museum, Greenwich) allowed his identity to be pinpointed.

61 West, 1810 letter. I have not identified this poem. Perhaps West was remembering a poem from *American Magazine and Monthly Chronicle* 1 (Sept. 1758) by Francis Hopkinson, which concluded with lines praising West: "Nor let the muse forget thy name O West;/Lov'd youth, with virtue as by nature blest!/If such the radiance of thy *early Morn*,/ What bright effulgence must thy *Noon* adorn?/Hail sacred Genius!"

62 Eagles, 1805 memo.

63 Galt, *West* (1816), 27–28.

64 Ibid., 45–49.

65 Benjamin Martin, *A New and Compendious System of Optics* (London, 1740), 161–62, 166.

66 Francesco Algarotti, *An Essay on Painting* (London, 1764), 60–66 (quotations in this paragraph: 82, 60, 62–63).

67 As quoted in Arthur K. Wheelock, Jr., *Vermeer and the Art of Painting* (New Haven and London: Yale University Press, 1995), 26.

68 Sir Joshua Reynolds, *Discourses on Art*, ed. Robert R. Wark (New Haven and London: Yale University Press for the Paul Mellon Centre for Studies in British Art, 1975), 237 (Discourse XIII, 1786). The statement that "Dutch Pictures are a representation of nature, just as it is seen in a Camera Obscura" appears in a letter from Reynolds to Edmund Burke, Aug. 14, 1781, quoted in John Ingamells and John Edgcumbe, eds., *The Letters of Sir Joshua Reynolds* (New Haven and London: Yale University Press for the Paul Mellon Centre for Studies in British Art, 2000), 100.

69 Horace Walpole to Rev William Mason, Sept. 21, 1777, in *The Yale Edition of Horace Walpole's Correspondence*, ed. W. S. Lewis et al., 48 vols. (New Haven: Yale University Press, 1937–83), 28: 328–31. Reynolds's cameras are in the collections of the Science Museum, London, and Harvard University, Cambridge, Mass. For analysis of later-eight-

eenth-century drawings by West that support his use of a camera, see Jenny Carson and Ann Shafer, "West, Copley, and the Camera Obscura," *American Art* 22 (Summer 2008): 31–34.

70 John Romney, *Memoirs of the Life and Works of George Romney* (London, 1830), 8–9. Romney's image as a natural genius arose much earlier but the author of his obituary in 1803 was sarcastic on the matter: the idea that "the obscure, untutored child of nature, who had never seen or heard any thing that could elicit his genius, or urge him to emulation, should at once become a painter without a prototype, seems, in the instance of Mr. Romney, a creation of his own"; Richard Cumberland, "Memoirs of Mr. George Romney," *European Magazine, and London Review* 43 (June 1803): 417.

71 This is only one aspect of the complex argument made by Ann Bermingham in "The Origin of Painting and the Ends of Art: Wright of Derby's *Corinthian Maid*," in *Painting and the Politics of Culture: New Essays on British Art, 1700–1850*, ed. John Barrell (Oxford and New York: Oxford University Press, 1992) 135–65. Bermingham reminds the reader that, although eighteenth-century images of the Corinthian maid routinely invoke the origin of painting or drawing, Pliny's story emphasizes the origin of modeling, as her father, the potter Dibutades, fills in the outline drawing with clay.

72 Eagles recalled that West stated, "He [Williams] first lent me the lives of the painters which confirm'd my inclination for the art"; Thomas Eagles, memorandum of a conversation with Benjamin West, July 10, 1805, Williams MSS. John Eagles embellished this remark considerably when quoting the document in "The Beggar's Legacy," *Blackwood's Edinburgh Magazine* 77 (Mar. 1855): 251–72, reprinted in John Eagles, *Essays Contributed to Blackwood's Magazine* (Edinburgh, 1857), 457–502 (quote at 488): "He first lent me *The Lives of the Painters*, which lighted up a fire in my breast which has never been extinguished, and confirmed my inclination for the art."

73 Galt, *West* (1816), 28.

74 Nicholas B. Wainwright, ed., "Notes and Documents: Conversations with Benjamin West," *Pennsylvania Magazine of History and Biography* 102 (Jan. 1978): 112. Galt was a practiced translator of Italian and, if he wanted to read Vasari, need not have depended on the eleven lives that Aglionby chose to include in his 1685 *Painting Illustrated in Three Diallogues*, reissued in 1719 as *Choice Observations upon the Art of Painting* (London, 1719).

75 James Northcote, *Memoirs of Sir Joshua Reynolds* (London, 1813), 10–11.

76 On the form of Richardson's writing, see Carol Gibson-Wood, *Jonathan Richardson: Art Theorist of the English Enlightenment* (New Haven and London: Yale University Press for the Paul Mellon Centre for Studies in British Art, 2000), 138–42.

77 [Jonathan Richardson, Jr., ed.], *Works of Mr. Jonathan Richardson* (London, 1773); the same text reappears in the 1792 edition, which bears an engraved profile portrait of Reynolds as its frontispiece; Northcote quoted this "very handsome compliment" in *Memoirs of Sir Joshua Reynolds* (London, 1813), 199.

78 Galt, *West* (1816), 29–31.

79 Jonathan Richardson, *An Essay on the Theory of Painting* (London, 1715), 19, 24.

80 John Eagles (whose father, Thomas, had died in 1812) composed the preface to *Penrose*. That text and the portions of Eagles's story "The Beggar's Legacy" pertaining to Williams are reprinted in James Thomas Flexner, "Benjamin West's American Neo-Classicism, with Documents on West and William Williams," *New-York Historical Society Quarterly* 36 (Jan. 1952): 34–41.

81 John Galt, *The Autobiography of John Galt*, 2 vols. (London: Cochrane and M'Crone, 1833), 2: 235–36.

82 In addition to his two-volume autobiography (1833), Galt wrote *The Literary Life and Miscellanies of John Galt*, 3 vols. (Edinburgh: William Blackwood; London: T. Cadell, 1834); vol. 1 offers an account of his life as a writer, while vols. 2 and 3 contain assorted, previously unpublished writings.

83 Galt's *Lawrie Todd, or The Settlers in the Woods*, 3 vols. (London: H. Colburn and R. Bentley, 1830) is the fictional "American" autobiography, which led to publication of its real prototype: Grant Thorburn, *Forty Years' Residence in America, or, The Doctrine of a Particular Providence Exemplified in the Life of Grant Thorburn, the Original Lawrie Todd, Seedsman*, introduction by John Galt, 2nd ed. (London: J. Fraser, 1834).

84 Abrams, *Valiant Hero*, 31. "A journeyman writer-for-hire" was Alberts's characterization, even though he concluded that Galt "fastened on a number of true but relatively minor incidents told him by West and used his creative imagination to develop them into major episodes" (*West*, 409, 410); Alberts did not consider Galt's incentive to do so.

85 Isaac D'Israeli, *A Dissertation on Anecdotes* (1793; New York: Garland, 1972), 32.

86 Coleridge's marginalia in his copy of Galt's *The Provost, or, Memoirs of his Own Times* (1822), in *The Collected Works of Samuel Taylor Coleridge: Marginalia*, vol. 12, pt. 2, ed. George Whalley (London: Routledge and Kegan Paul; Princeton: Princeton University Press, 1984), 840–41.

87 Galt has been the subject of three collections of essays: Christopher A. Whatley, ed., *John Galt, 1779–1979* (Edinburgh: Ramsay Head Press, 1979); Elizabeth Waterston, ed., *John Galt: Reappraisals* (Guelph, Ontario: University of Guelph, 1985); and Regina Hewitt, ed., *John Galt: Observations and Conjectures on Literary, History, and Society* (Lewisburg, Pa.: Bucknell University Press, 2012). The most recent volume, manifestly interdisciplinary, proposed to correct prior studies by examining Galt's work from the perspectives of literature, history, and social theory and various frames of reference within them.

88 "Galt wrote too much. The volume of what he had to write has always masked the importance and even the existence of the work he really wanted to write"; Ian A. Gordon, *John Galt: The Life of a Writer* (Toronto and Buffalo: University of Toronto Press, 1972), 142, 8.

89 "The term, KEEPING, in the Art of Painting, in general, is used to signify a just and proper subordination of all the parts of a Picture to the principal Object; in respect of Magnitude, Colour, and distinctness of Parts" and is "in great measure, synonymous with Aerial Perspective"; Thomas Malton, *A Complete Treatise on Perspective, in Theory and Practice; on the True Principles of Dr. Brook Taylor* (London, 1778), 295.

90 John Galt, *Voyages and Travels in the Years 1809, 1810, and 1811; Containing Statistical, Commercial, and Miscellaneous Observations on Gibraltar, Sardinia, Sicily, Malta, Serigo, and Turkey* (London: T. Cadell and W. Davies, 1812), 49–50, 60–61. Galt's "Erranti," the Sicilian painter, was Giuseppe Errante (1760–1821). The writer's visit to Albania gave him (as it did Byron) particularly rich material for imagining the evolution of societies, not least, by comparison, that of his native Scotland; see Massimiliano Demata, "From Caledonia to Albania: Byron, Galt, and the Progress of the Eastern Savage," *Scottish Studies Review* 2 (Autumn 2001): 61–76.

91 John Galt, "On the Fine Arts . . . ," *Philosophical Magazine* 42 (August 1813): 81–91. The word "decenere," now obsolete, comes from the Latin root *decerno*, to decide.

92 Galt, *Letters from the Levant*, 224–25.

93 West's encouragement must have meant a great deal to Galt, for he reissued the Sicilian "Discourse" yet again in 1814, now characterizing it as so "interwoven with his own ideas" as to be "in some degree an original essay"; "On the Principles of the Fine Arts," pts. 1, 2, *New Monthly Magazine* 1 (Feb. 1814): 23–26; 1 (Apr. 1814): 244–46.

94 John Galt, *The Tragedies of Maddelen, Agamemnon, Lady Macbeth, Antonia, and Clytemnestra* (London, 1812), reviewed in *Monthly Review* 73 (Mar. 1814): 264–71; John Galt, *Life and Administration of Cardinal Wolsey* (London: T. Cadell and W. Davies, 1812).

95 Galt, *Literary Life*, 1: 77. Galt paid printing costs for each of his books prior to *Life of West*, but he could not afford to do so in 1816, having by then a family to support; he sold the copyright on that volume to Cadell.

96 "Intelligence in Literature and the Arts and Sciences," *New Monthly Magazine* 1 (Apr. 1814): 262. Galt was an early and regular contributor to this newly launched magazine, which published his third, 1814 reworking of the Sicilian discourse, along with "Instructions in the Art of Rising in the World – A Satire," in the Feb. 1 (pp. 18–19) and Mar. 1 (pp. 127–29) issues, where that piece is ascribed to G. Haliton, Esq. Gordon (*John Galt*, 18) made the attribution to Galt.

97 On the vulgarity of Northcote's *Memoirs of Reynolds*, see *Farington Diary*, 12: 4414 (Aug. 20, 1813). West had read only extracts from the book in *Morning Chronicle* (Aug. 24, 1813), but said he "did not wish to see any more of it"; *Farington Diary*, 12: 4416 (Aug. 30, 1813). Review of *Memoirs of Sir Joshua Reynolds*, by James Northcote, *Critical Review*, 4th ser., 4 (Oct. 1813): 354, 369 ("irksomeness and insipidity" of the reader's task, 369); and *British Critic*, 2nd ser., 1 (Feb. 1814): 150.

98 *British Critic*, 2nd ser., 1 (Feb. 1814), 149–50, 157. Another critic of Northcote's book (in a long essay more tribute to Reynolds than review) thought the opportunity to represent an exemplary life – from which readers might learn – had been frittered away by an author more interested in the "circumstantial narratives of occurrences which happen to every man in society"; *Edinburgh Review* 45 (Sept. 1814): 262–92, at 263, 269. Benjamin Robert Haydon identified the writer as R. P. Knight; *Farington Diary*, 13: 4596 (Oct. 20, 1814). See also Northcote, *Life of Sir Joshua Reynolds*, intro. Lightbown.

99 West to J. S. Copley (who was not much better at spelling), June 20, 1767, *Copley–Pelham Letters*, 56.

100 "Fresnoy," *Middlesex Journal*, July 29, 1769.

101 Elizabeth West, in *Farington Diary*, 6: 2480 (Dec. 26, 1804); and Leigh Hunt, "Benjamin West," *Harper's New Monthly Magazine* 1 (July 1850): 194. Had West been a Quaker, as some (including Hunt) believed, his relative illiteracy would have constituted an anomaly given Quaker emphasis on education and writing. See James Walvin, *The Quakers: Money and Morals* (London: John Murray, 1997), 45–48, 91–104.

102 Hunt, "Benjamin West"; Beaumont's opinion noted in *Farington Diary*, 8: 3156 (Dec. 4, 1807). For other reports of West's mispronunciations: *Farington Diary*, 8: 3160 (Dec. 10, 1807); 12: 4364 (June 5, 1813); 13: 4492 (Apr. 18, 1814). Haydon, who had little respect for West, represented him as barely coherent in a devastating parody, "Dreams of a Somniator," in *Annals of the Fine Arts* 3 (1819): 7.

103 Nick Whistler, "Galt's Life and the *Autobiography*," in Waterston, ed., *Galt*, 48. Galt's sensitivity to language is nowhere more evident than in his Scottish novels, in which even individual characters engage in complex "dialect-switching" according to particular social and psychological situations; see J. Derrick McClure, "Scots and English in *Annals of the Parish* and *The Provost*," in Whatley, ed., *Galt*, 195–210.

104 "From the London Observer, March 19. Mr. West" (obituary), *Connecticut Journal*, May 23, 1820.

105 Galt, *Literary Life*, 2: 219. *Annals of the Parish* (Edinburgh: W. Blackwood, 1821) "is so void of any thing like a plot, that it lacks in the most material feature of the novel" (ibid., 1: 155).

106 Galt to David Wilkie, May 12, 1807, National Library of Scotland, Edinburgh, MS 9835, fols. 15–16, quoted in Gordon, *John Galt*, 10–11. According to a catalogue entry by H. A. D. Miles, Galt sent Wilkie "copies from drafts of two . . . verse descriptions of Scottish peasant life," one of which was published in 1833 as "The Penny Wedding," dedicated to Wilkie, who made a painting of the same title in 1818; Miles, in *Sir David Wilkie of Scotland*, ed. William J. Chiego et al. (Raleigh: North Carolina Museum of Art, 1987), 171. Galt's subjects, however, were usually drawn from the middle class. On the "ecstatic reception" of Wilkie's art in London, see David H. Solkin, "Crowds and Connoisseurs: Looking at Genre Painting at Somerset House," in *Art on the Line: The Royal Academy Exhibitions at Somerset House, 1780–1836*, ed. David H. Solkin (New Haven and London: Yale University Press for the Paul Mellon Centre for Studies in British Art and the Courtauld Institute Gallery, 2001), 157–71.

107 Galt's "impotent jokes upon academical education, and malicious sneers leveled against the clergy, for no other reason, as it should appear, than that they have been regularly educated," provoked a reviewer of *Letters from the Levant*. He facetiously proposed Galt's Scottishness as a way to "account for and excuse expressions which . . . in an Englishman who might be expected to have some acquaintance with the Universities, and not to be wholly without some tincture of academical learning, would have merited the severity of our censure"; *British Critic* 1 (Jan. 1814): 66–79. Nicholas Tromans has argued that there was little identifiably Scottish in early nineteenth-century painting, including Wilkie's, though the artist "conformed well enough . . . to London stereotypes about Scots in general for these to be trotted out with regularity"; *David Wilkie: Painter of Everyday Life* (London: Dulwich Picture Gallery, 2002), 22. One of those conceptions was that Scots were literal minded; Galt's best fictional works, however, are strongly ironical. On the shifting relationship over the eighteenth century between the Scottish and English, united as Britons since 1707, see Colley, *Britons*, 101–32.

108 Galt (*Autobiography*, 2: 227) indicated that the minister's tale, published as *Annals of the Parish* in 1821, was "nearly finished" when he approached Constable in 1813, but that state of completion is supposed to have been contradicted by his now-lost letter to Blackwood (the eventual publisher), which referred only to a proposal for a book. See Erik Frykman, *John Galt's Scottish Stories, 1820–1823* (Uppsala: Lundequistska, 1959), 31–32.

109 Galt, *Autobiography*, 2: 227–28.

110 Galt, *The Majolo: A Tale*, 2 vols. (London: H. Colburn, 1816).

111 Vol. 6 of *Blackwood's Edinburgh Magazine* included some half-dozen articles attributed to Galt (by Gordon, *John Galt*, 28), of which four addressed art topics: "The Scotchman in London" (Oct. 1819): 64–66 (a satirical tour of three sculptors' studios); and three articles headed "Transactions of the Dilettanti Society of Edinburgh" (Oct. 1819): 89–97, (Dec. 1819): 276–79, (March 1820): 660–63, on Greek to Renaissance sculpture, sixteenth-century Italian painting, and English architecture, respectively.

112 Martha Bohrer, "John Galt's *Annals of the Parish* and the Narrative Strategies of Tales of Locale," in Hewitt, *John Galt: Observations and Conjectures*, 98.

113 John Galt, *The Ayrshire Legatees, or The Pringle Family* (Edinburgh: William Blackwood; London: T. Cadell, 1821). Galt's name did

not appear on the title pages of his fictional works, which, following the success of his first-issued Scottish novel, gave credit to "the author of *Annals of the Parish*" and other works. As a businessman and parliamentary lobbyist, Galt did not want his name associated with fiction writing or his person identified with the narrators in his books; he was also following the custom of the most famous Scottish writer, Scott.

114 Wainwright, "Conversations with Benjamin West," 109.

115 Rembrandt Peale made clear his dislike of Galt, though in a way calculated to bring credit on himself. Galt "affected" to patronize an unnamed poet, finding him "a desk job that wore him down," but Peale persuaded the poet to leave "and thus had the satisfaction of having saved his life"; Peale, "Reminiscences: Exhibitions and Academies," *The Crayon* 1 (May 9, 1855): 290.

116 Galt, *Autobiography*, 2: 235–36. The often contentious relationship between the two painters was a focus of Neff with Weber, *American Adversaries*.

117 Eric Richards provided a solid overview of the importance of America for Scotland in "Scotland and the Uses of the Atlantic Empire," in *Strangers within the Realm: Cultural Margins of the First British Empire*, ed. Bernard Bailyn and Philip D. Morgan (Chapel Hill and London: University of North Carolina Press for the Institute of Early American History and Culture, Williamsburg, Va., 1991), 67–114.

118 J. B. Galt, "A Statistical Account of Upper Canada," *Philosophical Magazine* 29 (Oct. 1807): 7.

119 Galt later contributed to the British edition of another Pennsylvanian's life story, Alexander Graydon's *Memoirs of a Life Chiefly Passed in Pennsylvania within the Last Sixty Years* (Edinburgh: William Blackwood; London: T. Cadell, 1822) – roughly the same decades of social change that Galt traced in *Annals of the Parish*. He wrote the dedicatory preface (to the United States' ambassador to Great Britain, Richard Rush) and generally receives editorial credit from scholars, even though the verso of the title page identified the British edition as a reprint of the 1811 American publication. But perhaps Galt first brought the book to the attention of his publishers. Galt's conception of Providence had been shaped by Scottish Realist philosophers and historians, who believed that "it is in the everyday world, among the common activities of ordinary people that the 'laws' of historical development are to be found at work"; Keith M. Costain, "Theoretical History and the Novel: The Scottish Fiction of John Galt," *ELH* 43 (Autumn 1976): 347. See also Costain, "The Community of Man: Galt and Eighteenth-Century Scottish Realism," *Scottish Literary Journal* 8 (May 1981): 10–29. Galt borrowed the Realist term "theoretical history" to characterize certain of his fictional works, beginning with *Annals of the Parish*, of which he wrote: "To myself it has ever been a kind of treatise on the history of society in the West of Scotland during the reign of King George the Third"; Galt, *Literary Life*, 1: 155. Regina Hewitt, introducing a volume of nuanced essays, proposed a more complicated Galt, who "did not fully embrace the progress plot of conjectural history"; *John Galt: Observations and Conjectures*, 8.

120 Hoppner in *Quarterly Review* 2 (Nov. 1809): 433. Galt must have been aware of Hayley's biography, although the life and career of Romney (1734–1802), despite some early points of congruence with West's, unfolded quite differently.

121 Galt, *West* (1816), 4.

122 On *Port Folio*, see John T. Queenan, "The *Port Folio*: A Study of the History and Significance of an Early American Magazine" (Ph.D. dissertation University of Pennsylvania, 1955); Michael T. Gilmore, "Magazines, Criticism, and Essays," in *The Cambridge History of American Literature*, ed. Sacvan Bercovitch (Cambridge: Cambridge University Press, 1994), 558–72; Laura Rigal, *The American Manufactory: Art, Labor, and the World of Things in the Early Republic* (Princeton: Princeton University Press, 1998), 114–41; and William C. Dowling, *Literary Federalism in the Age of Jefferson: Joseph Dennie and "The Port Folio," 1801–1812* (Columbia: University of South Carolina Press, 1999). For an account of contributions to *Port Folio* by various members of one of America's most prominent political families, see Linda K. Kerber and Walter John Morris, "Politics and Literature: The Adams Family and the *Port Folio*," *William and Mary Quarterly*, 3rd ser., 23 (July 1966): 450–76.

123 "The Fine Arts," *Port Folio* 1 (Nov. 7, 1801): 355; emphasis in original for all quotations from *Port Folio*.

124 "The Fine Arts," *Port Folio* 4 (Feb. 11, 1804): 45–46.

125 C. W. Peale to West, Dec. 28, 1800, in *Peale Papers*, 2, pt. 1: 293–94; also 416–17.

126 "Biographical Sketch of Benjamin West, Esq. . . . ," *Port Folio* 5 (Oct. 26, 1805): 331–32; (Nov. 2): 347–48; (Nov. 9): 356–57; (Nov. 16): 363–65. Additional items on West during these years appear in *Port Folio* 2 (Aug. 28, 1802): 270; 3 (Jan. 8, 1803): 15; 3 (Mar. 12, 1803): 86.

127 "Anecdotes of American Painters: West," *Port Folio*, 3rd ser., 2 (Oct. 1809): 316–22. A reviewer of William Dunlap's *History* noted that author's correction of the persistent belief among Americans that West had been knighted; *The Knickerbocker, or New York Monthly Magazine* 4 (Dec. 1, 1834): 492. Dunlap made his contempt for the distinction clear, while implying that West's American sentiments prevented him from accepting an "empty title" – though the evidence did not permit him to state it outright (*History*, 1: 72–76). The third biography, "Benjamin West, Esq., President of the Royal Academy," appeared in *Port Folio*, 3rd ser., 6 (Sept. 1811): 245–57; (Oct. 1811): 329–41; (Nov. 1811): 445–56. See also "From La Belle Assemblée: The Artist – No. IV; A Correct Catalogue of the Works of Benjamin West, Esq., President of the Royal Academy," *Port Folio*, 3rd ser., 6 (Dec. 1811): 542–55.

128 "The Fine Arts – For the Port Folio: Original Letter from Sir Benjamin West to Charles W. Peale, Esq.," *Port Folio*, 3rd ser., 3 (Jan. 1810): 8–13; "For the Port Folio" (Mar. 1810): 231–33. Another letter from West – soliciting financial support for Thomas Sully, a native of Philadelphia then studying with him – appeared in vol. 3 (Apr. 1810): 329.

129 "Mr. West's Picture," *Poulson's American Daily Advertiser*, Sept. 9, 1811; and "Some Remarks on Mr. West's Picture," *Port Folio*, 3rd ser., 7 (Jan. 1812): 17–26. The writer for *Port Folio*, following custom, is not identified, but Dennie (who died Jan. 7, 1812) is known to have been closely involved with the production of that issue. A response by "R" appeared in *Port Folio*, 3rd ser., 7 (Feb. 1812): 142–44, with identification of the writer as Rembrandt Peale in papers of Nicholas Biddle, according to Queenan, "*Port Folio*," 336.

130 The author of the text reprinted in *Poulson's* is identified as Ange Denis Macquin in von Erffa and Staley, *West*, 346. The text appeared in the British newspaper *Phoenix* in 1811 and later was reissued in brochure form: A.D.M., *Description of the Picture, Christ Healing the Sick in the Temple, Painted by Benjamin West, Esq., President of the Royal Academy and Now in the British Gallery, Pall Mall* (London, 1812).

131 Laurence Sterne, *The Life and Opinions of Tristram Shandy, Gentleman* (1759–67), ed. James Aiken Work (Indianapolis: Odyssey Press; New York: Bobbs-Merrill, 1940), vol. 3, ch. 12. Sterne's character Parson Yorick, introduced in *Tristram Shandy*, inspired Dennie's imaginary persona in his *Lay Preacher* essays, written before 1801 but intermittently reprinted in *Port Folio*. On Dennie's affinity for Sterne's work, see Dowling, *Literary Federalism in the Age of Jefferson*, 28, 53–55.

132 "Mr. West's Picture of Christ Healing in the Temple," *Port Folio*, 3rd ser., 6 (Nov. 1811): 489–91.

133 West was aware of American responses to his *Christ Healing*. In 1818, during a visit to his studio by the American minister to Britain, West mentioned a pamphlet published in Philadelphia that was critical of the work; Richard Rush, *Memoranda of a Residence at the Court of London* (Philadelphia: Carey, Lea, & Blanchard, 1833), 151 (150–54 on Rush's visit with West).

134 "Remarks on Various Objects of the Fine Arts," *Port Folio*, 4th ser., 7 (June 1812): 538; "The Fine Arts," *Port Folio*, 4th ser., 4 (July 1814): 88–89 (letter from West praising C. R. Leslie).

135 As quoted in Wainwright, "Conversations with Benjamin West," 113.

136 "The Fine Arts," *Port Folio*, 3rd ser., 7 (Feb. 1812): 134; the last in the series of European artists' biographies appeared in *Port Folio*, 4th ser., 1 (Feb. 1813). Authorship of the articles on the fine arts during Biddle's tenure (which began after Dennie's death in January 1812) has been credited to his chief assistant, Paul Allen; Queenan, "*Port Folio*," 335.

137 This list of artist names concluded a brief defense of Philadelphians Adolf Wertmuller and Rembrandt Peale, as an effort to provide some perspective on their representation of female nudes in paintings of Danaë and Jupiter and Io, respectively; "For the Port Folio" *Port Folio*, 4th ser., 4 (Feb. 1814): 154–55.

138 *Port Folio*, 4th ser., 4 (July 1814): 100–3.

139 Ibid.

140 Review of *The Life of West*, by Galt, *Critical Review*, 5th ser., 3 (June 1816): 576–90. Much of this piece consists of summary and quotation, a traditional, but increasingly old-fashioned approach to book reviews, and even truer of a notice in *Monthly Review* 81 (Nov. 1816): 250–57. Following custom, all the reviews of Galt's book are anonymous.

141 *British Critic*, n.s., 6 (July–Dec. 1816): 500–16.

142 Review of *The Life of West*, by Galt, *Eclectic Review*, 2nd ser., 7 (Jan. 1817): 37–49. The writer blamed Galt for "impertinent digression" and a "propensity to theorize and dogmatize."

143 Allan Cunningham, *The Lives of the Most Eminent British Painters, Sculptors, and Architects*, 6 vols. (London, 1829–32), 2: 1, 24–27, 51, 56.

144 "Anecdote of Mr. West and an Italian Improvisatore," *Monthly Recorder* 1 (June 1813): 172–73. Dunlap claimed authorship when he reprinted that material in his *History*, 1: 48. Galt may not have conceived the character for West's biography, but he often used the figure of the improviser in his writings; see Angela Esterhammer, "Agency, Destiny, and National Character: John Galt and Europe," in Hewitt, *John Galt: Observations and Conjectures*, 323–43. Galt's account of West as the untutored natural artist became a blunt weapon against the artist in a scurrilously racist satire of members of the British Institution, which appeared in 1816. The preface, "Information Relative to the Arts in Africa," introduces "a young Hottentot Artist" "Bumjut" (a corruption of Benjamin), whose genius was first manifest "in the taste with which he was accustomed to ornament his own and his sister's face with the simple materials of his country, where, with the assistance of a brush, made of the tail of a lion, and a little yellow and red ochre, he produced an effect that perfectly electrified all the Connoisseurs for miles around"; [Smirke], *A Catalogue Raisonné of the Pictures Now Exhibiting in Pall Mall*, 2: "Preface."

145 Review of *The Life of West*, by Galt, *Analectic Magazine, and Naval Chronicle* 8 (Sept. 1816): 209–22, at 209–10; "Biographical Notice of Benjamin West, Esq. President of the Royal Academy of London," *Analectic Magazine* 8 (July 1816): 36–51; "Remarks on the Progress and Present State of the Fine Arts in the United States," *Analectic Magazine* 6 (Nov. 1815): 363–76 (American faculty of sight at 363).

146 Review of American edition of *The Life of West*, by Galt, *North American Review* 4 (Jan. 1817): 263–69, at 269.

147 "Review, *The Life and Studies of Benjamin West, Esq.*," *Portico* 3 (Jan. 1817): 1–7, at 4, 3. John Neal, an editor of this Baltimore journal and future art critic, was the likely reviewer.

148 Richard Brinsley Sheridan, *The Critic* (1779), 1.2. The character "Puff" lists variations on the type: "the puff direct, the puff preliminary, the puff collateral, the puff collusive, and the puff oblique, or puff by implication. These all assume, as circumstances require, the various forms of Letter to the Editor, Occasional Anecdote, Impartial Critique, Observation from Correspondent, or Advertisement from the Party"; Sheridan, *Plays*, ed. Clayton Hamilton (New York: Macmillan, 1926), 301, 300. *Port Folio* added to this list, by implication, any biography "compiled from materials furnished by" the subject, Galt's claim for *Life of West*. The review of Galt was not the first time the magazine had used this epigraph from Sheridan, see, e.g., "For the *Port Folio* – Review of Literature" (review of Martin Archer Shee, *Rhymes on Art*), *Port Folio*, 4th ser., 1 (June 1816): 511.

149 "For the *Port Folio* – Review of Literature," review of *The Life of West*, by Galt, *Port Folio*, 5th ser., 3 (Jan. 1817): 47–57.

150 John Neal, *Randolph: A Novel*, 2 vols. (Baltimore, 1823), 2: 109, 112, 61. Most convenient access to Neal's writings on art is in *Observations on American Art: Selections from the Writings of John Neal (1793–1876)*, ed. Harold Edward Dickson (State College: Pennsylvania State College, 1943).

151 [Neal], "North America," *Blackwood's Edinburgh Magazine* 16 (Aug. 1824): 131.

152 Walter Thornbury, *British Artists from Hogarth to Turner* (London, 1861), 100–1. Sir Thomas Lawrence, who succeeded West as Academy president, was gentler on the matter when he suggested in a public address that West, despite his eminence as a history painter, "would still have yielded the chief honours of the English School to our beloved Sir Joshua"; Lawrence, *Address to the Students of the Royal Academy, Delivered before the General Assembly at the Annual Distribution of Prizes, 10 December 1823* (London, 1824), 12.

153 Dunlap cast John Trumbull, president of the American Academy and himself once a West student, as the villain of the *History* and West as hero. Maura Lyons devoted a chapter to Dunlap's profiles of West and Trumbull, as expressions of 1830s art politics, in *William Dunlap and the Construction of an American Art History* (Amherst and Boston: University of Massachusetts Press, 2005), 89–120.

154 William Dunlap, *The Diary of William Dunlap, 1766–1839: The Memoirs of a Dramatist, Theatrical Manager, Painter, Critic, Novelist, and Historian*, ed. Dorothy C. Barck, 3 vols. in 1 (1930; repr., New York: Benjamin Blom, 1969), 3: 666 (Mar. 12, 1833); two days earlier, Dunlap noted that he looked over Galt's *Life of West*.

155 Dunlap, *History*, 1: 31 (where the name is spelled Smybert). At least one of the other eight artists who precede West in the *History*, Robert Feke (on whom Dunlap had little information), is now believed to have been born in the colonies – a circumstance that gave him high status in Wayne Craven's insistently nationalistic *Colonial American Portraiture: The Economic, Religious, Social, Cultural, Philosophical, Scientific, and Aesthetic Foundations* (Cambridge: Cambridge University Press, 1986), 281–95.

156 Dunlap, *History*, 1: 16. Similarly, and earlier: West "has not forgotten the republican land of his nativity . . . The claims of Great

Britain . . . cannot be substantiated in opposition to those of nature. He is emphatically an American: not merely born within the limits of our territories, but educated, and raised up to manhood on his native soil"; *The Hermit in America on a Visit to Philadelphia*, 2nd ed., ed. Peter Atall (Philadelphia: M. Thomas, 1819), 41.

157 Dunlap, *History*, 1: 34–35. In an anonymous assessment of Dunlap's book, one reviewer echoed the author's criticism of Galt, whose "love of fiction, or habit of writing fiction, has strangely adorned the simple history of the Quaker painter"; *North American Review* 41 (July 1835): 149. Even so, the review quoted lengthy passages from Dunlap's book of stories originating in Galt's 1816 volume.

158 Dunlap (*History*, 1: 95, 97–98) does not identify a context for Shee's remarks, which evidently continue with quoted text in the footnote (1: 97–98), where Shee further introduces "corroborative testimony of the highest artist and amateur authorities of our day." This included Beaumont's lament, from a letter to Sir Thomas Lawrence, on the decline of West's reputation (italicized in Dunlap).

159 Nationalist tribute barely masked pecuniary concerns when the artist's sons, Raphael West and Benjamin West, wrote J. W. Taylor, Speaker of the House of Representatives, with an offer to sell all works by their father then in their possession to the United States government. The acquisition, they argued, would provide "the foundation of a school for the growth of the fine arts in the rapidly advancing States of America" and serve as "an opportunity of commencing a truly National Gallery": "They are the productions of American born genius, and . . . the honor of having produced them belongs to the United States of America"; 19th Congress, House of Representatives, Doc. No. 8, West's Paintings: Letter from Sons of Benjamin West, Deceased, late President of the Royal Academy of London offering to sell the Government of the United States sundry paintings of that artist. December 11, 1826. Read, and laid upon the table. Washington, 1826; letter of Apr. 12, 1826, cited in Dillenberger, *West*, 198–99. The House did not act, and 181 paintings by West were offered at auction in London in 1829.

160 C. Edwards Lester, *The Artists of America: A Series of Biographical Sketches of American Artists with Portraits and Designs on Steel* (1846; repr., New York: Kennedy Galleries and Da Capo Press, 1970), 67, 113. In the preface to this idiosyncratic collection of eight artists' lives, Lester indicated that he had "drawn freely from Dunlap, who has written the only work which affords me aid," but his account of West is larded with quotations from Cunningham, *Lives of the Most Eminent British Painters*. Galt, whom Lester mentioned only a few times, was nevertheless the ultimate source for most of his anecdotes of West's youth. Henry T. Tuckerman, too, in his book on American artists, relied heavily on Galt's biography and echoed Lester's characterization of West as "the pioneer of American art." At the same time, Tuckerman resisted the tendency "to blend [West's] claims as an artist with those to which he is entitled as a man" and offered a balanced assessment of the painter's strengths and weaknesses; *Book of the Artists: American Artist Life Comprising Biographical and Critical Sketches of American Artists: Preceded by an Historical Account of the Rise & Progress of Art in America* (1867; repr., New York: James F. Carr, 1967), 96.

161 James Jackson Jarves, *The Art-Idea*, ed. Benjamin Rowland, Jr. (1864; Cambridge, Mass.: Belknap Press of Harvard University Press, 1960), 168–69.

162 James Thomas Flexner, *Maverick's Progress: An Autobiography* (New York: Fordham University Press, 1996), 242–43. An epilogue to Alberts's biography of West provides a solid overview of the history of West's reputation (*West*, 393–402). Henry E. Jackson composed a short monograph on West, the first published since Galt's (on which he drew): *Benjamin West: His Life and Work* (Philadelphia: John C. Winston, 1900).

163 Sadakichi Hartmann, *A History of American Art*, 2 vols. (Boston: L. C. Page, 1902), 1: 21–22; Suzanne LaFollette, *Art in America from Colonial Times to the Present Day* (New York: Harper & Bros., 1929), 52; Oskar Hagen, *Birth of the American Tradition in Art* (New York and London: Charles Scribner's Sons, 1940), 123. Eugen Neuhaus, equally critical of West but without invective, argued that "because of his antecedents and his early work in America he must be regarded as belonging to this country"; *The History and Ideals of American Art* (Stanford: Stanford University Press; London: H. Milford, Oxford University Press, 1931), 24. Elizabeth Johns offered a historiographic overview of these and other writers in "Scholarship in American Art," *American Studies International* 22 (Oct. 1984): 3–40. The bicentennial of West's birth brought the American artist further into focus, beginning with the exhibition *Benjamin West, 1738–1820* (Philadelphia: Philadelphia Museum of Art, 1938), the first since his death and notable for including nine colonial works among the sixty paintings. At the same time, William Sawitzky composed the first scholarly account of West's American work, together with a descriptive catalogue, "The American Work of Benjamin West," *Pennsylvania Magazine of History and Biography* 62 (Oct. 1938): 433–62. Sawitzky hoped to lend substance to a picture of the artist then colored almost entirely by the "romantic little stories" of Galt, Cunningham, and Dunlap – which, he observed, "have remained stock-in-trade with practically every subsequent writer on West" (435).

164 Samuel Isham, *The History of American Painting* (1905; new ed., New York: Macmillan, 1927), 40. As early as 1835, a reviewer of Dunlap's *History* deemed the outlines of West's career already "so familiar" as to "almost be called one of our school-boy lessons"; *American Quarterly Review* 17 (Mar. 1835): 146, 147. The tradition was even stronger thirty years later, when Tuckerman began his account of "the pioneer of American art" by asserting: "the extraordinary career of the Quaker boy who left the woods of America to become the President of the Royal Academy in London, is one of the memorable lessons of childhood" (*Book of the Artists*, 96). West's American youth, as first introduced by Galt, indeed proved an irresistible subject for juvenile literature. Edward Gallaudet's abridgement of the 1816 biography, *The Progress of Genius, or, Authentic Memoirs of the Early Life of Benjamin West, Esq., President of the Royal Academy, London* (Boston, 1831), was followed by Nathaniel Hawthorne's greatly condensed version in *Biographical Stories for Children* (1842), frequently reprinted in collections of Hawthorne stories. Twentieth-century renditions include Marguerite Henry and Wesley Dennis, *Benjamin West and his Cat Grimalkin* (New York: Bobbs-Merrill, 1947); Dorothea J. Snow, *Benjamin West: Gifted Young American Painter* (Indianapolis: Bobbs-Merrill, 1967); and a version for very young readers by Barbara Brenner, *The Boy Who Loved to Draw* (Boston: Houghton Mifflin, 1999), with illustrations by Olivier Dunrea that perfectly capture the marvelous tale.

165 Flexner, *America's Old Masters*, 5.

166 Robert Rosenblum, "What is American about American Art?" (1990), reprinted in Rosenblum, *On Modern American Art: Selected Essays* (New York: Abrams, 1999), 14. Not until David Solkin made West an important figure in his book *Painting for Money: The Visual Arts and the Public Sphere in Eighteenth-Century England* (New Haven and London: Yale University Press for the Paul Mellon Centre for Studies in British Art, 1993) did British scholars again begin to pay serious attention to West. Contemporary British art historians now fully incorporate him into narratives of British art; see, e.g., Myrone,

Bodybuilding; Hoock, *King's Artists*; and Holger Hoock, *Empires of the Imagination: Politics, War and the Arts in the British World, 1750–1850* (London: Profile Books, 2010).

167 Galt, *Autobiography*, 2: 236. Cadell and Davies evidently had not committed to a second volume when they published *The Life of West* in 1816. Letters in the National Library of Scotland, Edinburgh, establish that Galt first offered it to the Edinburgh publisher Constable (who declined the opportunity) and also to John Murray; Ian A. Gordon, "Galt and Constable: Two New Galt Attributions," *Scottish Literary Journal* 8 (May 1981): 7. *The Life and Works of Benjamin West*, issued jointly by Cadell and W. Blackwood, appeared shortly after the artist's demise in 1820, with W. T. Fry's engraving of West's 1793 self-portrait as the frontispiece.

CONCLUSION

1 William Dunlap, *A History of the Rise and Progress of the Arts of Design in the United States* (1834), 3 vols., ed. Rita Weiss (New York: Dover, 1969), 1: [6].

2 Peale had previously composed a brief history of American art, accounting for painters active during his formative years, in a remarkable letter to Rembrandt Peale, Oct. 28, 1812, *Peale Papers*, 3: 172–78. That document was private, but Peale told his son that he hoped to correspond with "West, Copley & others in[t]imate with the Arts practiced in America" so as to correct and expand on his own recollections. He either did not do so or never received replies, since no such letters survive. Peale's aim, in any case, must have been allied with his desire to publish his own life because his manuscript autobiography of the mid-1820s included these recollections of early American artists, *Peale Papers*, 5: 95–110.

3 Wayne Craven, *Colonial American Portraiture* (Cambridge: Cambridge University Press, 1986), 281–95.

4 Dunlap, *History*, 1: 14.

5 Trumbull, quoted in P. R. Weidner, ed., "The Journal of John Blake White," *South Carolina Historical and Genealogical Magazine* 40:2 (Apr. 1941): 63. Hogarth, embittered at the end of his life, had commented similarly on the "misery among the unsuccessfull [painters] how often have they wished they had been brought up cobblers"; quoted in Michael Kitson, "Hogarth's Apology for Painters," *Walpole Society* 41 (1966–68): 79.

6 R. Peale's advice to the American mother of London-born Charles Robert Leslie (who did become a notable Anglo-American artist), as related by Thomas Sully, "Recollections of an Old Painter," *Hours at Home* 10 (Nov. 1869): 72.

7 Frances Trollope, *Domestic Manners of the Americans* (1832; New York: A. A. Knopf, 1949), 268.

8 Stephen E. Patrick, "'I Have at Length Determined to Have My Picture Taken': An Eighteenth-Century Young Man's Thoughts about his Portrait by Henry Benbridge," *American Art Journal* 22 (Winter 1990): 79.

9 Morse, letter of Sept. 17, 1811, as quoted in *Samuel F. B. Morse: His Letters and Journals*, ed. Edward Lind Morse, 2 vols. (1914; repr., New York: Da Capo Press for Kennedy Galleries, Inc., 1973), 1: 46.

10 Ibid., 1: 132.

11 Dunlap, *History*, 2: 280.

12 Letter from Trumbull to Edward Everett, Jan. 12, 1827, as quoted in Theodore Sizer, "Trumbull's List of American Historical Painters," *Yale University Library Gazette* 26 (Apr. 1952): 193.

13 Quotations in Paul J. Staiti, *Samuel F. B. Morse* (Cambridge: Cambridge University Press, 1990), 158–59, from his chapter on "The National Academy of Design"; the second is from a review of the rival exhibitions: "The Two Academies," *New York Evening Post*, May 17, 1828.

14 "The Fine Arts: National Academy of Design," *New-York Mirror* 4 (June 2, 1827): 354, in reference to Thomas Doughty and Thomas Cole.

15 Not surprisingly the circumstances were a little more complicated than related by Dunlap, who also did not publicize the quick profit that he and Durand made after placing their pictures by Cole at the American Academy of Fine Arts exhibition and then promptly reselling them. See Carrie Rebora Barratt, "Mapping the Venues: New York City Art Exhibitions," in *Art and the Empire City: New York, 1825–1861*, ed. Catherine Hoover Voorsanger and John K. Howat (New York: Metropolitan Museum of Art; New Haven and London: Yale University Press, 2000), 47–50.

16 The identification of Cole's patron base with an American "aristocracy" arises from the work of art historian Alan Wallach, who saw Cole's fitness for such patrons (somewhat counterintuitively but persuasively) as a legacy of his middling-class English upbringing in industrial Lancashire. Wallach first explored this topic in "Thomas Cole and the Aristocracy," *Arts Magazine* 56 (Nov. 1981): 94–106, and greatly expanded on it in *Thomas Cole: Landscape into History*, ed. William H. Truettner and Alan Wallach (New Haven and London: Yale University Press; Washington, D.C.: National Museum of American Art, 1994), 23–111.

17 On Crawford Notch, see Theodore E. Stebbins, Jr., "Thomas Cole at Crawford Notch," *National Gallery of Art: Report and Studies in the History of Art* 2 (1968): 133–45, and Franklin Kelly, in Kelly et al., *American Paintings of the Nineteenth Century*, Collections of the National Gallery of Art Systematic Catalogue (New York and Oxford: Oxford University Press for the National Gallery of Art, 1996), part 1, 87–95 (quote at 89).

18 Nathaniel Hawthorne, "The Ambitious Guest," first published in *New-England Magazine* (June 1835), republished in *Twice-Told Tales* (1842), reprinted in *Hawthorne: Tales and Sketches* (New York: Literary Classics of the United States, 1982), 299–307.

19 Undated fragment, probably ca. 1845, Cole Papers (box 4, folder 2), New York State Library, Albany; as quoted in Wallach, "Cole and the Aristocracy," 104.

20 For comprehensive analysis of the painting, on which I have drawn, see Staiti, *Morse*, 175–206. "Morse had never been so proud to be an American and an American artist" as at that time, Staiti contended (188).

21 *First Annual Exhibition of the Society of Artists of the United States* (Philadelphia, 1811), 8 (cat. 105); Dunlap, *History*, 1:101.

22 Dunlap included Mount, then just thirty-one, in his *History*, 3: 451–53. Curiously, Mount – who wrote extensively about his artistic practices – declined to cooperate with two later authors who consequently did not include him in their books: Charles Edward Lester, *Artists of America* (1846) and Henry Tuckerman, *Artist-Life; or, Sketches of American Painters* (1847).

23 Elizabeth Johns, *American Genre Painting: The Politics of Everyday Life* (New Haven and London: Yale University Press, 1991), 42 and 217 n.30. Deborah J. Johnson reached a different conclusion in *William Sidney Mount: Painter of American Life* (New York: American Federation of Arts, 1998), 49, reading the fencing gesture as Mount's riposte to critics who venerated European traditions. Mount's work in portrai-

ture can be gauged from his record of works painted and payment received, reprinted in a volume of primary sources compiled by Alfred Frankenstein, *William Sidney Mount* (New York: Harry N. Abrams, 1975), 467–76.

24 Diary entries for Oct. 19, 1847, and Dec. 29, 1848, from Frankenstein, *Mount*, 180, 198.

25 Diary entry, Nov. 25, 1847, ibid., 181.

26 A. A. Harwood, "The Painter's Study," in *The Gift: A Christmas and New Year's Present for 1840*, ed. Miss Leslie (Philadelphia: Carey and Hart, 1839): 208–21. For a focused study of Mount's painting in this context, see especially William T. Oedel and Todd S. Gernes, "*The Painter's Triumph*: William Sidney Mount and the Formation of a Middle Class Art," *Winterthur Portfolio* 23 (Summer/Autumn 1988): 111–27. Their view that Mount was a populist is open to debate since his writings are contradictory on the matter; for an opposing view, see Elisabeth Louise Roark, "Artist as Subject: Images of Artists in American Painting, 1830–1860" (Ph.D. dissertation, University of Pittsburgh, 1991), 94–115.

27 See, in general, Elizabeth Johns, "The Farmer in the Works of William Sidney Mount," *Journal of Interdisciplinary History* 17 (Summer 1986): 257–81 (esp. 271–75). Royall Tyler's *The Contrast* (1787, published 1790), the first professionally produced American comedy in the United States, introduced the rustic Yankee "Jonathan" in opposition the dandified Billy Dimple, who is further corrupted by a trip to England. Association of the phrase "Yankee trick" with a deception was sufficiently well established by 1824 that Mount's uncle Micah Hawkins applied it to two men who merely posed as Yankees to gain property and wives in his popular ballad opera *The Saw-Mill, Or a Yankee Trick* (1824).

28 Nathaniel Hawthorne, "The Artist of the Beautiful" (1844), in *Mosses from an Old Manse*, 2 vols. (New York, 1846), 1: 164–91 (quotes at 175, 184).

29 The later nineteenth-century bookend to my study of colonial and early national American artists is an admired and antecedent publication, Sarah Burns's *Inventing the Modern Artist: Art and Culture in Gilded Age America* (New Haven and London: Yale University Press, 1996).

30 A. B. [John Neal], "North America," *Blackwood's Edinburgh Magazine* 16 (Aug. 1824): 131–36.

31 Neal, "American Painters – and Painting," *The Yankee and Boston Literary Gazette*, 2 (July 1829): 46–51 (quote at 46). As editor of that short-lived magazine following his return to America, Neal promised a survey of English painters, regrettably never executed; "Fine Arts in England," *The Yankee* 1 (Aug. 20, 1828), 270–71.

32 As quoted in John Durand, *The Life and Times of A. B. Durand* (New York: Charles Scribner's Sons, 1894), 164–65.

33 Ralph Waldo Emerson, "The American Scholar: An Oration Delivered before the Phi Beta Kappa Society, at Cambridge, Aug. 31, 1837," in *Nature: Addresses, and Lectures* (Boston and Cambridge, Mass.: James Monroe, 1849), 106.

34 Ignatius Loyola Robertson, *Sketches of Public Characters . . .* (New York: E. Bliss, 1830), 186–87.

INDEX

Numbers in **bold** indicate pages containing illustrations